Acclaim for Ronald Takaki's

A DIFFERENT MIRROR

"In our increasingly diverse society, the issues of race, ethnicity, and religion are often at the forefront of American consciousness, and always in the backs of our minds, shaping our own identity and our views of others. They reverberate in our voting booths, town halls, classrooms, and popular culture. In this timely update of *A Different Mirror: A History of Multicultural America,* Professor Ronald Takaki examines the challenges we face in reconciling our differences and forming a secure, sustainable future for our country. Now more than ever, it's essential that we understand and embrace our diversity if we are to grow together as a nation."
—President Bill Clinton

"A valuable contribution to the discussion of America as a multicultural society."
—*Boston Globe*

"Takaki's book is nothing less than an attempt to view all of American history from a multicultural perspective. It is a laudable effort—humane, well informed, accessible, and often incisive. It is clearly not intended to divide Americans but rather to teach them to value the nation's inescapable diversity."
—*New York Times Book Review*

"A groundbreaker.... It's fascinating to watch Takaki weave these multifaceted strands into a single narrative text."
—*San Francisco Chronicle*

"While Takaki's subtitle is 'a history of multicultural America,' his book is also a manifesto for the future."
—*New York Review of Books*

"*A Different Mirror* demonstrates that employing a multicultural approach to American history is a necessary first step toward the binding together of our disunited nation."   —*Detroit Free Press*

"*A Different Mirror* advances a truly humane sense of American possibility."
—Henry Louis Gates, Jr.

RONALD TAKAKI

A DIFFERENT MIRROR

*A History
of
Multicultural
America*

REVISED EDITION

FOREWORD BY CLINT SMITH

BACK BAY BOOKS
LITTLE, BROWN AND COMPANY
NEW YORK   BOSTON   LONDON

Back Bay Books / Little, Brown and Company
Hachette Book Group
1290 Avenue of the Americas, New York, NY 10104
littlebrown.com

Originally published in hardcover by Little, Brown and Company, June 1993
First Back Bay paperback edition, June 1994
First revised edition, December 2008
Revised edition with new foreword, March 2023

Back Bay Books is an imprint of Little, Brown and Company. The Back Bay Books name and logo are trademarks of Hachette Book Group, Inc.

The publisher is not responsible for websites (or their content) that are not owned by the publisher.

Library of Congress Cataloging-in-Publication Data
Takaki, Ronald T.
    A different mirror : a history of multicultural America / Ronald Takaki.
        p. cm.—(Back Bay nonfiction)
    "Originally published in hardcover by Little, Brown and Company, June 1993"—T.p. verso.
    Includes bibliographical references and index.
    ISBN 978-0-316-02236-1 (first revised pb) /
    978-0-316-49907-1 (pb with new foreword)
    1. Minorities—United States—History. 2. United States—Race relations. 3. United States—Ethnic relations. 4. Cultural pluralism—United States—History. I. Title.
E184.A1T335 2008
305.800973—dc22   2008032815

Printing 1, 2022

LSC-C

Printed in the United States of America

This book is dedicated to
my wife,
CAROL,
for our forty-nine years of friendship,
our joyous journey through a lifetime of scholarship,
and our ceaseless collaboration
in recovering and writing American
history's missing chapters.

CONTENTS

FOREWORD

Not long ago, I visited a prison camp in California where thousands of people of Japanese ancestry were incarcerated during World War II. It was my first time visiting such a place.

During the process of researching my own book *How the Word Is Passed,* I had spent several years visiting historical sites tied to slavery—plantations, prisons, cemeteries, monuments, memorials, museums—attempting to get a sense of how these sites of memory tell the story of what happened there. Spending so much time in these spaces made me more interested in understanding how other sites of memory, carrying notable pieces of American history, tell their story. How did they tell a story that for so long had not been told? Whose voices were included in the telling of this story and whose were not?

Here, at this former prison camp, I found myself transfixed by the watchtower—wooden beams crisscrossing one another in a wreath of haunting Xs and a floodlight that sat above the tower like an eye that never closed. I was unnerved by its singular protruding presence amid the flat desert land that surrounded it. I thought about the thousands of people who would have been surveilled under the eyes of watchtowers just like this one. I thought about the children who were held here, and what it meant to come of age in your own country surrounded by barbed wire and men with guns. I thought about how little I had known about the mass imprisonment of Japanese Americans until I opened up a book by a man who changed the way I understood this country. That book was *A Different Mirror* by Ronald Takaki.

I first encountered Ronald Takaki's *A Different Mirror* in graduate school as a teaching assistant in my university's Ethnic Studies course. The class, taught by the inimitable Dr. Christina

Villareal, had been a popular choice for many students, but the semester I joined the teaching team, it had taken on a particular salience amid the social and political turmoil unfolding all around us. It was the fall of 2015. The blood from Mike Brown's body still stained the concrete in Ferguson, Missouri. The wails of Tamir Rice's mother still shook the trees in Cleveland, Ohio. The decrescendo of Eric Garner's breath could still be heard hovering above Staten Island, New York.

Over the course of the preceding year, we had borne witness to the murders and abuse of what seemed like an endless cascade of Black men and women at the hands of law enforcement. We witnessed our political discourse become increasingly animated by explicit demagoguery and racism. We saw record numbers of immigrants from Central America attempt to make their way across the southern border of the United States, seeking refuge from violence and poverty. There was so much public discussion about what was happening in front of us, but it seemed there was relatively little discussion of the history that made these events possible. Takaki's book is one that helps establish the connection between the past and present in clear ways. It pushes the reader to ask pertinent questions about the country as it exists today. Can we understand contemporary police brutality without understanding the way American policing emerged from the residue of slavery and Jim Crow? Are we able to discern the xenophobic invectives from so many of our politicians without understanding the lineage of nationalism they are a part of? Can we fully comprehend why so many Central American migrants have sought asylum at our border without understanding how a history of American intervention in these countries contributed to the very instability they are attempting to flee?

In our Ethnic Studies course, students were encouraged to share their origin stories. If we were going to understand our collective relationship to American history, we had to understand how each of our individual lineages was an integral part of that collective fabric. It was important to understand where those histories overlapped, and where they diverged.

The class was filled with students who had protested in Ferguson, students who were undocumented, and students who had family members in prison. It was filled with students whose ancestors had been enslaved and those whose ancestors had been enslavers; students whose ancestors had built this country's railroads and those whose ancestors made a fortune from their construction; students whose grandparents had been incarcerated in prison camps on the West Coast during World War II, and students whose grandparents had fought on the shores of Normandy during D-Day. Amid the wide range of roots we carried, what brought us together was that we were all looking for the language to better understand where we came from; we were all looking for the history that might help us make sense of this country we called home.

A Different Mirror was the course's primary text; it was the book that would ground all of us in the underlying spirit of the class. I had never encountered Takaki's work before seeing it on the syllabus. I still remember, in the weeks before class began, sitting down to read *A Different Mirror* for the first time. I had arrived at the library early, found my favorite carrel in the corner of the second floor, and settled in. I opened a notebook, flipped to the first page of *A Different Mirror,* and began. Many hours later, as the summer sun had begun setting behind a thicket of campus tress, I was still there. I couldn't stop. An endless succession of paragraphs had been underlined, hundreds of pages had been dog-eared, and my notebook was full of revelations, observations, arrows, and exclamation points. It was as if I had been thirsty my entire life and had finally been given water to drink. Takaki's book was providing me with the tools I didn't know I needed; it gave me a new historical framework with which to understand the landscape of American life.

I had previously read books that outlined the histories of particular ethnic groups, but I had never encountered a book that put the experiences of so many different types of Americans in conversation with one another. Under Takaki's guidance, I was able to trace the intellectual throughlines that shaped Jefferson's conception of Black American inferiority and Roosevelt's belief in Japanese American disloyalty. I was able to establish clearer connections between the ideas that forced Native Americans off their land and those that brought in Chinese immigrants to build railroads across it. I was able to more fully understand the parallels of Mexican immigrants who generations ago had arrived at the southern border of the United States, and Irish immigrants who generations ago had arrived in the ports of Boston and New York.

With that said, one of the great strengths of *A Different Mirror* is that it does not allow comparison to slip into conflation. Takaki is careful as he threads his needle through history. He wants readers to understand the connections and overlapping histories that exist across different groups of Americans, but he is careful not to suggest that those histories are the same. It is the historical nuance and cultural dexterity with which Takaki writes that allows readers to make their own connections throughout the text.

Those coming to this book for the first time might assume from the subject matter that its tone may be an antagonistic one. But, in fact, Takaki is a generous usher through these different periods of American history. He is a guide, not a polemicist. The book is an invitation, not a diatribe. The generosity of spirit that emanates from the text is one of its greatest gifts. It allows readers to encounter new information in a way that expands their sense of curiosity rather than shuts them down.

Today we find ourselves in a moment when teaching history fully and accurately is being misrepresented by many as an ideological project rather than an honest one. There are state legislatures attempting to prevent teachers from teaching the very history that explains why our country looks the way that it does today. There are school boards banning books that provide students with perspectives from voices that are already on the peripheries of our country's collective consciousness. It is more essential than ever that we have books that explain the history of this country in clear and forthright ways—books that don't shirk from a certain part of history simply because some people might find it unsettling.

I grew up in New Orleans, Louisiana. It had once been the busiest slave market in the country. I didn't know that growing up. I didn't understand the history of slavery in any way that was commensurate with the impact it had on my city, my state, and my country. I knew next to nothing about the Indigenous Americans who first lived on this land. I was never taught about how the Irish were not considered white when they first arrived on these shores. I knew very little about the experiences of Chinese and Japanese immigrants and how essential their labor was in building America's early infrastructure. I had never encountered information that outlined the larger historical context that shaped Jewish resettlement. I was never taught much of anything about the shifting borders between Mexico and the United States. I think now of how transformational a book like *A Different Mirror* would have been if I had encountered it in my classroom. I think about how it would have given me clearer eyes to make sense of everything I saw around me.

"We have an obligation, but also an opportunity as teachers, to construct a new narrative of who we the people of the United States really are," Takaki said in a 2008 interview, just a year before he passed away.

Takaki's work has never been more important than it is right now. Reading *A Different Mirror* reminds us that learning the full history of the United States will make our lives richer, and gives us a better sense of how our histories fit into the ever-evolving American experiment.

—Clint Smith, August 2022

A Different Mirror

1

A DIFFERENT MIRROR

The Making of
Multicultural America

I HAD FLOWN from San Francisco to Norfolk and was riding in a taxi. The driver and I chatted about the weather and the tourists. The sky was cloudy, and twenty minutes away was Virginia Beach, where I was scheduled to give a keynote address to hundreds of teachers and administrators at a conference on multicultural education. The rearview mirror reflected a white man in his forties. "How long have you been in this country?" he asked. "All my life," I replied, wincing. His question was one I had been asked too many times, even by northerners with Ph.D.'s. "I was born in the United States," I added. He replied: "I was wondering because your English is excellent!" Then I explained: "My grandfather came here from Japan in the 1880s. My family has been here, in America, for over a hundred years." He glanced at me in the mirror. To him, I did not look like an American.

Suddenly, we both became uncomfortably conscious of a divide between us. An awkward silence turned my gaze from the mirror to the passing scenery. Here, at the eastern edge of the continent, I mused, was the site of the beginning of multicultural America. Our highway crossed land that Sir Walter Raleigh had renamed "Virginia" in honor of Elizabeth I, the Virgin Queen. Taking lands from the Indians, the English colonizers founded

Jamestown in 1607, and six years later they shipped the first four barrels of tobacco to London. Almost immediately, tobacco became an immensely profitable export crop, and the rise of the tobacco economy generated an insatiable demand for Indian land as well as for labor from England, Ireland, and Africa. In 1619, a year before the arrival of the Pilgrims at Plymouth Rock, a Dutch slave ship landed the first twenty Africans at Jamestown. Indeed, history saturated the surrounding landscape.

Questions like the one that my taxi driver asked me are always jarring. But it was not his fault that he did not see me as a fellow citizen: what had he learned about Asian Americans in courses called "U.S. history"? He saw me through a *filter*—what I call the Master Narrative of American History. According to this powerful and popular but inaccurate story, our country was settled by European immigrants, and Americans are white. "Race," observed Toni Morrison, has functioned as a "metaphor" necessary to the "construction of Americanness": in the creation of our national identity, "American" has been defined as "white."[1] Not to be "white" is to be designated as the "Other"—different, inferior, and unassimilable.

The Master Narrative is deeply embedded in our mainstream culture and can be found in the scholarship of a long list of preeminent historians. The father of the Master Narrative was Frederick Jackson Turner. In 1893, two years after the Census Bureau announced that Americans had settled the entire continent and that the frontier had come to an end, Turner gave a presentation at the meeting of the American Historical Association. Entitled "The Significance of the Frontier in American History," his paper would make him famous. Turner would become the dean of American history, his influence spanning generations of historians to come.

In what would be hailed as the "frontier thesis," Turner declared that the end of the frontier marked "the closing of a great historic movement"—the colonization of the Great West. He explained that the frontier had been "the meeting point between savagery and civilization." At this intersection, the Europeans had been "Americanized" by the wilderness. Initially, "the wilderness masters the colonist. It finds him a European in dress, industries, tools, modes of travel and thought. It takes him from the railroad car and puts him in a birch canoe. It strips off the garments of civilization, and arrays him in the hunting shirt and moccasin. It puts him in the log cabin of the Cherokee and Iroquois.... Before long he has gone to planting Indian corn and plowing with a sharp stick; he shouts the war cry and takes the scalp in orthodox Indian fashion." But "little by little he transforms the wilderness"; in "a series of Indian wars," the "stalwart and rugged" frontiersman takes land from the Indians for white settlement and the advance of "manufacturing civilization." "The outcome is not the Old Europe," Turner exclaimed. "The fact is that here is a new product that is American."[2]

In Turner's footsteps came Harvard historian Oscar Handlin. In his 1945 prizewinning study *The Uprooted*, Handlin presented—to use the book's subtitle—*The Epic Story of the Great Migrations That Made the American People*. In his introduction, Handlin wrote: "I once thought to write a history of immigrants in America. I discovered that the immigrants *were* American history."[3] However, Handlin studied only the migrations from Europe. His "epic story" overlooked the indigenous people of the continent and also the "uprooted" from Africa, Asia, and Latin America.

Contrary to the views of historians like Turner and Handlin, America is a nation peopled by the world, and we are all Americans.

The Master Narrative's narrow definition of who is an American reflects and reinforces a more general thinking that can be found in the curriculum, news and entertainment media, business practices, and public policies. Through this filter, interpretations of ourselves and the world have been constructed, leaving many of us feeling left out of history and America itself.

Today, our expanding racial diversity is challenging the Master Narrative. Demography is declaring: Not all of us came originally from Europe! Currently, one-third of the American people do not trace their ancestries to Europe; in California, minorities have become the majority. They already predominate in major cities across the country—Boston, New York, Chicago, Atlanta, Detroit, Houston, San Francisco, and Los Angeles. Diversity is emerging as America's "manifest destiny."

Within the lifetime of young people today, Americans of European ancestry will become a minority. Indeed, we will all be minorities. How can we prepare ourselves for this future, when the Master Narrative is such a powerful force in our thinking about the past? Analyzing the problem, fourteen-year-old Nicholas Takaki reported that his American history course had taught him "next to nothing about the significance of Asian Americans. I believe our education system as a whole has not integrated the histories of *all* people into our education system, just the Eurocentric view of itself, and the White-centered view of African Americans, and even this is slim to nonexistent. What I find is that most people don't know the fact that they don't know, because of the complete lack of information."[4]

Increasingly aware of this ignorance, educators everywhere have begun to recognize the need to recover the missing chapters of American history. In 1990, the Task Force on Minorities for New York stressed the importance of a culturally diverse education. "Essentially," the *New York Times* commented, "the issue is how to deal with both dimensions of the nation's motto: 'E pluribus unum' — 'Out of many, one.'" Universities from New Hampshire to Berkeley have established American cultural diversity graduation requirements. "Every student needs to know," explained University of Wisconsin chancellor Donna Shalala, "much more about the origins and history of the particular cultures which, as Americans, we will encounter during our lives." Even the University of Minnesota, located in a state that is 98 percent white, requires its students to take ethnic-studies courses. Asked why multiculturalism is so important, Dean Fred Lukermann answered: As a national university, Minnesota has to offer a national curriculum — one that includes all of the peoples of America. He added that after graduation many students move to cities like Chicago and Los Angeles and thus need to know about racial diversity. Moreover, many educators stress, multiculturalism has an intellectual purpose: a more inclusive curriculum is also a more accurate one.[5]

Indeed, the study of diversity is essential for understanding *how* and *why* America became what Walt Whitman called a "teeming nation of nations."[6]

Multicultural scholarship, however, has usually focused on just one minority. Thus, Cornel West in *Race Matters* covers only African Americans, Dee Brown in *Bury My Heart at Wounded Knee* only Native Americans, Irving Howe in *World of Our Fathers* only Jewish Americans, Mario Barrera in *Race and Class in the Southwest* only Mexican Americans, and even I myself in *Strangers from a Different Shore* only Asian Americans. While enriching and deepening our knowledge of a particular group, this approach examines a specific minority in isolation from the others and the whole. Missing is the bigger picture.

In our approach, we will instead study race and ethnicity inclusively and comparatively. While it would be impossible to cover all groups in one book, we will focus on several of them that illustrate and illuminate the landscape of our society's diversity — African Americans, Asian Americans, Irish Americans, Jewish Americans, Mexican Americans, Muslim Americans, and Native Americans.

African Americans have been the central minority throughout our country's history. Even fifty years after their first arrival in Virginia, Africans still represented only a tiny percentage of the colony's population. The planters preferred workers from their homeland, for they wanted their new society to be racially homogeneous. This thinking abruptly changed, however, in 1676, when the elite encountered an uprising of discontented and armed workers. After quelling the insurrection with reinforcements of British troops, the planters turned to Africa for their primary labor supply; the new workers would be enslaved and prohibited from owning arms. Subsequently, the African population spiked upward, and slavery spread across the South. African Americans would remain degraded as unpaid laborers and dehumanized as property until the Civil War. What President Abraham Lincoln called "this mighty scourge of war" finally ended "the bondsman's two hundred and fifty years of unrequited toil." But a grim future awaited African Americans: Jim Crow segregation, lynchings, race riots, and what W. E. B. Du Bois called "the problem of the color line." Still, they insistently struggled for freedom. Joined by people of other races in the sixties, African Americans marched and sang, "We shall overcome," winning significant victories that changed society. Indeed, the history of African Americans has been stitched into the history of America itself. Martin Luther King, Jr., clearly understood this truth when he wrote from a jail cell: "We will reach the goal of freedom in Birmingham and all over the nation, because the goal of America is freedom. Abused and scorned though we may be, our destiny is tied up with America's destiny."[7]

Asian Americans began arriving in America long before many European immigrants. Seeking "Gold Mountain," the Chinese were among the Forty-Niners. Then they worked on the railroad, in the agricultural fields of the West Coast states, and in the factories of California and even Massachusetts. As "strangers" coming from a "different shore," they were stereotyped as "heathen" and unassimilable. Wanted as sojourning laborers, the Chinese were not welcomed as settlers. During an economic depression, Congress passed the 1882 Chinese Exclusion Act—the first law that prohibited the entry of immigrants on the basis of nationality. The Chinese condemned this restriction as racist and tyrannical. "They call us 'Chink,'" complained a Chinese immigrant, cursing the "white demons." "They think we no good! America cut us off. No more come now, too bad!" The Japanese also painfully discovered that their accomplishments in America did not lead to acceptance.

During World War II, the government interned a hundred twenty thousand Japanese Americans, two-thirds of them citizens by birth. "How could I as a six-month-old child born in this country," asked Congressman Robert Matsui years later, "be declared by my own Government to be an enemy alien?"[8] In 1975, after the collapse of Saigon, tens of thousands of refugees fled to America from the tempest of the Vietnam War. Today, Asian Americans represent one of the fastest-growing ethnic groups in America, projected to represent 10 percent of the total U.S. population by 2050.

Initially, the Irish came here in the early seventeenth century. At that time, many of them were brought to Virginia involuntarily as captives of the English wars in Ireland and as indentured servants in the Irish "slave trade." During the nineteenth century, four million Irish emigrated to escape the hunger caused not only by the Potato Famine, but also by the rise of a ranching economy. In order to expand grazing lands, English landlords evicted Irish families from their farms. As beef exports from Ireland to England rose, so did the number of people leaving Ireland. In America, these immigrants became construction workers, maids, and factory workers in the textile mills of Lowell, Massachusetts. Representing a Catholic group seeking to settle in a fiercely Protestant society, the Irish became victims of nativist hostility. They came about the same time as the Chinese, but they had a distinct advantage: the Naturalization Law of 1790 had reserved citizenship for "whites" only. Consequently, the Irish became citizens, and, as voters, they pursued an "ethnic" strategy. They elected Irish to city councils and mayorships, and their elected officials made certain that Irish builders were given construction contracts and that Irish men were hired as firemen and policemen. By 1900, the Irish were entering the middle class.[9]

Fleeing pogroms in Russia, Jews were driven from what John Cuddihy described as the "Middle Ages into the Anglo-American world of the *goyim* 'beyond the pale.'" In America, they settled in the Lower East Side, a beehive of tenements and garment factories that exploited an army of Jewish women. To many Jews, America represented the Promised Land. This vision energized them to rise from "greenhorns" into middle-class Americans. Stressing the importance of education, they pooled family resources; the earnings of the daughters working in the sweatshops helped to support the education of their brothers in institutions like New York City College and Harvard. But as Jewish immigrants and their children were entering the mainstream, they found themselves facing the rise of Hitler and the horror of the ultimate pogrom. Safe in America, they asked themselves: What is our responsibility as Jews to Hitler's victims? What should we do to break America's "deafening silence" over the Holocaust? Demanding that America do everything it could to rescue people destined for the death camps, Jewish Americans encountered a tide of anti-Semitism and indifference. From the war emerged a Jewish-American activism for human rights and social justice. Jack Greenberg of the NAACP Legal Defense Fund recalled that Jews cheered when Jackie Robinson broke into the Brooklyn Dodgers in 1947. "He was adopted as the surrogate hero by many of us growing up at the time. He was the way we saw ourselves triumphing against the forces of bigotry and ignorance." Jews like Howard Zinn and Stanley Levison stood shoulder to shoulder with African Americans in the Civil Rights Movement.[10] During the 1964 Freedom Summer, over half of the white volunteers who went South were Jewish.

Mexican Americans were first incorporated into the United States by the 1846–48 war against Mexico. They did not come to America; instead, the border was moved when the United States annexed the Southwest. Most of the Mexican Americans today, however, have immigrant roots, having begun the trek to El Norte in the early twentieth century. "As I had heard a lot about the United States," Jesus Garza recalled, "it was my dream to come here." The Mexican-American experience has been different from that of other immigrants, for their homeland borders the United States — a proximity that has helped reinforce their language, identity, and culture. Today, Mexicans are still crossing the border, pushed by poverty from the south and pulled northward by employment opportunities. Most of the current twelve million "illegal immigrants" are from Mexico, and a burning public policy question is: What should the government do about them? One answer was given by *Time* magazine in its June 18, 2007, cover story: "Give them amnesty." The illegals are "by their sheer numbers undeportable. More important, they are too enmeshed in a healthy U.S. economy to be extracted." "Assimilation is slow, but inevitable." We must have "faith in America's undimmed ability to metabolize immigrants from around the world, to change them more than they change the U.S."[11] Indeed, like other immigrant groups, Mexican Americans have been learning English, applying for naturalized citizenship, voting, and becoming Americans.

Among Muslim Americans are the refugees from Afghanistan. After their country was invaded by the Russians in 1979, the United

States intervened, financing and arming the mujahideen—the anti-Soviet "freedom fighters." After the Russian defeat in 1989, civil war broke out, ending with the ascendancy of the religiously conservative and oppressive Taliban. Safe in America, the Afghan refugees were hardly noticed. On September 11, 2001, however, the terrorist attacks on the World Trade Center and the Pentagon suddenly changed the lives of Afghans in America. The hijackers were traced to Al-Qaeda, a terrorist organization headed by Osama bin Laden and based in Afghanistan. On that unforgettable day, Nadeem Saaed was afraid that Afghan Americans would be attacked and arrested. "Being Afghan American is not what people think it was before; now it's what people want to know about you and who you really are inside, an American or a terrorist."[12] In 2002, Western powers led by the United States invaded Afghanistan, seeking to destroy Al-Qaeda. The Taliban was quickly routed, but not vanquished. Omar Nourzaie summed up the challenge facing Afghan Americans: "The refugees know that a return to Afghanistan is not in their near future. They will have to change and make do in America."[13]

Native Americans represent a significant contrast to all of the other groups, for theirs was not an immigrant experience. They were the original Americans, here for thousands of years before the voyage of Columbus. They were on the shores of Massachusetts and Virginia when the English arrived in 1607. Indians had been farming the land for centuries, but the English colonizers stereotyped them as "savages" and seized their lands by warfare. Westward would be the course of empire, across Indian lands all the way to the Pacific. Leaders of military campaigns against the native people were celebrated as heroes. One of them was the Indian fighter and architect of Indian removal, President Andrew Jackson. In a message to Congress, he declared: "Humanity has often wept over the fate of the aborigines of this country, and Philanthropy has been long busily employed in devising means to avert it, but its progress has never for a moment been arrested, and one by one have many powerful tribes disappeared from the earth. To follow to the tomb the last of his race and tread on the graves of extinct nations excite melancholy reflections." But Indians had a different interpretation of what Jackson trumpeted as "progress." "The white man," Luther Standing Bear of the Sioux explained, "does not understand the Indian for the reason that he does not understand America. The man from Europe is still a foreigner and an alien. And he still hates the man who questioned his path across the continent."[14]

The "path" was designed to create a white America. The revolutionaries of 1776 founded a white republic, a democracy that was not for all people. In 1787, the Constitution legalized the institution of slavery. One of its provisions stated that the number of representatives each state sent to Congress was to be determined by the number of "free persons" and "three fifths of all other persons," the code phrase for slaves. In 1801, shortly before negotiating the Louisiana Purchase, President Thomas Jefferson wrote to James Madison that he looked forward to distant times when the American continent would be covered with "a people speaking the same language, governed in similar forms, and by similar laws."[15]

As it turned out, the economy would set a different agenda for who would be the people covering the continent. The War for Independence had been a struggle not only for political freedom from England but also for market freedom—freedom to trade without regulations from the mother country, to manufacture goods without restrictions, and to settle the land beyond the Appalachian Mountains. Unleashed, the new republic entered the era of the Market Revolution that would pull to America what Whitman welcomed as a "vast, surging hopeful army of workers."[16]

In America's expanding industrial economy, workers were often swept into ethnic antagonisms. Irish immigrants found themselves viewed as ignorant and inferior, and were forced to occupy the bottom rungs of employment. In the South, they were even made to do the jobs considered too hazardous and dangerous to be done by slaves, who were regarded by their owners as valuable property. In the North, Irish competed with blacks for jobs as waiters and longshoremen. As they pushed blacks out of the labor market, many Irish promoted their whiteness. "In a country of the whites where [white workers] find it difficult to earn a subsistence," they asked, "what right has the negro either to preference or to equality, or to admission?" Complaining that blacks did not know their place, many of the Irish newcomers shouted: "Down with the Nagurs!" "Let them go back to Africa, where they belong." Born in America, blacks complained that the Irish were taking jobs from them. "These impoverished and destitute beings, transported from the trans-Atlantic shores," a black observed, "are crowding themselves into every place of business and labor, and driving the poor colored American citizen out."[17]

Despite antagonisms, minorities also had much in common: labor experiences, hopeful dreams, and, above all, values.

Dynamically tied together in a complex interregional economy, workers found themselves in a robust industrial labyrinth of farms, factories, railroads, and mines stretching from Canada to Mexico and from the Atlantic to the Pacific. In the South, African Americans were cultivating cotton, which was shipped to New England, where "Irish factory girls" were operating machines in the textile mills, while Jewish women were sewing clothes in the garment factories of the Lower East Side. In the "New South" after the Civil War, African Americans were working in the steel mills of Birmingham, Alabama, while in the copper mines of Arizona, Mexican Americans were extracting the "red metal" used to manufacture electrical wires that made possible the illumination of America. In California, Chinese and Japanese immigrants were growing an agricultural garden to feed an industrializing urban society. By 1900, the United States was manufacturing more goods than England and France combined.

The greatest achievement of industrializing America was the Transcontinental Railroad. Together, the Chinese of the Central Pacific and the Irish of the Union Pacific built the ribbon of steel that connected the two coasts, making possible the movements of people, raw materials, and goods throughout the entire country. The construction of the nation's elaborate national railroad system required the hard work of an immense variety of workers. Their songs told the story of common experiences. Laying railroad ties, black laborers sang:

> *Down the railroad, um-huh*
> *Well, raise the iron, um-huh*
> *Raise the iron, um-huh.*

Irish railroad workers shouted as the sweat on their brows and backs glistened in the sun:

> *Then drill, my Paddies, drill—*
> *Drill, my heroes, drill,*
> *Drill all day, no sugar in your tay*
> *Workin' on the U.P. railway.*

Japanese laborers in the Northwest chorused as their bodies fought the fickle weather:

> *A railroad worker—*
> *That's me!*
> *I am great.*

> *Yes, I am a railroad worker.*
> *Complaining:*
> *"It is too hot!"*
> *"It is too cold!"*
> *"It rains too often!"*
> *"It snows too much!"*
> *They all ran off.*
> *I alone remained.*
> *I am a railroad worker!*

Mexican-American workers in the Southwest joined in as they swore at the punishing work:

> *Some unloaded rails*
> *Others unloaded ties,*
> *And others of my companions*
> *Threw out thousands of curses.*[18]

Shared class exploitation often led workers to struggle together. In 1870, Chinese immigrant laborers were transported to Massachusetts as scabs to break an Irish immigrant strike; in response, the Irish tried to organize a Chinese lodge of the Knights of St. Crispin, an Irish labor union. In 1903, Mexican and Japanese farm laborers went on strike together in California: their union officers had names like Yamaguchi and Lizarras, and strike meetings were conducted in Spanish and Japanese. The Mexican strikers declared that they were standing in solidarity with their "Japanese brothers."[19] In Hawaii, Japanese and Filipino laborers came together in "a solid body" during a 1920 strike. They had been pitted against each other by the planter class, but they realized they had a common class interest. To "effectively cope with the capitalists," the strikers declared, their "big, powerful union" had to bring together "laborers of all nationalities."[20] During its massive organizing drives in the 1930s, the Committee for Industrial Organization announced that its policy was "one of absolute racial equality in Union membership."[21] Describing a lesson learned by Mexican and Asian farm laborers in California, a Japanese immigrant conveyed in poetry the feeling of class connectedness across racial boundaries:

> *People harvesting*
> *work together unaware*
> *Of racial problems.*[22]

Regardless of their different complexions and origins, immigrants embraced similar hopeful dreams. In Ireland, people received letters from friends in the United States that glowingly described riches growing like grass and the boundlessness of a country where there were no oppressive English landlords. "My dear Father," wrote an Irish immigrant woman from New York in 1850, "any man or woman without a family would be fools that would not venture and come to this plentiful Country where no man or woman ever hungered." A witness in China reported the excitement generated by the news of the gold rush: "Letters from Chinese in San Francisco and further in the country have been circulated through all this part of the province. The accounts of the successful adventurers who have returned would, had the inhabitants possessed the means of paying their way across, have gone far to depopulate considerable towns."[23] Facing high taxes and difficulties making ends meet, Japanese farmers were enticed eastward. Excitedly they exclaimed:

> *Day of spacious dreams!*
> *I sailed for America,*
> *Overblown with hope.*

Fleeing from anti-Semitic persecution and violence in Russia, the cry "To America!" roared like "wild-fire" in Jewish communities. In the shtetls, a song floated in the air:

> *As the Russians mercilessly*
> *Took revenge on us,*
> *There is a land, America,*
> *Where everyone lives free.*

For Mexican immigrants crossing the border in the early twentieth century, El Norte became the stuff of fantasies:

> *If only you could see how nice*
> *the United States is;*
> *that is why the Mexicans*
> *are crazy about it.*[24]

Beyond their shared labor experiences and dreams, the diverse American people discovered a tie that binds—the Declaration of Independence, with equality as a principle for everyone, regardless of race or religion. Moreover, they were prepared to fight and even die for this "self-evident truth" in two of the nation's most horrendous conflicts—the Civil War and World War II.

The Civil War was initiated by the planter class of the South. Although they constituted only 5 percent of the southern white population, the slaveholders were dominant in politics. Defending their profitable "peculiar institution," this ruling elite took their states out of the Union in 1861. In his First Inaugural Address, President Lincoln declared: "One section of our country believes slavery is *right* and ought to be extended, while the other believes it is *wrong* and ought not to be extended." Southern secession, he argued, would mean anarchy. Lincoln sternly warned the South that he had taken a solemn oath to defend and preserve the Union. Americans were one people, he explained poetically, bound together by "the mystic chords of memory, stretching from every battlefield and patriot grave to every living heart and hearthstone all over this broad land." In the South, however, Lincoln's appeal for unity fell on deaf ears, and the war came.[25]

During the conflict, President Lincoln initially refused to allow the Union Army to enlist African Americans: he wanted to keep the border states in the Union and worried that whites would refuse to fight in an army that had black soldiers. In the spring of 1863, however, Lincoln faced a military crisis. "Manpower now posed a real problem," wrote historian David Herbert Donald. "There had been severe losses in a contest that had now lasted nearly two years. The terms for which many regiments had enlisted were about to expire, and soldiers wanted to go home. Thousands were absent without leave.... There were almost no new volunteers. It would be months before a new conscription act could bring in recruits."[26]

This shortage of military manpower meant that the North was on the terrifying edge of losing the war. At this critical point, Lincoln made a crucial decision. In a letter to the military governor of Tennessee, he wrote: "The colored population is the great available and yet unavailed of, force for restoring the Union. The bare sight of fifty thousand armed and drilled black soldiers on the banks of the Mississippi would end the rebellion at once." Lincoln gave his generals permission to enlist black men.[27] Tens of thousands of escaped slaves, desperate to liberate their families still in bondage, flocked to join the fight. "Now we sogers are men—men de first time in our lives," one of them declared. "Now we can look our old masters in de face. They used to sell and whip us, and we did not dare say one word. Now we ain't afraid, if they meet us, to run the bayonet through them."[28] In the Mississippi Valley, General Lorenzo Thomas enrolled twenty regiments of African Americans.

Altogether, a hundred eighty-six thousand blacks served in the Union Army. "Without the physical force which the colored people now give, and promise us," Lincoln explained, "neither the present, nor any coming administration, can save the Union." Without them, "we would be compelled to abandon the war in three weeks."[29] The Union Army pursued the war to victory. By then, one-third of the black soldiers were listed as killed or missing in action. But their sacrifice had not been in vain: the men that Lincoln praised as "black warriors" had made the decisive difference in determining that our "government of the people, by the people, for the people" did "not perish from the earth." Significantly, in his famous Gettysburg Address, Lincoln declared that the nation had been founded, "dedicated" to the "proposition" that "all men are created equal."[30]

World War II was also a significant fight for equality. Franklin D. Roosevelt had refused to desegregate the U.S. Armed Forces; thus we fought the Nazis with a Jim Crow army. The defense industry employed only white men until A. Philip Randolph threatened a march on Washington and forced the president to issue an executive order opening jobs to everyone, regardless of race or gender. After the attack on Pearl Harbor and the explosion of anti-Japanese hysteria, Roosevelt authorized the evacuation and internment of Japanese Americans. Facing Hitler's death factories, Jews in Europe frantically begged Roosevelt to let them seek refuge here; but heeding the polls showing widespread anti-Semitic opposition to the admission of Jews, Roosevelt refused to offer them sanctuary.

This contradiction between our professed principle of equality and our practice of prejudice was unshrouded by James G. Thompson in a letter to the *Pittsburgh Courier,* published on January 31, 1942:

> Being an American of dark complexion and some 26 years, these questions flash through my mind: "Should I sacrifice my life to live half American? Will things be better for the next generation in the peace to follow? Would it be demanding too much to demand full citizenship rights in exchange for the sacrificing of my life? Is the kind of America I know worth defending? Will America be a true and pure democracy after the war? Will colored Americans suffer still the indignities that have been heaped upon them in the past? These and other questions need answering; I want to know,

and I believe every colored American, who is thinking, wants to know.... The V for victory sign is being displayed prominently in all so-called democratic countries which are fighting for victory over aggression, slavery, and tyranny. If this V sign means that to those now engaged in this great conflict, then let we colored Americans adopt the double VV for a double victory.[31]

Thompson enlisted and served in the U.S. Armed Forces. So did 33,000 Japanese Americans. Leaving their families behind in the internment camps, they fought in the all-Japanese-American 442nd Regimental Combat Team. By the end of the war in Europe, these soldiers had suffered 9,486 casualties, including 600 killed. The 442nd, military observers agreed, was "probably the most decorated unit in United States military history."[32] Welcoming home these Japanese-American soldiers after the war, President Harry Truman acknowledged the country's indebtedness to them: "You fought for the free nations of the world...you fought not only the enemy, you fought prejudice—and you won."[33]

Actually, for Japanese Americans as well as other minorities, the fight against prejudice still had to be won. Out of the war came clamors for change. In 1952, under pressure from lobbying groups including Japanese-American veterans, Congress rescinded the "white"-only restriction of the 1790 Naturalization Law. A Japanese immigrant rejoiced in poetry:

> Going steadily to study English,
> Even through the rain at night,
> I thus attain,
> Late in life,
> American citizenship.[34]

Then came a casade of laws for social justice. At the 1963 March on Washington, Martin Luther King, Jr., declared: "I say to you today, my friends, that in spite of the difficulties and frustrations of the moment I still have a dream. It is a dream deeply rooted in the American dream. I have a dream that one day this nation will rise up and live out the true meaning of its creed: 'We hold these truths to be self-evident; that all men are created equal.'" A year later, Congress passed the Civil Rights Act, which, in turn, opened the way to the passage of the Immigration Act of 1965, which finally allowed the entry of Asian immigrants again.[35]

Two years later came a change that had been initiated by two ordinary individuals. Mildred and Richard Loving, an African-American woman and a white man, fell in love and married, but then they were arrested in Virginia for violating the state's anti-miscegenation law. They sued the state, and in 1967 the U.S. Supreme Court struck down the laws banning racially mixed marriages: "Restricting the freedom to marry solely because of racial classification violates the central meaning of the equal protection clause."[36]

In 1988, Congress passed a bill providing for an apology and a payment of $20,000 to each of the Japanese-American survivors of the World War II internment camps. When President Ronald Reagan signed the bill, he admitted that the United States had committed "a grave wrong." The nation needed, the president acknowledged, to end "a sad chapter in American history."[37]

Other chapters in history, both sad and joyful, hunger to be told. "It is very natural that the history written by the victim," said a Mexican in 1874, "does not altogether chime with the story of the victor." Sometimes the people of multicultural America have been hesitant to speak, thinking they were only "little people." "I don't know why anybody wants to hear my history," an Irish maid said apologetically in 1900. "Nothing ever happened to me worth the tellin'."[38]

But their stories are worthy. Native-American writer Leslie Marmon Silko explained why:

> *I will tell you something about stories...*
> *They aren't just entertainment.*
> *Don't be fooled.*

Indeed, the accounts given by the people in this book vibrantly re-create moments in history, capturing the complexities of human emotions and thoughts. They also provide the authenticity of experience. After she escaped from slavery, Harriet Jacobs wrote in her autobiography: "[My purpose] is not to tell you what I have heard but what I have seen—and what I have suffered."[39]

Their stories burst in the telling. "I hope this survey do a lot of good for Chinese people," an immigrant told an interviewer from Stanford University in the 1920s. "Make American people realize that Chinese people are humans. I think very few American people really know anything about Chinese." But the remembering is also for the sake of the children. "This story is dedicated to the descendants of Lazar and Goldie Glauberman," Jewish immigrant

Minnie Miller wrote in her autobiography. "My history is bound up in their history and the generations that follow should know where they came from to know better who they are." Similarly, Tomo Shoji, an elderly Japanese-American woman, urged Asian Americans to learn more about their roots: "We got such good, fantastic stories to tell. All our stories are different." Seeking to know how they fit into America, many young people want to hear the stories of their ancestors, unwilling to remain ignorant or ashamed of their identity and roots. One of them vowed to remember:

> *The story of your fight,*
> *Though not recorded*
> *In any history book,*
> *Yet lives engraved on my heart.*[40]

But what happens when historians do not "record" their stories, leaving out many of America's peoples? What happens, to borrow the words of Adrienne Rich, "when someone with the authority of a teacher" describes our society, and "you are not in it"? Such an experience can be disorienting—"a moment of psychic disequilibrium, as if you looked into a mirror and saw nothing." What should we do about our invisibility? Poet Audre Lorde answered:

> *It is a waste of time hating a mirror*
> *or its reflection*
> *instead of stopping the hand*
> *that makes glass with distortions.*[41]

Reflected in a mirror without distortions, the people of multicultural America belong to what Ishmael Reed described as a society "unique" in the world because "the world is here"—a place "where the cultures of the world crisscross."[42] Out of this intermingling arose a poem by Langston Hughes. So succinctly, so sonorously, the black poet laureate captured our multicultural memory:

> *Let America be America again,*
> *Let America be the dream the dreamers*
> *   dreamed,*
> *Say who are you that mumbles in the dark?*
> *I am the poor white, fooled and pushed*
> *   apart,*

I am the Negro bearing slavery's scars,
I am the red man driven from the land,
I am the immigrant clutching the hope
    I seek,
O, let my land be a land where,
Equality is in the air we breathe.[43]

The struggle to "let America be America" has been America's epic story. In the making of multicultural America, the continent's original inhabitants were joined by people pushed from their homelands by poverty and persecution in Asia, Latin America, and Europe, and pulled here by extravagant dreams. Others came here in chains from Africa, and still others fled here as refugees from countries like Vietnam and Afghanistan. And all of them belonged to "the great migrations that made the American people."

The men and women in this study might not have read John Locke, but they came to believe that "in the beginning, all the world was America." Like F. Scott Fitzgerald's Dutch sailors in the seventeenth century, they held their breath in the presence of this "fresh, green breast of the new world." They envisioned the emerging country as a place for a bold new start. Crossing borders not delineated by space, they broke the "cake of custom" as they transcended traditional fixed points of classification. Marginalized and degraded as the "Other," minorities came to believe even more fiercely and fervently than did the Founding Fathers in the "self-evident truths" that "all men are created equal," entitled to the "unalienable Rights" of "Life, Liberty, and the pursuit of Happiness."[44]

Together, "We the" diverse "people of the United States" transformed America into a mighty economy and an amazingly unique society of varied races, ethnicities, and religions. In the process, we transformed ourselves into Americans. Together, we composed "E pluribus unum"—a reality discerned by Herman Melville over one hundred years ago. Our country was settled by "the people of all nations," he wrote. "All nations may claim her for their own. You can not spill a drop of American blood, without spilling the blood of the whole world." Americans are "not a narrow tribe."[45]

This truth is reflected in "a different mirror." Remembered more inclusively, history offers all of us hopeful ties that bind—what Lincoln cherished as our "mystic chords of memory."

PART ONE

Foundations

Before Columbus: Vinland

FROM THE SHORE, the small band of Indians saw the floating island pulled by billowy clouds and the landing of the strangers. Never before had they seen such people. The newcomers looked like animals—monstrous, hairy, and pale skinned, their eyes the color of the sea and their hair the color of the sun. They carried shiny sharp sticks that looked like long, vicious claws. Their foreign speech sounded like gabble. Confused and frightened, the Indians quickly hid beneath their skin-covered boats, hoping to appear like three mounds on the beach. They could hear footsteps approaching; suddenly their boats were violently overturned. All but one of them were captured. Paddling away frantically, the lone survivor looked back and saw red stains darkening the beach.[1]

Led by Thorvald Eiriksson, son of Eirik the Red, the Vikings had sailed from Greenland to the New World. He had been told about this land by his brother, Leif, who had sailed south from Iceland about the year 1000 and reached a place he called "Vinland," an old Norse term for grassland or pasture. In the wonderful country to the south, Thorvald had learned, the grass tasted "sweet" and the rivers teemed with salmon. "This is a beautiful place," Thorvald exclaimed when he first saw what is now known as Newfoundland. "I should like to build myself a home here." After their initial encounter with the Indians on the beach, Thorvald and his men pitched camp and went to sleep. Suddenly, they were attacked by Indians armed with bows and arrows; Thorvald was wounded. "You must carry me out to the headland where I thought it would be good to live," the dying leader told his men. "You must bury me there, and put a cross at my head and another one at my feet, and from then on you must call the place Krossanes [Cross Head]."[2]

Shortly afterward, another group of Vikings sailed to Vinland.

Among them were Thorfinn Karlsefni and his wife, Gudrid. They found a land of great abundance: "Every stream was full of fish. They dug holes where sea and land met at high tide, and when the sea went down again, there was halibut lying in the holes. There were plenty of animals of all kinds in the forest." Then one day, the colonists were approached by some Indians. "Dark, ugly fellows, with ugly hair on their heads" and "large eyes and broad faces," the Beothuks, also named "Skraelings" by the Vikings, came out of the forest and were frightened by the bellowing of the cattle. "They ran towards Karlsefni's farm and wanted to get into the houses; but Karlsefni had the doors bolted. Neither of the two groups understood the other's language. Then the Skraelings took their packs off and undid their bundles and offered goods for sale; they wanted weapons more than anything else in exchange. But Karlsefni refused to sell any weapons." Instead, he offered them some cheese in exchange for pelts.[3]

The next year, the Beothuks returned to the site, rowing around the headland from the south. "There were so many of them that it looked as if charcoal had been strewn on the water." They wanted to trade for red cloth and swords. Suddenly, one of the Beothuks was killed as he tried to steal some weapons. During the fierce battle, the Vikings retreated up the riverbank, where they successfully resisted the Beothuk attacks. "Now it's hard to know what to do," Karlsefni said, "because I think they will come back a third time, and then they will come as enemies and there will be very many of them." The following spring, Karlsefni and his fellow Vikings abandoned the colony and returned to Greenland. They realized that, "although this was a good country, there would always be terror and trouble from the people who lived there."[4]

And so this first European settlement in the New World came to an end and remained virtually unknown to the Western world. The Norse people on Greenland had been cut off from their homeland, and when a Norwegian missionary arrived there in 1721, he found only the ruins of farms and churches. Only the Viking sagas, handed down orally and recorded in the fourteenth and fifteenth centuries, preserved the story of the first encounter. This Viking contact remained unacknowledged until 1960 when, on the northern point of Newfoundland at L'Anse aux Meadows, archeologists found a group of overgrown housesites with ancient Norse tools, and used carbon-14 analysis to date artifacts at about 1000 AD.

About five hundred years after Leif Eiriksson's voyage to Vinland, Christopher Columbus made his crossing and changed the course of history. Unlike the Viking expeditions, his project was sponsored by the king and queen of Spain and was the focus of immense and wide interest throughout Europe. Moreover, the printing press was now available to spread the exciting news of Columbus's amazing "discovery." The admiral thought he had reached Asia. After he sighted land on October 21, 1492, the explorer wrote in his journal: "I am determined to go to the mainland and to the city of *Quisay* [Hangchow] and to present Your Highnesses' letters to the Grand Khan." Two days later, he recorded: "I wish to depart today for the island of Cuba, which I believe should be *Cipango* [Japan], according to the description that this people give me of its size and wealth...." But Columbus was mistaken; actually, he had encountered a new land between Europe and Asia. This most momentous accident of history opened the way to efforts by Spain, Portugal, France, Holland, and England to colonize the continents that would be named the Americas. Unlike the Vikings, however, the new strangers stayed.[5]

2

❧⟨⟩❧

THE "TEMPEST" IN THE WILDERNESS

A Tale of Two Frontiers

T HE WHOLE EARTH is the Lord's garden," John Winthrop declared to his fellow English colonizers as they prepared to embark for America in 1629, "and he hath given it to the sons of men [to] increase and multiply and replentish the earth and subdue it. Why then should we stand starving here for the places of habitation...and in the meantime suffer a whole Continent as fruitful and convenient for the use of man to lie waste without any improvement." The Puritan "errand into the wilderness" was to create "a city upon a hill," with "the eyes of the world upon" their religious utopia. Beneath the English migrations was an economic reality—the increase in the population of their homeland from three to four million, the problems of famine, and the rise of the wool industry with its accompanying evictions of farmers. On this side of the Atlantic was a continent bursting with resources—timber, furs, fish, and especially land. The English settlement was given a religious meaning: "starving" in England, they would migrate to America where they would cultivate the "Lord's garden." The colonizers would not "suffer" the land to "lie waste without any improvement" by its original inhabitants.[1]

Shakespeare's Dream About America

In their first encounters with Europeans, the Indians tried to comprehend who the invaders were. Traditional Penobscot accounts had described the earth as flat and surrounded by ocean, the "great salt water," *ktci-sobe-k*. Beyond this body of water, there were other islands and countries inhabited by "tribes of strangers." The Indians of Massachusetts Bay, according to early reports by the English, "took the first ship they saw for a walking island, the mast to be a tree, the sail white clouds, and the discharging of ordnance for lightning and thunder." They were seized by curiosity. By word of mouth, the fantastic news spread, and the "shores for many miles were filled with this naked Nation, gazing at this wonder." Armed with bows and arrows, some of them approached the ship in their canoes, and "let fly their long shafts at her...some stuck fast, and others dropped into the water." They wondered why "it did not cry."[2]

Indian dreams had anticipated the coming of the strangers. In an old Wampanoag story, a wise chief foretold the arrival of Europeans: "On his death-bed he said that a strange white people would come to crowd out the red men, and that for a sign, after his death a great white whale would rise out of the witch pond below. That night he died...and the great white whale rose from the witch pond." Another version of this story added a warning from the chief: "That's a sign that another new people the color of the whale [would arrive], but don't let them have all the land because if you do the Indians will disappear." In Virginia, a Powhatan shaman predicted that "bearded men should come & take away their Country & that there should be none of the original Indians be left, within an hundred & fifty years." Similarly, an Ojibwa prophet had a dream many years before actual contact between the two peoples: "Men of strange appearance have come across the great water. Their skins are white like snow, and on their faces long hair grows. [They come here] in wonderfully large canoes which have great white wings like those of a giant bird. The men have long and sharp knives, and they have long black tubes which they point at birds and animals. The tubes make a smoke that rises into the air just like the smoke from our pipes. From them come fire and such terrific noise that I was frightened, even in my dream."[3]

Across the Atlantic, William Shakespeare also had a dream

about the arrival of the English in America. *The Tempest* was first performed in London in 1611, a time when the English were encountering what they viewed as strange inhabitants in new lands. A perspicacious few in the audience could have seen that this play was more than a mere story about how Prospero was sent into exile with his daughter, took possession of an island inhabited by Caliban, and plotted to redeem himself.[4]

Indeed, *The Tempest* can be approached as a fascinating tale that served as a masquerade for the creation of a new society in America. Seen in this light, the play invites us to view English expansion not only as imperialism, but also as a defining moment in the making of an English-American identity based on race. For the first time in the English theater, an Indian character was being presented. What did Shakespeare and his audience know about the native peoples of America, and what choices were they making in the ways they characterized Caliban? Although they saw him as a "savage," did they racialize savagery? Was the play a prologue for America?[5]

The Tempest, studied in relationship to its context, can help us answer these questions. The timing of the play was crucial: it was first performed after the English invasion of Ireland but before the colonization of New England, after John Smith's arrival in Virginia but before the beginning of the tobacco economy, and after the first contacts with Indians but before full-scale warfare against them. This was an era when the English were interacting with peoples that they would define as the "Other" in order to enable them to delineate the boundary between "civilization" and "savagery." The social constructions of both these terms were dynamically developing on two frontiers—Ireland and America.

English Over Irish

Attending the first performance of *The Tempest*, London theatergoers were familiar with the "wild Irish" on stage, for such images had been presented in plays like *Sir John Oldcastle* (1599) and *Honest Whore* (1605). To many in the audience, Caliban might have resembled the Irish. In the late sixteenth century, shortly before the beginning of the English migrations to America, Queen Elizabeth I encouraged some of her subjects to take up private colonization projects in Ireland. This island to the west posed a military threat, her advisers warned, because either Spain or France might use Catholic Ireland as a base from which to attack England. Among Elizabeth's chosen soldiers were Sir Humphrey Gilbert and his half-brother Sir Walter Raleigh. Both were ardent Protestants who believed the Irish Catholics to be pagan savages—a view shared by many of their countrymen.[6]

Like Caliban, the Irish were viewed as a people living outside of "civilization." They had tribal organizations, and their practice of herding seemed nomadic. Even their Christianity was said to be merely the exterior of strongly rooted paganism. "They are all Papists by their profession," claimed Edmund Spenser in 1596, "but in the same so blindly and brutishly informed for the most part as that you would rather think them atheists or infidels." To the English colonizers, the Irish lacked "knowledge of God or good manners." They had no sense of private property and did not "plant any Gardens or Orchards, Inclose or improve their lands, live together in setled Villages or Townes." The Irish were described as lazy, "naturally" given to "idleness," and unwilling to work for "their own bread." Dominated by "innate sloth," "loose, barbarous and most wicked," and living "like beasts," they were also thought to be criminals inclined to steal from the English. The colonizers complained that the Irish were not satisfied with the "fruit of the natural unlaboured earth" and therefore continually "invaded the fertile possessions" of the "English Pale."[7]

The English colonizers established a two-tiered social structure: "Every Irishman shall be forbidden to wear English apparel or weapon upon pain of death. That no Irishman, born of Irish race and brought up Irish, shall purchase land, bear office, be chosen of any jury or admitted witness in any real or personal action." To reinforce this social separation, British laws prohibited marriages between the Irish and the colonizers. The new world order was to be one of English over Irish.[8]

The Irish also became targets of English violence. "Nothing but fear and force can teach duty and obedience" to this "rebellious people," the invaders insisted. While the English were generally brutal in their warfare practices at that time, they seemed to have been particularly cruel toward the Irish. The colonizers burned the villages and crops of the inhabitants and relocated them on reservations. They slaughtered families, "man, woman and child," justifying their atrocities by arguing that families provided support for the rebels.[9]

The invaders took the heads of the slain Irish as trophies. Sir Humphrey Gilbert pursued a campaign of terror: he ordered that "the heads of all those...killed in the day, should be cut off from their bodies and brought to the place where he encamped at night, and should there be laid on the ground by each side of the way leading into his own tent so that none could come into his tent for any cause but commonly he must pass through a lane of heads.... [It brought] great terror to the people when they saw the heads of their dead fathers, brothers, children, kinsfolk, and friends." After seeing the head of his lord impaled on the walls of Dublin, Irish poet Angus O'Daly cried out:

> O body which I see without a head,
> It is the sight of thee which has withered up
>   my strength.
> Divided and impaled in Ath-cliath,
> The learned of Banba will feel its loss.
> Who will relieve the wants of the poor?
> Who will bestow cattle on the learned?
> O body, since thou art without a head,
> It is not life which we care to choose after
>   thee.[10]

After four years of bloody warfare in Munster, according to Edmund Spenser, the Irish had been reduced to wretchedness. "Out of every corner of the woods and glens they came creeping forth upon their hands, for their legs would not bear them. They looked anatomies of death; they spake like ghosts crying out of their graves." The death toll was so high that "in short space there were none almost left and a most populous and plentiful country suddenly left void of man and beast." The "void" meant vacant lands for English settlement.[11]

The atrocities that had been committed against the Irish would in fact be committed again against the Indians by English veterans of the wars in Ireland.

English Over Indian

Sir Humphrey Gilbert, Lord De La Warr, Sir Francis Drake, and Sir Walter Raleigh participated in both the invasion of Ireland and the colonization of the New World. The conquest of Ireland and the settlement of Virginia were bound so closely together that one correspondence, dated March 8, 1610, stated: "It is hoped the plantation of Ireland may shortly be settled. The Lord Delaware [Lord De La Warr] is preparing to depart for the plantation of

Virginia." Commander John Mason conducted military campaigns against the Irish before he sailed to New England, where he led troops against the Pequots of Connecticut. Samuel Gorton wrote a letter to John Winthrop, Jr., connecting the two frontiers: "I remember the time of the wars in Ireland (when I was young, in Queen Elizabeth's days of famous memory) where much English blood was spilt by a people much like unto these [Indians]. . . . And after these Irish were subdued by force, what treacherous and bloody massacres have they attempted is well known."[12]

The first English colonizers in the New World found that the Indians reminded them of the Irish. In Virginia, Captain John Smith observed that the deerskin robes worn by the Indians did not differ much "in fashion from the Irish mantels." Thomas Morton noticed that the "Natives of New England [were] accustomed to build themselves houses much like the wild Irish." Roger Williams reported that the thick woods and swamps of New England gave refuge to the Indians engaged in warfare, "like the bogs to the wild Irish." Thus, in their early encounters, the English projected the familiar onto the strange, their images of the Irish onto the native people of America. Initially, "savagery" was defined in relationship to the Irish, and the Indians were incorporated into this definition.[13]

The Tempest, the London audience knew, was not about Ireland but about the New World, for the reference to the "Bermoothes" [Bermuda] revealed the location of the island where Prospero landed. What was happening on stage was a metaphor for English expansion into America. The play's title was inspired by a recent incident: caught in a violent storm in 1609, the *Sea Adventure* had been separated from a fleet of ships bound for Virginia and had run aground in the Bermudas. Shakespeare knew many of the colonizers of Virginia, including Sir Humphrey Gilbert and Lord De La Warr. One of his personal friends was geographer Richard Hakluyt, author of widely read books about the New World. England's future was in America, proclaimed Hakluyt as he urged the English to "conquer a country" and "to man it, to plant it, and to keep it, and to continue the making of Wines and Oils able to serve England."[14]

In the play, the images of Caliban's island evoked descriptions of Virginia. "The air breathes upon us here most sweetly," the theatergoers were told. "Here is everything advantageous to life." "How lush and lusty the grass looks! how green!" Gonzalo praised the Edenic island as a retreat where everything was as yet unformed and unbounded, where letters, laws, metals, and occupations were yet unknown. In both imagery and language, it was almost as if Shakespeare had lifted his materials from contemporary documents about the New World. Tracts on Virginia had described the air as "most sweet" and as "virgin and temperate," and its soil *"lusty"* with meadows "full of *green grass*." In *A True Reportory of the Wracke,* published in 1609, William Strachey depicted Virginia's abundance: "no Country yieldeth goodlier *Corn,* nor more manifold increase.... We have thousands of goodly *Vines*."[15]

Moreover, the play offered a clue that the story was indeed about America: Caliban, one of the principal characters, was a New World inhabitant. "Carib," the name of an Indian tribe, came to mean a savage of America, and the term *cannibal* was a derivative. Shakespeare sometimes rearranged letters in words ("Amleth," the name of a prince in a Viking-era tale, for example, became "Hamlet"), and here he had created the word "Caliban."[16]

The English had heard or read reports about Indians who had been captured and brought to London. Indians had been displayed in Europe by Christopher Columbus. During his first voyage, he wrote: "Yesterday came [to] the ship a dugout with six young men, and five came on board; these I ordered to be detained and I am bringing them." When Columbus was received by the Spanish court after his triumphal return, he presented a collection of things he had brought back, including some gold nuggets, parrots in cages, and six Indians. During his second voyage, in 1493, Columbus again sent his men to kidnap Indians and returned to Spain with 550 Indian captives. "When we reached the waters around Spain," Michele de Cuneo reported, "about 200 of those Indians died, I believe because of the unaccustomed air, colder than theirs. We cast them into the sea."[17]

Similarly, English explorers engaged in this practice of kidnapping Indians. When Captain George Waymouth visited New England in 1605, he lured some Abenakis to his ship; taking three of them hostage, he sailed back to England to display them. An early-seventeenth-century pamphlet stated that a voyage to Virginia was expected to bring back its quota of captured Indians: "Thus we shipped five savages, two canoes, with all their bows and arrows." In 1611, according to a biographer of William Shakespeare, "a native of New England called Epenew was brought to England...and 'being a man of so great a stature' was showed up and down London for money as a monster." In the play, Stephano considered capturing Caliban: "If I can recover him, and keep him tame, and get to Naples with him, he's a present for any emperor." Such exhibitions of Indians were "profitable investments," literary scholar Frank Kermode noted, and were "a regular feature of colonial policy under James I. The exhibits rarely survived the experience."[18]

To the spectators of these "exhibits," Indians personified "savagery." They were depicted as "cruel, barbarous and most treacherous." They were thought to be cannibals, "being most furious in their rage and merciless...not being content only to kill and take away life, but delight to torment men in the most bloody manner...flaying some alive with the shells of fishes, cutting off the members and joints of others by piecemeal and broiling on the coals, eating the collops of their flesh in their sight whilst they live." According to Sir Walter Raleigh, Indians had "their eyes in their shoulders, and their mouths in the middle of their breasts." In *Nova Brittania,* published in 1609, Richard Johnson described the Indians in Virginia as "wild and savage people," living "like herds of deer in a forest." One of their striking physical characteristics was their skin color. John Brereton described the New England Indians as "of tall stature, broad and grim visage, of a blacke swart complexion."[19]

Like Caliban, Indians seemed to lack everything the English identified as civilized—Christianity, cities, letters, and clothing. Unlike the English, Indians were allegedly driven by their passions, especially their sexuality. Amerigo Vespucci was struck by how the natives embraced and enjoyed the pleasures of their bodies: "They...are libidinous beyond measure, and the women far more than the men.... When they had the opportunity of copulating with Christians, urged by excessive lust, they defiled and prostituted themselves."[20]

Could Caliban ever become civilized? The native seemed educable, for Prospero had taught him a European language: "I took pains to make thee speak, taught thee each hour one thing or other. When thou didst not, savage, know thine own meaning, but wouldst gabble like a thing most brutish." Defiantly, the slave retorted: "You taught me language, and my profit on't is, I know how to curse. The red plague rid you for learning me your language." A Virginia tract stated that the colonizers should take Indian children and "train them up with gentleness, teach them our English tongue." In the contract establishing the Virginia Company in 1606, the king endorsed a plan to propagate the

"Christian Religion to such people" who as yet lived in "darkness and miserable ignorance of the true knowledge and worship of God." Three years later, the Virginia Company in London instructed the colony's governor to encourage missionaries to convert Indian children. They should be taken from their parents if necessary, since they were "so wrapped up in the fog and misery of their iniquity." A Virginia promotional tract stated that it was "not the nature of men, but the education of men" that made them "barbarous and uncivil." Savage Indians could and should be educated.[21]

All of these cultural constructs of Indians at this point in time were either the fantasy of Shakespeare or the impressions of policymakers and tract writers in London. What would happen to these images on the stage called history?

Virginia: To "Root Out" Indians as a People

The first English settlement in the New World was in Virginia, the ancestral homeland of some fourteen thousand Powhatans. An agricultural people, they cultivated corn—the mainstay of their subsistence. Their cleared fields were as large as one hundred acres, and they lived in palisaded towns, with forts, storehouses, temples, and framed houses covered with bark and reed mats. They cooked their food in ceramic pots and used woven baskets for storing corn; some of their baskets were constructed so skillfully they could carry water in them. The Powhatans had a sophisticated numbering system for evaluating their harvests. According to John Smith, they had numbers from one to ten, after which counting was done by tens to one hundred. There was also a word for "one thousand." The Powhatan calendar had five seasons: "Their winter some call *Popanow,* the spring *Cattaapeuk,* the sommer *Cohattayough,* the earing of their Corne *Nepinough,* the harvest and fall of the leafe *Taquitock.* From September until the midst of November are the chief Feasts and sacrifice."[22]

In Virginia, the initial encounters between the English and the Indians opened possibilities for friendship and interdependency. After arriving in 1607, the first one hundred twenty colonizers set up camp. Then, John Smith reported, came "the starving time." A year later, only thirty-eight of them were still alive, hanging precariously on the very edge of survival. The reality of America did not match the imagery of the New World as a garden; the descriptions of its natural abundance turned out to be exaggerated. Many of the English were not prepared for survival in the wilderness. "Now was all our provision spent...all help abandoned, each hour expecting the fury of the savages," Smith wrote. Fortunately, in that moment of "desperate extremity," the Powhatans brought food and rescued the starving strangers.[23]

A year later, several hundred more settlers arrived, and again they quickly ran out of provisions. They were forced to eat "dogs, cats, rats, and mice," even "corpses" dug from graves. "Some have licked up the blood which hath fallen from their weak fellows," a survivor reported. "One [member] of our colony murdered his wife, ripped the child out of her womb and threw it into the river, and after chopped the mother in pieces and salted her for his food, the same not being discovered before he had eaten part thereof." "So great was our famine," John Smith stated, "that a savage we slew and buried, the poorer sort took him up again and ate him; and so did diverse one another boiled and stewed with roots and herbs."[24]

Hostilities soon broke out, however, as the English tried to extort food supplies by attacking the Indians and destroying their villages. In 1608, an Indian declared: "We hear you are come from under the World to take our World from us." A year later, Governor Thomas Gates arrived in Virginia with instructions that the Indians be forced to labor for the colonizers and also make annual payments of corn and skins. The orders were brutally carried out. During one of the raids, the English soldiers attacked an Indian town, killing fifteen people and forcing many others to flee. Then they burned the houses and destroyed the cornfields. According to a report by commander George Percy, they marched the captured queen and her children to the river where they "put the Children to death...by throwing them overboard and shooting out their brains in the water."[25]

Indians were beginning to doubt that the two peoples could live together in peace. One young Indian told Captain John Smith: "[We] are here to intreat and desire your friendship and to enjoy our houses and plant our fields, of whose fruits you shall participate." But he did not trust the strangers: "We perceive and well know you intend to destroy us." Chief Powhatan had come to the same conclusion, and he told Smith that the English were not in Virginia to trade but to "invade" and "possess" Indian lands.[26]

Indeed, Smith and his fellow colonizers were encouraged by their culture of expansionism to claim entitlement to the land. In the play, the theatergoers were told: "I think he will carry this island home in his pocket and give it his son for an apple." Prospero declared that he had been thrust forth from Milan and "most strangely" landed on this shore "to be the lord on't." Projecting his personal plans and dreams onto the wilderness, he colonized the island and dispossessed Caliban. Feeling robbed, Caliban protested: "As I told thee before, I am subject to a tyrant, a sorcerer, that by his cunning hath cheated me of the island." But the English in Virginia did not see their taking of land as robbery. In 1609, Robert Gray declared that "the greater part" of the earth was "possessed and wrongfully usurped by wild beasts...or by brutish savages." A Virginia pamphlet argued that it was "not unlawful" for the English to possess "part" of the Indians' land.[27]

The English colonizers soon wanted more than just a "part" of Indian territory. Their need for land was suddenly intensified by a new development after 1613—the cultivation of tobacco as an export crop. The settlers increasingly coveted Indian lands, especially the already cleared fields. Tobacco agriculture stimulated not only territorial expansion but also immigration. During the "Great Migration" of 1618–23, the colony grew from 400 to 4,500 people.

In 1622, the natives tried to drive out the intruders, killing some three hundred colonizers. John Smith denounced the "massacre" and described the "savages" as "cruel beasts," who possessed "a more unnatural brutishness" than wild animals. The English deaths, Samuel Purchas argued, established the colonizers' right to the land: "Their carcasses, the dispersed bones of their countrymen...speak, proclaim and cry, This our earth is truly English, and therefore this Land is justly yours O English." English blood had watered the soil, entitling them to the land.

In retaliation, the English waged total war. "Now by right of war," the colonizers declared, they would "invade the Country, and destroy them who sought to destroy us." They felt they could sweep away their enemies and take even their developed lands. "We shall enjoy their cultivated places.... Now their cleared grounds in all their villages (which are situated in the fruitfulest places of the land) shall be inhabited by us." Their tactics of warfare were vicious and treacherous, even sadistic. "Victory may be gained in many ways," a colonizer declared: "by force, by surprise, by famine in burning their Corn, by destroying and burning their Boats, Canoes, and Houses...by pursuing and chasing them with our horses, and bloodhounds to draw after them, and mastives to tear them." In 1623, Captain William Tucker led his soldiers to a

Powhatan village, presumably to negotiate a peace treaty. After concluding the treaty, he persuaded the Indians to drink a toast, but he served them poisoned wine. An estimated two hundred Indians died instantly, and Tucker's soldiers then killed another fifty and "brought home parts of their heads." In 1629, a colonizer reported, the English forced a hostile Indian leader to seek peace by "continual incursions" and by "yearly cutting down, and spoiling their corn." The goal of the war was to "root out [the Indians] from being any longer a people."[28]

New England: The "Utter Extirpation" of Indians

What occurred in New England was a different story, however; here again, the play was preview. The theatergoers were told that Caliban was "a devil, a born devil" and that he belonged to a "vile race." On the stage, they saw Caliban, with long, shaggy hair and with distinct racial markers—"freckled" and dark in complexion. His distinctive physical characteristics signified intellectual incapacity. Caliban was "a thing of darkness" whose "nature nurture [could] never stick." In other words, he had natural qualities that precluded the possibility of becoming civilized through "nurture," or education. The racial distance between Caliban and Prospero was inscribed geographically. The native was forced to live on a reservation located in a barren region. "Here you sty [to lodge, to place in a pigpen or sty] me in this hard rock," he complained, "whiles you do keep from me the rest o' the island." Prospero justified this segregation, charging that the "savage" possessed distasteful qualities "which good natures could not abide to be with. Therefore wast thou deservedly confined into this rock, who hadst deserved more than a prison." The theatergoers saw Caliban's "sty" located emblematically at the back of the stage, behind Prospero's "study," signifying a hierarchy of white over dark and cerebral over carnal.[29]

Prospero believed he could dispossess Caliban of his island because the "savage" was simply living there. The English colonizers in New England, however, found the Indians already farming the land. In 1616, Captain John Smith sailed north from Virginia to explore the New England coast, where he found not wild men but farmers. The "paradise" of Massachusetts, he reported, was "all planted with corn, groves, mulberries, savage gardens." "The sea Coast as you pass shews you all along large Corne fields." Indeed, the tribes in New England were horticultural. For example, the Wampanoags, whom the Pilgrims encountered in 1620, were a farming people, with a representative political system as well as a division of labor, with workers specializing in arrow making, woodwork, and leathercrafts.[30]

The Wampanoags as well as the Pequots, Massachusetts, Nausets, Nipmucks, and Narragansetts cultivated corn. As the main source of life for these tribes, corn was the focus of many legends. A Narragansett legend told how a crow had brought this grain to New England: "These Birds, although they do the corn also some hurt, yet scarce one Native amongst a hundred will kill them, because they have a tradition, that the Crow brought them at first an Indian Grain of Corn in one Ear, and an Indian or French bean in another, from the Great God Kautantouwits field in the Southwest from whence...came all their Corn and Beans." A Penobscot account celebrated the gift of Corn Mother: during a time of famine, an Indian woman fell in love with a snake in the forest. Her secret was discovered one day by her husband, and she told him that she had been chosen to save the tribe. She instructed him to kill her with a stone ax and then drag her body through a clearing. "After seven days he went to the clearing and found the corn plant rising above the ground.... When the corn had born fruit and the silk of the corn ear had turned yellow he recognized in it the resemblance of his dead wife. Thus originated the cultivation of corn."[31]

These Indians had a highly developed agricultural system. Samuel de Champlain found that "all along the shore" there was "a great deal of land cleared up and planted with Indian corn." Describing their agricultural practices, he wrote: "They put in each hill three or four Brazilian beans [kidney beans].... When they grow up, they interlace with the corn...and they keep the ground very free from weeds. We saw there many squashes, and pumkins, and tobacco, which they likewise cultivate." According to Thomas Morton, Indians "dung[ed] their ground" with fish to fertilize the soil and increase the harvest. After visiting the Narragansetts in Rhode Island, John Winthrop, Jr., noted that although the soil in that region was "sandy & rocky," the people were able to raise "good corn without fish" by rotating their crops. "They have every one 2 fields," he observed, "which after the first 2 years they let one field rest each year, & that keeps their ground continually [productive]." According to Roger Williams, when the Indians were ready to harvest the corn, "all the neighbours men and women, forty, fifty, a hundred," joined in the work and came "to help freely." During their green corn festival, the Narragansetts erected a long house, "sometimes a hundred, sometimes two hundred feet long upon a plain near the Court...where many thousands, men and women," gathered. Inside, dancers gave money, coats, and knives to the poor. After the harvest, the Indians stored their corn for the winter. "In the sand on the slope of hills," according to Champlain, "they dig holes, some five or six feet, more or less, and place their corn and other grains in large grass sacks, which they throw into the said holes, and cover them with sand to a depth of three or four feet above the surface of the ground. They take away their grain according to their need, and it is preserved as well as it be in our granaries." Contrary to the stereotype of Indians as hunters and therefore savages, these Indians were farmers.[32]

This reality led to antagonistic competition over resources between the original inhabitants and the English strangers. Within ten years after the arrival of Winthrop's group, twenty thousand more settlers came to New England. This growing English population had to be squeezed into a limited area of arable land. Less than 20 percent of the region was useful for agriculture, and the Indians had already established themselves on the prime lands.[33]

What opened the way for the English appropriation of Indian lands was the massive deaths of the indigenous people due to unseen pathogens. When the colonizers began arriving in New England, they found that the Indian population was already being reduced by European diseases. By 1616, epidemics had been ravaging Indian villages. Victims of "virgin soil epidemics," the Indians lacked immunological defenses against the diseases that had been introduced by European explorers. After he arrived at Plymouth Rock in 1620, William Bradford reported that the Indians living near the trading house "fell sick of the smallpox, and died most miserably." The condition of those still alive was "lamentable." Their bodies were covered with "the pox breaking and mattering and running one into another, their skin cleaving" to the mats beneath them. When they turned their bodies, they found "whole sides" of their skin flaying off. In this terrible way, they died "like rotten sheep." After one epidemic, William Bradford recorded in his diary: "For it pleased God to visit these Indians with a great sickness and such a mortality that of a thousand, above nine and a half hundred of them died, and many of them did rot above ground for want of burial."[34]

The colonizers interpreted these Indian deaths as divinely sanctioned opportunities to take the land. John Winthrop declared that the decimation of Indians by smallpox manifested a Puritan destiny: God was "making room" for the settlers and "hath hereby cleared our title to this place." After an epidemic had swept through Indian villages, John Cotton claimed that the destruction was a sign from God: when the Lord decided to transplant his people, he made the country vacant for them to settle. Edward Johnson pointed out that epidemics had desolated "those places, where the English afterward planted."[35]

Indeed, many New England towns were founded on the very lands the Indians had been living on before the epidemics. The Plymouth colony itself was located on the site of the Wampanoag village of Pawtuxet. The Pilgrims had noticed the village was empty and the cornfields overgrown with weeds. "There is a great deal of Land cleared," one of them reported, "and hath beene planted with Corne three or foure yeares agoe." "Thousands of men have lived there, which died in a great plague not long since," another Pilgrim wrote; "and pity it was and is to see so many goodly fields, and so well seated, without men to dress and manure the same." During their first spring, the Pilgrims went out into those fields to weed and manure them. Fortunately, they had some corn seed to plant. Earlier, when they landed on Cape Cod, they had come across some Indian graves and found caches of corn. They considered this find, wrote Bradford, as "a special providence of God, and a great mercy to this poor people, that here they got seed to plant them corn the next year, or else they might have starved." The survival of these pallid strangers was so precarious that they probably would have perished had it not been for the seeds they found stored in the Indian burial grounds. Ironically, Indian death came to mean life for the Pilgrims.[36]

As the English population increased and as their settlements expanded, the settlers needed even more land. To justify the taking of territory, the colonizers argued that the original inhabitants were not entitled to the land, for they lacked a work ethic. Native men were pursuing "no kind of labour but hunting, fishing and fowling." Ownership of the land required its utilization. "The *Indians* are not able to make use of the one fourth part of the Land," argued Reverend Francis Higginson in 1630, "neither have they any settled places, as Towns to dwell in, nor any ground as they challenge for their owne possession, but change their habitation from place to place." "Fettered in the chains of idleness," William Wood of Boston complained in 1634, Indians would rather starve than work. Indians were sinfully squandering America's resources. Under their irresponsible guardianship, the land had become "all spoils, rots," and was "marred for want of manuring, gathering, ordering, etc." Like the "foxes and wild beasts," Indians did nothing "but run over the grass." Ignoring the presence of Indian farms in New England and claiming the Indians were lazy and unproductive, the English colonizers were determined to transform Indian lands into Puritan farms.[37]

Over the years, the expansion of English settlements led to wars. During the Pequot War of 1637, some seven hundred Pequots were killed by the English and their Indian allies. Describing the massacre at Fort Mystic, an English officer wrote: "Many were burnt in the fort, both men, women, and children.... There were about four hundred souls in this fort, and not above five of them escaped out of our hands. Great and doleful was the bloody sight." Commander John Mason explained that God had pushed the Pequots into a "fiery oven," "filling the place with dead bodies." During King Philip's War of 1675–76, the Wampanoag leader Metacom, also known as King Philip, united several tribes in a widespread attack on the English settlements. "By August 1676," wrote historian Jill Lepore, "when Philip was shot to death near his home in Mount Hope, twenty-five English towns, more than half of all the colonists' settlements in New England, had been ruined and the line of English habitation had been pushed back almost to the coast. The struggling colonists had nearly been forced to abandon New England entirely, and their losses left them desperately dependent on England for support." With support from their home country, however, the colonizers fought back and defeated King Philip's forces. In the end, some six thousand Indians died from combat and disease, and thousands more were shipped out of New England as slaves. Victorious, the English soldiers decapitated King Philip and staked his head for public viewing in Plymouth.[38]

Ministers led the way in justifying the English violence and atrocities aimed at the original inhabitants. Warfare against the Indians, Reverend Cotton Mather explained, was a conflict between the Devil and God: "The Devil decoyed those miserable savages [to New England] in hopes that the Gospel of the Lord Jesus Christ would never come here to destroy or disturb His *absolute empire* over them." Indian deaths were viewed as the destruction of devil worshippers. The Indians, Reverend Increase

Mather observed, were "so *Devil-driven* as to begin an unjust and bloody war upon the English, which issued in their speedy and utter extirpation from the face of God's earth." What was forged in the violent dispossession of the original inhabitants was an ideology that demonized the "savages."[39]

This demonization of Indians served complicated ends. The enemy was not only external but also internal. To the Puritans, the Indians were like Caliban, a "born devil": they had failed to control their appetites, to create boundaries separating mind from body. They represented what English men and women in America thought they were not, and, more important—what they must not become. As exiles living in the wilderness far from "civilization," the Puritans used their negative images of Indians to delineate the moral requirements they had set up for themselves. As sociologist Kai Erikson explained, "Deviant forms of behavior, by marking the outer edges of group life, give the inner structure its special character and thus supply the framework within which the people of the group develop an orderly sense of their own cultural identity.... One of the surest ways to confirm an identity, for communities as well as for individuals, is to find some way of measuring what one is *not*." By depicting Indians as demonic and savage, the Puritans, like Prospero, were able to define more precisely what they perceived as the danger of becoming Calibanized.[40]

The Indians represented a threat to the Puritan errand in America. "The wilderness through which we are passing to the Promised Land is all over fill'd with fiery flying serpents. Our Indian wars are not over yet," warned Reverend Cotton Mather. "We have too far degenerated into Indian vices. The vices of the Indians are these: They are very lying wretches, and they are very lazy wretches; and they are out of measure indulgent unto their children; there is no family government among them. We have [become] shamefully Indianized in all those abominable things." The wars were now within the Puritan self and society; the dangers were internal. Vigilance against sin was required, or else the English would become like the Indians.[41]

To be "Indianized" meant to serve the Devil. Cotton Mather thought this was what had happened to Mercy Short, a young girl who had been a captive of the Indians and who was suffering from tormenting fits. According to Mather, Short had seen the Devil. "Hee was not of a Negro, but of a Tawney, or an Indian colour," she said; "he wore an high-crowned Hat, with straight Hair; and had one Cloven-foot." During a witchcraft trial, Mather reported,

George Burroughs had lifted an extremely heavy object with the help of the Devil, who resembled an Indian. Puritan authorities hanged an English woman for worshipping Indian "gods" and for taking the Indian devil-god Hobbamock for a husband.[42]

For the Puritans, to become Indian was the ultimate horror, for they believed Indians were "in very great subjection" of the Devil who "kept them in a continual slavish fear of him." Governor Bradford harshly condemned Thomas Morton and his fellow prodigals of the Merrymount settlement for their promiscuous partying with Indians: "They also set up a maypole, drinking and dancing about it many days together, inviting the Indian women for their consorts, dancing and frisking together like so many fairies." Interracial cavorting threatened to fracture a cultural and moral border—the frontier of Puritan identity. Congress of bodies, white and "tawney," signified defilement, a frightful boundlessness. If the Puritans were to become wayward like the Indians, it would mean that they had succumbed to savagery and failed to shrivel the sensuous parts of the self. To be "Indianized" meant to be decivilized, to be "Devil-driven."[43]

Indians came to personify the Devil and everything the Puritans feared—the body, sexuality, laziness, sin, and the loss of self-control. They had no place in a "new England." This was the Puritan triumph trumpeted by Edward Johnson in his *Wonder-Working Providence*. Where there had originally been "hideous Thickets" for wolves and bears, he proudly exclaimed in 1654, there were now streets "full of Girls and Boys sporting up and down, with a continued concourse of people." Initially, the colonizers themselves had lived in "wigwams" like Indians, but now they had "orderly, fair, and well-built houses...together with Orchards filled with goodly fruit trees, and gardens with variety of flowers." The settlers had also expanded the market, making New England a center of production and trade. The settlers had turned "this Wilderness" into "a mart." Merchants from Holland, France, Spain, and Portugal were coming here. "Thus," proclaimed Johnson, "hath the Lord been pleased to turn one of the most hideous, boundless, and unknown Wildernesses in the world in an instant...to a well-ordered Commonwealth."[44]

Within the English settlements, however, some misgivings about the violent English advance of "civilization" against "savagery" surfaced in a widely read book, *A True History of the Captivity and Restoration of Mrs. Mary Rowlandson,* published in 1682. Retaliating for English attacks on their villages during King Philip's War in 1676, a band of Narragansetts raided a small town, capturing several settlers, including Rowlandson. In her captivity story, she described living with the Indians for eleven weeks.

Although her account reflected and reinforced English stereotypes of Indians as "barbarous creatures," "merciless and cruel heathens," and "hellhounds," it also contained stories that challenged these negative images. Rowlandson related, for example, how some of the Indians had noticed that she lacked the strength to carry her wounded six-year-old daughter, so they put her on a horse with the child on her lap. One cold day, an Indian woman welcomed Rowlandson into her wigwam to give her warmth and some ground nuts. Afterward, she told the English woman to come back again sometime. Commenting on this hospitality, Rowlandson wrote: "Yet these were strangers to me that I never saw before." On another occasion, the Indian leader, King Philip, asked her to knit a shirt for his son and paid her a shilling for it. She also knitted a cap for the boy, and King Philip invited her to eat dinner with his family. Rowlandson contrasted the Indians in retreat with the English in pursuit. In the dead of winter, the Indians were able to survive by eating nuts, roots, and weeds as well as wild animals; whereas the English soldiers ran out of provisions and were forced to return to the settlements. Indian resourcefulness impressed Rowlandson: "I did not see (all the time I was among them) one man, woman, or child, dy with hunger."[45]

Rowlandson's observations, acknowledging the humanity of the Indians, offered possibilities for the English to understand, even empathize with, the people they were dispossessing. But the Prosperos in power would not allow such possibilities to be pursued. Instead, like Frederick Jackon Turner's frontiersman, they would continue their relentless conquest of the continent.

Stolen Lands: A World Turned "Upside Down"

Progress for white Americans was leading to poverty for indigenous Americans. In a 1789 petition to the Assembly of Connecticut, the Mohegans lamented that "the times" had been "Exceedingly alter'd":

Yea the Times have turn'd everything Upside down, or rather we have Chang'd the good Times, Chiefly by the help of the White People. For in Times past our Fore-Fathers lived in Peace, Love and great harmony, and had everything in Great plenty. When they

Wanted meat they would just run into the Bush a little ways with their Weapons and would Soon bring home good venison, Racoon, Bear and Fowl. If they Choose to have Fish, they Wo'd only go to the River or along the Sea Shore and they wou'd presently fill their Cannous With Veriety of Fish, both Scaled and shell Fish, and they had abundance of Nuts, Wild Fruit, Ground Nuts and Ground Beans, and they planted but little Corn and Beans and they kept no Cattle or Horses for they needed none. And they had no Contention about their Lands, it lay in Common to them all, and they had but one large Dish and they Cou'd all eat together in Peace and Love. But alas, it is not so now, all our Fishing, Hunting and Fowling is entirely gone. And we have now begun to Work on our Land, keep Cattle, Horses and Hogs And We Build Houses and fence in Lots, And now we plainly See that one Dish and one Fire will not do any longer for us. Some few there are Stronger than others and they will keep off the poor, weak, the halt and the Blind, And Will take the Dish to themselves. Yea, they will rather Call White People and Molattoes to eat With them out of our Dish, and poor Widows and Orphans Must be pushed one side and there they Must Set a Crying, Starving and die.[46]

Ever since the arrival of the English strangers in Jamestown in 1607 and at Plymouth Rock in 1620, the Indians' story had been one of stolen lands, sickness, suffering, starvation, and sadness. After the War of Independence in 1776 and the founding of a new nation, the original people of the land ominously asked: What would the future hold for them, with the advance of "civilization" against "savagery" westward across America to the Pacific?

This was the question addressed by one of the Founding Fathers—a young lawyer, Virginia planter, and author of the Declaration of Independence. In 1781, as governor of Virginia, Thomas Jefferson declared to the Kaskaskias that whites and Indians were both "Americans, born in the same land," and that he hoped the two peoples would "long continue to smoke in friendship together." At the same time, Jefferson advocated the removal and even the destruction of hostile Indians. "Nothing will reduce those wretches so soon as pushing the war into the heart of their country," he wrote to a colleague in 1776. "But I would not stop there. I would never cease pursuing them while one of them remained on this side [of] the Mississippi. We would never cease pursuing them with war while one remained on the face of the earth." In his view, Indians had to be civilized or exterminated.[47]

To become civilized, Jefferson believed, Indians had to give up their hunting way of life and transform themselves into farmers. As president, he explained to the Shawnees why they had no choice but to accept civilization: "When the white people first came to this land, they were few, and you were many; now we are many, and you few; and why? because, by cultivating the earth, we produce plenty to raise our children, while yours...suffer for want of food...are exposed to weather in your hunting camps, get diseases and die. Hence it is that your numbers lessen." They were, in other words, victims of their own culture, not of the introduction of unfamiliar diseases, the appropriation of their lands, and the brutal warfare waged against them.[48]

In blaming the Indians for their own decline, Jefferson was defensive, insisting that the transfer of Indian lands to whites had been done fairly and legally. "That the lands of this country were taken from them by conquest," he argued in *Notes on the State of Virginia,* "is not so general a truth as is supposed. I find in our historians and records, repeated proofs of purchase." If Jefferson's denial of guilt contained a quality of shrillness, there was a reason for it. In the original manuscript, he had written and then crossed out: "It is true that these purchases were sometimes made with the price in one hand and the sword in the other."[49]

In order to survive, Jefferson declared, Indians must adopt the culture of the white man. They must no longer live so boundlessly; instead, they must enclose farms as private property and learn arithmetic so they could keep accounts of their production. "My children," President Jefferson told the Cherokees, "I shall rejoice to see the day when the red man, our neighbors, become truly one people with us, enjoying all the rights and privileges we do, and living in peace and plenty as we do.... But are you prepared for this? Have you the resolution to leave off hunting for your living, to lay off a farm for each family to itself, to live by industry, the men working that farm with their hands...?" "Indians must learn how," Jefferson explained, "a little land, well cultivated, was superior in value to a great deal, unimproved." Jefferson assured the Indians that whites would respect their territorial possessions. "We take from no nation what belongs to it," he told them. "Our growing numbers make us always willing to buy lands from our red brethren, when they are willing to sell." He elaborated: "Your lands are your own; your right to them shall never be violated by us; they are yours to keep or to sell as you please.... When a want of land in a particular place induces us to ask you to sell, still you are always free to say 'No.'"[50]

While he offered these assurances, however, Jefferson worked to create conditions that would make Indians "willing to sell." In an 1803 "Confidential Message" to Congress, he explained how this could be done. First, encourage them to abandon hunting and turn to agriculture. "The extensive forests necessary in the hunting life will then become useless." Second, sell more manufactured goods to Indians by multiplying the trading houses and bring them into the market. This policy, Jefferson predicted, would lead the Indians to transfer their lands to whites. On February 27, 1803, in an "unofficial and private" letter to Indiana governor William Henry Harrison, Jefferson recommended: "To promote this disposition to exchange lands, which they have to spare and we want, we shall push our trading houses, and be glad to see the good and influential individuals among them run in debt, because we observe that when these debts get beyond what the individuals can pay, they become willing to lop them off by a cession of lands." To destroy Indians financially, Jefferson favored federal over private trading houses. While private business had to make profits, government enterprise could sell goods to Indians at prices "so low as merely to repay us cost and charges." By this process, he continued, white settlements would gradually "circumscribe" the Indians, and in time they would either "incorporate" with whites as "citizens" or retreat westward beyond civilization. In a letter to John Adams, Jefferson pointed out that Indians who rejected assimilation would face a dismal future. "These will relapse into barbarism and misery, lose numbers by war and want, and we shall be obliged to drive them, with the beasts of the forests into the Stony mountains."[51]

Ultimately, for Jefferson, Indians as Indians would not be allowed to remain within the borders of civilized society. In the seventeenth century, Edward Johnson had celebrated the disappearance of wolves and bears in "new" England; now Jefferson and men like him were clearing more wilderness for a new nation. The very transformation of the land emblematized progress, the distance whites in America had come from the time when barbarism had been dominant. In a letter to a friend written in the last year of his life, in 1824, Jefferson offered his vision of an American empire:

Let a philosophic observer commence a journey from the savages of the Rocky Mountains, eastwardly towards our sea-coast. There he would observe in the earliest stage of association living under no law but that of nature, subsisting and covering themselves with flesh and skins of wild beasts. He would next find those on our frontiers in the pastoral state, raising domestic animals to supply the defects of hunting. Then succeed our own semi-barbarous citizens, the pioneers of the advance of civilization, and so in progress he would meet the gradual shades of improving man until he would reach his, as yet, most improved state in our seaport towns. This, in fact, is equivalent to a survey, in time, of the progress of man from infancy to the present day.[52]

Here was a Jeffersonian version of John Winthrop's "city upon a hill." The land was not to be allowed to "lie waste without any improvement," the early forefathers had commanded, and now the republican "errand into the wilderness" was requiring the citizens of the new nation to subdue the land and advance their frontier westward. Such a view carried dire consequences for the Calibans of America called Indians. Like Prospero before him, Jefferson saw the westward advance of the frontier as the movement from "savagery" to "civilization."

3

⚜

THE HIDDEN ORIGINS
OF SLAVERY

BUT CALIBAN COULD have been African. As they watched *The Tempest* in London in 1611, theatergoers were told that Caliban was "freckled," dark in complexion. His father was a demon and his mother was Sycorax, a witch who had lived in Africa.[1]

Some people in the audience might have seen Africans in England. In 1554, according to trader William Towrson, five "Negroes" were transported to England where they were "kept till they could speak the language," and then they were taken back to Africa as translators for English traders. Two decades later, in 1578, voyager George Best stated: "I myself have seen an Ethiopian as black as coal brought into England, who taking a faire English woman to wife, begat a son in all respects as black as the father was...." Best speculated about the cause of the African's skin color: "It seemeth this blackness proceedeth rather of some natural infection of that man, which was so strong that neither the nature of the Clime, neither the good complexion of the mother concurring, could anything alter."[2]

What struck the English most about Africans was their color. "These people are all blacke, and are called Negros, without any apparell, saving before their privities," wrote an English traveler during his visit to Cape Verde in the 1560s. Similarly, Robert Baker described the Africans:

> And entering in [a river], we see
> a number of blacke soules,
> Whose likelinesse seem'd men to be,
> but all as blacke as coles.

In the English mind, the color black was freighted with an array of negative images: "deeply stained with dirt," "foul," "dark or deadly" in purpose, "malignant," "sinister," "wicked." The color white, on the other hand, signified purity, innocence, and goodness.[3]

"Brutish," Caliban seemed to personify what the English considered African traits. Travel reports described Africans as "a people of beastly living, without a God, law, religion." Their color allegedly made them "Devils incarnate." The Devil had "infused prodigious Idolatry into their hearts, enough to rellish his pallat and aggrandize their tortures," and to "fry their souls, as the raging Sun had already scorched their coal-black carcasses." Africans were also said to be cannibals: they allegedly ate human beings as the English would eat "befe or mutton."[4]

Belonging to a libidinous race, in Shakespeare's portrayal, Caliban was driven by the passions of his body. Prospero saw him as a sexual threat to the nubile Miranda, her "virgin-knot" yet unbroken. "I have used thee (filth as thou art) with humane care," Prospero scolded Caliban, "and lodged thee in mine own cell till thou didst seek to violate the honor of my child." And the surly native snapped: "O ho, O ho! Would't had been done! Thou didst prevent me; I had peopled else this isle with Calibans." In contrast, belonging to a civilized race, Prospero raised his mind or rationality to authority over his instinctual life.[5]

Like Prospero, the English colonists in the Virginia wilderness felt a great urgency to destroy, as historian Winthrop Jordan wrote so brilliantly and poetically, "the living image of primitive aggressions which they said was the Negro but was really their own." Far away from the security and surveillance of society in England, the colonists feared the possibility of losing self-control over their passions. "Intermixture and insurrection, violent sex and sexual violence, creation and destruction, life and death — the stuff of animal existence was rumbling at the gates of rational and moral judgment." If the gates fell, the colonists feared, so would civilization. Thus they projected onto blacks their hidden and rejected instinctual parts of human nature. Jordan imagined the English colonizers insisting: "We, therefore, we do not lust and destroy; it is someone else. We are not great black bucks of the fields. But a buck *is* loose, his great horns menacing to gore into us with life and destruction. Chain him, either chain him or expel his black shape from our midst, before we realize that he is ourselves."[6]

How did this English fear of sensuality play out in the history of Virginia? And how did it intersect with "the hidden origins of slavery"?

A View from the Cabins: Black and White Together

Again, *The Tempest* offers clues. In the theater, the audience heard Prospero refer to the African as "Caliban, my slave." "We cannot miss him. He does make our fire, fetch our wood, and serves in offices that profits us." When Shakespeare's play was first performed in London, there were no Africans in Virginia. Indeed, the introduction of Africans was something that had not even been considered at the time.[7]

In 1613, two years after the play was first performed in London, the colony sent its first shipment of tobacco to London, a small but significant four barrels. The exports grew dramatically from 2,300 pounds in 1616 to 19,000 the following year, and to 60,000 by 1620. Virginia's rapidly rising tobacco economy generated an insatiable demand for labor.

In 1619, a Virginia colonizer recorded a momentous event in the history of the English New World. "About the last of August," wrote John Rolfe in his diary, "came in a dutch man of warre that sold us twenty Negars."[8]

The first Africans to be landed in Virginia had probably been captured in wars or raids by enemy tribes before they were sold as slaves. Their ordeal must have been similar to the experience of Olaudah Equiano. After serving as a slave, he purchased his freedom and wrote an account of his captivity:

> The first object which saluted my eyes when I arrived on the coast was the sea, and a slaveship, which was then riding at anchor, and waiting for its cargo. These filled me with astonishment, which was soon converted into terror.... When I was carried on board I was immediately handled, and tossed up, to see if I were sound,

by some of the crew; and I was now persuaded that I had got into a world of bad spirits, and that they were going to kill me. Their complexions too differing so much from ours, their long hair, and the language they spoke, which was very different from any I had ever heard, united to confirm me in this belief.... When I looked round the ship too, and saw a large furnace or copper boiling, and a multitude of black people of every description chained together, every one of their countenances expressing dejection and sorrow, I no longer doubted of my fate; and, quite overpowered with horror and anguish, I fell motionless on the deck and fainted.... I was soon put down under the decks, and there I received such a salutation in my nostrils as I had never experienced in my life; so that, with the loathsomeness of the stench, and crying together, I became so sick and low that I was not able to eat.... [After a long voyage, the slaves finally sighted land.] We thought...we should be eaten by these ugly men...and...there was much dread and trembling among us, and nothing but bitter cries to be heard all the night from these apprehensions, insomuch that at last the white people got some old slaves from the land to pacify us. They told us we were not to be eaten, but to work.[9]

Though they had been "sold," the first Africans in Virginia probably were not slaves, persons reduced to property and required to work without wages for life. In 1619, Virginia had no law legalizing slavery. Like many English colonists, the Africans were sold as indentured servants, bound by contract to serve a master for four to seven years in order to repay the expense of their passage.

Curiously, for a long time, Africans remained a very small percentage of the work force.[10] The African population in Virginia increased very slowly—a contrast to the English colony in the Barbados of the West Indies, where there were 20,000 Africans by 1660, constituting a majority of the total population. In 1650, Africans constituted only 300 of Virginia's 15,000 inhabitants, or 2 percent. In 1675, of the colony's approximately 32,000 inhabitants, blacks totaled only 1,600, or 5 percent.[11]

Why were so few Africans being imported into Virginia when the demand for labor was so great and constantly inclining?

Carrying to Virginia negative images of Africans, English planters undoubtedly felt hesitant about peopling their colony with Calibans. Unlike their counterparts in the Barbados, they were not primarily businessmen seeking to make money and return to England. Rather, they had brought their families with them and were planning to stay. They had come to the colony intending to create a reproduction of English society in Virginia. Thus, in the early decades of the Virginia colony, planters chose to rely on white indentured servants. In the seventeenth century, 75 percent of the colonists came as servants. In 1664, the Council of Foreign Plantations reported that the colony's population had been "increased principally by sending of Servants." Tobacco agriculture and the generation of profits depended on these white workers. Describing how one planter with six indentured servants had made a thousand pounds with one crop of tobacco, John Pory of Virginia observed: "Our principal wealth...consisteth in servants."[12]

Recruited in England but also Germany and Ireland, these men and women were the outcasts of society. They included convicts, "rogues, vagabonds, whores, cheats, and rabble of all descriptions, raked from the gutter," as well as individuals who had been "decoyed, deceived, seduced, inveigled, or forcibly kidnapped and carried as servants to the plantations."[13] Like the Africans, many of the white indentured servants came involuntarily, "spirited" here by unscrupulous recruiters. The "spirits," an Englishman reported, "take up all the idle, lazie, simple people they can entice, such as have professed idleness, and will rather beg than work." In an English court, Christian Chacrett was accused of being "a Spirit, one that [took] up men and women and children and [sold] them on a ship to be conveyed beyond the sea" to Virginia. Some of the servants were victims of the Irish "slave trade." In Ireland, English poor laws for the correction and punishment of rogues and idle people led to the wholesale kidnapping of young women and men to supply the labor needs of the colonies. One of them, John King, recalled how he and others were "stolen in Ireland" by English soldiers. Taken from their beds at night "against their Consents," they were put on a ship. "Weeping and Crying," the Irish captives were kept on board until "a Lord's day morning" when the ship set sail for Virginia.[14]

Coming from different shores, white and black laborers had very limited understanding of each other. Mutual feelings of fear and hostility undoubtedly existed. Still, they shared a condition of exploitation and abuse. The workers were sometimes forced to wear iron collars around their necks, often beaten and even tortured for recalcitrance, and always required to have passes whenever they left their plantations. Together, these exploited men and women of two races experienced the day-to-day exhaustion and harshness of plantation labor. They had to cut trees and clear brush, plow the soil and prepare it for planting. In the hot and humid tobacco fields, they worked side by side—their backs bent over row after row of tobacco, their arms sore from topping young plants, their legs cramped from carrying heavy loads of tobacco leaves to the wagons, their nostrils filled with dust, and their ears stinging from the barking commands of their masters. Weary from a day of toil, they returned to their roughly built cabins and huts, where they were fed a dreary mess made from ground Indian corn called "loblolly." A white servant in Virginia was undoubtedly expressing the anguish of many laborers, whether from England or Africa, when he wrote: "I thought no head had been able to hold so much water as hath and doth daily flow from mine eyes."[15]

Occasionally, perhaps often, whites and blacks ran away together. In one case, the Virginia court declared: "Whereas [six English] Servants and Jno. a negro Servant hath Run away and Absented themselves from their masters Two months. It is ordered that the Sherriffe take Care that all of them be whipped...and Each of them have thirty nine lashes well layed on." The problem of absconding workers became so serious that the Virginia legislature complained about "English servants running away with Negroes."[16]

Some blacks and whites formed another kind of partnership. In 1630, the Virginia court decided that Hugh Davis was "to be soundly whipped before an assembly of negroes and others for abusing himself to the dishonor of God and the shame of Christianity by defiling his body in lying with a negro." Ten years later, the Virginia court punished a white man and a black woman: "Whereas Robert Sweat hath begotten with child a negro woman servant belonging unto Lieutenant Sheppard, the court hath therefore ordered that the said negro woman shall be whipped at the whipping post and the said Sweat shall tomorrow in the forenoon do public pennance for his offence at James city church in the time of divine service." Similarly, William Watts, a white man, and Mary, a black servant, were punished for fornication in 1649. A year later, a white man and black woman, found guilty of having sexual relations, were required to stand clad in white sheets before a congregation. In 1667, the court convicted Irish servant John Dorman of getting a "Negro woman" with child. Between 1690 and 1698 in Westmoreland County, fourteen white women were punished for having illegitimate children; at least four of the nineteen children were mulatto.[17]

Increasingly, black servants were singled out for special treatment. In 1640, for example, the Virginia legislature passed a law stating that masters should furnish arms to all men, "excepting negros." Blacks were also serving longer time periods for indenture as punishment for running away. In 1640, for example, three runaway servants—two white men and a black man—were captured and returned. They were each given thirty lashes. In addition, both white men were required to work for their masters for an additional year and for the colony for three more years. But the third runaway received the most severe punishment: "Being a Negro named John Punch shall serve his said master or his assigns for the time of his natural Life here or elsewhere." During the same year, six white men and a black man were arrested for running away. Communicating between two plantations, they had carefully planned their escape and gathered "corn powder and shot and guns"; after stealing a skiff and sailing down the Elizabeth River, they were apprehended. One of the white men, Christian Miller, received an especially harsh penalty—thirty lashes, an "R" (for Rogue) to be burned into his cheek, a shackle on his leg for at least a year, and seven years of service to the colony after he had completed his obligation to his master. The Negro Emanuel was given a similar punishment, except he was not ordered to serve additional time, implying he was required to labor for life.[18]

Some estate inventories showed that African laborers were more highly valued than English indentured servants, indicating that the former had a longer period of bound service. For example, the inventory of the estate of William Burdett, dated November 13, 1643, included this list:

	lb tobacco
Sarah Hickman to serve one year at	0700
John Gibbs to serve one year at	0650
Nehemia Coventon Aged 12 years to serve 8 years at	1000
Symon Caldron a boy very Lame and 14 years old to serve 7	0500
William Young another boy full of the scurvey to serve six years at	0600
Edward Southerne a little Boy very sick having seven years to serve at	0700
Michael Pacey a boy to serve six years at	1100
Caine the negro, very ancient at	3000

One negro girl about 8 years old at	2000
32 goats young and old at	2500
A parcel of hogs at	1800

What was happening was evident: Africans were being degraded into a condition of servitude for life.[19]

Other documents reveal they had also become property. According to the Virginia court records of 1642, Thomas Jacob transferred a "negro Woman Susan" to Bridgett Seaverne and her son: "I do hereby declare that I have given the negro unto them and their heirs and Assigns Freely forever." Two years later, William Hawley borrowed money from William Stone and provided as collateral "my Negro Mingo." In 1646, Francis Pott sold a Negro woman and boy to Stephen Charlton "to the use of him...forever." Wills provided that white servants were to serve their "full term of time" and Negroes "forever." A 1648 deed included a provision for a "Negro woman and all her increase (which for future time shall be born of her body)." In 1652, a Negro girl was sold to H. Armsteadinger "and his heirs...forever with all her increase both male and female." A year later, William Whittington sold John Pott "one Negro girl named Jowan; aged about Ten years and with her Issue and produce during her (or either of them) for their Life time. And their Successors forever." In 1645, Ralph Wormeley presented in court a certificate of a gift to Agatha Stubbings in "Consideration of Matrimony"—"Four Negro men and Two women...Ten Cows, six Draft Oxen." Africans had become classified as property: slaves as well as their future children could be inherited and also presented as gifts. By the 1650s, 70 percent of the blacks in Virginia were serving as de facto slaves.[20]

In 1661, the Virginia Assembly began to institutionalize slavery, to make it de jure. A law regarding the punishment of servants referred to "those Negroes who are incapable of making satisfaction by addition of time." In other words, they were required to serve for life. Eight years later, the Virginia legislature defined a slave as property, a part of the owner's "estate."[21]

Despite the fact that Africans had been reduced to slaves and that a system of upaid labor was more profitable than paid labor, planters still preferred to depend on white indentured servants. After 1670, there was a decrease in the number of indentured servants migrating to Virginia. The labor shortage, however, did not turn planters to Africa as a more reliable source of labor. "It was not until at least a decade after the decline in the supply of [white indentured] servants," historian Russell Menard observed, "that the number of blacks imported each year rose above a trickle." Why did the importation of Africans suddenly rise above "a trickle" in the late seventeenth century?[22]

"English and Negroes in Armes": Bacon's Rebellion

Here again, *The Tempest* can be illuminating. The theatergoers were given a scenario that was uncanny in its anticipation of what would happen in Virginia. What they saw on stage was an inter-racial class revolt to overthrow Prospero. When the jester, Trin-culo, and the butler, Stephano, first encountered Caliban, they found him repulsive—a fishlike monster and a devil. They gave him wine, and the inebriated islander offered to show Trinculo every "fertile inch o' the island." To his fellow servants, Caliban declared his desire to be free from Prospero's tyranny:

> *No dams I'll make for fish,*
> *Nor fetch in firing*
> *At requiring,*
> *Nor scrape trenchering, nor wash dish.*
> *'Ban, 'Ban, Ca-Caliban*
> *Has a new master. Get a new man.*
> *Freedom, highday! highday, freedom!*
> *freedom, highday, freedom!*

Seeking freedom, Caliban concocted a plot for rebellion. If Stephano would kill Prospero ("knock a nail into his head"), the butler would become the lord of the island and husband of Miranda. Caliban promised: "She will become thy bed." Stirred, the butler exclaimed: "Lead, monster; we'll follow." Warned in advance about the "foul conspiracy of the beast Caliban and his confederates," Prospero unleashed his hunting dogs against the rebels: "Fury, Fury! There, Tyrant, there! Go, charge my goblins that they grind their joints." Thus Prospero suppressed an interracial insurrection rooted in class, a condition shared by Caliban and Stephano as workers.[23]

Like Prospero, the English elite in Virginia erected a hierarchi-cal racial and class structure. Most English colonists had migrated to Virginia as indentured servants. They planned to complete their period of indenture and become landowners. According to Governor William Berkeley, white servants came with a "hope of bettering their condition in a Growing Country." The American expanse seemed to offer them the possibility of starting over, creating new selves and new lives. Land in Virginia, taken from the Indians, was available and cheap. After completing the time and terms of their servitude, indentured servants became freemen; as such, they could claim title to fifty acres of land. As landholders, they could nurture the hope of becoming wealthy through tobacco agriculture.[24]

The profitability of tobacco production, however, unleashed a land boom. Colonists with financial advantage scrambled to possess the best lands along the navigable rivers. Representing a landed elite, they dominated the Virginia assembly and began to enact legislation to advance and protect their class interests. They passed laws that extended the time of indentured servitude for whites and increased the length of service for white runaways. In this way, they minimized competition for lands and at the same time maximized the supply of white laborers by keeping them in servitude for as long as possible.[25]

Finding it increasingly difficult to become landowners, many white freemen and indentured servants were becoming angry and frustrated: they felt they had been duped into coming to America. In 1649, pamphleteer William Bullock warned planters about the men and women who, "not finding what was promised," had become "dejected." In England, they had been viewed as the "Surcharge of necessitous people, the matter or fuel of dangerous insurrections." In Virginia, they became an even greater threat to social order, joining what the planter elite fearfully called a "giddy multitude"—a discontented class of indentured servants, slaves, and landless freemen, both white and black, the Stephanos as well as the Calibans of Virginia. This unruly underclass constituted a volatile element. In the early 1660s, for example, indentured servant Isaac Friend led a conspiracy to band together forty servants and "get Arms." He issued the rebellious cry: "Who would be for Liberty, and free from bondage" join the revolt. Many others would flock to their armed campaign. Together they would "go through the Country and kill those that made any opposition," and would "either be free or die for it." The authorities were informed about Friend's plan and quickly suppressed the plot. Again, in 1663, a Gloucester court accused nine "Laborers" of conspiring to overthrow the Virginia government and sentenced several of them to be executed. This incident gave planters a frightening example of "the horror" in Virginia—the presence of "villains" engaged in a "barbarous design" to subvert "rights and privileges" in the colony.[26]

Unruliness and discontent, however, continued to grow. Fearing this landless class, the Virginia legislature restricted suffrage to landowners in 1670. Governor William Berkeley reported the explosive class conditions in his colony, where "six parts of seven" of the people were "Poor Indebted Discontented and Armed." The ownership of guns was widespread among whites, for every white man had a right to bear arms and was required by law to have a gun in order to help defend the colony. The landed elite distrusted this class of armed poor whites so much that they were even afraid to organize them for military service. On one occasion, in 1673, Governor Berkeley raised troops to defend Virginia against Dutch warships, but he did so very reluctantly. Of the men he enlisted in his army, Berkeley apprehensively noted, at least one-third were freemen or debtors. They could not be trusted, he cautioned, for in battle, they might revolt and join the enemy "in hopes of bettering their Condition by Sharing the Plunder of the Country with them."[27]

Three years later, the revolt Berkeley feared took place, led by Nathaniel Bacon, a planter in upcountry Virginia. To address the Indian threat in the back region of the colony, Bacon raised a militia from the ranks of the "giddy multitude." Bacon's actions shocked Berkeley and his council, who were more worried about armed white freemen than hostile Indians. In their view, Bacon's followers were a "Rabble Crew, only the Rascallity and meanest of the people...there being hardly two amongst them that we have heard of who have Estates or are persons of Reputation and indeed very few who can either write or read." Ignoring their concerns, Bacon led a march against the Indians, killing hostile Susquehannahs as well as friendly Occaneechees. He justified his expedition as a "Glorious" defense of the country. But Governor Berkeley angrily declared Bacon a rebel and charged him with treason, an act punishable by death. Bacon retaliated by marching five hundred armed men to Jamestown, the seat of government in Virginia.[28]

Furnished arms by the white rebels, black men joined Bacon's army. They realized that they had a greater stake in the rebellion than their fellow white rebels, for many of them were servants bound for life. Black and white together, Bacon's soldiers formed what contemporaries described as "an incredible Number of the meanest People," "every where Armed." They were the "tag, rag, and bobtayle," the "Rabble" against "the better sort of people." A colonial official reported that Bacon had raised an army of soldiers "whose fortunes & Inclinations" were "desperate." Bacon had unleashed an armed interracial "giddy multitude" that threatened the very foundations of social order in Virginia.[29]

The rebels forced Berkeley to escape by ship and burned Jamestown to the ground. Returning with armed reinforcements, the governor quickly and violently suppressed the biracial insurrection. At a rebel fortification on an island in the York River, Captain Thomas Grantham encountered some four hundred "English and Negroes in Armes." Lying to them, Grantham said they had been "pardoned and freed from their Slavery." Most of them accepted his offer, but eighty black and twenty white rebels refused to surrender. Promised safe passage across the river, the holdouts were captured when Grantham threatened to blow them out of the water. All of the captured "Negroes & Servants," Grantham reported, were returned "to their Masters."[30]

By force and deceit, the rebels of the "giddy multitude" had been defeated, but they had fought in what historian Edmund Morgan called "the largest rebellion" known in any American colony before the American Revolution. During the conflict, the specter of class revolution had become a reality, and the scare shook the elite landholders. Five years after the rebellion, planters continued to harbor fears of class disorder and urged the king to keep royal soldiers in Virginia to "prevent or suppress any Insurrection that may otherwise happen during the necessitous unsettled condition of the Colony." Large landowners saw that the social order would always be in danger so long as they relied on white labor.[31]

The planters had come to a crossroads. They could open economic opportunities to white workers and extend political privileges to them, but this would erode their own economic advantage and potentially undermine their political hegemony. Or they could try to reorganize society on the basis of class *and* race. By importing and buying more slaves, they could reduce their dependency on an armed white labor force and exploit workers from Africa, who could be denied the right to bear arms because of their race.

After Bacon's Rebellion, the planters made their choice: they turned to Africa as their primary source of labor and to slavery as their main system of labor. The growing African population can be measured decade by decade from the tax lists of Surry County. Slaves constituted 20 percent of households in 1674, 33 percent in 1686, and 48 percent in 1694. In other words, near the end of the century, slaves totaled nearly half the population in the county.[32]

From 5 percent of the colony's population in 1675, blacks increased sharply to 25 percent by 1715 and over 40 percent by 1750. "There were as many buyers as negros," Francis Nicholson commented on a sale of 230 slaves in Virginia in 1700, "and I think that, if 2,000 were imported, there would be substantial buyers for them." "The negroes are brought annually in large numbers," a visitor to Virginia reported. "They can be selected according to pleasure, young and old, men and women. They are entirely naked when they arrive, having only corals of different colors around their neck and arms." Unlike the first "twenty Negars," these Africans arrived as slaves.[33]

What the landed gentry systematically developed after the insurrection was a labor force based on caste. After 1680, the legislature enacted laws that denied slaves freedom of assembly and movement. The "frequent meeting of considerable number of negroe slaves under pretense of feasts and burials" was "judged of dangerous consequence." Masters and overseers were prohibited from allowing "any Negro or Slave not properly belonging to him or them, to Remain or be upon his or their Plantation above the space of four hours." Militia patrollers were authorized to visit "negro quarters and other places suspected of entertaining unlawful assemblies," and to "take up" those assembling "or any other, strolling about from one plantation to another, without a pass from his or her master, mistress, or overseer." The manumission of slaves was prohibited unless the master paid for transporting them out of the colony. Significantly, all blacks, free and slave, were disarmed: an act entitled "Preventing Negroes Insurrections" ordered that "it shall not be lawful for any negro or other slave to carry or arm himself with any club, staff, gun, sword or any other weapon."[34]

New legislation also sharpened the color line. Who was "black" was given expanded definition. Earlier, in 1662, the legislature had declared that children born in Virginia should be slave or free according to the condition of the mother. In 1691, a new law prohibited the "abominable mixture and spurious issue" of interracial unions and provided punishment of white women who violated the anti-miscegenation law: a white mother of a racially mixed child would be subject to banishment and the child would be enslaved. Whether fathered or mothered by whites, mulattoes became slaves; as such, they were implicitly classified as black. Thus was born the "one-drop rule."[35]

In their pursuit of their short-term class interests, the elite had made decisions that would have tragic consequences for centuries to come.

"White Over Black"

A hundred years after Bacon's Rebellion, one of the descendants of the planter class in Virginia was Thomas Jefferson. As a slave-owner, he actively participated in the buying and selling of slaves. "The value of our lands and slaves, taken conjunctly, doubles in about twenty years," he coolly calculated. "This arises from the multiplication of our slaves, from the extension of culture, and increased demands for lands." His observation was not merely theoretical: Jefferson's ownership of lands and slaves made him one of the wealthiest men in Virginia. Yet he continued to expand his slaveholdings. In 1805, he informed John Jordan that he was "endeavoring to purchase young and able negro men." In a letter to his manager regarding "a breeding woman," Jefferson referred to the "loss of 5 little ones in 4 years" and complained that the over-seers had not permitted the slave women to devote as much time as was necessary to care for their children. "They view their labor as the 1st object and the raising of their children but as secondary," he continued. "I consider the labor of a breeding woman as no object, and that a child raised every 2 years is of more profit than the crop of the best laboring man." By 1822, Jefferson owned 267 slaves.[36]

Jefferson was capable of punishing his slaves with great cruelty. He used James Hubbard, a captured runaway slave, as a lesson to discipline the other slaves: "I had him severely flogged in the presence of his old companions." On another occasion, Jefferson punished a slave in order to make an example of him in "terrorem" to others and then sold him to a slave trader from Georgia. Jefferson wanted him to be sent to a place "so distant as never more to be heard among us," and make it seem to the other slaves on his plantation "as if he were put out of the way by death."[37]

However, Jefferson also believed that slavery was an immoral institution. "The love of justice and the love of country plead equally the cause of these people [slaves]," Jefferson confessed, "and it is a moral reproach to us that they should have pleaded it so long in vain...." As a member of the Virginia legislature, he supported an effort for the emancipation of slaves. In his *Notes on the State of Virginia*, he recommended the gradual abolition of slavery, and in a letter to a friend written in 1788, he wrote: "You know that nobody wishes more ardently to see an abolition not only of the [African slave] trade but of the condition of slavery; and certainly nobody will be more willing to encounter every sacrifice for that object."[38]

Jefferson personally felt guilty about his ownership of slaves. In a letter to his brother-in-law, Francis Eppes, on July 30, 1787, he made a revealing slip. Once "my debts" have been cleared off, he promised, "I shall try some plan of making their [his slaves'] situation happier, determined to content myself with a small portion of their ~~liberty~~ labour." He tried to excuse himself for appropriating only their "labour," not their "liberty." In a letter to a friend written only a day earlier, Jefferson exploded with guilt: "The torment of mind, I will endure till the moment shall arrive when I shall not owe a shilling on earth is such really as to render life of little value." Dependent on the labor of his slaves to pay off his debts, he hoped to be able to free them, which he promised he would do the moment "they" had paid off the estate's debts, two-thirds of which had been "contracted by purchasing them." Unfortunately, for Jefferson and especially for his slaves, he remained in debt until his death.[39]

In Jefferson's view, slavery did more than deprive blacks of their liberty. It also had a pernicious and "unhappy" influence on the masters and their children:

> The whole commerce between master and slave is a perpetual exercise of the most boisterous passions, the most unremitting despotism on the one part, and degrading submissions on the other. Our children see this, and learn to imitate it; for man is an imitative animal. This quality is the germ of all education in him. From his cradle to his grave he is learning to do what he sees others do. If a parent could find no motive either in his philanthropy or his self-love, for restraining the intemperance of passion toward his slave, it should always be a sufficient one that his child is present. But generally it is not sufficient. The parent storms, the child looks on, catches the lineaments of wrath, puts on the same airs in the circle of smaller slaves, gives a loose to his worst of passions, and thus nursed, educated, and daily exercised in tyranny, cannot but be stamped by it with odious peculiarities. The man must be a prodigy who can retain his manners and morals undepraved by such circumstances.[40]

Slavery had to be abolished, Jefferson argued, but when freed, blacks would have to be removed from American society. This had to be done as soon as possible because slaves already composed nearly half of Virginia's population. "Under the mild treatment our slaves experience, and their wholesome, though coarse, food," Jefferson observed, "this blot in our country increases fast, or faster, than the whites." Delays for removal only meant the growth of the "blot." Jefferson impatiently insisted: "I can say, with conscious truth, that there is not a man on earth who would sacrifice more than I would to relieve us from this heavy reproach, in any practicable way. The cession of that kind of property... is a bagatelle which would not cost me a second thought, if, in that way, a general emancipation and expatriation could be effected."[41]

How could a million and a half slaves be expatriated? To send them away all at once, Jefferson answered, would not be "practicable." He estimated that such a removal would take twenty-five years, during which time the slave population would have doubled. Furthermore, the value of these slaves would amount to $600 million, and the cost of transportation and provisions an additional $300 million. "It cannot be done in this way," Jefferson decided. The only "practicable" plan, he thought, was to deport the future generation: black infants would be taken from their mothers and trained for occupations until they reached a proper age for deportation. Since an infant was worth only $22.50, Jefferson calculated, the loss of slave property would be reduced from $600 million to only $37.5 million. Jefferson suggested that slave children be shipped to the independent black nation of Haiti. The transportation of the children from America would lead to the eventual "disappearance" of the entire black population. Jefferson called the success of his plan "blessed." As for taking children from their mothers, Jefferson remarked: "The separation of infants from mothers... would produce some scruples of humanity. But this would be straining at a gnat, and swallowing a camel."[42]

One of the reasons why deportation would have to be a condition for emancipation was clear to Jefferson: blacks and whites could never coexist in America because of "the real distinctions" which "nature" had made between the two races. "The first difference which strikes us is that of color," Jefferson explained. This difference, "fixed in nature," was important. "Is it not the foundation of a greater or less share of beauty in the two races?" he asked rhetorically. "Are not the fine mixtures of red and white, the expressions of every passion by greater or less suffusions of color in the one, preferable to that eternal monotony, which reigns in the countenances, that immovable veil of black which covers the emotions of the other race?" The differences between the races, in Jefferson's view, also involved intelligence. He publicly stated his "opinion" that blacks were "inferior" in the faculty of reason. However, he conceded that such a claim had to be "hazarded with great diffidence" and that he would be willing to have it refuted.[43]

But Jefferson refused to consider evidence refuting his claim. For example, he would not acknowledge Phillis Wheatley as a poet. In 1773, this young black writer had published a book, *Poems on Various Subjects, Religious and Moral*. Her poems stirred interest and appreciation among many readers. Praising them, a French official living in America during the American Revolution wrote: "Phyllis is a negress, born in Africa, brought to Boston at the age of ten, and sold to a citizen of that city. She learned English with unusual ease, eagerly read and reread the Bible...became steeped in the poetic images of which it is full, and at the age of seventeen published a number of poems in which there is imagination, poetry, and zeal." In one of her poems, Wheatley insisted that Africans were just as capable of Christian virtue and salvation as whites:

> *'Twas mercy brought me from my* Pagan *land,*
> *Taught my benighted soul to understand*
> *That there's a God, that there's a* Saviour *too:*
> *Once I redemption neither sought nor knew.*
> *Some view our sable race with scornful eye,*
> *"Their colour is a diabolic die."*
> *Remember,* Christians, Negroes, *black as* Cain,
> *May be refin'd, and join th' angelic train.*

During the American Revolution, Wheatley proclaimed:

> *No more,* America, *in mournful strain*
> *Of wrongs, and grievance unredress'd complain,*
> *No longer shalt thou dread the iron chain,*
> *Which wanton* Tyranny *with lawless hand*
> *Had made, and with it meant t'enslave the land.*
> *Should you, my lord, while you peruse my song,*
> *Wonder from whence my love of* Freedom *sprung,*

Whence flow these wishes for the common good,
By feeling hearts alone best understood,
I, young in life, by seeming cruel fate
Was snatch'd from Afric's fancy'd happy seat:
What pangs excruciating must molest,
What sorrows labour in my parent's breast?
Steel'd was that soul and by no misery mov'd
That from a father seiz'd his babe belov'd:
Such, such my case. And can I then but pray
Others may never feel tyrannic sway?

Like Jefferson and many theoreticians of the American Revolution, Wheatley understood the meaning of the struggle for liberty. She, too, identified British tyranny as a form of slavery, but Wheatley reminded her readers that her understanding of freedom was not merely philosophical, for it tragically sprang from her own experience—the slave trade, forced separation from parents, and bondage in America.[44]

Jefferson contemptuously dismissed her writing: "The compositions published under her name are below the dignity of criticism." Considering blacks incapable of writing poetry, Jefferson caustically commented: "Religion, indeed, has produced a Phyllis Whately [*sic*]; but it could not produce a poet."[45]

Like Phillis Wheatley, Benjamin Banneker challenged Jefferson's "opinion" of black intellectual inferiority. On August 19, 1791, this free black mathematician from Maryland sent Jefferson a copy of the almanac he had compiled. "I suppose it is a truth too well attested to you, to need a proof here," Banncker wrote in his cover letter, "that we are a race of beings, who have long labored under the abuse and censure of the world...that we have long been considered rather as brutish than human, and scarcely capable of mental endowments." Noting that the almanac would soon be published, Banneker explained that he was sending Jefferson the "manuscript" of the work so that it could be viewed in his "own hand writing."[46]

Seeking to do more than demonstrate and affirm the intelligence of blacks, Banneker also scolded the author of the Declaration of Independence for his hypocrisy on the subject of slavery.

Sir, suffer me to recall to your mind that time, in which the arms of the British crown were exerted, with every powerful effort, in order to reduce you to a state of servitude: look back, I entreat you...you were then impressed with proper ideas of the great violation of liberty, and the free possession of those blessings, to which you were entitled by nature; but, Sir, how pitiable is it to reflect that although you were so fully convinced of the benevolence of the Father of Mankind, and of his equal and impartial distribution of these rights and privileges which he hath conferred upon them, that you should at the same time counteract his mercies, in detaining by fraud and violence, so numerous a part of my brethren under groaning captivity and cruel oppression, that you should at the same time be found guilty of that most criminal act, which you professedly detested in others.

The American Revolution, in Banneker's mind, had unleashed the idea that "liberty" was a natural right. Commitment to this principle demanded consistency. The overthrow of the British enslavement of the colonies required the abolition of slavery in the new republic.[47]

On August 30, 1791, Jefferson responded: "Nobody wishes more than I do to see such proofs as you exhibit, that nature has given to our black brethren, talent equal to those of the other colors of men; and that the appearance of a want of them is owing merely to the degraded condition of their existence...." But actually Jefferson did not take Banneker seriously. In a letter to Joel Harlow, Jefferson claimed that the mathematician had "a mind of very common stature," and that the black scholar had aid from Andrew Ellicot, a white neighbor who "never missed an opportunity of puffing him."[48]

Parsimonious toward Wheatley as a poet and skeptical toward Banneker as a mathematician, Jefferson was unable to free himself from his belief in black intellectual inferiority. Like Prospero, he insisted that, to borrow Shakespeare's poetic language, "nurture" could not improve the "nature" of blacks. Comparing Roman slavery and American black slavery, Jefferson pointed out: "Epictetus, Terence, and Phaedrus were slaves. But they were of the race of whites. It is not their condition then, but nature, which has produced the distinction." Black slaves in America, on the other hand, were mentally inferior: "In general, their existence appears to participate more of sensation than reflection.... It appears to me that in memory they are equal to the whites; in reason much inferior, as I think one could scarely be found capable of tracing and comprehending the investigations of Euclid; and that in imagination they are dull, tasteless, and anomalous."[49]

In Jefferson's view, blacks were not only inferior in intelligence but also belonged to a libidinous race. "They [black men] are more ardent after their female," he claimed; "but love seems with them to be more an eager desire, than a tender delicate mixture of sentiment and sensation." They "preferred" white women with their "flowing hair" and "more elegant symmetry of form." The black presence in America threatened white racial purity. "This unfortunate difference in color, and perhaps of faculty is a powerful obstacle to the emancipation of these people. Many of their advocates, while they wish to vindicate the liberty of human nature, are anxious to preserve its dignity and beauty.... Among the Romans emancipation required but one effort. The slave, when made free, might mix with, without staining the blood of his master." For Jefferson, interracial sex and racially mixed offspring would rupture the borders of caste. America must not become a nation of mulattoes. "Their amalgamation with the other color," he warned, "produces a degradation to which no lover of his country, no lover of excellence in the human character can innocently consent."[50]

Jefferson's abhorrence of interracial sex must have made the charges against his own misconduct extremely painful. In 1802, one of his political critics ignited a controversy; in the *Richmond Recorder,* James Callendar wrote: "It is well known that the man, *whome it delighteth the people to honor,* keeps and for many years has kept, as his concubine, one of his slaves. Her name is Sally. The name of her eldest son is Tom. His features are said to bear a striking though sable resemblance to those of the president himself. The boy is ten or twelve years of age. His mother went to France in the same vessel with Mr. Jefferson and his two daughters. The delicacy of this arrangement must strike every person of common sensibility. What a sublime pattern for an American ambassador to place before the eyes of two young ladies!" The editor of the *Richmond Examiner* dared Callendar to support his charge with explicit evidence. "I...have too much faith in Mr. Jefferson's virtuous actions and designs to be tremulous for his fame in a case like this," he declared. The editor argued that the child could be anyone's. "In gentlemen's houses everywhere, we know that the virtue of unfortunate slaves is assailed with impunity.... Is it strange therefore, that a servant of Mr. Jefferson's at a house where so many strangers resort...should have a mulatto child?

Certainly not." But the editor added: "If he [Jefferson] has acted improperly...let us see to what extent the evil goes, whether it is venial or whether it is so heinous, as to cut him off from the love of the people."[51]

The seeming scandal could not be contained. Newspapers published audacious poems mocking what they saw as their libidinous president.

> *In glaring red, and chalky white,*
> *   Let others beauty see;*
> *Me no such tawdry tints delight –*
> *   No black's the hue for me!*
>
> *Thick pouting lips! how sweet their grace!*
> *   When passion fires to kiss them!*
> *Wide spreading over half her face,*
> *   Impossible to miss them.*
>
> *Oh! Sally! harken to my vows!*
> *   Yield up thy sooty charms —*
> *My best belov'd! my more than spouse,*
> *   Oh! Take me to thy arms!*[52]

The editor of the *Boston Gazette* joined the chorus of critics. "We feel for the honor of our country," he declared. "And when the Chief Magistrate labours under the imputation of the most abandoned profligacy of private life, we do most honestly and sincerely wish to see the stain upon the nation wiped away, by the appearance at least of some colorable reason for believing in the purity of its highest character."[53]

Throughout the controversy over the charges of his relationship with Sally Hemings, Jefferson himself displayed a curious comportment. In a letter to James Madison, he offered an oblique denial. Describing how Callender had "intimated he was in possession of things he could and would make use of in a certain case" and how he had demanded "hush money," Jefferson added: "He knows nothing of me which I am not willing to declare to the world myself." But except for this one instance, Jefferson acted as if the controversy did not exist and as if there were no mulatto children resembling him on his plantation. Even his grandson, Thomas Randolph, admitted that the Hemings children looked so much like Jefferson that at some distance or in the dusk one of the grown slaves "might have been mistaken for Mr. Jefferson."

Yet, he added, Jefferson himself "never betrayed the least consciousness of the resemblance." Randolph stated that the resemblance was so striking that both he and his mother "would have been very glad to have them thus removed," but "venerated Mr. Jefferson too deeply to broach such a topic to him."[54]

Beneath the swirling controversy lay a hidden intimate past. In 1784, at the age of forty-one, the recently widowed Jefferson had gone to Paris as a special minister from the new republic. Accompanying him was his twelve-year-old daughter, Patsy. Three years later, Jefferson was joined by his daughter Polly, accompanied by her servant, the fifteen-year-old Sally Hemings. Hemings was one of the slaves Jefferson's wife had inherited from her father, John Wayles; this slave was also the offspring of Wayles and his mulatto slave mistress, Betty Hemings, making Sally Hemings three-quarters white and the half-sister of Jefferson's wife. "When Abigail Adams on June 26, 1787, met the sea captain who had brought Jefferson's eight-year-old Polly across the Atlantic," wrote historian Fawn Brodie, "she discovered with consternation that the slave accompanying the child was not a middle-aged woman, as she had expected, but an adolescent girl of considerable beauty." Known at Monticello as "Dashing Sally," recalled a slave who knew her, she was "mighty near white," with "long straight hair down her back."[55]

Reporting what his mother had told him, Madison Hemings wrote that his mother's stay in Paris was about eighteen months. "During that time my mother became Jefferson's concubine." In 1789, Jefferson wanted Sally Hemings to return with him to Virginia. "She was just beginning to understand the French language well, and in France she was free, while if she returned to Virginia she would be re-enslaved. So she refused to return with him. To induce her to do so he promised her extraordinary privileges, and made a solemn pledge that her children should be freed at the age of twenty-one years." She accepted his offer, and "soon after their arrival [in Virginia], she gave birth to a child, of whom Jefferson was the father. It lived but a short time." She gave birth to four more of Jefferson's children—Beverly, Harriet, Madison, and Eston. "We all became free agreeably to the treaty, entered into by our parents before we were born." In 1998, over two centuries after Sally Hemings's arrival in Paris, DNA evidence validated Madison Hemings's story.[56]

What worried Jefferson more than the threat of miscegenation or the controversy over Sally Hemings was the danger of race war. "Deep-rooted prejudices entertained by the whites," he anxiously explained, "ten thousand recollections, by the blacks, of the injuries they have sustained; new provocations; the real distinctions which nature has made and many other circumstances, will divide us into parties, and produce convulsions, which will probably never end but in the extermination of one or the other race."[57]

Unless slavery was abolished, Jefferson feared, whites would continue to face the threat of servile insurrection. Commenting on the slave revolt in Santo Domingo, he wrote to James Monroe in 1793: "It is high time we should foresee the bloody scenes which our children certainly, and possibly ourselves (south of Potomac) have to wade through, and try to avert them." In 1797, referring to the need for a plan for emancipation and removal, Jefferson anxiously confessed to a friend: "If something is not done, and soon done, we shall be the murderers of our children." Three years later, an attempted slave revolt shook Jefferson like "a fire bell in the night." The Gabriel Prosser conspiracy was crushed, and twenty-five blacks were hanged. Though the insurrectionary spirit among the slaves had been quelled in this instance, Jefferson warned, it would become general and more formidable. He predicted that slavery would be abolished—"whether brought on by the generous energy of our own minds" or "by the bloody process of St. Domingo." In Jefferson's nightmare, slaves would seize their freedom with daggers.[58]

By Jefferson's time, it had become clear that the seventeenth-century planters had failed to consider the tragic consequences of changing from white indentured servants to African slaves. Driven by immediate economic interests, the Virginia elite made choices that would ricochet down the corridors of time. They had created an enslaved black "giddy multitude" that would constantly threaten social order. "As it is," Jefferson cried out, "we have the wolf by the ears, and we can neither hold him, nor safely let him go. Justice is in one scale, and self-preservation in the other."[59] Jefferson wanted to abolish the institution that had denied "liberty" to the people he owned as property; it represented a "moral reproach" that "tormented" his conscience. But, by then, it was too late. Unlike Prospero, the slaveholders could not simply free their Calibans and leave the island. "All torment, trouble, wonder, and amazement inhabits here," the English theatergoers heard the old counselor Gonzalo pray. "Some heavenly power guide us out of this fearful country."[60]

PART TWO

Contradictions

The Rise of the Cotton Kingdom

EMBEDDED IN THE very birth of the United States in 1776 was a contradiction. The Founding Fathers had declared the "self-evident truth" that "all men are created equal," but in 1787, they wrote into the Constitution a provision that implicitly legalized slavery: the number of representatives each state would send to Congress would be determined by the number of "free persons" and "three fifths of all other persons," the code phrase for slaves.

By then, slavery had become a waning institution, offering hope that the contradiction between the nation's principles and what had come to be called the "peculiar institution" would resolve itself. The northern states proceeded to abolish slavery, and many slaveholders in the South were manumitting, or freeing, their slaves. Like Jefferson, they were feeling morally uncomfortable over slavery. Facing problems of soil exhaustion in the tobacco fields of Virginia, Maryland, and North Carolina, slaveholders were finding slavery unprofitable. In South Carolina and Georgia, slavery was confined to the coastal region where sea island cotton could be grown. This type of cotton had few seeds and was ideal to process into fiber for textile production. A second type of cotton, short staple cotton, could be grown in the upcountry region, but its abundance of seeds made it prohibitively expensive to extract by hand.

This static and even slumping economy changed in 1793: Eli Whitney's invention of the cotton gin made it viable to process short staple cotton. After 1800, slavery became enormously profitable not only in the cotton-producing states from Georgia to Texas but also in what became the slave-breeding states of Virginia and Maryland. In turn, cotton production ushered America into the era of the Market Revolution—the "take-off" years that transformed America into a highly complex industrial economy.[1] At the core of this economic boom was the ascendancy of the Cotton Kingdom.

In 1800, the United States had a population of six million, of which only three hundred twenty thousand were listed as urban. A large percentage of the rural population was engaged in subsistence farming, growing food crops mainly for their own needs. Living in the interior regions, many of these farmers found that the transportation of surplus crops to the market was too expensive. The cost of carrying a ton of goods only thirty miles overland was as much as shipping it three thousand miles from America to Europe. Thus, commercial activity was limited to the areas near the seaboard and navigable waterways.

By 1860, however, the U.S. economy had become complex and robust. Advances in transportation such as the steamboat and the railroad now linked the three major regions—the East, West, and South. Each region represented a division of production. New England and the Middle Atlantic states concentrated on manufacturing and commerce and relied on the West for foodstuffs for its growing urban population and the South for raw cotton to supply its textile factories. In 1860, the total value of manufactured goods in the East was $1,270,937,679, compared to only $540,137,811 for the other two regions combined. The western states of Ohio, Indiana, and Illinois exported grain and livestock to the East and South while depending on the East for manufactured goods. In 1860, the West shipped a million barrels of flour and thirty-one million barrels of grain through Buffalo to the East, and $185,211,254 worth of produce through New Orleans to the South. The South, mainly Georgia, South Carolina, Alabama, Mississippi, and Louisiana, produced fiber for the textile mills of the East and purchased food from the West and manufactured goods from the East.

The causes of this tremendous economic transformation were multiple. The shipping boom of the early 1800s had enabled merchants like Francis Lowell to accumulate capital to invest in manufacturing ventures. The proliferation of banks and the expansion of the credit system made it possible for farmers to borrow money and buy land for commercial agriculture. Introducing new machinery, technological progress paved the way for factory production. Government intervention in the form of protective tariffs and the development of transportation also contributed to the advance of the market. The transportation revolution laid vast networks of turnpikes, canals, and railroads across the country: between 1815 and 1860, freight charges for shipments overland had been reduced by 95 percent.[2]

But the most "decisive" impetus of the Market Revolution was cotton. "Cotton was strategic," observed economist Douglass C.

North, "because it was the major independent variable in the interdependent structure of internal and international trade. The demands for western foodstuffs and northeastern services and manufactures were basically dependent upon the income received from the cotton trade."[3] The tables below do the telling:

Table 1: Indian land sales and cotton production

Year	Land sales (acres)	Cotton (bales)
1833	1,816,083	559,210
1834	2,388,146	641,435
1835	5,522,474	760,923
1836	5,805,180	788,013
1837	1,259,814	916,960
1838	821,600	747,227
1839	851,586	911,913
1840	401,394	1,538,904
1841	228,699	1,231,334
1842	238,079	1,160,389

Table 2: Slave population

Year	Alabama	Mississippi	Louisiana
1820	41,879	32,814	69,064
1830	117,549	65,659	109,588
1840	253,523	195,211	168,452
1850	342,892	309,878	244,809

Table 3: Value of total exports and cotton exports

Year	Total exports	Cotton exports
1815	$52,557,000	$17,529,000
1830	$71,671,000	$29,674,883
1840	$123,669,000	$63,870,307
1850	$144,376,000	$71,984,616
1860	$333,576,000	$191,806,555

The development of the cotton export sector depended on the appropriation of Indian lands and the expansion of slavery. The major cotton-producing states—Alabama, Mississippi, and Louisiana—were carved out of Indian territory. Tribe after tribe in the South was forced to cede its lands to the federal government and move west of the Mississippi River. Eleven treaties of cession were negotiated with these tribes between 1814 and 1824; from these agreements the United States acquired millions of acres of lands, including one-fifth of Mississippi and three-quarters of Alabama. Sales of Indian lands were followed by increases in the slave population in Alabama, Mississippi, and Louisiana, and the slave population by increases in cotton production.

Dominant in the export trade, cotton was crucial in the development of interregional specialization. The capital derived from the export of cotton to England and France helped to finance enterprises throughout the economy and buttressed the industrialization of America.[4]

The Market Revolution created an even more diverse population, for it led to the massive influx of laborers from Ireland, the incorporation of Mexicans with the annexation of the Southwest territories, and then the migrations of the Chinese east to America. The inclusion of these new groups of Calibans led to a greater "pluribus," a more racially and culturally diverse "giddy multitude." The economy fastened these different peoples to each other, their histories woven into the tapestry of a greater "unum" called America. Working in the textile mills of New England, Irish immigrant women manufactured fabric made from cotton grown on former Indian lands and picked by enslaved African Americans; meanwhile, Irish immigrant men labored in New England shoe factories, making shoes from hides shipped by Mexican workers in California. Chinese and Irish railroad workers laid the transcontinental tracks that closed the frontier and changed forever the lives of Indians in the West. America was becoming a nation peopled by the world.

4

⚜

TOWARD "THE STONY MOUNTAINS"

From Removal to Reservation

*Andrew Jackson: "To... Tread on the
Graves of Extinct Nations"*

O N FEBRUARY 16, 1803, President Thomas Jefferson wrote a letter to Andrew Jackson, a young political leader in Tennessee: the government should advise the Indians to sell their "useless" forests and become farmers. Three decades later, as president himself, Jackson would forcibly remove even Indian farmers to the West, toward "the Stony mountains."[1]

Jackson's fortunes were tied to what happened to the Indians. In 1787, he moved from North Carolina to Nashville, where he practiced law, opened stores, and engaged in land speculation—lands that had originally belonged to Indians. Jackson paid $100 for twenty-five hundred acres at the Chickasaw bluffs on the Mississippi and immediately sold half of this property for $312. He kept the rest of the land until 1818, when he sold it for $5,000. Jackson had personally negotiated the Chickasaw treaty and opened the area to white settlement in 1814.

Meanwhile, General Jackson had led American troops against the Creeks in Mississippi, conquering "the cream of the Creek country" for the expansion of the "republick." During the war against the Creeks, Jackson called his enemies "savage bloodhounds" and "blood thirsty barbarians." When Jackson learned that hostile Creeks had killed more than two hundred whites at Fort Mims, he vowed revenge. "I know," he told his soldiers, "you will teach the cannibals who reveled in the carnage of our unoffending Citizens at Fort Meems that the thunder of our arms is more terrible than the Earth quakes of their Prophets, and that Heaven Dooms to inevitable destruction the wretch who Smiles at the torture he inflicts and who neither spares female innocence, declining age nor helpless infancy." Denouncing the Indian capture of a white woman who was confined to a post, "naked, lascerated," he urged the "brave sons of Tennessee" to wipe away this "blushing shame."[2]

Shortly before the battle of Horse Shoe Bend in March 1814, Jackson raged in letters to Major General Thomas Pinckney. "I must distroy those deluded victims doomed to distruction by their own restless and savage conduct." Calling them "savage dogs," he wrote: "It is by the charge I distroy from eight to ten of them...I have on all occasions preserved the scalps of my killed." At the battle of Horse Shoe Bend, Jackson and his troops surrounded eight hundred Creeks and killed almost all of them, including the women and children. Afterward, his soldiers made bridle reins from strips of skin taken from the corpses; they also cut off the tip of each dead Indian's nose for body count. Jackson sent clothing worn by the slain warriors to the ladies of Tennessee. In a letter to his wife, he wrote: "The *carnage* was *dreadful*.... I hope shortly to put an end to the war and return to your arms, kiss my little andrew for me, tell him I have a warriors bow and quiver for him." In a letter to Thomas Pinckney, Jackson boasted that he had conquered Indian lands, the "valuable country" west of the Cosee and north of the "allabama."[3]

Jackson shrouded the destruction of Indians and the appropriation of their lands in a metaphysical mantle of moral justification. After the bloody victory, Jackson told his troops:

> The fiends...will no longer murder our women and children, or disturb the quiet of our borders.... They have disappeared from the face of the Earth. In their places a new generation will arise who will know their duties better. The weapons of warfare will be exchanged for the utensils of husbandry; and the wilderness which now withers in sterility and seems to mourn the desolation which overspreads it, will blossom as the rose, and become the nursery of the arts.... How lamentable it is that the path to peace should

lead through blood, and over the carcases of the slain!! But it is in the dispensation of that providence, which inflicts partial evil to produce general good.

His soldiers, Jackson declared, were advancing civilization and progress.[4]

Revered as a hero of Indian wars, Jackson was elected to the presidency of the United States in 1828. He supported the efforts of Mississippi and Georgia to abolish Indian tribal units and allow white settlers to take cultivated Indian lands. As Jackson watched these states violate federal treaties with tribes, he pleaded presidential helplessness. "If the states chose to extend their laws over them," he told Congress, "it would not be in the power of the federal government to prevent it." Actually, treaties and federal laws had given authority over the Indians to Congress, not the states. The 1802 Indian Trade and Intercourse Act had provided that no land cessions could be made except by treaty with a tribe, and that federal rather than state law would operate in Indian territory. In 1832, after the Supreme Court ruled that states could not legally extend their jurisdiction into Indian territory, Jackson simply refused to enforce the Court's decision.[5]

Jackson's claim of presidential powerlessness and his failure to uphold the law functioned as a facade for collaboration and conspiracy. Behind the scene, he was actively working for Indian removal. General John Coffee laid out the strategy. "Deprive the chiefs of the power they now possess," he wrote to the president, "take from them their own code of laws, and reduce them to plain citizenship...and they will soon determine to move, and then there will be no difficulty in getting the poor Indians to give their consent. All this will be done by the State of Georgia if the United States do not interfere with her law." All Jackson had to do was stay out of the way.[6]

In Jackson's view, Indians could not survive living within white society. "The fate of the Mohigan, the Narragansett, and the Delaware is fast overtaking the Choctaw, the Cherokee, and the Creek. That this fate surely awaits them if they remain within the [states] does not admit of a doubt." Like the tribes before them, they would disappear. Driven by "feelings of justice," Jackson declared that he wanted "to preserve this much-injured race." He proposed a solution—the setting aside of a district west of the Mississippi "to be guaranteed to the Indian tribes as long as they shall occupy it." Beyond the borders of white society, Indians would be free to live in peace and to have their own governments "as long as the grass grows, or water runs." Jackson advised Indians to move to the West. Like whites, they should constantly seek to improve themselves and settle in new places. "Doubtless it will be painful [for Indians] to leave the graves of their fathers," Jackson declared in his first annual message to Congress. "But what do they more than our ancestors did or than our children are now doing? To better their condition in an unknown land our forefathers left all that was dear in earthly objects."[7]

Insisting that he wanted to be "just" and "humane," Jackson claimed his goal was to protect the Indians from the "mercenary influence of white men." Seeking to exercise "parental" control, he regarded himself as a "father," concerned about the welfare of his Indian "children." But if these "children" refused to accept his advice, Jackson warned, they would be responsible for the consequences. "I feel conscious of having done my duty to my red children, and if any failure of my good intentions arises, it will be attributable to their want of duty to themselves, not to me."[8]

Like the early Puritans, Jackson affirmed the "errand into the wilderness" in his justification for Indian removal and even death. What happened to the native people, he argued, was moral and inevitable. Indian graves represented progress—the advance of civilization across America. Nothing, Jackson insisted, was to be "regretted." "Humanity has often wept over the fate of the aborigines of this country, and Philanthropy has been long busily employed in devising means to avert it," Jackson explained in a message to Congress, "but its progress has never for a moment been arrested, and one by one have many powerful tribes disappeared from the earth. To follow to the tomb the last of his race and tread on the graves of extinct nations excite melancholy reflections." But "philanthropy could not wish to see this continent restored to the condition in which it was found by our forefathers." The president then asked: "What good man would prefer a country covered with forests and ranged by a few thousand savages to our extensive Republic, studded with cities, towns, and prosperous farms...filled with all the blessings of liberty, civilization, and religion?"[9]

Native Americans saw the chicanery of this metaphysics. Like Caliban cursing Prospero, Cherokee leader John Ross declared that "the perpetrator of a wrong" would never forgive "his victims." But President Jackson maintained a legal and moral posture. During his presidency, Jackson uprooted some seventy thousand Indians from their homes and drove them west of the Mississippi River. He was clearing the way for the rise of the Cotton Kingdom.[10]

The Embittered Human Heart: The Choctaws

Instituted by President Thomas Jefferson, the land-allotment program became the principal strategy for taking territory from the Creeks, Chickasaws, and Choctaws. In the 1805 Choctaw Treaty, the federal government had reserved certain tracts of land for individual Choctaws. Jefferson told a delegation of chiefs: "Let me entreat you...on the land now given to you, to begin to give every man a farm; let him enclose it, cultivate it, build a warm house on it, and when he dies, let it belong to his wife and children after him." The aim of Jefferson's policy was the transformation of the Choctaws into farmers.[11]

Actually, the Choctaws of Mississippi had been an agricultural people long before the arrival of whites. They employed the slash-and-burn method to clear areas for planting corn, beans, squash, pumpkins, and watermelons. To prepare the ground, they used a digging stick, a short heavy pole of hard wood with a sharp point. Then in the early summer, they celebrated the Green Corn Dance, a ceremony to bless the fields. After the harvest, they laid out the corn in small lots to dry, and then layered the corn between grass and clay mortar in little piles, "each covered and arranged side by side," looking "like a big mud dauber's nest." The Choctaws prepared the corn in various ways. "First they roast it in the fire and eat it so," a French traveler reported. "When it is very tender they pound it and make porridge of it, but the most esteemed among them is the cold meal."[12]

Before contact with the strangers from Europe, the Choctaws practiced communalism. After the harvest, the people erected a large granary. "To this each family carries and deposits a certain quantity, according to his ability or inclination, or none at all if he so chooses," reported a visitor. This "public treasury" supplied individual tribal members in need as well as neighboring towns suffering from crop failures. Critical of European individualism and possessiveness, they condemned the English for allowing their poor to suffer from hunger. Trader James Adair reported that the Choctaws were "very kind and liberal to every one of their own tribe, even to the last morsel of food they enjoy."[13]

By the early nineteenth century, many Choctaws had turned to raising cows and pigs in enclosed farms. Chief Franchimastabe explained that Choctaws would now have to raise cattle and live like white men, for the time of "hunting and living by the Gun" was nearly over. Choctaws also cultivated cotton for the market. Some of them had extensive operations: Greenwood LeFlore had

250 acres of cotton fields worked by thirty-two slaves, and David Folsom had 150 acres with a labor force of seventeen slaves. But these markers of civilization did not matter.[14]

In January 1830, the Mississippi state government abolished the sovereignty of the Choctaw nation. Any Choctaw who opposed state authority would be subjected to a thousand-dollar fine and a year in prison. In September, federal commissioners met with the Choctaws at Dancing Rabbit Creek to negotiate a treaty for acquiring their lands and removing them beyond the Mississippi. The Choctaw representatives turned down the offer: "It is the voice of a very large majority of the people here present not to sell the land of their forefathers." Thinking that the meeting was over, many Choctaws left. But the federal commissioners refused to accept no for an answer and bluntly told the remaining chiefs that the Choctaws must move or be governed by Mississippi state law. If they resisted, they would be destroyed by federal forces. A treaty was finally secured by intimidation.[15]

"We are exceedingly tired," wrote Chief David Folsom in a letter to Presbyterian missionaries. "We have just heard of the ratification of the Choctaw Treaty. Our doom is sealed. There is no other course for us but to turn our faces to our new homes toward the setting sun." Years later, Chief Cobb told Captain J. McRea, an officer in charge of removal: "Brother: Our hearts are full. Twelve winters ago our chiefs sold our country. Every warrior that you see here was opposed to the treaty. If the dead could have counted, it could never have been made, but alas! Though they stood around, they could not be seen or heard. Their tears came in the raindrops, and their voices in the wailing wind, but the pale faces knew it not, and our land was taken away."[16]

The Treaty of Dancing Rabbit Creek provided that the Choctaws cede all of their 10,423,130 acres to the federal government and migrate to lands west of the Mississippi River. Not all of the Choctaws were required to leave, however. Choctaw families and individuals were instructed to register with an Indian agent within six months after ratification of the treaty if they wished to remain in Mississippi and receive a land grant. Seemingly, the program gave Choctaws a fair chance to succeed in white society as individual landowners.[17]

Federal certifying agents, however, proceeded to collaborate with land speculators to transfer Indian tribal lands to individual Indians and then to whites. Speculators took Indians by groups from one agent to another and had them sign contracts for land grants. Often the speculators were the federal agents themselves. After securing lands for individual Indians, speculators made loans to them in exchange for their titles as collateral, and then they took over the deeds when the Indians failed to repay their debts.

Meanwhile, many white settlers simply took possession of Indian lands. "Owing to the law of the State of Mississippi passed at the last session, granting permission to the whites to settle in the Choctaw Nation," a contemporary reported, "hundreds have come in and are squatting on the lands in all directions." Once Indian lands were occupied, the squatters usually offered to pay for the property. "For the most part, every purchaser of cultivated reservations have made small advances to the Indians, with a promise to pay the balance when the Indians make a good title; which can hardly be effected, owing to the remote residence of the Indians when they remove to the west."[18]

The Treaty of Dancing Rabbit Creek and the land-allotment program unleashed white expansion: speculators, farmers, and planters proceeded to take Indian lands "legally," while absolving themselves from responsibility for Indian removal. Whites could not be blamed if Indians got into debt, lost their lands, and had to move beyond the Mississippi. "Our citizens were disposed to buy and the Indians to sell," explained Secretary of War Cass. "The improvident habits of the Indians cannot be controlled by [federal] regulations.... If they waste it, as waste it they too often will, it is deeply to be regretted yet still it is only exercising a right conferred upon them by the treaty." In other words, Indians were responsible for their own ruin. Behind the blame, however, was a hidden agenda. In a letter to General John Coffee, April 7, 1832, President Jackson wrote: "The object of the government now is, to have all their reservations surveyed and laid off as early as we can." Once Indians had been granted their individual land allotments, he added, they would "sell and move to the West."[19]

A year after the Treaty of Dancing Rabbit Creek, thousands of Choctaws began their trek to the territory west of the Mississippi River. "The feeling which many of them evince in separating, never to return again, from their own long cherished hills, poor as they are in this section of country," wrote an army officer, "is truly painful to witness...." But what was even more distressing to see was the suffering. While en route to their new homes, many Choctaws encountered terrible winter storms. One eyewitness recorded the experience of several hundred migrating Choctaws: "There were very aged persons and very young children in the company; many had nothing to shelter them from the storm by day or night. The weather was excessively cold, and yet not one in ten of the women had even a moccasin on their feet and the great majority of them were walking. One party came to us and begged for an ear of corn apiece [to relieve] their suffering." Not only the cold weather but also diseases like cholera stalked the migrants. Lieutenant Gabriel Rains reported to his general: "The Choctaws are dying to an alarming extent.... Near the agency there are 3,000 Indians and within the hearing of a gun from this spot 100 have died within five weeks. The mortality among these people since the beginning of fall as far as ascertained, amounts to one-fifth of the whole number."[20]

A French visitor witnessed the Choctaws crossing the Mississippi River on their way to the West. "It was then the middle of winter," reported Alexis de Tocqueville, "and the cold was unusually severe; the snow had frozen hard upon the ground, and the river was drifting huge masses of ice. The Indians had their families with them, and they brought in their train the wounded and the sick, with children newly born and old men upon the verge of death." Before his eyes was a microcosm of the epic story of Indian retreat before white expansion. "Three or four thousand soldiers drive before them the wandering races of the aborigines; these are followed by the pioneers, who pierce the woods, scare off the beasts of prey, explore the courses of the inland streams, and make ready the triumphal march of civilization across the desert." What struck Tocqueville was how whites were able to deprive Indians of their rights and exterminate them "with singular felicity, tranquilly, legally, philanthropically, without shedding blood, and without violating a single great principle of morality in the eyes of the world." Indeed, he wryly remarked, it was impossible to destroy men with "more respect for the laws of humanity."[21]

Uprooted, many Choctaws felt bitter and angry. "The privations of a whole nation before setting out, their turmoil and losses on the road, and settling their homes in a wild world," one of them declared, "are all calculated to embitter the human heart." In a "Farewell Letter to the American People, 1832," George W. Harkins explained why his people had left their ancestral lands: "We were hedged in by two evils, and we chose that which we thought least." The Mississippi legislators, he insisted, were not qualified to become lawmakers for a people so dissimilar in culture as the Choctaws were to whites. A "mountain of prejudice" would continue to obstruct "the streams of justice." Thus the Choctaws chose to "suffer and be free" rather than live under the degrading influence of laws where their voices could not be heard. They went unwillingly, however, for their attachment to their "native land" was strong. "That cord is now broken," Harkins cried out, "and we must now go forth as wanderers in a strange land!"[22]

The total cost of Choctaw removal, including salaries for the agents and fraudulent settlements, was $5,097,367.50. To pay for these expenses, the federal government sold the Choctaw lands to white settlers and received $8,095,614.89. In the Treaty of Dancing Rabbit Creek, the government had agreed that it would not make any profits from the sales of Choctaw lands. The Choctaws sued in federal court and won $2,981,247.39, but most of the awarded sum went to pay their lawyers.[23]

"The Trail of Tears": The Cherokees

In the beginning, according to Cherokee legend, water covered the earth and all of the animals lived in the sky. One day, a beaver dove into the ocean and created land by bringing mud to the surface and fastening it to the sky with four cords. Then the Great Buzzard flew to earth. "When he reached the Cherokee country, he was very tired, and his wings began to flap and strike the ground, and wherever they struck the earth there was a valley, and where they turned up again there was a mountain." This beautiful land of valleys and mountains became the home of the Cherokees.[24]

Like the Choctaws in Mississippi, the Cherokees in Georgia were also dispossessed, their lands "legally" moved into the "markett." In 1829, the Georgia legislature passed a law extending state authority over the territory of the Cherokee Nation. The Cherokees were given a choice—leave the state or be subjugated by white rule.[25]

Under the leadership of Chief John Ross, the Cherokees refused to abandon their homes and lands. The federal government, they insisted, was obligated to honor the treaties guaranteeing the sovereignty of the Cherokee Nation and the integrity of their territory. In a letter to Secretary of War Lewis Cass on February 6, 1834, Chief Ross condemned Georgia's lawlessness: "The right of property and even the life of the Cherokee is in jeopardy, and are at the mercy of the robber and the assassin. By these acts the citizen of Georgia is licensed to come into immediate collision with the Cherokee individual, by violence, if he chooses, for any and everything that is sacred to the existence of man upon earth. And the Cherokee is denied the right of appearing before the sanctuary of justice created by law for the redress of wrongs." A month later,

Chief Ross wrote directly to President Jackson: "The relations of peace and friendship so happily and so long established between the white and the red man...induces us, as representatives of the Cherokee nation, to address you [as] Father." By treaty, the Cherokee people had placed themselves under the protection of the federal government, which in turn had given "*assurances* of protection, good neighborhood and the solemn guarantee" for the territorial integrity of the Cherokee nation. A good father, the Cherokee chief insisted, should honor his promises to his children.[26]

But the appeals fell on deaf ears in Washington. Instead, President Jackson instructed Commissioner J. F. Schermerhorn to negotiate a treaty for Cherokee removal. Schermerhorn secured an agreement from John Ridge, the head of a small proremoval faction of Cherokees. According to the terms, the Cherokees would cede their land and be removed in exchange for a payment of $3,250,000. The treaty was signed in Washington on March 14, 1835, but it needed to be ratified by the tribe in full council to be valid.

Schermerhorn arranged to present the treaty to the Cherokee council at a meeting in New Echota, Georgia, to be held in December. To Secretary of War Lewis Cass, the commissioner wrote: "We shall make a treaty with those who attend, and rely upon it." What he meant was that only the proremoval faction would be permitted to attend. Before the meeting took place, the Georgia militia jailed Chief Ross and suppressed the Cherokee newspaper in order to restrict information about the meeting and to curb criticism. "The manner of seizure of the public press," Chief Ross protested in a letter to his people, "could not have been sanctioned for any other purpose than to stifle the voice of the Cherokee people, raised by their cries from the wounds inflicted upon them by the unsparing hand of their oppressors, and that the ear of humanity might thereby be prevented from hearing them." With the opposition to removal silenced, Schermerhorn procured a treaty at New Echota.[27]

The treaty was a sham: only a tiny fraction of the entire Cherokee Nation attended, and none of the tribal officers were present. According to Schermerhorn's own report, only about three to five hundred Cherokees out of a population of over seventeen thousand were present. Chief Ross and the antiremoval Cherokee leaders tried to block the treaty's approval in Congress. "This instrument," they declared to the Senate, "purports to be a contract with the Cherokee people, when in fact it has been agreed upon, in direct violation of their will, wishes, and interest, by a few unauthorized individuals of the [Cherokee] Nation." Some government officials confirmed that the treaty was indeed a fraud. In a letter to Secretary Cass, Major W. M. Davis described what had actually happened at New Echota: "Sir, that paper...called a treaty, is no treaty at all." It was "not sanctioned by the great body of the Cherokee" and was made "without their participation or assent." Davis charged that "Mr. Schermerhorn's apparent design was to conceal the real number present.... The delegation taken to Washington by Mr. Schermerhorn had no more authority to make a treaty than any other dozen Cherokee accidentally picked up for the purpose." Clearly, the treaty was chicanery; yet President Jackson "relied upon it," and Congress ratified it.[28]

The treaty let loose thousands of white settlers, who seized the "ceded" lands and forced many Cherokees to abandon their farms. In a letter to President Jackson, pro-removal leader Ridge complained about the injustice and abuse:

> We come now to address you on the subject of our griefs and afflictions from the acts of the white people. They have got our lands and now they are preparing to fleece us of the money accruing from the treaty. We found our plantations taken either in whole or in part by the Georgians—suits instituted against us for back rents for our own farms.... Even the Georgia laws, which deny us our oaths, are thrown aside, and notwithstanding the cries of our people...the lowest classes of the white people are flogging the Cherokees with cowhides, hickories, and clubs.[29]

Most of the Cherokees refused to migrate. In the spring of 1838, Chief Ross again protested against the treaty by presenting Congress with a petition signed by 15,665 Cherokees. But the federal government dismissed it and ordered the military to forcibly remove them.[30]

In command of seven thousand soldiers, General Winfield Scott warned the Cherokees: "My troops already occupy many positions...and thousands and thousands are approaching from every quarter to render assistance and escape alike hopeless. Will you, then by resistance compel us to resort to arms...or will you by flight seek to hide yourself in mountains and forests and thus oblige us to hunt you down?" The soldiers first erected internment camps and then rounded up the Cherokees. "Families at dinner were startled by the sudden gleam of bayonets in the doorway and rose up to be driven with blows and oaths along the weary miles of trail that led to the stockade. Men were seized in their fields...women were taken from their wheels and children from their play." The process of dispossession was violent and cruel. "The Cherokees are nearly all prisoners," the Reverend Evan Jones protested. "They had been dragged from their houses...allowed no time to take any thing with them, except the clothes they had on. Well-furnished houses were left prey to plunderers, who, like hungry wolves, follow in the train of the captors.... The property of many have been taken, and sold before their eyes for almost nothing—the sellers and buyers, in many cases having combined to cheat the poor Indians."[31]

From the internment camps, the Cherokees were marched westward. "We are now about to take our final leave and kind farewell to our native land the country that the Great Spirit gave our Fathers," a Cherokee informed Chief Ross. "We are on the eve of leaving that Country that gave us birth.... It is with [sorrow] that we are forced by the authority of the white man to quit the scenes of our childhood."[32]

The march took place in the dead of winter. "We are still nearly three hundred miles short of our destination," wrote Reverend Evan Jones in Little Prairie, Missouri. "It has been exceedingly cold...those thinly clad very uncomfortable...we have, since the cold set in so severely, sent on a company every morning, to make fires along the road, at short intervals.... At the Mississippi river, we were stopped from crossing, by the ice running so that boats could not pass...." The exiles were defenseless against the weather and disease. "Among the recent immigrants," wrote a witness near Little Rock, "there has been much sickness, and in some neighborhoods the mortality has been great.... Since last October about 2,000 immigrants have come. Twenty-five hundred more are on their way...much sickness and mortality among them." Quatie Ross, the wife of the chief, died of pneumonia at Little Rock. "Long time we travel on way to new land," one of the exiles recalled bitterly. "People feel bad when they leave Old Nation. Women cry and make sad wails. Children cry and many men cry, and all look sad when friends die, but they say nothing and just put heads down and keep on going towards West."[33]

Removal meant separation from a special and sacred place—their homeland created by the Great Buzzard. A Cherokee song acquired new and deeper meaning from the horror of removal:

> Toward the black coffin of the upland in the
> Darkening Land
> your paths shall stretch out.
> So shall it be for you....

Now your soul has faded away.
It has become blue.
When darkness comes your spirit shall
*   grow less and dwindle away, never to*
*   reappear.*

A Cherokee recalled how there were so many bodies to bury: "Looks like maybe all be dead before we get to new Indian country, but always we keep marching on." By the time they reached the new land west of the Mississippi, more than four thousand Cherokees—nearly one-fourth of this exiled Indian nation—died on what they have bitterly remembered as the "Trail of Tears."[34]

"American Progress": "Civilization" Over "Savagery"

Beyond the Mississippi River lived the Plains Indians—the Cheyenne, Arapaho, Kiowa, Sioux, and Pawnee. Inhabiting central Nebraska and northern Kansas, the Pawnees depended on buffalo and corn for their sustenance. Both sources of life were celebrated in Pawnee legends. When the Pawnee people were placed on the earth a long time ago, they wandered from place to place and lived on roots and berries. But food became scarce, and they suffered from hunger. Then one day, a young man looked into a cave and saw an old woman; he followed her into the cave and found another country with game and fields. "My son," she told him, "the gods have given you the buffalo. The buffalo are to run out of this cave, and the first buffalo that shall go out shall be killed by your people. Its hide must be tanned, the head must be cut off, and the skull set up on this high hill. When the meat and everything has been cut off from the skull, it must be taken to the village and put in the lodge." Next, the old woman gave the young man four bundles of corn of different colors, braided together: "These are the seeds for the people.... Now you must go and give the seeds to the people, and let them put them in the ground." With their buffalo and corn, the Pawnees were self-sufficient.[35]

The buffalo hunt was a sacred activity, and rituals guided the Pawnees in their migrations to the hunting grounds during the summers. Before the start of the hunt, they performed a ceremony. Pantomiming the buffalo, they chanted:

Listen, he said, yonder the buffalo are coming,
These are his sayings, yonder the buffalo are
*   coming,*

They walk, they stand, they are coming,
Yonder the buffalo are coming.
Now you are going to trot
Buffalo who are killed falling.

In another song, they described a herd of buffalo that had been sleeping on the plains. A calf, awakened by a frightening dream, warns grandfather buffalo:

Grandfather, I had a dream.
The people are gathering to surround us.
Truly they will surprise us....
They drove you near the village,
And then the playful boys killed you.
Truly they will surprise us....[36]

The hunt was highly organized. When the Pawnees located the buffalo, they would form a horseshoe with the open end facing the animals. At the two points, men on foot would begin the attack, shooting the buffalo at the edge of the herd. Then men on horses would charge. "When sufficient buffalo were killed for food and other needs, the butchering began," a Pawnee told his grandson years later. "This was neither a delicate or pleasant task." Skinning the buffalo in the winter was very difficult, for the "meat and skin would begin to freeze and the blood would cake and ice on the hands." In the summer, "the flies and gnats would become unbearable and it was then the young boys would offer to wave willow branches over the carcass, and at the same time drive away the dogs that would follow the hunters from the camp...."[37]

Strict taboos limited the buffalo kill to what the Pawnees were able to consume, thus conserving this crucial food supply. Nothing was wasted—the hides became tepees and robes, the horns spoons, the bones tools, the meat food. "The flesh, vitals, and even the intestines, all had their place in the Pawnee cuisine," reported John B. Dunbar in 1880. "The small entrails were carefully separated, freed from their contents by being pressed rapidly between the fingers, then braided together and dried with the adhering fat, forming in this condition a favorite relish. The integument of the paunch was preserved and eaten. The liver was frequently eaten raw while retaining its natural warmth, and was deemed a delicacy."[38]

The Pawnees were also farmers. In the spring, they planted corn. They knew the time had come, for they could smell "the dif-

ferent perfumes of the white weeds." "As soon as the frost was
out of the ground, these patches were cleared up and planted,"
reported a witness. During the ceremony to begin the planting,
women pantomimed the breaking of the ground with decorative
hoes made from the shoulder blades of buffalo. Songs thanking
Mother Corn and celebrating the growth of the plant accompanied their motions:

> *The ground now she clears....*
> *My mother the earth comes sidewise....*
> *Now the earth is dug into my mother....*
> *Earth lively Mother Corn....*
> *It is budding....*
> *The sprouts are coming out....*
> *The earth they are tossing it about....*
> *Life movement.*[39]

"The corn was hoed twice, the last time about the middle of
June," a contemporary reported. "Immediately thereafter they
started on the summer hunt and remained away till about the
first of September, when the young corn had attained sufficient
maturity for drying." In the fall, the Pawnees harvested their
crops and prepared for winter.[40]

During the early nineteenth century, the Pawnees began to
participate in the fur trade. "The foundations of Pawnee life were
undermined in the course of the fur trade, generally impercept-
ably, sometimes catastrophically," observed historian David J.
Wishart. "Pre-contact conceptions of nature were gradually supplanted: commercial motivations intervened and hunting was sec-
ularized; the idea of reciprocity with the environment was slowly
abandoned; wildlife overkill became more feasible and common."
Contact due to the fur trade also led to the introduction of new
diseases like smallpox which reduced the Pawnee population from
ten thousand in the 1830s to four thousand fifteen years later.[41]

By then, an even greater threat to the Pawnees had
emerged—the railroad. In his 1831 annual message to Congress,
President Andrew Jackson praised science for expanding man's
power over nature by linking cities and extending trade over
the mountains. The entire country had only 73 miles of railroad
tracks in 1830. Ten years later, track mileage measured 3,328
miles, then stretched to 8,879 in 1850 and 30,636 in 1860—more
than in all of Europe.[42]

As tracks traversed the continent, the railroad was ushering in a new era. In 1853, a newspaper editorial welcomed the ascendency of steam-driven transportation: "The human race very soon need not *toil,* but merely direct: hard work will be done by steam. Horses themselves are rapidly becoming obsolete. In a few years, like Indians, they will be merely traditional." Horses and also Indians would have no place in modern America. As the railroad crossed the plains and reached toward the Pacific coast, the iron horse was bringing the frontier to an end.[43]

"What shall we do with the Indians?" asked a writer for *The Nation* in 1867, as the Irish crews of the Union Pacific and the Chinese crews of the Central Pacific raced to complete the transcontinental railroad. The "highways to the Pacific" must not be obstructed. The Indians must either be "exterminated" or subjected to the "law and habits of industry." Civilizing the Indians, he suggested, would be "the easiest and cheapest as well as the only honorable way of securing peace." This would require the integration of Indians into white society. "We need only treat Indians like men, treat them as we do ourselves, putting on them the same responsibilities, letting them sue and be sued, and taxing them as fast as they settle down and have anything to tax."[44]

Two years later, in his annual message to Congress, President Ulysses S. Grant reflected on what the railroad portended for the Indians: "The building of railroads, and the access thereby given to all the agricultural and mineral regions of the country, is rapidly bringing civilized settlements into contact with all tribes of Indians. No matter what ought to be the relations between such settlements and the aborigines, the fact is they do not harmonize well, and one or the other has to give way in the end. A system which looks to the extinction of a race is too horrible for a nation to adopt without entailing upon itself the wrath of all Christendom and engendering in the citizen a disregard for human life and the rights of others, dangerous to society."[45]

In 1869, the transcontinental railroad was completed, and an iron line adorned the face of America from coast to coast. Secretary of Interior J. D. Cox boasted that the railroad had "totally changed" the nature of the westward migration. Previously, settlement had taken place gradually; but the railroad had "pierced" the "very center of the desert," and every station was becoming a "nucleus for a civilized settlement." Similarly, the editor of the *Cheyenne Leader* trumpeted the train as "the advance guard of empire": "The iron horse in his resistless 'march to the sea' surprises the aborigines upon their distant hunting grounds and frightens the buffalo from the plains where, for untold ages, his face has gazed in the eternal solitudes. The march of empire no longer proceeds with stately, measured strides, but has the wings of morning, and flies with the speed of lightning." As the railroad advanced to the Pacific, this mighty engine of technology was bespangling towns and cities across America, their lights glowing here and there on the horizon.[46]

Behind the "resistless" railroad were powerful corporate interests, deliberately planning the settlement of the West and the extension of the market. Railroad companies saw the tribes as obstacles to track construction and actively lobbied the government to secure rights-of-way through Indian territory. They pushed for the passage of the 1871 Indian Appropriation Act, which declared that "hereafter no Indian nation or tribe within the territory of the United States shall be acknowledged or recognized as an independent nation, tribe, or power, with whom the United States may contract by treaty." Explaining the law's significance, an attorney for a railroad corporation stated: "It is not a mere prohibition of the making of future treaties with these tribes. It goes beyond this, and destroys the political existence of the tribes." Armed with the 1871 Indian Appropriation Act, railroad companies rapidly threw tracks across America and opened the West to new settlement. All of this was seen by white settlers as the advance of civilization.[47]

Indians viewed the railroad very differently. They watched the iron horse transport white hunters to the plains, transforming the prairies into buffalo killing fields. They found carcasses littering and rotting along the railroad tracks, a trail of death for the buffalo—the main source of life for the Indians. Sioux chief Shakopee predicted ecological disaster and a grim future for his people: "The great herds that once covered the prairies are no more. The white men are like locusts when they fly so thick that the whole sky is like a snowstorm. You may kill one, two, ten; yes, as many as the leaves in the forest yonder, and their brothers will not miss them. Count your fingers all day long and white men with guns in their hands will come faster than you can count." The decimation of the buffalo signified the end of the Pawnee way of life.[48]

Along with the advance of the railroad and the increasing arrival of white settlers came a cry for Pawnee removal. "Pawnee Indians are in possession of some of the most valuable government land in the Territory," *The Nebraskian* editorialized. "The region of the country about the junction of Salt Creek and the Platte is very attractive and there would immediately grow up a thriving settlement were it not for the Pawnees. It is the duty of Uncle Sam to remove the Pawnee population."[49]

The Pawnees also found themselves under attack from the Sioux, who were moving south into their territory, also pushed by white settlers and driven by the decline of buffalo herds. Mainly a horticultural people, the Pawnees were militarily vulnerable. Women were murdered by the Sioux in the fields, earth lodges destroyed, corn crops burned, and food caches robbed. In 1873, a Pawnee hunting party was attacked by the Sioux at Massacre Canyon, and more than a hundred Pawnees were killed. Stunned by this tragedy, the Pawnees had to decide whether they should retreat to federal reservations for protection. "I do not want to leave this place," Chief Terrecowah declared. "God gave us these lands." Lone Chief echoed: "I have made up my mind to stay here on my land. I am not going where I have nothing."[50]

However, most Pawnees felt they had no choice, and migrated to a reservation in Kansas. One of their songs reminded them of their home in Nebraska:

> *It is there that our hearts are set,*
> *In the expanse of the heavens.*

The very identity and existence of the Pawnees had depended on the boundlessness of their sky and earth. But now railroad tracks cut across their land like long gashes, and fences enclosed their grasslands where buffalo once roamed. Indians had become a minority on lands they had occupied for thousands of years. "If the white man had stayed on the other side of the big water," Pawnee chief Likitaweelashar sadly reflected, "we Indians would have been better off for we are neither white men nor Indians now." Another Pawnee, Overtakes the Enemy, angrily exclaimed: "To do what they [whites] called civilizing us...was to destroy us. You know they thought that changing us, getting rid of our old ways and language and names would make us like white men. But why should we want to be like them, cheaters and greedy? Why should we change and abandon the ways that made us men and not the beggars we became?" A Pawnee chief told a white man who tried to offer gifts of blankets, guns, and knives: "You see, my brother, that the Ruler has given us all that we need; the buffalo for food and clothing; the corn to eat with our dried meat, or for cultivating the ground. Now go back to the country from whence you came. We do not want your presents, and we do not want you to come into our country."[51]

The world the Plains Indians had known was coming to an end. "The white men have surrounded me and have left me nothing but an island," protested Red Cloud. "When we first had this land we were strong. Now our nation is melting away like snow on the hillsides where the sun is warm; while the white people grow like blades of grass when summer is coming." The chief source of life and economic independence for them, the buffalo would no longer be roaming the plains. As he watched engineers surveying for a railroad in Wyoming, Red Cloud told them: "We do not want you here. You are scaring away the buffalo."[52]

In 1873, four years after the completion of the transcontinental railroad, an artist created a chromolithograph entitled *American Progress*. His painting dramatically depicted the tension between the new technology and the Indian. Twelve by sixteen inches in size, it was intended to decorate the homes of America—"from the miner's humble cabin to the stately marble mansion of the capitalist." At the center of this painting was a beautiful white woman, floating through the air and bearing on her forehead the "Star of Empire." In her right hand she carried a book, the emblem of education and knowledge, and held in her left hand telegraph wires that she was stringing across the plains. Behind her, in a clear lighted sky, were cities, factories, steamboats, and railroad trains. Three locomotives followed her. The ends of her long white gown, blowing in the wind, faded off into the tracks of the railroad, signifying the union of womanhood with technology. Beneath her, virtuous farmers plowed their fields, while pathfinders explored the "vacant lands." The course of empire was westward. Before the ethereal white woman, in a dark stormy sky, were buffalo, a bear, and Indians, in flight toward "the Stony mountains," yielding to her and the dynamic economic, cultural, and racial forces she represented. Twenty years before the presentation of Frederick Jackson Turner's paper "The Significance of the Frontier in American History," *American Progress* was offering a panoramic self-portrait of America's triumph of "civilization" over "savagery."

5

"NO MORE PECK O' CORN"
Slavery and Its Discontents

UNLIKE INDIANS, BLACKS were not outside of white society's borders; rather they were within what James Madison called the "bosom" of the republic, living in northern ghettos and on southern plantations. David Walker lived in both of these worlds. Born in North Carolina in 1785, he was the son of a slave father and a free mother. Inheriting the status of his mother, walker felt rage against the cruelty and injustice of slavery. Living below the Mason-Dixon Line was a painful contradiction for him: he saw people who shared his color defined as property. Somehow, Walker learned to read and write; he studied history and pondered why blacks in America were in such a wretched condition.[1]

Walker continued to reflect on this question after he moved to Boston, where he sold old clothes. Freedom in northern society, he realized, was only a facade for the reality of caste. Blacks were allowed only menial jobs. "Here we are—reduced to degradation," Walker observed. "Here we are cleaning the white man's shoes." Resentful of the stereotypes of blacks as savages, Walker countered that whites were the true barbarians: the enslavement of blacks, the selling and whipping of slaves—such practices were signs of savagery, not civilization.

Slavery, he believed, could only be destroyed through violence. "Masters want us for their slaves and think nothing of murdering us in order to subject us to that wretched condition—therefore, if there is an *attempt* made by us, kill or be killed."[2]

In 1829, Walker published his revolutionary thoughts in an *Appeal to the Colored Citizens of the World*. Southern legislators denounced the pamphlet as "seditious" and restricted its circulation; even northern white abolitionists like Benjamin Lundy and William Lloyd Garrison criticized it as "inflammatory" and "injudicious." A year later, Walker died, mysteriously. What he had presented was a candid, disturbing assessment of the condition of blacks: they had been reduced to slaves in the South and pariahs in the North.[3]

"North of Slavery"

In 1860, 225,000 African Americans lived in the North. They were "free," for the northern states had abolished slavery after the American Revolution. Their presence was far from pervasive, and blacks certainly did not threaten the racial homogeneity of white society. Yet they were the target of virulent racism. "The same schools do not receive the children of the black and European," Alexis de Tocqueville observed in the 1830s.

> In the theaters gold cannot procure a seat for the servile race beside their former masters; in the hospitals they lie apart; and although they are allowed to invoke the same God as the whites, it must be at a different altar and in their own churches, with their own clergy. The gates of heaven are not closed against them, but their inferiority is continued to the confines of the other world. When the Negro dies, his bones are cast aside, and the distinction of condition prevails even in the equality of death.[4]

As historian Leon Litwack described their situation, African Americans were only "north of slavery." Indeed, everywhere blacks experienced discrimination and segregation. They were barred from most hotels and restaurants and were forced to sit in separate sections in theaters and churches, invariably in the back. Black children usually attended separate and inferior schools. "The colored people are...charged with want of desire for education and improvement," a black protested, "yet, if a colored man comes to the door of our institutions of learning, with desires ever so strong, the lords of these institutions rise up and shut the door; and then you say we have not the desire nor the ability to acquire education. Thus, while the white youths enjoy all these advantages, we are excluded and shut out, and must remain ignorant." Transportation facilities were often segregated. In Philadelphia, blacks were allowed to ride only on the front platforms of streetcars, and New York City had separate buses—one exclusively for blacks. Told their presence in white residential districts would depreciate property values, blacks found themselves trapped in squalid slums.[5]

Although they were free, African Americans were restricted in their right to vote. Ironically, the political proscription of blacks often accompanied the advance of democacy for whites. In 1821, for example, the New York constitutional convention expanded suffrage for free "white" male citizens: to become voters, they could own property, or they could qualify in other ways such as paying taxes, serving in the militia, and working on the highways. On the other hand, blacks were required to be property owners in order to vote. The Pennsylvania constitutional convention of 1838 was more direct: it simply established universal "white" manhood suffrage and thus disenfranchised blacks completely.

Blacks also suffered from attacks by white workers. Time and again in northern cities, white mobs invaded black communities, killing people and destroying their homes and churches. Philadelphia, the "city of brotherly love," was the scene of several bloody antiblack riots. In 1834, rampaging whites forced blacks to flee the city. Seven years later in Cincinnati, white workers used a cannon against blacks, who armed themselves to defend their families. The mayor then persuaded about three hundred black men to be jailed for their own security, assuring them that their wives and children would be protected. But the white rioters attacked again, and order was not restored until the governor sent troops.

Victims of discrimination, segregation, and violence, northern African Americans encountered a powerful cluster of negative racial images. These stereotypes contributed to the conditions of racial degradation and poverty, which in turn, reinforced prejudice.

Blacks were denounced as "immature," "indolent," and "good-for-nothing." As one white Pennsylvanian charged, they were "simply unfit," "naturally lazy, childlike." Stereotypes of blacks as children were linked to notions of black intellectual inferiority. In his research on racial differences in intelligence, Dr. Samuel Morton of Philadelphia measured the cranial capacities of the skulls of whites and blacks. Finding that those of whites were larger, Dr. Morton concluded that whites were more intelligent. But the skulls of the whites that Morton examined belonged to men who had been hanged as criminals. Thus, as historian Thomas F. Gossett has remarked, it "would have been just as logical to conclude that a large head indicated criminal tendencies." This presumably "scientific evidence" of black mental inferiority was used to support the notion of white supremacy and to justify racial segregation. An Indiana senator, for example, declared in 1850: "The same power that has given him a black skin, with less weight or volume of brain, has given us a white skin, with greater volume of brain and intellect; and that we can never live together upon an equality is as certain as that no two antagonistic principles can exist together at the same time."[6]

While northern whites generally viewed blacks as childlike and mentally deficient, they also feared them as criminals. During the 1820s, Pennsylvania's governor expressed apprehension about the rising crime rate among blacks, and newspapers repeatedly reported Negro burglaries, Negro robberies, and Negro assaults against whites. The image of the black criminal led whites to restrict their migration into certain states. Ohio and Indiana required entering blacks to post a $500 bond as a guarantee against becoming a public charge and as a pledge of good behavior. The editor of an Indiana newspaper demanded that the law be enforced in order to "drive away a gang of pilferers."[7]

Moreover, blacks were seen as threats to racial purity. Indiana and Illinois prohibited interracial marriages. Everywhere, white social sentiment abhorred white and black relationships. "It is true," observed de Tocqueville, "that in the North...marriages may be contracted between Negroes and whites; but public opinion would stigmatize as infamous a man who should connect himself with a Negress, and it would be difficult to cite a single instance of such a union." In a petition to the Indiana legislature, whites called for the exclusion of blacks, warning that their wives and daughters would be "insulted and abused by those Africans." At the 1847 Illinois constitutional convention, a delegate explained that black migration should be restricted or else blacks would come into the state and "make proposals to marry our daughters." Efforts to disenfranchise blacks were often accompanied by denunciations of interracial sex. A delegate to the 1821 New York constitutional convention advocated the denial of suffrage to blacks in order to avoid the time "when the colors shall intermarry." In Wisconsin, opponents of black suffrage warned that political rights granted to blacks would encourage them to "marry our sisters and daughters." During an anti-Republican parade in New York in 1860, floats showed a thick-lipped Negro embracing a white woman and a Negro leading a white woman into the White House.[8]

School segregation was also fueled by fears of interracial unions. Whites petitioned the Indiana senate to establish segregated schools. The committee on education agreed that the Negro race was inferior and that the admission of Negro children "into our public schools would ultimately tend to bring about that feeling which favour their amalgamation with our own people." When Massachusetts prohibited racial discrimination in the public schools, a northern newspaper cried: "Now the blood of the Winthrops, the Otises, the Lymans, the Endicotts, and the Eliots, is in a fair way to be amalgamated with the Sambos, the Catos, and the Pompeys. The North is to be Africanized."[9]

The North for blacks was not the promised land. Although they were not slaves, they were hardly free. Under slavery, they were forced to work; as wage earners, they were excluded from many jobs. In New York, white dock workers attacked blacks seeking employment. In Cincinnati, white mechanics opposed the training of young blacks, and white cabinet shop workers demanded the dismissal of a recently hired black worker. Unable to find skilled jobs, many blacks were pushed into menial labor. In the 1850s, 87 percent of New York's gainfully employed blacks held menial jobs. Blacks were painfully aware of their grim prospects. "Why should I strive hard and acquire all the constituents of a man," a young man complained bitterly, "if the prevailing genius of the land admit me not as such, or but in an inferior degree! Pardon me if I feel insignificant and weak.... What are my prospects? To what shall I turn my hand? Shall I be a mechanic? No one will employ me; white boys won't work with me.... Drudgery and servitude, then, are my prospective portion."[10]

Was "Sambo" Real?

Meanwhile, in the South, four million African Americans were slaves, representing 35 percent of the total population in 1860. Like Caliban, they served the Prosperos of the master class. They constituted the essential labor force in southern agriculture for tobacco, hemp, rice, sugar, and especially cotton cultivation. The majority of the slaves worked on plantations, agricultural production units with more than twenty slaves.

Work on the plantations, according to historian Kenneth Stampp, began early in the morning when a horn awakened the slaves an hour before daylight. "All work-hands are [then] required to rise and prepare their cooking, etc. for the day," a plantation manual stated. "The second horn is blown just at good day-light, when it is the duty of the driver to visit every house and see that all have left for the field." Work was highly regimented. A glimpse of plantation labor was captured by a traveler in Mississippi: "First came, led by an old driver carrying a whip, forty of the largest and strongest women I ever saw together; they were all in a simple uniform dress of a bluish check stuff, the skirts reaching little below the knee; their legs and feet were bare; they carried themselves loftily, each having a hoe over the shoulder, and walking with a free, powerful swing, like *chasseurs* on the march. Behind came the cavalry, thirty strong, mostly men, but a few of them women, two of whom rode astride on the plow mules. A lean and vigilant white overseer, on a brisk pony, brought up the rear."[11]

A slave described the routine of a workday: "The hands are required to be in the cotton field as soon as it is light in the morning, and, with the exception of ten or fifteen minutes, which is given to them at noon to swallow their allowance of cold bacon, they are not permitted to be a moment idle until it is too dark to see, and when the moon is full, they often times labor till the middle of the night." After they left the fields, they had more work to do. "Each one must attend to his respective chores. One feeds the mules, another the swine—another cuts the wood, and so forth; besides the packing [of cotton] is all done by candle light. Finally, at a late hour, they reach the quarters, sleepy and overcome with the long day's toil."[12]

To manage this enslaved labor force, masters used various methods of discipline and control. They sometimes used kindness. "Now I contend that the surest and best method of managing negroes, is to love them," a Georgia planter explained. "We know...that if we love our horse, we will treat him well, and if we treat him well, he will become gentle, docile and obedient...and if this treatment has this effect upon all the animal creation...why will it not have the same effect upon slaves?" But masters also believed that strict discipline was essential and that power had to be based on fear. South Carolina's senator James Hammond, owner of more than three hundred slaves, fully understood the need for the absolute submission of a slave to his master: "We have to rely more and more on the power of fear. We are determined to continue masters, and to do so we have to draw the rein tighter and tighter day by day to be assured that we hold them in complete check." Completeness included psychological control: masters tried to brainwash their slaves into believing they were racially inferior and racially suited for bondage. Kept illiterate and ignorant, they were told they were incapable of caring for themselves.[13]

To many white southerners, slaves were childlike, irresponsible, lazy, affectionate, and happy. Altogether these alleged qualities represented a type of personality—the "Sambo."

"Slaves never become men or women," a traveler in the South commented. Slavemasters frequently referred to adult blacks as "grown-up children," or "boys" and "girls." Regarding themselves as guardians, they claimed their slaves had to be "governed as children."[14] Slavemasters repeatedly complained about the problem of laziness, saying their black laborers had to be supervised or they would not work. If slaves were freed, they would become "an insufferable burden to society." William Gilmore Simms gave this view literary expression; in his novel *The Yemassee,* Simms had the slave Hector respond to a proposal for his freedom. "I d——n to h——ll, massa, if I gwine to be free!" Hector protested. "De ting aint right; and enty I know wha' kind of ting freedom is wid black man? Ha! You make Hector free, he turn wuss more nor poor buckra—he tief out of de shop—he git drunk and lie in de ditch...." Obviously, slavemasters insisted, blacks had to be kept in slavery; otherwise they would surely become "indolent lazy thievish drunken," working only when they could not steal.[15]

But slavemasters also cherished the bonds of affection they claimed existed between themselves and their childlike slaves. In his *Black Diamonds Gathered in the Darkey Homes of the South,* Edward Pollard exclaimed: "I love to study his affectionate heart; I love to mark that peculiarity in him, which beneath all his buffoonery exhibits him as a creature of the tenderest sensibilities, mingling his joys and his sorrows with those of his master's home." Slaveholders described their slaves as the happiest people in the world, working little and spending the rest of their time "singing, dancing, laughing, chattering, and bringing up pigs and chickens." "At present we have in South Carolina," one slaveholder boasted, "two hundred and fifty thousand civilized and peaceable slaves, happy and contented...." In their private journals, masters recorded moments of closeness with their slaves. One of them scribbled into his diary on January 1, 1859: "The hands as usual came in to greet the New Year with their good wishes—the scene is well calculated to excite sympathies; notwithstanding bondage, affections find roots in the heart of the slave for the master."[16]

But the boast betrayed nervousness. The image of the slave as Sambo had special significance: the whole western world was ideologically opposed to American slavery, and therefore masters felt compelled to justify their peculiar institution as a "positive good." If they could show that their slaves were happy and satisfied with their condition, then perhaps they could defend themselves against their moral critics. They declared that "ours is a patriarchal institution now, founded in pity and protection on the one side, and dependence and gratitude on the other." There were moral misgivings among white southerners themselves. "We must satisfy them that slavery is of itself right," the defenders of the institution declared, "that it is not a sin against God." Time and again they insisted that the slavemaster was "enlightened," "humane," and "Christian," and that the slave was "submissive," "docile," "happy," "conscious of his own inferiority and proud of being owned & governed by a superior."[17]

Many masters had doubts about the morality of slavery. "Slavery," admitted the governor of Mississippi, "is an evil at best." Similarly, a white Virginian anxiously confessed: "This, sir, is a Christian community. Southerners read in their Bibles, 'Do unto all men as you would have them do unto you'; and this golden rule and slavery are hard to reconcile." One slaveholder jotted in his diary: "Oh what trouble,—running sore, constant pressing weight, perpetual wearing, dripping, is this patriarchal institution! What miserable folly for men to cling to it as something heaven-descended. And here we and our children after us must groan under the burden—our hands tied from freeing ourselves." Few slaveholders could "openly and honestly look the thing [slavery] in the face," a European traveler in the South observed. "They wind and turn about in all sorts of ways, and make use of every argument...to convince me that the slaves are the happiest people in the world."[18]

While claims that slaves were "Sambos" helped to comfort anguished consciences, they also offered the masters psychological assurances that their slaves were under control. Surely happy slaves would not come at night and slit the throats of their masters. In reality, slaveholders were terrified by the specter of slave rebellion. Aware of the bloody slave revolts in St. Domingo in the 1790s, they were warned by an American official in Haiti: "Negroes only cease to be *children* when they degenerate into *savages*." After the brutal suppression of the 1822 Denmark Vesey slave conspiracy in Charleston, a worried South Carolina slaveholder warned: our blacks were "barbarians who would, IF THEY COULD, become the DESTROYERS of our race."[19]

Holding what Thomas Jefferson had called the "wolf by the ears," masters lived in constant dread of slave insurrection. Southern newspapers frequently reported news of slave unrest and "evidences of a very unsettled state of mind among the servile population." The wife of a Georgia planter complained that slaves were "a threatening source of constant insecurity" and that "every southern *woman*" lived in terror of her slaves. A Louisiana slaveholder recalled tense times "when there was not a single planter who had a calm night's rest," and when every master went to bed with a gun at his side.[20]

Here was a society hysterically afraid of a black "giddy multitude." The master-slave relationship was dynamic, contradictory, and above all uncertain. "Sambo" existed and did not exist. What was the reality? How did the slaves themselves view their own behavior?

There were slaves who appeared to be "Sambos." Asked about whether he desired freedom, a slave replied to a curious visitor: "No, massa, me no want to be free, have good massa, take care of me when I sick, never 'buse nigger; no, me no want to be free." In a letter to his master who was away on a trip, a slave ended his report on plantation operations: "The respects of your affec. Svt. unto D[eath] in hopes ever to merit your esteem. Your most dutiful servant. Harford."[21]

But slaves who behaved like "Sambos" might not have actually been "Sambos": they might have been playing the role of loyal and congenial slaves in order to get favors or to survive, while keeping their inner selves hidden. Masters themselves sometimes had difficulty determining a slave's true personality. "So deceitful is the Negro," a master explained, "that as far as my own experience extends I could never in a single instance decipher his character.... We planters could never get at the truth." For many slaves, illusion protected them from their masters. "The only weapon of self defence that I could use successfuly, was that of deception," explained fugitive slave Henry Bibb. Another former slave explained that one had to "know the *heart* of the poor slave—learn his secret thoughts—thoughts he dare not utter in the hearing of the white man."[22]

Indeed, many slaves wore masks of docility and deference in order to shroud subversive plans. Every year thousands of slaves became fugitives, making their way north to freedom, and many of these runaways had seemed passive and cheerful before they escaped.

> *No more peck o' corn for me,*
> *No more, no more;*
> *No more peck o' corn for me,*
> *Many tousand go.*
>
> *No more driver's lash for me.*
> *No more pint o' salt for me.*
> *No more hundred lash for me.*
> *No more mistress call for me.*[23]

After his flight north, fugitive J. W. Loguen received a letter from his former slave mistress. "You know that we reared you as we reared our own children," wrote Mrs. Sarah Logue, "that you was never abused, and that shortly before you ran away, when your master asked you if you would like to be sold, you said you would not leave him to go with any body." In his reply, Loguen caustically remarked: "Woman, did you raise your *own children* for the market? Did you raise them for the whipping-post?" The ex-slave boldly proclaimed his love for liberty: "Wretched woman! Be it known to you that I value my freedom...more, indeed, than my own life; more than all the lives of all the slaveholders and tyrants under heaven."[24]

Sometimes a slave would play the role of "Sambo" and then strike directly at his tyrant. Slavemaster William Pearce told one of his erring slaves that he would be whipped after supper. When the slave was called out, he approached Pearce submissively. As soon as he was within striking distance, the slave pulled out a concealed ax and split his master's head. Nat Turner, according to historian Stampp, was "apparently as humble and docile as a slave was expected to be." In Virginia on August 22, 1831, he led seventy fellow slaves in a violent insurrection that lasted two days and left nearly sixty whites dead. After his arrest, Turner made a statement to the authorities. His master, he acknowledged, was "kind": "in fact, I had no cause to complain of his treatment to me." But Turner had had a religious experience: "I had a vision—and

I saw white spirits and black spirits engaged in battle...and blood flowed in streams...." A voice told him to wait for a sign from heaven: "And on the appearance of the sign (the eclipse of the sun last February), I should arise and prepare myself, and slay my enemies with their own weapons." Turner carried out his mission, and a white Virginian nervously observed: "It will long be remembered in the annals of our country, and many a mother as she presses her infant darling to her bosom, will shudder at the recollection of Nat Turner." The slave rebel's action was a frightening revelation to white southerners: smiling and holding his hat in his hand, "Sambo" could be planning their destruction.[25]

The reality for many slaves may have been even more complex and subtle than a duality of roles. Some "Sambo"-like behavior may have been, not so much a veil to hide inner emotions of rage and discontent, as a means of expressing them. Lying, stealing, laziness, immaturity, and ignorance all contained within them an aggressive quality: they constituted, in effect, resistance to efficiency, discipline, work, and productivity.

"Hands won't work unless I am in sight," a Virginia planter scribbled angrily in his diary. "I left the Field at 12 [with] all going on well, but very little done after [that]." Slaves occasionally destroyed tools and machinery and treated farm animals so brutally that they frequently crippled them. "They can neither hoe, nor ditch, chop wood, nor perform any kind of labor with a white man's skill," complained a master. "They break and destroy more farming utensils, ruin more carts, break more gates, spoil more cattle and horses, and commit more waste than five times the number of white laborers do." A continual problem for masters was the stealing of chickens and pigs. But slaves often viewed the matter differently: they were simply "taking" property (pigs) for use by other property (themselves). In other words, the master's "meat" was taken out of "one tub" and put in "another." "When I tuk the turkey and eat it," a slave said, "it got to be a part of me." This appropriation seemed justified because their weekly food allowance was so meager, and their masters were profiting from their labor. Even as they shucked corn, they sang:

> Massa in the great house, counting out his
>   money,
> Oh, shuck that corn and throw it in the barn.
> Missis in the parlor, eating bread and honey,
> Oh, shuck that corn and throw it in the barn.

Resenting the unfair appropriation of their labor, many slaves feigned illness and lied in order to avoid work. One planter complained that slaves were sick on workdays but not on Sundays. One slave managed to avoid work for many years by claiming he was nearly blind; after the Civil War, he was suddenly able to see again and became a successful farmer. Where masters perceived the destructiveness, lying, and laziness of their slaves as mischievous, childish, and irresponsible behavior, many slaves saw refusal to be exploited. Thus, the same action held different meanings, depending on whether one was the master or the slave.[26]

Unlike slaves on the plantation, slaves in the southern cities did not have to engage in such ambiguity. In 1860, there were seventy thousand urban slaves. They labored in textile mills, iron furnaces, and tobacco factories. Many of them had been "hired out" and were working as wage earners. The hiring-out system generally involved a contract that specified the wage, the length of service, some assurances concerning treatment, and the type of work to be performed. In a contract signed on January 1, 1832, for example, C. W. Thruston and his brother promised "to pay James Brown Ninety Dollars for the hire of Negro Phill until 25 Dec. next. And we agree to pay taxes & doctor bills. Clothe him during said time & return him...with good substantial cloth...shoes and socks and a blanket."[27]

In this case it appears that the master found the job for his slave, but this was not always the practice. Slavemasters would often simply let their slaves find their own jobs and require them to make weekly payments. In effect, slaves were renting their own labor from their masters. One Savannah slave used the hiring-out system imaginatively. First, he purchased his own time from his master at $250 a year, paying in monthly installments. Then he hired about seven or eight slaves to work for him.[28]

Hiring out weakened the slave system. No longer directly under the supervision of their masters, slaves could feel the loosening of reins. They were taking care of themselves and had many of the privileges of free persons. In fact, they were sometimes called "free slaves." Many of them were even permitted to "live out"—to make their own housing arrangements by renting a room or a house. Living away from their masters' watchful eyes, they enjoyed a degree of independence. Though they were slaves, they were in contact with free laborers, black and white, and learned what it meant to be free. "Hundreds of slaves in New Orleans," Frederick Law Olmsted reported, "must be constantly reflecting and saying to one another, 'I am as capable of taking care of myself as this Irish hod-carrier, or this German market-gardener; why can't I have the enjoyment of my labor as well as they? I am as capable of taking care of my own family as much as they of theirs; why should I be subject to have them taken from me by those men who call themselves our owners?'"[29]

No wonder one white southerner complained: "The cities is no place for niggers! They get strange notions into their heads and grow discontented. They ought, every one of them, be sent onto the plantations." A Louisville editor claimed that "negroes scarcely realize[d] the fact that they [were] slaves" in the city. They became "insolent, intractable, and in many cases wholly worthless." They made "free negroes their associates," "imbibing" their feelings and imitating their conduct. Another white southerner anxiously described the behavior of slaves in New Orleans: "It was not unusual for slaves to gather on street corners at night...where they challenged whites to attempt to pass, hurled taunts at white women, and kept whole neighborhoods disturbed by shouts and curses. Nor was it safe to accost them, as many went armed with knives and pistols in flagrant defiance of all the precautions of the Black Code." Apparently, urban slaves did not behave like "Sambos."[30]

Whether or not "Sambo" was real was revealed during the Civil War as Union troops were destroying the authority of the slave system. Everyone—white and black—sensed the momentousness of the conflict. "There is a war commenced between the North and the South," a planter told his slaves. "If the North whups, you will be as free a man as I is. If the South whups, you will be slaves all your days." Information about the war circulated through the slave quarters. Pretending indifference, house servants listened intently as their masters talked among themselves about the military and political events of the conflict. "We'se can't read, but we'se can listen," a South Carolina slave told Union soldiers.[31]

When slave Abram Harris heard that his master had been killed in the war, he felt loss and sorrow. "Us wus boys togedder, me en Marse Hampton, en wus jist er bout de same size," he said. "Hit so did hurt me when Marse Hampton got kilt kase I lubed dat white man." A former slave recalled: "I shall never forget the feeling of sickness which swept over me. I saw no reason for rejoicing as others were doing. It was my opinion that we were being driven from our homes and set adrift to wander, I knew not where. I did not relish the idea of parting with my young master who was as true a friend as I ever had." Occasionally, expressions of loyalty were accompanied by demands for respect. One slave told his master: "When you'all had de power you was good to me, and I'll protect you now. No nigger, nor Yankee, shall touch you. If you want anything, call for Sambo. I mean, call for Mr. Samuel—that's my name now."[32]

Other slaves, however, excitedly embraced their freedom. Slave Dora Franks overheard her master and mistress discussing the war: "He say he feared all de slaves 'ud be took away. She say if dat was true she feel lak jumpin' in de well. I hate to hear her say dat, but from dat minute I started prayin' for freedom." What was most striking was the way the presence of federal troops in an area stimulated noticeable changes in slave behavior. A few days after Union soldiers camped near her plantation, a slaveholder wrote in her diary: "The Negroes are going off in great numbers and are beginning to be very independent and impudent." In *The War Time Journal of a Georgia Girl*, Eliza Andrews described the strange behavior of one of her slaves. Alfred, "one of the most peaceful and humble negroes on the plantation," was charged with attacking a white man. "I hope there is some mistake," she commented fearfully, "though the negroes are getting unruly since the Yankees are so near." Mrs. Mary Jones recorded similar disillusionment in her diary. "The people are all idle on the plantations, most of them seeking their own pleasure," she wrote on January 6, 1865. "Susan, a Virginia Negro and nurse to my little Mary Ruth, went off with Mac, her husband, to Arcadia the night after the first day the Yankees appeared.... She has acted a faithless part as soon as she could." On January 21, she reported that her "faithful" cook, Kate, had suddenly left the plantation. Disappointed and angry, Jones concluded: "Their condition is one of perfect anarchy and rebellion."[33]

Indeed, during the war, plantation discipline generally disintegrated. "The wretches [are] trying all they can," complained a slaveholder in Texas, "it seems to me, to agrivate me, taking no interest, having no care about the future, neglecting their duty." Many slaves engaged in work slowdowns; others refused to work. Masters had difficulty extracting obedience. With the coercive power of the government focused on the battlefronts, many slaves became assertive, redefining their relationships with their masters.[34]

Slaves were impatient, ready to break for freedom. An old slave who had fled to the Union lines told the Yankees: "Ise eighty-eight year old. Too ole for come? Mas'r joking. Neber too ole for leave de land o' bondage." During the war, some five hundred thousand slaves ran off to the federal lines. In 1863, a northern clergyman asked a Virginia slave whether she had heard of the Emancipation Proclamation. "Oh, yes, massa!" she responded, "we all knows about it; only we darsn't let on. We pretends not to know. I said to my ole massa, 'What's this Massa Lincoln is going to do to the poor nigger? I hear he is going to cut 'em up awful bad. How is it, massa?' I just pretended foolish, sort of." Shortly after this conversation, she ran off to the Union lines. Another slave remembered the day the Union troops arrived at his master's plantation located on the coast of South Carolina: "De people was all a hoein'.... Dey was a hoein' in de rice-field, when de gunboats come. Den ebry man drap dem hoe, and leff de rice. De mas'r he stand and call, 'Run to de wood for hide. Yankee come, sell you to Cuba! run for hide!' Ebry man he run, and my God! run all toder way! Mas'r stand in de wood.... He say 'Run to de wood!' an ebry man run by him, straight to de boat."[35]

Watching their once loyal slaves suddenly bolt for the Union lines, many white southerners jettisoned their opinions about their slaves as "Sambos." Emily C. Douglas was shocked that her trusted slaves had deserted her: "They left without even a good-bye." Notions of slave docility were nullified. "You can form no idea of my situation and anxiety of mind," an overseer wrote to his employer in 1863. "All is anarchy and confusion here—everything going to destruction—and the negroes on the plantation insubordinate—My life has been several times in danger." In the minds of many whites, blacks had changed from children into savages. "The 'faithful slave' is about played out," a slaveholder observed bitterly. "They are the most treacherous, brutal, and ungrateful race on the globe." Similarly, a Georgia planter condemned the "ingratitude evinced by the African character." "This war has taught us the perfect impossibility of placing the least confidence in any Negro," he observed. "In too numerous instances, those we esteemed the most have been the first to desert us."[36]

Many of the deserters were women. For them, freedom had a different meaning, for they had experienced bondage in ways different than the men. As slaves, many of them found that more than their labor was appropriated: their bodies were regarded as property to be used to satisfy the erotic pleasures of their masters. As a fifteen-year-old slave, Harriet Jacobs had been sexually abused by her master. "He peopled my young mind with unclean images, such as only a vile monster could think of," she later wrote after she had escaped. "He told me I was his property; that I must be subject to his will in all things.... I shuddered to think of being the mother of children that should be owned by my tyrant." The presence of a large mulatto population stood as vivid visual proof of such sexual exploitation of slave women by slavemasters. "Like the patriarchs of old," a southern white woman bitterly complained, "our men live all in one house with their wives and their concubines; and the mulattoes one sees in every family partly resemble the white children. Any lady is ready to tell you who is the father of all the mulatto children in everybody's household but her own. These, she seems to think, drop from the clouds."[37]

Frederick Douglass: Son of His Master

One of these mulatto children was Frederick Douglass. As a young child on a Maryland plantation, he had been sent by his master, Thomas Auld, to live with his grandparents, Betsey and Isaac Bailey. Grandmother Bailey was in charge of the children of the younger slave women. Her cabin was isolated, located twelve miles from the plantation and far away psychologically from the reality of slavery. "I had always lived with my grandmother on the outskirts of the plantation," Douglass later recalled. "I had therefore been...out of the way of the bloody scenes that often occurred on the plantation."[38]

Douglass's childhood years at Grandmother Bailey's home were happy and secure. Frederick was never hungry, for his grandmother was skillful at fishing and farming. "Living here, with my dear old grandmother and grandfather," he noted later, "it was a long time before I knew myself to be a *slave*.... Grandmother and grandfather were the greatest people in the world to me; and being with them so snugly in their own little cabin—I supposed it to be their own—knowing no higher authority over me...than the authority of grandmamma, for a time there was nothing to disturb me."[39]

But this period turned out to be somewhat short. As a young boy, Douglass was placed in the home of Hugh Auld, his master's brother who lived in Baltimore. Sophia Auld had not owned slaves before, and she initially regarded him as "a child, like any other." Her own son, Tommy, and Frederick "got on swimmingly together." She was like a mother to him, the slave thought. Under

her care, he was "well-off": he had a straw bed with a cover, plenty
of food, and clean clothes. "Why should I hang down my head, and
speak with bated breath, when there was no pride to scorn me,
no coldness to repel me, and no hatred to inspire me with fear?"
Sophia seemed to say to him: "Look up, child; don't be afraid."[40]

But the slave system soon came down on both of them. Shortly
after Frederick joined the Auld household, he developed a strong
desire to learn to read, and Sophia gladly agreed to teach him.
The boy was precocious and learned quickly. Sophia seemed
proud of his progress, as if he had been "her own child," and told
her husband about her new pupil. Hugh Auld scolded her severely,
forbidding her to give the young slave any further lessons. "If
you give a nigger an inch he will take an ell," he angrily lectured
her. "Learning will spoil the best nigger in the world." Master
Auld's fury had a damaging effect on Sophia. Her husband's "iron
sentences, cold and harsh," disciplined her, and like "an obedient wife," she set herself like a "flint" against Frederick's education. "In ceasing to instruct me," he later wrote, "my mistress had
to seek to justify herself to herself.... She finally became even
more violent in her opposition to my learning to read than Mr.
Auld himself." She spied on Douglass and even interrogated him
about his activities. Whenever she caught him reading a book,
she would snatch it away.[41]

Still, the system of slavery could not completely crush Sophia's
sympathy for Douglass. A few years after the reading incident,
he went to work as an apprentice in the Baltimore shipyards and
was brutally beaten by white workers. When Sophia saw his swollen eye and blood-stained face, she was moved to tears. She gently
washed the blood from his face and covered his wounded eye with
a piece of fresh beef. "No mother's hand could have been more tender than hers.... Her affectionate heart was not yet dead, though
much hardened by time and circumstances."[42]

Meanwhile, Douglass had been influenced by his experiences
in Baltimore. Urban slavery was not as closed and coercive as
plantation slavery. Indeed, in Baltimore, which had a large population of free blacks, Douglass saw that not all blacks were slaves.
"I was living among freemen, and was in all respects equal to
them by nature and attainments. Why should I be a slave?"
On the wharves, the young slave met two Irishmen who told
him about the free society of the North, and he went home with
thoughts of escape and freedom pounding in his head. The city
also offered Douglass educational opportunities. Once he under-

stood that knowledge could be a path to freedom, he was determined to educate himself. He carried a copy of *Webster's Spelling Book* in his pocket when he went outside to play and took spelling lessons from his white playmates. He bought an antislavery book, *The Columbian Orator*, with money he had earned from blacking boots. In the urban environment, he had greater freedom of movement and contact with a wider variety of people and ideas than did slaves on the plantation. "It is quite probable," Douglass speculated, "that but for the mere circumstance of being thus removed [to Baltimore], before the rigors of slavery had been fully fastened upon me, before my young spirit had been crushed under the iron control of the slave driver, I might have continued in slavery until emancipated by the war."[43]

Master Thomas Auld realized he had made a mistake. He complained that "city life" had influenced Frederick "perniciously" and made him restless. Consequently, Auld placed the sixteen-year-old slave under the supervision of slave breaker Edward Covey. His instructions were simple and clear: Frederick was "to be broken," transformed psychologically into an obedient slave. "To make a contented slave," Douglass later explained, "you must make a thoughtless one.... He must be able to detect no inconsistencies in slavery. The man who takes his earnings must be able to convince him that he has a perfect right to do so. It must not depend on mere force—the slave must know no higher law than his master's will. The whole relationship must not only demonstrate to his mind its necessity, but its absolute rightfulness."[44]

Reduced to a field hand for the first time in his life, Douglass was so cruelly whipped and overworked that he felt Covey had indeed succeeded in breaking his spirit. "My natural elasticity was crushed; my intellect languished; the disposition to read departed; the cheerful spark that lingered about my eye died out; the dark night of slavery closed in upon me, and behold a man transformed to a brute!" But the young man did not realize how greatly Grandmother Bailey, Sophia Auld, and Baltimore had unfitted him for slavery. Thus, though he found himself in a "sort of beast-like stupor between sleeping and waking," he still gazed at the sailboats skimming across Chesapeake Bay and exclaimed: "You are loosed from your moorings, and free. I am fast in my chains, and am a slave!...O, that I were free!...I will run away.... I had as well be killed running as die standing."[45]

Covey sensed the slave's discontent and was determined to stamp out any thoughts of freedom. While working in the treading yard one hot August day, Douglass collapsed from heat and exhaustion. Too ill to respond to Covey's order to get up and work, he was savagely kicked. Bleeding profusely, he crawled to Master Auld, pleading for protection from the inhuman slave breaker. Instead, he was scolded and ordered to return to Covey. Douglass had not expected Auld to protect him "*as a man*," but he had hoped his master would at least protect him "*as his property*."[46]

Douglass knew he had to defend himself. Back at Covey's farm, he violently resisted the slave breaker's efforts to tie and whip him. "The fighting madness had come upon me, and I found my strong fingers firmly attached to the throat of the tyrant, as heedless of consequences, at the moment, as if we stood as equals before the law. The very color of the man was forgotten.... I held him so firmly by the throat that his blood followed my nails." In this supreme moment of physical confrontation, Douglass felt something profound. "I was a changed being after that fight. I was nothing before — I was a man now.... I had reached the point at which I was *not afraid to die*. This spirit made me a freeman in *fact*, though I still remained a slave in form."[47]

The fight with Covey taught him a lesson he would always remember: "A man without force is without the essential dignity of humanity." Years later, after Douglass escaped from slavery and was active in the abolitionist movement in the North, he broke from the moral suasion approach of William Lloyd Garrison and moved toward the violent strategy of the radical abolitionist John Brown. After his meeting with Brown in 1847, Douglass became less confident in the peaceful abolition of slavery. "My utterances became more and more tinged by the color of this man's strong impressions." Two years later, Douglass announced that he would welcome the news that the slaves had rebelled and were spreading "death and devastation" in the South. In 1859, he justified Brown's attack on Harpers Ferry — a bold attempt to seize arms from an arsenal and lead slaves in armed insurrection. "Capt. Brown has initiated a new mode of carrying on the crusade of freedom," Douglass declared, "and his blow has sent dread and terror throughout the entire ranks of the piratical army of slavery."[48]

Yet violence against the oppressor was not easy for Douglass to embrace. This was probably a crucial reason why he did not join John Brown and actually strike terror in the hearts of white southerners. While Douglass might have considered Brown's raid suicidal, he also believed every man should work for the abolition of slavery in his own way — "the tools to those who can use them."

His tools were the pen and podium. But slavery, as Douglass had experienced it, was too complicated and too contradictory for him to have a single and clear set of attitudes toward white southerners. The raised knife of revolt would be aimed not only at people tragically ensnared in a vicious system but also at people he cared about—Sophia Auld and perhaps even his own father.[49]

Douglass was never certain about his paternity. "In regard to the *time* of my birth, I cannot be definite as I have been respecting the *place*. Nor, indeed, can I impart much knowledge concerning my parents." But he thought that his father might have been Master Thomas Auld. "I was given away by my father [Thomas Auld], or the man who was called my father, to his own brother [Hugh Auld]." Told his father was a white man and possibly his owner, Douglass bitterly condemned slavery as a system that cruelly forced slavemasters to reject their slave children. Years later, after the Civil War and emancipation, Douglass visited Thomas Auld, and as he stood at the old man's bedside, he crossed a significant border separating them. Douglass insisted that Auld call him "Frederick," "as formerly," and asked his former master to satisfy an old, lingering, and anxious curiosity—his birth date. The date of his birth and his paternity were puzzling questions Douglass had linked in his mind. Reminiscing about his escape, Douglass assured Auld that he had not run away from him but from slavery. The two men had a warm reunion. "He was to me no longer a slaveholder either in fact or in spirit, and I regarded him as I did myself, a victim of the circumstances of birth, education, and custom."[50]

Douglass was intensely aware of his biracial ancestry. Time and again in his antislavery lectures he described himself as "the child of a white man" and "the son of a slaveholder." During an antislavery tour abroad, Douglass described England as "the land of my paternal ancestors." After the death of his wife Anna, he married Helen Pits, a white woman. In defense of this marriage, he remarked that his first wife "was the color of my mother and the second, the color of my father," and that "no one ever complained of my marriage to my former wife, though contrast of color was more decided and pronounced than in the present instance...." Angry over the racial exclusion of his daughter from a private school, Douglass told one of the parents responsible for the injustice: "We differ in color, it is true, (and not much in that respect)...."[51]

Descended from both white and black parents, Douglass hoped

for an integrated and interracial America, a society without racial borders. In his opposition to black emigration and separatism, Douglass argued that blacks were Americans and that they did not wish to return to Africa or form "a separate nation" in America. In his essay "The Future of the Colored Race," Douglass predicted that blacks would be "absorbed, assimilated," and would "only appear as the Phoenicians now appear on the shores of the Shannon in the features of a blended race."[52]

Martin Delany: Father of Black Nationalism

Douglass viewed the future of African Americans very differently than Martin Delany, the leading black nationalist of the nineteenth century. "I thank God for making me a man simply," Douglass observed, "but Delany always thanks him for making him a *black* man." Delany's pride in his blackness was reflected in his passionate interest in Africa. *"Africa for the African race,"* he declared, *"and black men to rule them.* By black men, I mean, men of African descent who claim an identity with the race."[53]

Delany's African identity was inspired by his parentage. He was born in 1812 in Charles Town, (West) Virginia, the son of a slave father and a free mother—Samuel and Pati Delany. His mother's father was a Mandingo prince, Shango, who had been captured as a youth during intertribal hostilities and brought to America with his betrothed, Graci. Shango was given his freedom because of his noble birth and returned to Africa; Graci was also freed but remained in America with their daughter, Pati. During his childhood, Martin had an intimate source of contact with Africa—his Mandingo grandmother (who died at the age of 107). Samuel Delany, the son of a Golah chieftain, managed to purchase his freedom when Martin was about ten years old. On his face, Samuel bore a scar from a wound he received while resisting arrest for striking his master.[54]

As a child, Martin learned that his membership in the black race made him the object of white scorn. Pati Delany's efforts to teach her children to read and write aroused angry opposition from white neighbors that was so intense that she felt compelled to move her family across the border to Pennsylvania.

But even north of slavery, racism was prevalent. As a journalist and an antislavery lecturer during the 1840s, Delany traveled widely throughout the North and often encountered racial hostility and violence. On one occasion, a white mob in Marseilles, Ohio, threatened to tar and feather him and burn him alive. Delany found that white children, even while involved in play, were never too busy to notice a black passing by and scream "nigger." "As the deportment of individuals is a characteristic evidence of their breeding," he noted, "so is the conduct of children generally observed as an evidence of the character of their parents." Delany found the racial epithets not only "an abuse of the feelings," but also "a blasting outrage on humanity."[55]

His bitterness toward northern society was sharpened by an admissions controversy at Harvard Medical School. In 1850, Delany, along with two other African Americans, had been admitted to the school. Their admission, however, was conditional: upon graduation, they would have to emigrate and practice medicine in Africa. Even so, their presence at Harvard provoked protests from white students. Demanding the dismissal of the blacks, they argued that integration would lower the "reputation" of Harvard and "lessen the value" of their diploma. The whites refused to attend classes with the blacks. Racial integration at Harvard, they warned, was "but the beginning of an Evil, which, if not checked will increase, and that the number of respectable *white* students will, in future, be in an inverse ratio, to that of *blacks*." Finally, the angry students attached a threat to their protest: if the faculty did not heed their demand, they would transfer to another school.[56]

The faculty quickly capitulated, ignoring a student counterpetition favoring the admission of the blacks. Deeming it "inexpedient" to allow blacks to attend lectures, the faculty defended their decision based on their commitment to teaching and academic excellence. They explained that the presence of blacks was a "source of irritation and distraction" that interfered with the "success of their teaching." Furthermore, the "intermixing" of the white and black races was "distasteful" to a large portion of the class and therefore "injurious" to the interests of the school. The incident filled Delany with rage. He was fully qualified for admission to Harvard Medical School. His letters of recommendation from his private instructors, Dr. Joseph Gazzam and Dr. Julius Le Moyne, provided evidence of his competence to study medicine.[57]

Two years later, Delany issued his manifesto for black emigration—*The Condition, Elevation, Emigration and Destiny of the Colored People of the United States.* Emerging as a leading theoretician of black nationalism, he organized the National

Emigration Convention; in 1859, Delany visited Africa to secure a land grant for the settlement of American blacks in the Niger Valley.

In his call for black emigration to Africa, Delany presented a detailed analysis of the degradation and despair blacks were experiencing in northern society. The inferior and dependent economic and social position blacks occupied in the North not only reinforced white prejudice but also inculcated feelings of inferiority and self-hatred among blacks. "Cast our eyes about us and reflect for a moment," Delany sadly declared, "and what do we behold! every thing that presents to view gives evidence of the skill of the white man. Should we purchase a pound of groceries, a yard of linen, a vessel of crockeryware, a piece of furniture, the very provisions that we eat,—all, all are the products of the white man." Delany argued that this condition of dependency with its constant reminders of their subordinate status had an insidious influence on black self-esteem. Born under oppression, black children could not "be raised in this country, without being stooped shouldered." Black men and women, moreover, appeared to be satisfied as menial workers, "accustomed" to being maids and cooks. They seemed to lack a sense of "self-respect." In Delany's judgment, blacks had been so broken by white oppression that they were actually helping to perpetuate their tragic condition.[58]

Blacks would never achieve acceptance and equality in America, Delany contended, unless they changed their condition and became self-reliant like whites—"a business, money-making people," educated for "the Store and Counting House." Black liberation, he believed, depended on entrepreneurial success. They must strive to acquire what had enabled whites to succeed—"a knowledge of all the various business enterprises, trades, professions, and sciences," a "practical Education" in business rather than a "Classical" education. "What did John Jacob Astor...know of Latin and Greek, and the Classics?"[59]

But Delany had no confidence that blacks would be able to change their condition in America. In his judgment, the oppression of blacks was essentially based on caste, not class. Although white laborers shared many class interests with blacks, the two groups would never join in common efforts to elevate themselves. The problem for blacks was "not a question of the rich against the poor" but of "white against black." Aware of antiblack hatred among white workers, Delany ruled out class struggle as a strategy for black liberation.[60]

Even if slavery was abolished, Delany believed, racism would persist as long as there were both whites and blacks living in America. The only way to rid society of race would be through amalgamation—for Americans to become a blended people. Delany believed this would never happen; moreover, he did not view racial mixture as desirable. Unlike Frederick Douglass, Delany did not want blacks to lose their "identity as a distinct race." "The truth is," he declared, "we are not identical with the Anglo-Saxon...and the sooner we know and acknowledge this truth, the better for ourselves and posterity." Blacks should be proud of themselves, for they possessed "the highest traits of civilization" and would someday instruct the world in the true principles of morals, religion, and law.[61]

To be redeemed, blacks had to emigrate to Africa in order to separate themselves from their white oppressors. "Were we content to remain as we are," Delany warned, "sparsely interspersed among our white fellow-countrymen, we might never be expected to equal them in any honorable or respectable competition for a livelihood." Therefore, the struggle had to focus on Africa. "No people can be free who themselves do not constitute an essential part of the *ruling element* of the country in which they live." If blacks were able to establish a proud and powerful black African nation, they would be able to win respect for blacks everywhere in the world and hasten the emancipation of slaves in America. "The claims of no people, according to established policy and usage," Delany insisted, "are respected by any nation, until they are presented in a national capacity."[62]

At the same time as Delany was celebrating Africa, he was also identifying with America. His book on emigration reflected this tension. It was "sincerely dedicated to the American people, North and South. By their most devout, and patriotic fellow-citizen, the author." Delany presented a strong case for black American citizenship by pointing to the immense contributions blacks had made to the American economy. Reminding readers about the black patriots of the American Revolution, he also argued: "Among the highest claims that an individual has upon his country, is that of serving in its cause, and assisting to fight its battles." America, for Delany, was home. "Here is our nativity," he observed, "and here have we the natural right to abide and be elevated through the measure of our own efforts.... Our common country is the United States. Here were we born, here raised and educated, here are the scenes of childhood...the sacred graves of our departed fathers and mothers." But here, too, Delany had experienced the abuse of white children, the violence of white mobs, and the scorn of the white students at Harvard. "We love our country, dearly love her," Delany cried, "but she [doesn't] love us — she despises us."[63]

This sense of agonizing ambivalence evoked complex and contradictory feelings within Delany during his visit to the Niger Valley in 1859. "The first sight and impressions of the coast of Africa are always inspiring, producing the most pleasant emotions," he scribbled in his diary. He was finally in the homeland described in his grandmother's Mandingo chants. During the first several days, Delany felt an "almost intense excitement," "a hilarity of feeling" approaching "intoxication." But then followed fatigue. This second "stage" of feeling, Delany thought, was "acclimation," often accompanied by nausea, chills, and violent headaches. During this period, he became homesick — "*a feeling of regret that you [had] left your native country for a strange one; an almost frantic desire to see friends and nativity; a despondency and loss of the hope of ever seeing those you [loved] at home again.*" Then Delany added in his diary: "These feelings, of course, must be resisted, and *regarded as a mere morbid affection of the mind* at the time, arising from an approaching disease." When he recovered from his psychosomatic malady, Delany felt an "ardent and abiding" love for Africa.[64]

An emotional storm was raging within Delany. He was in Africa, making arrangements for the settlement of American blacks. He was attempting to usher in a new era of African greatness and to affirm his blackness in African nationhood. Yet, as he stood on his ancestral soil, Delany experienced a mysterious despondency and found himself torn between an attachment to his "native country" and a love for this "strange" land. After he completed his negotiations for a land grant in the Niger Valley, Delany sailed for America, vowing he would return to Africa.

"Tell Linkum Dat We Wants Land"

Deliverance from slavery, for both Douglass and Delany, was to come from the barrel of a gun. Black men in blue, Douglass pointed out, were "on the battlefield mingling their blood with that of white men in one common effort to save the country." Through their participation in the war to save the Union, they were earning their right to claim full citizenship. Abandoning his dreams of emigrating to Africa, Delany volunteered for the Union Army and received an appointment as a major in the 104th Regiment of United States Colored Troops. "It is the duty of every colored man to vindicate his manhood by becoming a soldier," Delany declared, "and with his own stout arm to battle for the emancipation of his race."[65]

As armed soldiers, black men were not Sambos. "Now we sogers are men—men de first time in our lives," one of them declared. "Now we can look our old masters in de face. They used to sell and whip us, and we did not dare say one word. Now we ain't afraid, if they meet us, to run the bayonet through them." Their courage drove them to become instrumental in the saving of the Union, as noted in chapter one, and also in the liberating of some four million blacks.[66]

But what were the hopes and dreams of these newly freed people?

In 1865, General William Sherman asked twenty black leaders whether they preferred to live scattered among whites or in colonies by themselves. They replied that they preferred to have their own separate communities because racial prejudice would take years to overcome. When the agents of the Freedmen's Aid Commission arrived in the South, they found blacks asking: When will they open the schools? Blacks also wanted political power through the suffrage.

What the emancipated African Americans wanted most of all was economic independence. After the war, they demanded land. A freedman, Uncle Smart, told a northern teacher: "Do, my missus, tell Linkum dat we wants land—dis bery land dat is rich wid de sweat ob we face and de blood ob we back."[67] One of their songs vividly captured their dream:

> *Don't you see the lightning flashing in the*
> *cane brakes,*
> *Looks like we gonna have a storm*
> *Although you're mistaken it's the Yankee*
> *soldiers*
> *Going to fight for Uncle Sam.*
> *Old master was a colonel in the Rebel army*
> *Just before he had to run away—*
> *Look out the battle is a-falling*
> *The darkies gonna occupy the land.*[68]

Blacks felt they had already paid for the land "through a life of tears and groans, under the lash and yoke of tyranny." When a freedman named Cyrus was questioned by his former owner about his absence from the fields, he explained the new situation: "Seems lak we'uns do all the wuck and gits a part. Der ain't goin' ter be no more Master and Mistress, Miss Emma. All is equal. I done hear it from de cotehouse steps.... All de land belongs to de Yankees now, and dey gwine to divide it out 'mong de colored people."[69]

Some Radical Republicans, including Charles Sumner, Thaddeus Stevens, and George W. Julian, understood the need to grant land to the freed slaves. They argued that emancipation had to be accompanied by land confiscation from the planter class and land distribution to the newly freed blacks. The perpetuation of the large estates would mean the development of a semifeudal system based on the cheap labor of exploited and powerless blacks. But Congress was only willing to grant them civil and political rights through the Fourteenth and Fifteenth Amendments. The lawmakers rejected legislation for land distribution—known as the "40 acres and a mule" bill. Land should not be given to the freedmen, the *New York Times* argued, because they had to be taught the lessons of hard work, patience, and frugality. The *Nation* protested that land confiscation and distribution would violate the principle of property rights.[70]

During the war, however, forty thousand blacks had been granted land by military order. In 1864, after General Sherman completed his march to the sea, black leaders told him: "The way we can best take care of ourselves is to have land, and turn it and till it by our own labor." In response, General Sherman issued Special Field Order Number 15, which set aside large sections of South Carolina and Georgia for distribution to black people. They were given "possessory titles" to forty-acre lots until Congress could decide their final disposition. The blacks believed that they owned the lands. But after the planters were pardoned by President Andrew Johnson, they began to reclaim the lands and force their former slaves to work for them. The black landowners resisted: "To turn us off from the land that the Government has allowed us to occupy, is nothing less than returning us to involuntary servitude." "We own the land now. Put it out of your head that it will ever be yours again." In their protest to President Johnson, they pointed out how they had joined the Union Army and had fought to put down the southern rebellion: "Man that have stud upon the feal of battle & have shot there master and sons now going to ask ether one for bread or for shelter or comfortable for his wife & children sunch a thing the U S should not ought to expect a man [to do]." Some of them declared they were prepared to defend their property with guns. Federal troops quickly crushed the resistance: seizing the lands, they tore up the freedmen's title papers and restored the lands to the planter class.[71]

Thus ended the possibility of real freedom. A Union general explained to Congress: "I believe it is the policy of the majority of the farm owners to prevent negroes from becoming landholders. They desire to keep the negroes landless, and as nearly in a condition of slavery as it is possible for them to do." The newly freed blacks made this same point more directly and frankly: "Gib us our own land and we take care ourselves, but widout land, de ole massas can hire us or starve us, as dey please." Frederick Douglass explained the failure of Reconstruction: "Could the nation have been induced to listen to those Stalwart Republicans, Thaddeus Stevens and Charles Sumner, some of the evils which we now suffer would have been averted. The Negro would not today be on his knees, as he is, supplicating the old master class to give him leave to toil."[72]

Though the Civil War had led to the destruction of slavery, blacks in the South found themselves transformed from "property" to "freedmen," not "free" people. No longer slaves, they became wage earners or sharecroppers, working the land of their former master in exchange for a part of the crop. Forced to buy goods from the planter's store, they were trapped in a vicious economic cycle, making barely enough to pay off their debts. For example, according to an account book, the following transactions occurred between Polly and landowner Presley George:

Due Presley George by Polly:

For 4¾ cuts wool @ 75 cents/cut	$3.50
22 yds. cloth @ 50 cents/yd.	11.00
5 yds. thread @ 50 cents/yd.	2.50
Boarding one child (who didn't work) for 5 months	12.00
10 bushels corn @ $1.00/bushel	10.00
30 bushels corn @ $1.00/bushel	30.00
total	$69.00

Due Polly by Presley George:

For 3 months' work "by self" @ $4.00/month	$12.00
For 4 months' work by son Peter @ $8.00/month	32.00
For 4 months' work by son Burrel @ $4.00/month	16.00
For 4 months' work by daughter Siller @ $2.25/month	9.00
total	$69.00

Thus, the earnings of Polly and her family amounted to zero. All they had been able to do was to reimburse planter George for the debts they had incurred from their purchases.[73]

A black laborer described his condition of debt peonage: "I signed a contract—that is, I made my mark for one year. The Captain was to give me $3.50 a week, and furnish me a little house on the plantation...." A year later, he found himself in debt to the planter, and so he signed another contract, this one for ten years. During this time, he was "compelled" to buy his food, clothing, and other supplies from the plantation store. "We never used any money in our dealings with the commissary, only tickets or orders, and we had a general settlement once each year, in October. In this store we were charged all sorts of high prices for goods, because we seldom had more than $5 or $10 coming to us—and that for a whole year's work." At the end of his contract, he tried to leave the plantation but was told he owed $165 and consequently found himself reduced to a "lifetime slave." A black folk song lamented:

> *Slabery an' freedom*
> *Dey's mos' de same*
> *No difference hahdly*
> *Cep' in de name.*[74]

Meanwhile, the era known as the "New South" was emerging. Four years after the withdrawal of federal troops from the South in 1877, the editor of the *New Orleans Times-Democrat* reported that a "magic transformation" had occurred below the Mason-Dixon Line. The "stagnation of despair" had given way to the "buoyance" of hope and courage, and the "silence of inertia" to the "thrilling uproar of action." Southerners were a "new people," and the region was experiencing a "new birth." The vision of the "New South" was the industrialization of the old Cotton Kingdom.[75]

The signs of "progress" were especially evident in the rise of cities and the proliferation of factories. Atlanta, which had only 14,000 residents when General Sherman marched his army to the sea, had a population close to 40,000 in 1880, and 90,000 two decades later. The pride of the "New South"'s manufacturing was centered on its textile and iron production. The number of spindles had jumped from 600,000 in 1860 to 175,000,000 in 1890; the number of textile mills from 161 in 1880 to 400 in 1900. By the late 1880s, southern pig-iron production had surpassed the total output of the entire country in 1860. Jefferson County, the home of Birmingham, had only 22 factories in 1870; thirty years later it had 500 plants.

During this economic boom, blacks were drawn into the factories and mills of the "New South." Although they were systematically excluded from certain industries such as textiles and continued to be employed primarily in agriculture, blacks became an important source of industrial labor. In 1890, 6 percent of the total black workforce was employed in manufacturing, compared with 19 percent of the total native white workforce. Between 1890 and 1910, the number of black male workers in nonagricultural occupations increased by two-thirds, or to 400,000, due mainly to the expansion in sawmills, coal mining, and railroad construction. In 1880, 41 percent of Birmingham's industrial workers were black; thirty years later, blacks made up 39 percent of all steelworkers in the South.

Southern industrialists were eager to employ blacks. Richard H. Edmunds, editor of the *Manufacturers' Record*, regarded blacks as "the most important working factor in the development of the great and varied resources of our country." The manager of Shelby Iron Works insisted he would not exchange his black workers "for any other people on earth." After white workers struck at Chattanooga and Knoxville iron companies in 1883, management turned to black laborers and found them to be "fully as good as" white labor. Praising his black workers, the superintendent of the Saluda Cotton Factory stated that they not only worked as well as whites but were also less expensive and could be "easily controlled."[76]

One prominent symbol of the "New South" was the 1895 Atlanta Exposition. Thousands of visitors crowded into Atlanta to marvel at the industrial achievements of the postwar South. Included among the exhibits were the latest advances in technology, such as a battery of eight boilers and fourteen engines with a capacity of 2,250 horsepower. There was also a "Negro Building" designed and erected wholly by black mechanics and devoted to "showing the progress of the Negro since freedom." The main entrance of this building had relief work that depicted a "slave mammy" and a portrait of Frederick Douglass; inside was a steam engine built by students from the Tuskegee Normal and Industrial Institute.[77]

The most noted speaker at the opening of the exposition was Booker T. Washington, the thirty-nine-year-old principal of the Tuskegee Institute. The invitation to give the address had greatly moved him. From slave to honored guest, he had been given the opportunity to speak to an audience composed of the wealth and culture of the South, the representatives of his former masters. The event was momentous: it was the first time in southern history that a black had been asked to speak at such an important occasion. After his address, known as the "Atlanta Compromise," Washington suddenly found himself elevated by white men in power as the leader of his race.

Washington was catapulted into prominence within the context of both racial and class developments of the 1890s. Throughout much of the nineteenth century, Frederick Douglass had personified militancy in the struggle for racial equality, and his death in February 1895 had created a vacuum in black leadership. The southern movement to disenfranchise and segregate blacks as well as the increase in lynchings forced blacks to seek their rights more cautiously. Furthermore, northern and southern capitalists wanted a controllable black labor force, one they could pit against a new and troublesome white "giddy multitude"—now a largely European immigrant working class. They were concerned about the class tensions that had exploded in the 1877 Railroad Strike, the 1885 Haymarket Massacre, and the 1892 Homestead Strike. Within this context, an accommodationist African-American leadership emerged.

As Washington stood on the platform in Atlanta acknowledging "the flower and culture and beauty of the South," he told his black and white listeners in the segregated auditorium to "cast down their buckets" where they were. To blacks, he declared: "It is at the bottom of life we must begin, and not at the top." The agitation for "social equality" was the "extremest folly." "The opportunity to earn a dollar in a factory just now is worth infinitely more than the opportunity to spend a dollar in an opera-house." To whites, Washington recommended: cast down your bucket "among eight millions of Negroes whose habits you know, whose fidelity and love you have tested in days when to have proved treacherous meant the ruin of your firesides. Cast down your bucket among these people who have, without strikes and labour wars, tilled your fields, cleared your forests, built your railroads and cities." To both races, Washington dramatically advised: "In all things that are purely social we can be as separate as the fingers, yet one as the hand in all things essential to mutual progress." Washington's speech "electrified" the audience, drawing a "delirium of applause."[78]

Shortly after Washington's speech, President Grover Cleveland telegraphed a message of good wishes from Massachusetts to the Atlanta Exposition and then pulled a switch. Suddenly, geysers shot upward from a great fountain, and thousands of lights illuminated the entire exposition. In the electric incandescence, whites could be seen intermingling with what one visitor described as "hone-blowing Dahomeyans," "georgeous pig-tailed Chinamen," "American Indians," "sombre-eyed Mexicans," and "old-time Negroes in old-time costumes."[79]

Although Washington had publicly offered black cooperation to the southern elite, he was actually not an accommodationist. In Chicago five years later, he gave a speech condemning racism in American society. Congratulating the country for its recent victory in the Spanish-American War, he declared that Americans had won every conflict in history, "except the effort to conquer ourselves in blotting out racial prejudice.... Until we thus conquer ourselves I make no empty statement when I say that we shall have a cancer gnawing at the heart of this republic that shall some day prove to be as dangerous as an attack from an army without or within." When Washington arrived to speak at a hall in Tampa, Florida, and found that the audience had been divided into blacks and whites with a line of sheets separating the two groups, he refused to speak until the sheets were taken down. Behind the scenes, Washington strenuously fought against discrimination and disenfranchisement, covertly funding lawsuits against railroad segregation in Virginia and disenfranchisement legislation in Louisiana and Alabama.[80]

Moreover, Washington had always felt a sense of race pride. "From any point of view," he acknowledged in his autobiography,

"I had rather be what I am, a member of the Negro race, than be able to claim membership with the most favoured of any other race." African Americans, in Washington's view, should pursue a strategy of self-help, directing their own destiny, uplifting themselves, and establishing black institutions like Tuskegee and the Negro Business League. Like Delany, Washington urged blacks to pursue economic success. Before he sailed to Europe on a vacation in 1910, he resolved not to enter a single palace, gallery, cathedral, or museum. "I find markets more instructive than museums," he explained. As an educator, Washington had little respect for what he called "mere book education." He wanted his students to study "actual things," to acquire a practical education. Industrial training would be the path to economic independence and racial equality. "Let there be in a community," Washington predicted, "a Negro who by virtue of his superior knowledge of the chemistry of the soil, his acquaintance with the most improved tools and best breeds of stock, can raise fifty bushels of corn to the acre while his white neighbor only raises thirty, and the white man will come to the black man to learn. Further, they will sit down on the same train, in the same coach and on the same seat to talk about it."[81]

By the end of the nineteenth century, however, the possibility of progress for blacks was distressingly remote. Racial borders had been reinforced by class and caste. Most black farmers were sharecroppers or tenants, working a white man's land with a white man's plow and a white man's mule. "Every colored man will be a slave, & feel himself a slave," a black soldier had warned during the Civil War, "until he can raise him own bale of cotton & put him own mark upon it & say dis is mine!" By this measure of freedom, blacks were still "slaves." During the 1890s, new Jim Crow laws buttressed segregation by defining more precisely the "Negro's place" on trains and streetcars and in schools, parks, theaters, hotels, and hospitals. Proclaiming the doctrine of separate but equal in the 1896 ruling of *Plessy v. Ferguson*, the Supreme Court upheld the constitutionality of segregation. Poll taxes and literacy requirements for the suffrage were effectively disenfranchising blacks, and hundreds of blacks were annually being lynched. This era was brutally repressive—what historian Rayford Logan described as "the nadir."[82]

6

FLEEING
"THE TYRANT'S HEEL"

"Exiles" from Ireland

CALIBAN COULD ALSO have been Irish. As we noted in chapter two, like Caliban, the Irish were dispossessed of their island by the English Prosperos. The Irish, too, were depicted and degraded as the "Other"—as "savages," outside of "civilization," and "wild."

Fleeing English oppression in the nineteenth century, millions of Irish crossed the Atlantic to America. Thus, the age of Jackson witnessed not only Indian removal and the expansion of slavery, but also the great influx of immigrants from Ireland. Suddenly, blacks in the North were competing with Irish workers. "Every hour sees us elbowed out of some employment to make room perhaps for some newly arrived immigrants, whose hunger and color are thought to give them a title to special favor," Frederick Douglass complained. "White men are becoming house servants, cooks, stewards, common laborers and flunkeys to our gentry." Then he warned that Irish immigrants would soon find that in taking "our vocation," they had also assumed "our degradation." But Douglass found himself empathizing with the Irish. During a visit to Ireland in the 1840s, he witnessed the terrible suffering inflicted by the Potato Famine and was "much affected" on hearing the "wailing notes" of Irish ballads that reminded him of the "wild notes" of slave songs.[1]

Behind the Emigration: "John Bull Must Have the Beef"

The Irish described their migration to America in Gaelic terms: *deorai* or "exiles," *dithreabhach* or "homeless," and *dibeartach* or "banished people." "*Dob eigean dom imeacht go Meirice*," they explained, "I had to go to America," or "Going to America was a necessity for me." A contemporary noted: "There's such a clinging to the country that they would rather live on anything rather than go." But they were forced to leave their island. Their songs told mournful tales of exile in a foreign land:

> Such troubles we know that have often
> Caused stout Irish hearts to roam...
> And...sons from their homes were drove....
>
> The hills and the valleys so dear to my heart;
> It grieves me to think that from them I must
>   part.
> Compelled to emigrate far, far o'er the sea.[2]

Feeling like the "children of Israel," the Irish were driven from their beloved homeland by "English tyranny," the British "yoke" "enslaving" Ireland. The conquerors were seen as "savage tyrants" and "cursed intruders." The movement to America was "artificial," explained one Irish immigrant, because the poverty of Ireland had been created by English colonial policies. "Foul British laws," they declared, were the "whole cause" of their emigration. Time and again, the Irish complained that they were being pushed out of their country by their oppressors:

> I would not live in Ireland now, for she's a
>   fallen land,
> And the tyrant's heel is on her neck, with her
>   reeking blood-stained hand.
> There's not a foot of Irish ground, but's trodden
>   down by slaves,
> Who die unwept, and then are flung, like
>   dogs, into their graves.[3]

The emigration was rooted deeply in the history of English oppression. Beginning in the twelfth century, English conquest of Ireland led to the confiscation and transfer of lands to English colonizers. By 1700, the Irish owned only 14 percent of Ireland. As subsistence farmers, the Irish were forced to rent or lease land from English landlords. Then, in the late eighteenth century, the landlords decided to make their estates more profitable. Therefore, they initiated a campaign to transform the island's economy into a "cattle civilization." By enclosing their estates and evicting peasant families, landlords shifted from tillage agriculture to ranching. Between 1820 and 1840, livestock increased at a faster rate than the population, and cattle exports more than quadrupled. The conversion of land from tillage to grazing meant that 90 percent of the laborers previously needed for planting and harvesting had become superfluous.[4]

The landlords sought to bring Ireland into the British market. Due to increased beef production between 1750 and 1810, Irish exports rose from two million to six million British pounds. During a visit to Ireland in 1771, Benjamin Franklin reported that British colonialism and its emphasis on exports had reduced the Irish people to "extremely poor" tenants, "living in the most sordid wretchedness, in dirty Hovels of Mud and Straw, and clothed only in Rags." The Irish had been forced to survive on "Potatoes and Buttermilk, without Shirts," so that the "Merchants" could export "Beef" to England.

> . . . the Landlord calls for rent,
> The flood which over-spread the Land, has
> caused them to lament,
> And yet John Bull must have the Beef, let it
> be cooked or raw,
> We're told by each big English thief: we
> darsen't break the law.

By the 1830s, according to an observer, Ireland had developed a profitable export economy. But, he added, this commercialization of agriculture was accompanied by a "visible deterioration" in the condition of the "labouring classes and of the small farmers." "Progress" for the landlords meant pauperization for the peasants.

> Ireland's oppressors soon must know, they
> can't for ever last,
> Landlords [have] been cruel for generations
> past,

What right have they to claim the soil which
never was their own,
When thousands now are starving and
evicted from their home?[5]

"Misery, naked and famishing," reported visitor Gustave de Beaumont in the 1830s, was "everywhere, and at every hour of the day." The typical single-room cabin of an Irish family consisted of four walls of dried mud with a straw roof and a hole cut in the roof for the chimney. Inside lived the father, mother, children, and sometimes a grandfather or grandmother. There was no furniture in this "wretched hovel"; a single bed of straw served the entire family. "Five or six half-naked children [could] be seen crouched near a miserable fire, the ashes of which [covered] a few potatoes, the sole nourishment of the family." The squalor was oppressive, stifling. "What a Country this [was] to live in," a farmer complained, where Catholics were "only breathing, afraid & scarce able to raise their heads."[6]

But there was an alternative. Rather than "toil and starve like slaves," they could emigrate to "the Land of Promise." A song explained:

My father holds 5 acres of land, it was not
enough to support us all,
Which banished me from my native land, to
old Ireland dear I bid farewell.
My holdings here I can't endure since here
no longer I can stay.
I take my lot and leave this spot and try the
land of liberty.

By the thousands, Irish were leaving for America, where there was "room for all—employment for all and success for many." Letters from friends and family in the United States glowingly described riches "growing like grass" and the boundlessness of a country where there was no tyranny or oppression from landlords. Between 1815 and 1845, one million Irish came to America.[7]

During this period, however, most Irish endured their hardships at home. Rather than emigrate, many became *spalpeens*, or migratory workers, leaving their cottages each spring for agricultural or construction labor within Ireland, then returning to their families in the fall with "the rent money sewn inside their clothes." Their earnings, while meager, enabled many families to farm small plots and grow potatoes. By the early 1840s, the rural poor were existing mainly on potatoes; between late spring and the time of harvest, many were eating only one meal a day. Sometimes they cooked their potatoes only partially, keeping the cores or "bones" of the potatoes raw in order to digest their food more slowly. These hardy peasants believed they could survive in their homeland forever, for a family could produce a year's supply of potatoes on one acre of land. "What did we eat?" said an Irish immigrant. "Well, just potatoes."[8]

Then suddenly, a little-known fungus appeared and changed the course of Irish history. Although potato crops had been attacked by plant diseases in past years, a new blight destroyed about 40 percent of the crop in 1845. "Coming on the harvest time...the crops looked splendid," a farmer said as he recalled the beginning of the famine, "but one fine morning in July there was a cry around that some blight had struck the potato stalks." As the leaves blackened and crumbled, the air became "laden with a sickly odor of decay, as if the hand of death had stricken the potato field, and...everything growing in it was rotten." Returning annually, the deadly disease continued its relentless devastation. By 1855, some one million people had died from hunger and sickness.[9]

The Great Famine intensified the already terrible suffering. Unable to pay their rent, thousands of families were evicted. For many landlords, the famine offered an opportunity to convert more land into fields for grazing. The evicted peasants angrily denounced their oppressors:

> 'Twas famine's wasting breath,
> That winged the shaft of death,
> And the landlord, lost to feeling,
> Who drove us from our sheeling....[10]

During the famine years, Ireland continued to export grain and cattle to British markets. Half the people of Ireland could have been fed with the livestock exported in 1846: 186,483 cattle, 6,363 calves, 259,257 sheep, and 180,827 swine. Throughout the country, however, one could see "famished and ghastly skeletons," "cowering wretches almost naked in the savage weather," children with "their faces bloated yet wrinkled and of a pale greenish hue," and families eating seaweed and suffering from fevers and dysentery. According to an English visitor, the streets of one town were "crowded with gaunt wanderers, sauntering to and fro with hopeless air and hunger-struck look," while the poorhouse was surrounded by "a mob of starved, almost naked, women," "clamouring for soup tickets." So many people died that corpses were placed in reusable "trap-coffins" with hinged bottoms. For the living, the choice became clear: emigrate or face destitution and death.

> Desert a land of curse and slave,
> Of pauper woe...
> Poor Eire now is all a grave....[11]

In panic, one and a half million Irish fled to the United States during the Great Famine. More so than the earlier emigrants, these people were the "uprooted." The *Cork Examiner* reported that they were "running away from fever and disease and hunger, with money scarcely sufficient to pay passage for...the voyage." Their reason for coming to America was survival. It was not ambition, a ballad declared, but

> the blackening of the potatoes
> That drove us over the sea.[12]

With bundles on their shoulders, the departing men and women were "laving dear old Ireland without warnin'" to cross the "briny ocean." But before they left, they attended an "American wake" — a party hosted by their families. Sharing food and music, they said their good-byes and mourned what everyone knew would be a permanent separation.

> Sad was the day we said farewell,
> Dear native land, to thee;
> And wander'd forth to find a home,
> Beyond the stormy sea.
> Hard then our fate; fast flow'd the tears,
> We tried to hide in vain,
> At thought of those we left behind,
> And might ne'er see again.[13]

After the "wake," they traveled to Dublin and then to Liverpool, where they boarded crowded ships bound for America. The crossing was traumatic. "The emigrant is shown a berth," the *Times* reported, "a shelf of coarse pinewood, situated in a noisome dungeon, airless and lightless, in which several hundred persons of both sexes and all ages are stowed away on shelves two feet one inch above the other, three feet wide and six feet long, still reeking from the ineradicable stench left by the emigrants of the last voyage." On one ship, according to a witness, hundreds of passengers lay together like sacks, motionless. Some were dead, while others were sick, feverish and delirious, scarcely able to turn in their narrow berths. Tens of thousands of travelers died during the passage or immediately after arrival.[14]

The terrible blights finally ended in 1854, but the commercialization of agriculture, the eviction of families from their lands, and the decline of Irish crafts due to the importation of British manufactured goods continued to pauperize the Irish peasantry and depopulate Ireland. A contemporary described his country's melancholy condition: "This grass grown road, over which seemingly little, if any, traffic passes, is a type of solitude everywhere found. Tillage there is none; but in its stead one vast expanse of pasture land extends. Human habitations are rarer than the bare walls of roofless cottages. Where once a population dwelt...see how lonely and untrodden are these roads." In the 1860s, an American consul reported that there were "many thousands of strong young men" who sighed for "food & employment in the US," "and would gladly embrace *any* opportunity of removal from the misery & starvation" in Ireland. Between 1855 and 1900, two million more Irish came to America.[15]

An *"Immortal Irish Brigade"* of Workers

Pushed from Ireland by economic hardships and famine, the immigrants were pulled to America by prospects of jobs. They provided labor for the construction of canals and railroads, connecting the different economic regions of the country. Watching them work on the National Road in Pennsylvania, a farmer described them as an "immortal Irish brigade, a thousand strong, with their carts, wheelbarrows, shovels and blasting tools, grading the commons, and climbing the mountainside...leaving behind them a roadway good enough for an emperor to travel over." Irish laborers helped to build waterways, including Connecticut's Enfield Canal, Rhode Island's Blackstone Canal, and most important, New York's Erie Canal, described by Reverend Michael Buckley, a visitor from

Ireland, as "one of the grandest pieces of engineering ever seen in the world" and "proof" of "Irish talent." Standing knee-deep in water while cursing swarms of mosquitoes, the workers dug and shoveled earth as they sang:

> *When I came to this wonderful rampire, it*
> *   filled me with the greatest surprise,*
> *To see such a great undertaking, on the like I*
> *   never opened my eye.*
> *To see a full thousand brave fellows at work*
> *   among mountains so tall,*
> *To dig through the vallies so level, through*
> *   rocks for to cut a canal.*[16]

Irish workers built thousands of miles of rail lines such as the Western and Atlantic Railroad from Atlanta to Chattanooga and the Union Pacific segment of the transcontinental railroad. All day they were ordered: "Now Mick do this, and Mick do that." And they shouted back: "The divil take the railroad!" As they laid tracks, they tuned their bodies to the rhythms of a work song:

> *Then drill, my Paddies, drill—*
> *Drill, my heroes, drill,*
> *Drill all day, no sugar in your tay*
> *Workin' on the U. P. railway.*

At night, they continued to feel the vibrations of the sledgehammers in their hands and arms and to hear the pounding ringing in their heads. Exhausted, they tried to rest:

> *When I lay me down to sleep,*
> *   The ugly bugs around me creep;*
> *Bad luck to the wink that I can sleep,*
> *   While workin' on the railroad.*[17]

The Irish became disposable workers. The pervasive presence of the Irish in railroad work produced the popular saying that there was "an Irishman buried under every tie." Indeed, the Irish had high accident rates, for they were frequently assigned to the hazardous jobs. A Connecticut ax manufacturer explained that he employed the Irish as grinders because the death rate due to accidents was so high he had difficulty finding "Yankees" to do this dangerous work. "My father carried the mark of the quarry to his grave," wrote Elizabeth Gurley Flynn. "When he was a boy, working in a quarry in Maine, carrying tools, the sight of one eye was destroyed by a flying chip of granite." Time and again, newspapers reported accidents—"an Irishman drowned—an Irishman crushed by a beam—an Irishman suffocated in a pit—an Irishman blown to atoms by a steam engine—ten, twenty Irishmen buried alive in the sinking of a bank...." Yankees regarded the Irishman "as one made to work," reported Reverend Buckley. "Where they want labour they will engage Paddy as they would a drayhorse." An Irish worker recalled how he labored "so severely" digging cellars, "up before the Stars and working till darkness," "driven like horses" to be "a slave for the Americans." Working in the mines of Pennsylvania, Irish miners "sucked up" the black dust into their lungs as they dug the "bloody coal."[18]

Irish laborers, an immigrant complained, were "thought nothing of more than *dogs* ... despised & kicked about." They lived in "clumsy, rough and wretched hovels," made with "roofs of sod and grass" and "walls of mud," observed Charles Dickens during a visit to the United States. "Hideously ugly old women and very buxom young ones, pigs, dogs, men, children, babies, pots, kettles, dung hills, vile refuse, rank straw and standing water, all wallowing together in an inseparable heap, composed the furniture of every dark and dirty hut." America turned out to be a nightmare for many Irish immigrants. A song expressed their disappointment:

> *I got a letter from a relation*
> *Telling me to hasten across the sea,*
> *That gold was to be found in plenty there*
> *And that I'd never have a hard day or a poor*
> *   one again.*
>
> *Alas, when I landed*
> *I made for the city without delay;*
> *But I never saw gold on the street corners—*
> *Alas, I was a poor aimless person cast*
> *   adrift.*[19]

The Irish found themselves not only exploited as laborers but also pitted against workers of other races, including the Chinese.

In New England, Irish workers in the shoemaking industry were struggling against low wages and the introduction of labor-eliminating machines; consequently, they organized the Secret Order of the Knights of St. Crispin. The Crispins quickly became the largest labor organization in the United States; in 1870, it had a membership of fifty thousand. Demanding higher wages and an eight-hour day, the Crispins went on strike at a shoe factory in North Adams, Massachusetts. The owner, Calvin T. Sampson, fired the disgruntled workers and pursued a strategy of divide-and-control by driving a "wedge" between himself and the strikers.[20]

This "wedge" turned out to be a contingent of seventy-five Chinese workers from San Francisco. Brought to North Adams as scabs to break the Irish strike, they were housed in dormitories inside the locked and guarded gates of the factory yard. Within three months after their arrival, the Chinese workers were producing more shoes than the same number of white workers had been making before the strike. The success of Sampson's strategy was celebrated in the press. "The Chinese, and this especially annoys the Crispins," the editor of *The Nation* wrote, "show the usual quickness of their race in learning the process of their new business, and already do creditable hand and machine work."[21]

The Chinese were held up as a model for Irish laborers. Writing for *Scribner's Monthly*, William Shanks compared the Chinese to the Irish workers. The Chinese "labored regularly and constantly, losing no blue Mondays on account of Sunday's dissipations nor wasting hours on idle holidays," he reported. "The quality of the work was found to be fully equal to that of the Crispins." Through the use of Chinese labor, Sampson had widened his profit margin: the weekly saving in labor costs was $840, or $44,000 a year. These figures inspired Shanks to calculate: "There are 115 establishments in the State, employing 5,415 men...capable of producing 7,942 cases of shoes per week. Under the Chinese system of Mr. Sampson, a saving of $69,594 per week, or say $3,500,000 a year, would be effected, thus revolutionizing the trade."[22]

In their response to Sampson's "wedge," the striking Crispins tried to promote working-class solidarity by organizing a Chinese lodge of St. Crispin. Watching this initiative to build Irish-Chinese unity, the editor of *The Nation* commented: "Chinese lodges and strikes will come in time when enough Chinamen are collected together in any given place; but the prospect appears not immediately flattering at North Adams." Based on self-interest rather than an ideological commitment to class solidarity, this attempt to unionize the Chinese workers quickly collapsed. At a meeting in Boston, white workers turned against the Chinese laborers, condemning them for reducing "American labor" to "the Chinese standard of rice and rats."[23]

Sampson's daring action had a sobering effect on striking workers at nearby shoe factories. Ten days after the arrival of Sampson's "Mongolian battery," Parker Brothers, Cady Brothers, Millard and Whitman, and E. R. and N. L. Millard were able to force their laborers to return to work with a 10 percent wage cut. Commenting on the significance of Sampson's experiment of substituting Chinese for Irish laborers, a writer for *Scribner's Monthly* observed: "If for no other purpose than the breaking up of the incipient steps toward labor combinations and 'Trade Unions'...the advent of Chinese labor should be hailed with warm welcome." The "heathen Chinee," he concluded, could be the "final solution" to the labor problem in America.[24]

While they were contrasted with the Chinese, Irish immigrants found themselves compared to blacks. The Irish were stereotyped as "a race of savages," at the same level of intelligence as blacks. Pursuing the "lower" rather than the "higher" pleasures, seeking "vicious excitement" and "gratification merely animal," the Irish were said to be "slaves" of their "passions." Since sexual restraint was the most widely used method of birth control, the large families of these immigrants seemed to prove a lack of self-control: "Did wealth consist in children, it is well known, that the Irish would be rich people...." In a sermon called "The Dangerous Classes," Reverend Theodore Parker of Boston claimed that some people were "inferior in nature, some perhaps only behind us in development" on "a lower form in the great school of Providence—negroes, Indians, Mexicans, Irish, and the like." A southern planter stated that slaves were like the Irish in "their subserviency, their flattering, their lying, and their pilfering as traits common to the characters of both peoples." An English traveler reported that both the Irish and blacks were viewed as outcasts: "To be called an 'Irishman' is almost as great an insult as to be stigmatized as a 'nigger feller'...." Sometimes the immigrants were described as "Irish niggers."[25]

Like blacks, Irish workers were condemned for their alleged negative traits. They were dismissed from their jobs for laziness, gambling, drinking, and "other debaucheries," as well as for "levity" and "impudence." A saying claimed: "It's as natural for a

Hibernian to tipple as it is for a pig to grunt." Their "idleness" and "brutal leprosy of blue Monday habits," it was argued, rendered them unreliable as workers and kept them impoverished. Like the "giddy multitude" of seventeenth-century Virginia, the Irish were chastised as an unruly and disorderly class. In Jersey City, Irish workers were denounced by a newspaper editor as "a mongrel mass of ignorance and crime and superstition, as utterly unfit for its duties, as they [were] for the common courtesies and decencies of civilized life." Irish children, moreover, were seen as "undisciplined" and "uninstructed," "inheriting" the "stupidity of centuries of ignorant ancestors." At school, they allegedly emitted a "pungent odor"—the "fumes of New-England rum." The Massachusetts Board of State Charities calculated that it would take two or three generations to "correct the constitutional tendencies to disease and early decay." Worried about the alarming presence of a largely Irish working class, Horace Mann was determined to educate the children in order to save the masses from "falling back into the conditions of half-barbarous or of savage life."[26]

Many Irish saw parallels between themselves as a degraded people and blacks in bondage. In Ireland, they had identified themselves as the "slaves" of the British, and many supported the abolition of slavery in the United States. In 1842, thousands of them signed a petition that declared: "Irishmen and Irishwomen! treat the colored people as your equals, as brethren." But Irish sympathy for black slaves seemed to disappear with the Atlantic crossing. In America, many of them became antiblack. Frederick Douglass criticized the Irish immigrants for abandoning the idea of "liberty" they nurtured in their homeland by becoming "the oppressors of another race" in America. Irish freedom fighter Daniel O'Connell shared Douglass's disappointment. Chastising the immigrants for their racism, O'Connell declared: "It was not in Ireland you learned this cruelty."[27]

In America, the Irish found themselves stereotyped as ignorant and inferior, and forced to occupy the bottom rungs of employment. In the South, they were even made to do the dirty and hazardous jobs that masters were reluctant to assign to their slaves. A planter told a northern visitor that he had hired an Irish gang rather than use his own slaves to drain a flooded area. "It's dangerous work," he explained, "and a negro's life is too valuable to be risked at it. If a negro dies, it's a considerable loss, you know." In the North, Irish repeatedly fought blacks for jobs as waiters and longshoremen. During the 1830s, a Philadelphia newspaper reported that the Irish were displacing blacks as hackney coach-men, draymen, and stevedores.[28]

As they competed against blacks for employment, many Irish immigrants promoted their whiteness. "In a country of the whites where [white workers] find it difficult to earn a subsistence," they asked, "what right has the negro either to preference or to equality, or to admission?" Targets of Protestant nativist hatred identify-ing them as Catholic, outsiders, and foreigners, the Irish newcom-ers sought to become insiders, or Americans, by claiming their membership as whites. A powerful way to transform their own identity from "Irish" to "American" was to attack blacks. Thus, blacks as the "Other" served to facilitate their assimilation.[29]

Reacting to Irish hostility, blacks called their tormentors "white niggers." They resented being told by immigrants to leave the country of their birth and "go back" to Africa, a place they had never been.[30] Blacks complained that the Irish were taking jobs from them. "These impoverished and destitute beings, trans-ported from the trans-Atlantic shores," a black observed, "are crowding themselves into every place of business and labor, and driving the poor colored American citizen out. Along the wharves, where the colored man once done the whole business of shipping and unshipping—in stores where his services were once ren-dered, and in families where the chief places were filled by him, in all these situations there are substituted foreigners."[31]

As Americans, many blacks aimed nativist barbs against the Irish foreigners. "Pat O'Flannagan does not have the least thing in the world against Jim from Dixie," a black observed, "but it didn't take Pat long after passing the Statue of Liberty to learn that it is popular to give Jim a whack." Blacks scornfully described the Irish as "hyphenates" and mocked their accent as such "a heavy brogue that it sounded as if they had marbles in their mouths." "It is to be regretted," black journalist John E. Bruce observed, "that in [America] where the outcasts—the scum of European society—can come and enjoy the fullest social and political privi-leges, the Native Born American with wooly hair and dark com-plexion is made the Victim...of Social Ostracism."[32]

Victims of English prejudice and repression in Ireland, the Irish in America often redirected their rage in a pecking order. "They [the Irish] have been oppressed enough themselves to be oppressive whenever they have a chance," commented an observer, "and the despised and degraded condition of the blacks, presenting to them a very ugly resemblance of their own home circumstances, naturally excites in them the exercise of the disgust and contempt of which they themselves are very habitually the objects...." Viewing blacks as "a soulless race," some Irish said they "would shoot a black man with as little regard to moral consequences as they would a wild hog." The Irish opposed suffrage for blacks, fearful this would set "the Niggers high." Complaining that blacks did not know their place, they shouted: "Down with the Nagurs!"[33]

Irish antagonism toward blacks exploded during the Civil War. Many Irish were angry at President Abraham Lincoln for expanding the aims of the war to include emancipation. Condemning abolitionism as "Niggerology," many Irish immigrants were willing to support the war only to preserve the Union. "Let the niggers stay in the South!" Irish workers shouted. They had been warned by the Democrats during the 1860 election: "Vote against Abraham Lincoln, or you will have negro labor dragging you from your free labor." "Let the four millions of slaves in the South be set at liberty...and we should very soon have...a terrible conflict between white labor and black labor.... The unemployed slaves will be found among you in sufficient numbers to compete with you at your wharves and your docks, and in every branch of labor in which white people alone are now employed."[34]

During the Civil War, New York Democratic politicians warned that the Republicans were willing to "spend" Irish blood to win the abolitionist war and that freed blacks would be transported north to "steal the work and the bread of the honest Irish." Similarly, an Irish newspaper, the *Boston Pilot,* aroused the fears of its readers: "We have already upon us bloody contention between white and black labor.... The North is becoming black with refugee Negroes from the South. These *wretches* crowd our cities, and by overstocking the market of labor, do incalculable injury to white hands."[35]

The Irish became angry when a new draft law was enacted to bolster sagging enlistments in the Union Army. In July 1863, a mass meeting in New York City protested the law's provision that allowed a draftee to avoid military service by paying $300 or providing a substitute. This law clearly discriminated against the working class. Many of the first draftees were Irish, poor men unable to pay the fee. Irish rioters stormed and burned the draft office. Then they turned on blacks. "Vengence on every nigger in New York," the rampagers screamed as they assaulted blacks in the streets. One of the victims, William Green, said later: "They stripped me naked...they had a rope to hang me, and a man saved me." General rampage exploded as mobs vandalized and pillaged stores. "I saw the rioters in the street—100 or 150 of them," a passerby stated, describing the looting of a liquor store. "Some three or four stout boys with clubs attacked the windows and broke them in; they then smashed in the doors; then the crowd rushed in; they pitched out boxes of cigars and bottles, and in about 10 minutes the house was on fire." The riot continued for four days. Finally, an army regiment rushed to the city from Gettysburg and restored order. By then scores of people had been injured and 105 killed. Condemning the "revolting, fiendish, cowardly, cruel" treatment of "the poor unfortunate negroes," an Irish newspaper, the *Metropolitan Record,* declared that "a superior race should disdain to vent their passions on an inferior one."[36]

Irish "Maids" and "Factory Girls"

Labor competition between the Irish and blacks was fierce in the domestic services. According to an English visitor, employers were willing to "let negroes be servants, and if not negroes, let Irish fill their place." In 1830, the majority of the servants in New York City were black; twenty years later, they were Irish women. Daughters of farmers in Ireland, they had become maids in America. In the textile towns of Lowell and Providence, they became factory workers.

More than half of the Irish immigrants were women, compared to only 21 percent of southern Italians and 4 percent of Greeks. In New York City in 1860, Irish women outnumbered Irish men—117,000 to 87,000. This massive migration of women was saluted in a song:

> O brave, brave Irish girls,
> We well might call you brave
> Should the least of all your perils
> The Stormy ocean waves.[37]

In Ireland, the struggle for economic survival had a particular impact on women. Increasingly after 1815, farmers practiced impartible inheritance: their land was not divided among their sons but left to only one. Consequently, many sons had little choice but to emigrate. "If you divide a farm and give it to two sons, neither is going to have a heck of a lot," an Irish immigrant explained. "So I began to realize that [I] would have to go somewhere." Women, too, came to a similar realization. They found that many noninheriting sons lacked the resources to marry and that their own possibilities for marriage were extremely limited unless they had dowries. Marriage rates declined: by 1841, 44 percent of the men and 36 percent of the women aged twenty-six to thirty-five were single. Many young women felt gloomy about their futures in terms of marriage and family. "There is no fun in Ireland at all," lamented a young woman; "the times are very lonesome...there are no one getting married."[38]

The times were also hard on women economically. The commercialization of agriculture and the decline of Irish cottage manufacturing, such as weaving, left thousands of women excluded from the economy. "Laws made by men shut them out of all hope of inheritance in their native land," an observer noted. "Their male relatives exploited their labour and returned them never a penny as a reward, and finally, when at last their labour could not wring sufficient from the meagre soil to satisfy the exertions of all, these girls were incontinently packed across the ocean."[39]

To these daughters of Erin, possibilities for marriage and money were waiting for them across the ocean. "Every servant-maid thinks of [America as] the land of promise," the *Cork Examiner* announced, "where...husbands are thought more procurable than in Ireland." A dowry was not necessary here. "Over in Ireland people marry for riches," a woman wrote from Philadelphia, "but here in America we marry for love and work for riches." On this side of the Atlantic, women could find jobs, especially as maids. Guidebooks for prospective Irish immigrants announced that servant girls in America were paid from eight to sixteen dollars a month and offered enticing prospects: if a domestic worker saved half her wages and its accumulated interest, she would be rich within ten years. Indeed, many maids had "in the course of twenty or thirty years, by faithful industry and moderate economy become owners of from three to five thousand dollars."

> *She being inclined to Emigrate her wages*
>   *did demand,*
> *To seek a situation in America's FREE*
>   *LAND.*
> *This undaunted Female hearing that a ship*
>   *at Dublin Quay,*
> *Had advertised for Servants to go to*
>   *America,*
> *She bid farewell to all her friends....*[40]

Irish immigrant women became ubiquitous as maids. In the 1850s, they represented 80 percent of all female household laborers in New York City. Irish women went west to San Francisco where they, like many Chinese men, became servants. In California, Dennis Kearney led an anti-Chinese labor movement, charging that the Chinese threatened the employment of Irish women. "The Chinese Must Go!" shouted Kearney. "Our Women Are Degraded by Coolie Labor."[41]

Irish women entered domestic service in greater numbers and proportions than women of other immigrant groups. In 1900, 54 percent were classified as "servants and waitresses," compared to only 9 percent for Italian female workers. A Boston study reported that more than two-fifths of the immigrant women who entered the city in 1905 and 1906 became servants and that they were almost all Irish. Jewish and Italian women seldom became domestic workers. "Italian women were more likely to take in boarders because the men rarely permitted their wives to work as maids, cleaning women, or factory hands," explained historian Virginia Yans-McLaughlin. "The Italian ideal was to keep women at home."[42]

Unlike Italian women who came to America with their husbands or fathers, Irish immigrant women tended to be unmarried and unattached to families. Hence, they were attracted to work that offered housing and meals. "Single women can get along here better than men as they can get employment more readily than men," an Irish laborer in Philadelphia wrote home to his sisters. "For instance liveing out girls or as the[y] are called at home servant girls gets from eight to twelve shillings per week and keep, that is from two to three dollars of American money.... Labouring mens wages averages from six to nine dollars per week.... But their work is not near so steady as womens."[43]

For these women, service work offered more than shelter, sustenance, and money: it also provided an introduction to American culture. Irish women had come to settle permanently, and had to adapt to American society. "Certainly, they had to begin immediately the process of acculturation on their own terms," historian Hasia Diner noted, "and domestic service provided perhaps the most intimate glimpse of what middle-class America was really like."[44]

Some servants became attached to their employers and their families. "I got a place for general housework with Mrs. Carr," said an Irish woman. "I got $2 till I learned to cook good, and then $3 and then $4. I was in that house as cook and nurse for twenty-two years.... Mrs. Carr's interests was my interests. I took better care of her things than she did herself, and I loved the children as if they was my own." But, while they lived inside middle-class American homes, Irish maids were still outsiders. Their relationship to the family was a hierarchical one of upstairs and downstairs, masters and servants. They were present but invisible in a very intimate setting. Far from their own parents in Ireland, many of them hungered to belong to the families of their employers. "Ladies wonder how their girls can complain of loneliness in a house full of people, but oh! it is the worst kind of loneliness—their share is but the work of the house," a domestic servant said. "They do not share in the pleasures and delights of a home. One must remember that there is a difference between a *house,* a place of shelter, and a *home,* a place where all your affections are centered." Another servant echoed: "What I minded...was the awful lonesomeness. I went for general housework, because I knew all about it, and there were only three in the family." But the family members, "except to give orders," had "nothing to do with me. It got to feel sort of crushing at last."[45]

Moreover, the work itself was demanding and often demeaning. As they cooked, cleaned, laundered, and took care of the children, servants were required to wear caps and aprons, badges of social inferiority. Most worked as live-in servants, available on a beck-and-call schedule around the clock, usually for seven days a week. Their employers "bossed" them "everlastingly" and wanted them to be "on tap from six in the morning to 10 or 11 at night." One servant complained about her employer: "She had no more thought for me than if I had been a machine. She'd sit in her sitting-room on the second floor and ring for me twenty times a day to do little things, and she wanted me up till eleven to answer the bell, for she had a great deal of company." The servants felt like "prisoners," always "looked down upon." The daughter of a maid protested: "I hate the word service. We came to this country to better ourselves, and it's not bettering to have anybody ordering you around! If there was such a thing as fixed hours and some certain time to yourself, it might be different, but now I tell every girl I know, 'Whatever you do, don't go into service.'"[46]

The nature of domestic service involved what sociologist Stephen Steinberg termed "the exploitation of the whole person." The servant lacked privacy, for she lived and worked in her employer's home. Her character and manners were scrutinized for approval. In this sense, it was not just her labor that was purchased but the laborer herself. This lack of personal freedom was the reason why one Irish woman chose to work in a factory rather than in "the service":

> It's freedom that we want when the day's work is done. I know some nice girls…that make more money and dress better and everything for being in service. They're [house servants] and have Thursday afternoon out and part of every other Sunday. But they're never sure of one minute that's their own when they're in the house. Our day is ten hours long, but when it's done it's done, and we can do what we like with the evenings. That's what I've heard from every nice girl that ever tried service. You're never sure that your soul's your own except when you are out of the house, and I couldn't stand that a day.[47]

On the other hand, the factory worker had her labor appropriated only at the workplace. "Though the textile worker might be reduced to a commodity, paradoxically, her inner self was left intact." Factory work, however, was also difficult to "stand." Denouncing such labor as "especially fatal to women," Archbishop John Lancaster Spalding declared that there were "few sadder sights than the poor women of the cotton mills of New England," so many of them "Irish girls, whose cheeks once bloomed with health as fresh and fair as the purity of their hearts." Irish women were preponderant in the New England textile mills of Lawrence, Holyoke, Fall River, and other towns. In Lowell, the City of Spindles, they represented 58 percent of the total textile workforce. "The gray mills in Manchester [New Hampshire]," remembered Elizabeth Gurley Flynn, "stretched like prisons along the banks of the Merrimac River. Fifty percent of the workers were women…. Many lived in the antiquated 'corporation boarding houses,' relics of when the mills were built. Our neighbors, men and women, rushed to the mills before the sun rose on cold winter days and returned after dark. They were poorly dressed and poverty stricken."[48]

In the dusty and noisy mills, the women felt their heads had become "empty of sense and their ears…deaf." Constantly standing and tying knots, they suffered backaches "until they lost their minds and ran amuck." Far from the rural countryside of Ireland, they had become tenderers of machines, their activities routinized and measured by the clock.

When I set out for Lowell,
Some factory for to find,

I left my native country
And all my friends behind.

But now I am in Lowell,
And summon'd by the bell,
I think less of the factory
Than of my native dell.

The factory bell begins to ring
And we must all obey,
And to our old employment go,
Or else be turned away.

Come all ye weary factory girls,
I'll have you understand,
I'm going to leave the factory
And return to my native land.

The "factory girls" also worked in dangerous conditions. On January 10, 1860, a terrible tragedy occurred at Lowell's Pemberton Mill. A building suddenly collapsed, trapping nine hundred workers, mostly Irish women; then a fire broke out, adding to the terror and destruction. One hundred and sixteen women were seriously hurt while eighty-eight were killed. The list of victims included many daughters of Erin.[49]

Irish women were heavily employed in the sewing trades. "No female that can handle a needle need be idle," a young woman in Philadelphia wrote home. By 1900, a third of all seamstresses and dressmakers in the United States were Irish women. Work in the garment industry was repetitious and dirty, and the wages were pitifully low. "I am a good seamstress and work hard," one woman explained. "I try but I can not make over $1 per day. I pay rent for my machine, $2.50 per month. Am not able to afford to ride on street cars, therefore I have to walk, and if I happen to be one minute late, I have to walk up long flights of stairs and am not allowed to go on the elevator."[50]

Still, for many Irish women, America was a land of opportunity. "My dear Father," a daughter wrote from New York in 1850, "I must only say this is a good place and a good country.... Any man or woman without a family are fools that would not venture and come to this plentyful Country where no man or woman ever hungered or ever will and where you will not be seen naked...." Similarly, in the same year, Margaret McCarthy wrote home to her family: "Come you all Together Couragiously and bid adieu to that lovely land of our Birth" where there was so much misery, oppression, and degradation. She enclosed twenty dollars, urging her father to clear away from "that place all together and the Sooner the Better."[51]

For these women, America represented not only jobs and wages but also economic self-sufficiency—freedom from dependency on fathers or husbands. "I am getting along splendid and likes my work...it seems like a new life," one of them wrote to her younger sister in Ireland. "I will soon have a trade and be more independint.... You know it was always what I wanted so I have reached my highest ambition." Thomas McCann wrote home about his sister: "Maggie is well and likes this Country. She would not go back to old Ireland for any money." What Maggie especially valued was the "independence" she had found in America.[52]

"Green Power": The Irish "Ethnic" Strategy

Immigrant women were mainly confined to domestic service and factory work. Their daughters, on the other hand, did not follow in their occupational footsteps. In 1900, only 19 percent of the Irish women born in America worked as servants or laundresses, compared to 61 percent of the immigrant generation. An employment agent reported that most immigrant Irish women were illiterate: "In fact they are the only class I know of that cannot read or write." But their daughters, he added, were educated and shunned domestic service. Increasingly, young women were entering white-collar employment as secretaries, nurses, and teachers. By 1910, Irish-American women constituted one-fifth of all public school teachers in northern cities and one-third in Chicago alone.[53]

These advances for Irish women reflected a broader pattern of Irish success—a rise out of the ranks of "the giddy multitude." By 1900, two-thirds of the Irish were citizens by birth, and they were better educated and had greater occupational mobility than their parents. In Boston, for example, 40 percent of those born in America had white-collar jobs in 1890, compared to only 10 percent for the immigrants. The family of John Kearney of Poughkeepsie, New York, represented this pattern. After arriving in America, Kearney worked as an unskilled laborer and then became a junk dealer; one of his sons rose from postal clerk to superintendent of city streets, and another son went from grocery clerk to inspector of the city's waterworks. "My children [are] doing first rate," an

Irish immigrant proudly declared, but "if they were back there [in Ireland] what would they be?"[54]

By the early 1900s, Irish Americans were attending college in greater proportion than their Protestant counterparts. They had even begun to enter Harvard University in substantial numbers. Initially, the students at this elite school resented the Irish presence, but gradually they came to accept the newcomers. President Abbott Lawrence Lowell viewed the Irish favorably and highlighted Harvard's role in assimilating them into American society. "What we need," he had explained earlier, "is not to dominate the Irish but to absorb them." We want them to become "rich," he added, "send their sons to our colleges, and share our prosperity and our sentiments." In his opinion, however, such inclusionism should be reserved for certain groups. The "theory of universal political equality," he argued, should not be applied to "tribal Indians," "Chinese," or "negroes under all conditions, [but] only to our own race, and to those people whom we can assimilate rapidly." Lowell added that the Irish were unlike Jewish immigrants: they were Christian as well as culturally similar to Americans of English origin. The Irish could, therefore, become "so merged in the American people" that they would not be "distinguished as a class."[55]

What greatly enabled the Irish to "merge" into the mainstream was the fact that they were "white" and hence eligible for naturalized citizenship. Their rates for becoming citizens and voters were the highest of all immigrant groups. They wanted to become Americans, for they had come here as settlers rather than as sojourners: only 10 percent of them went back to Ireland, while Italians had a return rate ranging from 40 to 60 percent. "The outstanding fact" about the Irish "return tide was its minuteness," observed historian Arnold Schrier. "Compared with the vast numbers who left Ireland it was a mere trickle." The Irish entry into citizenship and politics was facilitated by their language skills. "The Irish had one advantage which other immigrants did not share—they did not have to learn to speak English," recalled Elizabeth Gurley Flynn. Thus "they more easily became citizens."[56]

Unlike the Chinese immigrants who were barred from naturalized citizenship and the blacks who were largely disenfranchised, the Irish possessed the suffrage. The rise of Irish political power was rooted in their pattern of settlement. A rural people in Ireland, they became urban in America. In 1850, one in three Irish immigrants lived in fifteen cities, including 134,000 in New York City, 72,000 in Philadelphia, and 35,000 in Boston. Thirty years later, one-third of

New York City's population was Irish. By 1885, Boston's Irish Catholic children outnumbered white Protestant children. This city was no longer the "Boston of the Endicotts and the Winthrops" but had become "the Boston of the Collinses and the O'Briens."[57]

As voters, they consciously cultivated and promoted their "Green Power." Led by politicians like John Kelly, New York's Tammany Hall helped elect the city's first Irish Catholic mayor, William R. Grace. By 1890, the Irish had captured most of the Democratic party organizations in northern cities. In New York, Boston, Chicago, and San Francisco, Irish political machines functioned like "Robin Hoods," taking taxes from the Yankee middle class and giving revenues to the Irish through the public payrolls. By 1900, the Irish represented 30 percent of the municipal employees in these cities. Through political machines, the Irish were able to get jobs in the fire and police departments as well as municipally owned utilities, subways, street railways, waterworks, port facilities, and in city hall itself. The "Irish cop" and "Irish fireman" became ubiquitous at this time. Irish political bosses also awarded public works projects to Irish building contractors. As early as 1870, Irish building contractors constituted a fifth of all contractors in the country. An "Irish ethic" led these contractors to give preferential treatment to compatriot subcontractors and workers.[58]

Meanwhile, ethnic associations like the Ancient Order of Hibernians and the Clan na Gael functioned as networks for employment, while skilled Irish workers monopolized many trades and shared job opportunities only with their countrymen. Emigration was no longer "like going into a City where you don't know anybody," a worker wrote to a relative in Ireland. "Should your Brother Paddy Come to America, he can rely on his Cousins to promote his interests in Procuring work." Heavily concentrated in the building trades, Irish workers became highly unionized. Many of the prominent leaders in the labor movement were Irish—Terence Powderly of the Knights of Labor, Mary Kenny O'Sullivan of the American Federation of Labor, and Cork-born Mary Harris, the legendary labor activist known as "Mother Jones." Through this leadership and the unions, many Irish were able to experience what historian David Montgomery described as "the much celebrated rise from rags to riches."[59]

By 1900, the Irish occupied a significant niche in the skilled labor market: 1.2 million were employed in the blue-collar trades, representing 65 percent of all Irish workers. Most of these blue-collar laborers—78 percent—were skilled. While the Irish composed only 7.5 percent of the entire male workforce, they were disproportionately represented in the elite construction and industrial occupations—one-third of the plumbers and steamfitters, one-fifth of the stonecutters and brass workers, and one-sixth of the teamsters and steelworkers. Once they became members of the privileged stratum of the workforce, they monopolized the better jobs. Irish workers campaigned to make American labor equal "white" labor. Irish "ethnic solidarity" and influence in the unions enabled them to exclude the "others" such as the Chinese and blacks. This Irish exclusion of racial minorities from the skilled and high-waged jobs represented what historian David Roediger called "the wages of whiteness."[60]

Ironically, Irish social and economic success challenged their ethnicity and sense of group unity. "How shall we preserve our identity?" asked an Irish immigrant in 1872. "How shall we preserve our faith and nationality, through our posterity, and leave our impress on the civilization of this country?" The *Irish American* urged its readers to learn Gaelic so they could "feel more proud and manly as Irish, and be more respected as American citizens." Even as the Irish immigrants took possession of America, many of them reaffirmed their Irish identity by telling and retelling stories about British oppression in the homeland. Elizabeth Gurley Flynn, for example, remembered how in the 1890s "the awareness of being Irish came to us as small children, through plaintive song and heroic story. The Irish people fought to wrest their native soil from foreign landlords, to speak their native Gaelic tongue, to worship in the church of their choice, to have their own schools, to be independent and self-governing. We drew in a burning hatred of British rule with our mother's milk. Until my father died at over eighty, he never said *England* without adding, 'God damn her!'"[61]

The immigrants had hoped to return to their beloved Emerald Isle, but most of them stayed and struggled to make America their new homeland. Working as "factory girls" and railroad builders, entering politics and businesses, and speaking English with an "American accent," they transformed themselves into Americans. "The second generation here are not interested in their ancestors," an immigrant stated, because "we have never told them of the realities of life [in Ireland], and would not encourage any of them to visit. When we left there, we left the old world behind, we are all American citizens and proud of it." For them, the ocean was a psychological border, protecting them from bitter memories. "We have too many loved ones in the Cemetary here to leave them," an immigrant wrote to her brother in Ireland. "We have been here a long time—and it is home to us now."[62]

7

⠀

"FOREIGNERS IN THEIR NATIVE LAND"

The War Against Mexico

A S IRISH WOMEN were working in Lowell's textile mills and as Irish men were helping to build a national system of transportation, America's frontier was advancing westward toward the Pacific Ocean. The Market Revolution was setting in motion forces that would lead to the violent acquisition of territory from Mexico. During the war against Mexico in the 1840s, many Irish immigrants served in the U.S. Armed Forces. Ironically, the Irish had been pushed from their homeland by British imperialism, and here they found themselves becoming Americans by participating in the conquest of Mexico. Jefferson's vision of a continent covered with "a people speaking the same language, governed in similar forms, and by similar laws" was being realized. In the expanding American empire, however, the "people" were actually becoming more diverse: added to the blacks, Indians, and Irish were Mexicans.[1]

"We Must Be Conquerors or We Are Robbers"

The Market Revolution stimulated the expansion of the Cotton Kingdom into Mexico, a sovereign nation bordering the United States in the Southwest. During the 1820s, Americans crossed the Mexican border, settling in a territory known as Tejas. Many of them were slaveholders from the South in search of new lands for cotton cultivation. In 1826, President John Quincy Adams tried to purchase Texas for a million dollars, but Mexico refused the offer.

A year later, worried about U.S. westward expansion, the Mexican government sent a commission to investigate the influx of Americans into Texas. In his diary, Lieutenant Jose Maria Sanchez described how the foreign intruders were growing in number and defying Mexican laws. "The Americans from the north have taken possession of practically all the eastern part of Texas, in most cases without the permission of the authorities. They immigrate constantly, finding no one to prevent them, and take possession of the *sitio* [location] that best suits them without either asking leave or going through any formality other than that of building their homes." While visiting the American settlement of San Felipe de Austin, Sanchez predicted: "In my judgment, the spark that will start the conflagration that will deprive us of Texas, will start from this colony." Similarly, Commissioner Manuel Mier y Teran reported: "The incoming stream of new settlers is unceasing." As the military commander of Mexico's eastern interior provinces in 1829, Mier y Teran expressed apprehension: "The department of Texas is contiguous to the most avid nation in the world. The North Americans have conquered whatever territory adjoins them." Then he added ominously: "They incite uprisings in the territory in question."[2]

In 1830, the Mexican government outlawed the institution of slavery and prohibited further American immigration into Texas. The new policy, however, provoked opposition among some Mexicans in the territory. The council of San Antonio, composed of members of the Mexican elite, favored keeping the border open to Americans. "The industrious, honest North Americans settlers have made great improvements in the past seven or eight years," the council declared. "They have raised cotton and cane and erected gins and sawmills."[3]

American foreigners in Texas were furious about the new restrictions. As slaveholders, many of them were determined to defy the Mexican law abolishing slavery. Americans continued to cross the border as illegal aliens. By 1835, there were some twenty thousand Americans in Texas, greatly outnumbering the four thousand Mexicans. Tensions were escalating. Stephen Austin urged his countrymen to "Americanize" Texas and bring the territory under the U.S. flag. He stated that his "sole and only desire" since he first saw Texas was to "redeem it from the wilderness—to settle it with an intelligent honorable and enterprising people." He invited compatriots to come to Texas, "each man with his rifle," "passports or no passports." Viewing the conflict as one between a "mongrel Spanish-Indian and negro race" and "civilization and the Anglo-American race," Austin declared that violence was inevitable: "War is our only recourse. There is no other remedy."[4]

War came in 1836 when some Americans in Texas began an armed insurrection against Mexican authority. The center of the rebellion for independence was San Antonio, where a mission had been converted into a fort that would become the stuff of American legend. Barricading themselves in the Alamo, 175 Texas rebels initiated hostilities in a struggle for what would be called the Lone Star Republic. The Mexican government declared the action illegal and sent troops to suppress the rebellion. Surrounded by Mexican soldiers, the rebels refused to surrender. According to one story, their leader, William Barret Travis, dramatically drew "a line in the sand." All the men who crossed it, he declared, would fight to the death.[5]

Led by General Antonio Lopez de Santa Anna, the Mexican soldiers stormed the Alamo and killed most of the rebels, including Jim Bowie and Davy Crockett. Among the men slain were a few Mexicans, including Juan Abamillo, Carlos Espalier, and Antonio Fuentes, who had decided to side with the Americans. The conflict even pitted brother against brother—Gregorio Esparza defended the fort while Francisco Esparza was one of the attacking soldiers. Santa Anna's army then captured the town of Goliad, where four hundred American prisoners were executed. Rallying around the cry, "Remember the Alamo," Sam Houston organized a counterattack. Houston's troops surprised Santa Anna's forces at San Jacinto. According to historian Carlos Castañeda, they "clubbed and stabbed" Mexican soldiers seeking to surrender, "some on their knees." The slaughter became "methodical" as the Texan riflemen "poured a steady fire into the packed, jostling ranks." After the battle, two Americans and 630 Mexicans lay dead.[6]

Houston forced Santa Anna to cede Texas. Mexico repudiated the treaty, but Houston declared Texas an independent republic and was subsequently elected its president. In his inaugural address, Houston claimed that the Lone Star Republic reflected "glory on the Anglo-Saxon race." He insisted that their struggle was against Mexican "tyranny" and for American "democracy": "With these principles we will march across the Rio Grande, and...ere the banner of Mexico shall triumphantly float upon the banks of the Sabine, the Texan standard of the single star, borne by the Anglo-Saxon race, shall display its bright folds in Liberty's triumph, on the isthmus of Darien."[7]

In 1845, the United States annexed the Lone Star Republic, and Mexico broke off diplomatic relations. Tensions between the two countries then focused on a border dispute: the United States claimed that the southern border of Texas was the Rio Grande River, but Mexico insisted that it was 150 miles to the north at the Nueces River. In early January 1846, President James K. Polk ordered General Zachary Taylor to take his troops into the disputed territory. The American forces occupied an area near the mouth of the Rio Grande and blockaded the river—an act of war under international law. On May 9, an armed skirmish between American and Mexican forces provided the pretext for a declaration of war. In his war message, Polk declared that Mexican troops had "passed the boundary of the United States...invaded our territory and shed American blood upon American soil." He added: "War exists notwithstanding all our efforts to avoid it."[8]

The border dispute shrouded the real reason behind the war. A key U.S. objective was the annexation of California. This territory was an important source of raw material for the Market Revolution: it exported cattle hides to New England, where Irish factory laborers manufactured boots and shoes. More important, California had strategic harbors. Sperm oil from whales was a crucial fuel and lubricant in the growing economy, and the American whaling industry was sending its ships to the Pacific Ocean. The ports of California were needed for repairs and supplies. Policymakers also wanted to promote American trade with the Pacific Rim. In a message to Congress, President James K. Polk explained that California's harbors "would afford shelter for our navy, for our numerous whale ships, and other merchant vessels employed in the Pacific ocean, and would in a short period become the marts of an extensive and profitable commerce with China, and other countries of the East."[9]

In California, the war began in the small town of Sonoma. There, on June 6, 1846, General Mariano Vallejo was rudely awakened at his home by thirty armed Americans. They had arrived "before it was quite light," one of them recalled. "We knocked on the front of his dwelling and one of his servants came out. We was standing all a-horseback." So began the revolt to wrest California from Mexico and establish what would be called the "Bear Flag Republic." The rebels were mostly uncouth frontiersmen, viewed by the Mexicans as strangers, "grimy adventurers," and "exiles from civilization." Some of them had crossed the border after the Mexican government had prohibited American immigration and hence were illegal aliens. Most of the intruders had been in California for less than a year, and now they were claiming the territory as theirs. Their homemade flag displayed the image of a grizzly bear facing a lone star, suggesting an analogy to the Texas Republic. To the Mexicans, the bear was a thief, a plunderer of their cattle; they would call the armed intruders *los Osos* (the Bears).[10]

Commandante Vallejo represented Mexican authority in the region of California north of San Francisco, and the American rebels had come to "arrest" him. Actually, Vallejo was no longer on active duty, and there were no Mexican troops at the fort. The ragtag rebels entered the general's elegant home with its handsome mahogany chairs and fine piano; a gentleman always, Vallejo offered them wine before returning to his bedroom to change his clothes. A striking contrast to the Americans, Vallejo was educated and cultured, the possessor of a vast library. The general, his brother Salvador, and his brother-in-law Jacob Leese were then taken as prisoners to Fort Sutter near Sacramento. Salvador Vallejo bitterly recalled that his captors would check on them and comment: "Let me see if my Greasers are safe."[11]

Two months later, General Vallejo was freed and allowed to return home, only to find his rancho stripped. "I left Sacramento half dead, and arrived here [Sonoma] almost without life, but am now much better," Vallejo wrote to an American friend in San Francisco. "The political change has cost a great deal to my person and mind, and likewise to my property. I have lost more than one thousand live horned cattle, six hundred tame horses, and many other things of value.... All is lost."[12]

Unlike his immigrant captors, Don Vallejo was a Californian by birth. As the commander of the Sonoma fort, he represented a long history of Spanish and Mexican efforts to secure the California territory against American and Russian expansion. Three centuries earlier, believing that Asia was close to Mexico, Hernan Cortes had sent an expedition to California, and in 1542, Juan Rodriguez Cabrillo sailed along its coast. The Spanish colonization of this region began in 1769, when Father Junipero Serra founded the mission of San Diego de Alcala. The plan was to extend the Spanish frontier northward as the colonizers took Indian lands and converted the native peoples. During the next half century, twenty-one missions were established, stretching five hundred miles along the California coast northward to Los Angeles, Santa Barbara, Monterey, San Jose, San Francisco, and Sonoma.

While some of the settlers came from Spain, most were from Mexico, recruited from the ranks of the desperately poor. They were generally mestizo: the forty-six settlers sent to Los Angeles, for example, were "a mixture of Indian and Negro with here and there a trace of Spanish." The government promised the colonists equipment and food, including herds of cattle. By 1781, however, there were only about six hundred settlers in Alta California. Trying to bolster immigration, Governor Diego de Borica reported: "This is a great country, the most peaceful and quiet country in the world... [with] good bread, excellent meat, tolerable fish." But California failed to attract settlers: by 1821, there were only three thousand Mexicans, most of them the offspring of the first colonists. Meanwhile, Spain had overextended its empire; overthrowing Spanish rule, Mexico became an independent country.[13]

The owner of a vast estate, Vallejo belonged to the Mexican elite. Like other rancheros, he had been granted vast tracts of land by the Spanish and Mexican governments. In Don Vallejo's stratified society, the *gente de razon* were at the top. The Spanish term for "people of reason" generally meant Spanish and Castilian-speaking people, although it did come to include mestizos who were properly educated. "Throughout all California," John Marsh reported in 1836, "the Indians are the principal laborers; without them the business of the country could hardly be carried on." The laborers worked not only on the range but also in the hacienda. "Each one of my children, boys and girls, has a servant who has no other duty than to care for him or her," Dona Francisca Vallejo, the mother of sixteen children, told a visitor. "I have two for my own personal service. Four or five grind the corn for the tortillas; for here we entertain so many guests that three could not furnish enough meals to feed them all. About six or seven are set apart for service in the kitchen. Five or six are continually occupied in washing clothes of the children and the rest employed in the house; and finally, nearly a dozen are charged to attend the sewing and spinning." Vallejo and his fellow rancheros practiced a patriarchical culture. "All our servants are very much attached to us," explained Dona Vallejo. "They do not ask for money, nor do they have a fixed wage; we give them all they need, and if they are ill we care for them like members of the family. If they have children we stand as godparents and see to their education. We treat our servants rather as friends than as servants."[14]

In Vallejo's California, there were also a few Anglos from the United States. The early American newcomers were generally accepted, even offered land grants by the Mexican government if they converted to Catholicism and became naturalized citizens. For example, Jacob Leese married Rosalia Vallejo, a sister of Mariano Vallejo. Don Abel Stearns of Massachusetts married into the wealthy Bandini family and became a large landowner and cattle rancher. These American men became "Dons," a title signifying high status and membership in the California landed elite. Learning Spanish and practicing the local customs, they became part of their adopted society. "While here [in San Gabriel]," an American visitor reported, "I met with a Yankee—Daniel A. Hill [from Santa Barbara]...who had been a resident in the country for many years, and who had become, in manner and appearance, a complete Californian."[15]

By the 1840s, more Yankees were entering Vallejo's world, driven there by dreams of wealth and landownership generated by pamphlets and books about California. Entering California illegally, many of them might have read Richard Henry Dana's bestselling book, *Two Years Before the Mast,* published in 1840. In his report on his travels to California, Dana noted that some of the Mexicans were "even as fair" as the English, of "pure Spanish blood." Below them was the laboring class. Racially, the laborers went "down by regular shades," "growing more and more dark and muddy" with "pure" Indians at the bottom rung. Dana characterized Mexicans as "an idle, thriftless people." He disdainfully noticed that many Americans were marrying "natives" and bringing up their children as Catholics and Mexicans. Perhaps he had in mind his uncle. After his arrival in Santa Barbara in 1826, William G. Dana of Boston converted to Catholicism and married sixteen-year-old Josefa Carillo after delaying the nuptial ceremony for two years in order to complete naturalization formalities. Don "Guillermo" and Dona Josefa had twenty-one children. Richard never visited his uncle during his stay in California. If the "California fever" [laziness] spared the first generation, the younger Dana warned, it was likely to "attack" the second, for

Mexicans lacked the enterprise and calculating mentality of Americans. Inefficient in moneymaking, they spent their time in pleasure-giving activities such as festive parties called fandangos. What distinguished Anglos from Mexicans, in Dana's opinion, was their Yankeeness—their industry, frugality, sobriety, and work ethic. Impressed with California's natural resources—its forests, grazing land, and harbors—Dana exclaimed: "In the hands of an enterprising people, what a country this might be!"[16]

Determined to place California in their own hands, the intruders were now coming in groups; many brought their families and saw themselves as Americans, not future Mexicans. They were a different sort from the first Americanos. "Many [of these early immigrants] settled among us and contributed with their intelligence and industry to the progress of my beloved country," Governor Juan Alvarado observed and then added unhappily: "Would that the foreigners that came to settle in Alta California after 1841 had been of the same quality as those who preceded them!" Mexicans complained about the new settlers: "The idea these gentlemen have formed for themselves is, that God made the world and them also, therefore what there is in the world belongs to them as sons of God." "These Americans are so contriving that some day they will build ladders to touch the sky, and once in the heavens they will change the whole face of the universe and even the color of the stars." Governor Pio Pico nervously complained: "We find ourselves threatened by hordes of Yankee immigrants who have already begun to flock into our country and whose progress we cannot arrest."[17]

Many of these Yankees had come west fully intending to take the territory from Mexico. The leader of Vallejo's captors, Benjamin Ide, told his men: "We must be conquerors or we are robbers." The rebels insisted that they were defending the interests of American settlers against unfair and arbitrary Mexican rule. But the manager of Fort Sutter where Vallejo was imprisoned refuted this claim. "This was simply a pretense," John Bidwell charged, "to justify the premature beginning of the war [in California], which henceforth was to be carried in the name of the United States." What Vallejo's armed captors were doing, he added, was playing "the Texas game."[18]

Shortly after the rebels arrested General Vallejo and established the Bear Flag Republic, Commander John D. Sloat initiated the war in California: he sailed his ship into Monterey Bay and declared California a possession of the United States.

The taking of California turned out to be almost nonviolent. Elsewhere in the Southwest, however, the war unleashed a brutal, unrestrained military campaign. American soldiers themselves documented the atrocities committed against the Mexican civilian population. "Since we have been in Matamoros a great many murders have been committed," a young captain, Ulysses S. Grant, wrote in a private letter. "Some of the volunteers and about all the Texans seem to think it perfectly right to impose on the people of a conquered city to any extent, and even to murder them where the act can be covered by dark. And how much they seem to enjoy acts of violence too!" Another officer, George G. Meade, wrote in a letter: "They [the volunteers] have killed five or six innocent people walking in the street, for no other object than their own amusement. They rob and steal the cattle and corn of the poor farmers." General Winfield Scott admitted that American soldiers had "committed atrocities to make Heaven weep and every American of Christian morals blush for his country. Murder, robbery and rape of mothers and daughters in the presence of tied-up males of the families have been common all along the Rio Grande." A Mexican newspaper denounced the outrages, describing the American invaders as "the horde of banditti, of drunkards, of fornicators...vandals vomited from hell, monsters who bid defiance to the laws of nature, shameless, daring, ignorant, ragged, bad-smelling, long-bearded men with hats turned up at the brim, thirsty with the desire to appropriate our riches and our beautiful damsels."[19]

The horror ended in early 1848, a few months after General Winfield Scott's army occupied Mexico City. In the Treaty of Guadalupe Hidalgo, signed on February 2, Mexico accepted the Rio Grande River as the Texas border and ceded the Southwest territories to the United States for fifteen million dollars. The acquisition included the present-day states of California, New Mexico, Arizona, Nevada, and parts of Colorado and Utah, a total of over one million square miles. Together with Texas, the area amounted to one-half of Mexico.

To many Americans, the war and the conquest had extended their "errand into the wilderness" to the Pacific. In 1845, *Democratic Review* editor John L. O'Sullivan announced that "to overspread the continent allotted by Providence for the free development of our yearly multiplying millions" was America's "manifest destiny." Like John Winthrop's "city upon a hill," this vision depicted the national mission as *divinely* designed.[20]

The doctrine of "manifest destiny" embraced a belief in American Anglo-Saxon superiority. As the editor of the *Brooklyn Daily Eagle,* Walt Whitman exclaimed: "We pant to see our country and its rule far-reaching.... What has miserable, inefficient Mexico...to do with the great mission of peopling the New World with a noble race?" Whitman praised General Zachary Taylor's conquest of Monterey as "another clinching proof of the indomitable energy of the Anglo-Saxon character." "This continent," a congressman chimed, "was intended by Providence as a vast theatre on which to work out the grand experiment of Republican government, under the auspices of the Anglo-Saxon race." Former secretary of state of the Texas Republic Ashbel Smith confidently predicted: "The two races, the Americans distinctively so called, and the Spanish Americans or Mexicans, are now brought by the war into inseparable contact. No treaties can henceforth dissever them; and the inferior must give way before the superior race. After the war, when the 40,000 soldiers now in Mexico shall be withdrawn, their places will be soon more than supplied by a still greater number of merchants, mechanics, physicians, lawyers, preachers, schoolmasters, and printers."[21]

In an essay entitled "The Conquest of California," the editor of the *Southern Quarterly Review* proudly explained: "There are some nations that have a doom upon them.... The nation that makes no onward progress...that wastes its treasures wantonly—that cherishes not its resources—such a nation will burn out...will become the easy prey of the more adventurous enemy." Enterprising Americans, the editor reported, had already begun to "penetrate" the remote territory of California, extracting her vast and hidden riches, and would soon make her resources "useful" by opening her "swollen veins" of precious metals.[22]

Anglo Over Mexican

Mexicans had a different view of the Anglo conquest. Suddenly, they were "thrown among those who were strangers to their language, customs, laws, and habits." The border had been moved, and now thousands of Mexicans found themselves inside the United States. The treaty permitted them to remain in the United States or to move across the new southern border. If they stayed, they would be guaranteed "the enjoyment of all the rights of citizens of the United States according to the principles of the Constitution."[23]

Most remained, but they felt a peculiar alienation. "Our race, our unfortunate people will have to wander in search of hospitality in a strange land, only to be ejected later," Mexican diplomat Manuel Crescion Rejon predicted. "Descendents of the Indians that we are, the North Americans hate us, their spokesmen depreciate us, even if they recognize the justice of our cause, and they consider us unworthy to form with them one nation and one society; they clearly manifest that their future expansion begins with the territory that they take from us and pushing aside our citizens who inhabit the land." A few years later, Pablo de la Guerra vented his frustrations before the California senate. The "conquered" Mexicans, he complained, did not understand the new language, English, which was now "prevalent" on "their native soil." They had become *foreigners in their own land*."[24]

What this meant for many Mexicans was political vulnerability and powerlessness. In California, for example, while Mexicans were granted suffrage, they found that democracy was essentially for Anglos only. At first, they greatly outnumbered Anglos by about ten to one. But the conquered people suddenly became a minority. In January 1848, gold was discovered near John Sutter's mill; the gold rush ignited a massive migration into California. By 1849, the Anglo population reached one hundred thousand compared to only thirteen thousand Mexicans.

Dominant in the state legislature, Anglos enacted laws aimed at Mexicans. An antivagrancy act, known as the "Greaser Act," defined vagrants as "all persons who [were] commonly known as 'Greasers' or the issue of Spanish or Indian blood...and who [went] armed and [were] not peaceable and quiet persons." In 1850, the legislature passed a foreign miners' tax. This law was actually a "Mexican Miners' Tax," for the tax collectors took fees mainly from Spanish-speaking miners, including American citizens of Mexican ancestry.[25]

Many of these miners had come from Mexico, where techniques for extracting gold had been developed. In California, they shared this knowledge with Anglo miners, introducing Spanish mining terms such as *bonanza* (rich ore) and *placer* (deposits containing gold particles). But Anglos resented the Mexicans as competitors, making no distinction between Mexicans and Mexican Americans. "The Yankee regarded every man but a native American as an interloper," observed a contemporary, "who had no right to come to California and pick up the gold of 'free and enlightened citizens.'" Anglo miners sometimes violently defended what they regarded as their "right" to the gold In his memoir, Antonio Franco Coronel described one frightening experience: "I arrived at the Placer Seco [about March 1849] and began to work at a regular digging.... Presently news was circulated that it had been resolved to evict all those who were not American citizens from the placers because it was believed that the foreigners did not have the right to exploit the placers." Shortly afterward, a hundred Anglos invaded the diggings of Coronel and some other Mexicans, forcing them to flee for their lives. "All of these men raised their pistols, their Bowie knives; some had rifles, others pickaxes and shovels."[26]

Though Mexicans were a minority of the state population, they continued to represent a sizable presence in Southern California. In Santa Barbara, for example, Mexicans represented a majority of the voters and dominated local elections. "The Americans have very little influence in the elections," complained Charles Huse in the 1850s. "The Californians have a majority of the votes. When they are united, they can elect whomever they wish." However, Huse predicted that Anglos would have "all the power" in a few years and would not "consult the Californians about anything." Indeed, Mexicans soon became a minority as Anglos flocked into Santa Barbara. In 1873, Mexican voters were overwhelmed at the polls. Though they elected Nicolas Covarrubias as county sheriff, they lost the positions of county assessor, clerk, treasurer, and district attorney. Politically, the Anglos were now in command. "The native population wear a wondering, bewildered look at the sudden change of affairs," a visitor noted, "yet seem resigned to their unexpected situation, while the conquerors are proud and elated with their conquest." Mexican political participation declined precipitously in Santa Barbara—to only 15 percent of registered voters in 1904 and only 3 percent in 1920.[27]

Compared to California, the political proscription of Mexicans in Texas was more direct. There, Mexicans were granted suffrage but only in principle. A merchant in Corpus Christi reported that the practice in several counties was to withhold the franchise from Mexicans. A traveler observed that the Mexicans in San Antonio could elect a government of their own if they voted but added: "Such a step would be followed, however, by a summary revolution." In 1863, after a closely contested election, the *Fort Brown Flag* editorialized: "We are opposed to allowing an ignorant crowd of Mexicans to determine the political questions in this country, where a man is supposed to vote knowingly and thoughtfully." During the 1890s, many counties established "white primaries" to disenfranchise Mexicans as well as blacks, and the legislature instituted additional measures like the poll tax to reduce Mexican political participation.[28]

Political restrictions lessened the ability of Mexicans not only to claim their rights as citizens but also to protect their rights as landowners. The original version of the Treaty of Guadalupe Hidalgo had contained a provision, Article X, which guaranteed protection of "all prior and pending titles to property of every description." In ratifying the treaty, however, the U.S. Senate omitted this article. Instead, American emissaries offered the Mexican government a "Statement of Protocol" to reassure Mexicans that "the American government by suppressing the Xth article...did not in any way intend to annul the grants of lands made by Mexico in the ceded territories." Grantees would be allowed to have their legitimate titles acknowledged in American courts.[29]

But whether the courts would in fact confirm their land titles was another matter. In New Mexico, the Court of Private Land Claims was established in 1891. Dominated by Anglo legal officials, the court confirmed the grants of only 2,051,526 acres, turning down claims for 33,439,493 acres. The court's actions led to Anglo ownership of four-fifths of the Mexican land grants. Similarly, in California, Mexican land titles were contested. Three years after the Treaty of Guadalupe Hidalgo, Congress passed a land law establishing a commission to review the validity of land grants made under Spanish and Mexican rule. The boundaries for these land grants had been drawn without surveying instruments and were loosely marked on maps indicating a notched tree, a spot "between the hills at the head of a running water," a pile of stones, and the like. Frequently, land was measured with the expression *poco más o menos* (a little more or less). The entire Pomona Valley, for example, was described as "the place being vacant which is known by the name of [Rancho] San Jose, distant some six leagues, more or less, from the Ex-Mission of San Gabriel." U.S. land law, however, required accurate boundaries and proof of legitimate titles.[30]

Such evidence, Mexican landholders discovered, was very difficult to provide. Unfamiliar with American law and lacking English-language skills, they became prey to Anglo lawyers. If they were successfully able to prove their claim, they would often be required to pay their lawyers one-quarter of their land. Others borrowed money at high interest rates in order to pay legal fees; after they won their cases, many rancheros were forced to sell their land to pay off their debts. "The *average* length of time required to secure evidence of ownership," historian Walton Bean calculated, "was 17 *years* from the time of submitting a claim to the board." In the end, whether or not they won their claims, most of the great rancheros in northern California lost their lands. "When they [the rancheros] receive patent," *El Clamor Publico* of Los Angeles observed, "if they are not already ruined, they will be very close to it." In an 1859 petition to Congress, sixty rancheros protested that they had been forced to sell their lands to pay interests, taxes, and litigation expenses. "Some, who at one time had been the richest landholders," they observed, "today find themselves without a foot of ground, living as objects of charity."[31]

After paying his lawyers $80,000, Salvador Vallejo managed to prove his land claim before the Land Commission; during his appeal in the district court, however, squatters settled on his rancho. They kept burning his crops, and he finally sold his property for $160,000 and moved to San Francisco. Although Mariano Vallejo lost his Soscol land claim, he won his Petaluma land claim in appeals to the U.S. Supreme Court. But squatters had occupied his land and refused to move; they also ran off his Indian laborers and destroyed his crops. Vallejo was forced to sell parts of his vast estate, which had originally totaled more than 100,000 acres, until he was down to only 280 acres in Sonoma. Bitter over the loss of his land, Vallejo cursed the new Anglo order: "The language now spoken in our country, the laws which govern us, the faces which we encounter daily are those of the masters of the land, and of course antagonistic to our interests and rights, but what does that matter to the conqueror? He wishes his own well-being and not ours!"[32]

Meanwhile, the "play of the market" contributed to the dispossession of the Mexican landed class. The cattle industry in California had begun to decline in the late 1850s; lacking the financial resources to convert their ranches from grazing to agriculture, many rancheros were forced to sell their land. In Texas, the cattle industry was extremely unstable and volatile. The periodic falls in the cattle market generated sales and transfers of property from Mexican to Anglo ranchers. "During the ten-year boom of 1875–1885, the King ranch purchased nearly 58,000 acres of Mexican-owned land," historian David Montejano calculated, "but the ranch would acquire nearly as much, 54,000 acres, in the following five years, a time of market collapse (1886–1891)."[33]

During periods of drought, Anglo ranchers had an advantage: they were able to protect their ranches better than their Mexican competitors because they had greater access to bank credit and could obtain funds to dig deeper wells. After droughts, they were financially stronger and able to purchase land from economically distressed rancheros. For example, the drought of the 1890s financially devastated rancher Victoriano Chapa of Texas. In 1901, at the age of eighty-nine years, Chapa was persuaded to sell his stock and lease his land. The approaching transfer made him depressed. Chapa told historian J. Frank Dobie, whose family owned a nearby ranch: "Why have we been talked into this evil trade? We belong here. My roots go deeper than those of any mesquite growing up and down this long arroyo. We do not need money. When a man belongs to a place and lives there, all the money in the world cannot buy him anything else so good. *Valgame Dios,* why, why, why?" Chapa took his life two days before the transfer of his land.[34]

What made the market especially destructive for rancheros was the introduction of a new system of taxation. Previously, under Mexican rule, the products of the land were taxed. This policy made sense in a region where climatic conditions caused income from agriculture to fluctuate; ranchers and farmers paid taxes only when their cattle or crops yielded profits. Under the new order, however, the land itself was taxed. While this tax system was color-blind and applied to all landowners, it assisted the dispossession of Mexican landowners. Many Mexican farmers borrowed money to pay their taxes only to be forced to sell their property to pay off debts incurred by the interest. In Southern California, for example, Julio Verdugo mortgaged his Rancho San Rafael to Jacob Elias for $3,445 at 3 percent interest per month. After eight years, Verdugo owed $58,000 and had to sell his entire rancho to Alfred B. Chapman. Chapman, feeling sorry for Verdugo, gave the old ranchero some land for a residence.[35]

As Mexicans told and retold stories about the loss of their land, they created a community of the dispossessed. They recalled how "the native Californians were an agricultural people" and had "wished to continue so." But then they "encountered the obstacle of the enterprising genius of the Americans, who... assumed possession of their lands, [took] their cattle, and destroyed their woods." In Santa Barbara, a Mexican old-timer recounted the decline of the rancheros who had fallen into debt to Anglo merchants and lost their ranches: "The Spanish people had to live and as the dwindling herds would not pay their bills, they mortgaged their land to the *Americanos*. They got much of our lands."[36] A Mexican woman remembered her grandmother's bitterness: "Grandmother would not trust any gringo, because they did take their land grants away and it still was a memory to her. She always used to say, 'Stay with your race, stay with your own.'" A Mexican song poignantly expressed how it felt to be dispossessed and alienated on their native soil:

> *The Mexico-Texan, he's one fonny man*
> *Who lives in the region that's north of the*
>   *Gran';*
> *Of Mexican father, he born in thees part.*
> *For the Mexico-Texan, he no gotta lan';*
> *And sometimes he rues it, deep down in hees*
>   *heart.*
> *He stomped on da neck on both sides of the*
>   *Gran';*
> *The dam gringo lingo no cannot spick,*
> *It twista da tong and it maka heem sik;*
> *A cit'zen of Texas they say that he ees!*
> *But then,—why they call heem da Mexican*
>   *Grease?*
> *Soft talk and hard action, he can't*
>   *understan',*
> *The Mexico-Texan, he no gotta lan'.*[37]

In 1910, the Laredo *La Cronica* described the degradation of many Mexicans from landholders to laborers: "The Mexicans have sold the great share of their landholdings and some work as day laborers on what once belonged to them. How sad this truth!" Like Caliban, Mexicans found themselves now working for strangers: they were serving in "offices that profited" the Anglo Prosperos who had come to possess their country.[38]

Mexicans were extensively used as workers in ranching and agriculture. In Texas, Mexican cowboys, vaqueros, helped to drive the cattle herds on the Chisholm and Western trails to the railroad centers in Abilene and Dodge City. Vaqueros taught Anglo cowboys and ranchers their time-tested techniques of roping, branding, and handling cattle. Rancher C. C. Cox described a roundup: "Once a week or oftener we would make a rodeo or round up the cattle. The plan is to have one herding ground on the Ranch—the cattle soon learn to run together at that place when they see the vaqueros on the wing—and when those on the outskirts of the range are started, the movement becomes general, and no prettier or more interesting sight can be imagined than a rodeo in full progress—every cow catches the alarm and starts off at a brisk trot headed for the herding ground."[39]

But Mexican cowboys soon began to vanish. The extension of rail lines into Texas eliminated the cattle drives, and agriculture in the state shifted from grazing to tillage. Mexican cowboys had looked down on farm laborers with "mingled contempt and pity," rancher J. Frank Dobie observed in the 1920s, but "more and more of the vaqueros" were turning to "cotton picking each fall."[40]

Mexican farm laborers had been in the cotton fields even before Texan independence. As cotton cultivation expanded during the second half of the nineteenth century, they became the mainstay of agricultural labor. "Soil and climate are suitable and cheap labor is at hand," announced the *Corpus Christi Weekly Caller* in 1885. "Mexican farm labor can be utilized in the cultivation of cotton as well during the picking season." They cleared the lands for planting. "Grubbing bush," many Anglos said, "is a Mexican job." They dug irrigation ditches, bringing water from rivers and streams to parched areas. Some of the irrigation methods had originally been developed by the Moors in Africa before the tenth century and had been brought to the Southwest by the Spanish. Other techniques had come from the Pueblo Indians, who had developed irrigation systems in the region long before the arrival of the first Spaniards. Mexican laborers would level the land, then divide the fields into squares with low embankments to hold the water. After soaking a block, they would make a hole in one of the walls, permitting the water to flow into the next square. This method of irrigation came to be known as "the Mexican system." Over the years, these laborers transformed the Texas terrain from scrub bush to the green fields of the Lower Valley known as the "winter garden."[41]

Mexicans also served as an important workforce in railroad construction. During the 1880s, they constituted a majority of the laborers laying tracks for the Texas and Mexican Railroad. An Arizona newspaper stated: "It is difficult to get white men to work, the wages being only $1.50 a day, and board $5 per week with some minor charges, which reduce a man's net earnings." When the first Mexican section crew began working in Santa Barbara in 1894, the *Morning Press* reported that the "Chinamen section hands" of the Southern Pacific had been replaced by "a gang of Mexicans." By 1900, the Southern Pacific Railroad had forty-five hundred Mexican employees in California.[42]

Railroad construction work was migratory. Railroad workers and their families lived in boxcars and were shunted to the places where they were needed. "Their abode," a manager said, "is where these cars are placed." In the torrid heat of summer and the freezing cold of winter, the workers laid tracks as they sang:

> Some unloaded rails
> Others unloaded ties.

An army of bending backs and swinging arms, they connected the cities of the Southwest with ribbons of steel.

> Those who knew the work
> Went repairing the jack
> With sledge hammers and shovels,
> Throwing earth up the track.

They shoveled up not only dirt but also complaints about the low wages and exhausting work.

> And others of my companions
> Threw out thousands of curses.[43]

Meanwhile, Mexicans were working in the mining industries. In the New Almaden Quicksilver Mine in California, Mexican miners labored deep in the bowels of the earth. To bring the ore to the surface, each worker carried a two-hundred-pound pack strapped to his shoulders and forehead. Their nerves straining and muscles quivering, hundreds of these carriers ascended perpendicular steps, "winding through deep caverns" in darkness lit by candles on the walls. They wore pantaloons with the legs cut above the knees, calico shirts, and leather sandals fastened at their ankles. Emerging into the daylight at the entrance of the mine, they deposited their burdens into cars and then took time to smoke their *cigarros* before descending again. In the copper mines of Arizona, Mexicans extracted the "red metal" used to manufacture electrical wires. "One might say," observed historian Carey McWilliams, "...that Mexican miners in the copper mines of Arizona, Utah, and Nevada, have played an important role in making possible the illumination of America by electricity."[44]

Mexican laborers found themselves in a caste labor system—a racially stratified occupational hierarchy. On the Anglo-owned cattle ranches in Texas, for example, the managers and foremen were Anglo, while the cowhands were Mexican. In the New Mexico mines, Anglo workers operated the machines, while Mexican miners did the manual and dangerous work. In Santa Barbara, building contractors hired Anglos as skilled carpenters and Mexicans as unskilled ditch diggers. Sixty-one percent of the Mexican laborers in San Antonio were unskilled in 1870, compared to only 24 percent of the Anglos. In Southern California cities like Santa Barbara and Los Angeles, 75 percent of the Mexican workers were crowded into low blue-collar occupations such as service and unskilled labor, compared to 30 percent of the Anglos.[45]

Even where Mexicans did the same work as Anglos, they were paid less than their counterparts. In the silver mining industry of Arizona, for example, Mexican workers received between $12 and $30 a month plus a weekly ration of flour, while "American" miners got between $30 and $70 a month plus board. In the copper industry, companies listed their Mexican employees on their payrolls under the special heading of "Mexican labor," paying them at lower rates than Anglo laborers for the same job classifications. "The differences in the wages paid Mexicans and the native-born and north Europeans employed as general laborers," a congressional investigation reported, "...are largely accounted for by discrimination against the Mexicans in payment of wages." Trapped in this dual wage system, Mexican miners were especially vulnerable to debt peonage. Forced to live in company towns, they had no choice but to buy necessities from the company store where they had to use their low wages to pay high prices for food and clothing. Allowed to make purchases on credit, these miners frequently found themselves financially chained to the company.[46]

Justifying this racial hierarchy, mine owner Sylvester Mowry invoked the images as well as language used earlier by slavemasters to describe the affection and loyalty of their slaves. "My own experience has taught me that the lower class of Mexicans...," Mowry declared, "are docile, faithful, good servants, capable of strong attachments when firmly and kindly treated. They have been 'peons' for generations. They will always remain so, as it is their natural condition."[47]

But, like the enslaved blacks of the Old South, Mexican workers demonstrated that they were capable of defying these stereotypes of docility and submissiveness. Demanding self-respect and better wages, they repeatedly went on strike. In 1901, two hundred Mexican construction workers of the El Paso Electric Street Car Company struck, demanding a wage increase and an end to management's practice of replacing them with lower-paid workers recruited from Juarez, Mexico. While they did not win a raise, they successfully protected their jobs against imported laborers. Two years later, Mexican members of the United Mine Workers won strike demands for a pay increase and an eight-hour day from the Texas and Pacific Coal Company in Thurber, Texas.[48]

Protesting wage cuts in 1903, hundreds of Mexican and Japanese farmworkers went on strike together in Oxnard, California. Together, they organized the Japanese-Mexican Labor Association (JMLA). The strikers elected Kosaburo Baba as president, Y. Yamaguchi as secretary of the Japanese branch, and J. M. Lizarras as secretary of the Mexican branch. At their union meetings, discussions were conducted in both Spanish and Japanese, with English serving as a common language for both groups. For the first time in the history of California, two minority groups, feeling a solidarity based on class, had come together to form a union. Here was a West Coast version of the "giddy multitude."

In a statement written jointly by Yamaguchi and Lizarras, the union declared: "Many of us have family, were born in the country, and are lawfully seeking to protect the only property that we have—our labor. It is just as necessary for the welfare of the valley that we get a decent living wage, as it is that the machines in the great sugar factory be properly oiled—if the machines stop, the wealth of the valley stops, and likewise if the laborers are not given a decent wage, they too, must stop work and the whole people of this country suffer with them." The strikers successfully forced the farmers to pay union laborers a piecework rate of five dollars per acre for thinning beets. The JMLA had emerged as a victorious and powerful force for organizing farm laborers.[49]

Flushed with victory, J. M. Lizarras petitioned the American Federation of Labor to charter their organization as the Sugar Beet Farm Laborers' Union of Oxnard. Samuel Gompers, the president of the federation, agreed to issue a charter to Lizarras on one condition: "Your union will under no circumstance accept membership of any Chinese or Japanese." Believing that this requirement contradicted the very principles of the Oxnard strike, the Mexican strikers refused the charter. Lizarras protested:

> We beg to say in reply that our Japanese brothers here were the first to recognize the importance of cooperating and uniting in demanding a fair wage scale. In the past we have counseled, fought and lived on very short rations with our Japanese brothers, and toiled with them in the fields, and they have been uniformly kind and considerate. We would be false to them and to ourselves and to the cause of unionism if we now accepted privileges for ourselves which are not accorded to them.... We will refuse any other kind of charter, except one which will wipe out race prejudice and recognize our fellow workers as being as good as ourselves. I am ordered by the Mexican union to write this letter to you and they fully approve its words.

Without the AFL charter and the general support of organized labor, the Japanese and Mexican union passed out of existence within a few years. Their strike, however, had demonstrated that Mexican laborers were ready to stand with fellow Japanese in a movement based on interethnic class unity.[50]

The most powerful Mexican workers' show of force occurred in Arizona. At the Clifton-Morenci mines in 1903, some thirty-five hundred miners went out on strike, 80 percent of them Mexican. The strikers demanded an eight-hour day, free hospitalization, paid life insurance, fair prices at the company stores, and the abolition of the dual wage system. Italian and Slavonian workers joined them in demanding wages equal to those paid to Anglo Americans and northern Europeans. The strikers successfully shut down the mines, but they were forced to return to work after heavy rains and flooding destroyed many of their homes. Several strike leaders were convicted of inciting a riot and sent to prison. Twelve years later, however, the miners struck again. To thwart the actions of the five thousand strikers, the company sealed the mine entrances with cement and told them "to go back to Mexico." Hundreds of strikers were arrested during the nineteen-week conflict. The National Guard was ordered to break the strike, but in the end, the strikers managed to extract wage increases. "Everyone knows," commented the *Los Angeles Labor Press,* "that it was the Mexican miners that won the strike at Clifton and Morenci by standing like a stone wall until the bosses came to terms."[51]

These strikes reflected a feeling of Mexican ethnic solidarity. *"Abajo los Gerentes,"* the workers chanted, "down with the bosses." Mexican musicians provided entertainment for the parades and meetings, while Mexican merchants, *comerciantes,* offered food and clothing to the strikers. More important, the *huelgas* (strikes) were often supported by Mexican *mutualistas* (benevolent associations). "The Mexicans belong to numerous societies and through these they can exert some sort of organizational stand together," reported a local newspaper during the 1903 strike at the Clifton-Morenci mines.[52]

The *mutualistas* reinforced this consciousness of being Mexican north of the border. Everywhere in the barrios of Arizona, Texas, New Mexico, and California, there were organizations like Sociedad Benevolencia, Miguel Hidalgo, Sociedad Mutualistia, Sociedad Obreros, and Sociedad Mutualista Mexicana. Members of the *mutualistas* were laborers as well as shopkeepers and professionals such as lawyers, newspaper editors, and doctors. These associations helped individual members cover hospitalization and funeral expenses, provided low-interest loans, and raised money for people in time of dire need. Taking some of their names from national heroes and conducting their meetings in Spanish, they reminded Mexicans of their common origins as children of "the same mother: Mexico."[53]

The *mutualistas* dispelled the myth of Mexicans as a quiet, siesta-loving, sombreroed people. Through these ethnic organizations, Mexicans were resisting labor exploitation and racism. In 1911, several Texas *mutualistas* came together in a statewide convention, the Congreso Mexicanista. Concerned about anti-Mexican hostility and violence, the congress called for ethnic solidarity: *"Por la raza y para la raza,"* "All for one and one for all." One of the delegates, the Reverend Pedro Grado, defined their struggle as that of class and race: "The Mexican braceros who work in a mill, on a hacienda, or in a plantation would do well to establish Ligas Mexicanistas, and see that their neighbors form them." United, they would have the strength to "strike back at the hatred of some bad sons of Uncle Sam, who believe themselves better than the Mexicans because of the magic that surrounds the word *white."* The *mutualistas* reflected a dynamic Mexican-American identity — a proud attachment to the culture south of the border as well as a fierce determination to claim their rights and dignity in "occupied" Mexico.[54]

8

⊰⧉⋯⧉⊱

SEARCHING FOR GOLD
MOUNTAIN

Strangers from a Different Shore

CALIBAN ALSO COULD have been Asian. "Have we devils here?" the theatergoers heard Stephano declare in *The Tempest*. "Do you put tricks upon's with savages and men of Inde, ha?" The war against Mexico reflected America's quest for a passage to India. During the nineteenth century, this vision inspired Senator Thomas Hart Benton of Missouri to proclaim the movement toward Asia as America's manifest destiny. The "White" race was obeying the "divine command, to subdue and replenish the earth," as it searched for new and distant lands. As whites migrated westward, Benton pointed out, they were destroying "savagery." As civilization advanced, the "Capitol" had replaced the "wigwam," "Christians" had replaced "savages," and "white matrons" had replaced "red squaws." Under the "touch" of an "American road to India," Benton exclaimed, the western wilderness would "start" into life, creating a long line of cities across the continent. Crossing the Rocky Mountains and reaching the Pacific, whites were finally circumnavigating the earth to bring civilization to the "Yellow" race. "Orientalized," to use the concept of Edward Said, Asians had become the "Other."[1]

The annexation of California led to not only American expansion toward Asia but also the migration of Asians to America. In a plan sent to Congress in 1848 shortly after the Treaty of Guadalupe Hidalgo, policymaker Aaron H. Palmer predicted that San Francisco, connected by railroad to the Atlantic states, would become the "great emporium of our commerce on the Pacific." Chinese laborers, he proposed, should be imported to build the transcontinental railroad as well as to bring the fertile lands of California under cultivation. "No people in all the East are so well adapted for clearing wild lands and raising every species of agricultural product...as the Chinese."[2]

Pioneers from Asia

A year later, Chinese migrants began arriving in America, but they came for their own reasons. Many sought sanctuary from intense conflicts in China caused by the British Opium Wars. Significantly, while British colonialism was pushing Irish westward across the Atlantic, it was also driving Chinese eastward across the Pacific. Many migrants were also fleeing from the turmoil of peasant rebellions such as the Taiping Rebellion and the bloody strife between the Punti ("Local People") and the Hakkas ("Guest People") over possession of the fertile delta lands. "Ever since the disturbances caused by the Red bandits and the Kejia bandits," a Chinese government report noted, "dealings with foreigners have increased greatly. The able-bodied go abroad."[3]

Harsh economic conditions also drove Chinese migrants to seek survival in America. Forced to pay large indemnities to Western imperialist powers, the Qing government imposed high taxes on peasant farmers; unable to pay these taxes, many of them lost their lands. Floods intensified the suffering. "The rains have been falling for forty days," an 1847 report to the emperor stated, "until the rivers, and the sea, and the lakes, and the streams have joined in one sheet over the land [for miles]." Behind the emigrating spirit was starvation. "The population is extremely dense," an observer explained; "the means of subsistence, in ordinary times, are seldom above the demand, and consequently, the least failure of the rice crop produces wretchedness."[4]

Learning about Gam Saan, "Gold Mountain," many of the younger, more impatient, and more daring Chinese left their villages for America. The migrants were mostly men, planning to work abroad temporarily. They were illiterate or had very little schooling, but they dreamed of new possibilities inspired by stories of the "gold hills." To these hopeful migrants, America possessed an alluring boundlessness, promising not only gold but also opportunities for employment. Sixteen-year-old Lee Chew recalled the triumphant return of a fellow villager from the "country of the American wizards." With the money he had earned overseas, he bought land as spacious as "four city blocks" and built a palace on it. Then he invited his family and friends to a grand party where they were served a hundred roasted pigs, chickens, ducks, geese, and an abundance of dainties. Young Lee was inspired, eager to leave for this fabulous country.[5]

America seemed so beckoning. During the 1860s, a Chinese laborer might earn three to five dollars a month in China; in California, he could work for the railroad and make thirty dollars a month. A folk song expressed the emotions of many migrants:

> *In the second reign year of Haamfung [1852],*
> *a trip to Gold Mountain was made.*
> *With a pillow on my shoulder, I began my*
> *perilous journey:*
> *Sailing a boat with bamboo poles across the*
> *sea,*
> *Leaving behind wife and sisters in search of*
> *money,*
> *No longer lingering with the woman in the*
> *bedroom,*
> *No longer paying respect to parents at home.*[6]

The immigrants migrated to America voluntarily as free laborers: some of them paid their own way, and probably most of them borrowed the necessary funding under the credit-ticket system. Under this arrangement, an individual borrowed money from a broker to cover the cost of transportation and then paid off the loan plus interest out of his earnings in the new country. The majority of the migrants were married. As they prepared to leave their farms and villages, they realized that they would probably not see their wives again for years. But they promised to return someday.[7]

And so they left China, by the hundreds of thousands. Three hundred and twenty-five Chinese migrants joined the "Forty-Niners" rushing to California. Like their counterparts from the eastern United States and elsewhere, they came to search for gold. A year later, 450 more Chinese arrived in California; then suddenly, they came in greatly increasing numbers—2,716 in 1851, and 20,026 in 1852. By 1870, there were 63,000 Chinese in the United States. Most of them—77 percent—were living in California, but they were elsewhere in the West as well as in the Southwest, New England, and the South. The Chinese constituted a sizable proportion of the population in certain areas: 29 percent in Idaho, 10 percent in Montana, and 9 percent in California. By 1930, about 400,000 had made the Pacific crossing to America. Significantly, about half of them stayed and made the United States their permanent home.

At first, there were signs that the Chinese were welcome in California. "Quite a large number of the Celestials have arrived among us of late, enticed thither by the golden romance that has filled the world," the *Daily Alta California* reported in 1852. "Scarcely a ship arrives that does not bring an increase to this worthy integer of our population." The paper predicted that "the China boys will yet vote at the same polls, study at the same schools and bow at the same altar as our own countrymen." Three years later, merchant Chun-Chuen Lai of San Francisco sanguinely observed that "the people of the Flowery land [China] were received like guests," and "greeted with favor. Each treated the other with politeness. From far and near we came and were pleased."[8]

But Lai failed to notice the rapidly changing political climate that had begun to turn against his fellow immigrants. From the goldfields of the Sierras came the nativist cry: "California for Americans." In 1852, the California legislature enacted a second foreign miners' tax. Aimed mainly at the Chinese, this tax required a monthly payment of three dollars from every foreign miner who did not desire to become a citizen. Even if they had wanted to, the Chinese could not have become citizens, for they had been rendered ineligible to citizenship by a 1790 federal law that reserved naturalized citizenship for "whites." By 1870, California had collected five million dollars from the Chinese, a sum representing between 25 to 50 percent of all state revenue.[9]

During the 1860s, twenty-four thousand Chinese, two-thirds of the Chinese population in America, were working in the California mines. Most of these miners were independent prospectors. Many organized themselves into small groups and formed their own companies. A newspaper correspondent described companies of twenty or thirty Chinese "inhabiting close cabins, so small that one...would not be of sufficient size to allow a couple of Americans to breathe in it. Chinamen, stools, tables, cooking utensils, bunks, etc., all huddled up together in indiscriminate confusion, and enwreathed with dense smoke, presented a spectacle." These miners worked mainly placer claims. To extract the gold, they shoveled sand from the stream into a pan or rocker and then washed away the sand and dirt until only the heavy particles of gold remained. Chinese miners became a common sight in the California foothills, especially along the Yuba River and its tributaries and in towns like Long Bar, North-east Bar, and Foster Bar. They wore blue cotton shirts, baggy pants, wooden shoes, and wide-brimmed hats and had queues hanging down their backs.[10]

As mining profits declined, however, the Chinese began leaving the goldfields. Thousands of them joined other Chinese migrants to work on the railroad. In February 1865, fifty Chinese workers were hired by the Central Pacific Railroad to help lay tracks for the transcontinental line leading east from Sacramento; shortly afterward, fifty more were hired. The immigrant laborers were praised by company president Leland Stanford as "quiet, peaceable, industrious, economical—ready and apt to learn all the different kinds of work" required in railroad building. "They prove nearly equal to white men in the amount of labor they perform, and are much more reliable," company superintendent Charles Crocker reported. "No danger of strikes among them. We are training them to do all kinds of labor: blasting, driving horses, handling rock as well as pick and shovel." When white workers demanded that the company stop hiring Chinese laborers, Crocker retorted: "We can't get enough white labor to build this railroad, and build it we must, so we're forced to hire them. If you can't get along with them, we have only one alternative. We'll let you go and hire nobody but them." Within two years, Crocker had hired twelve thousand Chinese, representing 90 percent of the entire workforce. The savings derived from the employment of Chinese rather than white workers was enormous. The company paid the Chinese workers thirty-one dollars a month; had management used white workers, they would have had to pay the same wages plus board and lodging, which would have increased labor costs by one-third.[11]

The construction of the Central Pacific Railroad line was a Chinese achievement. They performed the physical labor required to lay the tracks and provided important technical labor such as operating power drills and handling explosives for boring the tunnels through Donner Summit. The Chinese workers were, in one observer's description, "a great army laying siege to Nature in her strongest citadel. The rugged mountains looked like stupendous ant-hills. They swarmed with Celestials, shoveling, wheeling, carting, drilling and blasting rocks and earth." Time was critical to the company's interest, for the amount of payment it received in land and subsidy from the federal government was based on the miles of track it built. Determined to accelerate construction, the managers forced the Chinese laborers to work through the winter of 1866. Snowdrifts, over sixty feet tall, covered construction operations. The workers lived and worked in tunnels under the snow, with shafts for air and lanterns for light. Work was dangerous, occasionally deadly. "The snow slides carried away our camps and we lost a good many men in those slides," a company official reported matter-of-factly; "many of them we did not find until the next season when the snow melted."[12]

The Chinese workers went on strike that spring. Demanding wages of forty-five dollars a month and an eight-hour day, five thousand laborers walked out "as one man." The company offered to raise their wages from thirty-one to thirty-five dollars a month, but the strikers stood by their original demands. "Eight hours a day good for white men, all the same good for Chinamen," they declared. In response, the managers moved to break the strike. They wired New York to inquire about the feasibility of transporting ten thousand blacks to replace the striking Chinese. Superintendent Crocker isolated the strikers and cut off their food supply. "I stopped the provisions on them," he stated, "stopped the butchers from butchering, and used such coercive measures." Coercion worked. Virtually imprisoned in their camps in the Sierras and starving, the strikers surrendered within a week.[13]

Forced to return to work, the Chinese completed the railroad, the "new highway to the commerce of Asia." After they were released by the Central Pacific Railroad in 1869, thousands of them went to San Francisco, where their compatriots were already heavily involved in manufacturing. The formation of an urban Chinese community and the industrial development of the city paralleled each other. In 1860, only 2,719 Chinese resided in San Francisco, representing 7.8 percent of the Chinese population in California. Ten years later, the Chinese population in the city had soared to 12,022, a 343 percent increase. Meanwhile, San Francisco had begun to develop as a locus of industry: in 1860, it had about two hundred manufacturing firms employing some fifteen hundred workers. Ten years later, with nearly one-fourth of California's Chinese population living there, San Francisco had more than twelve thousand laborers employed in industrial production and was the ninth leading manufacturing city in the United States. Half of the labor force in the city's four key industries—boot and shoe, woolens, cigar and tobacco, and sewing—was Chinese.[14]

Meanwhile, in the rural regions the Chinese were helping to develop California's agriculture. Between 1860 and 1880, hundreds of Chinese were able to become farmers through tenancy, which offered a way to enter the business with minimum capital. "We found the broad fields apportioned off and rented to separate companies of Chinamen who were working them upon shares—each little company having its own cabin," an observer reported in 1869. "Teams being furnished them, they do all the working, preparing the ground, seeding, tending the crop, and gathering the fruit, leaving nothing for the proprietor to do but to attend to the marketing, and to put into his own pocket half of the proceeds."[15]

Most of the Chinese engaged in agriculture were laborers. They helped to transform farming in California from wheat to fruit. "They were a vital factor," historian Carey McWilliams wrote, "one is inclined to state *the* vital factor, in making the transition possible." Experienced farmers in the Pearl River Delta before coming to America, the Chinese shared their agricultural knowledge with their white employers, teaching them how to plant, cultivate, and harvest orchard and garden crops.[16]

Indeed, the Chinese built the agricultural industry of California. In the San Joaquin and Sacramento river deltas, they constructed networks of irrigation canals and miles of dikes and ditches. Wielding shovels and working waist-deep in water, they drained the tule swamps and transformed the marshes into agricultural lands. In 1869, a writer for the *Overland Monthly* acknowledged the change in the landscape wrought by the Chinese: "The ditches and dykes which at present protect only a few little patches here and there of the most fruitful soil that the sun shines on, may be made to perform a like service all over the Tulare swamps; and the descendants of the people who drained those almost limitless marshes on either side of their own swiftly-flowing Yellow River, and turned them into luxuriant fields, are able to do the same thing on the banks of the Sacramento and the San Joaquin." In the Salinas Valley, Chinese laborers dug six miles of ditches to drain the land, cutting the peat soil "with huge knife-like spades and pitching it out with steel forks and hooks." Their work boosted the value of the land from $28 per acre in 1875 to $100 per acre two years later.[17]

In 1869, the *Overland Monthly* described the ubiquitous presence of Chinese laborers in California agriculture: "Visit a hop plantation in the picking season, and count its 50, 60, or 70 pickers in the garb of the eastern Asiatics, working steadily and noiselessly on from morning till night, gathering, curing and sacking the crop.... Go through the fields of strawberries...the vineyards and orchards, and you will learn that most of these fruits are gathered or boxed for market by this same people." In 1880, the Chinese represented 86 percent of the agricultural labor force in Sacramento County, 85 percent in Yuba, and 67 percent in Solano.[18]

Though they were paid low wages, Chinese farm laborers did not always passively accept what their employers offered them. In 1880, fruit pickers in Santa Clara County went out on strike for higher wages. After the 1882 Chinese Exclusion Act reduced the supply of farm labor, Chinese agricultural workers demanded higher rates for their wages. In 1900, the Bureau of Labor Statistics reported: "Relieved, by the operation of the Exclusion Acts, in great measure from the pressing competition of his fellow-countrymen, the Chinese worker was not slow to take advantage of circumstances and demand in exchange for his labor a higher price, and, as time went on, even becoming Americanized to the extent of enforcing such demands in some cases through the medium of labor organization."[19]

Meanwhile, Chinese workers became targets of white labor resentment, especially during hard times. "White men and women who desire to earn a living," the *Los Angeles Times* reported on August 14, 1893, "have for some time been entering quiet protests against vineyardists and packers employing Chinese in preference to whites." Their protests soon became violent as economic depression led to brutal anti-Chinese riots by unemployed white workers throughout California. From Ukiah to the Napa Valley to Fresno to Redlands, Chinese were beaten and shot by white workers and often loaded onto trains and shipped out of town. These immigrants bitterly remember this violence and expulsion as the "driving out."[20]

"Ethnic antagonism" in the mines, factories, and fields forced thousands of Chinese into self-employment—stores, restaurants, and especially laundries. Chinese washhouses were a common sight as early as the 1850s. By 1890, there were sixty-four hundred Chinese laundry workers in California, representing 69 percent of all laundry workers. During this period, the ratio of Chinese laundry workers to all Chinese workers jumped from one out of every seventeen to one out of every twelve.[21]

The "Chinese laundryman" was an American phenomenon. "The Chinese laundryman does not learn his trade in China; there are no laundries in China," stated Lee Chew who came to America in the early 1860s. "The women there do the washing in tubs and have no washboards or flat irons. All the Chinese laundrymen here were taught in the first place by American women just as I was taught." In China, observed Chin Foo Wong of New York, laundry work was a "woman's occupation," and men did not "step into it for fear of losing their social standing."[22]

Why did Chinese men in America enter this line of work? Unlike the retail or restaurant business, a laundry could be opened with a small capital outlay of from seventy-five to two hundred dollars. The requirements were minimal: a stove, trough, dry room, sleeping apartment, and a sign. A Chinese laundryman did not need to speak much English to operate his business. "In this sort of menial labor," said one, "I can get along speaking only 'yes' and 'no.'" He could also manage without knowing numbers. "Being illiterate, he could not write the numbers," another laundryman said, describing a fellow operator. "He had a way and what a way! See, he would draw a circle as big as a half dollar coin to represent a half dollar, and a circle as big as a dime for a dime, and so on. When the customers came in to call for their laundry, they would catch on to the meaning of the circles and pay accordingly."[23]

But "Chinese laundrymen" were also "pushed" into their occupation. Laundry work was one of the few opportunities that were open to Chinese. "Men of other nationalities who are jealous of the Chinese have raised such a great outcry about Chinese cheap labor that they have shut him out of working on farms or in factories or building railroads or making streets or digging sewers," explained Lee Chew. "So he opens a laundry." Thus the "Chinese laundry" represented a retreat into self-employment from a narrowly restricted labor market. "You couldn't work in the cigar factories or the jute or woolen mills any more—all the Chinese had been driven out," old Chinese men later sadly recalled. "About all they could be was laundrymen or vegetable peddlers then." Racial discrimination drove Chinese into work they disdained as degrading to them as men.[24]

While most Chinese lived in the West, they were present elsewhere in the United States, including the South. A year after the end of the Civil War, a planter declared: "We can drive the niggers out and import coolies that will work better at less expense, and relieve us from the cursed nigger impudence." The plan was to turn from black to Chinese labor. "Emancipation has spoiled the negro and carried him away from the fields of agriculture," the editor of the *Vicksburg Times* in Mississippi complained in 1869. "Our prosperity depends entirely upon the recovery of lost ground, and we therefore say let the Coolies come." That same year, the southern planters' convention in Memphis announced that it was "desirable and necessary to look to the teeming population of Asia for assistance in the cultivation of our soil and the development of our industrial interests." In his address to the convention, labor contractor Cornelius Koopmanshoop announced that his company had imported thirty thousand Chinese laborers into California and offered to make them available in the South.[25]

Planters soon saw that the Chinese could be employed as models for black workers: hardworking and frugal, the Chinese would be the "educators" of former slaves. During the 1870s, Louisiana and Mississippi planters imported several hundred Chinese laborers and pitted them against black workers. They praised the foreign workers for outproducing blacks and for "regulating" the "detestable system of black labor." A southern governor frankly explained: "Undoubtedly the underlying motive for this effort to bring in Chinese laborers was to punish the negro for having abandoned the control of his old master, and to regulate the conditions of his employment and the scale of wages to be paid him." An editor in Kentucky spoke even more bluntly when he predicted that the introduction of Chinese labor would change the "tune" from "'forty acres and a mule'" to "'work nigger or starve.'" Planters welcomed their new workers. "Messrs. Ferris and Estell, who are cultivating on the Hughs place, near Prentiss," a Mississippi newspaper reported in 1870, "recently imported direct from Hong Kong, a lot of Chinese, sixteen in number, with whom as laborers, they are well pleased."[26]

The Chinese did not stay long on the plantations, however. As early as 1871, the *New Orleans Times* noted that the Chinese preferred to work in the city rather than do the "plodding work of the plantations." In 1880, about a hundred Chinese were living in New Orleans, where they worked as laundrymen, cigar makers, shoemakers, cooks, and woodcarvers. By then the southern planters had overthrown Reconstruction; with their political power over blacks restored, they quickly lost interest in Chinese labor.[27]

The use of Chinese labor and its success raised two crucial questions. "What shall we do with them is not quite clear yet," remarked Samuel Bowles in 1869 in his book *Our New West*. "How they are to rank, socially, civilly, and politically, among us is one of the nuts for our social science students to crack,—if they can." And what would happen to white workers as America's industrial development depended more and more on Chinese labor?[28]

One answer to both questions was the concept of a yellow proletariat in America. According to this view, the Chinese would constitute a permanently degraded caste labor force. They would be in effect a unique "industrial reserve army" of migrant laborers forced to be foreigners forever. Thus, unlike European immigrant laborers, the Chinese would be a politically proscribed labor force. Serving the needs of American employers, they would be here only on a temporary basis. "I do not believe they are going to remain here long enough to become good citizens," Central Pacific manager Charles Crocker told a legislative committee, "and I would not admit them to citizenship." The employers of Chinese labor argued that they did not intend to allow the migrants to remain and become "thick" (to use Crocker's term) in American society.[29]

The advocates of Chinese labor offered assurances to white laborers. They explained that Chinese "cheap" labor would reduce production costs, and the resulting low prices for goods would be equivalent to a wage increase for white workers. They also argued that Chinese labor would upgrade white labor, for whites would be elevated to foremen and directors. "If society must have 'mudsills,'" they elaborated, "it is certainly better to take them from a race which would be benefited by even that position in a civilized community, than subject a portion of our own race to a position which they have outgrown." Charles Crocker explained:

> I believe that the effect of Chinese labor upon white labor has an elevating instead of degrading tendency. I think that every white man who is intelligent and able to work, who is more than a digger in a ditch...who has the capacity of being something else, can get to be something else by the presence of Chinese labor.... There is proof of that in the fact that after we got Chinamen to work, we took the more intelligent of the white laborers and made foremen of them. I know of several of them now who never expected, never had a dream that they were going to be anything but shovelers

of dirt, hewers of wood and drawers of water, and they are now respectable farmers, owning farms. They got their start by controlling Chinese labor on our railroad.[30]

What enabled businessmen like Crocker to degrade the Chinese into a subservient laboring caste was the dominant ideology that defined America as a racially homogeneous society and Americans as white. The status of racial inferiority assigned to the Chinese had been prefigured in the black and Indian past.[31]

Indeed, the newcomers from a Pacific shore found that racial qualities previously assigned to blacks had become "Chinese" characteristics. Calling for Chinese exclusion, the *San Francisco Alta* warned: "Every reason that exists against the toleration of free blacks in Illinois may be argued against that of the Chinese here." White workers referred to the Chinese as "nagurs," and a magazine cartoon in California depicted the Chinese as a bloodsucking vampire with slanted eyes, a pigtail, dark skin, and thick lips. The Chinese were described as heathen, morally inferior, savage, childlike, and lustful. Chinese women were condemned as a "depraved class," their immorality associated with a physical appearance "but a slight removal from the African race."[32]

Like blacks, Chinese men were viewed as threats to white racial purity. At the 1878 California Constitutional Convention, John F. Miller warned: "Were the Chinese to amalgamate at all with our people, it would be the lowest, most vile and degraded of our race, and the result of that amalgamation would be a hybrid of the most despicable, a mongrel of the most detestable that has ever afflicted the earth." Two years later, lawmakers prohibited marriage between a white person and a "negro, mulatto, or Mongolian."[33]

In the minds of many whites, the Chinese were also sometimes associated with Indians. The editor of the *California Marin Journal* declared that the winning of the West from the "red man" would be in vain if whites were now to surrender the conquered land to a "horde of Chinese." Policies toward Indians suggested a way to solve the "Chinese Problem." "We do not let the Indian stand in the way of civilization," stated former New York governor Horatio Seymour, "so why let the Chinese barbarian?" In a letter published in the *New York Times,* Seymour continued: "Today we are dividing the lands of the native Indians into states, counties, and townships. We are driving off from their property the game upon which they live, by railroads. We tell them plainly, they must give up their homes and property, and live upon corners of their own territories, because they are in the way of our civilization. If we can do this, then we can keep away another form of barbarism which has no right to be here." A U.S. senator from Alabama "likened" the Chinese to Indians, "inferior" socially and subject to federal government control. The government, he argued, should do to the Chinese what it had already done to the Indians—put them on reservations.[34]

All three groups—blacks, Indians, and Chinese—shared a common identity: they were all Calibans of color. This view was made explicit in the 1854 California Supreme Court decision of *People v. Hall*. A year before, George W. Hall and two others were tried for murdering Ling Sing. During the trial, one Caucasian and three Chinese witnesses testified for the prosecution. After the jury returned a guilty verdict, the judge sentenced Hall to be hanged. Hall's lawyer then appealed the verdict, arguing that the Chinese witnesses should not have been permitted to testify against Hall. An existing California statute provided that "no black or mulatto person, or Indian, shall be permitted to give evidence in favor of, or against, any white person," and the question was whether this restriction included the Chinese. In its review, the California Supreme Court reversed Hall's conviction, declaring that the words "Indian, Negro, Black, and White" were "generic terms, designating races," and that therefore "Chinese and other people not white" could not testify against whites.[35]

This view of a shared racial status among all three groups led President Rutherford B. Hayes to warn Americans about the "Chinese Problem." The "present Chinese invasion," he argued in 1879, was "pernicious and should be discouraged. Our experience in dealing with the weaker races—the Negroes and Indians—is not encouraging. I would consider with favor any suitable measures to discourage the Chinese from coming to our shores."[36]

Three years later, Congress passed the Chinese Exclusionary Act, which prohibited the entry of Chinese laborers. Actually, there was very little objective basis for viewing Chinese immigrants as a threat to a homogeneous white society. The Chinese constituted a mere .002 percent of the U.S. population in 1880. Restriction was rooted in racism.

Behind the exclusion act were fears and forces that had little relationship to the Chinese. Something had gone wrong in America, and an age of economic opportunity seemed to be coming to an end. This country had been a place where an abundance of land and jobs had always been available. But suddenly, during the closing decades of the nineteenth century, society was experiencing what historian John A. Garraty called "the discovery of unemployment." This new reality plunged America into a national crisis. Enormous expansions of the economy had been followed by intense and painful contractions: tens of thousands of men and women were thrown out of work, and social convulsions such as the violent 1877 Railroad Strike rocked the nation.[37]

Within this context of economic crisis and social strife, Congress made it unlawful for Chinese laborers to enter the United States for the next ten years and denied naturalized citizenship to the Chinese already here. Support for exclusion was overwhelming. In the debate, lawmakers revealed fears that went much deeper than race. They warned that the presence of an "industrial army of Asiatic laborers" was exacerbating class conflict between labor and capital within white society. They claimed that white workers had been "forced to the wall" by corporations employing Chinese. The struggle between labor unions and the industrial "nabobs" and "grandees" was erupting into "disorder, strikes, riot and bloodshed." "The gate," nervous men in Congress declared, "must be closed." The specter of the "giddy multitude" was haunting American society again. Six years later, the prohibition was broadened to include "all persons of the Chinese race," although exemptions were provided for Chinese officials, teachers, students, tourists, and merchants. Renewed in 1892, the Chinese Exclusion Act was extended indefinitely in 1902.[38]

Meanwhile, contrary to the stereotype of Chinese passivity, the Chinese fought discrimination. Time and again, they took their struggle for civil rights to court. Believing that the Chinese should be entitled to citizenship, they challenged the 1790 Naturalization Law. In 1855, Yong Chan applied for citizenship in San Francisco's federal district court. The local newspapers noted that he was more "white" in appearance than most Chinese. The court denied him citizenship, however, ruling that the 1790 law restricted citizenship to "whites" and that the Chinese were not "white." Seeking federal legislation to abolish discriminatory state laws, Chinese merchants successfully lobbied Congress to include protections for them in the 1870 Civil Rights Act, which declared that "all persons" within the jurisdiction of the United States shall have "the same right" to "make and enforce contracts, to sue, be parties, give evidence, and to the full and equal benefit of all laws and proceedings for the security of person and property as is enjoyed by white citizens." Furthermore, "no tax" shall be imposed "by any State upon any person immigrating thereto from a foreign country which is not equally imposed and enforced upon every person emigrating to such State from any other foreign country, and any law of any State from any other foreign country is hereby declared null and void." The new federal law voided the foreign miners' tax.[39]

But guarantees of equal protection by federal law had little effect on what actually happened in society. The Chinese continued to be vulnerable, victims of racial violence. Blamed as "the source of the troubles" of white workingmen, the Chinese suffered from racial attacks. They had to flee from boys who threw rocks at them and screamed, "God Damn Chinamen." "When I first came," Andrew Kan recounted, "Chinese treated worse than dog. Oh, it was terrible, terrible. At that time all Chinese have queue and dress same as in China. The hoodlums, roughnecks and young boys pull your queue, slap your face, throw all kind of old vegetables and rotten eggs at you." "The Chinese were in a pitiable condition in those days," recalled Kin Huie in his account of San Francisco's Chinatown during the 1870s. "We were simply terrified; we kept indoors after dark for fear of being shot in the back. Children spit upon us as we passed by and called us rats."[40]

In general, the unwelcome newcomers were apprehensive about settling in America. As a Chinese merchant in San Francisco explained, the immigrants did not find "peace in their hearts in regard to bringing families."[41]

Twice a Minority: Chinese Women in America

A few Chinese women did come to Gold Mountain. In 1852, of the 11,794 Chinese in California, only seven were women. Eighteen years later, of 63,199 Chinese in the United States, 4,566 were female—a ratio of fourteen to one. In 1900, of the 89,863 Chinese on the United States mainland, only 4,522, or 5 percent, were female.

Chinese tradition and culture limited migration for women. Confucianism defined the place of a woman: she was instructed to obey her father as a daughter, her husband as a wife, and her eldest son as a widow. According to custom, the afterbirths of children were buried in different places, depending on the sex of the baby—in the floor by the bed for boys and outside the window for girls. This practice symbolized what was expected to happen to a woman: she would leave her home to join the family of her husband. As a daughter-in-law, she would take care of her husband's aging parents. "A boy is born facing in; a girl is born facing out," said a proverb. A daughter's name was not recorded on her family tree; it was entered later next to her husband's name in his genealogy.[42]

Women were also left behind because it would have been too expensive for them to accompany their husbands, and the men thought they would be gone only temporarily. Moreover, according to an explanation sometimes known as the "hostage theory," women were kept home in order to ensure that their absent husbands would not become prodigal sons in America. The Chinese system of patrilineal descent provided for the equal division of a family's land among all adult sons and the sharing of responsibility for their elderly parents. By keeping the wives and children of their sons at home, parents hoped they would be able to buttress family ties and filial obligations: their wandering sons would send money home and also return someday. "The mother wanted her son to come back," explained Mau Yun Len, a Chinese immigrant woman. Married to Too Shing Len, she continued: "If wife go to America, then son no go back home and no send money."[43]

There were also conditions in America that discouraged women from joining their husbands. In California, Chinese men entered a society of harsh frontier conditions and racial hostility. As railroad and farm workers, they were viewed by employers as temporary and migratory. The very nature of their work rendered it difficult to have families here. But even if they had wanted to bring their wives, the men discovered that many whites viewed America as a "white man's country" and perceived the entry of Chinese women and families as threatening to racial homogeneity. Federal immigration policies had been enacted to bar Chinese women. Passed in 1875 to prohibit the entry of prostitutes, the Page Law was enforced so strictly and broadly that it excluded not only Chinese prostitutes but also Chinese wives. The 1882 prohibition of "Chinese laborers" included women.[44]

Earlier, however, some Chinese men had been able to bring their wives to America or to have women sent here to become their wives. Ah Chew came to California in 1854 when he was fifteen years old. After he decided to settle down in the Sacramento Delta, his grandson explained, he went back to "China on a sailboat to marry, and then brought his wife over here." Similarly, in 1862, Gee-Hee Chin came to Washington where he worked in a lumber mill. Within a few years, he sent for a wife and got her a job as a cook in the mill's cookhouse. In 1875, Mrs. Chin gave birth to their son, Lem Chin, believed to be the first Chinese born in the Washington Territory. In 1869, A. W. Loomis reported the case of "a wife coming all the way alone across the stormy sea" to be with her husband. "Friends at home besought her not to do a thing so in conflict with Chinese custom; the husband and his relatives in this country, when they heard of her purpose, wrote entreating her not to expose herself to the hardships and perils on the sea, and to the trials which would be liable to befall her here; but she answered that where the husband was there she had a right to be." She came to California where she supported herself and her child by sewing garments and making cigarettes while her husband worked for a mining company in the Kern River area. In America, Chinese families were gradually forming as men began to leave mining and railroad construction and enter more stable pursuits like farming and shopkeeping. As early as 1876, in its memorial to President Ulysses S. Grant, the Chinese Six Companies noted the presence of "a few hundred Chinese families" in the country, and added: "There are also among us a few hundred, perhaps a thousand, Chinese children born in America."[45]

During the early decades, most of the Chinese women came alone, often forcibly transported to America as prostitutes. After arriving, they were compelled to sign contracts to pay for the cost of transportation and became sexual indentured servants. One of them, Ah So Wong, described her tragic experience: "I was nineteen when this man came to my mother and said that in America there was a great deal of gold.... He was a laundryman, but said he earned plenty of money. He was very nice to me, and my mother liked him, so my mother was glad to have me go with him as his wife. I thought that I was his wife, and was very grateful that he was taking me to such a grand, free country, where everyone was rich and happy." Then two weeks after Ah So Wong arrived in San Francisco, she was shocked to learn that her companion had taken her to America as a "slave" and that she would be forced to work as a prostitute.[46]

Chinese prostitutes worked in the mining outposts, agricultural villages, and in the Chinatowns of Sacramento, Marysville, and San Francisco. Dressed in fancy clothes and jewelry, some prostitutes worked in high-class brothels. "And every night, seven o'clock, all these girls were dressed in silk and satin, and sat in front of a big window," recalled Lilac Chen who had been brought to San Francisco in 1893 by a brothel owner, "and the men would look in and choose their girls who they'd want for the night." Most prostitutes worked in lower-grade brothels or in "cribs"—4-by-6-foot street-level compartments with their windowed doors covered with bars or heavy screens. Dressed in cotton tunics and trousers, women peered from the windows, promising men pleasure for twenty-five or forty cents: "Lookee two bits, feelee floor bits, doee six bits." They were fed two or three times a day, their dinner usually consisting of rice and a stew of pork, eggs, liver, and kidneys.[47]

Virtual slaves, many of the prostitutes became opium addicts, seeking a drug-induced psychic sanctuary from the daily abuse and degradation. Disease was a constant threat: syphilis and gonorrhea were widespread. Life was dangerous and sometimes short. Occasionally, prostitutes were beaten to death by their customers or owners, and others committed suicide by taking an overdose of drugs or drowning themselves in San Francisco Bay.[48]

In the 1870 census manuscripts, 61 percent of the 3,536 Chinese women in California listed their occupation as "prostitute." But the number of Chinese prostitutes in California decreased significantly. By 1880, only 24 percent of the 3,171 Chinese women in the state were designated as "prostitute" in the census. The number of adult Chinese females listed as "housekeepers" more than doubled from 21 percent in 1870 to 46 percent in 1880. Many prostitutes had been able to pay off their debts of indentured servitude and free themselves. Marriages and children became possibilities for them. A Chinese folk song urged Chinese prostitutes to seek husbands and a safer life:

> Prostitution ruins the body most harmfully.
> My advice is to get hitched to a man.
> We've all witnessed the frequent raids of
>   brothels in the Golden Gate;
> You need not to worry about these rough-
>   necks once you live with a man.[49]

The problem for Chinese men was that there were too few Chinese women. "In all New York there are less than forty Chinese women," Lee Chew commented bitterly, "and it is impossible to get a Chinese woman out here [to the United States] unless one goes to China and marries her there, and then he must collect affidavits to prove that she is really his wife. That is in the case of a merchant. A laundryman can't bring his wife here under any circumstances." Protesting the legislation prohibiting the entry of Chinese women, a Chinese man asked: "What Chinese going do for wife?" For the overwhelming majority of Chinese men, their future would not include a family in their adopted country. "Pathetic the lonely bachelors stranded in a foreign land," reflected a Cantonese rhyme.[50]

A Colony of "Bachelors"

Though they generally considered themselves sojourners, the Chinese showed signs of settling down from the very beginning. During the 1850s, Chinatown in San Francisco was already a bustling colony of thirty-three general merchandise stores, fifteen apothecaries, five restaurants, five herb shops, three boarding houses, five butcher stores, and three tailor shops. A traveler reported that the stores were "stocked with hams, tea, dried fish, dried ducks, and other Chinese eatables, besides copper pots and kettles, fans, shawls, chessmen, and all sorts of curiosities. Suspended over the doors were brilliantly-colored boards covered with Chinese writings, and with several yards of red ribbon streaming from them, while the streets thronged with Celestials, chattering vociferously as they rushed about from store to store." A Chinese immigrant, arriving in San Francisco in 1868, found a thriving and colorful Chinatown, "made up of stores catering to the Chinese only." The people were "all in their native costume, with queues down their backs," and the entire street fronts of the stores were open, with groceries and vegetables overflowing on the sidewalks. Every morning, vegetable peddlers could be seen in the streets, wearing "loose pajamalike" clothes and "carrying two deep baskets of greens, fruits, and melons, balanced on their shoulders with the help of a pole."[51]

Nine years later, the Chinese quarter of San Francisco was six blocks long, running from California Street to Broadway. Travelers' reports described a foreign community. All day long and often until late at night, the streets were crowded with people. With shaven crowns and neatly braided queues, men sauntered "lazily along, talking, visiting, trading, laughing, and scolding in the strangest, and, to an American, the most discordant jargon." The stores and shops had signs with euphonious and poetic names. Adorning the entrances of wholesale houses were signs for "everlasting harmony, producing wealth," "unitedly prospering," "the flowery fountain," and "ten thousand profits." Apothecary shops offered assurances: "The hall of the approved medicines of every province and of every land." Restaurants described their culinary delights: "Fragrant almond chamber." "Chamber of the odors of distant lands." "Fragrant tea chamber." Fan Tan saloons enticed men with dreams of quick wealth: "Get rich, please come in," "Riches ever flowing." On the glass windows and doors of their stalls, opium dealers pasted red cards: "Opium dipped up in fractional quantities. Foreign smoke in broken parcels. No. 2 Opium to be sold at all times." Scrolls on the walls of stores announced: "Ten thousand customers constantly arriving. Let rich customers continually come."[52]

The immigrants also built Chinatowns in rural towns like Sacramento, Marysville, and Stockton, where these business communities served the needs of Chinese miners and farmers. By 1860, there were 121 Chinese merchants, storekeepers, and grocers in the three counties of Sacramento, Yuba, and San Joaquin. Twenty years later, their number had increased by 44 percent to 174. In addition, there were 22 restaurant keepers, 54 butchers and fish sellers, and 564 laundrymen and laundresses.[53]

Organizations abounded in the Chinatowns. Tongs were present almost from the very beginning: in 1852, the first secret society, the Kwang-tek-tong, was founded in California. Originally underground antigovernment movements in the homeland, the tongs served a particular need in Chinese America. "We are strangers in a strange country," explained a tong member. "We must have an organization to control our country fellows and develop our friendship." A laundry worker said he had decided to join a tong because it offered friendship and support to Chinese migrants in an unfamiliar land. Tongs also provided protection. "Occasionally members of the tongs use their organization to take advantage of non-members of tongs," said a Chinese. Meeting the needs of immigrants, tongs proliferated in the United States. Extending their activities beyond mutual assistance, they came to control the opium trade as well as gambling and prostitution in the Chinese communities.[54]

The immigrants also formed fongs, organizations composed of family and village members, and clans, larger groups of village associations. These associations maintained clubhouses that functioned as residences and social centers. They established temples, transmitted letters to villages in China, and shipped home the bodies or bones of the deceased. In addition, district associations were responsible for receiving newcomers, providing initial housing, finding employment, and administering the "credit-ticket" system to make certain all the migrant's debts had been paid before he returned to China. In San Francisco, the district associations were later organized into the Chung Wai Wui Koon, known popularly as the Chinese Six Companies. This organization helped settle interdistrict conflicts and provided educational and health services to the community. The leaders of the Chinese Six Companies were merchants who interacted with the city's white business community and had access to public officials.

Gradually, the Chinese were creating their own communities in America. They built altars to honor their gods and celebrated traditional holidays. During Chinese New Year in January or February, they ushered in the New Year with lion dances and firecrackers. During the celebration, whites also joined the festive throngs in Chinatown. "The merchants," said Loomis, "appear highly delighted to see and to welcome all of our citizens whom they can recognize as friends, and all with whom they have had any kind of business connections." As soon as the clock tolled off the last minute of the departing year, firecrackers exploded in a roaring, crackling din, filling entire streets with columns of smoke and sheets of fire to frighten away the evil spirits for the new year.[55]

For recreation, many men attended the Chinese theater. The first Chinese play in America was presented in 1852, when 123 actors of the Hong Fook Tong performed at the American Theater in San Francisco. In 1879, a Chinese theater was erected, a three-story brick building with a seating capacity of twenty-five hundred people. The price of admission was thirty-five cents. During performances, the men—sometimes a few hundred, sometimes a thousand—sat on benches in the gallery. Smoking cigars and cigarettes and eating mandarin oranges and melon seeds, they listened to the Chinese orchestra and watched the drama.

On Sundays, most of the men had no families to take on outings. They had "no *homes* in this country," observed Otis Gibson of San Francisco. They strolled the streets, he added, for they had "nothing to do, and nowhere else to go." When asked about what he did during his free time, a waiter at a restaurant replied: "Yes, go to theater. When I no work? I sleep. Sometimes gamble a little." At night and during the weekends, men played mah-jongg, fantan, and "baakgapbiu," a game similar to keno. "Gambling is mostly fan tan," reported Lee Chew, "but there is a good deal of poker, which the Chinese have learned from Americans and can play very well.

They also gamble with dominoes and dice." Tom Lee, a cook and houseboy, said: "No get lonely for home China, many China boys all same one family. Sometime have holiday. Put on Merican hat, shoe, tie, all same White man, walk to Stockton have good time."[56]

Mostly, the men spent their leisure hours in the back rooms of stores. There "all Chinese came," a migrant recalled. "Not just relatives. They all just like to get together. They talk together." Cut off from their wives, men spent endless hours talking about their lives. Sometimes "Letters for the colony" would arrive from China, directed in care of the store that served as a community post office. "Our village had something to do—they send a letter over here, we get together and talk it over—and send it back," a migrant stated. "We communicate, see, otherwise you're alone. You know nothing." One sojourner received a letter from his mother, a wailing reminder to fulfill his filial obligations:

> I hear that you, _____, my son, are acting the prodigal.... For many months there has arrived no letter, nor money. My supplies are exhausted. I am old; too infirm to work; too lame to beg. Your father in the mines of the mountains suffers from a crushed foot. He is weak, and unable to accumulate money. Hereafter, my son, change your course; be industrious and frugal, and remit to me your earnings; and within the year let me welcome home both your father and yourself.[57]

Married men received letters from their "widows" in China. Stranded sojourners, they read "letters of love, soaked with tears" that complained about their long absence. Since most of the men were illiterate, they relied on the store proprietors to use their calligraphy skills to write letters for them. One migrant dictated a letter that began, "My Beloved Wife":

> It has been several autumns now since your dull husband left you for a far remote alien land. Thanks to my hearty body I am all right. Therefore stop your embroidering worries about me.
>
> Yesterday I received another of your letters. I could not keep tears from running down my cheeks when thinking about the miserable and needy circumstances of our home, and thinking back to the time of our separation.
>
> Because of our destitution I went out, trying to make a living. Who could know that the Fate is always opposite to man's design?

Because I can get no gold, I am detained in this secluded corner of a strange land. Furthermore, my beauty, you are implicated in an endless misfortune. I wish this paper would console you a little. This is all what I can do for now.

This letter was never finished and never mailed, left in a desk drawer of the Kam Wah Chung Store in John Day, Oregon.[58]

What happened to the nameless writer of this unmailed letter probably paralleled the life stories of the owners of the store where it was found. On Lung and Hay Ing had come to America as sojourners in the 1880s. At first, they worked as wage earners and then opened their own general store. Gradually over the years, as they built their business and developed personal and social ties to their new community, they came to feel detached from their homeland and their families. In 1899, Lung's father commanded in a letter: "Come home as soon as you can. Don't say 'no' to me any more.... You are my only son. You have no brothers and your age is near forty.... You have been away from home for seventeen years, you know nothing about our domestic situation.... Come back, let our family be reunited and enjoy the rest of our lives." In a letter to "My Husband-lord," Lung's wife scolded her absent mate: "According to Mr. Wang, you are indulging in sensuality, and have no desire to return home. On hearing this I am shocked and pained. I have been expecting your return day after day.... But, alas, I don't know what kind of substance your heart is made of.... Your daughter is now at the age of bethrothal and it is your responsibility to arrange her marriage." Her appeal must have moved her husband, for Lung wrote to his cousin Kwang-jin Liang on March 2, 1905: "We are fine here, thank you. Tell my family that I will go back as soon as I accumulate enough money to pay the fare." But a few weeks later, Lung learned in a letter from his cousin, dated March 4, that certain family events had already passed him by: "Two years ago your mother died. Last year your daughter married. Your aged father is immobile. He will pass away any time now. Your wife feels left out and hurt.... Come back as soon as you receive this message." Meanwhile, Ing's father had also written to his son in 1903: "Men go abroad so that they might make money for support of their families, but you have sent neither money nor a letter since you left."[59]

Like Lung and Ing, thousands of men had come to America in search of Gold Mountain. But they never returned.

My life's half gone, but I'm still unsettled;
I've erred, I'm an expert at whoring and
    gambling.
Syphilis almost ended my life.
Ashamed, frightened —
Now, I must wake up after this long night-
    mare.... [60]

In America, the Chinese found their lives circumscribed in new and different ways. As strangers from a different shore, they had been denied equality of opportunity and were separated from their homeland by the "tyrannical laws" of exclusion. "They call us 'Chink,'" complained an old laundryman, cursing the "white demons." "They think we no good! America cut us off. No more come now, too bad!" Though they could not become citizens, they felt they had earned the right to claim their adopted country. "Since I have lived and made money in this country," Andrew Kan argued, "I should be able to become an American citizen."[61]

A Sudden Change in Fortune: The San Francisco Earthquake

Back in their homeland, Chinese women fingered and studied old yellowing photographs of their men, so young and so handsome. Look at these dreamers and the twinkle in their eyes, filled with possibilities and promises, they said proudly. But, what did they look like now, after decades in Gam Saan? A folk song conveyed the widening emotional distances that had developed between Chinese men in America and their wives in China:

Pitiful is the twenty-year sojourner,
Unable to make it home.
Always obstacles along the way, pain knitting
    my brows.
A reflection on the mirror, a sudden fright:
    hair, half frost-white.
Frequent letters from home, all filled with
    much complaint.[62]

Desperate to be reunited with their loved ones, some men looked for loopholes in the law. Aware that Chinese merchants were permitted to bring their families here, Chinese laundrymen, restaurant owners, and even common laborers sometimes tried to pose as "paper merchants." A Chinese who had sworn in his oath to the immigration authorities that he was a "merchant" turned out to be a hotel cook; another was actually a gardener. Other Chinese would bribe merchants to list them as partners or would buy business shares in order to claim they were merchants. "A number of the stores in the cities are organized just for that purpose," explained an immigration commissioner. "They are organized just to give the Chinese a chance to be a merchant."[63]

Most Chinese men, however, thought they would never be able to bring their wives to America. Then suddenly a natural disaster occurred that changed the course of Chinese-American history. Early in the morning of April 18, 1906, an earthquake shook San Francisco. "*Aih yah, dai loong jen, aih yah dai loong jen,*" residents of Chinatown screamed, "the earth dragon is wriggling." In terror, they jumped out of their beds, fled from collapsing buildings, and ran down buckling streets. "I remember how everything fell off the shelf," said eighty-three-year-old Alice Fun who was born in San Francisco in 1899. "We had one of those stoves made out of brick and the stove had crumbled. So my father was going to put it back together again. But very soon we had to evacuate the place." Leland Chin was asleep when the earthquake hit: "I wake up, and here everything is shaking. Then here went everything tumbling down!" He looked out onto California Street and saw "a big crack" in the earth. Then came the fires, roaring down along Montgomery Street and the financial district.[64]

The fires destroyed almost all of the municipal records and opened the way for a new Chinese immigration. Chinese men could now claim they had been born in San Francisco, and as citizens they could bring their wives to the United States. Before the earthquake, women consistently remained at 5 percent or less of the Chinese population. In 1900 there were only 4,522 Chinese females in America. Only handfuls of them entered the country each year: between 1900 and 1906, their numbers ranged from 12 to 145 annually. But after the catastrophe in San Francisco, they began arriving in increasing numbers—from 219 in 1910, to 356 in 1915, to 573 in 1920, to 1,050 in 1922, and 1,893 two years later. One of every four Chinese immigrants was female during this period, compared to only one of twenty during the nineteenth century. Altogether 10,048 Chinese females came between 1907 and 1928. By 1930, women represented 20 percent of the Chinese population, providing the beginning of a viable base for the formation of Chinese-American families.[65]

Chinese sons also began coming to America. According to U.S. law, the children of American citizens were automatically U.S. citizens, even if they were born in a foreign country. Thus children in China fathered by Chinese-American citizens were American citizens by birth and eligible for entry to the United States. Many of them came here as bona fide sons of American citizens. Others came as imposters, or "paper sons." Hay Ming Lee explained how the process worked: "In the beginning my father came in as a laborer. But the 1906 earthquake came along and destroyed all those immigration things. So that was a big chance for a lot of Chinese. They forged themselves certificates saying they were born in this country, and then when the time came, they could go back to China and bring back four or five sons, just like that!" Exactly how many boys falsely claimed citizenship as "paper sons" will never be known, but it was later calculated that if every claim to natural-born citizenship were valid, every Chinese woman living in San Francisco before 1906 would have had to have given birth to eight hundred children.[66]

By the thousands Chinese began entering the United States again. After sailing through the Golden Gate and disembarking on Angel Island in San Francisco Bay, the newcomers were placed in the barracks of the immigration station. Their quarters were crowded and unsanitary, resembling a slum. "When we arrived," said one of them, "they locked us up like criminals in compartments like the cages in the zoo. They counted us and then took us upstairs to our rooms. There were two to three rooms in the women's section.... Each of the rooms could fit twenty or thirty persons." The men were placed in one large room. There were 190 "small boys up to old men, all together in the same room," a visitor reported in 1922. "Some were sleeping in the hammock like beds with their belongings hanging in every possible way...while others were smoking or gambling." The days were long and tedious, and "lights went out at a certain hour, about 9 P.M." But their "intestines agitated," many could not fall asleep. The inmates could see San Francisco to the west and Oakland to the east; they had journeyed so far to come to America and yet they were not allowed to enter.[67]

The purchase of a birth certificate, many of the "paper sons" discovered, did not guarantee entry, for they had to pass an examination and prove their American identity. To prepare for the examination, they studied "crib sheets," or *hau-kung*, and memorized information about the families of their "fathers": they had to remember "everyone's name, the birthday, and if they passed away, when." When they approached the Golden Gate, they tore up their crib sheets and threw them overboard. Paper son Jim Quock recalled: "The only way I could come was to buy a paper, buy a citizen paper. I paid quite a bit of money, too. I paid $102 gold!" Quock was given a two-hundred-page book about his "paper" family to study. After his arrival at the Angel Island Immigration Station, he was detained for three weeks for the interrogation. "They ask you questions like how many steps in your house?" Quock recalled. "Your house had a clock? Where do you sleep at your house? I said, 'I sleep with my grandmother and brother.' They say, 'Okay, which position do you sleep?' All kinds of questions; you got to think." Sometimes "paper sons" had to think quickly during the examination. Two young men, seeking admission as the sons of a merchant, were questioned by the inspectors. The first applicant was asked if there were a dog in the house and he answered, "Yes." Later, they asked the second applicant the same question and he said, "No, no dog." The inspectors then recalled the first applicant, pressing him about the existence of the dog. "Yes," he replied smartly, "well, we had a dog, but we knew we were coming to the United States, so we ate the dog."[68]

The newcomers were not released until they had convinced the authorities their papers were legitimate. Not everyone passed the examination. Approximately 10 percent of all the Chinese who landed on Angel Island were forced to return to China. On the walls of the barracks, they carved poems of protest and disappointment.

> *Barred from land, I really am to be pitied.*
> *My heart trembles at being deported back to*
>   *China....*
> *I came to seek wealth but instead reaped*
>   *poverty.*[69]

The lucky ones were allowed to hurry onto ferries and sail happily to San Francisco. By 1943, some fifty thousand Chinese had entered America through Angel Island.

"Caught in Between": Chinese Born in America

From Angel Island, the newcomers went to the cities, seeking shelter and employment in the Chinatowns of Los Angeles, Oakland,

Chicago, Seattle, Portland, Sacramento, New York, and Boston. By 1940, 40 percent of all Chinese lived in two cities—San Francisco and New York. The metropolitan Chinatowns developed a different character and purpose from the nineteenth-century Chinatowns. They were no longer way stations to service single male workers in transit to the goldfields, farms, and railroads. Chinatowns had become residential communities for families, Chinese economic enclaves, and tourist centers. "Wherever the Chinese are," observed Rose Hum Lee in 1942, "it has been possible to count the variations in the ways they can earn their living on the fingers of the hand—chop suey and chow mein restaurants, Chinese art and gift shops, native grocery stores that sell foodstuffs imported from China to the local Chinese community and Chinese laundries."[70]

Chinatown also became a place where children lived. The immigration of Chinese women after the 1906 San Francisco earthquake led to the formation of families in the Chinese community. In 1900, only 11 percent of the Chinese population were American born. Children were rare: only 3.5 percent of the Chinese were under fifteen years old, compared to 34.7 percent of the general population. "The greatest impression I have of my childhood in those days was that at that time there were very few families in Chinatown," recalled a resident. "Babies were looked on with a kind of wonder." Children were "petted" by the Chinese bachelors. But the American-born Chinese group grew quickly to 41 percent of the population in 1930 and 52 percent ten years later.[71]

In their Chinatown world, children watched their parents at work—laundrymen expertly wielding hot irons over *hong-choong* (ironing beds), seamstresses operating sewing machines in noisy garment factories, and cooks chopping carrots and celery in cramped restaurant kitchens. The youngsters noticed how their parents had to work long hours: "My father would get up and leave the house about six in the morning and not close the store until almost nine at night. So what's that? Fifteen hours?" Younger children accompanied their mothers to the factory. "My mother tied me to her back and sewed," recalled Victor Wong, who was a child in San Francisco's Chinatown during the 1930s. "The constant drum of sewing machines. The chatter of Cantonese. The F car rolling and rumbling from somewhere through Stockton Street near the tunnel. Stop; screeching and ding-ding off again to somewhere not Chinatown." The children were urged by their parents to study hard so that they could have better lives.

"I've worked my fingers to the bones for you boys to get yourself an education," an immigrant father told his son. "If you cannot be better than they [whites] are, try to be their equal anyway, because that way, one of these days, you can be up there too."[72]

For the second-generation Chinese, education was viewed as the way to get "up there." The children went to the public schools, where they said the Pledge of Allegiance to the flag of the United States and learned about American culture. In the essay "Problems of Second Generation Chinese" published in 1932, Kit King Louis wrote that in the home the two cultures met and sometimes also clashed. Many American-born Chinese, especially the more educated youngsters, simply wanted more independence and more choice for themselves than their parents allowed. Betty Lee Sung, the daughter of a Chinese laundryman in Baltimore, broke from the expectations of her father: "My father did not want me to go on to college at all. He thought girls shouldn't have an education. He wanted me to get married; he wanted to match me with all sorts of men. And I didn't want to do that. I wanted to go to school. And he said, 'If you want to go to school and you disobey me, I'll disown you.' And I said, 'Well, I'll just have to leave. Good-bye, papa.'" But in reality the choice—to be Chinese or American—was not so simple, so clear-cut. Many youngsters experienced stormy and at times subtle ambivalence. "There was endless discussion about what to do about the dilemma of being caught in between... being loyal to the parents and their ways and yet trying to assess the good from both sides," commented Victor Wong. "We used to call ourselves just a 'marginal man,' caught between two cultures."[73]

World War II would change the conditions of the Chinese in America, especially of the second generation. When Jade Snow Wong graduated from Mills College, she found herself worrying about her future career. She had assumed she would enter graduate studies for a master's degree in social work. "But Pearl Harbor had been bombed," she wrote in her autobiography, "and the students, like everyone else, were caught in the war fever."[74]

PART THREE

Transitions

The End of the Frontier:
The Emergence of an American Empire

IN 1891, THE CENSUS BUREAU announced that the frontier no longer existed. Americans now reached beyond what Jefferson called the "Stony mountains" and were settling the entire continent from the Atlantic to the Pacific. This conquest over nature had led to the building of what Max Weber called "the tremendous cosmos of the modern economic order." What had happened was the explosive formation of an industrial economy. Between 1815 and 1860, the value of manufactured goods increased eightfold. By 1890, U.S. manufacturing production had surpassed the combined total of England and Germany. American labor patterns reflected these economic changes. In 1840, agricultural workers had constituted 70 percent of the labor force, while those in manufacturing, trades, and construction represented only 15 percent. Sixty years later, the number of workers in agriculture decreased to 37 percent, while those in manufacturing and related areas such as transportation and public utilities increased to 35 percent.[1]

This dynamic industrial order generated cycles of economic instability, massive unemployment, and production gluts. Businessmen had been expanding the operation of their plants beyond the needs of the market. "It is incontrovertible," reported the chief of the National Bureau of Labor, "that the present manufacturing and mechanical plant of the United States is greater — far greater—than is needed to supply the demand; yet it is constantly being enlarged, and there is no way of preventing the enlargement." Expansion was not accompanied by an increase of employment, however. During the 1894 depression, 18 percent of the labor force was unemployed, and Secretary of State Walter Gresham warned: "We cannot afford constant employment for our labor.... Our mills and factories can supply the demand by running seven or eight months out of twelve." Then he added anxiously: "It is surprising to me that thoughtful men do not see the danger in the present conditions." Social unrest and violent class conflicts had become increasingly prevalent. The Railroad Strike of 1877, the Haymarket Massacre of 1886, and the bloody Homestead Strike of 1892 shook society. Time and again, hundreds of thousands of workers went out on strike. In confrontations between labor and capital in Chicago, Pittsburgh, New York, and other cities, dozens of protesting workers were killed and hundreds were wounded by the police, militia, and Pinkerton detectives.[2]

These industrial class tensions alarmed the Reverend Josiah Strong, author of the 1885 bestseller, *Our Country: Its Possible Future and Its Present Crisis*. In his jeremiad on the grave peril facing America, this leading Protestant minister warned that class conflict was hardening and that cities were becoming huge, festering sores of social ills. Catholic immigrants from southern Europe were flooding the land and threatening to overwhelm society. An illiterate, ignorant, immoral, and "criminal" population, dominated by their "appetites," was swelling the ranks of the working class. Factory workers were laboring in "unsanitary" conditions, in "confined" situations where they did "one thing over and over again." Living in congested cities, these exploited workers constituted a "tenement population," a class attracted to "socialism." On their backs, men of great wealth were rising—millionaires who possessed "oppressive" and "despotic" power to raise prices and close factories. This new elite represented a "modern and republican feudalism." The cause of the "crisis" was the ending of the frontier. The West had historically provided an "abundance of cheap land," the basis of the "general welfare and contentment" of the people. "When the supply [of land] is exhausted," Strong predicted gloomily, "we shall enter upon a new era, and shall more rapidly approximate European conditions of life."[3]

What would the future hold for a frontierless America? During this time of social disintegration and urban turmoil, there emerged a leader with a solution. In 1890, Admiral Alfred Thayer Mahan published *The Influence of Sea Power upon History,* which went through fifteen editions in eight years and was read all over the world. His aim was to boost funding for a "New Navy." Its impact was immediate: that year, Congress authorized the construction of three battleships and the rebuilding of the navy.

In his carefully constructed study, Mahan observed that before the end of the frontier, the energies of the nation had been directed inward. The settlement of the West and the cultivation of the wilderness had turned the "eyes of the country" away from the sea. But now the nation stretched from coast to coast, and the time had arrived for America to turn outward, beyond the continent. Americans had the character and capacity for colonization—"the instinct for commerce, bold enterprise in the pursuit of gain, and a keen scent for the trails" to new territories. With the end of the frontier and the need for new markets overseas, Mahan argued, the United States should develop "colonies" to serve as coaling stations for the navy and increase the country's commerce. The history of sea power was largely a narrative of conflicts and wars between nations seeking to expand their wealth through international commerce. Thus, in Mahan's view, it was critical for the United States to become a major sea power and build "an armed navy, of a size commensurate with the growth of its shipping," and to pursue "warlike preparation."[4]

Embedded in his naval and commercial strategy was Mahan's view on race. The "distant unsettled commercial regions" were located in Asia. In seeking "possession" and "control" of territory in the Far East, the "civilized" and "virile" men of the United States would enter a "region rich in possibilities, but unfruitful through the incapacity or negligence" of its inhabitants, where the "inferior race" would fall back and disappear before "the persistent impact of the superior." No one had a "natural right" to land: the right to own and control territory depended on "political fitness." Only men who utilized the land were entitled to it. Here Mahan was echoing John Winthrop's solemn pledge not to let the earth's natural resources lie in "waste." What had happened to the American Indian was, in Mahan's judgment, a consequence of a civilized people trespassing upon the inhabitants' "technical" rights of possession. Like Andrew Jackson, Mahan asked: "Will anyone seriously contend that the North American continent should have been left forever in the hands of tribes whose sole use of their territory was to contravene the purposes of human life?" The dispossession of the Indian in the winning of the West was a model for the colonization of Asia: both expansions represented the triumph of the superior white race.[5]

Beneath what Mahan called his "race patriotism" and his aggressive militarism was a rage rooted in what he considered the degradation of the navy. Only eight years before the publication of his book on sea power, the navy had only one first-rate ship. The remaining ones were inferior. Due to a budget cut, Mahan, along with a number of other officers, had been relieved from duty. Humiliated, he protested bitterly in letters to a friend: "In a healthy condition of naval affairs, I should by this [time] be going to sea but the low ebb to which the navy is now reduced...gives me no hope of even such commands as we have for some time to come." "Immersed as our people are in peaceful and material pursuits, the military establishment is necessarily one of our lesser interests.... Practically we have nothing. Never before has the navy sunk so low."[6]

Determined to restore the honor and status of the navy through the rearming of America, Mahan became a strident imperialist.

Mahan was the chief architect of the 1898 war against Spain. In 1890, *The Influence of Sea Power upon History* was read by an emerging political leader named Theodore Roosevelt. In a letter to Mahan, Roosevelt praised the study as "the clearest and most instructive general work of the kind, and wished that "the whole book could be placed where it could be read by the navy's foes, especially in Congress." A working relationship developed between the two men. After Roosevelt had been appointed Assistant Secretary of the Navy in 1897, Mahan advised him: "I would suggest...that the real significance of the Nicaragua canal now is that it advances our Atlantic frontier by so much to the Pacific." Asia, not Europe, had become vital to America's interests. Mahan also urged Roosevelt to place the "best admiral" in the Pacific, for "much more initiative may be thrown on him than can be on the Atlantic man." Roosevelt disseminated Mahan's advice in circles of power. A month before the United States declared war on Spain, on March 21, 1898, Roosevelt thanked Mahan for his guidance: "There is no question that you stand head and shoulders above the rest of us! You have given us just the suggestions we want.... You probably don't know how much your letter has really helped me clearly to formulate certain things which I had only vaguely in mind. I think I have studied your books to pretty good purpose."[7] At the end of the Spanish-American War, Mahan realized his dream of empire, with the annexation of the Philippines, where a coaling station would be built for his "New Navy." But he had also helped to set the United States on a collision course with Japan, a clashing of two great sea powers that would lead to the attack on Pearl Harbor and the dropping of the atomic bomb on Hiroshima.

The 1890s was a time of transitions to the twentieth century—not only the emergence of America as an overseas empire, but also the beginning of the influx of new immigrants from Russia and Japan as well as the early migrations of Mexicans to El Norte and of African-American migrations to northern cities. One of the significant changes was the end of the frontier, symbolized by the massacre at Wounded Knee.

9

❧❧❧

THE "INDIAN QUESTION"

From Reservation to Reorganization

The Massacre at Wounded Knee

TEN YEARS BEFORE the U.S. war against Spain, from the shores of Pyramid Lake in Nevada there came an Indian prophet. Claiming he was the messiah, Wovoka of the Paiutes called for Indians everywhere to dance the Ghost Dance, for Christ had returned to earth as an Indian. As they danced, Wovoka's followers wore muslin "ghost shirts," decorated with sacred symbols of blue and yellow lines. They believed that the garments would protect them against bullets. Wovoka's message promised the restoration of Indian ways as well as their land and the buffalo:

> All Indians must dance, everywhere, keep on dancing. Pretty soon in next spring Big Man [Great Spirit] come. He bring back all game of every kind. The game be thick everywhere. All dead Indians come back and live again. When Old Man [God] comes this way, then all the Indians go to mountains, high up away from whites. Whites can't hurt Indians then. Then while Indians way up high, big flood comes like water and all white people die, get drowned. After that water go away and then nobody but Indians everywhere and game all kinds thick.[1]

Wovoka's vision of a world without whites spread like prairie fire through Indian country. On Sioux reservations, Ghost Dancing became the rage, seizing Indian imaginations and mobilizing their frustrations. In the winter of 1890, an agent at Pine Ridge Reservation in South Dakota sent a warning to Washington: "Indians are dancing in the snow and are wild and crazy. We need protection and we need it now. The leaders should be arrested and confined at some military post until the matter is quieted, and this should be done at once."[2]

The Indian Bureau in Washington quickly identified the Ghost Dance "fomenters of disturbances" and ordered the army to arrest them, including Chiefs Sitting Bull and Big Foot. Indian policemen were sent to Sitting Bull's cabin; after arresting him, they were confronted by angry and armed Sioux. During an exchange of gunfire, the police shot and killed the chief. The news of Sitting Bull's murder alarmed Big Foot, chief of another group of Sioux. While trying to escape, Big Foot and his people, mostly women and children, were intercepted by the cavalry. They surrendered and were escorted to a camp near a frozen creek called Wounded Knee.[3]

As the Indians set up their tepees for the night, they saw two manned Hotchkiss guns on the ridge above them. "That evening I noticed that they were erecting cannons up [there]," Wasu Maza recalled, "also hauling up quite a lot of ammunition." The guns were trained on the Indian camps, and the scene became terribly ominous. In the morning, under a clear blue sky, the Indians heard a bugle call. Surrounded by mounted soldiers, the men were instructed to assemble at the center of camp. Suffering from pneumonia, Big Foot was carried to the meeting.[4]

The captives were ordered to turn over their weapons. "They called for guns and arms," White Lance recounted, "so all of us gave the guns and they were stacked up in the center." Thinking there were more arms hidden in the tepees, the soldiers began a search. The situation became tense and volatile. Medicine man Yellow Bird began dancing the Ghost Dance to reassure the worried Indians. He urged them to wear their sacred shirts: "The bullets will not hurt you." Suddenly, a shot rang out. Instantly, the troops began shooting indiscriminately at the Indians. "There were only about a hundred warriors and there were nearly five hundred soldiers," Black Elk reported. "The warriors rushed to where they had piled their guns and knives."[5]

The Indians tried to defend themselves, but then they heard an "awful roar," the death sounds of the Hotchkiss guns. Shells hailed down upon them, at the rate of fifty per minute, each missile carrying a two-pound charge that exploded into thousands of shrapnel. The smoke was so dense it was like fog, blinding the Indians. "My father ran and fell down and the blood came out of his mouth [he was shot through the head]," recalled Yellow Bird's son, who was four years old at the time. Blue Whirlwind received fourteen wounds, while her two children running at her sides were also shot. "We tried to run, but they shot us like we were buffalo," said Louise Weasel Bear. "I know there are some good white people, but the soldiers must be mean to shoot children and women."[6]

Fleeing the camp, the Indians were pursued by the soldiers. "I saw some of the other Indians running up the coulee so I ran with them, but the soldiers kept shooting at us and the bullets flew all around us," reported Mrs. Rough Feathers. "My father, my grandmother, my older brother and my younger brother were all killed. My son who was two years old was shot in the mouth that later caused his death." Trails marked by blood and bodies radiated outward from the camp. "Dead and wounded women and children and little babies were scattered all along there where they had been trying to run away," Black Elk reported. "The soldiers had followed them along the gulch as they ran, and murdered them in there."[7]

When the Hotchkiss guns stopped spewing their deadly charges, a terrible silence descended on the bloody scene. Hundreds of Indians lay dead or wounded on the icy ground, along with scores of soldiers, most of them hit by their own fire. Shortly afterward, clouds rolled across the sky and "a heavy snow began to fall," covering the corpses like a white blanket as if Nature were trying to shroud or cleanse the gore and blood. After the storm passed, the soldiers threw the dead Indians into a long trench, their frozen bodies "piled one upon another like so much cordwood, until the pit was full." Many of the corpses were naked: the "ghost shirts" had been stripped from the dead as souvenirs. A photograph of Big Foot lying in the snow showed the contorted body of the chief, his hands still trying to shield himself and his pained face fixed in a grotesque grimace by the massacre he had witnessed at Wounded Knee.[8]

Where the Buffalo No Longer Roam

Like the heroic frontiersman celebrated by Frederick Jackson Turner in his 1893 paper on the significance of the frontier in American history, General George Armstrong Custer personified the advance of "civilization" against "savagery."

In the winter of 1868, Custer had tracked Black Kettle's band of Cheyennes to the Washita River; as he quietly surveyed the Indian encampment in the darkness and heard the cry of an infant, he knew he had his enemy trapped. Custer divided his eight hundred soldiers into four groups and ordered them to surround the sleeping Indians. Then, at dawn, with his band playing "Gary Owen," Custer and his troops mounted a four-pronged attack, destroying the lodges, killing 103 Cheyenne men, and capturing 53 women and children. Marching triumphantly into Camp Supply, Custer's soldiers waved the scalps of Black Kettle and the slain men.

Eight years later, Custer met his own violent death at the Battle of the Little Big Horn in Montana territory. News of Custer's death provoked shrill cries for revenge. Buffalo Bill Cody was so angry he closed his Wild West Show and pledged to go west and take the "first scalp for Custer." Demanding that the federal government avenge Custer's defeat, the editor of the *Bismarck Weekly Tribune* called for the establishment of reservations for all Indians. In their loud clamor for retaliation, both Buffalo Bill and the editor failed to discern the special irony that Custer's death contained, for they did not know that the general in many ways had identified with the Indians.[9]

In his prolific writings on the West and the Indian character, Custer revealed his complicated and often contradictory feelings. He portrayed the land's original people as "infesting" the plains, their "cruel and ferocious nature" far exceeding that of any "wild beast." At the same time, Custer felt a certain empathy for them. When the Europeans arrived in America, he wrote, they found the natives in their homes of "peace and plenty," the "favored sons of nature." Indians stood in their "native strength and beauty, stamped with the proud majesty of free born men." But what were they now, these "monarchs of the west"? Their homes and their forests had been swept away by the ax of the woodsman; they had been driven to the "verge of extinction," resolved to die amid the "horrors of slaughter." Interacting with Indians in the West, he found much to be admired—their "remarkable taciturnity," "perseverance" for revenge and conquest, "stoical courage," and the "wonderful power and subtlety" of their senses.[10]

What would happen to Indians in an advancing technological society? Custer believed that their options were limited and degrading. To locate them on reservations would make them "grovel in beggary" and deny them the qualities derived from the

wilderness. To civilize Indians would be to require them to abandon their way of life as warriors, and to sacrifice their manhood
by working for a living.[11]

Custer thought that "if" he were an Indian, he would choose
the "free open plains" rather than submit to the "confined limits
of a reservation." Death would be preferable to life in a cage.[12]

Deep within Custer was a rage against the very modern society he was helping to extend into the West. The eastern settlement was to Custer what the reservation was to the Indian. He
wanted to be free from the restraints of white society, its com-
mercialism, "luxuries," and "easy comforts." Beyond civilization
in the West, Custer could still "indulge in the wild Western life
with all its pleasures and excitements" and recover the "virtues of
real manhood." There, like the Indian, he could roam the plains
and experience the thrill of a buffalo chase.[13]

In the wilderness, Custer was able to enter a "new world, a
Wonderland." The beauty of the Wichita Mountains mesmerized
him: "The air is pure and fragrant, and as exhilarating as the
purest of wine; the climate entrancingly mild; the sky clear, and
blue as the most beautiful sapphire, with here and there clouds of
rarest loveliness, presenting to the eye the richest commingling
of bright and varied colors; delightful odors are constantly being
wafted by." And everywhere were sounds—the singing of the
mockingbird, the colibri, hummingbird, and thrush. Swept away
by the magnificence of nature, he felt an intoxication. Riding
across the plains, with its horizon after horizon of grass, Custer
was hypnotized, drawn irresistibly into its awesome vastness. Its
undulations reminded him of the ocean: they were like "gigantic
waves," "standing silent and immovable." Here was the ultimate
expanse of "vacant lands." The West offered Custer what his wife,
Libby, described as an "escape"—a world still beyond the noises
of the machine and the constraints of modern society.[14]

At the Little Big Horn on that fateful day in 1876, General
Custer knew his troops were outnumbered and surrounded
by Crazy Horse and his Lakota and Cheyenne warriors. Yet he
refused to surrender. Instead the general ordered his soldiers to
take a last stand on that grassy hillside, and all of them were
killed. In that final clash, perhaps Custer understood only too
clearly and too profoundly how much he and the Indian shared a
common fate in a world where the buffalo no longer roamed.

As Commissioner of Indian Affairs during the 1870s, Francis
Amasa Walker had tried to avoid the use of armed force against

Indians. American soldiers, he recommended, should not surprise Indian "camps on winter nights" and shoot down "men, women, and children together in the snow." Instead, Walker believed the government should pursue a "Peace Policy"—buy off and feed the Indians in order to avoid violent conflict.[15]

Unlike Custer, Walker had very limited personal contact with Indians. He made only one visit of inquiry and inspection to the agencies of the Sioux in the Wyoming and Nebraska territories. But Walker believed that he knew what was best for the Indians. What gave Commissioner Walker such confidence was his belief in technology and the market as civilizing forces. He observed:

> The labor that is made free by discoveries and inventions is applied to overcome the difficulties which withstand the gratification of newly-felt desires. The hut is pulled down to make room for the cottage; the cottage gives way to the mansion, the mansion to the palace. The rude covering of skins is replaced by the comely garment of woven stuffs; and these, in the progress of luxury, by the most splendid fabrics of human skill. In a thousand forms wealth is created by the whole energy of the community, quickened by a zeal greater than that which animated the exertions of their rude forefathers to obtain a scanty and squalid subsistence.[16]

Progress was bringing an end to the frontier and the Indian way of life. The railroad—"the great plough of industrial civilization"—had drawn its "deep furrow" across the continent, Walker explained, and Americans were now migrating to the Great Plains, "creeping along the course of every stream, seeking out every habitable valley, following up every indication of gold among the ravines and mountains...and even making lodgement at a hundred points on lands secured by treaty to the Indians." Indians were facing a grim future in this rapidly changing world. Thus the "friends of humanity should exert themselves in this juncture, and lose not time" in order to save the Indians. For Walker, the "Indian Question" had become urgent: what should be done to ensure the survival of the Plains Indians?[17]

Walker believed in social engineering: government should scientifically manage the welfare of Indians. Since industrial "progress" had cut them off from their traditional means of livelihood, Indians should be given temporary support to help them make the necessary adjustments for entering civilization. To accomplish this transition, Walker conceived a plan: Indian tribes would be consolidated into one or two "grand reservations" with railroads cutting through them here and there, leaving the rest of the territory open for white settlement, free from Indian "obstruction or molestation." Warlike tribes would be corraled onto reservations, and all Indian bands outside their boundaries would be "liable to be struck by the military at any time, without warning." Such areas would, in effect, be free fire zones.[18]

The ultimate goal, Walker explained, was the eventual assimilation of Indians. On the reservations, the government would subject them to "a rigid reformatory discipline." Not allowed to "escape work," they would be "required" to learn industrial skills until at least one generation had been placed on a course of "self-improvement." "Unused to manual labor" and accustomed to "the habits of the chase," Indians lacked "forethought" and self-discipline. Unless the government planned their education, Walker predicted, the "now roving Indians" would become "vagabonds" and "festering sores" within civilization. Trained and reformed on the reservations, Indians would be prepared to enter civilized society.[19]

What he hoped his reservation system would do, Walker insisted, was to help the Indians over the rough places on "the white man's road." He believed he knew, from his own experience, what was required. He once told a friend that Indians were like "children" who disliked school and preferred to "play truant at pleasure." Then he added: "I used to have to be whipped myself to get me to school and keep me there, yet I always liked to study when once within the school-room walls." Grateful for the "whipping" he had received as a child and the self-discipline he had developed, Walker was certain "wild Indians" would become "industrious" and "frugal" through "a severe course of industrial instruction and exercise under restraint." Indians should not be left alone, "letting such as will, go to the dogs, letting such as can, find a place for themselves in the social and industrial order." In Walker's view, Indians should not be allowed to remain Indians. There was no longer a West, no longer the "vacant lands" of the continent. Indians everywhere would eventually have to settle down to farming and urban labor.[20]

Allotment and Assimilation

Other white reformers had a different solution to the "Indian Question," however. Regarding themselves as "friends" of the

Indians, they believed that the reservations only served to segregate native peoples from white society and postpone their assimilation. Their viewpoint became policy in 1887, when Congress passed the Dawes Act. Hailed by the reformers as the "Indian Emancipation Act," the law reversed Walker's strategy, seeking instead to break up the reservations and accelerate the transformation of Indians into property owners and U.S. citizens. Under the Dawes Act, the president was granted the power, at his discretion and without the Indians' consent, to allot reservation lands to individual heads of families in the amount of 160 acres. These lands would be ineligible for sale, or "inalienable," for twenty-five years. This would protect the Indians from landgrabbers and also give them time to become farmers. The federal government was authorized to sell "surplus" reservation land—land that remained after allotment—to white settlers in 160-acre tracts. The money derived from the sales would be held in trust for the Indians to be used for their "education and civilization." In the allotment program, Indians would be granted U.S. citizenship.[21]

During the debate over the bill, a senator from Texas declared his opposition to Indian citizenship: "Look at your Chinamen, are they not specifically excepted from the naturalization laws?" But Indians, unlike the Chinese, were generally seen as capable of assimilation. "The new law," observed historian Frederick Hoxie, "was made possible by the belief that Indians did not have the 'deficiencies' of other groups: they were fewer in number, the beneficiaries of a public sympathy and pity, and capable of advancement."[22]

To advance and civilize the Indians, Senator Henry Dawes contended, the tribal system had to be destroyed, for it was perpetuating "habits of nomadic barbarism" and "savagery." As members of tribes, Indians would continue to live in idleness, frivolity, and debauchery. As owners of lands in common, they would lack "selfishness," which was "at the bottom of civilization." The key to civilizing Indians would be to convert them into individual landowners. Repeatedly, the "friends" of the Indians declared that allotment was designed to make them independent and self-reliant. With the breakup of the reservations and the sale of "surplus" lands to whites, they would learn the "habits of thrift and industry" from their white neighbors. "The aggressive and enterprising Anglo-Saxons" would set up their farms "side by side" with Indian farms, and "in a little while contact alone" would lead Indians to emulate the work ethic of their white neighbors.

"With white settlers on every alternative section of Indian lands," allotment supporters predicted, "there will be a school-house built, with Indian children and white children together; there will be churches at which there will be an attendance of Indian and white people alike. They will readily learn the tongue of the white race. They will for a while speak their own language, but they will readily learn the ways of civilization."[23]

This conversion of Indians into individual landowners was ceremonialized at "last-arrow" pageants. On these occasions, the Indians were ordered by the government to attend a large assembly on the reservation. Dressed in traditional costume and carrying a bow and arrow, Indians were individually summoned from a tepee and told to shoot an arrow. Each one then retreated to the tepee and reemerged wearing "civilized" clothing, symbolizing a crossing from the primitive to the modern world. Made to stand before a plow, the Indian was told: "Take the handle of this plow, this act means that you have chosen to live the life of the white man—and the white man lives by work." At the close of the ceremony, each Indian was given an American flag and a purse with the instruction: "This purse will always say to you that the money you gain from your labor must be wisely kept."[24]

While giving Indians what they already owned, their land, the Dawes Act also took lands away from them. White farmers and business interests were well aware of the economic advantages that the allotment program offered. In 1880, Secretary of the Interior Carl Schurz predicted that allotment would "eventually open to settlement by white men the large tracts of land now belonging to the reservations, but not used by the Indians." Shortly after Congress passed his bill, Senator Henry Dawes recounted an experience he had while traveling by train on a recently completed railroad track across five hundred miles of Indian territory. The potential of the terrain impressed Dawes. "The land I passed through was as fine a wheat-growing country as it could be. The railroad has gone through there, and it was black with emigrants ready to take advantage of it." In his recommendation for allotment on the White Earth Reservation in Minnesota, a government official pointed out that the present Chippewa lands were "valuable for the pine timber growing thereon, for which, if the Indian title should be extinguished, a ready sale could be found."[25]

Legislation that granted railroad corporations right-of-way through Indian lands coincided with the enactment of the Dawes law: in 1886–87, Congress made six land grants to railroad interests. "The past year," the Indian affairs commissioner observed that September, "has been one of unusual activity in the projection and building of numerous additional railroads through Indian lands." During the next two sessions, Congress enacted twenty-three laws granting railroad right-of-ways through Indian territories.[26]

Four years after the passage of the Dawes Act, Indian commissioner Thomas Morgan calculated that Indian land reductions for the year 1891 alone totaled 17,400,000 acres, or one-seventh of all Indian lands. "This might seem like a somewhat rapid reduction of the land estate of the Indians," he noted. But the Indians were not "using" most of the relinquished land "for any purpose whatever" and had "scarcely any of it...in cultivation," and therefore they "did not need it." Moreover, they had been "reasonably well paid" for the land. "The sooner the tribal relations are broken up and the reservation system done away with," Morgan added, "the better it will be for all concerned. If there were no other reason for this change, the fact that individual ownership of property is the universal custom among civilized people of this country would be a sufficient reason for urging the handful of Indians to adopt it."[27]

In 1902, Congress accelerated the transfer of lands from Indians to whites: a new law required that all allotted lands, upon the death of the owners, be sold at public auctions by the heirs. Unless they were able to purchase their own family lands, Indians would lose what had been their property. "Under the present system," a government official informed President Theodore Roosevelt, "every Indian's land comes into the market at his death, so that it will be but a few years at most before all the Indians' land will have passed into the possession of the settlers." Four years later, Congress passed the Burke Act, which nullified the twenty-five-year trust provision in the Dawes Act and granted the secretary of the interior the power to issue fee-simple title to any allottee "competent and capable of managing his or her affairs." Thus, Indian allotments were no longer protected from white land purchasers.[28]

Native Americans resisted these efforts to usurp their lands. Chief Lone Wolf of the Kiowas, for example, insisted in court that the 1868 Treaty of Medicine Lodge Creek had provided for tribal approval of all land cessions. But in 1903, the Supreme Court decided that the federal government had the power to abrogate the provisions of an Indian treaty. An official of the Indian affairs welcomed the *Lone Wolf* decision, for it allowed the government to dispose of Indian land without their consent. If their consent were required, he asserted, it would take fifty years to eliminate the reservations. Now the government had the power to allot reservation lands and sell "the balance" of reservation lands in order to make "homes for white farmers."[29]

What would be the future for the Indians if they no longer had any land? "When the last acre and last dollar are gone," Indian Affairs Commissioner Francis Leupp answered, "the Indians will be where the Negro freedmen started thirty-five years ago." Therefore, it was the government's duty to transform Indians into wage earners. In order to train Indians to become agricultural workers, Leupp arranged for the leasing of tribal lands to sugar-beet companies willing to employ Indians. As a field laborer, the commissioner explained, the Indian would acquire valuable work habits. "In this process the sensible course is to tempt him to the pursuit of a gainful occupation by choosing for him at the outset the sort of work which he finds the pleasantest; and the Indian takes to beet farming as naturally as the Italian takes to art or the German to science.... Even the little papoose can be taught to weed the rows just as the pickaninny in the South can be used as a cotton picker."[30]

But allotment led neither to self-sufficient Indian farmers nor to wage earners. Most reservations were located in the plains region where land could be effectively used only for ranching or large-scale farming. Plots of 160 acres were hardly realistic. What happened to the Cheyennes and Arapahoes illustrated a general pattern of dispossession and pauperization. The reservation lands of both tribes had been allotted in 1891, and the "surplus" lands sold to whites. Sixteen years later, the combined income of the Cheyennes and Arapahoes totaled $217,312. About two-thirds of this revenue came from the sale of inherited lands and the remainder from leasing allotments; only $5,312 came from farming. Per capita tribal income for that year was just $78.[31]

Forty years after the Dawes Act, the Brookings Institution reported that 55 percent of all Indians had a per capita annual income of less than two hundred dollars, and that only 2 percent had incomes of more than five hundred dollars per year. In 1933, the federal government found that almost half of the Indians living on reservations that had been subject to allotment were landless. By then, the Indians had lost about 60 percent of the 138 million–acre land base they had owned at the time of the Dawes Act. Allotment had been transforming Indians into a landless people.[32]

The Indian "New Deal": What Kind of a "Deal" Was It?

The allotment program was suddenly halted in 1934 by the Indian Reorganization Act, a policy devised by John Collier. As the Indian affairs commissioner appointed by President Franklin D. Roosevelt, he offered Indians a "New Deal."

A critic of individualism, Collier admired the sense of community he found among the Indians of New Mexico. "Only the Indians," he observed, "...were still the possessors and users of the fundamental secret of human life—the secret of building great personality through the instrumentality of social institutions." This valuable knowledge should be preserved. Defining "the individual and his society as wholly reciprocal," the Indian way of life had much to teach whites and should be appreciated "as a gift for us all." Allow Indians to remain Indians, Collier insisted. "*Assimilation*, not into our culture but into modern life, and *preservation and intensification of heritage* are not hostile choices, excluding one another, but are interdependent through and through." Collier's philosophy called for cultural pluralism: "Modernity and white Americanism are not identical. If the Indian life is a good life, then we should be proud and glad to have this different and native culture going on by the side of ours.... America is coming to understand this, and to know that in helping the Indian to save himself, we are helping to save something that is precious to us as well as to him."[33]

In Collier's view, allotment was destroying the Indian communal way of life. By breaking the tribal domain into individual holdings, allotment had been "much more than just a huge white land grab; it was a blow, meant to be fatal, at Indian tribal existence." The goal of government policy, Collier contended, should not be the absorption of Indians into the white population, but the maintenance of Indian cultures on their communally owned lands. Thus, as the architect of the Indian reorganization bill, Collier proposed the abolition of allotment and the establishment of Indian self-government as well as the preservation of "Indian civilization," including their arts, crafts, and traditions.[34]

After reading a draft of the bill, President Roosevelt noted on the margin: "Great stuff." On June 18, 1934, he signed the Indian Reorganization Act. While the final version of the law did not include a provision for the preservation of Indian culture, it abolished the allotment program and authorized federal funding for tribes to purchase lands, reversing policy dating back not only to 1887 but to 1607. Indians on reservations would be allowed to establish local self-governments. Reorganization, however, would apply only to those tribes in which a majority of members had voted to accept it. "This was...a further means of throwing back upon the tribes the control over their own destinies—of placing Indian salvation firmly in Indian hands," Collier explained. "The role of government was to help, but not coerce, the tribal efforts." The following year, 172 tribes representing 132,426 people voted in favor of the law, while 73 tribes with a combined population of 63,467 chose to be excluded.[35]

One of the tribes that turned down the Indian Reorganization Act was the Navajo. The Navajos' negative vote reflected their opposition to Collier and the Indian New Deal. To them, Collier belonged to a tradition reaching back to Jefferson and Walker: though he was articulating a philosophy of Indian autonomy, Collier was telling them what was in their interest and making decisions for them.[36]

Navajos remembered decisions that whites had made for them in the 1860s. Since the seventeenth century, when they acquired sheep from the Spanish, Navajos had been herders. After the war against Mexico and the American annexation of the Southwest, they began to encounter white intruders. In 1863, they surrendered to Kit Carson after his troops destroyed their orchards and sheep herds. According to a Navajo account, "those who escaped were driven to the Grand Canyon and the Painted Desert, where they hid in the rocks like wild animals, but all except a few were rounded up and caught and taken away to Hwalte [Bosque Redondo]." Navajos have remembered this march as the "Long Walk."[37]

"A majority of the Navajos," according to a member of the tribe, "didn't know the reason why they were being rounded up and different stories went around among the people." Many feared that they "would be put to death eventually." When they arrived at Bosque Redondo, they were told by the government to irrigate the land and become farmers. The general in charge of removal explained that the Navajos had to be taken away from "the haunts and hills and hiding places of their country" in order to teach them "the art of peace" and "the truths of Christianity." On their new lands, they would acquire "new habits, new ideas, new modes of life" as they ceased to be "nomads" and became "an agricultural people." But the Navajos refused to switch from herding to farming. Five years later, the government resettled the Navajos on a reservation in their original homeland

and issued sheep to replace the stock Kit Carson's forces had destroyed.[38]

Now in the 1930s, their instructions were coming, not from a soldier like Kit Carson, but from a liberal government administrator. Although Collier was proposing to give Indians self-rule, he was also trying to socially engineer the Indian world—what he called an "ethnic laboratory." Collier's policy reflected the broad philosophy of the New Deal with its faith in government planning. "To this extent," observed historian Graham D. Taylor, "it resembled earlier Indian policies in that it proposed to manipulate Indian behavior in ways which their white 'guardians' thought best for them."[39]

In 1933, Collier decided that it was best for the Navajos to reduce their stock. Government studies had determined that the Navajo reservation had half a million more livestock than their range could support, and that this excess had produced overgrazing and severe soil erosion. Unless the problem of erosion was controlled soon, Collier feared, the sheep-raising Navajos would experience great hardship and suffering. The government had to intervene for the sake of the tribe's survival. "The future of the Navajo is in our hands," stated an official. "His very economy is dependent upon our solution of his land problems." Using a revealing metaphor to describe the relationship between the government and the Navajos, he explained: "When formerly the parents placated the children with a stick of candy when it cried, now the parents are attempting to find the cause of the tears and to take such corrective measures as are necessary.... The youngster will not always understand a dose of castor oil may sometimes be more efficacious than a stick of candy."[40]

While Collier was concerned about Navajo survival, he was also worried about white interests. He had received reports that silt from erosion on Navajo land was filling the Colorado River and threatening to clog Boulder Dam. Under construction during the early 1930s, the dam was designed to supply water to California's Imperial Valley and electricity to Los Angeles. The United States Geological Survey had studied the silt problem and located its origin on the Navajo reservation: "Briefly in the main Colorado system, the Little Colorado and the San Juan are major silt problems, while within each of these basins the Navajo Reservation's tributaries are the major silt problem. The fact is the... Navajo Reservation is practically 'Public Enemy No. 1' in causing the

Colorado Silt problem." Unless Navajo sheep overgrazing and hence erosion were controlled, the silt would block economic development in the Southwest. Collier told the Navajo council that soil erosion must be stopped, or else Boulder Dam would be damaged and not able to supply water and electric power to Southern California.[41]

Thus Collier initiated a stock reduction program on the Navajo reservation. The federal government would purchase four hundred thousand sheep and goats, and would compensate for any loss of income resulting from this stock reduction by employing Navajos on federal work projects. Collier flew to the Navajo reservation seventeen times over the next five years to explain and promote the program. But the Navajos were not receptive. "The Council members, and hundreds, even thousands, of Navajos listened and answered back," Collier recalled. "In my long life of social effort and struggle, I have not experienced among any other Indian group, or any group whatsoever, an anxiety-ridden and anguished hostility even approaching that which the Navajos were undergoing."[42]

Determined to have his way, Collier brought in a federal government expert to explain to the Navajos how herd reduction would actually mean increased livelihood. Using a chart to present his ideas, A. C. Cooley showed a blue line for the number of stock, a yellow line for wages from federal projects, and a red line for income derived from stock. He then argued that as the blue and yellow lines fell over the next few years, the red line would rise with improved grazing conditions, livestock breeding, and management. The Navajos were not impressed. One of them asked Cooley why all three lines could not rise together.[43]

Collier kept pushing his agenda for stock reduction and finally managed to secure the support of the Navajo tribal council. But the Navajos themselves, Collier found, "resisted with a bitterness sometimes sad, sometimes wild, but always angry." Indeed, many Navajos felt Collier had manipulated the council.[44]

What worried the Navajos was the fact that they depended on sheep for their livelihood. For them, sheep and survival were the same. "Remember what I've told you," a Navajo father instructed his son, "you must not lose, kill or give away young ewes, young mares and cows, because...there's a million in one of those." He warned: "So with anyone who comes to you and tells you to let the herd go. You mustn't let the herd go, because as soon as you do there'll be nothing left of them.... The herd is money. It gives you clothing and different kinds of food.... Everything comes from the sheep."[45]

Raising sheep was a way of life for the Navajos. The animals were a part of their world. "When the sheep are grazing," said Haske Chamiso, "I always walked right in the middle of the sheep. I didn't turn the sheep back. I just go along with the sheep. When I get tired, I just lay down in the middle of the sheep and go to sleep and finally my sister would find me." Navajo boys grew up caring for the flocks. Herding represented the closeness of the family and the teaching of values. "All I was doing was herding sheep all the time," explained Ted Chamiso. "I was raised right there at my home, with my mother and father all the time. Then my father used to teach me once in a while. Told me never to steal anything. So I never steal horses, sheep, or goats that don't belong to me. So I never steal all my life since I know myself. I never do any of those bad things my father told me not to do. Not to laugh or make fun of people."[46]

Now the government was ordering the Navajos to reduce their stock. In a letter to a Navajo minister, a group of Navajos denounced the Indian affairs commissioner: "John Collier promised to help us more than any other white man, but before he made these promises he forced us to agree to some hard things that we didn't like. We Indians don't think it is right for Collier to tell us we should govern ourselves, and then tell us how to do it. Why does he want to fool us that way and make us believe we are running our country, when he makes us do what he wants."[47]

Collier proceeded to carry out his stock reduction program. "No Washington people came here to reduce the goats," a Navajo reported. "But policemen told us those were orders from Washington and we had to be rid of the goats. The poorest people were scared and they just reduced the goats and sheep." As they watched the agents take their animals, the Navajos anxiously wondered how they would live without their stock. They issued a chorus of complaints: "The poorest people owned goats—the easiest people to take away from. The pressure was so great the little fellow sold, everyone sold. A goat sold for one dollar. The money doesn't mean half so much to the family as having the goat to kill and eat for several days." "I sure don't understand why he wants us to be poor. They reduce all sheep. They say they only goin' to let Indians have five sheep, three goats, one cattle, and one horse." "A great number of the people's livestock was taken away. Although we were told that it was to restore the land, the fact remains that hunger and poverty stood with their mouths wide open to devour us." After his sheep had been taken away from him, a herder cursed the officials: "You people are indeed heartless. You have now killed me. You have cut off my arms. You have cut off my legs. You have taken my head off. There is nothing left for me. This is the end of the trail."[48]

By 1935, the stock had been reduced by 400,000 sheep and goats; still Collier was not satisfied. Noting that 1,269,910 animals were still grazing on land capable of supporting only 560,000, he impatiently stated: "This means that a further reduction of 56 percent would be necessary in order to reduce the stock to the carrying capacity of the range." A Navajo complained: "The sheep business gives us the only decent living. When we have no more sheep then Mr. Collier will dance the jig and be happy."[49]

Meanwhile, Navajos found themselves becoming increasingly dependent on wage income: nearly 40 percent of their annual per capita income of $128 came from wage earnings, mostly from temporary government employment. The stock reduction program had reduced many Navajos to dependency on the federal government as employees in New Deal work programs. They denounced Collier's project as "the most devastating experience in Navaho history" since their imprisonment at Bosque Redondo in the 1860s.[50]

Tragically, the stock reduction program was unnecessary as an erosion control program. Scientists would do further research on silt settlement and determine that overgrazing was not the source of the problem. "By the 1950s, although 5 percent of the Lake Mead reservoir had already silted up," according to historian Richard White, "scientists were far more hesitant in attributing blame for the situation than their colleagues in the 1930s." But the Navajos had been telling this to the government all along. They argued that erosion had been reported as early as the 1890s and was related more to drought than to overgrazing. Trying to explain this cycle of dry weather and subsequent erosion to the government experts, Navajos had pointed out that the 1930s were also years with little rain and predicted that the range would recover when the drought ended. They reminded the government bureaucrats: "We know something about that by nature because we were born here and raised here and we knew about the pro-

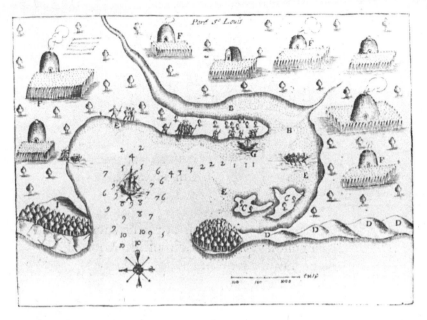

A map of Wampanoag villages and cornfields on Cape Cod drawn by Samuel de Champlain. (Des Sauvages: ou Voyage de Samuel de Champlain de Brouage faict en la France Nouvelle *[Paris, 1604]*)

Irish immigrants boarding ships at Queenstown, Cork, 1851. (Illustrated London News, *May 10, 1851*)

Learning about "Gold Mountain," many of the younger, more impatient, and more daring Chinese left their villages for America. *(Asian American Studies Library, University of California, Berkeley)*

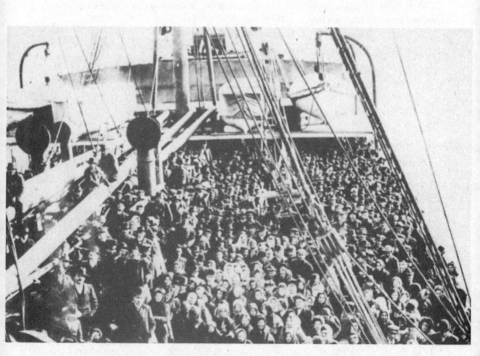

European immigrants packed on a ship bound for America. *(Library of Congress)*

Black Union soldiers, mustered out at Little Rock, Arkansas. (Harper's Weekly, *vol. 10 [May 19, 1866]*)

Arrival of Japanese immigrants. *(Hawaii State Archives)*

Left: Red Cloud, photograph by Charles M. Bell, 1880 *(Smithsonian Institution)*

Below: "Chinese Cheap Labor" in Louisiana. (Every Saturday 3, no. 83 [July 29, 1871])

Facing page, above: Chinese railroad workers building the transcontinental railroad, circa 1866. *(Asian American Studies Library, University of California, Berkeley)*

Facing page, below: Irish railroad workers building the transcontinental railroad, circa 1866. *(Union Pacific Railroad Museum Collection, Omaha, Nebraska)*

Left: Big Foot lying in the snow after the massacre at Wounded Knee, 1890. *(Smithsonian Institution)*

Below: Many Chinese men spent their leisure hours in the back rooms of stores. *(Asian American Studies Library, University of California, Berkeley)*

Facing page: Hester Street, Lower East Side. Pushcarts lined the streets, and a cacophony of Yiddish voices rose from the crowds. *(Brown Brothers)*

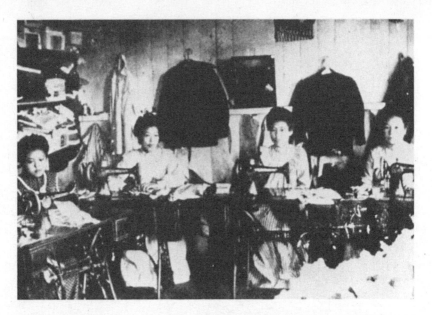

Japanese immigrant women sewing clothing for laborers in a garment shop on a plantation in Hawaii. *(Hawaii State Archives) Below:* Jewish immigrant women working in a garment factory. "The machines were all in a row. And it was so hot, not even a decent fan. And you worked, and you sweated." *(Brown Brothers)*

Irish immigrant maids. As they cooked, laundered, and took care of the children, servants were required to wear aprons. *(State Historical Society of Wisconsin) Below:* Mexican workers in San Antonio, Texas, 1924. *(Goldbeck Collection, Humanities Research Center, University of Texas, Austin)*

The Triangle Shirtwaist Factory fire, 1911. "They hit the pavement just like hail," a fireman reported. *(Brown Brothers)*

Mexican miners in Arizona. *(Arizona Historical Society)*

Chicano laborers shelling pecans in San Antonio, Texas, in the 1930s. *(National Archives)*

Striking Jewish shirtwaist workers, 1909. (Munsey's Magazine, *1910*)

One of "MacArthur's boys," Marine Ira Hayes of the Pima tribe participated in the landing at Iwo Jima in 1945. *(U.S. Department of the Army)*

Mrs. Emily Lee Shek became the first Chinese woman to join the WAACS. She is pictured here with Eleanor Roosevelt. *(U.S. Department of the Army)*

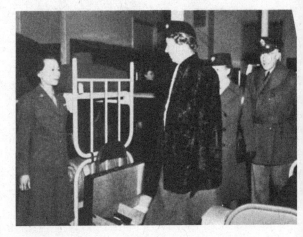

At Dachau, Jewish prisoners were liberated by U.S. troops, including Japanese-American soldiers. *(Photograph by Sus Ito. Courtesy of the Japanese American Resource Center and Rudy Tokiwa)*

Black female worker in a shipyard during World War II. *(National Archives)*

Mexican-American railroad workers during World War II. *(Library of Congress)*

Frederick Douglass. *(Reproduced in Frederick Douglass,
My Bondage and My Free-
dom [New York, 1855])*

Martin Delany, Union
officer. *(Howard University
Library. Reproduced in* Martin
Robinson Delany *[New York:
Doubleday, 1971])*

Marcus Garvey, 1922.
(United Press Photo)

The three civil rights workers murdered in Mississippi — Michael Schwerner, James Chaney, and Andrew Goodman. *(AP/Wide World)*

Sit-in at the Greensboro Woolworth's lunch counter, February 2, 1960 — Joseph McNeil, Franklin McCain, Billy Smith, and Clarence Henderson. (Greensboro News & Record *Library*)

Martin Luther King, Jr., and Malcolm X. *(Library of Congress)*

American Progress, ca. 1873, chromolithograph by George A. Crofutt (Courtesy of the Library of Congress)

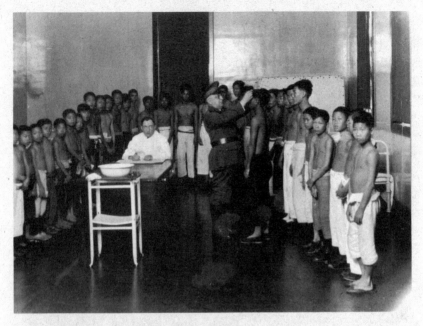

Angel Island Immigration Station (Courtesy of the National Archives)

Minnie Miller (née Glauberman); her husband, Abraham; her father, Lazar; and her daughter, Sarah—Jewish immigrants from Poland, 1920s (Courtesy of Rick Balkin)

Sikh farmworkers in California, 1912, (From H. A. Millis, "East Indian Immigration to the Pacific Coast," *Survey* XXVIII)

African American soldiers at Buchenwald, April 1, 1945 (Courtesy of the United States Holocaust Memorial Museum, Washington, D. C.)

Fatema Nourzaie, the American-born daughter of Afghan refugees who fled from their war-torn homeland (Photograph by the author)

Alexis Lopez and his mother at his graduation, University of California, Berkley, 2007. The grandson of a Mexican immigrant who worked in the fields of California, Alexis is planning to pursue his dream of becoming a doctor. (Courtesy of Alexis Lopez)

cesses of nature on our range." One of their ancient songs told them about their land's dependency on rain:

> *House made of dawn,*
> *House made of the dark cloud,*
> *The zigzag lightning stands high upon it,*
> *Happily, with abundant showers, may I*
> *walk.*

Problems of erosion had always gone away when the grass returned along with the rain, Navajos knew, as they searched the skies for dark clouds in the dawn and evening, hopeful that showers would bless the land and their people.[51]

10

❧❦☙

PACIFIC CROSSINGS

From Japan to the Land of "Money Trees"

W ITH THE END of the frontier in the 1890s, America witnessed the arrival of a new group of immigrants. Like the Irish, the Japanese were pushed here by external influences. During the nineteenth century, America's expansionist thrust had reached all the way across the Pacific Ocean. In 1853, Commodore Matthew C. Perry sailed his armed naval ships into Tokyo Bay and forcefully opened Japan's doors to the West. As Japanese leaders watched Western powers colonizing China, they worried that their country would be the next victim. Thus, in 1868, they restored the Meiji emperor and established a strong centralized government. To defend Japan, they pursued a twin strategy of industrialization and militarization and levied heavy taxes to finance their program.

Bearing the burden of this taxation, farmers suffered severe economic hardships during the 1880s. "The distress among the agricultural class has reached a point never before attained," the *Japan Weekly Mail* reported. "Most of the farmers have been unable to pay their taxes, and hundreds of families in one village alone have been compelled to sell their property in order to liquidate their debts." Thousands of farmers lost their lands, and hunger stalked many parts of the country. "What strikes me most is the hardships paupers are having in surviving," reported a journalist. "Their regular fare consists of rice husk or buckwheat chaff ground into powder and the dregs of bean curd mixed with leaves and grass."[1]

Searching for a way out of this terrible plight, impoverished farmers were seized by an emigration *netsu*, or fever. Fabulous stories of high wages abroad stirred their imaginations. A plantation laborer in the Kingdom of Hawaii could earn six times more than in Japan; in three years, a worker might save four hundred yen—an amount equal to ten years of earnings in Japan. When the Japanese government first announced it would be filling six hundred emigrant slots for the first shipment of laborers to Hawaii, it received 28,000 applications. Stories about wages in the United States seemed even more fantastic—about a dollar a day, or more than two yen. This meant that in one year a worker could save almost a thousand yen—an amount equal to the income of a governor in Japan. No wonder a young man begged his parents: "By all means let me go to America." Between 1885 and 1924, 200,000 left for Hawaii and 180,000 for the U.S. mainland. In haiku, one Japanese migrant captured the feeling of expectation and excitement:

> *Hugh dreams of fortune*
> *Go with me to foreign lands,*
> *Across the ocean.*

Prospective Japanese immigrants exclaimed, "In America, money grew on trees."[2]

Picture Brides in America

Like the Chinese, the Japanese crossed the Pacific driven by dreams of making money. But the two migrations differed significantly. The Japanese flow east to America included an abundance of women. By 1920, women represented 46 percent of the Japanese in Hawaii and 35 percent in the Golden State, compared with only 5 percent for the Chinese. Why did proportionally more women emigrate from Japan than China?

Unlike China, Japan was ruled by a strong central government that was able to regulate emigration. Seeking to avoid the problems of prostitution, gambling, and drunkenness that reportedly plagued the predominantly male Chinese community in the United States, the Japanese government promoted female emigration. The 1882 Chinese Exclusion Act had prohibited the entry of "laborers," both men and women, but the militarily strong Japan was able to negotiate the 1907 Gentlemen's Agreement. While this treaty prohibited the entry of Japanese "laborers," it allowed the Japanese government to permit women to emigrate as family members.[3]

Through this loophole in immigration policy came over sixty thousand women, many as "picture brides." The picture bride system was based on the established custom of arranged marriage. In Japanese society, marriage was not an individual matter but rather a family concern, and parents consulted go-betweens to help them select partners for their sons and daughters. In situations involving families located far away, the prospective bride and groom would exchange photographs before the initial customary meeting. This traditional practice lent itself readily to the needs of Japanese migrants. "When I told my parents about my desire to go to a foreign land, the story spread throughout the town," picture bride Ai Miyasaki later recalled. "From here and there requests for marriage came pouring in just like rain!" Similarly, Riyo Orite had a "picture marriage." Her marriage to a Japanese man in America had been arranged through a relative. "All agreed to our marriage, but I didn't get married immediately," she recalled. "I was engaged at the age of sixteen and didn't meet Orite until I was almost eighteen. I had seen him only in a picture at first.... Being young, I was unromantic. I just believed that girls should get married. I felt he was a little old, about thirty, but the people around me praised the match. His brother in Tokyo sent me a lot of beautiful pictures [taken in the United States].... My name was entered in the Orites' *koseki* [family register]. Thus we were married."[4]

The emigration of Japanese women occurred within the context of internal economic developments. While women in China were restricted to farm and home, Japanese women were increasingly entering the wage-earning workforce. Thousands of them were employed in construction work as well as in the coal mines, where they carried heavy loads on their backs out of the tunnels. Young women were also working in textile mills, where they had sixteen-hour shifts and lived in dormitories. By 1900, 60 percent of Japan's industrial laborers were women. While it is not known how many of the women who emigrated had been wage earners, this proletarianization of women already well under way in Japan paved the way for them to consider working in America.[5]

Japanese women were also more receptive to the idea of traveling overseas than Chinese women. The Meiji government required the education of female children, stipulating that "girls should be educated...alongside boys." Emperor Meiji himself promoted female education. Japanese youth, "boys as well as girls," he declared, should learn about foreign countries and become "enlightened as to ideas of the world." Japanese women, unlike their Chinese counterparts, were more likely to be literate. "We studied English and Japanese, mathematics, literature, writing, and religion," recalled Michiko Tanaka. Under the reorganization of the school system in 1876, English was adopted as a major subject in middle school. Women also heard stories describing America as "heavenly," and some of the picture brides were more eager to see the new land than to meet their husbands. "I wanted to see foreign countries and besides I had consented to marriage with Papa because I had the dream of seeing America," Michiko Tanaka revealed to her daughter years later. "I was bubbling over with great expectations," said another picture bride. "My young heart, 19 years and 8 months old, burned, not so much with the prospects of uniting with my new husband, but with the thought of the New World."[6]

The emigration of women was also influenced by Japanese views on gender. A daughter was expected to marry and enter her husband's family. "Once you become someone's wife you belong to his family," explained Tsuru Yamauchi. "My parents said once I went over to be married, I should treat his parents as my own and be good to them." One day, Yamauchi was told that she would be going to Hawaii to join her future husband: "I learned about the marriage proposal when we had to exchange pictures." Emigration for her was not a choice but an obligation.[7]

Whether a Japanese woman went to America often depended on which son she married. Unlike the Chinese, Japanese farmers had an inheritance system based on impartible inheritance and primogeniture. Usually the first son inherited the family's holdings. In the mountainous island nation of Japan, arable land was limited, and most of the farm holdings were small, less than two and a half acres. Division of a tiny family holding would mean disaster for the family. As the inheritor of the family farm, the eldest son had the responsibility of caring for his aged parents and hence was required to stay home. The other sons would have to leave the family farm and find employment in town. This practice of relocating within Japan could easily be applied to moving abroad. Thus, although the immigrants included some first sons, they tended to be the younger ones. Unlike Chinese sons who had to share responsibility for their parents, these Japanese men were not as tightly bound to their parents and were allowed to take their wives and children with them to America.[8]

But whether or not women migrated was also influenced by needs in the receiving countries. In Hawaii, the government initially stipulated that 40 percent of the contract labor emigrants from Japan were to be women. During the government-sponsored contract labor period from 1885 to 1894, women constituted 20 percent of the emigrants. During the period from 1894 to 1907, thousands of additional women sailed to Hawaii as private contract laborers. Planters assigned 72 percent of them to field labor. Furthermore, they promoted the Japanese family as a mechanism of labor control. In 1886, Hawaii's inspector-general of immigration reported that Japanese men were better workers on plantations where they had their wives. After 1900, when Hawaii became a territory of the United States, planters became even more anxious to bring Japanese women to Hawaii. Since the American law prohibiting contract labor now applied to the islands, planters had to find ways to stabilize their labor force. Realizing that men with families were more likely to stay on the plantations, managers asked their business agents in Honolulu to send "men with families."[9]

Meanwhile, Japanese women were pulled to the United States mainland, where their husbands needed them as workers. Shopkeepers and farmers sent for their wives, thinking they could assist as unpaid family labor. Wives were particularly useful on farms where production was labor intensive. "Nearly all of these tenant farmers are married and have their families with them," a researcher noted in 1915. "The wives do much work in the fields."[10]

As they prepared to leave their villages for Hawaii and America, many women felt separation anxieties. One woman remembered her husband's brother saying farewell: "Don't stay in the [United] States too long. Come back in five years and farm with us." But her father quickly remarked: "Are you kidding? They can't learn anything in five years. They'll even have a baby over there.... Be patient for twenty years." Her father's words shocked her: suddenly she realized how long the separation could be. Another woman recalled the painful moment she experienced when her parents came to see her off: "They did not join the crowd, but quietly stood in front of the wall. They didn't say 'good luck,' or 'take care,' or anything…. They couldn't say anything because they knew, as I did, that I would never return." As their ships sailed from the harbor, many women gazed at the diminishing shore:

> *With tears in my eyes*
> *I turn back to my homeland,*
> *Taking one last look.*[11]

Tears in the Canefields

"Get labor first," sugar planters in Hawaii declared, "and capital will follow." By pursuing this strategy, they successfully developed a profitable sugar export economy. Between 1875 and 1910, cultivated land multiplied nearly eighteen times, or from 12,000 to 214,000 acres. To achieve this triumph, planters had to find workers, and their chief source was Japan. To their labor suppliers, they sent requisitions for needed supplies. In a letter to a plantation manager, July 2, 1890, the Davies Company of Honolulu acknowledged receipt of an order for:

bonemeal
canvas
Japanese laborers
macaroni
Chinaman

In another letter, January 3, 1898, the Davies Company confirmed a list of orders which included:

DRIED BLOOD [fertilizer].
LABORERS. We will book your order for 75 Japanese
to come as soon as possible.
MULES & HORSES.[12]

Though they imported workers along with supplies, planters were conscious of the nationalities of their laborers. They were systematically developing an ethnically diverse labor force in order to create divisions among their workers and reinforce management control. Complaining about the frequency of strikes on plantations where the workers were mostly from the same country, plantation managers recommended: "Keep a variety of laborers, that is different nationalities, and thus prevent any concerted action in case of strikes, for there are few, if any, cases of Japs, Chinese, and Portuguese entering into a strike as a unit." In a "confidential" letter to planter George Wilcox, a labor supply company wrote: "Regarding the proportion of Chinese and Japanese laborers we beg to advise, that the Hawaiian Sugar Planters' Association and the Bureau of Immigration have agreed upon 2/3rd of the former and 1/3 of the latter. For your *private* information we mention, that the reason for this increasing the percentage of the Chinese laborers is due to the desire of breaking up the preponderance of the Japanese element."[13]

Planters explained that they preferred to divide the workforce "about equally between two Oriental nationalities." In 1903, they began importing Korean laborers in order to "pit" them against the Japanese. Aware of the antagonism between these two groups, planters believed that the Koreans were "not likely to combine with the Japanese at any attempt at strikes." After receiving a demand for higher wages from Japanese laborers, a planter asked a labor supplier to send a shipment of Korean laborers: "In our opinion, it would be advisable, as soon as circumstances permit, to get a large number of Koreans in the country...and drive the Japs out."[14]

But the Korean labor supply was cut off in 1905. Informed about abuses suffered by the Koreans on the plantations, the Korean government prohibited further emigration to Hawaii. A year later, planters began bringing laborers from the Philippines, a territory acquired by the United States after the Spanish-American War. Again the purpose was to diversify and discipline the labor force. On July 28, 1909, the Hawaiian Sugar Planters' Association reported that several hundred Filipino laborers were en route to Hawaii: "It may be too soon to say that the Jap is to be supplanted, but it is certainly in order to take steps to clip his wings," and to give "encouragement to a new class [Filipinos]...to keep the more belligerent element in its proper place." Planters anxiously asked the labor suppliers to hurry the delivery of the Filipino workers. On August 7, for example, one of them complained about the high wages demanded by the Japanese laborers on his plantation: "If possible for you to arrange it I should very much like to get say 25 new Filipinos to put into our day gang.... In this way perhaps we can stir the Japs a bit." Twenty days later, he wrote again, stating that he was very pleased to receive the shipment of thirty Filipinos, and that he planned to use them to bring the Japanese workers to "their senses."[15]

To strengthen their authority over their ethnically diverse

workforce, planters stratified tasks according to race: whites occupied the skilled and supervisory positions, while Asian immigrants were the unskilled field laborers. In 1904, the Hawaiian Sugar Planters' Association passed a resolution that restricted skilled positions to "American citizens, or those eligible for citizenship." Asian immigrants were excluded, for they were not "white" and therefore ineligible to become naturalized citizens. In 1915, Japanese laborers were mostly field hands and mill laborers. Of 45 mill engineers, 41 were of European ancestry, three were Hawaiian or part-Hawaiian, and only one was Japanese. A racial division was particularly evident in supervisory positions: of the 377 overseers, only 2 were Chinese and 17 Japanese, while 313 were white. A Japanese worker told an interviewer how he was frustrated by racial discrimination. "I haven't got a chance" to get ahead in employment, he explained. "You can't go very high up and get big money unless your skin is white. You can work here all your life and yet a *haole* [white] who doesn't know a thing about the work can be ahead of you in no time."[16]

On the plantations, Japanese workers found themselves in a world of regimented labor. Early in the morning, they were jarred from their sleep by the loud scream of the plantation siren. A work song captured the beginning of the workday:

> *"Awake! stir your bones! Rouse up!"*
> *Shrieks the Five o'Clock Whistle.*
> *"Don't dream you can nestle*
> *For one more sweet nap.*
> *Or your ear-drums I'll rap*
> *With my steam-hammer tap*
> *Till they burst.*
> *Br-r-row-aw-i-e-ur-ur-rup!*
> *Wake up! wake up! wake up!*
> *w-a-k-e-u-u-u-up!"*

> *"Filipino and Japanee;*
> *Porto Rican and Portugee;*
> *Korean, Kanaka and Chinese;*
> *Everybody whoever you be*
> *On the whole plantation—*
> *Wake up! wake up! wake up!*
> *w-a-k-e-u-u-u-up!*
> *Br-r-row-aw-i-e-ur-ur-rup!"*[17]

When the whistle stopped shrieking, *lunas,* or foremen, strode through the camps. "Get up, get up," they shouted as they knocked on the doors of the cottages and barracks. "*Hana-hana, hana-hana,* work, work."[18]

"All the workers on a plantation in all their tongues and kindreds, 'rolled out' sometime in the early morn, before the break of day," reported a visitor. One by one and two by two, laborers appeared from "the shadows, like a brigade of ghosts." From the labor camps, they came by train, "car after car of silent figures," their cigarettes glowing in the darkness. In front of the mill, they lined up, shouldering their hoes. As the sun rose, its rays striking the tall mill stack, "quietly the word was passed from somewhere in the dimness. Suddenly and silently the gang started for its work, dividing themselves with one accord to the four quarters of the compass, each heading toward his daily task." The workers were grouped into gangs of twenty to thirty workers and marched to the fields. Each gang was supervised by an "overseer, almost always a white man." The ethnicity of the gangs varied: some were composed of one nationality, while others included Hawaiians, Filipinos, Puerto Ricans, Chinese, Japanese, Portuguese, and Koreans.[19]

There were gangs of women workers, too. In 1920, 14 percent of the plantation labor force was female, mostly Japanese. Women were concentrated in field operations such as hoeing, stripping leaves, and harvesting. Though they were given many of the same assignments as men, women were paid less than their male counterparts. Female field hands, for example, received an average wage of only fifty-five cents per day in 1915, compared to the seventy-eight cents for male field hands.[20]

Field work was punishing and brutal. "We worked like machines," a laborer complained. "For 200 of us workers, there were seven or eight *lunas* and above them was a field boss on a horse. We were watched constantly." A Japanese woman recalled: "We had to work in the canefields, cutting cane, being afraid, not knowing the language. When any *haole* or Portuguese luna came, we got frightened and thought we had to work harder or get fired." "The *luna* carried a whip and rode a horse," another Japanese laborer recounted. "If we talked too much the man swung the whip. He did not actually whip us but just swung his whip so that we would work harder."[21]

The *lunas* "never called a man by his name," the workers grumbled. "Every worker was called by number," one of them complained. "Always by the *bango*, 7209 or 6508 in that manner. And that was the thing I objected to. I wanted my name, not the number." Carried on chains around their necks, the *bangos* were small brass disks with stamped identification. In the old country, workers had names that connected them to family and community; but in Hawaii, they had become numbers. They resented this new impersonal identity. Laborers were "treated no better than cows or horses," one of them recalled. The *bango* seemed to emblematize a distance between themselves and their humanity.[22]

The laborers cursed the overseers, "talking stink" about the driving pace of the work: "It burns us up to have an ignorant *luna* stand around and holler and swear at us all the time for not working fast enough. Every so often, just to show how good he is, he'll come up and grab a hoe and work like hell for about two minutes and then say sarcastically, 'Why you no work like that?' He knows and we know he couldn't work for ten minutes at that pace." The *lunas* were just plain mean.

> *Hawaii, Hawaii*
> *But when I came*
> *What I saw*
> *Was hell*
> *The boss was Satan*
> *The* lunas
> *His helpers.*[23]

In the cane fields, workers hoed weeds, one of the most tedious and backbreaking tasks. They had to "hoe hoe hoe... for four hours in a straight line and no talking," said a worker. "Hoe every weed along the way to your three rows. Hoe—chop chop chop, one chop for one small weed, two for all big ones." When the cane was ripe, *lunas* on horseback led the workers into the fields to harvest the crop. The cutting of the cane caught the eye of a visitor: "Just beyond these Chinese huts were canefields, an intense yellow-green, the long, slender leaves tossing in the breeze like a maize-field before the harvest. There were great bands of Japanese at work in the field." They worked with "incredible rapidity, the line of men crossing a field, levelling the cane."[24]

Harvesting the cane was dirty and exhausting work. As the workers mechanically swung their machetes, they felt the pain of blistered hands and scratched arms. "When you cutting the cane and you pulling the cane back," a worker said, "sometimes you get scratched with the leaves from the cane because they have a little edge just like a saw blade." Their heavy arms and their bent backs begged for a break, a moment of rest.

> Becoming weary
> I sit for a while to rest
> In the cane field,
> And whistle
> To call the breezes.[25]

Sometimes the breezes failed to come. Twelve feet high, the cane enclosed and dwarfed the Japanese workers. As they cut the stalks, they sweated from the terrible heat and humidity. Surrounded by clouds of red dust, the laborers covered their faces with handkerchiefs. The mucus they cleared from their noses looked like blood.

> My husband cuts the cane stalks
> And I trim their leaves
> With sweat and tears we both work
> For our means.[26]

After collecting the cane stalks, the workers tied them into bundles and loaded them onto railway cars. A train then pulled the cane to the mill where engines, presses, furnaces, boilers, vacuum pans, and centrifugal drums crushed the cane and boiled its juices into molasses and sugar. Inside the mill, laborers felt as if they were in the "hold of a steamer." The constant loud clanking and whirring of the machinery were deafening. "It was so hot with steam in the mill," Bashiro Tamashiro recalled, "that I became just like *pupule* [crazy]."[27]

At four-thirty in the afternoon, the plantation whistle shrieked the signal to stop working. "*Pau hana*," the laborers sighed, "finished working." Though they were too tired to hoe another row or carry another bundle of stalks, they felt a sudden final burst of energy and eagerly scrambled to their camps.

Contrary to the stereotype of the Japanese immigrants as quiet and accommodating, they aggressively protested against the unfair labor conditions and often engaged in strikes. Divided by their diverse national identities, laborers of different groups initially tended to define their class interests in terms of their particular ethnicity. Thus, Japanese workers organized themselves into "blood unions" based on ethnic membership. The most important manifestation of "blood unionism" was the Japanese strike of 1909. Protesting against a differential wage system based on ethnicity, the strikers demanded higher wages and equal pay for equal work. They angrily pointed out that Portuguese laborers were paid $22.50 per month, while Japanese laborers received only $18.00 for the same work. "The wage is a reward for services done," they argued, "and a just wage is that which compensates the laborer to the full value of the service rendered by him.... If a laborer comes from Japan and he performs the same quantity of work of the same quality within the same period of time as those who hail from the opposite side of the world, what good reason is there to discriminate one as against the other? It is not the color of skin that grows cane in the field. It is labor that grows cane."[28]

Seven thousand Japanese plantation laborers halted operations on Oahu, while their compatriots on the other islands provided support by sending money and food. Japanese business organizations such as the Honolulu Retail Merchants Association contributed to the strike fund, and the Japanese Physicians Association gave free medical service to the strikers and their families. A strong sense of ethnic solidarity inspired the strikers. Stridently shouting *banzais* at rallies, they declared their determination to "stick together" as Japanese.[29]

The strike reflected an awakening consciousness among the workers, a transformation from sojourners to settlers, from Japanese to Japanese Americans. In their demand for a higher wage, the strikers explained: "We have decided to permanently settle here, to incorporate ourselves with the body politique [*sic*] of Hawaii—to unite our destiny with that of Hawaii, sharing the prosperity and adversity of Hawaii with other citizens of Hawaii." Significantly, the Japanese were framing their demands in "American" terms. They argued that the deplorable conditions on the plantations perpetuated an "undemocratic and un-American" society of "plutocrats and coolies." Fair wages would encourage laborers to work more industriously and productively. The goal of the strike was to create "a thriving and contented middle class—the realization of the high ideal of Americanism."[30]

The planters responded by pressuring the government to arrest the strike leaders for "conspiracy." Then they hired Koreans, Hawaiians, Chinese, Portuguese, and Filipinos as scabs.

The strikers held out for four months before they were forced to return to work. But they had actually scored a victory, for shortly afterward, the planters eliminated the differential wage system and raised the wages of the Japanese workers.

A strike based on ethnicity seemed to make sense to Japanese plantation laborers in 1909, for they constituted about 70 percent of the workforce, while Filipinos represented less than 1 percent. But this ethnic solidarity also made it possible for the planters to use laborers of other nationalities to undermine the "Japanese" strike. After the 1909 strike was broken, planters imported Filipino laborers in massive numbers. Eleven years later, Japanese workers represented only 44 percent of the labor force, while Filipino workers had risen to 30 percent. Organized into separate "blood" unions, workers of both nationalities began to realize that the labor movement in Hawaii would have to be based on interethnic working-class unity.

In December 1919, the Japanese Federation of Labor and the Filipino Federation of Labor submitted separate demands to the Hawaiian Sugar Planters' Association. The workers wanted higher wages, an eight-hour day, an insurance fund for retired employees, and paid maternity leaves. Their demands were promptly rejected by the planters. The Japanese union thought that both groups should plan for a long strike. Feeling that the time for action had arrived, however, the Filipino Federation of Labor unilaterally issued an order for the Filipinos to strike and urged the Japanese to join them. "This is the opportunity that the Japanese should grasp," declared the leader of the Filipino union, "to show that they are in harmony with and willing to cooperate with other nationalities in this territory, concerning the principles of organized labor.... We should work on this strike shoulder to shoulder."[31]

Three thousand Filipino workers went out on strike. They set up picket lines and called for labor solidarity. "What's the matter? Why you *hana-hana* [work]?" the Filipino strikers asked their Japanese co-workers. Several Japanese newspapers urged the Japanese laborers to support the Filipinos. The *Hawaii Shimpo* scolded Japanese workers for their hesitation: "Our sincere and desperate voices are also their voices. Their righteous indignation is our righteous indignation.... Fellow Japanese laborers! Don't be a race of unreliable dishonest people! Their problem is your problem!" The *Hawaii Hochi* advised Japanese laborers to strike immediately: "Laborers from different countries" should take "action together." Between Filipinos and Japanese, the *Hawaii Choho* declared, there should be "no barriers of nationality, race, or color." Sensing the will of the community, the Japanese Federation of Labor ordered its members to join the strike. United in struggle, eight thousand Filipino and Japanese strikers—77 percent of the entire plantation workforce on Oahu—brought production to a sudden stop. Here was a Hawaiian version of the "giddy multitude." *"Pau hana,"* they told each other, "no go work." *"Pau hana,"* they declared defiantly, "we on strike."[32]

During the strike, the leaders of the Japanese Federation of Labor questioned the wisdom of having two separate unions and consequently formed the Hawaii Laborers' Association—a name that conveyed multiethnic class camaraderie. They insisted that all workers, regardless of ethnicity, should cooperate in safeguarding their standard of living. The fact that the "capitalists were *haoles* [Caucasians]" and the "laborers Japanese and Filipinos" was a "mere coincidence," explained Takashi Tsutsumi. The fundamental distance was class. Japanese and Filipinos were acting as "laborers" in "a solid body" during the 1920 strike. What the workers were learning from their struggle, Tsutsumi continued, was the need to build "a big, powerful and non-racial labor organization" which could "effectively cope with the capitalists." Such a union would bring together "laborers of all nationalities."[33]

The strikers were learning a valuable lesson. Filipinos and Japanese, joined by Spanish, Portuguese, and Chinese, had participated in the first major interethnic working-class struggle in Hawaii. They had all been awakened by the 5:00 A.M. whistle and had labored together in the fields and mills; now they were fighting for a common goal. As they walked the picket lines and protested at mass rallies, they understood more deeply the contributions they had made as workers to Hawaii's economic development. "When we first came to Hawaii," they proudly declared, "these islands were covered with ohia forests, guava fields and areas of wild grass. Day and night did we work, cutting trees and burning grass, clearing lands and cultivating fields until we made the plantations what they are today."[34]

Confronted by this interethnic challenge, the planters turned to their time-tested strategy of divide-and-control. The president of one sugar corporation explained: "We are inclined to think that the best prospect, in connection with this strike, is the fact that two organizations, not entirely in harmony with each other, are connected with it, and if either of them falls out of line, the end will be in sight." The planters fomented distrust between the two nationalities. They offered a bribe to Filipino union leader Pablo Manlapit. Suddenly, to the surprise of both the Filipino and Japanese strikers, Manlapit called off the strike, condemning it as a Japanese action to cripple the economy of Hawaii. But, at the rank-and-file level, many Filipinos continued to strike. Escalating their attack, the planters launched a "program of propaganda": they claimed that the Japanese strikers were puppets of Japan and were seeking to "Japanise" the islands.[35]

Meanwhile, the planters enlisted Hawaiians, Portuguese, and Koreans as strikebreakers. They also served forty-eight-hour eviction notices to the strikers, forcing them to leave their homes and find makeshift shelters in Honolulu's empty lots. Homeless during the height of an influenza epidemic, thousands of workers and their family members became sick, and one hundred and fifty died. "My brother and mother had a high fever," Tadao Okada recalled, "but all of us were kicked out of our home." Tired, hungry, and ill, the strikers gave up their struggle in July. The planters claimed a complete victory, but three months later, they discretely increased wages by 50 percent.[36]

The strikes represented only the surface of a contested terrain. Beneath the conflict over who would control labor and benefit from the wealth it created was a quiet struggle over the content of culture in Hawaii. Would the culture be dominated by the Anglo-American planter class, or would it be enriched with the traditions and customs of the Japanese as well as of the other nationalities in Hawaii? Culture was critical, for it had the power to deny or provide a way for people to affirm their individual self-esteem and positive group identity.

In the camps, Japanese workers were conscious of the racial and class hierarchy symbolized by the plantation housing pattern. According to the graphic description by Milton Murayama in his novel, *All I Asking For Is My Body*, the manager's house was on the top of the hill. Below it were the nice-looking homes of the Portuguese and Japanese *lunas,* then the identical wooden frame houses of the Japanese camp, and finally the more run-down Filipino camp. This stratified system was laid out around its sewage system. The concrete ditches that serviced the toilets and outhouses ran from the manager's house on the highest slope down to the Filipino camp on the lowest perimeter of the plantation. The tiered housing pattern and sewage system seemed emblematic: "Shit too was organized according to the plantation pyramid."[37]

Workers of different nationalities were usually housed in separate camps. "There were the Japanese camps," recalled Richard Okawa, describing the Hawi Plantation on the Big Island, "and the Chinese and Filipino camps, and one camp for the Puerto Ricans." The Puunene Plantation on Maui had sixteen camps, including many Japanese and Filipino camps, said Minoru Takaki, who worked all his life on the Puunene Plantation. There were also "Young Hee Camp," "Ah Fong Camp," "Spanish A Camp," "Spanish B Camp," and "Alabama Camp." "Yeah," he said, "we used to have Negroes on the plantation."[38]

Generally, the early camps were crowded and unsanitary. According to a contemporary observer, workers were housed in dwellings that resembled "pig sties," and several hundred laborers "swarmed together" in one-story "tenements." A Japanese laborer recalled: "Fifty of us, both bachelors and married couples, lived together in a humble shed—a long ten-foot-wide hallway made of wattle and lined along the sides with a slightly raised floor covered with a grass rug, and two *tatami* mats to be shared among us." Another worker described the "large partitioned house" she inhabited: "The type of room for married people was small, no bed or anything.... It was just a space to lay the futon down and sleep. We didn't have any household things, only our one wicker trunk, not even a closet. We just pounded a nail by the place we slept, a hook where I hung my *muumuu*, the old *kanaka* [Hawaiian] style."[39]

As planters employed men with families rather than single men, they began replacing the barracks with cottages for families. Planters decided that "dependable married men" were "preferred" as workers and authorized the building of cottages for married laborers. In 1920, the Hawaiian Sugar Planters' Association promoted the development of family housing units: "Housing conditions on the plantations have changed greatly during the past few years, lately on account of the change in labor from single to married men." But planters also had self-interested reasons for improving the camps. They wanted to "stimulate" a "home feeling" in order to make their workers happier and more productive. "Pleasant surroundings, with some of the modern comforts and conveniences," explained a plantation official, "go a long way to make the worker healthier and more efficient in his work."[40]

The laborers had their own reasons for beautifying their camps. Seeking to add a reminder of their homeland, Japanese workers placed bonsai plants on the steps of their cottages. They also created artistic gardens; a mainland visitor observed that the flowers and "miniature gardens with little rocky pools and goldfish" suggested "a corner of Japan." Determined to have their traditional hot baths, Japanese workers also built *furos*. "The bath was communal," Tokusuke Oshiro said. "We all took a bath together. If, however, you got in last, it would be very dirty."[41]

Meanwhile, the workers were transforming their camps into ethnic communities. "There was another thing I'd come to like about the camp," remarked Kiyoshi in Milton Murayama's novel about plantation life. "The hundred Japanese families were like one big family. Everybody knew everybody else, everybody was friendly."[42]

On every plantation, Japanese immigrants established Buddhist temples and Japanese-language schools for their children. The camps became the sites for their traditional celebrations. During the midsummer, Japanese held their traditional *obon*, or festival of souls. Dressed in kimonos, they danced in circles to the beat of *taiko* drums to honor the reunion of the living with the spirits of the dead. In early November, they observed the Mikado's birthday. Irritated by the interruption of the plantation production schedule, plantation managers found they had no choice but to let their Japanese workers have the day off. "There is an old custom here among the Japs of observing the 3rd of November as a holiday," a plantation manager complained. "The Emperor's Birthday was celebrated everywhere," Tokusuke Oshiro recalled. "Mainly there was *sumo....* Several young men, usually the good ones, got together at a camp and had Japanese-style *sumo* matches."[43]

The Japanese immigrants also enjoyed sharing their ethnic foods. The daughter of a Portuguese laborer remembered how her mother would make gifts of her bread and "little buns for the children in the camp. The Japanese families gave us sushis and the Hawaiians would give us fish." "Everybody took their own lunches" to school, Lucy Robello of the Waialua plantation said. "And like the Japanese used to take their little riceballs with an *ume* [pickled plum] inside and little *daikon*[radish]. And us Portuguese, we used to take bread with butter and jelly or bread with cheese inside." Then, at noon, Japanese and Portuguese children would trade their *kaukaus* [lunches] with each other. Meanwhile, in the fields, their parents were also sharing their lunches. "We get in a group," William Rego recalled. "We pick from this guy's lunch and that guy'll pick from my lunch and so forth." Crossing ethnic lines, workers would taste each other's foods and exclaim in Hawaiian: "*Ono, ono!*" "Tasty, tasty!"[44]

Initially, the laborers of each ethnic group spoke only their native language. Language gave each group a sense of community within the plantation camps, enabling its members to maintain ties with each other as they shared memories of their distant homelands and stories of their experiences in the new country. But soon workers of different nationalities began to acquire a common language. Planters wanted the immigrant laborers to be taught a functional spoken English so they could give commands to their multilingual workforce. "By this," explained a planter, "we do not mean the English of Shakespeare but the terms used in everyday plantation life. A great many of the small troubles arise from the imperfect understanding between overseers and laborers." Over the years, a plantation dialect developed called "pidgin English"—a simple English that incorporated Hawaiian, Japanese, Portuguese, and Chinese phrases as well as their rhythms and intonations. Though it had begun as "the language of command," this hybrid language with its luxuriant cadences, lyrical sounds, and expressive hand gestures soon became the language of the community. "The language we used had to be either pidgin English or broken English," explained a Filipino laborer describing the communication of different ethnic groups on the plantation. "And when we don't understand each other, we had to add some other words that would help to explain ourselves. That's how this pidgin English comes out beautiful."45

As pidgin English became the common language of the camps, it enabled people from different countries to communicate with each other and thus helped them create a new identity associated with Hawaii. This acquisition of a new language reflected a deeper change in their outlook toward themselves and their new land. They had come to Hawaii intending to earn money and then return to Japan. Of the 200,000 Japanese who entered Hawaii between 1885 and 1924, 110,000, or 55 percent, went home. What is so striking and so significant is the fact that so many sojourners stayed.

Gradually, over the years, Japanese immigrant workers found themselves establishing families in the new land. By 1920, 45 percent of the Japanese in Hawaii were nineteen years old and younger. The immigrants were planting new roots in Hawaii through their children. In a letter to his brother, Asakichi Inouye explained why he had decided not to return to Japan: "My children are here, and my grandson [Daniel, who would later be elected to the U.S. Senate], and it is here that I have passed most of the days of my life. I do not believe that my wife and I, in our last years, could find contentment in Yokoyama, which has become for us a strange place." When Shokichi and Matsu Fukuda migrated to Maui in 1900, they were sojourners. Some twenty years later, they decided they would return to Japan and take their Hawaiian-born children with them. But their son, Minoru, was a teenager by then, and Hawaii was his home, the only world he knew. "He refused to go," remembered his niece Aiko Mifune. "Japan was a foreign country to him. He was very adamant that the family should stay in Hawaii." Mitsue Takaki also found herself planting new roots in Hawaii. She had come as a picture bride in 1920; eleven years later, her husband injured his knee on the plantation and returned to Japan for medical treatment. When he tried to reenter Hawaii, the immigration authorities refused to grant him permission. Mitsue chose to remain in the islands with her three small children—Minoru, Susumu, and Kimiyo. She went to night school to learn English and worked as a maid in the plantation clubhouse to support her children. She wanted them to be educated and have opportunities in the land of their birth.[46]

The planters, however, did not want the children of immigrant workers to have opportunities: they needed the second generation as plantation laborers. In their view, these children should not be taught beyond the sixth or eighth grade, and their education should be vocational training. A sugar corporation president declared that teachers should prepare their students to enter plantation work like their parents. Pointing to the need for agricultural labor, a plantation manager complained: "Why blindly continue a ruinous system that keeps a boy and girl in school at the taxpayers' expense long after they have mastered more than sufficient learning for all ordinary purposes?" A visitor from the mainland noticed the presence of Japanese children on the plantations and asked a manager whether he thought the coming generation of Japanese would make intelligent citizens. "Oh, yes," he replied, "they'll make intelligent citizens all right enough, but not plantation laborers—and that's what we want."[47]

In many schools, however, students were learning about freedom and equality as they recited the Gettysburg Address and the Declaration of Independence. "Here the children learned about democracy or at least the theory of it," said a University of Hawaii student. They were taught that honest labor, fair play, and industriousness were virtues. But they "saw that it wasn't so on the plantation." They saw whites on the top and Asians on the bottom. Returning from school to their camps, students noticed the wide "disparity between theory and practice." This contradiction was glaring. "The public school system perhaps without realizing it," the university student observed, "created unrest."[48]

Seeing their parents suffering from drudgery, low wages, and discrimination, many second-generation Japanese Americans refused to be tracked into plantation labor. Education, they believed, was the key to employment opportunity and freedom from the plantation. "Father made up his mind to send his children to school so far as he possibly could," said the daughter of a Japanese plantation worker. "Yet he had no idea of forcing us. Instead he employed different methods which made us want to go to school. We were made to work in the cane fields at a very early age.... After a day's work in the fields dad used to ask: 'Are you tired? Would you want to work in the fields when you are old enough to leave school?'...My father did everything in his power to make us realize that going to school would be to our advantage."[49]

Young Japanese Americans aspired to be something more than field laborers. Toshio Takaki, who had come to the Puunene Plantation from Japan at the age of 13, felt this restlessness. Initially he worked as a field laborer, but he had an artistic passion and developed an interest in photography. "The cottages in camp were small and he used the closet as a darkroom," neighbor Ellen Kasai recalled. He went around the plantation carrying a camera and taking pictures, and impressed the people in McGerrow Camp as an odd and interesting young man. The plantation could not hold him down, and sometime in the 1920s he left to study with the photographer Jerome Baker in Honolulu. The 1926 Honolulu city directory's entry for Toshio Takaki listed him as a finisher for the Honolulu Photo Supply Company; six years later he was listed as Harry T. Takaki, photographer, with a studio on Bethel Street.[50]

Japanese immigrants had labored to build the great sugar industry in Hawaii. Their sweat had watered the canefields. As they spoke pidgin English and as they watched their children grow up in the camps and attend American schools, they began to realize that they had become settlers and that Hawaii had become their home.

> *With one woven basket*
> *Alone I came*
> *Now I have children*
> *And even grandchildren too.*[51]

Transforming California: From Deserts to Farms

During a visit to California in the 1920s, a young Japanese man from Hawaii was shocked by the pervasiveness and intensity of anti-Japanese hostility. He had heard "various rumors" about the terrible ways whites treated the Japanese there. "But I didn't realize the true situation until I had a personal experience," he said. "In one instance, I went to a barber shop to get my hair trimmed. On entering the shop, one of the barbers approached me and asked for my nationality. I answered that I was Japanese, and as soon as he heard that I was of the yellow race, he drove me out of the place as if he were driving away a cat or a dog."[52]

Compared with their counterparts in Hawaii, where the Japanese represented 40 percent of the population in 1920, the Japanese on the mainland were a tiny racial minority, totaling only 2 percent of the California population. They were scorned by white society and had become the target of hostile and violent white workers. Denied access to employment in the industrial labor market, many Japanese entered entrepreneurial activity. "When I was in Japan, I was an apprentice to a carpenter," explained an immigrant, "but in America at that time the carpenters' union wouldn't admit me, so I became a farmer."[53]

Most of the immigrants had been farmers in Japan: for centuries their families had cultivated small plots, irrigating the land and relying on intensive labor. To become a farmer in America was their dream. Initially, the Japanese worked in agriculture, railroad construction, and canneries. Within two decades after first arriving, however, thousands of them were becoming farmers.[54]

To obtain land, the Japanese used four methods—contract, share, lease, and ownership. The contract system was a simple arrangement: the farmer agreed to plant and harvest a crop for a set amount to be paid by the landowner when the crop was sold. The share system involved greater risks as well as the possibility of greater remuneration because the farmer received a certain percentage of the crop's profit. The contract and share systems enabled the Japanese immigrant to raise himself from field laborer to farmer without much capital. Under both arrangements, the landowner provided the tools, seed, fertilizer, and everything else necessary for the production of the crop; the Japanese farmer, in turn, was responsible for the labor. In order to feed himself and his workers, he purchased supplies on credit from storekeepers and merchants. After the crop was harvested and sold, he paid for his expenses—wages owed to his laborers and bills owed to his creditors. Under the lease arrangement, the Japanese farmer rented the land. He could obtain capital through loans from brokers and shippers. At the end of the season, if he harvested a bountiful crop and received a good price for it, he would pay his rent and clear his debts.[55] The eventual goal was to become a landowning farmer.

What enabled the Japanese to become farmers so rapidly was their timely entry into agriculture. Beginning in the late nineteenth century, industrialization and urbanization had led to increased demands for fresh produce in the cities. The development of irrigation in California at this time opened the way for intensive agriculture and a shift from grain to fruit and vegetable production: between 1879 and 1909, the value of crops representing intensive agriculture skyrocketed from just 4 percent to 50 percent of all crops grown in California. This tremendous expansion occurred under a market stimulus created by two extremely important technological achievements—the completion of the national railroad lines and the invention of the refrigerated car. Now farmers were able to ship their perishable fruits and vegetables to almost anywhere in the United States.[56]

Japanese farmers were in the right place at the right time, and they rapidly flourished. As early as 1910, they produced 70 percent of California's strawberries, and by 1940 they grew 95 percent of the fresh snap beans, 67 percent of the fresh tomatoes, 95 percent of the celery, 44 percent of the onions, and 40 percent of the fresh green peas. In 1900, California's Japanese farmers owned or leased twenty-nine farms totaling 4,698 acres. Within five years, the acreage had jumped to 61,858 and increased again to 194,742 by 1910 and to 458,056 acres ten year later.

The workday on the farms was long and demanding. Stooped over the rows of plants, husbands and wives worked side by side, their hands in constant motion as they felt the hot sun on their backs.

> *Both of my hands grimy,*
> *Unable to wipe away*
> *The sweat from my brow,*
> *Using one arm as towel—*
> *That I was…working…working.*

Remembering the relentless pace of farm work, Yoshiko Ueda said: "I got up at 4:30 A.M. and after preparing breakfast I went to the fields. I went with my husband to do jobs such as picking potatoes and sacking onions. Since I worked apace with ruffians I was tired out and limp as a rag, and when I went to the toilet I couldn't stoop down. Coming back from the fields, the first thing I had to do was start the fire [to cook dinner]." Ueda worked so hard she became extremely thin. "At one time I got down to 85 pounds, though my normal weight had been 150."[57]

Women had double duty — field work and housework. "I got up before dawn with my husband and picked tomatoes in the greenhouse," Kimiko Ono recounted. "At around 6:30 A.M. I prepared breakfast, awakened the children, and all the family sat down at the breakfast table together. Then my husband took the tomatoes to Pike Market. I watered the plants in the greenhouses, taking the children along with me.... My husband came back at about 7 P.M. and I worked with him for a while, then we had dinner and put the children to bed. Then I sorted the tomatoes which I had picked in the morning and put them into boxes. When I was finally through with the boxing, it was midnight — if I finished early — or 1:30 A.M. if I did not."

> *Face black from the sun*
> *Even though creamed and powdered,*
> *No lighter for that!*

"We worked from morning till night, blackened by the sun. My husband was a Meiji man; he didn't even glance at the house work or child care. No matter how busy I was, he would never change a diaper." Another woman described how after a long day laboring in the greenhouse and taking care of the children, she had to work at night: "I did miscellaneous chores until about midnight. However tired I was, the 'Meiji man' wouldn't let me sleep before him."[58]

Driven by their dreams of making the land yield rich harvests, these pioneering men and women converted marginal lands like the hog wallow lands in the San Joaquin Valley, the dusty lands in the Sacramento Valley, and the desert lands in the Imperial Valley into lush and profitable agricultural fields and orchards. "Much of what you call willow forests then," farmer S. Nitta proudly told an interviewer in 1924, "Japanese took that land, cleared it and made it fine farming land." In 1920, the agricultural production of Japanese farms was valued at $67,000,000 — approximately 10 percent of the total value of California's crops.[59]

One of the most successful Japanese farmers was Kinji Ushijima, better known as George Shima. After arriving in 1887, he worked as a potato picker in the San Joaquin Valley and then became a labor contractor, supplying Japanese workers to white farmers. Shima wanted to become a farmer himself and began by leasing fifteen acres. To expand his operations, he leased and purchased undeveloped swamplands in the delta; diking and draining his lands, he converted them into fertile farmlands. A fleet of a dozen steamboats, barges, tugboats, and launches transported Shima's potatoes from Stockton to San Francisco. By 1912, Shima controlled 10,000 acres of potatoes valued at $500,000 and was regarded as a Japanese Horatio Alger. The *San Francisco Chronicle* praised Shima as a model: his success "pointed to the opportunities here to anybody with pluck and intelligence." Wealth did not immunize Shima from racism, however. When he purchased a house in an attractive residential section close to the university in Berkeley, he was told by protesters led by a classics professor to move to the "Oriental" neighborhood. The local newspapers announced: "Jap Invades Fashionable Quarters" and "Yellow Peril in College Town." But Shima refused to move. America was his home, he insisted; he had lived in this country so long that he felt "more at home here than in Japan." Widely known as "the Potato King," Shima had an estate worth $15 million when he died in 1926. His pallbearers included David Starr Jordan, the chancellor of Stanford University, and James Rolph, Jr., the mayor of San Francisco.[60]

Many Japanese immigrants believed that their success, especially in agriculture, would help them become accepted into American society. This was the vision of Kyutaro Abiko. His mother had died giving birth to him in 1865, and Abiko was raised by his grandparents. When he was fourteen years old, he ran away to Tokyo, where he was converted to Christianity. Separated from his family, Abiko lacked the usual ties binding him to Japan. Feeling his "ambitions were stifled" there, Abiko departed for America. In 1885, he arrived in San Francisco, with only a dollar in his pocket. While doing menial jobs to make ends meet, he attended the University of California but did not complete his degree. By the early 1890s, Japanese immigrants were arriving in increasing numbers, and Abiko saw opportunities in the service business. During the 1890s, he operated several enterprises, including a restaurant and a laundry, and began publishing a newspaper, the *Nichibei Shimbun*. Fluent in English and familiar with business, Abiko became a labor contractor and one of the founders of the Japanese American Industrial Corporation. His company quickly became one of the largest labor contracting agencies in California, supplying Japanese labor to agriculture, mining, and the railroads.[61]

A thoughtful man, Abiko worried about the future of the Japanese in America. They were coming as sojourners, and he believed that this mentality was one source of their problems. They were driven by a single purpose—to make money and return to Japan as soon as possible. Thinking they would be here only temporarily, they did not care about their shabby living conditions and indiscreet behavior such as drinking, gambling, and carousing with prostitutes. Neither did they feel a desire or a responsibility to contribute to American society. The sojourner identity, in turn, was contributing to an anti-Japanese exclusionist movement, for it seemed to confirm hostile claims that they were foreign and unassimilable.

In Abiko's view, the Japanese should bring their families and settle in America. Abiko personally set an example: in 1909, he returned to Japan to marry Yonako and brought her back to his new homeland. But the Japanese immigrants had to do more than establish families here, Abiko argued. They had to become farmers. A student of American history and culture, Abiko realized that farming had been the path for many European immigrants to become Americans. He was certain the Japanese were suited to become Americans through agriculture, for most of them had been farmers in the old country. His newspaper, the *Nichibei Shimbun*, became the voice of his message: go into farming, own land, be productive, put down roots in America.[62]

An activist, Abiko took his crusade beyond words. He decided to create an actual model of his ideal Japanese farming community. In 1906, he founded the American Land and Produce Company which purchased 3,200 acres of undeveloped desert land near Livingston in the San Joaquin Valley and parcelled the land into forty-acre lots for sale to Japanese farmers. "We believe that the Japanese must settle permanently with their countrymen on large pieces of land," Abiko declared, "if they are to succeed in America." The settlement was called the Yamato Colony. "Yamato," the ancient name for "Japan," was to be a "new Japan," Abiko's "city upon a hill" in the San Joaquin Valley of California.[63]

A handful of Japanese pioneers responded to the invitation in 1907 and moved to this desolate site where they were greeted by clouds of fine sand blowing in the wind. The colonists settled as families and planted grapevines, which took four seasons to mature—a sign they were planning to stay. Significantly, the pioneers chose a site for a cemetery. "If there was to be a permanent colony," Seinosuke Okuye wrote in his diary in 1907, "the spot for the cemetery should be chosen from the beginning." Abiko's faithful followers had left the graves of their ancestors in Japan, and now they were preparing to become literally one with the soil of their adopted land.[64]

The nearby Merced River had been dammed, and the Yamato colonists constructed a system of irrigation canals and ditches to tap this life-giving supply of water. By 1910, they had planted 1,064 acres of grapes, 507 acres of fruit trees, 100 acres of alfalfa, and 500 acres of hay. "In the eleven years since the Japanese founded their colony," reported the *San Francisco Chronicle* in 1918, "fruit shipments from Livingston have increased from nothing in 1906 to 260 carloads in 1917." By then, the Yamato Colony was home for forty-two farmers, all with families. They were mixing their labor with the soil and becoming Americans.

> *A wasted grassland*
> *Turned to fertile fields by sweat*
> *Of cultivation:*
> *But I, made dry and fallow*
> *By tolerating insults.*

Fertile fields moistened by sweat, Abiko hoped, would bring respect to the Japanese and an end to the insults directed against them as "strangers."[65]

But this strategy of acceptance through agriculture failed to recognize the depth of racial exclusionism. Their very success provoked a backlash. In 1907, the federal government pressured Japan to prohibit the emigration of laborers to the United States. Six years later, California enacted the Alien Land Law, which prohibited landownership to "aliens ineligible to naturalized citizenship." Aimed at Japanese immigrants, this restriction was based on the 1790 federal law providing that only "white" persons could become citizens.

Determined to prove his right and fitness for citizenship, Takao Ozawa filed an application for United States citizenship on October 14, 1914. Ozawa was confident he was qualified. After arriving here as a student in 1894, he graduated from high school in Berkeley, California, and had attended the University of California for three years. He then moved to Honolulu, where he worked for an American company and settled down to raise a family. When his application was denied, Ozawa challenged the rejection in the U.S. District Court for the Territory of Hawaii in 1916. But the court ruled that Ozawa was not eligible for naturalized citizenship. The petitioner was, the court declared, "in every way eminently qualified under the statutes to become an American citizen," "except" one—he was not white. Six years later, the case went before the Supreme Court. Ozawa informed the Court that he was a person of good character. Honest and industrious, he did not drink liquor, smoke, or gamble. More important, "at heart" he was "a true American." He did not have any connection with the government of Japan or with any Japanese churches, schools, or organizations. His family belonged to an American church and his children attended an American school. He spoke the "American (English) language" at home so that his children could not speak Japanese. Ozawa lost his appeal: he was not entitled to naturalized citizenship, the Supreme Court held, because he "clearly" was "not Caucasian."[66]

Two years later, Congress enacted a general immigration law that included a provision prohibiting the entry of all "aliens ineligible to citizenship," the code phrase for Japanese. In an editorial on the 1924 law, the *Rafu Shimpo* of Los Angeles scolded the lawmakers for betraying America's own ideals and dishonoring its best traditions. Congress had "planted the seeds" of possible future "cataclysmic racial strife," the newspaper warned, by "branding" the Japanese people as inferior. Asked by an interviewer what he thought about the new exclusion law, a Japanese immigrant exploded: "That's not right. It's all right if they treat all countries like that, but just Japan, that's not right." Another immigrant explained: "We try hard to be American but Americans always say you always Japanese. Irish become American and all time talk about Ireland; Italians become Americans even if do all time like in Italy; but Japanese can never be anything but Jap."[67] Over thirty years of hard work seemed to be "ending darkly."

> *America ... once*
> *A dream of hope and longing,*
> *Now a life of tears.*[68]

The Nisei: Americans by Birth

The immigrants had hoped that their lands, transformed from deserts to farmlands, would entitle them to settlement in America. But now the Issei, the first generation, feared they would have no future in their adopted land, except through their children—the Nisei, the second generation. Representing a rapidly growing group within the Japanese community, the Nisei constituted 27 percent of the mainland Japanese population in 1920 and 63 percent twenty years later, on the eve of World War II.[69]

Because their children were Americans by birth, the Issei hoped the Nisei would be able to secure the dignity and equality of opportunity denied to them. "You are American citizens," they reminded their children time and again like a litany. "You have an opportunity your parents never had. Go to school and study. Don't miss that opportunity when it comes." Education would give the second generation access to employment opportunities denied to the immigrants. The parents were willing to give up their own comforts, even necessities, for the education of their children.

> Alien hardships
> Made bearable by the hope
> I hold for my children.[70]

But citizenship and education, the second generation soon discovered, did not immunize them from racial discrimination. Even they, American citizens by birth, were told to "go back" to Japan and called "Japs." Walking home from school, Japanese children were often attacked by white boys throwing stones at them. Often perceived as foreigners, Nisei winced when asked: "You speak English well; how long have you been in this country?"[71]

The Nisei also experienced difficulty finding jobs in the mainstream economy. Generally, Japanese Americans graduated from high school with good grades, even honors, and many had completed college. The average educational level of the Nisei was two years of college, well above the national average. Still they found themselves denied employment opportunities in the larger economy. Many came of age during the Depression—a time of massive unemployment in the country. Job possibilities were especially limited for them because of racial discrimination. A study of 161 Nisei who graduated from the University of California between 1925 and 1935 found that only 25 percent were employed in professional vocations for which they had been trained. Twenty-five percent worked in family businesses or trades that did not require a college education, and 40 percent had "blind alley" jobs. In Los Angeles, the vast majority of Nisei worked in small Japanese shops, laundries, hotels, fruit stands, and produce stores. "I am a fruitstand worker," a Nisei explained. "It is not a very attractive nor distinguished occupation. I would much rather it were doctor or lawyer...but my aspirations of developing into such [were] frustrated long ago by circumstances [and] I am only what I am, a professional carrot washer."[72]

To grow up Japanese American was to feel a sense of twoness, an experience described by Monica Sone in her autobiography, *Nisei Daughter*. As a child living with her family in Seattle, she was surrounded by a cultural duality. She ate pickled *daikon* and rice as well as ham and eggs. Monica played games like *jan-ken-po* and jacks, and studied Japanese *odori* dance and ballet. To be Japanese, Monica learned, involved an identity with Japan. Seattle's Japanese celebrated *Tenchosetsu*, the emperor's birthday, shouting *banzai, banzai, banzai* and singing "Kimi Gayo," the Japanese national anthem. They would attend sumo wrestling matches and performances of Japanese classical plays. Every June, Seattle's Japanese held a community gathering—the *Nihon Gakko* picnic where they played games, sang *naniya bushi* songs, danced, and stuffed themselves with sushi, barbecued teriyaki meats, and *musubi* rice balls.[73]

Monica knew she was not just Japanese. While she enjoyed many of the activities of her parents, she was also being a kid in American society. She was a member of the Mickey Mouse Club, which met every Saturday morning at the Coliseum Theater. "We sang Mickey Mouse songs," she recalled, "we saw Mickey Mouse pictures, we wore Mickey Mouse sweaters, we owned Mickey Mouse wrist watches."[74]

As she grew up, Monica found that the Japanese were not welcome in America. She heard whites call her father "Shorty" and "Jap." Even the second-generation Japanese, Monica painfully noticed, were denied a claim to the land of their birth. As a teenager, she drove out to the country with some friends to swim at the Antler's Lodge. But the manager blocked their entrance, saying, "Sorry, we don't want any Japs around here." "We're not Japs. We're American citizens," the angry teenagers yelled as they sped away in their car.[75]

The most anxious problem Monica and her fellow Nisei faced

was employment discrimination. Their job prospects seemed dim. "A future here! Bah!" exploded one of her father's friends. "How many sons of ours with a beautiful bachelor's degree are accepted into American life? Men with degrees in chemistry and physics do research in the fruit stands of the public market. And they all rot away inside." After graduation from high school, Monica applied for secretarial training at Washington State Vocational School and was told by the counselor: "We are accepting six of you Japanese-American girls this year. I don't want you to think that we are discriminating against people of your ancestry, but from our past experiences, we have found it next to impossible to find jobs for you in the business offices downtown."[76]

The problem for Monica Sone and her fellow Nisei went far beyond the mere matter of jobs. It was profoundly cultural, involving the very definition of who was an American. Deep in their hearts, Nisei did not wish to be completely assimilated, to become simply "American." They felt they were a complex combination of the two cultures, and they wanted to embrace their dual identity. But their hope to be both Japanese and American would be violently shattered on a December morning in 1941.

11

❦

THE EXODUS FROM RUSSIA

Pushed by Pogroms

ALIBAN COULD ALSO have been Jewish. In Russia, Jews were degraded as the "Other." Coming from a different shore than the Japanese, they began their migration to America during the 1880s. A persecuted ethnic minority, they were forced to leave as settlers rather than sojourners; unlike the Japanese immigrants, they felt they could not return to their homeland. In an important sense, they were political refugees. "The government itself had set off the pogroms in order to save the throne from a revolutionary upheaval," observed immigrant Abraham Cahan. "By making the Jews the scapegoats, it had confused the common people so that in the end the peasants were certain that the Jews and not the Czar were the cause of their troubles." Almost everywhere, government officials encouraged acts of violence against Jews.[1]

The repression in Russia was pervasive. Jews were required to live in the Pale of Settlement, a region stretching from the Baltic to the Black Sea. "Within this area the Czar commanded me to stay, with my father and mother and friends, and all other people like us." recalled Mary Antin, who emigrated to America in the 1890s. "We must not be found outside the Pale, because we were Jews." Special borders contained them; like Caliban, they had been "styed." Prohibited from owning land, most Jews were forced to live in the urban areas where they earned their livelihoods as merchants and artisans. In 1879, 38 percent of the Jews were employed in manufacturing or crafts, 32 percent in commerce, and only 3 percent in agriculture. Their concentration in crafts made many of them especially vulnerable. "It was not easy to live, with such bitter competition as the congestion of the population made inevitable," an immigrant explained. "There were ten times as many stores as there should have been, ten times as many tailors, cobblers, barbers, tinsmiths. A Gentile, if he failed in Polotzk, could go elsewhere, where there was less competition. A Jew could make the circle of the Pale, only to find the same conditions as at home."[2]

Life in the shtetls, Jewish towns and villages, was also intensely insecure, for anti-Semitic violence was a ubiquitous reality. Especially dreaded were the pogroms—massacres of Jews and the destruction of their shops and synagogues. "I feel that every cobblestone in Russia is filled with Jewish blood," an immigrant bitterly recalled. "Absolutely every year, there was a *pogrom* before *Pesach* [Passover]. In big cities during the *pogroms*, they used any reason to get rid of you. As many Jews as they could kill, they did; but there were some Gentiles who would save you. We survived because Pa was a *gildikupets* [merchant] and knew many wealthy Gentiles. But he was hurt many times." Golda Meir never forgot the persecution her family experienced: "We lived then on the first floor of a small house in Kiev, and I can still recall distinctly hearing about a pogrom that was to descend on us. I didn't know then, of course, what a pogrom was, but I knew it had something to do with being Jewish and with the rabble that used to surge through town, brandishing knives and huge sticks, screaming 'Christ killers' as they looked for the Jews, and who were now going to do terrible things to me and to my family." Similarly, Mollie Linker was only a child when her father left Russia: "I remember sitting by the window...and looking out. When it got dark, you closed the shutters, you were afraid. You were actually always in fear because of big *pogroms*.... I remember that scare...was in us all the time." The pogroms, observed Abraham Cahan, forced Jews to realize that "Russia was not their homeland and that a true home must be found for Jews. But where?"[3]

Spreading from shtetl to shtetl across Russia, a song pointed the way:

> As the Russians, mercilessly
> Took revenge on us.

There is a land, America,
Where everyone lives free....[4]

By the beginning of World War I, one-third of all Jews in Russia and eastern Europe had emigrated, most of them to the United States. America had caught their "fancy." Stories about freedom and a better life there were "buzzing" all around them. The distant land was viewed as a "Garden of Eden," "the golden land," where Jews would no longer be enslaved by "dead drudgery." The cry "To America!" roared like "wild-fire." "America was in everybody's mouth. Businessmen talked of it over their accounts; the market women made up their quarrels that they might discuss it from stall to stall; people who had relatives in the famous land went around reading their letters." At a sewing school in Minsk, Jewish girls received letters from America describing astonishingly high wages—the starting pay for a seamstress in New York was four dollars a week, a sum equal to a month's earnings in rubles. In Abraham Cahan's autobiographical novel, David Levinsky was seized by this emigration fever: "It was one of these letters from America, in fact, which put the notion of emigrating to the New World definitely in my mind. An illiterate woman brought it to the synagogue to have it read to her, and I happened to be the one to whom she addressed her request. The concrete details of that letter gave New York tangible form in my imagination. It haunted me ever after." While reading a letter from her father who had gone to America ahead of his family, Mary Antin felt "a stirring, a straining." "It was there, even though my mother stumbled over strange words.... My father was inspired by a vision. He saw something—he promised us something. It was this 'America.' And 'America' became my dream." In her dream, America became the Promised Land.[5]

Hopeful possibilities exploded in their heads. Fannie Edelman wanted to escape to America where she could "fall in love and marry." "I was fourteen years old when I heard that people were leaving for the United States," she recalled. "I used to think of running away from our little town and from my severe father and coming to a free world called America." Another young woman, after deciding she wanted to emigrate, had difficulty eating and sleeping: "I was fighting to death for the money to go to America. I used to see the people going to the train to leave. I used to envy those people like anything. They said, 'You'll get married and then you'll go to America.' I says, 'I need a shlepper [a dragger] to America? I can shlep myself!' Who didn't want to go to America?" The country also offered educational opportunities. "I heard so much about America as a free country for the Jews," said Fannie Shapiro, "and you...didn't have to pay for schooling, so I came." Children "played at emigrating," and a mother's lullaby told children:

> Your daddy's in America
> Little son of mine
> But you are just a child now
> So hush and go to sleep.
> America is for everyone
> They say, it's the greatest piece of luck
> For Jews, it's a garden of Eden
> A rare and precious place.
> People there eat challah
> In the middle of the week.[6]

Their fears of persecution and their extravagant dreams gave them the courage to uproot themselves and leave their birthplace forever. On the streets of the shtetl, Jewish women sold their beds, chairs, kitchen tables, and other belongings in order to raise money for transportation to America. Taking only their personal possessions, Jews left familiar little towns with their cobbled streets and alleys, their smells and sounds of crowded and colorful marketplaces. "The last I saw of Polotzk was an agitated mass of people, waving handkerchiefs and other frantic bits of calico, madly gesticulating, falling on each other's necks, gone wild altogether," recalled an immigrant. "Then the station became invisible." Another explained that when he left Velizh, he had not realized that he was starting such a long journey: "This was the point at which I was cutting myself off from my past, from those I loved. Would I ever see them again?"[7]

As they boarded the ships, the voyagers "were all herded together in a dark, filthy compartment in the steerage." "We learned that our vessel had formerly been a cattle ship and had just been converted into a passenger boat," Alexander Harkavy wrote. "Our compartment was enormously large, and wooden bunks had been put up in two tiers, one on top of the other." The passengers felt the engine's vibrations and smelled the "choking, salty odor." As often as possible, they went up on deck, especially to see the sunset. "But as the wonderful colors sank with the sun, [their] hearts would fill with a terrible longing for home. Then [they] would draw together and sing Russian folk songs filled with nostalgia and yearning." The sea was stormy and the ship rocked, remembered Samuel Cohen. "I kept tossing about. I stuck my head out of the bunk a little. A shower of vomit came down from the upper bunk on my face."[8]

At night, the passengers thought about the world that they had left behind and the new one that awaited them. They had embarked on an exodus. "Every emigrating Jew moving westward realized he was involved in something more than a personal expedition," said Abraham Cahan. "Every Jew...came to feel that he was part of a historic event in the life of the Jewish people." Jews were a "countryless people." Their migration to America seemed to be a continuation of a journey that had begun thousands of years earlier in Egypt, for as historian Irving Howe explained, "the events of Jewish life were divided in two endless days, the Biblical yesterday and the exile of today."[9]

Finally, after a long Atlantic crossing, the passengers sighted land. The moment was a deeply moving experience for Cahan's David Levinsky: "When the ship reached Sandy Hook [New Jersey] I was literally overcome with the beauty of the landscape. The immigrant's arrival in his new home is like a second birth to him." Levinsky stood breathless before "the magnificent verdure of Staten Island, the tender blue of sea and sky, the dignified bustle of passing craft." In a trance, he excitedly murmured: "This, then, is America!" "Everybody was on deck," recalled Emma Goldman, who was only seventeen years old when she arrived. "[My sister] Helena and I stood pressed to each other, enraptured by the sight of the harbor and the Statue of Liberty suddenly emerging from the mist. Ah, there she was, the symbol of hope, of freedom, of opportunity!" After a long voyage in a packed steerage of seasick people, a Polish girl climbed to the deck and saw "the big beautiful bay and the big woman with the spikes on her head and the lamp that [was] lighted at night in her hand." Suddenly, the passengers began shouting, "Ellis Island." Their bodies leaned forward, and their hands gripped the railing of the ship as they saw the immigration station.[10]

Who were they, these newcomers searching for a door to America? "The immigrants who had been forced to abandon their homes in Eastern Europe were a hardy lot," declared Gilbert Klaperman in *The Story of Yeshiva.* "With rare exceptions, they arrived penniless and inadequately trained in a profession or handicraft. They did possess, however, indomitable faith in themselves and unflagging courage to face all difficulties. They dug their roots deep into the alien soil until it became home to them. They founded families and raised children and children's children who enriched America with invaluable contributions. This immigrant generation of the post-1881 decades may be called, indeed, the heroic generation."[11]

Actually, these Jewish immigrants were a highly select group. They were educated: 80 percent of the men and 63 percent of the women who came between 1908 and 1912 were literate. While most of them were poor, they were not "inadequately trained in a profession or handicraft." Two-thirds of the Jews specifying an occupation were skilled workers, compared to only 16 percent of the Italians. But, as Klaperman correctly noted, the Jews came to America as settlers. Unlike most other European immigrant groups, they planned to stay. Sixty percent of the southern Italian migrants returned to their homeland, whereas the return rate for Jews was only 3 percent. Significantly, Jews emigrated mainly as families. Almost half of them were women, compared to only about 20 percent for southern Italians. Children represented one out of every four Jews. These immigrants saw themselves as exiles, unable to return to Russia as long as religious persecution persisted. The Jews had to make America their new home.[12]

A Shtetl in America

From Ellis Island, most of the immigrants headed for New York City's Lower East Side. During the early nineteenth century, German Jews had settled in this area. A new Jewish community blossomed as massive waves of Russian Jews began arriving in the 1880s; by 1905, the Lower East Side had a population of a half-million Jews. Unlike the mostly "bachelor" community of nearby Chinatown, the Jewish colony had throngs of children.

The laughter of children joined "a symphony of discordant noises" filling the air. Pushcarts lined the streets, and a cacophony of Yiddish voices, "a continual roar," rose from the crowds. "Shopkeepers grabbed the arms of passers-by and with torrents of cajolery endeavored to pull them inside their stores, cursing those who had escaped their clutching hands." In this colony, Jews seemed to be living just like they had in Russia: they resided and worked "within that small compass, meeting only people of their own nationality." Rose Cohen found that the Lower East Side was

like living in "practically the same environment" as in the homeland. It was as though "we were still in our village in Russia."[13]
But the ethnic enclave of the Lower East Side was also different in significant ways. There was an "American atmosphere of
breathless enterprise and breakneck speed." Crowds of people
were on "the streets, shouting, going in all directions." Life did
not seem "normal," for "everybody was in a hurry and money was
the main thing in life." The "scurry and hustle of the people" were
"overwhelmingly greater, both in volume and intensity," than in
the native towns of their homeland. They seemed like "a new race
in the world." Pent up in the old country, their energies were being
unleashed in this new land of boundlessness. The "swing and
step of the pedestrians, the voices and manner of the street peddlers," seemed to testify to far "more self-confidence and energy,
to larger ambitions and wider scopes, than did the appearance of
the crowds" back home.[14]

The colony was also a ghetto. At the turn of the century, the
Lower East Side was the most densely populated section of the
city. Walking the streets during warm evenings, pedestrians
found all the windows open and were able to see "the life inside
with all its filth and sadness. Bare, scarred tables. Countless beds,
with tangled sheets and blankets. The yellow gaslight, and so
many, many children, and nakedness and noise." The tenth ward,
located in the Jewish colony, housed over five hundred people per
acre; on Rivington Street, a contemporary reported, "the archi-
tecture seemed to sweat humanity at every window and door."[15]

The residents were just trying to find sunlight and fresh air,
to escape from the dark and stifling interiors of the "dumbbell"
tenements. Six to seven stories in height, this type of apartment
resembled a dumbbell: on every floor there were two apartments
at each end connected by a hallway. A narrow, five-foot-wide air
shaft separated the buildings. A window facing the street or a
small backyard offered the only direct light for each apartment.
Writing for the *American Magazine* in 1888, a journalist described
these dumbbell tenements:

> They are great prison-like structures of brick, with narrow doors
> and windows, cramped passages and steep rickety stairs. They are
> built through from one street to the other with a somewhat nar-
> rower building connecting them.... The narrow court-yard...in
> the middle is a damp foul-smelling place, supposed to do duty as
> an airshaft; had the foul fiend designed these great barracks they

could not have been more villainously arranged to avoid any chance of ventilation....In case of fire they would be perfect death-traps, for it would be impossible for the occupants of the crowded rooms to escape by the narrow stairways, and the flimsy fire-escapes...are so laden with broken furniture, bales and boxes that they would be worse than useless. In the hot summer months...these fire-escape balconies are used as sleeping-rooms by the poor wretches who are fortunate enough to have windows opening upon them.[16]

Typically, each apartment was packed with people, family members, and also boarders. "At the hour of retiring," a witness told the United States Immigration Commission, "cots or folded beds and in many instances simply mattresses are spread about the floor, resembling very much a lot of bunks in the steerage of an ocean steamer." A 1908 survey of 250 Lower East Side families found that about 50 percent slept three or four persons to a room, and nearly 25 percent had five or more persons. Most of the tenements lacked baths. "I cannot get along without a 'sweat' [Russian bath] at least once a week," an immigrant complained. Occupants competed to use the toilet: each tenement had only two facilities for each floor. "A five-story house of this character contain[ed] apartments for eighteen or twenty families," counted Jacob Riis in the 1890s, "a population frequently amounting to 100 people, and sometimes increased by boarders and lodgers to 150 or more."[17]

To escape from the confinement of the tenements, the immigrants would retreat to the park. "On hot summer nights [we would] seek relief from the heat in Jackson Street Park," one of them remembered. "The park, innocent of grass and trees, was a large area close to the East River, with many lanes of benches... and a stone pavilion like a Greek temple, where a small band occasionally played and milk was dispensed at a penny a glass. The park was always crowded. The men were in their undershirts. The women, more fully dressed, carried newspapers for fans. Hordes of barefoot children played games, weaving in and out of the always thick mass of promenaders."[18]

As they settled in the Lower East Side, the Jews began to establish organizations and create community. They formed networks or lodges, *landsmanshafts,* composed of people from the same town or district in Russia, seeking the company of friends from *di alte heym,* "the old home village." They also found community and conversation in the public bathhouses as well as in the neighborhood delicatessens and candy stores that had become gathering places. In cafés like Schreibers on Canal Street and Café Royale on Second Avenue, Jewish intellectuals drank tea as they debated philosophical and political issues before rushing off to hear lectures regularly presented by the Educational Alliance and the People's Institute at Cooper Union. "There were scores of lectures every week," said Marcus Ravage. "One night it was Darwin and the next it might be the principle of air pressure. On a Saturday night there were sometimes two meetings so arranged that both could be attended by the same audience." Others preferred the movie theaters, where for five cents they could watch a half-hour film. "If it's not too busy, you can see it several times," an immigrant said. "They open at one in the afternoon, and customers, mostly women and children, gossip, eat fruit and nuts, and have a good time."[19]

Everywhere outside the cafés and theaters, there were peddlers. Carrying packs or pushing carts, they knocked on doors and cajoled housewives to buy their goods. Shortly after Isaac Raboy arrived at Ellis Island, he found himself on Delancey Street, where peddlers were hawking their wares as they pushed their carts filled with "exotic" things. Streams of people flowed down the streets. "Suspenders, collah buttons, 'lastic, matches, hankeches—please, lady, buy," peddlers shouted. "Bandannas and tin cups at two cents, peaches at a cent a quart, damaged eggs for a song, hats for a quarter, and spectacles warranted to suit the eye...for thirty-five cents." A contemporary observed: "There are few more pathetic sights than an old man with a long beard, a little black cap on his head and a venerable face—a man who had been perhaps a Hebraic or Talmudic scholar in the old country...standing for sixteen hours a day by his push-cart in one of the dozen crowded streets of the Ghetto...selling...apples, garden stuff, fish and second-hand shirts."[20]

The Jewish peddler soon became a figure of Jewish-American folklore. In one of Anzia Yezierska's stories, Gedalyeh Mindel wrote to his family: "My sun is beginning to shine in America. I am becoming a person—a businessman. I have for myself a stand in the most crowded part of America, where...every day is like market day by a fair. My business is from bananas and apples. The day begins with my pushcart full of fruit, and the day never ends before I count up at least two dollars' profit—that means...four rubles a day, twenty-four rubles a week!...White bread and meat I eat every day just like the millionaires." Historian Moses Rischin noted that "the peddler's pack...provided the most direct introduction to American ways, the most promising school for the study of the country's speech, tastes and economic needs, and the broadest field for the play of the aspiring tradesman's imagination." The peddler personified the transformation of the Jewish immigrant from scholar to salesman.[21]

This journey was described in Cahan's novel. An old man who had been a Talmudic scholar in Russia found that his wife was not willing to support him in America. Insisting that he go out and peddle, she snapped: "America is not Russia. A man must make a living here." The husband told David Levinsky: "America is a topsy-turvy country." A quick learner, Levinsky abandoned his dream of becoming a scholar and turned to peddling: "I rented a push-cart and tried to sell remnants of dress-goods, linen, and oil cloth.... I would announce to the passers-by the glad news that I had struck a miraculous bargain at a wholesale bankruptcy sale...and exhort them not to miss their golden opportunity." In this way, Levinsky began his "rise."[22]

But while Jewish peddlers appeared ubiquitous, they actually represented only a very small proportion of working Jews. A survey of gainfully employed Jews living in New York City in 1890 revealed that only 10 percent were peddlers. On the other hand, 60 percent worked in the garment industry.[23]

In the Sweatshops: An Army of Garment Workers

For the Jewish "rise" in America, what mattered more than a frenetic entrepreneurial spirit was the fact that many Jewish immigrants brought something useful—their skills, especially in the sewing trades. "I am a tailor," recalled an immigrant years later at the age of eighty-two, "and I was working piecework on Russian officers' uniforms. I saved up a few dollars and figured the best thing was to go to the U.S.A. Those days everybody's dream in the old country was to go to America. We heard people were free and we heard about better living."[24]

The arrival of these skilled immigrants was timely, for they were needed in New York's expanding garment industry. In earlier times, clothes had been tailor-made, but the Civil War had transformed garment manufacturing. In order to meet the Union Army's demand for clothing, tailors established uniform standards and measurements. This innovation enabled them to mass-produce garments in factories, utilizing new inventions such as the Singer sewing machine, the electric cutting knife, and the but-tonhole machine. Between 1880 and 1890, the number of men's clothing factories doubled from 736 to 1,554, and women's cloak factories tripled from 236 to 740. The center of this growing new industry was New York City. Between 1880 and 1910, the number of clothing factories jumped from 10 percent of the city's factories to 47 percent, and garment workers from 28 percent to almost half of its industrial workers.[25]

German Jews had initially dominated the garment industry. Having come to America earlier, many of them had established themselves economically and socially by the time of the great Jewish migration from Russia. German-Jewish firms like Blumenthal Brothers, Kuppenheimers, and Hart, Schaffner & Marx were prominent in clothing manufacturing. Gradually, many Jewish newcomers from Russia became contractors and manufacturers themselves. Together, the German and Russian Jewish garment makers revolutionized the way clothes were made and what Americans wore. In his novel, Cahan described this triumph: "Foreigners ourselves, and mostly unable to speak English, we had Americanized the system of providing clothes for the American woman of moderate or humble means." The Jewish garment makers had democratized dress in America, offering the masses machine-made classy clothes. They had done away with "prohibitive prices and greatly improved the popular taste. Indeed, the Russian Jew had made the average American girl 'a tailor-made' girl."[26]

The Jewish garment makers transformed the Lower East Side into a huge, spreading industrial beehive. On the Second Avenue elevated train, a passenger could ride half a mile through the sweater district. "Every open window of the big tenements, that [stood] like a continuous brick wall on both sides of the way, [gave] you a glimpse of one of these shops.... Men and women bending over their machines or ironing clothes at the window, half-naked. Morning, noon, or night, it made no difference." From block after block of sweatshops came the "whir of a thousand sewing-machines, worked at high pressure from the earliest dawn till mind and muscle [gave] out together."[27]

In 1914, about 60 percent of the businesses were small shops, employing fewer than thirty workers. Contractors did not need much capital, only about $50, to start shops with foot-power machines. Once their workers and machines were in place, they could bid for contracts from the manufacturers. Buyers provided cloth to the contractors and paid as little as possible for the finished clothes "The shop was not the manufacturer's," wrote Cahan, describing the place where Levinsky worked. "It belonged to one of his contractors, who received from him 'bundles' of material which his employees...made up into cloaks or jackets. The cheaper goods were made entirely by operators; the better grades partly by tailors, partly by operators, or wholly by tailors; but these were mostly made 'inside,' in the manufacturer's own establishment." The nature of the industry pushed both workers and contractors. The laborers dared not stop working, "knowing that there were plenty of other men ready instantly to take their places," journalist Ray Stannard Baker explained; "and the contractor, himself the victim of frightful competition and the tool of the manufacturer, always playing upon their ready fears, always demanding a swifter pace, forced the price constantly downward."[28]

To increase production, many contractors used the task system, assigning a quota to a team of ten or twenty workers—family members, boarders, or *lanslite,* neighbors from the old country. They worked as a unit, with specific tasks assigned to a sewing-machine operator, a baster, a presser, and a finisher. A team received a group wage based on the number of garments produced, with each member paid a certain percentage. This system drove everyone on the team, for each worker wanted to increase the pace of production for the group. "The highest speed of one was in substance made the minimum speed of others," an immigrant worker explained, "since no man could get ahead in his work without his fellow workmen keeping the same speed in the productive formation." Larger shops employed the "section" system of production: work was subdivided into several steps, and workers performed one task repeatedly. This system reduced skilled tailors and seamstresses to assembly-line workers. "When I came here," complained Bella Feiner, "I knew more than I know now. I knew how to make a whole dress." But this fragmentation of production also opened employment to unskilled immigrants. "The foreman asked me what I could do," remembered Lottie Spitzer. "And I said, 'I don't know anything.' In fact, I couldn't even handle a needle. But he taught me and [soon] I was basting sleeve linings."[29]

In the sweatshops, the work was physically punishing. The section system gave the bosses power to set the pace of their workers, who sat in long rows with their "bodies bent over the machines."

Each person completed an assigned task and then passed her part of the garment to the next worker on the line, while the foreman nagged them to hurry. "Most of them smoke cigarettes while they work," observed a contemporary; "beer and cheap whiskey are brought in several times a day by a peddler. Some sing Yiddish songs—while they race. The women chat and laugh sometimes—while they race." But many women were forced to work silently. "We were like slaves. You couldn't pick your head up. You couldn't talk. We used to go to the bathroom. The forelady used to go after us, we shouldn't stay too long."[30]

"The machines were all in a row. And it was so hot, not even a decent fan. And you...worked, and you sweated. Windows were open, of course; flies too. You had a little half hour for lunch (we worked close to ten hours). And you talked. But you were kept so busy and the machines were roaring.... You had to be careful not to stitch your fingers in." Accidents did happen. "The machines go like mad all day, because the faster you work the more money you get. Sometimes in my haste, I get my finger caught and the needle goes right through it. It goes so quick, though, that it does not hurt much. I bind the finger up with a piece of cotton and go on working.... Where the needle goes through the nail it makes a sore finger, or where it splinters a bone it does much harm."[31]

The long hours and the repetitious stitching made workers feel like appendages of their sewing machines. "You don't have to think," said Mollie Wexler, who worked in a dress factory. All you have to do is "pin together and put together," "just sit and shoot like the machine itself." Anzia Yezierska related a story about a young Jewish woman who had "dreamed of free schools, free colleges" where she could learn to give out her "innermost thoughts and feelings" to the world. But no sooner had she come off the ship than hunger drove her to the sweatshop, "to become a 'hand'—not a brain—not a soul—not a spirit—but just a 'hand'—cramped, deadened into a part of the machine." A Yiddish poet described the numbness workers felt as they toiled, trapped in the sweatshops:

> *I work, and I work, without rhyme, without reason*
> *produce, and produce, and produce without end.*
> *For what? and for whom? I don't know, I don't wonder*
> *since when can a whirling machine comprehend?*
>
> *No feelings, no thoughts, not the least understanding;*
> *this bitter, this murderous drudgery drains*

the noblest, the finest, the best and the richest,
the deepest, the highest that living contains.

Away rush the seconds, the minutes and hours;
each day and each night like a wind-driven sail;
I drive the machine, as though eager to catch them,
I drive without reason — no hope, no avail.[32]

The workday was long, from eleven to fifteen hours. "My work was sewing on buttons. While the morning was still dark I walked into a dark basement. And darkness met me when I turned out of the basement." The workers had to wait until night to begin living. "At the end of the day one feels so weak that there is a great temptation to lie right down and sleep," said a seamstress. "But you must go out and get air, and have some pleasure.... Sometimes we go to Coney Island, where there are good dancing places, and sometimes we go to Ulmer Park to picnics. I am very fond of dancing, and, in fact, all sorts of pleasure."[33]

Daughters of the Colony

Thousands of these garment workers were young women. Many of them had come first, before their families. "In growing numbers," observed historian Susan A. Glenn, "Jewish families were willing and found it practicable to send one or more children including their working-age daughters, in advance." What made it "practicable" to send them ahead was the fact that many possessed sewing skills. In the Pale of Settlement in the 1890s, over fifty thousand Jewish women worked in the sewing trades, constituting 70 percent of all registered female artisans. The first sewing machines had been introduced in Russia two decades earlier, and the Singer sewing machine came to symbolize a guarantee of a good livelihood. Fannie Shapiro recalled that in each small Russian town there were little shops where "two, three, four, or five girls in a house, [were] working, making dresses and things. And they had a Singer's, a sewing machine." Girls reaching the age of thirteen were usually apprenticed to a seamstress. One of them, Sarah Rozner, had to work hard to learn how to operate the sewing machine: "I finally got it, and believe me it helped a lot when I came to this country."[34]

In America, most of the young Jewish women working in the garment industry were single, planning to work for a few years before marriage. One of them told an interviewer: "Henry has seen me home every night for a long time and makes love to me. He wants me to marry him, but I am not seventeen yet, and I think that is too young.... Lately he has been urging me more and more to get married—but I think I'll wait." In 1910, over 70 percent of the Jewish daughters sixteen years old or over were working for wages. "Right after Passover, I entered school," remembered one of them. "When school was out in June, I knew I couldn't go back any more, so coming home I cried all the way....My father had a job for me. I couldn't do any thing—at that age, you know, you couldn't work till you were sixteen, but kids worked at fourteen and thirteen."[35]

Constituting over one-third of the garment industry's workforce in 1910, these young women labored in dangerous and cramped conditions. In the sweatshops, they were literally packed together. On floor after floor, they worked elbow to elbow at sewing machines on row after row of long tables. "We are so crowded together that there is not an inch of space," they complained. "The machines are so close together that there is no way to escape in case of immergansie."[36]

An emergency did happen on March 26, 1911, when a fire suddenly exploded at the Triangle Shirtwaist Company. Eight hundred workers, mostly young women, were trapped in the burning building. "A stream of fire tore up through the elevator shaft and stairways to the upper floors. Fire instantly appeared at all windows, and tongues of flames crept higher and higher along the walls to where little groups of terrified girls, workers, stood in confusion." Screaming, struggling, they jumped from windows, some from the ninth floor, their bodies smashing on the sidewalks. "One girl after another fell, like shot birds, from above, from the burning floors," wrote Morris Rosenfeld in his account based on eyewitness reports. "They hit the pavement just like hail," a fireman at the scene reported. "We could hear the thuds faster than we could [see] the bodies fall." Jumping from the higher floors, the girls came down with such force that they tore the nets from the grasps of firemen or snapped the cords. Unable to escape, 146 young workers—mostly Jewish and Italian—died in the smoke and heat of the inferno. There were so many bodies they could not all be taken away in ambulances and patrol wagons; grocers and peddlers offered their wagons and pushcarts.[37]

Mothers rushed to the scene, where they saw the blackened

bodies of their daughters laid out on the sidewalks. Tearing their hair, they screamed: *"Oy vey, kindenyu!"* "Oy vey, my child!" "For a piece of bread, a terrible death, robbed me of my only child." "My little girl lies dead, shrouds instead of a wedding gown." The tragedy stunned the colony: fifty thousand people marched silently in a mass memorial parade to grieve for their dead daughters. The charred bodies were buried together in the Workmen's Circle Cemetery.

> *Over whom shall we weep first?*
> *Over the burned ones?*
> *Over those beyond recognition?*
> *Over those who have been crippled?*
> *Or driven senseless?*
> *Or smashed?...*
> *This is our funeral,*
> *These our graves,*
> *Our children....*[38]

News of the horror rapidly spread to the shtetls of Russia. "I still remember what a panic that news caused in our town when it first came," said Elizabeth Hasanovitz. "Many a family had their young daughters in all parts of the United States who worked in shops. And as most of these old parents had an idea of America as one big town, each of them was almost sure that their daughter was a victim of that terrible catastrophe." In his description of the grisly scene, a reporter wrote: "I looked upon the dead bodies and I remembered these girls were the shirtwaist makers. I remembered their great strike of last year in which the same girls had demanded more sanitary conditions and more safety precautions in the shops. Their dead bodies were the answer."[39]

Indeed, many of the dead women had gone out on strike in 1909–10, participating in the famous "uprising of twenty thousand." In July, a spontaneous strike had erupted at Rosen Brothers, and then in September at Leiserson's and the Triangle Shirtwaist Factory. The striking women asked for assistance from the Ladies' Waist Makers Union Local 25. With only a hundred dues-paying members and four dollars in its treasury, Local 25 appealed to the International Ladies' Garment Workers' Union, requesting a call for a general strike in the shirtwaist industry. But the ILGWU, founded in 1909, had only a few thousand members and lacked the resources to mobilize such a massive action.

The power to do so had to come from the people themselves. On the night of November 22, 1909, thousands of workers crowded into the Cooper Union to attend a mass meeting organized by the striking women. They had come to demonstrate their support for the strikers and to denounce the intransigence of the bosses and the brutality inflicted against the picketers by hired thugs and the police. In the packed hall, their bodies restless and taut with anger, they heard speaker after speaker advise them to be patient and act cautiously. Frustrated by the urgings of restraint, a fragile-looking teenager suddenly rushed to the platform. "I am a working girl," Clara Lemlich declared in Yiddish, "one of those striking against intolerable conditions." The charismatic leader passionately articulated the pent-up feelings of the audience. She compared the abuse of the garment workers to the experience of blacks: "[The bosses] yell at the girls and 'call them down' even worse than I imagine the Negro slaves were in the South." She urged action: "I am tired of listening to speakers who talk in generalities. What we are here for is to decide whether or not to strike. I offer a resolution that a general strike be declared—now." Her brave words and her call to action touched off a thunderous applause. Meeting chairman Benjamin Feigenbaum jumped to the platform and joined hands with Lemlich. Their arms held high together, he asked the crowd in Yiddish to support her call for a general strike, framing it as a Jewish struggle: "Do you mean faith? Will you take the old Jewish Oath?" Aroused, the people raised their right hands and pledged: "If I turn traitor to the cause I now pledge, may this hand wither from the arm I now raise." The next morning, fifteen thousand shirtwaist workers were on strike.[40]

"The East Side was a seething mass of excited women, girls, and men." Strikers attending packed meeting halls spilled out into the streets. "All over the East Side a sea of excited faces, a mass of gesticulating women and men, blocked the streets." "Vast crowds" were "wildly demonstrative," marching through the streets and breaking into "storms of applause as the word that another boss had settled with the strikers was passed along." The strikers swelled in numbers, to over twenty thousand; they were overwhelmingly Jewish, with Italian women constituting about 6 percent. The demands of the strikers included a fifty-two-hour workweek, overtime pay, and union recognition.[41]

As they picketed, the strikers were arrested by the police and beaten by thugs. Still, according to one contemporary, "neither the police, nor the hooligan hirelings of the bosses nor the biting frost and chilling snow of December and January dampened their willingness to picket the shops from early morn till late at night."

In the black winter of 1909
When we froze and bled on the picket line
We showed the world that women could fight
And we rose and we won with women's might.

Hail the waist makers of 1909
Making their stand on the picket line
Breaking the power of those who reign
Pointing the way and smashing the chain.

The courageous strikers impressed the community: they were proudly described as "*unzere vunderbare farbrente meydlekh,*" "our wonderful fervent girls." The strike was powerful, intimidating, and by February, more than 300 of the some 450 firms in the New York industry had been forced to make some kind of settlement.[42]

Several months later, another strike exploded as fifty thousand cloak and suit workers walked off their jobs. The strikers wanted higher wages, a forty-nine-hour workweek, and a "closed shop," the hiring of union members only. Both sides reached an agreement in September with the signing of a "Protocol of Peace." Among the gains the workers received were a fifty-hour workweek, wage increases, and preferential hiring for union members.[43]

These labor struggles represented a watershed in Jewish-American history. They initiated "a decade of labor unrest in the garment trades," noted historian Susan A. Glenn. "Between 1909 and 1920 a wave of strikes and mass organizational campaigns swept through the garment trades, changing a largely unorganized industry into a union stronghold.... By the end of World War I clothing workers were among the best-organized members of the American labor force." The International Ladies' Garments Workers' Union had one hundred thousand dues-paying members in 1920, and one hundred seventy thousand workers belonged to the Amalgamated Clothing Workers of America.[44]

These labor triumphs had ethnic as well as class significance. In their struggles, the workers had created a broadly based radical Jewish consciousness. "Until now there had been no more than a large scattering of Jewish immigrant workers who would sometimes cohere for a fierce outbreak and then crumble into isolated persons," Irving Howe noted. "The Jewish community in the United States was not really a Jewish community," remarked leftist Paul Novick, "it was just something in fermentation until the labor movement came along." The strikes were "Jewish" strikes: the workers received support and sustenance from the Jewish community. Jewish neighborhood organizations donated food and clothing, and Jewish shopkeepers allowed striking workers and families to purchase goods on credit. "The major topics most frequently bantered about concerned the union meetings and sometimes... strikes in the needle trades in which everyone worked," an immigrant remembered. The "uprisings" of this era sharpened a shared sense of ethnicity, an immigrant Jewish identity in America.[45]

Up from "Greenhorns": Crossing Delancey Street

The Jews had come to make new homes in America, and their strikes had given them a sense of belonging to the new land. They were making a claim on their adopted country and demanding wages that would allow them to enjoy America's bounties. Their labor struggles, while springing from ethnic solidarity, were also transforming them from "greenhorns" into Americans.

"Oysgrinen zikh," Jewish immigrants said to themselves; "Don't be a greenhorn." When they arrived in America, they were foreigners in their dress, language, and thinking. "I just didn't know how to cope with it all," a Jewish immigrant recalled. "I was unhappy because I didn't know anything, and I was frightened.... When they used to call me names like 'greenhorn,' I felt that I would rather die than hear it again."[46]

The passion to become American was reflected in one of the most frequently asked questions in the Lower East Side: "How long have you been in America?" How long was measured by their degree of assimilation. The Jewish immigrants began learning American ways in a process they called "purification." To become American meant to acquire "civility"—a quality of middle-class refinement in behavior and tastes. According to scholar John Cuddihy, they had been driven by the pogroms in Russia "out of their Middle Ages into the Anglo-American world of the *goyim* 'beyond the pale.' " In America, they were swept into a process of modernization and assimilation.[47]

This process required what Cuddihy termed the "price of admission": they had to give up certain customs and cultural traits that had been tied to their ethnicity. Wearing the proper clothing was crucial in acquiring the appearance of civility. "I was such a greenhorn, you wouldn't believe," said Sophie Abrams. "My first day in America I went with my aunt to buy some American clothes. She bought me a shirtwaist...a blue print with red buttons and a hat, such a hat I had never seen. I took my old brown dress and shawl and threw them away!...When I looked in the mirror, I couldn't get over it. I said, boy, Sophie, look at you now. Just like an American." Immediately after arriving in the Lower East Side, Cahan's Levinsky noticed that the people were better dressed than people back home. "The poorest-looking man wore a hat (instead of a cap), a stiff collar and a necktie, and the poorest woman wore a hat or bonnet." Passersby looked at Levinsky and exclaimed: "There goes a green one!" The remark stung him, for he understood what they were implying: "We are not, of course. We are Americanized." Shortly afterward, a friend bought Levinsky a suit, a hat, handkerchiefs, collars, shoes, and a necktie. "That will make you look American," said his benefactor. Levinsky gazed at himself in the mirror, "bewildered," scarcely recognizing himself in his "modern" outfit. To dress fashionably became a necessity. "Some of the women blame me very much because I spend so much money on clothes," said a garment worker. "But a girl must have clothes if she is to go into good society at Ulmer Park or Coney Island or the theater. Those who blame me are the old country people who have old-fashioned notions, but people who have been here a long time know better. A girl who does not dress well is stuck in a corner, even if she is pretty."48

Language was also an indicator of assimilation. In Russia, most Jews had made no effort to learn the dominant language, but as immigrants in America they were eager to learn English. "Today," observed a resident of New York's Jewish community in 1905, "English is more and more the language spoken on the East Side, whereas eight years ago it was rare to hear that tongue." In a letter to the *Jewish Daily Forward*, a mother complained about her daughter who had preceded her family to America: "During the few years she was here without us she became a regular Yankee and forgot how to talk Yiddish.... She says it is not nice to talk Yiddish and that I am a greenhorn." As a student at a public evening school, Levinsky was impressed by his teacher's facility in English: "I would hang on his lips, striving to memorize every English word I could catch and watching intently, not only his enunciation, but also his gestures, manners, and mannerisms, and accepting it all as part and parcel of the American way of speaking." More than dress, Levinsky believed, good English was a requirement for assimilation: "People who were born to speak English were superior beings. Even among the fallen women I would seek those who were real Americans." Learning English was a way for the immigrants to become "regular Yankees" and lessen the ethnic distance between themselves and native-born Americans.[49]

The quest to become American also led to the changing of names for some, possibly many. "They [immigrant Jews] themselves seemed ready to accept the idea that they were nobodies," recalled the son of an immigrant. "They were so scared that they even dropped the pride of a family name." Russian -skis and -vitches were dropped, and names like Levinsky became Levin. But names were also Anglicized: from Bochlowitz to Buckley, Jacobson to Jackson, and Stepinsky to Stevens. Many young people happily adopted "American" first names in school: Dvoirah became Dora; Hyman, Howard; Moishe, Morris; Breina, Beatrice; and Rivka became Ruth. "My Hebrew name being Maryashe in full, Mashke for short, Russianized in Marya (*Mary-ya*)," said Mary Antin, "my friends said that it would hold good in English as *Mary;* which was very disappointing, as I longed to possess a strange-sounding American name."[50]

American holidays and consumerism became popular in the Jewish colony. The Yiddish daily *Forward* noted that Jews enjoyed giving presents at Christmastime and that this practice was "the first thing" that demonstrated one was not a "greenhorn." For many newcomers, historian Andrew R. Heinze observed, the goal was to become an "allrightnik," "the successful Jewish immigrant who adopted American habits, particularly habits of consumption, so thoroughly as to blend into the group of cosmopolitan Jews who had attained a high degree of cultural assimilation." Ownership of luxury goods proclaimed silently that the newcomer was a prospective citizen, and not Europe's "wretched refuse" coming to America's "teeming shore." By adapting to abundance, the immigrants were adopting America.[51]

Not to be a "greenhorn" also meant to take summer vacations at resorts, especially in the Catskill Mountains. As Jewish immigrants raised themselves economically and socially, they began flocking to cottages and hotels in small towns like Tannersville and Hunter. "One of the latest fashions among the poor people of the East Side," the *Commercial Advertiser* reported in 1899, "is for the father of a family to send his wife and children to the mountains for the summer. Not that East Side prosperity has placed some of the luxuries within reach of the poor. On the contrary, board in the Catskills has come down to a point where the 'keep' of a workingman's family in a boardinghouse is almost as cheap as it is at home in the city." The resorts also offered opportunities to flaunt newly acquired accoutrements that trumpeted their success. "The only good thing about the Catskills is the fresh air," observed the *Forward* wryly, "but instead of taking advantage of it, the women sit on the porch like a fashion show, each one showing off her clothes and jewelry."

> *And here in the Catskill what do Jews believe?*
> *In kosher, certainly; in Shabbes, less,*
> *(But somewhat, for they smoke in secret then.)*
> *In Rosh Hashanah and in Yom Kippur,*
> *In charity and in America;*
> *But most of all in pinochle and poker,*
> *In dancing and in jazz, in risqué stories,*
> *And everything that's smart and up-to-date.*

As Jewish businessmen, wives, garment workers, teachers, shopkeepers, and children spent their summers in the Catskills, they were participating in "a distinctly Jewish version of the American vacation," an extravagant custom "fulfilling the vision of the earthly paradise" that the immigrants had carried to America.[52]

One of the "allrightniks" who vacationed in the Catskills was David Levinsky. He had gone there like the others—the "cloak-manufacturers, shirt-manufacturers, ladies'-waist-manufacturers, cigar-manufacturers, clothiers, furriers, jewelers, leather-goods men, real-estate men, physicians, dentists, lawyers" and their families. In most cases, these vacationers were "people who had blossomed out into nabobs in the course of the last few years," Levinsky reported. "The crowd was ablaze with diamonds, painted cheeks, and bright-colored silks," "a babel of self-consciousness," a minature of "parvenu smugness." As a wealthy garment manufacturer, Levinsky "paraded" his newly acquired manners, his neckties, and his English vocabulary.[53]

For Jewish men to be "American" meant to participate in the world of business. But for married Jewish immigrant women, it meant to stay at home. A government study conducted in 1907–8 found that only 8 percent of Russian-Jewish wives were wage earners, compared with 17 percent for southern Italians. Actually, many Jewish wives had incomes—the rent from their boarders: 56 percent of Jewish immigrant households in 1911 had boarders. Wives could also work in family businesses, and many of them could be seen and heard hawking from pushcarts. "At the time when girls were married it was terrible [for them] to go to work.... That was forbidden," recalled an immigrant woman. "[But] if they worked in their own business, they could have worked day and night."[54]

Not encouraged, perhaps not even permitted to be wage-earning workers, the Jewish wife was expected to be a *baleboste,* an "owner of the home," taking care of domestic responsibilities such as preparing meals and paying the bills. "We were high class with low-class means," an immigrant daughter recalled. "We just didn't let a woman like my mother go to work, even if she wanted to." Marriage meant the end of working outside the home. "When I came here I was thirteen and a half," said Mollie Linker. At the age of fifteen years, she was working and took "almost three hundred people [out] on strike." "I got married at eighteen.... Then the babies came." Mollie Linker's father-in-law told her that as a mother it was "a shame to go to work." Similarly, Ruth Katz recalled: "At the time I came [to America], the woman was home cooking and cleaning and raising the children. Women weren't supposed to go out and work.... That I think we brought from Europe, that a Jewish wife should not go to work."[55]

While the role of the *baleboste* was imported, staying home for Jewish wives and mothers represented an American adaptation. In Russia, it had reflected the traditional notion of the husband's economic importance; here it acquired a new veneer. An Old World tradition had become a signature of bourgeois success in the New World. "Over time," wrote the historian Susan A. Glenn, "Jewish immigrants became increasingly sensitive to bourgeois notions of respectability." Seeking to identify themselves with "upwardly mobile, assimilated Americans," many insisted that a wife should "devote herself exclusively to her domestic obligations and leave the task of breadwinning to the husband." To have the luxury of not working meant that Jewish wives and their families were no longer "greenhorns" and that they had "made it" socially and economically. They had entered the world of "civility."[56]

But Jewish "success" was earned. "Most New York City Jews

did not make the leap from poverty to the middle class by going to college," historian Selma C. Berrol found. "Rather, widespread utilization of secondary and higher education *followed* improvements in economic status and was as much a result as a cause of upward mobility." As skilled workers, as unionized laborers, and as businessmen, many Jewish immigrants had already begun their "rise" and had the economic means to support the education of their children.[57]

Jewish immigrant fathers and mothers were driven by a determination to have their children become professionals rather than peddlers, tailors, merchants, and garment factory workers. Parents wanted their children to get out of blue-collar jobs and into white-collar employment, to have occupations "higher than the dirty work in a factory." Describing the Jewish commitment to education, the *Daily Forward* editorialized: "The Jew undergoes privation, spills blood, to educate his child. In [this] is reflected one of the finest qualities of the Jewish people. It shows our capacity to make sacrifices for our children...as well as our love for education, for intellectual efforts."[58]

However, the beneficiaries of this determination to educate the American-born generation were mainly the sons, and many of the "sacrifices" were made by their sisters, earning money in the sweatshops of the Lower East Side. After the Triangle Shirtwaist Factory fire, Elizabeth Dutcher of the Women's Trade Union League spoke to the families of the victims and was surprised to learn how much these young women had been contributing to family budgets. They had been "supporting old fathers and mothers, both in this country and abroad; mothering and supporting younger brothers and sisters, sending brothers to high school, to art school, to dental college, to engineering courses." In 1910, the income of working daughters amounted to nearly 40 percent of the family's yearly earnings.[59]

With young Jewish women working, their brothers were able to go to college. A 1910 survey of the working-class sections of New York City found that there were more Jews above the age of sixteen still in school than any other ethnic group. Soon Jewish students began crowding into the colleges and universities in New York and elsewhere on the East Coast. "The thirst for knowledge," the *New York Evening Post* reported in 1905, "...fills our city colleges and Columbia's halls with the sons of Hebrews who came over in steerage." By 1916, Jewish students were ubiquitous on college campuses in the city—44 percent of the enrollment at Hunter College and 73 percent at City College. A government report noted how City College was "practically filled with Jewish pupils, a considerable proportion of them children of Russian or Polish immigrants on the East Side." Jewish students had also begun to enter Harvard, and by 1920 this elite school's population was 20 percent Jewish.[60]

But the increasing presence of Jewish students at Harvard provoked a backlash. In 1923, a writer for *The Nation* complained that the upwardly mobile Jew sent "his children to college a generation or two sooner than other stocks," and that consequently there were "in fact more dirty Jews and tactless Jews in college than dirty and tactless Italians, Armenians, or Slovaks." Anti-Semitic murmurs and complaints swept across the campus. A dormitory at Harvard was called "Little Jerusalem" because of its large number of Jewish students. Expressions of resentment and ethnic epithets began to circulate: "Jews are an unassimilable race, as dangerous to a college as indigestible food to man." "They are governed by selfishness." "They do not mix. They destroy the unity of the college." "They memorize their books! Thus they keep the average of scholarship so high that others with a degree of common sense, but less parrot-knowledge, are prevented from attaining a representative grade."[61]

President Abbott Lawrence Lowell announced that the college had a "Jewish problem" and led efforts to curb their enrollment. "It is the duty of Harvard," he wrote privately in a letter to a member of the Board of Overseers on March 29, 1922, "to receive just as many boys who have come, or whose parents have come, to this country without our background as we can effectively educate; including in education the imparting, not only of book knowledge, but of ideas and traditions of our people. Experience seems to place that proportion at about 15%." He was planning to place a quota on Jewish-American admissions. Two months later, President Lowell expressed concern that what had happened to resort hotels could happen to Harvard: "The summer hotel that is ruined by admitting Jews meets its fate, not because the Jews it admits are of bad character, but because they drive away the Gentiles.... This happened to a friend of mine with a school in New York, who thought, on principle, that he ought to admit Jews, but discovered in a few years that he had no school at all. A similar thing has happened in the case of Columbia College."[62]

In a letter to the *New York Times* published in June, Lowell offered another reason why he felt it was important for Harvard to keep Jewish enrollment stable: "There is perhaps no body of men in the United States...with so little anti-Semitic feeling as the instructing staff of Harvard University. There is, most unfortunately, a rapidly growing anti-Semitic feeling in this country...fraught with very great evils for the Jews." Arguing that quotas would help reduce anti-Semitism on campus, Lowell continued: "The anti-Semitic feeling among students is increasing, and it grows in proportion to the increase in the number of Jews."[63]

Meanwhile, Harvard instituted new admissions criteria and procedures. The new policies stressed the need for well-rounded rather than strictly studious students and for "regional balance" from the interior regions rather than overrepresentation from New York City. In addition, applicants were required to submit a passport-sized photograph "for purposes of identification and for later use by the Dean's office." What was meant by "identification" and what that "use" would be were not explained. But it was known that some Jews had changed their family names, and it was thought that Jews could be identified by their "Semitic" facial features. After the establishment of these new policies, Jewish admissions to Harvard declined, fluctuating between 10 and 16 percent of each freshman class during the 1920s and 1930s.[64]

Not everyone agreed with President Lowell. At a banquet of the Bunker Hill Knights of Columbus, Boston mayor James Curley criticized Harvard for seeking to bar students because of "an accident of birth." An Irish American, he denounced discrimination against the Jews: "God gave them their parents and their race, as he has given me mine. All of us under the Constitution are guaranteed equality, without regard to race, creed, or color." Then Mayor Curley warned: "If the Jew is barred today, the Italian will be to-morrow, then the Spaniard and Pole, and at some future date the Irish."[65]

The restrictions at Harvard were part of a larger nativist movement. In 1924, Congress passed a severely restrictionist immigration act. Among the bill's supporters was Harvard's President Lowell. The law established immigration quotas designed to reduce immigration from southern and eastern Europe. These quotas were based on 2 percent of the number of foreign-born persons of each nationality in the United States in 1890—before the height of Jewish immigration. The principle of restricting immigration according to nationality, first introduced with the 1882 Chinese Exclusion Act, was now given broader application, and Jewish immigration sharply declined after 1924.

What made Jews seem threatening to American society was the integration of a culturally different group that was growing in numbers. "As the Jewish population increases," observed Abraham Cahan, "animosity grows with it. Nations love only themselves, not strangers. If we get too close to the Americans with our language and customs, they will be annoyed.... The chasm between *shtetl* Jews and Yankees—it's like two different worlds. When there are only a few Jews, gentiles go slumming to inspect the novelty. When the Jews fill up the streetcars and parks, we are resented."[66]

Earlier, representing a small group, immigrant German Jews had been welcomed in American society. "Wherever there is a chance for enterprise and energy the Jew is to be found," declared the *Philadelphia Evening Telegraph* appreciatively in 1872. "He brings into every community wealth and qualities which materially assist to strengthen and consolidate its polity.... No other element in the community is so orderly."[67]

As Russian Jewish immigrants began arriving in massive waves, however, this favorable view quickly faded. "Numerous complaints have been made in regard to the Hebrew immigrants who lounge about Battery Park, obstructing the walks and sitting on the chains," the *New York Tribune* reported in 1882. "Their filthy condition has caused many of the people who are accustomed to go to the park to seek a little recreation and fresh air to give up this practice." Because many of the new immigrants had become peddlers and businessmen, they were seen as Shylocks. In "a society of Jews and brokers," lamented Henry Adams in 1893, "I have no place." In *The Passing of the Great Race*, published in 1916, Madison Grant warned that the Jewish "dwarf stature, peculiar mentality, and ruthless concentration on self-interest" were being "engrafted upon the stock of the nation." During the 1920s, Henry Ford led an anti-Semitic campaign against "international Jews," whose loyalties were allegedly not to America but only to their greedy interests. "Jewish financiers" were not building "anything," Ford argued, and Jewish labor leaders were organizing unions in order "to interrupt work." Anti-Semitism also surfaced among workers. "The Russian Jews and the other Jews will completely control the finances and Government of this country in ten years, or they will all be dead," a workingman declared in a letter to the *New York Sun* in 1895. "The hatred with which they are regarded...ought to be a warning to them. The people of this country...won't be starved and driven to the wall by Jews who are guilty of all the crimes, tricks, and wiles that have hitherto been unknown and unthought of by civilized humanity." At the street level, "Jew-baiting" frequently occurred as rowdies taunted, stoned, and pulled the beards of Jewish peddlers.[68]

Ironically, the very success of Jews in America seemed to fuel anti-Semitism. The Jews "reaped more and more dislike as they bettered themselves," noted historian John Higham. "The more avidly they reached out for acceptance and participation in American life, the more their reputation seemed to suffer." "It is not the failure of Jews to be assimilated into undergraduate society which troubles them [President Lowell and the supporters of quotas]," observed Horace Kallen in 1923. "They do not want Jews to be assimilated into undergraduate society. What troubles them is the completeness with which the Jews want to and have been assimilated." Indeed, as second-generation Jews became educated and began seeking white-collar employment in gentile companies, they often encountered discrimination. Classified job listings sometimes specified "Christians only." Many hospitals turned away Jewish doctors for internships, and prestigious law firms refused to hire Jewish lawyers. The doors to university faculty appointments were often closed to Jews. A young Jewish-American professor of literature at Columbia University, Lionel Trilling, was told by his chairman in 1936 that his department was not prepared to keep "a Freudian, a Marxist, and a Jew...at our kind of institution."[69]

Antagonism against Jews sharpened as they began moving out of the Lower East Side, closing the distances between them and gentile America. Seeking new homes in more middle-class areas, they often encountered restrictive covenants—clauses in deeds that explicitly prohibited selling of the property to Jews. Around the turn of the century, Jews began moving uptown to Harlem. "For rent" signs warned that they were not welcome: *Keine Juden, und keine Hunde*" ("No Jews, No Dogs"). But the Jews kept settling in Harlem, and one of its neighborhoods eventually came to be known as "Little Russia." "Calvary Presbyterian Church," the *New York Times* reported, "is now one of the prettiest little Jewish synagogues in...New York."[70]

During the 1920s, over one hundred thousand Jews left the Lower East Side, crossing Delancey Street as they spread into the Bronx and Brooklyn. There in "the wilds of the Bronx," the "country" at the end of a long subway ride, they could live on tree-lined streets still bordered by open fields and vacant lots. As a young boy, Michael Gold accompanied his father to see a house for sale in Brooklyn. "The suburb was a place of half-finished skeleton houses and piles of lumber and brick," he later wrote. "Paved streets ran in rows between empty fields where only the weeds rattled. Real estate signs were stuck everywhere. In the midst of some rusty cans and muck would be a sign shouting, 'This Wonderful Apartment House Site for Sale!'" Similarly, Zalman Yoffeh recalled: "When I was nine years old, my mother heard of a wonderful bargain in the then sparsely-populated Brownsville [in Brooklyn]—four rooms with a private bathroom. We moved there."[71]

While it was not like the movement out of Egypt or Russia, another exodus had begun. "The young married people are going to the outlying districts of the Bronx and Brooklyn," observed a settlement house worker in 1925. "Their standards of living are higher than those of their parents. They seek better homes...for the price they can afford to pay." They wanted to leave the dingy and dirty alleys of the Lower East Side where some "greenhorns" still lived and reside in "American" neighborhoods. "The generation that entered the immigrant ghetto," wrote historian Ben Halpern, "was confronted by one overwhelming task: to get out, or to enable the next generation to get out."[72]

Many Jews managed to get out of the colony, but their migrations led to "concentrated dispersal." They settled together in the newer neighborhoods and suburbs of New York. During the 1920s, the percentage of New York's Jews living in neighborhoods which were at least 40 percent Jewish increased from 54 to 72 percent. This new residential pattern was shaped not only by anti-Semitic housing discrimination, but also by Jewish networks of friends and family who shared information about available housing in Jewish neighborhoods. Also assisting them in their quest for new homes were Jewish real estate brokers and Jewish builders. Russian Jewish contractors, "with hosts of carpenters, bricklayers, plumbers," observed Abraham Cahan, built housing in the Bronx and Brooklyn. "Vast areas of meadowland and rock were turned by them, as by a magic wand, into densely populated avenues and streets of brick and mortar. Under the spell of their activity, cities...sprang up within the confines of Greater New York in the course of three or four years."[73]

They were migrating again, this time from the Lower East Side. Years earlier, the refugees had fled the shtetls of Russia to what they called the Promised Land. Like F. Scott Fitzgerald's imagined Dutch sailors, they saw America as a "fresh, green breast of the new world," where Gatz could reinvent himself into Gatsby.[77] Determined to rise from "greenhorns," Jews passionately embraced the country's possibilities, striving to assimilate and become Americans. But as they made their journey into their adopted homeland, they fearfully watched the emergence of an evil empire in Europe that would lead to a ghastly defining moment in Jewish history.[74]

12

❧❦❧

EL NORTE
Up from Mexico

TO THE JEWISH exiles, America was "the Promised Land," and to the immigrants from Mexico, it was "El Norte."

Unlike the immigrants from Asia and Europe, Mexicans lived in a country that bordered the United States. Entry was easy. "All you had to do coming from Mexico, if you were a Mexican citizen," recalled Cleofas Calleros, who came with his family in the early 1900s, "was to report at the immigration office on the American side...give your name, the place of your birth, and where you were going to." Most of the immigrants did not even bother to report to the immigration authority. They simply walked across the shallow Rio Grande. A federal official observed: "These immigrants appear at the border in *sombrero, sarape,* and sandals, which, before crossing the river, they usually exchange for a suit of 'American' clothing, shoes, and a less conspicuous hat."[1]

Like the Japanese immigrants who were arriving about the same time, Mexicans saw America as a land of opportunity. In villages and towns where they had been born and expected to live out their lives, they welcomed their brothers and friends returning from work in the United States. A song filled their imaginations with extravagant hopes and vivid images of success:

> *If only you could see how nice*
> *the United States is;*

that is why the Mexicans
are crazy about it.
Your watch is on its chain
and your scarf-pin in your tie
and your pockets always filled
with plenty of silver.[2]

From El Norte, immigrants wrote to friends and relatives back home: "Come! come! come over it is good here." The news set off a chain reaction that brought "others and others." In this way, just one person coming here led to the migration of twenty-eight families from his village. "Since I was very small I had the idea of going out to know the world," Jesus Garza recalled. "As I had heard a lot about the United States it was my dream to come here."[3]

Such dreams created a tremendous pull to the north. "If anyone has any doubt about the volume of this class of immigrant," an American reporter wrote in 1914, "a visit to South Texas would reveal the situation. In a day's journey by automobile through that region one passes hundreds of Mexicans, all journeying northward on foot, on burroback and in primitive two-wheel carts. They are so numerous as to almost fill the highways and byways. When questioned many of them will tell you that they fled from Mexico to escape starvation. In a great number of instances the refugees have friends or relatives in this country who have told them of the wealth and prosperity of the wonderful *ESTADOS UNIDOS*."[4]

Mexicans were also pushed from their homeland. Large landholders and speculators had been expropriating small farms and uprooting rural families. An 1883 land law allowed private land-development companies to receive up to one-third of any land they surveyed and subdivided. Forced to become tenant farmers and sharecroppers, the peasants had become especially vulnerable to exploitation. "The owners gave us the seeds, the animals, and the land," recalled Elias Garza after he had moved to Los Angeles, "but it turned out that when the crop was harvested there wasn't anything left for us even if we had worked very hard. That was terrible. Those land owners were robbers." Migrating to cities, Mexican peasants suffered from cyclical unemployment as industries expanded and contracted. "The Mexican people, with industries dying...," Marcelo Villegas observed, "are crushed, starved, and driven out of their country."[5]

In addition to poverty, there was the danger of violence. The 1910 Mexican Revolution forced tens of thousands of refugees to flee northward. "We were running away from the rebellion," said Jesus Moreno, who arrived in Los Angeles with his family in 1915. "There were a lot of people coming to that city [El Paso] because of the Revolution.... We came to the United States to wait out the conclusion of the Revolution. We thought it would be over in a few months." These political refugees had planned to return to Mexico. "I would rather cut my throat before changing my Mexican nationality," explained Carlos Ibanez. "I am only waiting until conditions get better, until there is absolute peace before I go back." But the waiting stretched into years and years. "Of course I have never thought of changing my citizenship," sighed Fernando Sanchez in the 1920s, "but the truth is that I don't know when I will go back to Mexico for things are getting worse there day by day on account of the revolutions."[6]

And so Mexicans went northward in search of safety and work. "We left Durango because work was very scarce," Pedro Villamil recalled, "and we were told that one could get good money in the United States and there was work for whoever wanted it." An immigrant construction worker in Santa Barbara explained: "Where I came from I used to work ten hours for $1.25.... Then I came here and they paid $1.25 for eight hours—it was good." "It is only natural," the Mexican newspaper *El Paso del Norte* commented, "that the 'Supreme Law of Necessity' obliges all these people to emigrate to a foreign land in search of higher wages." A contemporary reported that there was a "steady drift of labor from south to north," drawn by American wages two to three times higher than wages in Mexico. Carlos Ibanez explained he was paid so little for his labor in Zacatecas that he did not "even remember how much it was." So he decided to leave Mexico "in search of fortune" in California.[7]

What accelerated the movement of Mexicans to the United States was the development of transportation: in 1895, the Mexican International Railroad had extended a line nine hundred miles into Mexico, linking the Texas border town of Eagle Pass with Durango. The railroad triggered a mass migration. "There is not a day in which passenger trains do not leave for the border, full of Mexican men who are going in gangs to work on railroad lines in the United States," reported a Mexican newspaper in 1904. "Each week five or six trains are run from Laredo," the *Los Angeles Times* reported in 1916, "carrying Mexicans who have been employed by labor agents, and similar shipments are being made from other border points."[8]

Traveling by rail overnight, the migrants traversed great geographical as well as cultural distances. One of their songs told what it felt like to cross the border by train:

> *The fleeting engine*
> *Can't do anything good*
> *Because at dusk it is at home*
> *And at dawn in a strange country.*[9]

When they woke up, they found themselves far from familiar sights and sounds. A somberness swept over them as they wondered what crossing the border would mean for them.

Most of the immigrants were from the agricultural labor class, and they were predominantly young—between the ages of fifteen and forty-four. They included women: either a man brought his family with him, or he migrated first to find a job and a place to live and then sent for his family. Between 1900 and 1930, the Mexican population in the Southwest grew from an estimated 375,000 to 1,160,000, the majority of them born in Mexico. The new immigrants settled in Texas, Arizona, New Mexico, and California, and spread as far away as Michigan and Illinois.[10] As the migrants crossed the border, they sang:

> *Good-bye, my beloved country,*
> *now I am going away....*
> *I go to the United States*
> *to seek to earn a living.*
> *Good-bye, my beloved land;*
> *I bear you in my heart.*[11]

Sprinkling the Fields with the Sweat of Their Brows

During the early twentieth century, Mexicans were enticed across the border because their labor was needed. "I have had to work very hard where I have found work," said one of them, "whether it was on the railroad, in the cotton fields or beet fields, in the hotels as a waiter, as an elevator man, or in the asphalt." Indeed, Mexicans worked in a wide range of jobs.[12]

A rural people in Mexico, many of the newcomers became urban industrial workers in America. "In southern California and in Texas," a researcher found in 1908, "Mexicans do most of the excavating and road building, and are otherwise employed on public works." In 1928, a Texas official estimated that Mexicans represented about 75 percent of all construction labor in the state. Mexicans were hired mainly as manual laborers. White labor unions jealously protected the skilled jobs by creating a two-tiered labor market that reflected a racial division. "I have gone from one place to another working as a laborer," Policarpo Castro said in the 1920s, "for I haven't found anything else because the masons' union don't want to admit Mexicans.... But although I have worked as a laborer I have always tried to learn everything that I could. I have worked in cement, in a brick-yard, laying pipes...and have learned all that sort of work, even how to make entrances and walks for a garage with an incline. All that will do me some good in Mexico.... I know that if I want to amount to something in any work I will have to do it there in Mexico, because the Americans only despise us." A Mexican bluntly explained why he was not able to be a carpenter: "They [whites] wouldn't let me on account of my race—discrimination."[13]

In Los Angeles, 70 percent of the Mexicans were unskilled blue-collar workers in 1918, compared to only 6 percent for Anglos. "In...many communities," a journalist observed in 1929, "it is the Mexicans who do the common labor. In fact, we have imported them for that very purpose." In El Paso, only 5 percent of the Mexicans were in professional and managerial occupations in 1920, compared to 30 percent of the Anglos. "There were no Mexican men or women, boys or girls, working in the banks," Cleofas Calleros recalled. "American offices, like insurance offices...they never hired Mexicans." Most workers were locked into low blue-collar occupations. Mexican heads of households living in Santa Barbara in 1900, for example, were still employed in the same jobs thirty years later.[14]

The urban Mexican workforce included women, employed in garment factories, food processing plants, and canneries. Working in the canneries was especially punishing. A "harsh cannery whistle" shattered the "air at midnight" or the "frozen black hours of the near dawn" to rouse the workers from their beds. Then they rushed to the cannery as they buttoned their clothes, their "teeth chattering all the way." Inside the cannery, they felt the cold of the salt wind as they cut the heads and guts from the sardines. The fish kept coming down the chute, and they had to work faster and faster. Finally, the "silver stream" stopped flowing, and they went home tired, splattered with fish blood. But they had some money to buy food and pay the rent.[15]

In the Midwest and East, Mexicans worked in steel mills,

packing houses, and automobile assembly plants. In the South-west, they found employment in the railroad companies. "[They] are not subject to agitators," a labor supplier stated. "They're not organized. They're peaceable... and will work on the desert or anywhere the Santa Fe wants to put them." The chief engineer of the Santa Fe Railroad commented: "The Mexican cannot be driven like the Negro, but anyone who knows how to manage the Mexicans can get more work out of them than any other class." A federal official listed the reasons why Mexicans made good rail-road workers: "As a laborer the Mexican immigrant is said to be unambitious, physically not strong, and somewhat [indigent] and irregular, but against this is put the fact that he is docile, patient, orderly in camp, fairly intelligent under competent supervision, obedient, and cheap. His strongest point with the employers is his willingness to work for a low wage."[16]

Most Mexicans, however, worked in agriculture. In Califor-nia, farmers turned increasingly to Mexican labor as immigra-tion laws such as the 1907 Gentlemen's Agreement and the 1924 Immigration Act excluded Asian labor. "We have no Chinamen; we have not the Japs," farmers argued. "The Hindu is worthless; the Filipino is nothing, and the white man will not do the work." "Due to their crouching and bending habits," claimed Dr. George Clements of the Los Angeles Chamber of Commerce's Agricul-tural Department, the "oriental and Mexican" were suited to tasks in the fields, while whites were "physically unable to adapt" themselves to such work. A cotton grower in California's Imperial Valley declared that the farmers needed Mexicans as stoop labor-ers: "We mean to get Mexicans for the work and get all we need." By the 1920s, at least three-fourths of California's two hundred thousand farm laborers were Mexican.[17]

Mexican agricultural laborers also became indispensable in Texas. The state employment service estimated that of the three hundred thousand full-time migrant workers in the state, 10 per-cent were Anglo, 5 percent black, and 85 percent Mexican. An official of the San Antonio Chamber of Commerce declared: "Yes, sir, we are dependent on the Mexican farm-labor supply, and we know it. Mexican farm-labor is rapidly proving the making of this State." A newspaper described the widespread agricultural employment of Mexicans: "To meet the demand agents have been sent across the border into Mexico. Many of those [recruited Mex-ican workers] going into the cotton fields of Texas are accompa-nied by their entire families. This is to the liking of the planters, for it is maintained that children as a rule will pick as much cotton as the grown-ups." Texas farmers repeatedly offered similar explanations for the widespread employment of Mexicans: "The white people won't do the work and they won't live as the Mexicans do on beans and tortillas and in one room shacks." "Whites cannot be as easily domineered, led, or directed as the Mexicans." "I prefer Mexican labor to other classes of labor. It is more humble and you get more for your money." "No other class we could bring to Texas could take his place. He's a natural farm laborer."[18]

But there was nothing natural about doing backbreaking work. Rosaura Valdez described how much work it took to pick a hundred pounds of cotton: "I'd have a twelve foot sack, about this wide. I'd tie the sack around my waist and the sack would go between my legs and I'd go on the cotton row, picking cotton and just putting it in there. So when we finally got it filled real good then we would pick up the sack, toss it up on our shoulders, and then I would walk, put it up there on the scale and have it weighed, put in back on my shoulder, climb up a ladder on a wagon and empty that sack in."[19]

Farm work was seasonal and migratory, with laborers following the crops. "Each family traveling on its own, they came in trucks piled with household goods or packed in the secondhand *fotingos* [travel-worn Fords] and chevees. The trucks and cars were ancient models, fresh out of a used-car lot, with license tags of many states." Where they would be living at any given time was determined by where the jobs were. "We went to Calipatria [California] and the whole family of us engaged in cotton picking," said Anastacio Torres. "They paid very well at the time. They paid us $2.00 or $1.75 for every 100 pounds of cotton which we picked and as all of the family picked we managed to make a good amount every day. When the cotton crop of 1919 was finished we went to Los Angeles and then I got a job as a laborer with a paper manufacturing company. They paid me $3.40 a day for eight hours' work. I was at that work for some time and then returned to the Imperial Valley for lemon picking."[20]

Conditions in the migrant labor camps were squalid and degrading. "Shelters were made of almost every conceivable thing—burlap, canvas, palm branches," reported a minister describing a camp in the Imperial Valley. There were no wooden floors, and chicken yards adjoined the shelters. Next to the houses was a huge pile of manure with children tumbling in it as though it were a haystack. "There were flies everywhere.... We found one woman carrying water in large milk pails from the irrigation ditch. The water was brown with mud, but we were assured that after it had been allowed to settle that it would be clear and pure.... There were no baths." The growers felt no responsibility for the housing conditions or the welfare of their workers. They thought of Mexicans as "here today and elsewhere tomorrow." Commenting on the Mexican laborers, a farmer bluntly stated: "They have finished harvesting my crops, I will kick them out on the country road. My obligation is ended."[21]

Feeling they were entitled to dignity as well as better working conditions and higher wages, Mexicans actively participated in labor struggles, especially during the Great Depression. Between 1928 and 1933, Mexican farm laborers in California had their wages cut from 35 cents to 14 cents an hour. In response, they supported strikes led by trade unions such as the Confederacion de Uniones de Obreras Mexicanas (Confederation of Mexican Labor Unions) and La Union de Trabajadores del Valle Imperial (the Imperial Valley Workers' Union). Their labor militancy contradicted and challenged stereotypes of Mexican passivity. "The growers became genuinely alarmed," reported an investigator for the California Department of Industrial Relations during one of the strikes. "Heretofore they have been accustomed to considering the Mexican workers as bovine and tractable individuals, best adapted to the climatic conditions in the Imperial Valley and therefore the most desirable workers in the valley. The organization of a union of Mexican laborers seems to have evoked in the growers an ardent wish for its earliest demise."[22]

One of the most powerful Mexican strikes occurred in 1933 when twelve thousand laborers in the San Joaquin Valley resisted wage reductions. The mostly Mexican workforce turned down the growers' wage rate of 60 cents per hundredweight of picked cotton and struck for a rate of $1.00. To break the strike, employers evicted the strikers from their camps and dumped their belongings on the highway; they also used the local police to arrest the strike leaders and disrupt the picket lines. "We protect our farmers here in Kern County," a deputy sheriff told an interviewer. "They are our best people. They are always with us. They keep the country going. They put us here and they can put us out again, so we serve them. But the Mexicans are trash. They have no standard of living. We herd them like pigs." The local media also joined the attack on the strikers. "If the strike continues, it is more than likely that every last one of you will be gathered into one huge bull pen," a newspaper threatened. "Many of you don't know how the United States government can run a concentration camp.... Do you want to face the bull pen? Do you want to be deported to Mexico?"[23]

Mexican strikers refused to be intimidated. Striking women were particularly active: they posted picket lines daily, the older women in rebozos (shawls) and the younger women wearing flapper styles. They urged the strikebreakers to support their struggle. "Don't be sell outs!" they shouted. "Join the strike. We also have to eat and we also have family." Lydia Ramos experienced a tremendous sense of solidarity: "We didn't know what union it was or who was organizing or nothing. We just knew that there was a strike and that *we* were not going to break a strike." Asked why not, she answered: "Well, we believe in justice. So I want everything that's good for me and I want everything that's good for somebody else. Not just for them...but equality and justice. If you're going to break somebody's strike, that's just going against your beliefs." In the end, the strikers won a compromise wage rate of 75 cents per hundredweight.[24]

The strikes reflected a deep discontent in El Norte. One of the strikers, Juan Berzunzolo, had come here in 1908 and worked on the tracks of the Southern Pacific and in the beet fields of Colorado. "I have left the best of my life and my strength here," he said, "sprinkling with the sweat of my brow the fields and factories of these gringos."[25]

Tortillas and Rotis: Mixed Marriages

Sprinkling the fields with the sweat of their brows alongside Mexican workers were immigrants from India. At the beginning of the twentieth century, workers from the Punjab region of India began arriving on the West Coast. By 1920, some sixty-four hundred had entered the United States. Most of them were Sikhs. Their religion of Sikhism had been founded in the sixteenth century by Guru Nanak in his effort to unite Muslims and all castes of Hindus. Wearing their traditional headdress, the newcomers were described as "the tide of turbans." "Always the turban remains," a witness wrote, "the badge and symbol of their native land, their native customs and religion." Picking fruit in the orchards of California, the men with their twisted white turbans were seen as "an exotic thing in the western landscape."[26]

The Indian immigrants had been farmers or farm laborers in

the Punjab: 80 percent came from the "Jat," or farmer caste. After the 1882 Exclusion Act prohibited the entry of Chinese workers and the 1907 Gentlemen's Agreement cut off the supply of Japanese labor, growers turned to Asian Indians along with Mexicans, to reduce the labor shortage.[27]

Like the Mexican laborers, the Sikhs followed the harvesting of the different crops. The "turbaned" workers "were continually on the wing," reported Annette Thackwell Johnson for the *Independent* magazine in 1922, "coming from the melon and cotton fields in the Imperial Valley, en route to the fig orchards and vineyards of Fresno, or the rice fields near Sacramento." Farm work was one of constant movement. "During the grape picking season great numbers of them are in Fresno County," a Stockton lawyer said. "At the time of rice harvesting there will be about a thousand of them near Willows; during the cotton season in Imperial Valley (this being when the weather is very hot), they go to that place for work." The workday was long and the work backbreaking. "We got up at half past three," said a Sikh, "and before the first faint daylight was visible we were ready for work. Periodically the boss—an American foreman—would come into the fields and yell, 'Hurry up! Hurry up!'"[28]

The Sikh farm laborers constituted a community without women. In 1914, women represented only 00.24 percent of the 5,000 Asian Indians in California. Very few Asian Indian women emigrated, and after the enactment of the 1917 exclusion law, men with wives in India could not bring them to the United States. The men thought about returning to India and bringing their wives back. "I knew that if I went back to India to join her, we would never be allowed to come back to the United States," said Bagga Singh Sunga of El Centro. "If we had our women here," said a fellow countryman, "our whole life would be different."[29]

Anti-miscegenation laws had prohibited Punjabi men from marrying white women, so many of them married Mexicans. In central California, 76 percent of the Sikhs had Mexican wives, most of them twelve to twenty years younger. They had met each other while working in the fields and orchards and developed relationships leading to marriage.

Love was not the only reason why Sikhs married Mexican women. Most of them had been farmers in India, and they wanted to become farmers in California. But the Alien Land Act of 1913 had prohibited landownership to "aliens ineligible to naturalized citizenship," and Asian Indians were not "white." Sikhs discovered that they could own land through their Mexican wives. Lohar Bupara married Teresa, a Mexican immigrant, and purchased land for farming near Delano under her name. Inder Singh, a farmer in the Imperial Valley, told an interviewer in 1924: "Two years ago I married a Mexican woman and through her I am able to secure land for farming. Your land law can't get rid of me now; I am going to stay." Many Sikh-Mexican marriages involved sisters: one sister would marry an Asian Indian man and then introduce her sister to a friend of her husband. Mir Dad, for example, married Susana Lopez in 1924. He had met her while visiting his friend Mir Alam Khan, the husband of Susana's younger sister, Maria. Similarly, Moola Singh married Maria La Tocharia in 1932, then her sister Julia married Mota Singh and another sister, Hortencia, married Natha Singh. Their marriages to Mexican women were generally not accepted by their families in India. "It used to be that our folks in India objected to such marriages," said Sucha Singh in 1924. He himself had not written to his family about his marriage to a Mexican. "I suppose others have told them about it, but I do not care even if they should be 'sour' about it."[30]

In these Sikh-Mexican families, cultural traditions were often melded. Foods, for example, were interchanged — tortillas for rotis or jalapeños for Punjabi chili peppers. Languages were also mixed together. The Mexican wives generally understood some Punjabi, but the children spoke English and Spanish in the home. Punjabi fathers learned to speak Spanish. The children were usually given Spanish first names like Armando, Jose, and Rudolfo. A few of the sons had Indian names, but they went by Spanish names or nicknames. Mexican mothers told an interviewer: "Gurbachen? Oh, you mean Bacho," and "Kishen? That's Domingo." Lohar and Teresa Bupara named their three children Sarjit, Oscar, and Ana Luisa. The oldest, Sarjit, spoke Spanish, English, and Punjabi. The children were baptized Catholic and were raised under the *compadrazgo* (godparents) system of the Spanish culture and the Catholic Church.[31]

On the Other Side of the Tracks

Included as laborers, Mexicans were excluded from Anglo society. They knew that public buildings were considered "Anglo territory" and that they were permitted to shop in the Anglo business section of town only on Saturdays. They could patronize Anglo cafés, but only at the counter or for carry-out service. "A group of us Mexicans who were well dressed once went to a restaurant in Amarillo," complained Wenceslao Iglesias in the 1920s, "and they told us that if we wanted to eat we should go to the special department where it said 'For Colored People.' I told my friend that I would rather die from starvation than to humiliate myself before the Americans by eating with the Negroes." At sunset, Mexicans had to retreat to their barrios on the other side of the tracks from where the Anglos lived.[32]

In the morning, Mexican parents sent their children to segregated schools. "There would be a revolution in the community if the Mexicans wanted to come to the white schools," an educator said. "Sentiment is bitterly against it. It is based on racial inferiority." The wife of an Anglo ranch manager in Texas put it this way: "Let him [the Mexican] have as good an education but still let him know he is not as good as a white man. God did not intend him to be; He would have made them white if He had." For many Anglos, Mexicans also represented a threat to their daughters. "Why don't we let the Mexicans come to the white school?" an Anglo sharecropper angrily declared. "Because a damned greaser is not fit to sit side of a white girl."[33]

In the segregated schools, Mexican children were trained to become obedient workers. Like the sugar planters in Hawaii who wanted to keep the American-born generation of Japanese on the plantations, Anglo farmers in Texas wanted the schools to help reproduce the labor force. "If every [Mexican] child has a high school education," beet sugar growers asked, "who will labor?" A farmer in Texas explained: "If I wanted a man I would want one of the more ignorant ones.... Educated Mexicans are the hardest to handle.... It is all right to educate them no higher than we educate them here in these little towns. I will be frank. They would make more desirable citizens if they would stop about the seventh grade."[34]

Serving the interests of the growers, Anglo educators were preparing Mexican children to follow in the footsteps of their parents. "It isn't a matter of what is the best way to handle the education here to make citizens of them," a school trustee in Texas stated frankly. "It is politics." School policy was influenced by the needs of the local growers, he elaborated. "We don't need skilled or white-collared Mexicans. The farmers are not interested in educating Mexicans. They know that then they can get better wages and conditions." A Texas superintendent explained why schools should not educate Mexican children: "You have doubtless heard that ignorance is bliss; it seems that it is so when one has to transplant onions. If a man has very much sense or education either, he is not going to stick to this kind of work. So you see it is up to the white population to keep the Mexican on his knees in an onion patch."[35]

"The Mexican children almost don't receive any education," Alonso Galvan complained to an interviewer in the 1920s. "They are taught hardly anything at the schools to which the Mexican children go, and I have heard many teachers, farmers and members of a School Board say, 'What do the Mexicans want to study for when they won't be needed as lawyers? They should be taught to be good; they are needed for cotton picking and work on the railroads.'" A student remembered his sixth-grade teacher advising him not to continue his education and attend high school. "Your people are here to dig ditches," the teacher said, "to do pick and shovel work. I don't think any of you should plan to go to high school."[36]

There were, however, some teachers who tried to give Mexican children a sense of dignity and self-respect. Ernesto Galarza recalled how his school principal "Miss Hopley and her teachers never let us forget why we were at Lincoln; for those who were alien, to become good Americans; for those who were so born, to accept the rest of us." In his school, Americanization did not mean "scrubbing away" what made them Mexican. "No one was ever scolded or punished for speaking in his native tongue on the playground." The teachers tried to pronounce their Spanish names. "Becoming a proud American," Galarza said, "did not mean feeling ashamed of being a Mexican."[37]

Mexican parents wanted their children to have an education in order to get better opportunities and jobs than they had. Isidro Osorio, who had worked on the railroad and in agriculture, described his hope for his children's future: "What I know is that I have worked very hard to earn my $4.00 a day, and that I am an ignorant laborer, but that is why I want to give a little schooling to my children so that they won't stay like I am and can earn more so that they won't have to kill themselves working." Similarly, Jesus Mendizabal told sociologist Manuel Gamio in the 1920s: "I have three children now; they are quite large and they are all going to school. One of them helps me a little now working during vacations and at times when he doesn't go to school. I pray to God that He may give me life to go on working, for I would rather die than take them out of school. I want them to amount to some-

thing, to learn all that they can, since I didn't learn anything."
A boy explained why his parents emphasized the importance of
education: "They want me to go to school so that I won't have to
work beets."[38]

Beginning in the 1920s, however, Mexicans found that they
were not wanted to work in the beet fields or even to stay in America. In 1924, legally admitted Mexicans totaled 87,648—equal to
45 percent of the immigrants from southern and eastern Europe.
This large share reflected the fact that the National Origins Act
limited immigration from southern and eastern Europe but did
not apply to nations in the Western Hemisphere.

This dramatic change in the racial composition of immigration set off nativist alarms. To many Anglos, this new influx represented an invasion, its magnitude so large that it seemed to
threaten "a reconquest of the Southwest." In an obvious reference
to Mexicans as a racially mixed group, Madison Grant warned:
"From the racial point of view, it is not logical to limit the number
of Europeans while we throw the country open without limitation
to Negroes, Indians, and half-breeds." Besides entering the country in great numbers, Mexicans were increasing rapidly in numbers because of their high birthrate. The danger was Mexican
fecundity, C. M. Goethe declared. "The average American family has three children," he calculated. "Mexican laborers average
between nine and ten children to the family. At the three-child
rate a couple would have twenty-seven great-grandchildren. At
the nine-child rate 729 would be produced. Twenty-seven American children and 729 hybrids or Amerinds!" Another nativist
charged that Mexican men constituted a miscegenationist threat
to white racial purity: "If the time ever comes when men with
a small fraction of colored blood can readily find mates among
white women, the gates would be thrown open to a final radical
race mixture of the whole population." In a petition to Congress
sent in 1927, thirty-four prominent educators demanded the preservation of the nation's genetic purity by including Mexico in the
national origins quota system. One of the signatories was A. Lawrence Lowell, president of Harvard University.[39]

Mexican immigration also seemed to be endangering America's cultural identity. Vanderbilt University economics professor
Roy Garis urged white Americans to guard against the "Mexi-
canization" of the Southwest. The region should be the "future
home for millions of the white race" rather than the "dumping
ground for the human hordes of poverty striken peon Indians of

Mexico." The benefits derived from the "restriction of European and the exclusion of Oriental immigration" should not be nullified by allowing Mexican immigration to create a "race problem" that would "dwarf the negro problem of the South," destroying all that was "worthwhile" in "our white civilization."[40]

Mainstream magazines and newspapers joined the hysterical denunciation of racial and ethnic diversity, aiming barbs at Mexican immigrants. "The simple truth is that the dilution of the people and the institutions of this country has already gone too far," the *Saturday Evening Post* editorialized in March 1930. "The country is groping, must grope, toward more rather than less homogeneity. With the Mexicans already here, with the as yet unassimilated immigrants from certain European countries, and finally with the vast and growing negro population, we already have an almost superhuman task to bring about requisite national unity. We are under no obligation to continue to make this country an asylum for the Mexican peon, and we should not do so." Two months later, the *New York Times* echoed this call for the restriction of Mexican immigration: "It is folly to pretend that the more recently arrived Mexicans, who are largely of Indian blood, can be absorbed and incorporated into the American race."[41]

The demand for Mexican exclusion resonated among Anglo workers. Viewing Mexicans as a competitive labor force, they clamored for the closing of the border. In 1910, the American Federation of Labor's *Advocate* asked: "Is it a pretty sight to see men, brawny American men with callouses on their hands and empty stomachs — sitting idly on benches in the plaza, while slim-legged peons with tortillas in their stomachs, work in the tall building across the way? Do you prefer the name Fernandez, alien, to the name, James, citizen, on your payroll?" Five years later, the *Advocate* again denounced the employment of Mexicans as cheap laborers: "True Americans do not want or advocate the importation of any people who cannot be absorbed into full citizenship, who cannot eventually be raised to our highest social standard."[42] Clearly, race was being used as a weapon by the American Federation of Labor: Mexicans not only constituted "cheap labor" but were regarded as incapable of becoming fully American.

Then came the Great Depression. Rendered superfluous as laborers and blamed for white unemployment, Mexicans became the targets of repatriation programs. Hungry Mexicans were sometimes granted temporary relief by welfare agencies only if they promised to return to Mexico. "Many Mexican immigrants are returning to Mexico under a sense of pressure," reported sociologist Emory Bogardus in 1933. "They fear that all welfare aid will be withdrawn if they do not accept the offer to take them out of our country."[43]

In their repatriation efforts, private charities and government agencies provided railroad transportation for tens of thousands of Mexicans to their "homeland." In Santa Barbara, Mexicans were literally shipped out from the Southern Pacific depot. "They [the immigration officials] put all the people...in boxcars instead of inside the trains," a witness recalled. "They sent a lot of people from around here too.... A big exodus.... They were in here illegally but the moral part of it, like separation and putting them in boxcars.... I'll never forget as long as I live." Many of the "repatriates" were children who had been born in the United States. The Los Angeles Chamber of Commerce estimated that 60 percent of the "repatriated" children were American citizens "without very much hope of ever coming back into the United States." Altogether about 400,000 Mexicans were "repatriated."[44]

The Barrio: A Mexican-American World

For many Mexicans, the border was only an imaginary line between Mexico and the United States — one that could be crossed and recrossed at will. Living in El Norte, they created a Mexican-American world called the barrio.

In their ethnic enclaves located in cities and rural towns, they did not feel like aliens in a foreign land as they did whenever they crossed the railroad tracks and ventured uptown into the Anglo world. Though their neighborhood was a slum, a concentration of shacks and dilapidated houses, without sidewalks or even paved streets, the barrio was home to its residents. The people had come from different places in Mexico and had been here for different lengths of time, but together they formed "the *colonia mexicana*." "We came to know families from Chihuahua, Sonora, Jalisco, and Durango," remembered one of them. "Some had come to the United States even before the revolution, living in Texas before migrating to California. Like ourselves, our Mexican neighbors had come this far moving step by step, working and waiting."[45] Originally from different parts of Mexico, they were inventing a new identity: they were becoming Mexican American.

In their communities, the newcomers celebrated national holidays like the Sixteenth of September, Mexican Independence

Day. "We are Mexicans," declared a speaker at one of the celebrations, "almost all of us here...by our fathers or ancestors, although we are now under a neighboring nation's flag to which we owe respect. Notwithstanding, this respect does not prevent us from remembering our Mexican anniversary." The celebrations, Ernesto Galarza recalled, "stirred everyone in the barrio" and gave them the feeling that they were "still Mexicans." At these festive occasions, there were parades in the plazas attended by city and county officials as well as Mexican consuls. The entire town became a fandango. Colorful musicians strolled, and people danced in the streets. Excited crowds shouted "viva Mexico" and sang Mexican songs as fireworks exploded and muchachos (kids) listened to stories about Mexico told by the *viejitos* (old ones). Bands played the national anthems of both countries. The flags and the colors of the United States and Mexico were displayed together—red, white, and blue as well as red, white, and green.[46]

Their religion was a uniquely Mexican version of Catholicism, a blending of a faith brought from the Old World and beliefs that had been in the New World for thousands of years before Columbus. For the Mexicans, God was deeply personal, caring for each of them through their saints. In their homes, they decorated their altars with *santitos,* images of saints dear to them. They had a special relationship with the Virgen de Guadalupe: according to their account, she had appeared to a poor Indian in Mexico. "I have with me an amulet which my mother gave to me before dying," a Mexican told an interviewer. "This amulet has the Virgin of Guadalupe on it and it is she who always protects me." Their Virgin Mary was Mexican: many paintings and statues represented her as dark in complexion.[47]

What bound the people together was not only ethnicity but also class. "We were all poor," a Mexican said, "we were all in the same situation." The barrio was a "grapevine of job information." A frequently heard word was *trabajo* (work), and "the community was divided in two—the many who were looking for it and the few who had it to offer." Field hands, railroad workers, cannery workers, construction laborers, and maids came back to the barrio after work to tell one another where the jobs were and how much they were paid and what the food and living quarters were like.[48]

In the colony, unskilled workers from Mexico were welcomed. "These Mexicans are hired on this side of the Rio Grande by agents of the larger farms, and are shipped in car load lots, with windows and doors locked, to their destination," a local newspaper reported. "After the cotton season the majority will work their way back to the border and into Mexico." But the barrio offered these migrant workers a place to stay north of the border. "Beds and meals, if the newcomers had no money at all, were provided—in one way or another—on trust, until they found jobs." Aid was given freely, for everyone knew what it meant to be in need. "It was not charity or social welfare," Ernesto Galarza explained, "but something my mother called *asistencia,* a helping given and received on trust, to be repaid because those who had given it were themselves in need of what they had given. [Newcomers] who had found work on farms or in railroad camps came back to pay us a few dollars for *asistencia* we had provided weeks or months before."[49]

People helped each other, for survival depended on solidarity and mutual assistance. For example, Bonifacio Ortega had dislocated his arm while working in Los Angeles. "I was laid up and had to be in the hospital about three months," he recalled. "Fortunately my countrymen helped me a lot, for those who were working got something together every Saturday and took it to me at the hospital for whatever I needed. They also visited me and made me presents." Ortega's arm healed, and he returned to work at a brickyard. "We help one another, we fellow countrymen. We are almost all from the same town or from the nearby farms. The wife of one of the countrymen died the other day and we got enough money together to buy a coffin and enough so that he could go and take the body to Jalisco."[50]

Moreover, "the *colonia mexicana*" was a place where Mexicans could feel at home in simple, day-to-day ways. Women wearing rebozos were seen everywhere, just like in Mexico. There were Mexican plays and *carpas*—acrobats and traveling sideshows. Stands and cafés offered tamales and other favorites such as frijoles, tortillas, *menudo* (tripe stew), and *dulces* made with *piloncillo* (Mexican sugar). Cantinas and bars were places to hang out and drink beer. *Mercados* (grocery stores) stocked Mexican foods like chorizo (sausage), while *panderias* baked fresh bread. Shopping in the *tiendas* (small shops) was familiar. "In the second-hand shops, where the barrio people sold and bought furniture and clothing, there were Mexican clerks who knew the Mexican ways of making a sale."[51]

In the early evenings, as the sun began to set, the people sat outside their homes, as they had in villages on the other side of the border. The air still carried the smells of suppertime—"tortillas baking, beans boiling, chile roasting, coffee steaming, and kerosene stenching." The men "squatted on the ground, hunched against the wall of the house and smoked. The women and the girls... put away the kitchen things, the *candiles* turned down to save kerosene. They listened to the tales of the day if the men were in a talking mood." They spoke in two languages—"Spanish and with gestures."[52]

As darkness descended, men and women shared stories about life in El Norte. "They [Anglos] would rant at public meetings and declare that this was an American country and the Mexicans ought to be run out." "You can't forget those things [acts of discrimination]. You try to forget because you should forgive and forget, but there is still a pain in there that another human being could do that to you." "I haven't wanted to, nor do I want to learn English, for I am not thinking of living in this country all my life. I don't even like it here." "They talk to us about becoming citizens, but if we become citizens we are still Mexicans. They look at our hair, and listen to our speech and call us Mexicans." "I have always had and now have my home in El Paso, but I shall never change my [Mexican] citizenship in spite of the fact that [here] I have greater opportunities and protection." "I want to go back to Leon because it is my country and I love Mexico. But I like it better here for one can work more satisfactory. No one interferes with one and one doesn't have to fear that there will be or won't be revolutions."[53] Their stories did the telling: despite their complaints about racism in America and their attachments to Mexico, they were in fact making El Norte their homeland.

As the night air became chilly, the barrio people pulled their serapes and rebozos around their shoulders, and their hunched figures blended into the darkness. But no one was sleepy yet, so the people continued to sit in front of their homes. The stars were brighter above Mexico, someone commented, and there were more of them. *Sí*, yes, another added, and there were coyotes howling nearby. As in their old villages, the streets in the barrio had no lights, and now only their voices could be heard. "When they pulled on their cigarettes, they made ruby dots in the dark, as if they were putting periods in the low-toned conversation."[54]

13

꙰

TO "THE LAND OF HOPE"

Blacks in the Urban North

L IKE THE MEXICANS trekking to El Norte, southern blacks were migrating northward by the tens of thousands during the early twentieth century. They were going to the cities of the Midwest and the Northeast, where they joined European immigrants, including the Irish and Jews. Describing the powerful spirit behind this great black migration, the daughter of a sharecropper wrote: "And Black men's feet learned roads. Some said good-bye cheerfully...others fearfully, with terrors of unknown dangers in their mouths...others in their eagerness for distance said nothing. The daybreak found them gone. The wind said North. Trains said North. The tides and tongues said North, and men moved like the great herds before the glaciers." Blacks listened and heard the message:

> Some are coming on the passenger,
> Some are coming on the freight,
> Others will be found walking,
> For none have time to wait.[1]

An exodus was under way. "The Afro-American population of the large cities of the North and West," the New York Age reported in 1907, "is being constantly fed by a steady stream of new people from the Southern States." Between 1910 and 1920, the black population jumped from 5,700 to 40,800 in Detroit, 8,400 to 34,400 in Cleveland, 44,000 to 109,400 in Chicago, and 91,700 to 152,400 in New York. W. E. B. Du Bois noted: "There can be no doubt of the drift of the black South northward."[2]

"The Wind Said North"

All over the South, blacks went to bed at night and woke up in the morning thinking and talking about the message of the wind, and then suddenly one day, they found themselves swept up in the migration "fever." Nothing could restrain their boundlessness. "Everybody seems to be asleep about what is going on right under their noses," a Georgia newspaper stated. "That is, everybody but those farmers who have awakened up of mornings recently to find every male Negro over 21 gone—to Cleveland, to Pittsburgh, to Chicago." After half the black population left her little town in Mississippi, a woman said: "If I stay here any longer, I'll go wild. Every time I go home I have to pass house after house of all my friends who are in the North and prospering. I've been trying to hold on here and keep my property. There ain't enough people here I now know to give me a decent burial." To be left behind was to feel a sudden loneliness:

> I've watched the trains as they disappeared
> Behind the clouds of smoke,
> Carrying the crowds of working men
> To the land of hope.[3]

On one Georgia plantation, a landlord was surprised to find all of his tenants gone, except two old men. Uncle Ben and Uncle Joe were too poor to purchase train tickets. They sorrowfully told their landlord that everyone else had abandoned him, but that they had loyally remained behind on the plantation. The landlord gave the two men some money because they promised to stay and work the crops. Immediately after he left, the old-timers took the money and boarded the train to join their companions in the North.[4]

Like the immigrants from Asia, Mexico, and Europe, southern blacks were driven by particular "pushes." After emancipation, most blacks had been forced to become sharecroppers and tenant farmers. Dependent on white landlords and enslaved by debts, they complained:

> *Working hard on southern soil,*
> *Someone softly spoke;*
> *'Toil and toil and toil and toil,*
> *And yet I'm always broke.'*

The ordeal of sharecropping was crushing: at the end of the harvest, tenant farmers were often disappointed to find themselves only deeper in debt. Though they were free, many were in economic bondage. "There was," they had painfully come to realize, "no rise to the thing."

> *Where I come from*
> *folks work hard*
> *all their lives*
> *until they die*
> *and never own no part*
> *of earth nor sky.*

Their economic situation became extremely dire as floods destroyed their farms and insects ravaged their cotton crops.

> *Boll-weevil in de cotton*
> *Cut worm in de cotton,*
> *Debil in de white man,*
> *Wah's goin' on.*[5]

Meanwhile, there were "pulls" from the North. World War I had virtually cut off the flow of European immigrants, reducing their numbers from 1,200,000 in 1914 to only 110,000 in 1918. Facing tremendous labor shortages, factory managers dispatched labor recruiters to the South. "These same factories, mills and workshops that have been closed to us, through necessity are being opened to us," a black newspaper in Chicago reported. "We are to be given a chance, not through choice but because it is expedient. Prejudice vanishes when the almighty dollar is on the wrong side of the balance sheet." Traveling in the South, journalist Ray Stannard Baker reported: "Trains were backed into several Southern cities and hundreds of Negroes were gathered up in a day, loaded into the cars, and whirled away to the North. I was told of instances in which Negro teamsters left their horses standing in the streets, or deserted their jobs and went to the trains without notifying their employers or even going home." A black worker told Baker: "The

best wages I could make [in Georgia] was $1.25 or $1.50 a day. I
went to work at a dye house at Newark, N.J., at $2.75 a day, with a
rent-free room to live in. The company paid my fare North."[6]

Like Mexicans, blacks were following the jobs. "More positions
open than men for them," announced the headlines of the *Chicago Defender,* which was owned by black editor Robert Abbott.
Article after article described the great labor shortage and the
willingness of employers to "give men a chance to learn the trade
at $2.25 a day." Classified job listings beckoned:

> Men wanted at once. Good steady employment for colored. Thirty
> and 39½ cents per hour. Weekly payments. Good warm sanitary
> quarters free.... Towns of Newark and Jersey City.
>
> Laborers wanted for foundry, warehouse and yard work. Excel-
> lent opportunity to learn trades, paying good money. Start $2.50–
> $2.75 per day. Extra for overtime.[7]

A young black woman asked the *Defender* to send her information about employment in the North:

> *Dear Sirs:* I am writeing to you all asking a favor of you all. I am a
> girl of seventeen. I now feel like I aught to go to work. And I would
> like very very well for you all to please forward me to a good job. I
> am tired of down hear in this _____/ I am afraid to say.[8]

Meanwhile, from the North, blacks sent home glowing reports
about their jobs. "M_____, old boy," one of them wrote, "I was promoted on the first of the month. I was made first assistant to the
head carpenter...and was raised to $95 a month. I should have
been here 20 years ago. I just begin to feel like a man. It's a great
deal of pleasure in knowing that you have got some privilege. My
children are going to the same school with the whites and I dont
have to umble to no one. I have registered—Will vote the next
election and there isnt any 'ye sir' and 'no sir'—its all yes and
no and Sam and Bill." "I am well and thankful to say I am doing
well," wrote a black woman who had recently arrived in Chicago.
"I work in Swifts packing Co., in the sausage department.... We
get $1.50 a day.... Tell your husband work is plentiful here and he
wont have to loaf if he want to work." A South Carolina newspaper
described the good fortune of a Greenwood County farm boy who
had gone North to work for twenty-five dollars a week. "He came
home last week to assist his people on the farm and brought more

than one hundred dollars and plenty of nice clothes. He gave his mother fifty dollars, and put fifty dollars in the Greenwood bank and had some pocket change left."⁹

But there was something more, something deeper than economics: a new generation of blacks was coming of age. "I have men," a white plantation owner stated, "who were slaves on the place.... They have always lived there and will probably die there, right on the plantation where they were born." The old former slaves were passing away, however, and so was the racial etiquette of deference and subordination they represented. "The South," W. E. B. Du Bois observed, "laments to-day the slow, steady disappearance of a certain type of Negro—the faithful, courteous slave of other days, with his dignified...humility."¹⁰

In place of such old-time Negroes, there were younger blacks, born after the Civil War and after slavery, an institution and way of life that seemed to them in the far distant past. To them, accounts of slavery "were but childhood tales." Slavery was not something they had experienced, something they could remember. They did not feel, as did the older generation, the lingering vividness and sedimentary power of the peculiar institution. White southerners frequently complained that this new generation was "worthless." Lacking the habits of "diligence, order, faithfulness" of those who had been born in slavery, they "rarely remain[ed] long enough under the supervision of any planter to allow him sufficient time to teach them." Compared to the "older class of colored labor," men who were "pretty well up in years" and who constituted a "first rate class of labor," the blacks of the "younger class" were "discontented and wanted to be roaming."¹¹

Most of the blacks moving north belonged to this post–Civil War generation, restless, dissatisfied, unwilling to mask their true selves and accommodate to traditional subservient roles. In a statement to a Labor Department investigator in 1916, a black man explained this generational difference:

> My father was born and brought up as a slave. He never knew anything else until after I was born. He was taught his place and was content to keep it. But when he brought me up he let some of the old customs slip by. But I know there are certain things that I must do and I do them, and it doesn't worry me; yet in bringing up my own son, I let some more of the old customs slip by. For a year I have been keeping him from going to Chicago; but he tells me this is his last crop; that in the fall he's going. He says, "When a young white

man talks rough to me, I can't talk rough to him. You can stand that; I can't. I have some education, and inside I has the feelings of a white man. I'm going."[12]

"Tired of the South," these young blacks "wanted to make a change." A migrant declared that he could not live in North Carolina "and be a man and be treated like a man." A black in Mississippi told Ray Stannard Baker that he was planning to move to Indiana: "They're Jim Crowin' us down here too much; there's no chance for a coloured man who has any self-respect." "The exodus...of colored people from the sunny South to the colder states of the North," the *Richmond Reformer* explained, "has its very birth out of the 'Jim Crow' and 'Segregation' conditions which now exist in the cities of the South and which have crowded colored people into narrow unsanitary or unhealthy quarters...segregating them like cattle, hogs or sheep." More intolerable than segregation was racial violence. "For every lynching that takes place," noted Booker T. Washington in 1903, "...a score of colored people leave...for the city."

> *Yes, we are going to the north!*
> *I don't care to what state,*
> *Just so I cross the Dixon Line,*
> *From this southern land of hate,*
> *Lynched and burned and shot and hung,*
> *And not a word is said.*[13]

Young blacks spoke loudly with their feet: they left the South in search of what Du Bois called "the possibility of escaping caste at least in its most aggravating personal features." Possessing "a certain sort of soul, a certain kind of spirit," they found the "narrow repression and provincialism of the South simply unbearable." Why stay in the South, declared the *Chicago Defender*, "where your mother, sister and daughter are raped and burned at the stake; where your father, brother and sons are treated with contempt and hung to a pole, riddled with bullets at the least mention that he does not like the way he is treated"? In letters to the *Defender,* blacks described their flight from southern racism:

Dear Sir Bro.... I seen in the Defender where you was helping us a long in securing a posission as brickmason plaster cementers stone mason. I am writing to you for advice about comeing north.... We expect to do whatever you says. There is nothing here for the colored man but a hard time wich these southern crackers gives us.

They refused to be victimized by southern police abuse:

Dear Sir: I am writing you for information to come north [and] to see if there is any way that you can help me by giving me the names of some of the firms that will send me a transportation as we are down here where we have to be shot down lik rabbits for every little orfence as I seen an orcurince hapen down here this after noon when three depties from the shrief office...come out and found some of our raice mens in a crap game and it makes me want to leave the south worse than I ever did.

And they demanded their dignity:

Dear Sir: wanted to leave the South and Go and Place where a man will Be any thing Except A Ker I thought would write you for Advise As where would be a Good Place for a Comporedly young man That want to Better his Standing who has a very Promising young Family. I am 30 years old and have Good Experience in Freight Handler and Can fill Position from Truck to Agt. would like Chicago or Philadelphia But I dont Care where so long as I Go where a man is a man.[14]

Free from the shadow of slavery, these young people were able to imagine new possibilities for themselves in the North. "I didn't want to remain in one little place all my days," one of them stated. "I wanted to get out and see something of the world." Hoping to become a writer, a young black man went North during the 1920s. "I went to Chicago as a migrant from Mississippi," Richard Wright recalled. "And there in that great iron city, that impersonal, mechanical city, amid the steam, the smoke...there in that self-conscious city, that city so deadly dramatic and stimulating, we caught whispers of the meanings that life could have, and we were pushed and pounded by facts much too big for us." Like novelist Toni Morrison's Joe and Violet, country people who moved from Virginia to New York City, these migrants were responding to the inner urges of "their stronger, riskier selves." Arriving in the northern cities, they shouted: "At last, at last, everything's ahead."[15]

By 1930, some two million blacks had migrated to the cities of the North and changed the course of history. "The migration is probably, next to emancipation, the most noteworthy event which has ever happened to the Negro in America," observed Ray Stannard Baker in 1917. "Negroes are acting for themselves, self-consciously, almost for the first time in their history. They did not win their freedom: it was a gift thrust upon them by the North. But in the present migration..., they are moving of their own accord."[16]

As they traveled to the North, they spoke excitedly about the "Flight out of Egypt," "Bound for the Promised Land," and "Going into Canaan." Jeremiah Taylor of Mississippi had been resigned to remain on his farm until his son returned from town one day and told him that folks were leaving "like Judgment day." After a group of migrants crossed the Ohio River, they knelt down in prayer and then sang: "I Done Come out of the Land of Egypt with the Good News." "The cry of 'Goin' Nawth' hung over the land like the wail over Egypt at the death of the first-born," reported a sharecropper's daughter.[17]

"Railroads, hardroads, dirt roads, side roads, roads were in the minds of the black South and all roads led North."[18]

The Crucible of the City

As they journeyed to "the land of hope," the migrants carried not only hope but also uncertainties. Richard Wright recalled how he had left the South to fling himself into the "unknown." The *Defender* described the migrants' feelings of "trembling and fear": "They were going—they didn't know where—among strange people, strange customs." A song captured their mood of ambivalence:

> *I'm a poor boy and I'm a stranger blowed in*
> *   your town,*
> *Yes I am,*
> *I'm a poor boy and I'm a stranger blowed*
> *   in your town,*
> *I'm a poor boy and I'm a stranger blowed in*
> *   your town,*
> *I'm goin' where a friend can be found.*

But their expectations of freedom exceeded their uneasiness about becoming strangers. And so they went to northern cities, especially to Chicago and New York.[19]

Chicago was "the mouth of the stream of Negroes from the South." Emmett J. Scott's metaphor aptly described this brawling midwestern city—the home of the *Defender,* which had been urging young blacks to come north. Chicago was also the terminus of the Illinois Central Railroad, with its rail lines connected to the small towns of Mississippi, Arkansas, and Louisiana. Chicago was a dynamic industrial center, spawning jobs and inspiring dreams.[20]

In 1900, Chicago had a black population of only 30,000. "I lived on Lincoln Street—there were foreigners there," a black resident remembered, describing the integrated neighborhoods of the time. "My children used to go to white kids' parties, for where we lived there was nothing much but foreigners. There was only one other colored family in that block." Only one ward in the entire city was 25 percent black, while 19 out of 35 wards were about .5 percent black. Twenty years later, the black population jumped to 109,000, concentrated in the predominantly black neighborhoods of the South Side.[21]

The black migration to Chicago sparked an explosion of white resistance. "A new problem, demanding early solution, is facing Chicago," the *Tribune* warned. "It pertains to the sudden and unprecedented influx of southern Negro laborers." The newspaper depicted the newcomers as carefree and lazy: "In a house at Thirty-second and Wabash eight or ten Negroes were lying about on the floor, and one was picking a banjo and singing a song the chorus of which ended 'Mo' rain, mo' rest, / Mo' niggers sleep in de nest.'" Determined to repel this Negro "invasion," several hundred white residents organized the Hyde Park Improvement Protective Club, which announced that real estate agents must not sell homes to blacks in white blocks. "The districts which are now white," a leader of the organization declared, "must remain white. There will be no compromise."[22]

The conflict over housing intensified during World War I as blacks responded to the labor needs of Chicago's war-related industries. In 1917, the Chicago Real Estate Board pointed out that southern blacks were "pouring into Chicago at the rate of ten thousand a month," and warned that this influx would precipitate a decline in property values. A year later, the Kenwood and Hyde Park Property Owners' Association urged whites not to sell or rent to blacks. Whites "won't be driven out," the association vowed; they would prevent a Negro "take-over" and keep their neighborhood "clear of undesirables at all cost."[23]

Meanwhile, the schools became racial battlegrounds. An African American recalled: "The Italian boys were so low morally. They made several attempts to rape some of the girls...[they] used to gang us.... We were always able to have a good fight and have some blood shed." "I remember how I used to fight with the white children, especially the Dago children," said another black. "They would call out to us colored children, 'Nigger, nigger, never die, black face and China eye,' and when I catch one and get through with him he would think *he* was black."[24]

Similarly, the workplace became a terrain of competition and conflict. Before the war, blacks were largely restricted to employment as servants. In 1910, over 60 percent of the women were domestic servants or laundresses; close to half of all the employed men worked as porters, servants, waiters, and janitors. Though generally excluded from industrial employment, blacks were allowed to cross caste labor lines occasionally as strikebreakers. Managers used them as scabs during the 1904 stockyards strike and the teamsters strike a year later. The *Broad Ax,* a black weekly, criticized employers for "bringing hundreds and hundreds of colored men here from the remote parts of the South...to temporarily serve as strikebreakers for such Negro-hating concerns as Marshall Field and Company, Mandel Brothers and Montgomery Ward and Company, who [had] no use for Negroes in general except to use them as brutish clubs to beat their white help over the head." After the settlement of both strikes, the black workers were discharged.[25]

The war, however, generated a sharp demand for labor and opened expanded opportunities for blacks in industries. By 1920, the majority of black men were employed in factories rather than domestic and personal services. Women made similar, although smaller, inroads—15 percent of them had become factory operatives. They had been eager to get out of domestic work. Employers "almost make you a slave," complained a woman who had quit her job as a maid to work in a mail-order house. Personal service reminded blacks of the South, where they had been dependent on whites and closely supervised. Like the Irish maids who left the "service" for factory work, many black women wanted more autonomy. "I'll never work in nobody's kitchen but my own any more," exclaimed one of them who was employed in a box factory. "No indeed! That's the one thing that makes me stick to this job. You do have some time to call your own." For the first time in their lives, black men and women were working in industries, making what they considered good wages—42 cents an hour in the packing houses and even higher rates in manufacturing.[26]

In the stockyards and packing houses, managers deliberately employed African Americans in order to subvert the union activities of white workers. Seeking to keep the workforce racially divided, they hired a black promoter, Richard Parker, to set up a black company union, the American Unity Labor Union. As the front man for the interests of management, Parker played on black suspicions of the white labor movement and pitted the company union blacks against the white workers. He distributed twenty thousand handbills warning blacks not to join the "white man's union." One of his advertisements published in a black newspaper declared:

GET A SQUARE DEAL WITH YOUR OWN RACE

Time has come for Negroes to do now or never. Get together and stick together is the call of the Negro. Like all other races, make your own way; other races have made their unions for themselves. They are not going to give it to you just because you join his union. Make a union of your own race; union is strength....

This union does not *believe in strikes.* We believe all differences between laborers and capitalists can be arbitrated. Strike is our last motive if any at all.[27]

The Stockyards Labor Council, a white union, tried to counter management's divide-and-conquer campaign by launching its own recruitment drive among black workers. They issued appeals for interracial working-class unity: "The bosses think that because we are of different color and different nationalities we should fight each other. We're going to fool them and fight for a common cause—a square deal for all." At a union rally of black and white workers, a council leader declared: "It does me good to see such a checkerboard crowd—by that I mean all of the workers here are not standing apart in groups, one race huddled in one bunch, one nationality in another. You are all standing shoulder to shoulder as men, regardless of whether your face is white or black."[28]

The council failed to organize the black laborers. "To be frank," an official conceded, "we have not had the support from the colored workers which we expected. Our method of propaganda may have been weak somewhere; probably we do not understand the colored workers as we do ourselves.... Be that as it may, the colored worker has not responded to the call of unionism." Actually, blacks did not respond because they lacked familiarity with unions, and many did not trust the white union.[29]

Racial competition in the workplace added fuel to social antagonisms in the neighborhoods where tensions were literally beginning to explode. In 1917, bombs destroyed the homes of several black families; a year later, a letter warned black tenants on Vincennes Avenue: "We are going to BLOW these FLATS TO HELL and if you don't want to go with them you had better move at once." Shortly after, three bombs went off in the neighborhood. In 1919, several bombings were aimed at the offices of real estate agents who had sold homes to blacks in white neighborhoods. Altogether scores of bombings resulted in two deaths and many injuries as well as the destruction of property worth thousands of dollars.[30]

To add to the terror, white gangs like Ragan's Colts attacked blacks in the streets and parks, especially Washington Park, which separated the black neighborhoods from the white neighborhoods of Hyde Park. On June 21, 1919, white hoodlums killed two black men, reportedly because they wanted to "get a nigger." White gangs posted notices on the boundaries between white and black neighborhoods, threatening to "get all the niggers on the Fourth of July." Afraid and angry, blacks prepared to defend themselves. African-American lawyer Beauregard Moseley warned that blacks had been pushed to the limit by racial violence and were "resolved to meet force with force."[31]

The Fourth of July passed, apparently without incident, but then the tinderbox of race hatred exploded on July 27. On that Sunday afternoon, Eugene Williams had been swimming at the segregated Twenty-ninth Street beach. Williams, who was clinging to a floating railroad tie, had drifted over to the white side of the beach. Somehow he drowned. Blacks at the scene claimed that Williams went down after he had been hit by stones thrown by whites. A cry swept across the beach: "White people have killed a Negro." Frustrated because the police refused to make any arrests, some blacks attacked several white men. Hours later, in retaliation, white gangs beat some blacks who had wandered into white neighborhoods. General rioting broke out, leaving two people dead and over fifty injured. The next day, violence flared up again. As blacks tried to return home from work at the stockyards, they were dragged from streetcars and assaulted by white mobs; armed whites in cars invaded black neighborhoods, shooting indiscriminately at homes. Innocent whites working at businesses located in the black areas were beaten by blacks seeking revenge. The rioting continued throughout the week until the militia was finally able to restore order. The casualty figures were grimly high—23 blacks and 15 whites were killed, while 342 blacks and 178 whites were injured.[32]

In response to racism in Chicago, African Americans decided to promote black solidarity and ethnic enterprise. "We should hasten to build up our own marts and trades," a black minister told his congregation, "so we can give employment and help to provide against such a day as we are now experiencing." Political and business leaders advised blacks to turn inward and develop their own communities with earnings from the steel mills, stockyards, and factories: "Why should these dollars be spent with white men? If white men are so determined that Negroes must live separate and apart, why not beat them at their own game?" Blacks were encouraged to establish their own banks, insurance companies, and stores.[33]

Chicago was the "Black Metropolis," but New York City was the home of Harlem, "the Negro Capital of the World." Blacks had been there since the seventeenth century: as slaves, they had constructed the original wagon road on Manhattan and also worked on farms and estates in what was called New Amsterdam. Their presence continued after the transfer of the Dutch colony to England and after the American Revolution. In 1790, African Americans constituted nearly a third of the population living in a section known as Harlem. But their presence gradually decreased over the years, and by 1890, Harlem had become predominantly white and wealthy. The community was soon to be rapidly transformed. Just as the black exodus from the South was beginning, a housing boom in Harlem collapsed.

The glut of vacant apartments attracted the attention of black real estate agents, especially Philip A. Payton, Jr. His strategy was simple: lease apartment houses from white landlords and then rent them to blacks at a profit. One of his advertisements in a real estate journal announced:

Colored Tenements Wanted

Colored man makes a speciality of managing colored tenements; references; bond. Philip A. Payton, Jr., agent and broker, 67 West 134th.

Payton explained: "By opening for colored tenants first a house on one block and then a house in another I have finally succeeded in securing over two hundred and fifty first class flats and private dwellings."[34]

Payton's penetration, however, encountered resistance from white residents. "Harlem has been devastated as a result of the steady influx of Negroes," a longtime resident complained in 1913. Some white homeowners organized to counter the black "invasion" and the "black hordes." They signed restrictive covenants which stated that their buildings not be leased or sold to "colored" persons. The president of the Harlem Property Owners' Improvement Corporation declared: "It is the question of whether the white man will rule Harlem or the negro." He urged whites to drive the blacks out of Harlem and "send them to the slums where they belonged." But white property owners often found that their choice was to rent to blacks or not rent at all. In order to make their own loan payments, many of them had to yield; reluctantly, they posted notices on their buildings:

NOTICE

We have endeavored for some time to avoid turning over this house to colored tenants, but as a result of…rapid changes in conditions…this issue has been forced upon us.[35]

"The 'border line' which separated whites and Negroes 'rapidly receded' each year," observed historian Gilbert Osofsky, "and by 1914 some 50,000 Negroes lived in the neighborhood." The border kept moving: between 1920 and 1930, 118,792 whites left the neighborhood, while 87,417 blacks arrived. Symbolically, Temple Israel of Harlem became Mount Olivet Baptist Church. Harlem had become the home of more than two-thirds of all the blacks living in Manhattan—the "largest colony of colored people, in similar limits, in the world."[36]

Soon Harlem became overcrowded. In 1925, the population density was 336 persons per acre compared to only 223 for Manhattan as a whole. Meanwhile, landlords were allowing their apartments to deteriorate, and tenants were complaining about broken pipes, leaking roofs, unsanitary conditions, and rats. Unable to move to other areas of the city because of discrimination, blacks were forced to pay higher rents, spending approximately 33 percent of their income on rent, compared to 20 percent for working-class whites. Housing costs were especially burdensome for Harlem blacks because they were confined to low-wage employment.

According to sociologist E. Franklin Frazier, New York had two types of businesses—those that employed "Negroes in menial positions" and those that employed "no Negroes at all." While some black women worked in the garment industry, most of them were domestic servants. The men generally worked as longshoremen and teamsters or as elevator operators, janitors, porters, chauffeurs, and waiters.[37]

Though African Americans lived in congested housing and were employed in low-wage jobs, they felt a surge of power and a sense of pride. Coming to Harlem in search of "the land of hope," they had broken the chains of racial subordination forged by centuries of slavery. Harlem seemed to be a place where black people could begin anew in America. "I sit on my stoop on Seventh Avenue," one migrant declared, "and gaze at the sunkissed folk strolling up and down and think that surely Mississippi is here in New York, in Harlem, yes." This feeling of freedom inspired them to create a community that represented more than just a place where blacks lived. Restless and hopeful, they were ready, eager to listen to a charismatic leader articulate what was on fire within them—fierce dreams of dignity refusing to be deferred. Suddenly, in 1916, Marcus Garvey arrived in Harlem. "Up, you mighty race," he declared, "you can accomplish what you will."[38]

Black Pride in Harlem

Garvey personified a new stirring, a vision of black pride sweeping through Harlem like a fresh breeze blowing north from Jamaica. In his autobiography, he recalled how he was unaware of race as a young child on the Caribbean island: "To me, at home in my early days, there was no difference between white and black." One of his friends was a "little white girl." "We were two innocent fools who never dreamed of a race feeling and problem. As a child, I went to school with white boys and girls, like all other negroes. We were not called negroes then." But at the age of fourteen, Garvey was told by his friend that her parents had decided to send her away to school and that she was not to write to him because he was a "nigger." The incident shook Garvey: "It was then that I found for the first time that there was some difference in humanity, and that there were different races, each having its own separate and distinct social life."[39]

A few years later, during a trip to Europe, Garvey began to formulate his ideology of black nationalism. "You are black," meaning inferior, he had been told. The insult led Garvey to ask: "Where is the black man's Government? Where is his King and his kingdom? Where is his President, his country, and his ambassador, his army, his navy, his men of big affairs?" Unable to find these symbols of power, Garvey declared: "I will help to make them." His imagination began to soar as he envisioned "a new world of black men, not peons, serfs, dogs and slaves, but a nation of sturdy men making their impress upon civilization and causing a new light to dawn upon the human race." In 1914, Garvey returned to Jamaica, where he founded the Universal Negro Improvement Association (UNIA) to unite all the "Negro peoples of the world" and establish a black nation in Africa.[40]

In 1916, Garvey decided to relocate the base for his movement in Harlem. The UNIA exploded with activity—colorful parades in Harlem led by Garvey dressed in military uniform, the publication of *The Negro World,* the establishment of small-business enterprises like grocery stores and laundries in the community, and the launching of the Black Star Line. During the 1920s, Garvey's organization had 9,000 members in Chicago, 6,000 in Philadelphia and Cincinnati, 4,000 in Detroit, and over 30,000 in New York.[41]

Garvey offered a message that electrified many blacks in Harlem and many other ghettos of urban America: the color of their skin was beautiful, and Africa had a glorious past. "When Europe was inhabited by a race of cannibals, a race of savages, naked men, heathens and pagans, Africa was peopled with a race of cultured black men, who were masters in art, science, and literature." Many Harlemites found their voices in their new leader. "Now we have started to speak," Garvey declared, "and I am only the forerunner of an awakened Africa that shall never go back to sleep." Garvey depicted a glorious future for blacks: "We are the descendants of a suffering people; we are the descendants of a people determined to suffer no more." To overthrow oppression, they must reclaim their continent: "If Europe is for the Europeans, then Africa shall be for the black peoples of the world. We say it; we mean it.... The other races have countries of their own and it is time for the 400,000,000 Negroes to claim Africa for themselves." A song of the Garvey movement urged:

> *Advance, advance to victory,*
> *Let Africa be free;*
> *Advance to meet the foe*
> *With the might*
> *Of the red, the black, and the green.*

Red symbolized the blood of the race, black their color, and green the greatness of Africa's future.[42]

Influenced by Booker T. Washington's philosophy of black self-help and independence, Garvey promoted black capitalism and called upon his followers to invest in his shipping company: "The Black Star Line Corporation presents to every Black Man, Woman, and Child the opportunity to climb the great ladder of industrial and commercial progress. If you have ten dollars, one hundred dollars, or one or five thousand dollars to invest for profit, then take out shares in the Black Star Line, Inc. This corporation is chartered to trade on every sea and all waters. The Black Star Line will turn over large profits and dividends to stockholders, and operate to their interest even whilst they will be asleep." Some 40,000 blacks bought 155,510 shares amounting to three-quarters of a million dollars.[43]

The most prominent symbol of the UNIA, the Black Star Line became a slippery slope for Garvey. In 1922, the leader was arrested, charged with using the mails to defraud by advertising and selling stock for a nonexistent ship. According to Garvey, "a sum of $25,000 was paid by one of the officers of the corporation to a man to purchase a ship, but the ship was never obtained and the money was never returned." Garvey's managers had also made mistakes in their purchase of ships that required very costly repairs, and the corporation became mired in debt. The government's case was weak, for it could not prove intent to commit fraud. But Garvey was found guilty and sentenced to five years in prison. From the Atlanta penitentiary, Garvey sent a message: "My work is just begun. Be assured that I planted well the seed of Negro or black nationalism which cannot be destroyed even by the foul play that has been meted out to me." Released two years later by a presidential pardon, Garvey was deported to Jamaica as an undesirable alien.[44]

Garvey was gone, but the powerful dreams he represented remained in the hearts of Harlemites. The *New York News* declared that Garvey had "awakened the race consciousness and race pride of the masses of Africans everywhere as no man ever did...save Booker T. Washington." The *Spokesman,* a black publication, echoed: "Garvey made thousands think, who had never thought before. Thousands who merely dreamed dreams, now see visions."[45]

In the visions of black intellectuals, Harlem became what Langston Hughes called the center of the "New Negro Renaissance," "a great magnet" pulling them from everywhere. "More than Paris, or the Shakespeare country, or Berlin, or the Alps," Hughes said, "I wanted to see Harlem, the greatest Negro city in the world." Hughes would remember the "thrill of the underground ride to Harlem": "I went up the steps and out into the bright September sunlight. Harlem! I stood there, dropped my bags, took a deep breath and felt happy again."[46]

Drawing their inspiration and materials from black folks and their culture, Harlem's black intellectuals created a literature that rebelled against Middletown America. Actually, many of them had come from the black middle class. In his sociological profile of these writers, Robert Bone found that "the parents of the Renaissance novelists were 55 percent professional and 45 percent white collar." Hughes complained that his father, a wealthy rancher, was "interested only in making money." Many of the writers had attended college, and they felt especially hurt by the stings of discrimination and inequality. Educational and economic success, they had come to realize, did not mean social acceptance. To these middle-class black intellectuals, Harlem held out the promise of what Alain Locke called the "New Negro." The "mass movement of the urban immigration of Negroes" was "projected on the plane of an increasingly articulate elite." In the "largest Negro community in the world," "the peasant, the student, the business man, the professional man, artist, poet, musician, adventurer and worker, preacher and criminal, exploiter and social outcast" were coming together. They were forming an imagined community based on a vision of black pride. "In Harlem," Locke announced, "Negro life is seizing upon its first chances for group expression and self-determination. It is—or promises at least to be—a race capital."[47]

The "New Negro" would be "a collaborator and participant in American civilization," and black intellectuals would be in the forefront of this great movement. But first blacks had to learn how to accept themselves. In his essay "The Negro Artist and the Racial Mountain," Hughes explained that the tragic problem of black intellectuals was denial: they did not want to be black or write about black life. "One of the most promising of the young Negro poets said to me once, 'I want to be a poet—not a Negro poet,' meaning I believe, 'I want to write like a white poet'; meaning subconsciously, 'I would like to be a white poet'; meaning behind that, 'I would like to be white.'" Such a flight from black identity was bound to undermine his artistic creativity. "I was sorry the young man said that," Hughes continued, "for no great poet has ever been afraid of being himself. And I doubted then that, with his desire to run away spiritually from his race, this boy would ever be a great poet." Hughes understood this denial, for he knew that there was a "mountain standing in the way of any true Negro art in America—this urge within the race toward whiteness, this desire to pour racial identity into the mold of American standardization, and to be as little Negro and as much American as possible."⁴⁸

To overcome the "racial mountain," Hughes insisted, black writers had to declare boldly: "I am a Negro—and beautiful!" The lives of black folks had to be celebrated, for theirs was a counterculture affirming the joy of life rather than the fear of spontaneity. Simple people, they had their songs and a nip of gin on Saturday nights; they did not care to be like whites, obsessed with work and materialistic success. Black folks, Hughes insisted, furnished a "wealth of colorful, distinctive material for any artist" because they had been able to preserve their "own individuality in the face of American standardizations." "Perhaps these common people will give to the world its truly great Negro artist," Hughes declared, "the one who is not afraid to be himself."⁴⁹

In his own poems, Hughes described his search for identity. Was he African? he had wondered. "So long, so far away" was Africa; "not even memories" were "alive." "I did not feel the rhythms of the primitive surging through me," he explained apologetically. "I was only an American Negro—who had loved the surface of Africa and the rhythms of Africa—but I was not Africa. I was Chicago and Kansas City and Broadway and Harlem." Still, though the drums were "subdued and time-lost," Hughes felt he could hear a song of Africa through "some vast mist of race."⁵⁰ Hughes was struggling to create an identity that was both African and American, a racial self symbolized by the rivers of both continents.

> I've known rivers:
> I've known rivers ancient as the world and older than
>   the flow of human blood in human veins.
> My soul has grown deep like the rivers.
> I bathed in the Euphrates when dawns were young.
> I built my hut near the Congo and it lulled me to sleep.

I looked upon the Nile and raised pyramids above it.
I heard the singing of the Mississippi when Abe Lincoln
went down to New Orleans, and I've seen its muddy
bosom turn all golden in the sunset.
I've known rivers:
Ancient, dusky rivers.[51]

In contrast to Hughes, Jean Toomer decided that his struggle against the "racial mountain" compelled him to go not to Harlem, but to the rural South. As a young writer searching for his roots, Toomer wandered from university to university—Wisconsin, Chicago, New York University, City College of New York. He was the son of a white father and a mulatto mother. His father, a planter, had abandoned the family shortly after Toomer was born, and Jean and his mother lived in Washington, D.C. In 1921, he left New York to teach in a black school in rural Georgia. In the South, black folk culture beckoned, and Toomer felt something irresistible surge within him. In a letter to a friend in 1922, Toomer described the epiphany he had experienced:

Within the last two or three years...my growing need for artistic expression has pulled me deeper and deeper into the Negro group.... It has stimulated and fertilized whatever creative talent I may contain within me. A visit to Georgia last fall was the starting point of almost everything of worth that I have done. I heard folk-songs come from the lips of Negro peasants. I saw the rich dusky beauty that I had heard many false accounts about, and of which till then, I was somewhat skeptical. And a deep part of my nature, a part that I had repressed, sprang suddenly to life and responded to them."[52]

What came out of this powerful encounter was the lyrical novel *Cane*. The story opens in rural Georgia, where the soil is a rich red, and the black people are strong and beautiful. The roots of black culture reach all the way back to a continent across the Atlantic. The Dixie Pike is described as a road that "has grown from a goat path in Africa." But something tragic and evil haunts the land. The people are prisoners of slavery's past. One of the characters, Kabnis, moves from the North to Georgia. The hills, valleys, folk songs, and red soil surround him, but he is unable to appreciate this beauty. Middle class and mulatto, he has become separated from black folks and their culture. He wants to connect himself to them but cannot come to terms with that part of his own black past symbolized by the old ex-slave Father John. When Kabnis sees Father John, he recoils, insisting: "An besides, he aint my past. My ancestors were Southern blue-bloods." His denial keeps him "suspended a few feet above the soil whose touch would resurrect him." To recover his wholeness would require his acknowledgment of slavery as well as his black ancestry.[53]

Toomer painfully understood this truth. Like Kabnis, he was never able to resolve the dilemma of his biracial identity. In 1924, the same year as the publication of *Cane,* he went to France to study at the Georges Gurdjieff Institute, seeking to develop a cosmic consciousness. "I am," he told friends, "what I am, and what I may become I am trying to find out." "What was I?" Toomer asked. "I thought about it independently, and, on the basis of fact, concluded I was neither white nor black, but simply an American." A year later, Toomer returned to Harlem, where he set up a Gurdjieff group and gave lectures on Gurdjieff methods. In 1930, James Weldon Johnson requested Toomer's permisson to publish some of his poems in a book entitled *American Negro Poetry.* Toomer refused, explaining: "My poems are not Negro poems. My prose likewise. They are, first, mine. And, second, in so far as general race or stock is concerned, they spring from the result of racial blending here in America which has produced a new race or stock. We may call this stock American." A "blended" individual, Toomer, unlike Hughes, could not uniformly celebrate his blackness.[54]

Like Toomer, Zora Neale Hurston felt compelled to touch the "soil" of black folk culture in the South. Born and raised in the all-black town of Eatonville, Florida, she initially attended Howard University, where she began writing and publishing short stories. As a young writer, she realized that Harlem was the place to be: "So, beginning to feel the urge to write, I wanted to be in New York." There she could set her hat "at a certain angle and saunter down Seventh Avenue, Harlem City, feeling as snooty as the lions in front of the Forty-Second Street Library." During the 1920s, Hurston studied anthropology with Franz Boas at Barnard College and Columbia University. In 1927, she returned to the South to do research on black folks and write about them. Out of her research came a novel, published in 1937, *Their Eyes Were Watching God.*[55]

In this novel, Hurston's main character, Janie, runs off with a young man. She finds Joe Starks exciting, for he is ambitious and has a dream of building an all-black town. "De man dat built things oughta boss it," he declares. "Let colored folks build things too if dey wants to crow over somethin'." Starks has his own idea of what Janie should be: "A pretty doll-baby lak you is made to sit on de front porch and rock and fan yo'self and eat p'taters dat other folks plant just special for you." Janie discovers she has become "Mrs. Mayor Starks," a possession for "*him* to look at." She tries to rebel: "You sho loves to tell me whut to do, but Ah can't tell you nothin' Ah see!" And Starks retorts: "Dat's 'cause you need tellin'. It would be pitiful if Ah didn't. Somebody got to think for women and chillun and chickens and cows. I god, they sho don't think none themselves." Forced into submission, Janie learns to hush, but the "spirit of the marriage" leaves the bedroom.[56]

Like Toomer, Hurston found Hughes's concept of the "racial mountain" too simplistic, too one-dimensional. What rendered race especially complex for her was gender. The "Negro Renaissance" seemed stifling to Hurston as an artist and as a woman. "From what I had read and heard," she complained, "Negroes were supposed to write about the Race Problem. I was and am thoroughly sick of the subject. My interest lies in what makes a man or a woman do such-and-so, regardless of...color." Indeed, within the world of blacks, as she saw it, there was a gender mountain.[57]

"But a Few Pegs to Fall": The Great Depression

By the 1920s, Harlem had become a slum, the home of poor people desperately clinging to deferred dreams. The Harlem Renaissance, with its cabarets and literary lights, hid much of the ghetto's squalor. Then came the Great Crash of 1929 and the shattering of the economy, unshrouding the grim reality behind this veil of glamor. "The depression brought everybody down a peg or two," Langston Hughes observed. "And the Negroes had but a few pegs to fall."[58]

African Americans fell into deeper poverty everywhere, in the South as well as the North. In 1930, despite the great migration, the majority of them still lived below the Mason-Dixon Line, growing cotton as sharecroppers and tenant farmers. Their livelihoods crumpled along with the stock market: cotton prices had dropped sharply from 18 cents per pound in 1929 to 6 cents in 1933. That year, two-thirds of the blacks cultivating cotton only broke even or went deeper into debt. Moving to southern cities in search of work, blacks encountered angry unemployed whites, shouting: "No Jobs for Niggers Until Every White Man Has a Job!" "Niggers, back to the cotton fields—city jobs are for white folks." By 1932, more than 50 percent of blacks living in southern cities were unemployed.[59]

In northern cities, unemployment rates among African Americans soared to similar levels. In 1932, sociologist Kelley Miller described the black worker as "the surplus man, the last to be hired and the first to be fired." In Harlem, according to social worker Anna Arnold Hedgeman, blacks were "faced with the reality of starvation and they turned sadly to public relief.... Meanwhile, men, women, and children combed the streets and searched in garbage cans for food, foraging with dogs and cats.... Many families had been reduced to living below street level. It was estimated that more than ten thousand Negroes lived in cellars and basements which had been converted into makeshift flats. Packed in damp, ratridden dungeons, they existed in squalor not too different from that of Arkansas sharecroppers."[60]

The statistics told the story of hardship and hunger for blacks. In its survey of 106 cities, the Urban League found that "with a few notable exceptions...the proportion of Negroes unemployed was from 30 to 60 percent greater than for whites." Similarly, government reports showed that blacks joined the relief rolls two times more frequently than whites due to unemployment. In October 1933, 18 percent of the black population was on relief, compared to 10 percent for whites. "Heretofore [the black's] employment problem has been chiefly one of advancement to positions commensurate with his ability," an Urban League leader explained. "Today he is endeavoring to hold the line against advancing armies of white workers intent upon gaining and content to accept occupations which were once thought too menial for white hands." Even the jobs once viewed as degrading were now coveted by whites.[61]

The New Deal offered little relief to blacks. Federal programs designed to provide a safety net for people in distress forced blacks to take a back seat. The Agricultural Adjustment Administration gave white farmers and workers higher rates of support than their black counterparts. "The AAA was no new deal for blacks," wrote historian Harvard Sitkoff; "it was a continuation of the same old raw deal." Similarly, the National Recovery Administration failed to protect black workers from discrimination in employment and wages. Blacks denounced the NRA as "Negroes Ruined Again" and "Negro Removal Act." In 1935, at a conference called "The Position of the Negro in the Present Economic Crisis," black leaders and intellectuals declared disappointment in the Roosevelt administration: "The Negro worker has good reason to feel that his government has betrayed him under the New Deal."[62]

The economic crisis and the failure of the New Deal generated strategy debates among blacks, especially within the NAACP. Feeling that blacks had been battered economically and politically, W. E. B. Du Bois decided that they should consider "voluntary segregation." As a leader of the NAACP and the editor of *The Crisis,* Du Bois had long been a fighter for integration. But the Great Depression led him to urge blacks to "herd together" and "segregate" themselves, at least on an interim basis, in order to survive. They should view themselves as black consumers and producers, committed to working together to build a black "economic nation within a nation." They should create a "closed economic circle"—shop at Negro-owned stores stocked with Negro-grown food, transported by Negro shippers, and processed by Negroes. What Du Bois had in mind was not capitalism but a "cooperative and socialistic state" within the black community, "a collective system on a non-profit basis" with the consumers at "the center and the beginning of the organization." Du Bois argued that such a separatist strategy was only "common sense." Blacks should "face the fact quite calmly that most white Americans [did] not like them." Criticized harshly by the NAACP for his segregationist proposal, Du Bois resigned as editor. Declaring that segregation was an evil, the NAACP called for "the building of a labor movement, industrial in character, which will unite all labor, white and black, skilled and unskilled, agricultural and industrial."[63]

Indeed, as the NAACP recognized, blacks had begun to enter industrial employment and the labor unions. In 1933, the United Mine Workers led by John L. Lewis launched a campaign to bring black workers into the union by employing black organizers and demanding equal pay, regardless of race. Known as "the U.M.W. Formula," this strategy was adopted by the Committee for Industrial Organization (CIO), which initiated massive organizing drives across the country. Led by Philip Murray, the Steel Workers Organizing Committee announced that its policy was "one of absolute racial equality in Union membership." In St. Louis in 1937, an Urban League official reported: "The S.W.O.C. organizers are making it a point to have a Negro officer in each lodge, composed from a plant in which there are Negro workers." In the auto industry, the United Auto Workers urged blacks to join, pledging its opposition to racial discrimination. In 1941, after it enrolled black workers, who constituted 12 percent of Ford Motor Company's labor force, the UAW won union recognition and wage increases. While these achievements did not mean the end of racism among white workers, they demonstrated that interracial labor solidarity was essential, especially in the struggle against management during a time of economic crisis. Like the "giddy multitude" of Bacon's Rebellion, these black and white workers understood their common class interests.[64]

Meanwhile, seeking to attract black voters, New Deal policymakers were beginning to address the needs of blacks. The Public Works Administration, for example, mandated the proviso: "There shall be no discrimination on account of race, creed or color." Blacks praised the WPA for prohibiting racial discrimination and for giving them a chance to participate in the program. "In the northern communities, particularly the urban centers," a black journal editorialized, "the Negro has been afforded his first real opportunity for employment in white-collar occupations." The Democratic Party's strategy of appealing to blacks paid off. The massive migration of blacks to northern cities had led to a national political realignment. A contemporary political analyst calculated that black voters held the power to control elections in northern states totaling 157 electoral votes, 31 more than the southern states. During the Depression, disillusioned with Herbert Hoover and the Republicans, African Americans were starting to abandon the party of Lincoln. In the 1936 presidential election, according to George Gallup, over three-fourths of northern blacks voted for Franklin D. Roosevelt, who had been promoted among them as the second "Emancipator."[65]

Blacks were becoming players in a newly emerging Democratic coalition, but their advances in labor and politics would soon be swept into the powerful international currents of World War II.

PART FOUR

Transformations

The Problem of the Color Lines

IN 1903, THE PERSPICACIOUS public intellectual W. E. B. Du Bois wrote in the opening of *The Souls of Black Folk:* "Herein lie buried many things which if read with patience may show the strange meaning of being black here at the dawning of the Twentieth Century. This meaning is not without interest to you, Gentle Reader; for the problem of the Twentieth Century is the problem of the color line."[1]

Forty years later, World War II forced America to confront the problem of the twentieth century. Social scientists took the lead in pointing out the problem of the color line. In *Man's Most Dangerous Myth: The Fallacy of Race,* published in 1942, Ashley Montagu framed the war as a conflict between the "spirit of the Nazi racist" and the "spirit of democracy." Nazism reflected the wrongheaded and dangerous thinking that "the shape of the nose or the color of skin" had something "to do with human values and culture." A year later, in *The Races of Mankind,* Ruth Benedict denounced racism as unscientific and urged the United States to "clean its own house" and "stand unashamed before the Nazis and condemn, without confusion, their doctrines of a Master Race."[2]

Policymakers and pundits also depicted the war as a defense of democracy and a campaign against racism. "By making this a 'people's' war for freedom," it was argued, "we can help clear up the alien problem, the negro problem, the anti-Semitic problem." Republican leader Wendell Willkie echoed: "Today it is becoming increasingly apparent to thoughtful Americans that we cannot fight the forces of imperialism abroad and maintain a form of imperialism at home.... Our very proclamations of what we are fighting for have rendered our own inequities self-evident. When we talk of freedom of opportunity for all nations, the mocking paradoxes in our own society become so clear that they can no longer be ignored." "We are behind the times I admit," Frank

Dixon, a former governor of Alabama, confessed to a friend. "The Huns have wrecked the theories of the master race with which we were so contented so long." The *New York Times* editorialized in May 1941: "A nation making an all-out effort cannot neglect any element in its population. If it is engaged on the side of democracy it must leave open the doors of opportunity to all, regardless of race."[3]

During the war, the most eloquent call for American society to confront its own racism appeared in Gunnar Myrdal's *An American Dilemma: The Negro Problem and Modern Democracy.* In fighting this "ideological war," he argued, Americans must apply the principle of democracy more explicitly to race. "Fascism and nazism are based on a racial superiority dogma—not unlike the old hackneyed American caste theory—and they came to power by means of racial persecution and oppression." Therefore, Americans must stand before the whole world in support of racial tolerance and equality. "When in this crucial time the international leadership passes to America," Myrdal observed, "the great reason for hope is that this country has a national experience of uniting racial and cultural diversities and a national theory, if not a consistent practice, of freedom and equality for all.... The main trend in [this country's] history is the gradual realization of the American Creed."[4]

Indeed, during World War II, Hitler's Nazism with its ideology of Aryan racial supremacy forced Americans to look critically at the color lines within their own society. For different racial and ethnic minorities, the contradictions between the reality of prejudice and the principle of equality became American dilemmas.

14

⛤⛤

WORLD WAR II

American Dilemmas

A S WORLD WAR II raged in Europe and Asia, President Franklin D. Roosevelt issued a warning to the American people. In a speech to Congress delivered on January 6, 1941, he declared: "This nation has placed its destiny in the hands and heads and hearts of its millions of free men and women, and its faith in freedom under the guidance of God. Freedom means the supremacy of *human rights* everywhere. Our support goes to those who struggle to gain those rights and keep them. Our strength is our unity of purpose. To that high concept there can be no end save victory."[1]

Eleven months later, on the Sunday morning of December 7, 1941, Japanese planes shattered the quiet sky and swooped down from the clouds to drop bombs on the ships anchored in the U.S. naval base of Pearl Harbor, Hawaii. The surprise attack was devastating. Altogether, 21 ships were sunk or damaged, 164 planes destroyed, 1,178 soldiers and sailors wounded, and 2,388 killed. Before Congress the next day, President Roosevelt gravely announced: "Yesterday...a date which will live in infamy—the United States was suddenly and deliberately attacked by naval and air forces of the Empire of Japan.... I ask that Congress declare that since the unprovoked and dastardly attack...a state of war has existed."[2]

Suddenly, President Roosevelt became the leader of a democracy at war, and "American dilemmas" would besiege his presidency.

Japanese Americans: "A Tremendous Hole" in the Constitution

Shortly after inspecting the still smoking ruins at Pearl Harbor, Navy Secretary Frank Knox issued a statement to the press: "I think the most effective fifth column work of the entire war was done in Hawaii, with the possible exception of Norway." At a cabinet meeting on December 19, Knox recommended the internment of all Japanese aliens on an outer island.[3]

However, in a radio address aired two days after the Japanese attack on Pearl Harbor, General Delos Emmons as military governor of Hawaii declared: "There is no intention or desire on the part of the federal authorities to operate mass concentration camps. No person, be he citizen or alien, need worry, provided he is not connected with subversive elements...While we have been subjected to a serious attack by a ruthless and treacherous enemy, we must remember that this is America and we must do things the American Way. We must distinguish between loyalty and disloyalty among our people." For General Emmons, the "American way" required him to respect and enforce the U.S. Constitution.[4]

On March 13, 1942, President Roosevelt, acting on the advice of the Joint Chiefs of Staff, approved a recommendation for the evacuation of 20,000 "dangerous" Japanese from Hawaii to the mainland. Two weeks later, General Emmons reduced the number to 1,550 Japanese who constituted a potential threat. Irritated by Emmons, the president wrote to Secretary of War Henry L. Stimson on November 2: "I think that General Emmons should be told that the only consideration is that of the safety of the Islands and that the labor situation is not only a secondary matter but should not be given any consideration whatsoever."[5]

General Emmons countered that such a removal of Japanese would severely disrupt both the economy and the defense of Hawaii. The Japanese, he explained, represented over 90 percent of the carpenters, nearly all of the transportation workers, and a significant proportion of the agricultural laborers. Japanese were "absolutely essential" for rebuilding Pearl Harbor. Commenting on the charges of Japanese-American fifth-column activities, General Emmons declared: "There have been no known acts of sabotage committed in Hawaii." In the end, he ordered the internment of only 1,444 Japanese.[6]

And so, the 158,000 Japanese Americans living in Hawaii did not become victims of mass internment, even though military action between the United States and Japan had in fact occurred in the islands and even though there were more of them living there than on the mainland.

But what happened to the 120,000 Japanese Americans living on the West Coast turned out to be a different story.

Three days after the attack on Pearl Harbor, FBI director J. Edgar Hoover informed Washington that "practically all" suspected individuals were in custody: 1,291 Japanese (367 in Hawaii, 924 on the mainland), 857 Germans, and 147 Italians. In a report to the attorney general submitted in early February, Hoover concluded that a mass internment of the Japanese could not be justified for security reasons.[7]

Despite these intelligence findings, Lieutenant General John L. DeWitt, head of the Western Defense Command, behaved very differently from his counterpart, General Emmons in Hawaii. DeWitt wanted to exclude Japanese aliens as well as U.S.-born Americans of Japanese ancestry from certain areas. On January 4, 1942, at a meeting of federal and state officials, DeWitt argued that military necessity justified exclusion: "We are at war and this area—eight states—has been designated as a theater of operations." He declared that he had no confidence in the loyalty of the Japanese living on the West Coast: "A Jap is a Jap is a Jap." On February 5, after he had received DeWitt's assessment of the need to remove all Japanese, aliens as well as citizens, Provost Marshal General Allen Gullion drafted a War Department proposal for the exclusion of "all persons, whether aliens or citizens...deemed dangerous as potential saboteurs" from designated "military areas."[8]

But a decision on evacuation still had not been made in Washington. During lunch with President Roosevelt on February 7, Attorney General Francis Biddle declared that "there were no reasons for mass evacuation." In his diary on February 10, Secretary of War Stimson wrote: "The second generation Japanese can only be evacuated either as part of a total evacuation...or by frankly trying to put them out on the ground that their racial characteristics are such that we cannot understand or trust even the citizen Japanese. This latter is the fact but I am afraid it will make a tremendous hole in our constitutional system to apply it."[9]

On February 14, 1942, General DeWitt sent Stimson his formal recommendation for removal, buttressing it with a racial justification: "In the war in which we are now engaged racial affinities are not severed by migration. The Japanese race is an enemy race and while many second and third generation Japanese born on United States soil, possessed of United States citizenship, have become 'Americanized,' the racial strains are undiluted.... It, therefore, follows that along the vital Pacific Coast over 112,000 potential enemies, of Japanese extraction, are at large today." On February 19, President Roosevelt signed Executive Order 9066, which directed the secretary of war to prescribe military areas "with respect to which, the right of any person to enter, remain in, or leave shall be subject to whatever restrictions the Secretary of War or the appropriate Military Commander may impose in his discretion." The order did not specify the Japanese as the group to be excluded, but they were the target. A few months later, when President Roosevelt learned about discussions in the War Department to apply the order to Germans and Italians on the East Coast, he wrote to inform Stimson that he considered enemy alien control to be "primarily a civilian matter except in the case of the Japanese mass evacuation on the Pacific Coast." Unlike the Germans and Italians, the Japanese had been singled out.[10]

Under General DeWitt's command, the military posted an order: "Pursuant to the provisions of Civilian Exclusion Order No. 27, this Headquarters, dated April 30, 1942, all persons of Japanese ancestry, both alien and non-alien, will be evacuated from the above area by 12 o' clock noon, P. W. T., Thursday May 7, 1942." Years later, Congressman Robert Matsui, who was a baby in 1942, asked: "How could I as a 6-month-old child born in this country be declared by my own Government to be an enemy alien?" The evacuees were instructed to bring their bedding, toilet articles, extra clothing, and utensils. In silent numbness, Japanese stood before the notices. "Soldiers came around and posted notices on telephone poles," said Takae Washizu. Reading the evacuation notice with disbelief, a Japanese American wrote:

> Notice of evacuation
> One spring night
> The image of my wife
> Holding the hands of my mother.[11]

Believing the military orders were unconstitutional, Minoru Yasui of Portland refused to obey the curfew order: "It was my belief that no military authority has the right to subject any United States citizen to any requirement that does not equally apply to all other U.S. citizens. If we believe in America, if we believe in equality and democracy, if we believe in law and justice, then each of us, when we see or believe errors are being made, has an obligation to make every effort to correct them." Meanwhile, Fred Korematsu in California and Gordon Hirabayashi in Washington refused to report to the evacuation center. "As an American citizen," Hirabayashi explained, "I wanted to uphold the principles of the Constitution, and the curfew and evacuation orders which singled out a group on the basis of ethnicity violated them. It was not acceptable to me to be less than a full citizen in a white man's country." The three men were arrested and convicted; sent to prison, they took their cases to the Supreme Court, which upheld their convictions, saying the government's policies were based on military necessity. Most Japanese, however, felt they had no choice but to comply with the evacuation orders.[12]

Instructed that they would be allowed to take only what they could carry, they were forced to sell most of their possessions—their refrigerators, cars, furniture, radios, pianos, and houses. At the control centers, the men, women, and children were registered and each family was given a number, and they found themselves surrounded by soldiers with rifles and bayonets. In poetry, one of the evacuees captured the humiliation:

> *Like a dog*
> *I am commanded*
> *At a bayonet point.*
> *My heart is inflamed*
> *With burning anguish.*

From there they were taken to the assembly centers. "I looked at Santa Clara's streets from the train over the subway," wrote Norman Mineta's father in a letter to friends in San Jose. "I thought this might be the last look at my loved home city. My heart almost broke, and suddenly hot tears just came pouring out." They knew that more than their homes and possessions had been taken from them. "On May 16, 1942, my mother, two sisters, niece, nephew, and I left...by train," said Teru Watanabe. "Father joined us later. Brother left earlier by bus. We took whatever we could carry. So much we left behind, but the most valuable thing I lost was my freedom."[13]

After a brief stay in assembly centers, the evacuees were herded into 171 special trains, 500 in each train. One of the passengers distilled his distress in poetry:

> *Snow in mountain pass*
> *Unable to sleep*
> *The prison train.*

They had no idea where they were going. The trains took them to ten internment camps: Topaz in Utah, Poston and Gila River in Arizona, Amache in Colorado, Jerome and Rohwer in Arkansas, Minidoka in Idaho, Manzanar and Tule Lake in California, and Heart Mountain in Wyoming.[14]

Most of the camps were located in remote desert areas. "We did not know where we were," remembered an internee. "No houses were in sight, no trees or anything green—only scrubby sagebrush and an occasional low cactus, and mostly dry, baked earth." They looked around them and saw hundreds of miles of wasteland, "beyond the end of the horizon and again over the mountain—again, more wasteland." They were surrounded by dust and sand.[15]

In the camps, the internees were assigned to barracks, each about 20 by 120 feet, divided into four or six rooms. Usually a family was housed in one room, 20 by 20 feet. The room had "a pot bellied stove, a single electric light hanging from the ceiling, an Army cot for each person and a blanket for the bed." An internee painfully conveyed the confinement's unbearableness:

> *Birds,*
> *Living in a cage,*
> *The human spirit.*

The barracks were lined in orderly rows; barbed-wire fences with guard towers defined space for the internees.[16]

They found themselves in a world of military-like routine. Every morning at seven, the internees were awakened by a siren blast. After breakfast in a cafeteria, the children went to school, where they began the day by saluting the flag of the United States and then singing "My country, 'tis of thee, sweet land of liberty." Looking beyond the flagpole, they saw the barbed wire, the watchtowers, and the armed guards. "I was too young to understand," stated George Takei years later, "but I remember soldiers carrying rifles, and I remember being afraid."[17]

Camp life was oppressive and regimented, each day boring and tedious. Forced to abandon the values of self-reliance and activity, shopkeepers and farmers suddenly found themselves working for the government for wages. Young married couples worried about having children born in the camps. "When I was pregnant with my second child, that's when I flipped," said a Nisei woman. "I guess that's when the reality really hit me. I thought to myself, gosh, what am I doing getting pregnant. I told my husband, 'This is crazy. You realize there's no future for us and what are we having kids for?'"[18]

In September 1942, the Selective Service classified all young Japanese men as IV-C, enemy aliens. A month later, however, the director of the Office of War Information urged President Roosevelt to authorize the enlistment of American-born Japanese: "Loyal American citizens of Japanese descent should be permitted, after an individual test, to enlist in the Army and Navy. This matter is of great interest to OWI. Japanese propaganda to the Philippines, Burma, and elsewhere insists that this is a racial war. We can combat this effectively with counter propaganda only if our deeds permit us to tell the truth." President Roosevelt understood the need to neutralize "Japanese propaganda." In December the army developed a plan for forming an all-Japanese-American combat team. On February 1, 1943, hypocritically ignoring the evacuation order he had signed a year earlier, Roosevelt wrote to Secretary of War Stimson: "No loyal citizen of the United States should be denied the democratic right to exercise the responsibilities of his citizenship, regardless of his ancestry.... Americanism is not, and never was, a matter of race or ancestry. Every loyal American citizen should be given the opportunity to serve this country...in the ranks of our armed forces."[19]

Five days later, the government required all internees to answer loyalty questionnaires. The questionnaires had two purposes: to enable camp authorities to process individual internees for work furloughs as well as for resettlement outside the restricted zones, and to register young men for the draft. Question 27 asked draft-age males: "Are you willing to serve in the armed forces of the United States on combat duty, wherever ordered?" Question 28 asked all internees: "Will you swear unqualified allegiance to the United States of America and faithfully defend the United States from any or all attack by foreign or domestic forces, and forswear any form of allegiance or obedience to the Japanese emperor, or any other foreign government, power or organization?"

Forced to fill out and sign the loyalty questionnaire, internees stared at the form. One of them agonized:

> *Loyalty, disloyalty,*
> *If asked,*
> *What should I answer?*

Some 4,600, or 22 percent, of the 21,000 males eligible to register for the draft, answered with a "no," a qualified answer, or no response. Many of them said they were not expressing disloyalty but were protesting against the internment. In January 1944, the Selective Service began reclassifying to I-A men who had answered "yes" to the two questions and serving draft registration notices. Thirty-three thousand Japanese Americans enlisted in the United States Armed Forces. They believed participation in the defense of their country was the best way to express their loyalty and to fulfill their obligation as citizens.[20]

Several thousand of them were members of the Military Intelligence Service (MIS), functioning as interpreters and translators on the Pacific front. Armed with Japanese-language skills, the soldiers of the MIS provided an invaluable service: they translated captured Japanese documents, including battle plans, lists of Imperial Navy ships, and Japanese secret codes. One of their officers described their heroic work: "During battles they crawled up close enough to be able to hear Jap officers' commands and to make verbal translations to our soldiers. They tapped lines, listened in on radios, translated documents and papers, made spot translations of messages and field orders." General Charles Willoughby, chief of intelligence in the Pacific, estimated that the contributions of the Japanese Americans of the MIS shortened the Pacific war by two years.[21]

Japanese-American soldiers also helped to win the war in Europe. In 1942, General Emmons in Hawaii formed a battalion of Japanese Americans—the 100th Battalion. In response to Emmons's call for Japanese Americans to serve in the U.S. Armed Forces, 9,507 American-born Japanese volunteered. "I wanted to show something, to contribute to America," explained Minoru Hinahara. "My parents could not become citizens but they told me, 'You fight for your country.'" After military training, 1,400 men of this battalion were sent to North Africa and then to Italy in September 1943. They participated in the Italian campaign until the following March: 300 of them were killed and 650 wounded.

The 100th was called the "Purple Heart Battalion." In June, the 100th Battalion merged with the newly arrived 442nd Regimental Combat Team, composed of Japanese Americans from Hawaii as well as from the internment camps on the mainland. These soldiers experienced bloody fighting at Luciana, Livorno, and the Arno River, where casualities totaled 1,272 men—more than one-fourth of the regiment. After the battle at the Arno River, they were sent to France, where they took the town of Bruyeres from the German troops in heavy house-to-house fighting.[22]

Then in April 1945, the Japanese-American soldiers assaulted German troops on Mount Nebbione. "Come on, you guys, go for broke!" they shouted as they charged directly into the fire of enemy machine guns. One of them, Captain Daniel Inouye, crawled to the flank of an emplacement and pulled the pin on his grenade. "As I drew my arm back, all in a flash of light and dark I saw him, that faceless German," he remembered. "And even as I cocked my arm to throw, he fired and his rifle grenade smashed into my right elbow and exploded and all but tore my arm off. I looked at it, stunned and unbelieving. It dangled there by a few bloody shreds of tissue, my grenade still clenched in a fist that suddenly didn't belong to me any more.... I swung around to pry the grenade out of that dead fist with my left hand. Then I had it free and I turned to throw and the German was reloading his rifle. But this time I beat him. My grenade blew up in his face and I stumbled to my feet, closing on the bunker, firing my tommy gun left-handed, the useless right arm slapping red and wet against my side."[23]

Inouye had given one of his limbs in defense of his country. By the end of the war in Europe, the soldiers of the 442nd had suffered 9,486 casualties, including 600 killed. The 442nd, military observers agreed, was "probably the most decorated unit in United States military history." They had earned 18,143 individual decorations—including 1 Congressional Medal of Honor, 47 Distinguished Service Crosses, 350 Silver Stars, 810 Bronze Stars, and more than 3,600 Purple Hearts. They had given their lives and limbs to prove their loyalty.[24]

After the war, on July 15, 1946, on the lawn of the White House, President Harry Truman welcomed home the Nisei soldiers of the 442nd: "You fought for the free nations of the world...you fought not only the enemy, you fought prejudice—and you won." As they stood on the land of their birth, however, they could not be certain they had defeated prejudice in America. Captain Inouye discovered they had not won the war at home. He was on his way back to Hawaii in 1945 when he tried to get a haircut in San Francisco. Entering the barbershop with his empty right sleeve pinned to his army jacket covered with ribbons and medals for his military heroism, Captain Inouye was told: "We don't serve Japs here."[25]

Even before the end of the war, the government had begun to close the internment camps. "My parents did not know what to do or where to go after they had been let out of camp," said Aiko Mifune. Her mother, Fusayo Fukuda Kaya, had come to America as a picture bride in 1919; she and her husband, Yokichi, had been tenant farmers in California before they were interned in Poston, Arizona. "But everything they had worked for was gone; they seemed listless and they stayed in Arizona and tried to grow potatoes there." Most of the internees wanted to go home to the West Coast, and they boarded trains bound for Los Angeles, Seattle, and San Francisco. At many train stations, the returning internees were met with hostile signs: "No Japs allowed, no Japs welcome." Many found their houses damaged and their fields ruined. Some of them were never able to return home: too old, too ill, or too broken in spirit, they died in the internment camps. Tragically, they had come all the way to America only to be buried in forlorn and windswept cemeteries of desert camps. Seeking solace in poetry, a camp survivor wrote:

> When the war is over
> And after we are gone
> Who will visit
> This lonely grave in the wild
> Where my friend lies buried?[26]

African Americans: "Bomb the Color Line"

Altogether, some nine hundred thousand African Americans enlisted in the U.S. Armed Forces during World War II. But they served in a Jim Crow, or segregated, military. Four years before the attack on Pearl Harbor, Charles H. Houston of the NAACP demanded that Franklin D. Roosevelt issue an executive order banning all racial discrimination in the armed forces. But in 1940, the president signed the Selective Service Act, which included a provision that prohibited intermingling between "colored and white" army personnel in the same regiments.[27]

Roosevelt's refusal to integrate the armed forces provoked disbelief and anger across black America. In a telegram to the

White House, A. Philip Randolph of the Brotherhood of Sleeping Car Porters declared: "We are inexpressibly shocked that a President of the United States at a time of national peril should surrender so completely to enemies of democracy who would destroy national unity by advocating segregation. Official approval by the Commander-in-Chief of the Army and Navy of such discrimination and segregation is a stab in the back of democracy." On October 9, 1940, the *Crisis* carried the headline: "WHITE HOUSE BLESSES JIM CROW."[28]

Roosevelt's segregationist policy quickly became a symbol of America's hypocrisy. "Democracy must wage a two-fold battle—a battle on far flung foreign fields against Hitler, and a battle on the home front against Hitlerism," insisted Adam Clayton Powell, Jr., a New York City councilman. African-American columnist George Schuyler also castigated the Jim Crow army: "Our war is not against Hitler in Europe, but against Hitler in America. Our war is not to defend democracy, but to get a democracy we have never had." In his protest against segregation in the U.S. Armed Forces, the editor of the *Chicago Defender* urged America to "bomb the color line."[29]

"Prove to us," African Americans challenged Roosevelt and other policymakers, "that you are not hypocrites when you say this is a war for freedom." The war for freedom had to be fought in the country's backyard. "The Army jim-crows us," complained a student. "The Navy lets us serve only as messmen.... Employers and labor unions shut us out. Lynchings continue. We are disfranchised...spat upon. What more can Hitler do than that." In a letter to the NAACP, a soldier wrote: "I am a Negro soldier 22 years old. I won't fight or die in vain. If I fight, suffer or die it will be for the freedom of every black man to live equally with other races." Scheduled to be drafted into the army, a black youth declared: "Just carve on my tombstone, 'Here lies a black man killed fighting a yellow man for the protection of a white man.'"[30]

The army training camps were segregated. In a letter to Truman K. Gibson, the black civilian aide to the secretary of war, private Bert Babero described the toilets at Camp Barkeley, Texas. He noticed a sign in the latrine, designating a section for "Negro soldiers" and another section for "white soldiers." The German prisoners of war held at this army base were allowed to use the white facility. "Seeing this was honestly disheartening," Babero wrote. "It made me feel, here, the tyrant is actually placed over the liberator." In a letter to the *Baltimore Afro-American*, a soldier described the extensiveness of segregation in the training facility. "We cannot go to the church services on the camp. We have to be told when we can go and worship God." Entering the service clubs for sandwiches, they were told: "We don't serve colored."[31]

After training, African Americans were often given degrading work assignments. Writing to the *Richmond Afro-American*, blacks in the 328th Aviation Squadron based in Pampa, Texas, protested against job discrimination within the army: "We are a group of permanent K.P.'s [kitchen police]. We are allowed no other advancement whatsoever. It is true that K.P. pushers (Head K.P.) are made Cpl. and Sgt. but the K.P.'s themselves are a miserable group that will be worked like slaves. We are confined to this job not because we are not fit for anything else but because we are dark. We are referred to on this post as 'that nigger squadron at the end of the field.'"[32]

African Americans wanted equal opportunity to fight in combat, but most of them found themselves assigned to service and support duties. In Europe, blacks composed half of the Transportation Corps. On the beaches of Normandy during the D-Day invasion, they unloaded supplies from ships and transported them to the fighting troops. "We were really stevedores," recalled Timuel Black. "I went into Normandy with combat troops. We serviced them." Their work was especially dangerous. "The Germans aimed at our supplies," explained Black. "We were direct targets. I'd been on six-by-six trucks many nights when the Luftwaffe was strafing us, dropping those small bombs and firing those machine guns at us." Their biggest task was feeding an enormous army in movement. "We were in Belgium during the Battle of the Bulge," Black boasted. "We were at one time feeding three million soldiers: the First, the Third, the Ninth, and the British Seventh." No food, no fighting, the African American soldiers knew. Without their vital support, the Allies would have been beaten back to the beaches by this fierce Nazi counterattack.[33]

When given the chance, African Americans seized opportunities to be in combat as skilled fighters. Initially, the commander of the U.S. Air Service, General H. H. "Hap" Arnold, had refused to allow African Americans to serve as pilots. In his view, they should be laborers and waiters. "Black pilots could not be used," he said, "since this would result in having Negro officers serving over white enlisted men. This would create an impossible social problem." "They didn't want blacks to fly," recalled Fred

Smith of Chicago. "They said blacks were not smart enough to be pilots."[34]

African Americans protested their exclusion from the air force. Insisting that blacks were capable of becoming aviators, the editor of the *Pittsburgh Courier* declared: "How can we excuse refusal to abolish the disuniting COLOR LINE when the life of this nation is threatened?" In response to this criticism, Secretary of War Henry L. Stimson authorized the training of black aviation cadets in a segregated unit at Tuskegee Air Force Base. The War Department defended its segregationist policy, claiming that it could not ignore the social relationships between the races that had been established "through custom and habit."[35]

Sent to Europe as members of the segregated 99th Pursuit Squadron and 332nd Fighter Group, the Tuskegee pilots fought the German Luftwaffe in aerial combat. For their heroic service in Sicily and Italy, two of them were awarded the Distinguished Unit Citation, the military's highest commendation. When General Ira C. Aeker, commanding officer of the Mediterranean Air Force, inspected the 99th Pursuit Squadron on April 20, 1944, he declared: "By the magnificent showing your fliers have made since coming into this theatre, and especially in the Anzio beachhead operations, you have not only won the plaudits of the Air Force, but have earned the opportunity to apply your talents to much more advanced work than was at one time planned for you." The chance for "advanced work" came when the pilots of the 99th Pursuit Squadron and the 332nd Fighter Group escorted bombers first over France and then over Berlin itself.[36]

As the protectors of white pilots flying bombers en route to enemy targets, the Tuskegee pilots dubbed themselves the "Lonely Eagles." Their nickname signified their segregated status even in the sky. "We flew alone," explained Coleman Young, "because our 332nd was not readily accepted when we were sent overseas and attached to white groups. A group was usually composed of three squadrons; so our one black squadron was attached to three white squadrons. They still kept us segregated." But the skills and sharpness of the Tuskegee pilots earned them respect, and bombing groups began requesting them as escorts. "They all wanted us," said Young, "because we were the only fighter group in the entire air force that did not lose a bomber to enemy action. Oh, we were much in demand."[37]

Trained as tankers, the African Americans of the 761st Battalion were also in demand. "When General Patton sent for us," said

E. G. McConnell, "he asked for the best tank unit in the country. Hot dog it, were we proud, proud! I was in a unit I was damn proud of, and I knew that the things we did would shape the future for my children and grandchildren. We were so proud and dedicated to the cause of progress...going ahead so everyone would be able to live like an American." The black tankers participated in the first offensive after the D-Day invasion; then they found themselves fighting in one of the fiercest battles of World War II.[38]

"They put us on flatcars in France and shipped us to Belgium, where the fighting was," recalled Johnie Stevens. "We got off the flatcars, took our tanks off the flatcars, and went right into combat. But that Battle of the Bulge was something. I'm telling you! We never fell back. We never lost an inch of ground during the whole campaign. You can't find nothing in the record that says the 761st lost any of their ground. One of our tank crews that was knocked out, they got out of their tank and fought with machine guns—a captured German officer said he'd never seen anything like that before. Because we stood our ground up there, we really didn't give it up." On January 10, 1945, Stevens was wounded. "Well, here I am in the hospital again," he wrote in his journal: "I was not hit as bad as I was the first time, but I received my Oak Leaf Cluster today and believe me, I earned it. The whole outfit has earned a citation. They stayed on the line for 96 days without relief which is a damn good record for one tank battalion."[39]

African-American women also served in the military. A student at New York University when she enlisted, Elaine Bennett explained: "I wanted to prove to myself, and maybe the world, that we [African Americans] would give what we had back to the United States as a confirmation that we were full-fledged citizens." They represented 4 percent of the 150,000 members of the Women's Army Corps; 855 of them worked in Europe as members of the 6888th Central Postal Directory Battalion.[40]

"The job of our battalion," Lucia M. Pitts recalled, "was to keep up with the addresses of our fighting men, who were constantly on the move, and see that their mail reached them. An average of 30,000 address changes had to be made every day." Margaret Y. Jackson vividly described the frenzied work of processing the mail. "As we labored at long tables, piled high with mail, we were more than objectively impressed by the stacks of letters which we sought to place in the hands of the individuals to whom they were sent. Many of these letters were from the same loved ones.... After weeks—even months—they finally wound up on the floor of the auditorium in the Central Postal Directory. Many of us were as pleased as the soldiers must have been when stacks of letters were distributed to them at mail call." Working together with white WACs in the auditorium, the busy mail processors took satisfaction in seeing "mountains of mail dwindle to small hills." Wherever the WACs went in Birmingham after work, they were constantly approached by servicemen profusely thanking them for getting their long-awaited letters and packages to them. The WACs took pride in their motto: "No mail, no morale."[41]

Meanwhile, at the home front, blacks discovered that the "Arsenal for Democracy" was not democratic: defense-industry jobs were reserved for whites only. Even before its entry into the war, the United States began to increase production of military goods. At a 1941 meeting in Chicago, a black woman called for a mass demonstration in Washington: "We ought to throw 50,000 Negroes around the White House, bring them from all over the country, in jalopies, in trains and any way they can get there, and throw them around the White House and keep them there until we can get some action from the White House." The idea of a march on Washington seized the imagination of A. Philip Randolph, president of the Brotherhood of Sleeping Car Porters. "Let the Negro masses speak," he declared. "Negroes have a stake in National Defense.... It involves equal employment opportunities. Let us tear the mask of hypocrisy from America's Democracy!" In his "Call to the March on Washington," Randolph declared: "Negroes, by the mobilization and coordination of their mass power, can cause President Roosevelt to issue an executive order abolishing discrimination in all government departments, army, navy, air corps and national defense jobs."[42]

Randolph's threat of a mass demonstration alarmed Washington officials. The march was scheduled for July 1. At the White House on June 18, Roosevelt met with civil rights leaders, including Randolph. Roosevelt began by entertaining his guests with old political anecdotes. Impatient, Randolph respectfully interrupted: "Mr. President, time is running on. You are quite busy, I know. But what we want to talk with you about is the problem of jobs for Negroes in defense industries. Our people are being turned away at factory gates because they are colored. They can't live with this thing. Now, what are you going to do about it?" Roosevelt asked Randolph how many people would be at the march. "One hundred thousand, Mr. President."[43]

A week later, Roosevelt signed Executive Order 8802: "There

shall be no discrimination in the employment of workers in defense industries or Government because of race, creed, color, or national origin... and it is the duty of employers and of labor organizations... to provide for the full and equitable participation of all workers in defense industries, without discrimination because of race, creed, color, or national origin." His order also established the Committee on Fair Employment Practice to investigate complaints of discrimination and take appropriate steps to redress valid grievances. The march was canceled. But Roosevelt's new policy for the defense industry was designed for failure. The committee had no power to penalize companies that violated the non-discrimination order.[44]

Ultimately, the real pressure for the integration of the defense industries came from the sheer need for labor in America's "Arsenal for Democracy." At the beginning of 1942, only 3 percent of defense workers were black; by November 1944, that number had jumped to 8.3 percent. Blacks constituted 25 percent of the labor force in foundries, 12 percent in shipbuilding and steel mills. During the war years, the wages of black families increased from 40 percent to 60 percent of that of white families.[45]

The military's demand for men created labor shortages and opened industrial employment opportunities to women, including black women. Of the one million African Americans employed in the defense industries, 600,000 were women. Between 1940 and 1944, the percentage of black women in industry increased from 6.5 percent to 18 percent of the female workforce. Between 1940 and 1944, their numbers in Detroit's factories rose sharply, from 14,451 to 46,750. In the aircraft plants of Los Angeles, 2,000 black women were employed by North American Aviation alone. In "Negro Women on the Production Front," published in a 1943 issue of *Opportunity: Journal of Negro Life,* Mary Anderson wrote: "At the same time that Negro women are contributing to the war effort in essential war and civilian jobs, they are broadening their occupational experience. They are developing skills needed now and after the war. We must use the highest skills and the full strength of all our people, men and women, to win the war and to win the peace."[46]

"When we first got into the war," recalled San Francisco shipworker Lyn Childs, "the country wasn't prepared. And as the manpower in the country was getting pulled into the service, all of the industries were wide open. So they decided, 'Well, we better let some of those blacks come in.' Then after the source of men dried up, they began to let women come in. The doors were opened." Childs described the excitement black women felt over the opportunity to work in the defense industry. "Do you think that if you did domestic work all of your life, where you'd clean somebody's toilets and did all the cooking for some lazy characters who were sitting on top, and you finally got a chance where you can get a dignified job, you wouldn't fly through the door?"[47]

Between 1940 and 1944, the proportion of black women employed in housecleaning declined from 60 percent to 45 percent. One of these women was Fanny Christina Hill. Moving from Tyler, Texas, to Los Angeles in 1943, she had planned to continue working as a housecleaner. "Well, I better get me a good job around here working in a hotel or motel," Hill told her sister. "No," said her sister, "you just come on out and go in the war plants and work and maybe you'll make enough money where you won't have to work in the hotels or motels." Hill applied for a job at North American Aviation. "There was a black girl that was hired with me," she recalled. "I went to work the next day, sixty cents an hour. The war made me live better, it really did." "My sister always said that Hitler was the one that got us out of the white folks' kitchen."[48]

However, as African Americans followed the defense jobs into the cities, they often found themselves targeted by hate crimes and violence. In 1943, at the height of industrial production for the war, urban race riots exploded across the country — 242 racial battles in 47 cities. The center of the "Arsenal for Democracy," Detroit was also the scene of the bloodiest conflict. At the beginning of the war, African Americans totaled 150,000 of this city's population of 1.6 million. Between 1940 and 1943, half a million people, including more than 50,000 blacks, moved into the city. Although jobs in the defense industry were abundant, white workers were determined to continue the exclusion of blacks from the factories. Competition between whites and blacks intensified not only in the workplace but also in housing. The tremendous influx of newcomers into Detroit had created crowded living conditions, and black newcomers were forced to live in segregated ghettos.

Racial tensions in Detroit were volatile. As chief counsel for the NAACP, Thurgood Marshall tried to warn Roosevelt about Detroit's powder keg of racial tensions. "In those days," he told Carl T. Rowan years later, "I would lie awake some nights worrying that Detroit and other cities that had industries that were critical to the war effort were becoming tinderboxes because whites, from the Roosevelt brain trust to the unions, wanted to

keep Negroes out of the mobilization jobs. The tragedy was that
Roosevelt didn't have a fucking clue as to the explosive tensions
that were building up."[49]

Actually, the president was fully aware of the razor-sharp
edges of racial tensions in Detroit. In a "Special Report on Negro
Housing Situation in Detroit," March 5, 1942, marked "Confidential," the federal government's Office of Facts and Figures
had noted the escalating racial antagonisms in Detroit. "It now
appears," the report stated, "that only the direct intervention of
the President can prevent not only a violent race riot in Detroit
but a steadily widening fissure that will create havoc in the working force of every Northern industrial city." A clear warning was
given: "Unless strong and quick active intervention by some high
official, preferably the President, is not taken at once, hell is going
to be let loose."[50]

Hell was actually let loose in the summer of 1943, when Detroit
exploded in fire and violence as white and black mobs attacked
each other. At the end of three days of burning, looting, and murdering, millions in property had been destroyed and nine whites
and twenty-five blacks had been killed. John Sengstacke of the
Negro Publishers' Association asked Roosevelt to appeal to the
conscience of the nation in one of his famous "fire-side chats": "We
urge you to call attention of all Americans through the radio and
the press to the unpatriotic activities of those who subvert the
constitutional guarantee of equal opportunity for all." Roosevelt
felt the pressure to speak out. "Don't you think it is about time,"
he asked his press secretary, Steve Early, "for me to issue a statement about racial riots?" In the end, the president decided not
to make a public address on the crisis. He realized, Eleanor Roosevelt explained, that "he must not irritate the southern leaders,"
whose votes he needed for essential war bills.[51]

President Roosevelt did not speak out against the racial violence in Detroit, but a group of wounded American soldiers did. In
a letter to a newspaper in their home city of Detroit, they wrote
that the riot made "us fighters think—what are we fighting for?"
They declared they were fighting and willing to die for the "principles that gave birth to the United States of America. In this
hospital ward, we eat, laugh, and sleep uncomplaining together."
They signed their letter: "Jim Stanley, Negro; Joe Wakamatsu,
Japanese; Eng Yu, Chinese; John Brennan, Irish; Paul Colosi,
Italian; Don Holzheimer, German; Joe Wojiechowski, Polish; and
Mike Cohen, Jewish."[52]

Their names with their ethnic identities said it all: the war for freedom still needed to be won at home.

Chinese Americans: To "Silence the Distorted Japanese Propaganda"

"I remember December 7th so clearly," said Lonnie Quan of San Francisco. "I was living at Gum Moon Residence Club on Washington Street. It was Sunday. I didn't have a radio in the room." When her boyfriend arrived, he exclaimed: "This is it. Pearl Harbor was attacked!" The news was overwhelming: "I just couldn't believe it—it was a shock. I remember going to work in a restaurant, Cathay House, and everybody was just kinda glued to the radio." The next day, the United States and the Republic of China declared war on Japan, and the two countries became allies.[53]

America's entry into the war ignited patriotic explosions in Chinatowns across the country. In New York's Chinatown, excited crowds cheered themselves hoarse when the first draft numbers drawn were for Chinese Americans. According to a New York City survey, approximately 40 percent of the Chinese population was drafted, the highest of all nationalities. The Chinese wanted to join the army in order to gain respect in America. "To men of my generation," explained Charlie Leong of San Francisco's Chinatown, "World War II was the most important historic event of our times. For the first time we felt we could make it in American society." The war had given them the opportunity to get out of Chinatown, don army uniforms, and be sent overseas, where they felt "they were part of the great patriotic United States war machine out to do battle with the enemy." Similarly Harold Liu recalled: "In the 1940s for the first time Chinese were accepted by Americans as being friends because at that time, Chinese and Americans were fighting against the Japanese and the Germans and the Nazis. Therefore, all of a sudden, we became part of an American dream." Altogether 13,499 Chinese were drafted or enlisted in the U.S. Armed Forces—22 percent of Chinese adult males.[54]

Confined for decades to a Chinese ethnic labor market composed mainly of restaurants and laundries, Chinese workers welcomed the new and higher-paying employment opportunities, especially in the defense industries, where labor shortages were acute. Waiters left the restaurants and rushed to the industrial jobs. In Los Angeles some three hundred Chinese laundry workers closed their shops to work on the construction of the ship *China Victory*.

"At Douglas, home of the A-20 attack planes and dive bombers," the *Chinese Press* noted in 1943, "there are approximately 100 Chinese working at its three plants—Santa Monica, Long Beach, and El Segundo." Chinese workers constituted 15 percent of the shipyard workforce in the San Francisco Bay Area in 1943. Chinese also found employment in the defense industries at the Seattle-Tacoma Shipbuilding Corporation, the shipyards of Delaware and Mississippi, and the airplane factories on Long Island. One of these new defense-industry workers was Arthur Wong. After arriving in New York's Chinatown in 1930 at the age of seventeen, he found himself confined to the ethnic labor market. "I worked five and a half days in the laundry and worked the whole weekend in the restaurant," he said. "And then came the war, and defense work opened up; and some of my friends went to work in a defense plant, and they recommended that I should apply for defense work. So I went to work for Curtiss-Wright, making airplanes. I started out as an assembler, as a riveter."[55]

Chinese-American women also flocked to the defense industries. Several hundred "alert young Chinese-American girls," the *Chinese Press* reported in 1942, "have gone to the defense industries as office workers." The paper proudly presented a partial roster of these workers in the Bay Area—including Fannie Yee, Rosalind Woo, and Jessie Wong of Bethlehem Steel, and Anita Chew, Mildred Lew, and Evelyn Lee of Mare Island's Navy Yard. "They're part of the millions who stand behind the man behind the gun." A year later, the *Chinese Press* informed its readers about Alice Yick, Boston Navy Yard's only Chinese woman mechanical trainee, who could run light lathes, grinders, shapers, planers, and other machine tools. "Helen Young, Lucy Young, and Hilda Lee," the paper continued, "were the first Chinese women aircraft workers in California. They help build B-24 bombers in San Diego."[56]

Fighting the war in the Pacific, the United States had to face the problem of anti-American propaganda by the Japanese government. Japan had been appealing to Asia to unite in a race war against white America. Tokyo broadcasts aimed at China described how the Chinese in the United States suffered from "a campaign of venomous vilification of the character of the Chinese people." "Far from waging this war to liberate the oppressed peoples of the world," Tokyo argued on the airwaves, "the Anglo-American leaders are trying to restore the obsolete system of imperialism."[57]

Alarmed by the Japanese condemnation of America's anti-Chinese laws and sentiment, many policymakers felt the need to "spike" the propaganda guns of Japan. A retired Navy officer told Congress that the Chinese exclusion laws were worth "twenty divisions" to the Japanese army. Supporters of the repeal bill expressed fears of the war turning into a racial conflict. "The Japanese have been carrying on a propaganda campaign seeking...to set the oriental world against the occidental world," one congressman warned. "They have called it a campaign of Asia for Asiatics." Another congressman predicted: "Suppose the Chinese do capitulate and join Japan; then all Asia is apt to go with her. Then you will have a race struggle in which we are hopelessly outnumbered that will last, not for 1 year or 5 years, but throughout generations to come."[58]

In 1943, Congress began considering a bill to repeal the Chinese exclusion laws and to allow a quota for Chinese immigration. President Roosevelt sent Congress a message favoring the repeal bill. "China is our ally," Roosevelt wrote on October 11, 1943. "For many long years she stood alone in the fight against aggression. Today we fight at her side. She has continued her gallant struggle against very great odds." Aware that the act would be essential to the war effort in Asia, the president urged Congress to "be big enough" to acknowledge an error of the past: "By the repeal of the Chinese exclusion laws, we can correct a historic mistake and silence the distorted Japanese propaganda."[59]

Shortly afterward, Congress repealed the exclusion acts and provided a quota for Chinese immigration. Hypocritically, the law allowed only a tiny trickle of 105 Chinese immigrants to be admitted annually. But Chinese Americans also won a long-awaited victory: immigrants from China, the new law provided, were eligible for naturalized citizenship, even though they were not "white."

Mexican Americans: Up from the Barrio

When he heard the news of the Japanese attack on Pearl Harbor, Alex Romandia was stunned. As a Mexican American, he felt righteous indignation. "Our country had been attacked," he told his brother Roberto, "and we had to defend it." Twenty-seven years old, Romandia was working in Hollywood as a stunt man and had befriended many Jewish intellectuals. Feeling rejected by the larger society, Romandia and several of his Jewish friends decided to volunteer for the army. "All of us," he said, "had to prove ourselves—to show that we were more American than the Anglos."[60]

Altogether, half a million Mexican Americans enlisted in the U.S. armed services—a significant proportion of this group's population of 2,690,000. The war offered Mexican Americans a chance to claim the United States as their country, too. Soldier Anthony Navarro explained: "We wanted to prove that while our cultural ties were deeply rooted in Mexico, our home was here in this country." A Mexican-American soldier explained what it meant for America to be his homeland: "We, too, were entitled to work, play, and to live as we pleased. Weren't *all* Americans entitled to the same opportunities?"[61]

From the barrios arose the war slogan in English, "Americans All." "All around us," Socorro Díaz Blanchard recalled, "boys were going into the service." Many families had several members in the armed forces. "When the Second World War started, my brother, José, my brother-in-law, my cousins, and my cousins' husbands served," said Socorro Delgado. "At one time there were as many as fifteen of our immediate family who had gone to war! Every Friday Father Burns and Father Rossetti had a novena for the Sorrowful Mother. We would go and mention the names of the boys who were in the war. There was a victory candelabra with seven candles, and the candles would be lit. They lasted for a week."[62]

At home, families waited anxiously for news about husband, sons, and brothers at the battlefront. "It was very depressing when the men went off to war because it shattered our community," recalled Juanita Vasquez. "Whenever a young man was killed in action, we all felt the same pain because we all went to school together and were close friends." Margaret Villanueva Lambert worked on an assembly line in a defense factory. "I remember a few times during the war," she said, "when I was working and all of a sudden there would be a loud scream followed by uncontrollable crying of a woman who had learned that her husband or son was dead. We all feared that moment when we, too, could be requested to go to the front office and find a representative of the military with an attaché case tucked under his arm with a letter for the next of kin. The workers would always collect a fund for these women."[63]

The Mexican-American casualty rates were extremely high. California congressman Jerry Voorhis pointed out the debt America owed to the people of the barrio: "As I read the casualty lists from my state, I find anywhere from one-fourth to one-third of those names are names such as Gonzales or Sanchez, names indicating that the very lifeblood of our citizens of Latin-American descent in the uniform of the armed forces of the United States is being poured out to win victory in the war." One of the Mexican-American soldiers who returned home wounded was Raul Morin. With casts on both legs, Morin was sent to De Witt General Hospital near Auburn, California. "Among the patients there from Los Angeles I met 'Memo' Terrazas, who was slowly recovering from a brain injury, partially paralyzed, and loss of speech. I also met Frank Carrillo, and Florencio Rodriguez, both veterans of the North African campaign; Vincent Gonzales, Ernie Ochoa, Larry Vasquez, George Yorba.... There must have been over one thousand Mexican Americans in that hospital."[64]

Mexican-American soldiers served with distinction. *La Opinión* proudly published news of military awards: "Sergeant José Lopez was awarded the highest honor in the military—the Congressional Medal of Honor—after killing 100 Germans. He is from Mission, Texas, and is referred to as a 'one man army.'" "Sergeant Francisco Navarro of the U.S. Air Force is currently enjoying a well-earned rest after flying 295 missions (800 hours of flight) aboard a C-47 in India-Burma. He has earned the Distinguished Flying Cross, two Oak Leaves." "The Congressional Medal of Honor was awarded to Macario Garcia from Camp Hood, Texas, for bravery in combat. Garcia, a Mexican national, became a U.S. citizen. He lived in Sugarland, Texas, growing and picking cotton."[65]

One Mexican American was given a military award for a unique battle achievement. As a boy living in the barrio of East Los Angeles, Guy Louis Gabaldon had been one of seven children crowded into a small house. On the streets, he was befriended by two Japanese-American brothers, Lane and Lyle Nakano, and eventually moved into their home. "More and more I was with them than I was with my natural parents," recalled Gabaldon. He lived with the Nakanos for six years and learned Japanese. But then the war came, and the family was taken away to an internment camp.[66]

Only seventeen years old at the time, Gabaldon joined the marines and was sent to the Pacific front. On his first day of combat on Saipan, he killed thirty-three Japanese soldiers. Perhaps they reminded him of the sons of his Japanese foster family. Filled with remorse, Gabaldon decided he would go out alone and try to persuade the Japanese soldiers to surrender, for they were completely surrounded and cut off from the Japanese navy. He captured six soldiers. Speaking in Japanese, he told them that they would be given medical care and food. "I'm keeping three of you here," Gabaldon said. "The other three can leave and bring some friends back." But he warned them that if they did not return, he would shoot his hostages. The three came back with six more soldiers. Gabaldon kept repeating this tactic, and within seven hours, he had eight hundred prisoners. For his bravery, Gabaldon was awarded the Navy Cross. "Working alone in the front of the lines," read his citation, "he daringly entered enemy caves, pillboxes, buildings and jungle brush, frequently in the face of hostile fire, and succeeded not only in obtaining vital military information but in capturing well over 1,000 civilians and troops."[67]

Meanwhile, on the home front, Mexicans were contributing to the war effort. To meet new demands for agricultural production, the federal government initiated the bracero program (from the Spanish word *brazos*, or arms). Recruited in Mexico, guest laborers would work in the United States under contract and then be returned at the end of their term. On September 29, 1942, the first fifteen hundred braceros were brought to California by train. During the war years, the federal government recruited workers by the thousands: 4,000 in 1942, 52,000 in 1943, 62,000 in 1944, and 120,000 a year later. By 1947, 200,000 of them had worked in the United States.[68]

Also a "war industry," agriculture contributed a vital military need: food. The braceros worked in twenty-one states, where in 1944 alone they harvested crops worth $432 million. "They're all right, good workers," a Washington farmer commented. "I only hope I can get them again." Other farmers agreed: "These Mexicans are as good as any help I ever had." "We wouldn't trade one of these Mexicans for ten of the kind of help we have had on this job before." But the good workers complained that the farmers were not good bosses. A farm laborer protested: "We come here like *animales rentados* [rented animals], not like men."[69]

While the braceros labored in the fields, Mexican Americans in the cities worked in the factories of the defense industry. The rapidly inclining demand for labor in the defense industries forced employers to turn to Mexican labor. In 1941, the number of Mexicans employed in the Los Angeles shipyards was zero; by 1944, it had jumped to seventeen thousand. Employment opportunities for them expanded throughout the defense industries—steel, armaments, and aircraft. *La Opinión* carried advertisements in Spanish: "Martin Ship Service Company needs Mexican Workers for repair and maintenance work. You don't need to speak English. We have Mexican supervisors. You only need a birth certificate. You don't need to be a U.S. citizen." On January 23, 1944, *La Opinión* reported that twelve thousand Mexicans were employed by Douglas Aircraft in Southern California.[70]

Many of these new workers were women. On April 1, 1942, *La Opinión* announced: "Roosevelt High School will open an aviation class for national defense, especially for women, on Tuesday and Thursday nights. This class will teach mounting, perforation, etc. as is taught by the various aircraft production companies." For the first time in their lives, Mexican-American women were no longer forced to be farm laborers, maids, or garment workers. "Prior to the war," recalled Natalie Martinez Sterling, "the only jobs available to young Mexican women were nonskilled types of occupations such as making cardboard boxes and sewing clothes. The war allowed us job opportunities as sales clerks and defense workers. The government was actually training us with job skills that would help us after the war." Felisa Ruiz welcomed the chance to work in the defense industry. "During the depression," she said, "the only jobs available to young Mexican-American women were limited primarily to sewing and laundry work, hotel maids, and as domestics. These jobs both were physically demanding and paid very little. When the war broke out, defense jobs were all of a sudden open to us because of the labor shortage with the men off to war. Many of us left these menial jobs into highly skilled occupations with good to excellent pay with overtime."[71]

During the tremendous employment expansion, thousands of Mexican-American women became riveters. One of them was Margarita Salazar. In 1942, she was twenty-five years old, working in Molly's Beauty Shop, where customers were telling fantastic stories about women assembling airplanes. "I quit Molly's and went to work for defense," Salazar recalled. "I could make more money. I could see that I wasn't going to make that much money working as an operator and the money was in defense. Everybody would talk about the overtime and how much money it was. And it was exciting. Being involved in that era you figured you were doing something for your country—and at the same time making money." She applied for a job at a Lockheed assembly plant and was hired immediately. An Italian worker taught Salazar how to drill: "Jeanette broke me in," she said.[72]

Working on the assembly lines, Mexican-American women learned not only how to rivet but also how to get along with workers of other races. "Aircraft work generally required a team of two women for riveting—one person working outside the plane and the other person inside," recalled Carmen Caudillo. "At one particular plant, there were many white women from Missouri who refused to have anything to do with the Black workers. One supervisor decided to pair several Black and Mexican women together. At first, there was some prejudice on both sides, but as time passed, we became good friends both in and out of the plant."[73]

Women of different ethnicities also became friends in the factory cafeterias. "There were other Mexican women," said Margarita Salazar, "but I don't recall too many colored girls, not in our little section. But when we'd go to lunch, I'd see a lot of them. We all blended in—men, women, Mexican, Italian." At another plant, Antonia Molina also had affirming experiences. "I remember one day when some new Black workers came to our factory. From the start, some white workers absolutely refused to even say hello. The next day, some of us Mexican women invited the Black women over to our table for lunch. We did so because we knew what it was like to be discriminated against. By the end of the week, several white workers also joined us for lunch. We soon realized that we had to set aside our differences in order to win the war."[74]

"Through earning our own wages," Carmen Chavez said, "we had a taste of independence we hadn't known before the war. The women of my neighborhood had changed as much as the men who went to war. We developed a feeling of self-confidence and a sense of worth." Alicia Mendeola Shelit experienced a similar feeling. With her earnings as a worker at Douglas Aircraft, this single parent purchased her first home. Shelit was proud that she was bringing "the money in to feed [her] kids, like a man."[75]

For Mexican Americans in the defense industry, the war represented a convergence of patriotism and personal growth. "We didn't understand the international politics that led to the war," said a woman who had worked in a factory. "We did know, however, that the Japanese had cowardly bombed Pearl Harbor and had killed hundreds of young American boys—boys who were my brothers' ages. The Japanese had attacked our country. I say our country because I was born here. My generation went proudly to war because this country, despite the discrimination, had provided my family with a better life than my relatives had in Mexico." A better life meant a different one. "All of us were definitely changed by the four years of defense work," observed Victoria Morales. "Prior to the war, we were young women with few social and job skills. But the war altered these conditions very quickly.

By the end of the war, we had been transformed into young, mature women with new job skills, self-confidence, and a sense of worth as a result of our wartime contributions."[76]

As soldier warriors overseas and as worker warriors in the "Arsenal for Democracy" on the home front, they were fighting for the dignity they were entitled to as Americans.

Native Americans: "Why Fight the White Man's War?"

"Why fight the white man's war?" asked young Indians after the Japanese attack on Pearl Harbor. Why enlist in the U.S. Armed Forces, when the Indian people had been losing their lands ever since the arrival of the English colonizers at Jamestown in 1607? Now they were being asked to help defend their conquerers. "Why do you have to go?" an Indian mother asked her son. "It's not your war." "We had lost our own country to foreigners," said a Navajo. Navajos bitterly remembered the "Long Walk"—how in 1863 Kit Carson's forces had marched the Navajo tribe at bayonet point to the Bosque Redondo Reservation in New Mexico.[77]

Yet, during World War II, Navajos enlisted. Almost 20 percent of all reservation Native Americans in the military came from the Navajo Nation in the Southwest. Raymond Nakai was asked why Navajos enlisted: "Our answer is that we are proud to be American. We're proud to be American Indians. We always stand ready when our country needs us." The Navajo Nation declared: "We resolve that the Navajo Indians stand ready to aid and defend our government and its institutions against all subversive and armed conflict and pledge our loyalty to the system which recognizes minority rights and a way of life that has placed us among the greatest people of our race." In 1943, a Navajo soldier wrote to his tribal council: "I don't know anything about the white man's way. I never went outside the reservation. I am proud to be in a suit like this now. It is to protect my country, my people, the head men, the chiefs of my people."[78]

Another reason why so many Navajos enlisted was poverty. By the time of Pearl Harbor, the federal government's stock reduction program had made the Navajos dependent on wage income: nearly 40 percent of their annual per capita income of $128 came from wages, mostly from temporary government employment. "I went to war," said Wilson Keedah, "because there were no jobs on the reservation." Eugene Crawford also saw the marines as a way out of squalor. "One of the recruiters," he recalled, "tried to attract me into signing up by saying that becoming a marine would be much better than staying on the reservation."[79]

Pushed by poverty, the Navajos were also pulled into the military because they possessed something uniquely valuable to the U.S. military. "The marines recruited Navajos for our language," explained Cozy Stanley Brown. "They liked to use our language in war to carry messages." In May the first group of code talkers were sent to the marine base in San Diego for training.[80]

The Navajos who were selected to be code talkers had to be proficient in both their tribal language and English. Minimally, they had to have a tenth-grade education. The code talker, explained Navajo Jimmy King, had "to spell 'artillery,' and then 'bivouac,' 'reconnaissance,' and then words like 'strafing' and some other military terms. You had to know the English language well enough you could spell whatever you were saying, and the terms accurately so that you can carry on your code talking efficiently and effectively." Accuracy was an absolute necessity. "There are thousands and thousands of lives involved," said King. "Let's say bombing, or strafing, shelling so many *xxx* yards from a certain point. Suppose he gets one digit wrong. Now, that digit might mean shelling, strafing, bombing of our own men."[81]

At the marine base, recalled Cozy Stanley Brown, "we were taught to use the radio. We had to do that in a hurry. I guess that was why they forced us to complete the training in eight weeks." Then the code talkers had to creatively adapt their language for use in the Pacific war. "We got together and discussed how we would do it. We decided to change the name of the airplanes, ships, and the English ABC's into the Navajo language. We did the changing. For instance, we named the airplanes 'dive bombers' for *ginitsoh* (sparrow hawk), because the sparrow hawk is like an airplane—it charges downward at a very fast pace." Many Navajo words were converted into military terms: *a-ye-shi* (eggs) for bombs, *jas-chizzie* (swallow) for torpedo plane, *ne-as-jah* (owl) for observation plane, and *jay-sho* (buzzard) for bomber. The Navajo language could not be understood or mimicked by the Japanese military. Many words had sounds that could be heard only by a native speaker, and its verb forms were so complex that they had to be composed by someone who had grown up with the language. The Navajo code talkers had developed what came to be admired by the U.S. military as "the unbreakable code."[82]

The code talkers hit every beach from Guadalcanal to Okinawa. Altogether there were 420 Navajo code talkers, sending and receiving reports from the field commanders. Their secret messages carried information on enemy gun locations, movements of American troops, artillery fire, plane bombardments, and the sites of enemy entrenchments and strategic lookout points.

In February 1945, the Navajo code talkers participated in one of the most important Pacific battles: the fight for Iwo Jima. "It just seemed like the island was burning early in the morning," one of them recalled. "This shelling was coming down just like rain." Teddy Draper never forgot the fear he felt during the beach landing: "There were a lot of machine guns going along all the way around Suribachi about 50 feet apart from the bottom to the top. Just flying shells, all over. You couldn't see. And I thought, 'I don't know if I'm going to live or not.'" During the first two days of the invasion, Navajo code talkers worked around the clock, sending more than eight hundred battle messages without an error.[83]

On the third day, the fighting focused on Mount Suribachi, a vital observation post for the Japanese defense of the island. Navajo code talker Teddy Draper recalled that on the third day of fierce fighting, "I was close to 100 feet down on the north slope when Sergeant Ray told me to send a message that Suribachi had been secured and at what time and get it down to headquarters. I didn't see the flag go up, but I passed the message when it happened." The message read: "Naastsosi Thanzie Dibeh Shida Dahnesta Tkin Shush Wollachee Moasi Lin Achi." When the message was received on a ship, a Navajo translater announced that the American flag was flying over Mount Suribachi.[84]

Casualty rates for the battle of Iwo Jima were enormous: twenty thousand Japanese soldiers were killed, while seven thousand marines were killed and nineteen thousand wounded. The American dead included four Navajo code talkers—Peter Johnson, Paul Kinlahcheeny, Sam Morgan, and Willie Notah. Signal officer Major Howard Conner declared: "Without the Navajos the marines would never have taken Iwo Jima."[85]

After returning to the reservation, many Navajo veterans found that they had been wounded psychologically by the war. George Kirk kept having dreams of enemy soldiers jumping into his foxhole, so he went to see a medicine man for a ceremony called the "Enemy Way," a symbolic slaying of the "enemy presence." Coming home after his imprisonment in a Japanese POW camp for three years, Claude Hatch had a ceremony to help him heal from his traumatic battle experiences. "My father passed away shortly before I was liberated," he recalled, "but after returning home my relatives decided to have the Enemy Way ceremony for me because of all the things that had happened to me." Keats Begay said that he had a Squaw Dance ceremony performed on him, but he noted that there were some veterans who were still emotionally ill and were "receiving disability income." Indeed, there were veterans who did not easily recover from the psychic wounds of the war.[86]

One such veteran was described in a letter a woman had written to a marine commanding officer:

> I don't know I do rite in writin you this but no harm try. It about Big Bill _____, can he be kept from comin home to he family, he was a fine guy till he got to be Marine, got big Head so many stripes on sleeve and decorate in front, first time come home got heap drunk, was maybe sick, cold not so bad, no want go back, next time staid over got wife take back, and made lie for him, she no like, she scared of him, all time want take car, her need live 1/4 mile out of town, she work hard, he all time send for money, talk he got woman, want car is talk, last week sends from town off far, her come after him, she no money, no gas, no go, he cot ride, made hell all time, argue, argue, car, money, he hit her maby broke nose, black both eyes, kick her round, he sure bad umbra, now take car, no paid for, how he pay, she works for his two chilen and one with till school out, and he put other woman fore her for spite. Bill no not me I get this from friends, they say fraid we write, he kill them and her maby. I going away tomorrow, try not let him know where, you get these army police here, maby you say they told. Her land woman for over one year, I sure will back this up.
>
> Mrs. B _____
>
> No like bad man buse woman.[87]

Why men like this veteran had become drunken and abusive husbands was explained by Oliver La Farge of the Association of American Indian Affairs. Writing in *Harper's Magazine* in 1947, he described how a Navajo had returned from the war only to feel he was "in a box" of poverty. The land was too dry for farming, and his welfare check was too meager. "He knew what he was going to do now," La Farge wrote. "He was going to hook a ride into town, sell his coat, buy a pint of bootleg rotgut, and get drunk. He hated what he was doing, but he could not help himself. He could not get out of the box; he could only momentarily forget it."[88]

The problem for many despondent Navajo veterans was not simply the post-traumatic stresses of the war. There was little economic opportunity on the reservation waiting for these military heroes. A year after the war, the New Mexico Association on Indian Affairs reported that the average male on the Navajo reservation was earning less than $100 a year. The association concluded: "The poor economic situation of the Navajo is beyond belief." The reason for this devastating suffering was revealed in a single set of statistics: the tribal population had reached sixty thousand in 1946, and the reservation lands could support only thirty-five thousand people.[89]

Still, the war had revived a Navajo spirit. Embedded in the deployment of their language as a weapon was an irony. "When I was going to boarding school," said Teddy Draper, Sr., "the U.S. government told us not to speak Navajo, but during the war, they *wanted* us to speak it!" Recalling how he was not allowed to speak Navajo in his boarding school, Keith Little said he viewed his code-talking contribution as a fight for Navajo "freedom," including the cultural right to have their tribal language. On the blood-soaked beaches of Pacific islands, the Navajos had demonstrated the value of America's cultural diversity. "We, the Navajo people," declared Kee Etsicitty, "were very fortunate to contribute our language as a code for our country's victory. For this I strongly recommend we teach our children the language our ancestors were blessed with at the beginning of time. It is very sacred and represents the power of life."[90]

Jewish Americans: A "Deafening Silence"

After World War II, the still molten memory of their near extermination as a people made Jewish Americans wonder what they should tell their children about the Nazi "heart of darkness." This was the question a father raised in a 1956 letter to the "Bintel Brief" (similar to "Dear Abby") editor of the *Jewish Daily Forward*. The editor advised the parents to wait until their children had grown old enough to understand the "massacres" of six million Jews. "Certainly we should tell our children about the holocaust," he answered, "and about the fact that the whole world was silent."[91]

That "whole world" included the United States. When Hitler came to power in 1933, four and a half million Jews were living in the United States. Safe from Nazism on this side of the Atlantic Ocean, they found themselves facing an agonizing dilemma: how should they respond to the unfolding genocide in Europe?

In 1933, representative Samuel Dickstein of New York offered a congressional resolution for the admission of all German Jews who were related to American citizens and were fleeing from persecution in Germany. Unexpectedly, Dickstein encountered opposition from three of the leading Jewish-American organizations. The American Jewish Committee voiced the strongest criticism of his resolution. Founded in 1906 by wealthy German-Jewish immigrants, the committee believed that Jews in this country should simply be loyal Americans, and warned that Dickstein's proposal was provoking the anti-Semitic charge that Jews in America were willing to sacrifice American interests in order to help Jews in Germany. B'nai B'rith asserted that the immigration restrictions should be enforced to protect American labor. The American Jewish Congress also called for keeping the gates closed. Composed of Eastern European Jews, the Congress was led by Rabbi Stephen Wise of New York City. Speaking against the passage of "special amendments to American immigration laws" or "new legislation" for Jewish victims of Nazi Germany, Wise argued that the existing restrictions were needed to keep out immigrants who would take jobs away from American workers. Jews in this country, the rabbi declared, were "Americans, first, last, and all the time."[92]

But, in 1938, Jewish Americans realized that they could not be just "Americans." During one terrifying night, rampaging mobs murdered scores of Jews in Germany. According to the *New York Times,* in Berlin "raiding squads of young men roamed unhindered through the principal shopping districts, breaking shop windows with metal weapons, looting or tossing merchandise into the streets or into passing vehicles and leaving the unprotected Jewish shops to the mercy of vandals who followed in this unprecedented show of violence." The night of fear and breaking glass came to be known as "Kristallnacht."[93]

At a press conference, Roosevelt condemned the night of mayhem and murder: "The news of the past few days from Germany has deeply shocked public opinion in the United States…. I myself could scarcely believe that such things could occur in a twentieth-century civilization." Asked if he had considered a possible mass transfer of Kristallnacht victims to the United States, Roosevelt replied: "I have given a great deal of thought to it." Then he added: "The time is not ripe for that." Roosevelt was also asked if he would relax the immigration laws for Jewish refugees. "That is not in contemplation," he answered; "we have the quota system." Roosevelt was empathetic to the plight of Jews in Europe: he himself had appointed a Jewish American to his cabinet, Henry Morgenthau, secretary of the treasury. But the president was heeding the polls. A Gallup poll conducted after Kristallnacht in November 1938 showed that 77 percent of the Americans surveyed opposed increasing the immigration quota for Germany. Although Roosevelt extended the visas for twelve thousand refugees already in the United States, he refused to open the gates to new refugees.[94]

Senator Robert Wagner of New York and Representative Edith Rogers of Massachusetts hoped that Americans would at least have the heart to save Jewish children. In 1939, they jointly introduced a bill that would allow the nonquota entry of twenty thousand refugee children from Germany over a two-year period. The children would be admitted on the condition that they would be supported by responsible private agencies or individuals and would not become public charges. The bill quickly came under attack from restrictionists. John B. Trevor of the American Coalition of Patriotic Societies scolded Wagner and Rogers for sponsoring such legislation in view of the needs of a million "neglected boys and girls, descendants of American pioneers, undernourished, ragged and ill."[95]

The Wagner-Rogers bill needed support from the president. While on a Caribbean cruise in February 1939, Roosevelt received a cable from Mrs. Roosevelt: "Are you willing I should talk to Sumner [Wells] and say we approve passage of Child Refugee Bill. Hope you are having grand time. Much love. Eleanor." Roosevelt replied: "It is all right for you to support the child refugee bill, but it is best for me to say nothing till I get back." After he returned, Roosevelt maintained his silence. Trying to get the president to issue a statement on the proposed legislation, Representative Caroline O'Day wrote to ask him for his view on the bill. Instead, Roosevelt penciled on her letter the following instructions to Secretary "Pa" Watson: "File, no action. FDR."[96]

Roosevelt was aware of widespread public opposition to the bill. A Gallup poll revealed that 66 percent of those questioned did not want the government to admit the children. Eleanor Roosevelt understood her husband's sensitivity to the pulse of the people. "While I often felt strongly on various subjects," she wrote in *This I Remember*, "Franklin frequently refrained from supporting causes in which he believed, because of political realities."[97]

The Wagner-Rogers proposal also turned out to be an extremely sensitive political issue for Jewish-American leaders. During the congressional hearings on the legislation, Rabbi Wise stated that he would be willing to admit "a rather limited number of children," but that he wanted the immigration restrictions to remain.

"If there is a conflict between our duty to those children and our duty to our country, speaking for myself as a citizen, I should say, of course, that our country comes first; and if children cannot be helped, they cannot be helped, because we should not undertake to do anything that would be hurtful to the interests of our country." The Wagner-Rogers bill failed to leave the committees, and even frightened refugee children would not be saved.[98]

A few months later, 907 German Jewish refugees tried to rescue themselves. They boarded the steamship *St. Louis* bound for Cuba, where they expected to find asylum. When their ship reached Havana, however, the Cuban government suddenly invalidated their immigration visas. Turned away at the dock, they remained on board while their ship steamed in circles between Cuba and Florida. The passengers saw the lights and beaches of Miami, but the U.S. Coast Guard escorted their ship out of American waters. Frantically, they pleaded for permission to land in the United States. Describing the *St. Louis* as "the saddest ship afloat today," carrying a "cargo of dispair," the *New York Times* editorialized: "We can only hope that some hearts will soften somewhere and some refuge found. The cruise of the *St. Louis* cries high to heaven of man's inhumanity to man." The *Jewish Daily Forward* printed a scream for help from the passengers: "We appeal to world Jewry. We are being sent back. How can you be peaceful? How can you be silent? Help! Do everything you can! Some on the ship have committed suicide. Help! Do not allow the ship to go back to Germany!"[99]

As the ship sailed along the U.S. coastline, a Jewish-American organization, the Joint Distribution Committee, tried to post a bond of $500,000 guaranteeing that the refugees would not become public charges in Cuba. The Cuban government refused the offer. The rejected refugees now focused all of their hope on Roosevelt. "The desperate passengers on the *St. Louis* telegraphed the President," wrote historian Arthur Hertzberg, "but he ignored them." They were forced to sail back to Europe where a ghastly future awaited them.[100]

The *St. Louis* incident unleashed a sense of frustration within Jewish-American communities. "Let our leaders lead!" demanded Samuel Margoshes impatiently in the Yiddish daily, *The Day.* "Let them not delay and postpone. Let the General Jewish Council meet and deliberate immediately. The Jewish masses are waiting to go out into the streets, to close their places of business, to stop all work, to declare a fast and to demonstrate to the entire world that we will no longer allow ourselves to be slaughtered by a barbaric regime."[101]

The anguish intensified in September 1939 when Germany occupied Poland, and three million more Jews came under Nazi rule. "In the matter of the treatment of Jews in Nazi-overrun Poland," Wise wrote in *Opinion* in February 1940, "we face a spectacle of daily torture and horror such as men have not beheld since the days of Genghis Khan."[102]

But what awaited the Jews of Europe would surpass the atrocities of Genghis Khan. Hitler's homicidal plan was unshrouded during the German invasion of Russia. Following the advancing German army, Nazi execution squads, known as the Einsatzgruppen, began murdering Jews by the hundreds of thousands. The atrocities were reported in newspapers throughout the West. The shocking revelations forced Wise to reassess his reluctance to give special consideration to the Jewish victims.[103]

News of the mass murders continued to reach the United States, and on July 21, 1942, twenty thousand people gathered at Madison Square Garden to protest the Nazi atrocities. In a message sent to the rally, Roosevelt urged the people there to support his rescue-through-victory strategy. "Americans who love justice and hate oppression," he declared, "will hail the solemn commemoration in Madison Square Garden as an expression of the determination of the Jewish people to make every sacrifice for victory over the Axis powers." At the mass meeting, Rabbi Wise endorsed Roosevelt's strategy when he declared that the "salvation of our people" could come only through a "speedy and complete" victory.[104]

At this point, Americans were still unaware of the extent of the Nazi extermination effort—the systematic and complex apparatus of trains, barracks, factories, gas chambers, and crematoria. But within weeks, they would no longer be able to claim that they did not know. On August 28, 1942, Wise received a cable from Gerhart Riegner, the World Jewish Congress representative in Geneva. The message stated: "Received alarming report that in Fuhrer's headquarters plan discussed and under consideration according to which all Jews in countries occupied or controlled by Germany numbering 3½–4 millions should after deportation and concentration in East be exterminated at one blow to resolve once for all the Jewish question in Europe." The Reigner report made one thing absolutely clear: there was no longer a reason for doubting the genocide, or an excuse for hesitating to make every effort to rescue Jews. Hitler had, in fact, unleashed his ultimate pogrom—the "Final Solution."[105]

Wise took the incriminating cable to Under-Secretary of State

Sumner Wells, only to be told that he should wait until the information could be confirmed. The wait for Wells's response was agonizing for Wise, for he knew that Jews were being murdered by the thousands daily. "I have had the unhappiest days of my life," the rabbi wrote to Reverend John Hayes Holmes. "Think of what it means to hear, as I have heard, through a coded message—first from Geneva, then from Berne, through the British Foreign Office,—that Hitler plans the extermination at one time of the whole Jewish population of Europe; and prussic acid is mentioned as the medium." Wise writhed in anguish: "I don't want to turn my heart inside out, but I am almost demented over my people's grief."[106]

Three months later, after the Nazis had murdered an additional one million Jews, Wise was finally summoned by Wells. "I hold in my hands documents which have come to me from our legation in Berne," the under-secretary of state said. "I regret to tell you, Dr. Wise, that these documents confirm and justify your deepest fears."[107]

At once, Wise held a press conference to report the evidence of the official Nazi policy of genocide. Incredibly, the press did not cover the shocking news as a major story. In order to arouse the American public from its moral lethargy, Jewish leaders organized a Day of Mourning and Prayer on December 2, 1942. In New York City, half a million Jewish union laborers stopped production for ten minutes, and special services were held in synagogues. NBC broadcast a quarter-hour memorial service. "In every country where Hitler's edicts run, every day is a day of mourning for Jews," editorialized the *New York Times*. "Today has been set aside, by action of the chief Rabbinate of Palestine, supported by the Jewish organizations of the United States, as a day of mourning, prayer and fasting among Jews throughout the free countries of the world."[108]

That day, Wise requested a meeting with President Roosevelt: "Dear Boss: I do not wish to add an atom to the awful burden which you are bearing with magic and, as I believe, heaven-inspired strength at this time. But you do know that the most overwhelming disaster of Jewish history has befallen Jews in the form of the Hitler mass-massacres...and it is indisputable that as many as two million civilian Jews have been slain."[109]

Six days later, Wise and delegates from major Jewish organizations met with Roosevelt. The meeting turned out to be a great disappointment. The meeting lasted twenty-nine minutes, and Roosevelt engaged in casual conversation for nearly the entire time. Finally, the discussion turned to the Jewish crisis in Europe. "The entire conversation lasted only a minute or two," wrote one of the participants in his diary. In a letter to Sumner Wells, the Joint Emergency Committee on European Jewish Affairs charged that the relegation of Jews to "the day of victory" was "virtually to doom them to the fate" that Hitler had designed for them.[110]

The most militant criticism of Roosevelt's rescue-through-victory strategy came from the Committee for a Jewish Army of Stateless and Palestinian Jews. To stir the moral conscience of America, this committee turned to drama to break the intolerable silence of the White House. In March 1943, they sponsored a tour of Ben Hecht's pageant *We Will Never Die*. Forty thousand people attended the opening presentation at Madison Square Garden. The performance presented the history of Jews, their contributions to civilization, and the genocide they were experiencing. Hecht's powerful dramatization of the Jews caught in the jaws of genocide conveyed a passionate plea to Americans: do everything possible to rescue the remaining four million Jews.[111]

Determined to help save his Jewish brethren in Europe, Secretary of the Treasury Henry Morgenthau decided to prod Roosevelt into action. At a meeting with the president on January 16, 1944, he presented a report on the mass murders of Jews. The opening sentence expressed moral indignation: "One of the greatest crimes in history, the slaughter of the Jewish people in Europe, is continuing unabated." Morgenthau called for immediate measures. "The matter of rescuing the Jews from extermination is a trust too great to remain in the hands of men who are indifferent, callous and perhaps even hostile. The task is filled with difficulties. Only a fervent will to accomplish, backed by persistent and untiring effort, can succeed where time is so precious."[112]

Six days later, Roosevelt signed an executive order establishing the War Refugee Board, a government agency that would be responsible for "the development of plans and programs and the inauguration of effective measures for a) the rescue, transportation and maintenance and relief of the victims of enemy oppression, and b) the establishment of havens of temporary refuge for such victims."[113]

Welcoming the creation of the War Refugee Board, Jewish leaders urged the government to create havens of refuge in the United States. "Every surviving Jewish man, woman and child who can escape from the Hitlerite fury into the territories of the United Nations," the American Jewish Congress declared, should have "the right of temporary asylum."[114]

Roosevelt rejected these proposals. He defended his administration's policies by explaining that the government was transporting to North Africa all of the refugees who had been able to escape from Nazi control. In the end, Roosevelt offered a small concession: he agreed to create an emergency shelter near Oswego, New York, for one thousand refugees representing "a reasonable proportion of various categories of persecuted people." At Auschwitz the gas chambers were murdering twelve thousand people daily.[115]

In June 1945, Roosevelt's rescue-through-victory strategy came to a conclusion as Allied military forces swept across Germany and liberated the prisoners of Hitler's death camps. By then, six million Jews had been exterminated.

What the liberating U.S. troops witnessed in the camps was the heart of a ghastly darkness. An African-American soldier recalled the sickening sensation he experienced as he scanned the searing scene—the survivors looking like ghosts, the ovens still warm. "Why Jews?" Paul Parks asked. "It doesn't make sense. Why were they killed?" A prisoner explained: "They were killed because they were Jews." Park commented: "I understand that." Then he added: "I understand that because I've seen people lynched just because they were black." Park compared the experiences of the two groups: "There's one other great incident of humanity that I'm very familiar with, the three hundred years of slavery in my own country, where people for generations were not allowed to be free, subject to the dictates of another race. Held in bondage, forced to work, and forced to do what another person wanted you to do. And if you didn't obey, there were no laws against killing you and destroying your family. So I said, 'As you talk, I see there's a close parallel between the history of my people in America and what's happened to the Jews in Europe.'"[116]

The liberators also included Japanese-American soldiers. With their families in internment camps in the United States, they had fought their way through Italy and France, and had reached Dachau. In his diary, Ichiro Imamura gave an eye-level account: "When the gates swung open, we got our first good look at the prisoners. Many of them were Jews. They were wearing black and white striped prison suits and round caps. A few had shredded blanket rags draped over their shoulders. The prisoners struggled to their feet [and] shuffled weakly out of the compound. They were like skeletons—all skin and bones." Initially, the Jewish prisoners were surprised and confused to see soldiers of Japanese ancestry. "When they first came in, we thought they were allies of the Germans," a prisoner stated years later. "We believed they were there to torture us." Indeed, Japanese-American soldiers had to explain who they were. One of them recalled that at first the Jewish prisoners thought that their liberators did not look like "Americans." "I am an American soldier," he reassured them, "and you are free."[117]

Also among the liberators were Jewish-American soldiers. Entering one of the barracks at Buchenwald, Chaplain Rabbi Herschel Schacter saw hundreds of survivors lying on shelves from the floor to the ceiling. They were "strewn over scraggly straw sacks," looking down at him out of dazed eyes. Schacter then shouted in Yiddish, "Sholem Aleychem, Yiden, yir zent frey!" "You are free." Schacter felt a special empathy for this pitiful humanity before him: "If my own father had not caught the boat on time, I would have been there."[118]

During an inspection of the camp at Dachau, Walter J. Fellenz visited one of the gas chambers. He noticed that over its entrance, written in Yiddish, was the word "Showers." The room itself was inlaid with high-quality brown tile and had two hundred chrome shower nozzles. Chaplain Judah Nadich tried to picture what it was like to be in the gas chamber with chrome shower nozzles. The rabbi then noticed thousands of scratches on the inside of the door, "scratches that must have been made by the fingernails of so many men and women and children."[119]

The "scratches" told the story of a "deafening silence."[120]

Listening, American Zionists were determined that Jews had to have a homeland: a Jewish nation in Palestine would be their Promised Land. Before the rise of Hitler, Jewish Americans had little interest in Zionism. In 1930, the Zionist Organization of America had such a dwindling membership that Rabbi Stephen Wise observed: "There is a complete lull in things Zionistic in America." When Hitler came to power, however, "the dire developments" of Nazism, as historian Henry Feingold noted, would do for "the Zionist movement what it had been unable to do for itself." Membership in the Zionist Organization of America jumped from 18,000 in 1929 to 52,000 in 1939, and 136,000 by 1945. In 1947, the General Assembly of the United Nations scheduled a vote on the proposal to partition Palestine into a Jewish state and an Arab state. But President Truman hesitated on the issue when his secretary of defense, James Forrestal, informed him that enforcing the partition would require 160,000 U.S. ground troops. At this point, one of Truman's Jewish-American friends begged the president to meet with Chaim Weizmann, chief of the World Zionist Organization. At a meeting with Weizmann on March 18, 1948, Truman agreed to "press forward with partition." On May 14, 1948, the British withdrew from Palestine, and in Tel Aviv, David Ben-Gurion declared the existence of the Jewish State of Israel. In Washington, President Truman signed the document recognizing Israel.[121]

A Holocaust Called Hiroshima

In a poem written in 1946, Robert Frost reflected on America's use of the atomic bomb as a weapon of mass destruction:

> *Having invented a new Holocaust,*
> *And been the first with it to win a war,*
> *How they make haste to cry with fingers crossed,*
> *King's X—no fairs to use it anymore!*[122]

A year earlier, on April 12, 1945, President Franklin D. Roosevelt suddenly died, and Vice President Harry S. Truman was sworn into office. That night, the new president wrote in his diary: "I was very much shocked. I am not easily shocked but was certainly shocked when I was told of the President's death and the weight of the government had fallen on my shoulders." The former senator from Missouri felt most anxious about the tremendous burden of international responsibility and his ignorance of foreign affairs.[123]

Feeling inadequate to fill the shoes of the great F.D.R., he confided to his friend Senator George D. Aiken of Vermont: "I'm not big enough. I'm not big enough for this job." What made his new job especially difficult was the sting of personal indignities and sarcasms. *Time* magazine described the new president as "a man of distinct limitations, especially in high level politics." Margaret Truman recalled that her father "snorted with indignation when someone called him the 'little man in the White House.'" But Truman hid his insecurity behind a facade of toughness. Publicly, he presented himself as a man of the frontier. He blustered: "The buck stops here."[124]

As a southerner coming from a family of slaveholders and supporters of the Confederacy, Truman brought to his bluster strongly held ideas about race. Long before his sudden ascendancy to the presidency, he had written to his future wife, Bess:

I think one man is as good as another so long as he's honest and decent and not a nigger or a Chinaman. Uncle Will [Young, the Confederate veteran] says the Lord made a white man of dust, a nigger from mud, then threw up what was left and it came down a Chinaman. He does hate Chinese and Japs. So do I. It is race prejudice I guess. But I am strongly of the opinion that Negroes ought to be in Africa, yellow men in Asia, and white men in Europe and America.[125]

Like many Americans, Truman was swept into a revenge-seeking rage over the treacherous attack on Pearl Harbor. Unlike the war in Europe, the violent conflict in the Pacific was a war of racial hatreds. The Japanese military denounced the American enemy as white "brutes" and "devils." On this side, the American military depicted the enemy as "yellow apes" and "yellow sub-humans." *Time* magazine declared: "The ordinary unreasoning Jap is ignorant. Perhaps he is human. Nothing...indicates it." In American society, the term "Jap" was widely used, implicitly identifying the enemy as the Japanese people, in contrast to the term "Nazis," referring only to the followers of Hitler, not the German people. Disturbed by Pearl Harbor and the Bataan Death March, Truman argued: "When you have to deal with a beast you have to treat him as a beast." In his diary entries written at the Potsdam Conference in July 1945, Truman expressed hatred for the "Japs—savages, ruthless and fanatic."[126]

Intersecting with each other, these personal and cultural dynamics drove Truman to insist on unconditional surrender. At the Potsdam Conference in July, the president rejected Winston Churchill's suggestion to let Japan surrender, with the condition that they be allowed to keep the emperor system. Truman also refused to heed the recommendation of the Joint Chiefs of Staff and Secretary of War Stimson that the United States let the already defeated Japan surrender on a conditional basis. They knew from intercepted messages from Tokyo to Moscow that the Japanese government was asking Russia to help negotiate a surrender. On July 18, in his diary at Potsdam, Truman wrote: "Stalin had told P.M. [Churchill] of telegram from Jap emperor asking for peace."[127]

In that same diary entry, he excitedly recorded: "Manhattan (it is a success)." Truman had received a top-secret message that the atomic bomb had been successfully tested by the Manhattan Project in New Mexico. Buoyed by the sudden possession of twenty thousand tons of TNT, he decided to act unilaterally, independent of both England and Russia. In the Potsdam Declaration of July 26, Truman issued a fierce ultimatum: Japan had to accept "unconditional surrender" or face "utter devastation."[128]

Japan refused, and Truman ordered the atomic attack. The first bomb was dropped on Hiroshima on August 6. Some seventy thousand people were instantly incinerated, most of them women and children. Three days later, the second atomic bomb was dropped on Nagasaki.

But the Japanese government still refused to surrender unconditionally. On August 10, Washington received from Japan an acceptance of the Potsdam Declaration, except on one crucial condition: that it "does not comprise any demand which prejudices the prerogatives of His Majesty as a Sovereign Ruler." At that point, Truman realized that his ultimatum had not worked. He ordered that the third atomic bomb not be dropped, and accepted a surrender with the stipulated condition. That day, Truman had privately told cabinet member Henry Wallace an admission he would never acknowledge publicly. He confided that "the thought of wiping out another 100,000 people was too horrible," and that he did not like "the idea of killing all those kids."[129]

Shortly after the earth-shattering event, W. E. B. Du Bois condemned the atomic attack on the "colored nation" of Japan. "We have seen in this war, to our amazement and distress, a marriage between science and destruction.... We have always thought of science as the emancipator. We see it now as the enslaver of mankind." For America's leading black intellectual, the atomic flash over Hiroshima illuminated in a ghastly way "the problem of the color line."[130]

For Du Bois, Hiroshima was a tragic way for the war to end. Before the attack on Pearl Harbor, the men and women of different racial and ethnic minorities had felt little in common and lacked a shared sense of national purpose. Suddenly swept into the already raging international conflict, they came to find themselves fighting as one people against fascism in Europe and Asia, bound by what Abraham Lincoln had described as the "mystic chords of memory" stretching from every battlefield and patriot grave to every "living heart and hearthstone" all over America. They also fought to make their country live up to its founding principles for all Americans. The war, Du Bois declared, was a struggle for "democracy not only for white folks but for yellow, brown, and black."[131]

15

❧◆❧

OUT OF THE WAR

Clamors for Change

Rising Winds for Social Justice

AT THE END of World War II, Walter White of the NAACP declared: "A wind *is* rising, a wind of determination by the have-nots of the world to share the benefits of freedom and prosperity which the haves of the earth have tried to keep exclusively for themselves. That wind blows all over the world. Whether that wind develops into a hurricane is a decision which we must make now and in the days when we form the peace."[1]

During the war, millions of men and women of different racial and ethnic minorities had challenged America's contradiction of the color lines, and in the process reinvented themselves. One of them was Maya Angelou. As an African-American teenager, she had been encouraged by the demand for labor to apply for a job as a streetcar operator in San Francisco. "I'd picture myself, dressed in neat blue serge suit, my money changer swinging jauntily at my waist, and a cheery smile for the passengers which would make their own work day brighter," she recalled. At the Market Street Railway Company office, the receptionist told Angelou that they were accepting applicants only from agencies. Suspicious, Angelou pointed out that the job was listed in that morning's newspaper; demanding to see the manager, she was told that he was out of the office. Angelou refused to be denied. *"I WOULD HAVE THE*

JOB. I WOULD BE A CONDUCTORETTE AND SLING A FULL MONEY CHANGER FROM MY BELT. I WOULD," she insisted. Returning time and again to the office, she was finally allowed to fill out an application form. "I was given blood tests, aptitude tests, physical coordination tests, and Rorschachs; then on a blissful day I was hired as the first Negro on the San Francisco streetcars."[2] Angelou had discovered a spirit within her destined to soar; she would be a literary conductorette, slinging poems and stories from her heart.

Ermelinda Murillo also reinvented herself during the war. Her family had emigrated from Jalisco, Mexico; in 1923, when she was three years old, they moved to Chicago. Twenty years later, a widow with a two-year-old daughter, Murillo was hired by Inland Steel Company in Indiana. She worked as a heat chaser, hot shear expediter, hotbed operator, and stocker of steel bars. "I speak some Spanish, Polish, Serbian, Croatian," Murillo said. "I learned bits of each language by working with people with various ethnic backgrounds. If I can't get a point across in one language, I simply try another. We worked hard, argued, shared a sandwich and had coffee together. To me it was a real world inside the mill." After the war, Inland Steel asked Murillo to continue working for the company. Her hard hat read: "MELA — QUEEN OF THE 12-INCH."[3]

One of the first Chinese-American women to volunteer for the Army Nurse Corps, Helen Pon Onyett had also earned respect during the war. She was twenty-five-years-old, with four years of nursing experience, when she enlisted in 1942. Onyett nursed wounded soldiers aboard transports off North Africa. "I can't swim, so I wore my Mae West [life jacket] twenty-four hours a day. It was very scary, especially when some of the ships you would be traveling with would be sunk right under your nose." On board, she found that she was appreciated as an army nurse. Her experience was so affirming that she served in the military reserve for more than thirty years after the war. "I wouldn't have done half the things I did if I hadn't been in the service.... I had a chance to go to school on the G.I. Bill and to improve my standing." In 1971, Onyett was promoted to the rank of full colonel. "When I spoke before audiences, people gawked at me, saying, 'Oh, my God, she's a colonel,' not 'She's Oriental.'"[4]

African-American Mary Daniels Williams was also changed by the war. Asked by an interviewer about her military service, Williams said that she had been a housecleaner with only a ninth-grade education when Japan attacked Pearl Harbor. She had given birth to a stillborn child and had an unsuccessful marriage. "I had no skills. I was going nowhere fast. I was getting older and I could just see us living in the slum forever. I could see myself living in two or three rooms for the rest of my life, and I decided for myself I wasn't going to do it." At a post office a military recruiter promised her "education, new places to go and to visit — well, just a totally new life." Williams enlisted in the Women's Army Corps and served in England and France. After the war, she used the G.I. Bill to attend college; she completed her bachelor's degree and worked for twenty years as a social worker in Cincinnati. "I knew what I wanted," said Williams, "and I knew that I was never gonna scrub another floor."[5]

At the end of the war, African Americans were determined that they were "never gonna" serve again in a segregated armed forces. In 1948, while threatening to lead massive civil disobedience, A. Philip Randolph demanded the end of this shameful practice. At a meeting with President Harry Truman, Randolph declared: "Negroes are in no mood to shoulder guns for democracy abroad, while they are denied democracy here at home." Under pressure, Truman issued an executive order that required "equality of treatment and opportunity for all persons in the armed services."[6]

After they had returned to California from the internment camps, Kajiro and Kohide Oyama petitioned the court to overturn the Alien Land Law, which denied the right to landownership to Japanese immigrants because they were not "white." They took their case all the way to the U.S. Supreme Court, and in 1948 the Court ruled that the law prohibiting the Japanese from owning land was "nothing more than outright racial discrimination" and therefore "unconstitutional." The Fourteenth Amendment was "designed to bar States from denying to some groups, on account of race or color, any rights, privileges, and opportunities accorded to other groups." Referring to the war against Nazi Germany, the Court declared that the Alien Land Law was "an unhappy facsimile, a disheartening reminder, of the racial policy pursued by those forces of evil whose destruction recently necessitated a devastating war." A Japanese immigrant welcomed the Court decision:

> *Land laws faded out,*
> *It is comfortable now —*
> *This America.*

Four years later, under pressure from lobbying groups including Japanese-American veterans, Congress rescinded the "white"-only restriction of the 1790 Naturalization Law. Winning citizenship for the immigrant generation "was the culmination of our dreams," exclaimed Harry Takagi. "The bill established our parents as the legal equal of other Americans; it gave the Japanese equality with all other immigrants." By 1965, forty-six thousand Japanese immigrants had taken their citizenship oaths. Although they were now in their twilight years, many of them were eager to become citizens of their adopted country. One of them rejoiced in poetry:

> Going steadily to study English,
> Even through the rain at night,
> I thus attain,
> Late in life,
> American citizenship.[7]

There was still another ghost from the past that needed to be exorcised—the mass internment of Japanese Americans during World War II. "Stigmatized" by the experience, the ex-internees had been silently carrying a "burden of shame." During the 1970s, however, many third-generation Japanese Americans were feeling the need to break the silence. Inspired by the Black Power movement and a growing sense of ethnic pride, they were searching for their roots. Now they wanted their elders to tell them about the internment experience. "Why? Why!" their parents would ask defensively. "Why would you want to know about it? It's not important, we don't need to talk about it." Young Japanese Americans replied that they needed to tell the world what happened during those years of infamy, and urged their parents to join pilgrimages to the camps at Manzanar and Tule Lake. The questions and the pilgrimages inspired a demand for redress and reparations. During the congressional hearings, scores of former internees came forward and told their stories. "For over thirty-five years I have been the stereotype Japanese American," Alice Tanabe Nehira told the commission. "I've kept quiet, hoping in due time we will be justly compensated and recognized for our years of patient effort. By my passive attitude, I can reflect on my past years to conclude that it doesn't pay to remain silent."[8]

Finally, Japanese Americans had spoken, and their voices persuaded lawmakers to redress the injustice of internment. In 1988, led by Congressman Robert Matsui and Senator Daniel Inouye, Congress passed a bill providing for an apology and a payment of $20,000 to each of the survivors of the internment camps. When President Ronald Reagan signed the bill, he admitted that the United States had committed "a grave wrong." During World War II, Japanese Americans had remained "utterly loyal" to this country, he pointed out. "Indeed, scores of Japanese Americans volunteered for our Armed Forces—many stepping forward in the internment camps themselves. The 442nd Regimental Combat Team, made up entirely of Japanese Americans, served with immense distinction—to defend this nation, their nation. Yet, back at home, the soldiers' families were being denied the very freedom for which so many of the soldiers themselves were laying down their lives." The nation needed, the president acknowledged, to end "a sad chapter in American history."[9]

The winds of protest also swept through the barrios. "During the war," stated defense worker Juana Caudillo, "there was a lessening of discrimination by some public places because they needed our money.... After the war, some restaurants, stores, and taverns again refused to serve us on an equal basis with whites. We knew this was totally unfair because we had worked hard to win the war." Determined to win a "double victory," Mexican-American veterans founded the American GI Forum in Corpus Christi, Texas, in 1948. Membership in this civil rights organization rose rapidly. Over one hundred forum chapters were organized within a year, spreading to twenty-three states and reaching a membership of over twenty thousand. The GI Forum organized the boycott against Coors for employment discrimination and also demanded bilingual education and the end of the bracero program.[10]

The war had changed Mexican Americans. After veteran Cesar Chavez returned home from fighting fascism overseas, he dedicated himself to the struggle of farm workers. His mission was to combat prejudice and win decent wages for Mexican-American agricultural laborers. As the leader of the United Farm Workers, he declared: "Our struggle is not easy. Those who oppose our cause are rich and powerful, and they have many allies in high places. We are poor. Our allies are few. But we have something the rich do not own. We have our own bodies and spirits and the justice of our cause as our weapons." Sabine R. Ulibarri of New Mexico declared: "Those of us who went to war didn't return the same. We had earned our credentials as American citizens. We had paid our dues on the counters of conviction and faith. We were not about to take any crap." "When our young men came home from the war," recalled Eva Hernandez, "they didn't want to be treated as second-class citizens anymore. We women didn't want to turn the clock back either regarding the social positions of women before the war. The war had provided us the unique chance to be socially and economically independent, and we didn't want to give up this experience simply because the war ended. We, too, wanted to be first-class citizens in our communities."[11]

This resolve to fight discrimination inspired demands to end segregated education. In the 1946 case of *Mendez v. Westminster School District of Orange County*, the U.S. Circuit Court of Southern California declared that the segregation of Mexican children violated their right to equal protection of the law guaranteed to them under the Fourteenth Amendment and therefore was unconstitutional. To support the Mendez case, amicus curiae briefs were filed by the American Jewish Congress, the National Association for the Advancement of Colored People, and the Japanese American Citizens League. This victory in court led the state legislature, a year later, to repeal section 8003, the law that permitted school districts to segregate Indian, Chinese, and Japanese children.[12]

The *Mendez* decision set a precedent for the historic Supreme Court 1954 *Brown v. Board of Education* decision. As chief counsel for the NAACP, African-American Thurgood Marshall presented the legal argument against the 1896 "separate but equal" doctrine of *Plessy v. Ferguson*. Behind his passion for social justice was Marshall's memory of World War II. "War is hell in every place and time," he told Carl T. Rowan, "but it was a special hell for people who were forced to fight for freedoms they had never known, for liberties that thousands of them would die without knowing it." Marshall was certain, however, that there would be a reckoning after the war. "I watched the bravery and patriotism of blacks, of the Japanese in World War Two, and I couldn't believe white Americans would continue to treat them as semislaves. People who died flying fighter planes in an Air Force that didn't welcome them. Japanese boys who fought valiantly even though their parents were behind the barbed wire of our concentration camps." Marshall said he was willing to bet "a bundle" that white Americans would respect the Fourteenth Amendment after the war and "that this country would move to place the colored race, in respect to civil rights, upon a level equal to whites."[13]

Marshall won his bet: the Supreme Court ruled that separate

educational facilities were "inherently unequal" and that school segregation was "a denial of the equal protection of the laws." The decision was hailed as a victory for all Americans. "We look upon this memorable decision not as a victory for Negroes alone," the NAACP announced, "but for the whole American people and as a vindication of America's leadership in the free world." Robert Williams recalled the elation he experienced when the Court announced its decision: "I felt that at last the government was willing to assert itself on behalf of first-class citizenship, even for Negroes. I experienced a sense of loyalty that I had never felt before. I was sure that this was the beginning of a new era of American democracy." A year later, the Supreme Court delivered a supplementary ruling, instructing the lower courts to implement the *Brown* decision "with all deliberate speed."[14]

Integration remained largely a court ruling on paper, however, while segregation persisted as a reality in society. Pressure for change would have to come not from judicial pronouncements, but from a people's movement for civil rights. A year after the *Brown* decision, blacks shifted the focus of their struggle from the courts to the community. What would turn out to be a momentous stirring for racial justice began on December 1, 1955, when a forty-two-year-old African-American seamstress boarded a bus in Montgomery, Alabama. Rosa Parks had been an activist in civil rights protests during the war, and had attended an antisegregation program that past summer at the Highland Folk School in Tennessee. She decided the time had come for action against what Du Bois had denounced as the "Problem of the Color Line." After entering the bus, Parks sat down in the row behind the section reserved for whites. City law stipulated that the first four rows were reserved for whites, and that if whites filled up their section, blacks would have to move to make room for them. The bus became full, and the driver ordered Parks to stand up so that a white man could sit down. "Are you going to stand up?" he asked. "No," she replied. "Go on and have me arrested." Her arrest led to an explosive protest—the Montgomery bus boycott. Although blacks were dependent on buses to get to and from work, thousands of them refused to take the bus. A song declared defiance:

> *Ain't gonna ride them buses no more*
> *Ain't gonna ride no more*
> *Why in the hell don't the white folk know*
> *That I ain't gonna ride no more.*

Instead they shared rides, rode in black-owned taxis, and walked. "My feets is tired," a woman said, "but my soul is rested." Another walker, an elderly woman, explained: "I'm not walking for myself. I'm walking for my children and my grandchildren."[15]

In this history-making moment, a young minister found himself suddenly catapulted into the leadership of the struggle. When he arrived in Montgomery a year earlier to become the pastor of the Dexter Avenue Baptist Church, Martin Luther King, Jr., noticed that blacks represented almost half of the city's population. Confined to domestic service and common labor, they were surrounded by the walls of segregation. "The schools of course were segregated," King noted; "and the United States Supreme Court decision on school integration, handed down in May 1954, appeared to have no effect on Montgomery's determination to keep them that way." But, more than the schools, the buses had become an especially disliked symbol of segregation. King personally knew what it meant to be humiliated by discrimination on a bus. When he was in the eleventh grade, he had traveled with a teacher to a distant town in Georgia to give a speech at a contest. After winning a prize for his presentation "The Negro and the Constitution," he boarded the bus for Atlanta with his teacher. When the bus filled up, the white driver told them to give up their seats for some white passengers. At first King refused and was called "a black son-of-a-bitch." Advised by his teacher to avoid a confrontation, King reluctantly surrendered his seat. "That night will never leave my mind," King recalled. "It was the angriest I have ever been in my life."[16]

As the leader of the Montgomery bus boycott, King gave voice to black frustration. In his first speech to the boycotters, he declared: "There comes a time when people get tired. We are here this evening to say to those who have mistreated us so long that we are tired—tired of being segregated and humiliated; tired of being kicked about by the brutal feet of oppression." What should be the course of resistance? "Our actions must be guided by the deepest principles of our Christian faith," King declared. "Love must be our regulating ideal. Once again we must hear the words of Jesus echoing across the centuries: 'Love your enemies, bless them that curse you, and pray for them that despitefully use you.'" In the struggle for freedom, King fused together this Christian doctrine and Mahatma Gandhi's tactic of nonviolence. The boycott ended more than a year later when the court ordered the desegregation of the bus system. The victory affirmed the power of blacks to transform the conditions of their lives through a grassroots movement. Their courageous action inspired an inner transformation—a hard-won sense of self-esteem. "We got our heads up now," exclaimed a black janitor proudly, "and we won't ever bow down again—no, sir—except before God."[17]

After the Montgomery protest came other confrontations with America's contradictions. First there were the sit-ins of black students at the Woolworth's lunch counter in Greensboro, North Carolina, in 1960. "We're trying to eradicate the whole stigma of being inferior," the students explained. "We do not picket just because we want to eat. We do picket to protest the lack of dignity and respect shown us as human beings." One of the students, Franklin McCain, recalled: "I probably felt better that day than I've ever felt in my life. I felt as though I had gained my manhood, so to speak, and not only gained it, but had developed quite a lot of respect for it." Out of the lunch counter sit-ins emerged the Student Nonviolent Coordinating Committee (SNCC). The student sit-ins spread across the South. "I myself desegregated a lunch counter, not somebody else, not some big man, some powerful man, but me, little me," a black student boasted. "I walked the picket line and I sat in and the walls of segregation toppled. Now all people can eat there." The students were standing tall against history-entrenched humiliations. "A generation of young people," King observed, "has come out of decades of shadows to face naked state power; it has lost its fears, and experienced the majestic dignity of a direct struggle for its own liberation. These young people have connected up with their own history—the slave revolts, the incomplete revolution of the Civil War, the brotherhood of colonial colored men in Africa and Asia. They are an integral part of the history which is reshaping the world, replacing a dying order with a modern democracy." In their songs, the students expressed their determination to break the chains of discrimination:

> Ain't gonna let nobody turn me 'round,
> turn me 'round, turn me 'round,
> Ain't gonna let nobody turn me 'round,
> I'm gonna keep on walkin', keep on a-talkin'
> Marching up to freedom land.[18]

A year after the Greensboro sit-ins came the "freedom rides"— acts of civil disobedience to integrate the interstate buses and bus terminals of the South. Led by the Congress of Racial Equality

(CORE), black and white civil rights supporters defiantly and bravely rode together in buses, singing:

> *Hallelujah, I'm traveling*
> *Hallelujah, ain't it fine,*
> *Hallelujah, I'm traveling*
> *Down Freedom's main line.*

In the South, the freedom riders were yanked from the buses and brutally beaten by racist white mobs before television cameras. "Every Freedom Rider on that bus was beaten pretty bad," recalled Isaac Reynolds. "I'm still feeling the effect. I received a damaged ear." They faced injury and even death, but they knew they could not allow violence to turn them back. "I was afraid *not* to continue the Freedom Ride," explained Diane Nash. "If the signal was given to the opposition that violence could stop us...if we let the Freedom Ride stop then, whenever we tried to do anything in the Movement in the future, we were going to meet with a lot of violence. And we would probably have to get a number of people killed before we could reverse that message."[19]

Then, in 1963, came the famous March on Washington. The idea that had originally been proposed during World War II became a reality. On August 28, addressing the gathering of two hundred thousand people at the Lincoln Memorial, A. Philip Randolph reiterated the 1941 demands he had submitted to President Roosevelt: "We are the advance guard of a massive moral revolution for jobs and freedom. All who deplore our militancy, who exhort patience in the name of false peace, are in fact supporting segregation and exploitation. They would have social peace at the expense of social and racial justice."[20]

After his speech, Randolph introduced Martin Luther King, Jr., as the man who personified "the moral leadership of the civil rights revolution." Speaking to the marchers, the nation, and the world, King shared his vision of freedom in America. "Five score years ago, a great American, in whose symbolic shadow we stand, signed the Emancipation Proclamation," King declared. "I say to you today, my friends, that in spite of the difficulties and frustrations of the moment I still have a dream. It is a dream deeply rooted in the American dream. I have a dream that one day this nation will rise up and live out the true meaning of its creed: 'We hold these truths to be self-evident; that all men are created equal.'"[21]

Also speaking at the March on Washington, Rabbi Joachim

Prinz wove together King's dream and the still-molten memory of the Holocaust. A death camp survivor, he shared a lesson he had learned from Hitler's murderous rampage against Jews. The "most urgent" problem was not bigotry and hatred; "the most urgent, the most disgraceful, the most shameful and the most tragic problem [was] silence." The rabbi appealed to his listeners: "America must not become a nation of onlookers." The memory of the Holocaust carried a moral lesson: as a response to racial injustice, silence constituted complicity.[22]

"Black and white together," the marchers sang, "we shall overcome someday." Indeed, whites were involved in the Civil Rights Movement, and many of them were Jews. Over half of the white students who went south to organize voter-registration drives during Freedom Summer of 1964 were Jewish. The two white civil rights workers who were murdered with African-American James Chaney in Mississippi that summer were Jewish—Andrew Goodman and Michael Schwerner. Jewish supporters wrote many of the checks that financed Martin Luther King's Southern Christian Leadership Conference as well as SNCC and CORE.[23]

Jewish involvement in the movement for black freedom had deep roots in American history. During the 1850s, three Jewish immigrants joined John Brown's armed struggle against slavery in "Bloody Kansas." Remembering the pogroms in Russia, Jewish immigrants identified with the victims of antiblack race riots in urban America. After the killing of thirty-eight blacks during the 1917 East St. Louis riot, the Jewish newspaper *Forward* compared the violence to a 1903 pogrom in Russia: "Kishinev and St. Louis—the same soil, the same people. It is a distance of four and a half thousand miles between these two cities and yet they are so close and so similar to each other." Jews contributed leadership to the NAACP: its chairman for most of the years between 1914 and 1939 was Joel E. Spingarn. The head of the NAACP Legal Defense and Education Fund was Jack Greenberg, and the NAACP's fiery labor director was Herbert Hill, a graduate of an orthodox Yeshiva. One of Martin Luther King's closest personal advisers was Stanley Levison; Howard Zinn, a professor at Spelman College, was a counselor to SNCC. Over half of the white lawyers who went south to defend the civil rights protesters were Jewish.[24]

In joining the crusade for justice for African Americans, Jewish Americans remembered the persecution and violence they had experienced in Russia, and they knew that the border between racism and anti-Semitism often blurred. A society that opposed discrimination, they realized, would also allow Jews equality of opportunity. Even as a ten-year-old kid cheering for Jackie Robinson when he broke into major league baseball in 1947, Jack Greenberg understood what this victory meant for Jews. Robinson was "adopted as the surrogate hero by many of us growing up at the time," the civil rights lawyer recalled. "He was the way we saw ourselves triumphing against the forces of bigotry and ignorance." Those forces had curbed Jewish admissions at Harvard and were continuing to discriminate against the appointment of Jews to the faculties of elite universities. The frontline of the battle for equality for everyone, including Jews, was the civil rights struggle for blacks. Indeed, as historian Jonathan Kaufman noted in hindsight, "Jews benefited enormously from the terrain shaped by the civil rights movement. Jews were the first to use antidiscrimination laws to gain access to restricted apartment buildings in large cities. The growing tide of tolerance left by the civil rights movement opened opportunities for Jews as well as for blacks in law firms, corporations, and universities."[25]

"The civil rights movement spoke to the Jewish head," Kaufman pointed out, "but it also spoke to Jewish hearts." Though many Jews had left the Lower East Side for the suburbs and had entered the mainstream of the Promised Land, they carried in their hearts a religion that compelled them to be concerned about oppression. The American Dream had worked for them; now they felt a duty as well as a memory of their own hardships to help make this promise work for blacks. Jewish civil rights workers often referred to "that quote"—the ancient pronouncement by Rabbi Hillel: "If I am not for myself, who will be for me? But if I am only for myself, what am I? And if not now, when?" Nazi genocide had unshrouded the horrible inhumanity of racism. As Jews, they nurtured a special understanding of what it meant to be degraded and victimized as the "Other."[26]

This black-Jewish "alliance," however, was soon "broken." As the focus of the struggle for black equality moved to the North, the relationship between blacks and Jews became increasingly strained. The Civil Rights Movement was shifting from demands for political rights to demands for economic equality. Until then, Kaufman noted, "the price of racial change had been taken out of the hide of the South. Northerners, including northern Jews, did not have to deal with consequences directly." In the North, the racial terrain was different: Jews owned about 30 percent of the stores in Harlem, Watts, and other black communities. During the 1964 Harlem riot, blacks looted many Jewish-owned stores. A class divide separated the two groups. Ghetto blacks were also noticing that many of their landlords were Jewish. At a school integration meeting in Boston, a young black questioned whether blacks could work with Jews when Jewish landlords were exploiting them. According to Kaufman, a popular saying in the 1960s went: "Of the five people that a black meets in the course of the day—his landlord, the storeowner, the social worker, the teacher, the cop—one, the cop, is Irish. The other four are Jews."[27]

At a deeper level, the split between Jews and blacks reflected a larger ideological divide, as conflicting visions of equality emerged. The Civil Rights Movement had begun as a struggle for equality for blacks through integration, which was often defined as a condition of equality. To "overcome" meant to integrate the schools, buses, lunch counters, and other public facilities; this goal was expanded to include equality of opportunity for voting and employment. But in 1966, like earlier black nationalists such as Marcus Garvey, Stokely Carmichael and other young militant blacks issued a clarion call for Black Power. Increasingly, they viewed racial oppression in America as "internal colonialism." Identifying themselves with the Third World, they saw themselves as members of Frantz Fanon's "wretched of the earth," the subjugated peoples of Africa, Latin America, and Asia engaged in struggles for liberation against white colonial domination. Equality, for many black militants, now meant self-determination for blacks as a colonized people in America. The cry of black nationalism was for separatism rather than integration, and there was no place for whites, including Jews, in the movement for black liberation.[28]

But the Civil Rights Movement, composed of blacks and whites fighting together against discrimination, had led to successes. In 1964, Congress prohibited discrimination in public accommodations and employment and established the Fair Employment Opportunity Commission. A year later, lawmakers authorized federal examiners to register qualified voters and abolished obstacles like literacy tests designed to deny voting rights to blacks. Also in 1965, the demand for equality pushed President Lyndon Johnson to promote the right of equal employment by issuing Executive Order 11246. This law required firms with federal contracts to take "affirmative action" in hiring minorities. Companies had to set "good faith goals and timetables" for employing "underutilized" qualified minority workers. At Howard University, Johnson declared: "This is the next and more profound stage of the battle for civil rights. We seek not just freedom but opportunity—not just legal equity but human ability—not just equality as a right and a theory but equality as a fact and equality as a result."[29]

"We shall overcome," the Civil Rights Movement's diverse people sang, "we shall overcome." Indeed, in many significant ways, they did overcome. What emerged was a different America, less saturated with discrimination.

Raisins in the Sun: Dreams Deferred

Meanwhile, however, the Civil Rights Movement was unable to overcome the structural economic foundations of racial inequality for African Americans. While the laws and court orders prohibited discrimination, they failed to relieve poverty among blacks. African Americans had won the right to sit at a lunch counter and order a hamburger, but many of them did not have the money to pay for their meal. Blacks were told that the law now prohibited discrimination in employment, but they also saw that jobs for them were scarce. The desperation was especially acute in the inner cities of the North. "You know the average young person out here don't have a job, man, they don't have anything to do," an African American explained angrily in the early 1960s. "You go down to the employment agency and you can't get a job. They have you waiting all day, but you can't get a job."[30]

Explaining the reason they could not get jobs, scholar Kenneth Clark wrote in *Dark Ghetto*: "Those who are required to live in congested and rat-infested homes are aware that others are not so dehumanized. Young people in the ghetto are aware that other young people have been taught to read, that they have been prepared for college, and can compete successfully for white-collar, managerial, and executive jobs." One of these alienated blacks predicted in 1962: "When the time comes, it is going to be too late. Everything will explode because the people live under tension now; they going to a point where they can't stand it no more." This point was dramatically reached in Los Angeles during the long hot summer of 1965.[31]

"The fire bombs of Watts blasted the civil rights movement into a new phase," declared Martin Luther King, Jr. Ultimately, the struggle to realize the American Dream had to advance beyond antidiscrimination laws and confront what King called the "airtight cage of poverty." The underlying economic basis of racial inequality was a far more elusive and formidable foe than the lynch mobs and police attack dogs. "Jobs are harder and costlier to create than voting rolls," King explained. "The eradication of slums housing millions is complex far beyond integrating buses and lunch counters." This harsh reality of urban squalor and despair was reflected in the jagged mirrors of every northern ghetto. "I see a young Negro boy," King wrote in 1963. "He is sitting on a stoop in front of a vermin-infested apartment house in Harlem. The stench of garbage is in the halls. The drunks, the jobless, the junkies are shadow figures of his everyday world."[32]

This impoverished and depressing world was familiar to Malcolm X. "I don't see any American dream," he declared in 1964; "I see an American nightmare." Growing up in the ghettos of the North, Malcolm Little had pursued a life of drugs and crime. Arrested and found guilty of burglary, he was given an eight-year sentence. As Malcolm X later explained, his "high school" had been the "black ghetto of Roxbury" in Boston, his "college" the "streets of Harlem," and his graduate school the "prison." While serving time, he was converted to Elijah Muhammed's Nation of Islam. As a leader of the Black Muslims, Malcolm X advocated a separatist ideology and mocked King for his faith in integration as well as his strategy of nonviolence. Like David Walker, who had issued his revolutionary appeal in the early nineteenth century, Malcolm X urged blacks to use violence to defend their rights. As the struggle for racial justice shifted from the South to the urban North, Malcolm X's message exposed the failure of the Civil Rights Movement to address the problems of joblessness and poverty."[33]

The Civil Rights Movement was hitting the walls of inequality based on class as well as race—what King called the "inseparable twins" of economic injustice and racial injustice. Beginning in the 1960s, black America became deeply splintered into two classes. On the one hand, the middle class experienced gains: the percentage of families earning $25,000 or more increased from 10 percent in 1960 to 25 percent in 1982, and the number of blacks in college nearly doubled between 1970 and 1980 (from 522,000 to over 1 million). On the other hand, there emerged what has been called a "black underclass." The distressing situation of this group could be measured by the persistence of intergenerational poverty, the increasing unemployment rates for young black men, and the dramatic rise in black female-headed families. Between 1960 and 1980, the percentage of such families doubled, reaching

40 percent, compared to an increase from 8 to 12 percent for white families. While blacks composed only 12 percent of the American population in 1980, they constituted 43 percent of all welfare families. "By now my wife was pregnant," said African-American John Godfrey. "And I was unemployed. So push came to shove. We went down to welfare. I needed medical protection for her and the baby. It was a sobering experience. I felt—I don't know how to put it into words—I was totally disgusted with myself. I felt I had failed myself, because I was unable to take care of myself and my family."[34]

Survival for many black women, even for those with husbands, became difficult on welfare. Trapped in a catch-22 situation, they wanted to get off welfare but found themselves forced by low wages to remain dependent on government subsidy. "None of my jobs ever paid more than minimum wage," said Alice Grady. "As soon as I can get a babysitter, I intend to go back to work. But it won't be easy. There is a bus stop right out front, but according to where your job is, you'd probably need two or three buses to get to work. You'd have to leave early in the morning, and you'd be leaving your children because they're not supposed to be at school until eight or nine o'clock. Then you'd have to find a babysitter for them in the evening until you got home. But I'm hoping to get off welfare and get me a good job. Right now they're helping me, but it's just making ends meet. You don't have anything left. Right now my husband is looking for a job. We vote. This year we couldn't because we were homeless. You know, the homeless can't vote. You have to have an address. It's just rough on welfare. It's just not enough. What can I do for school clothes for the kids? When my husband gets a job, we'll be cut back on welfare." A world of barriers surrounded women like Alice Grady, keeping them impoverished and blocking their avenues of exit. At several different points, they were frustrated by a cycle of poverty generated by low wages and reinforced by inadequate childcare, poor public transportation, lack of affordable housing, and political disenfranchisement.[35]

Moreover, the employment situation of both black women and black men was devastated by major changes in the economy. The movement of plants and offices to the suburbs isolated many urban blacks from places of employment: in 1980, 71 percent of them lived in central cities, whereas 66 percent of whites resided in suburbs. Illustrating the dynamic interaction of the suburbanization of production, unemployment, and welfare, Chicago lost

229,000 jobs and enrolled 290,000 new welfare recipients in the sixties, while its suburbs gained 500,000 jobs. Meanwhile, blacks also suffered from the effects of the "deindustrialization of America." Due to the relocation of production to low-wage countries like South Korea and Mexico, some 22 million American workers lost their jobs between 1969 and 1976. "Blacks have been severely hurt by deindustrialization," William Julius Wilson explained, "because of their heavy concentration in the automobile, rubber, steel, and other smokestack industries."[36]

African-American blue-collar workers had been rendered economically superfluous. One of them was Jimmy Morse. After working for U.S. Steel in Gary, Indiana, for thirty years, he voluntarily retired in 1983 rather than wait for the imminent layoff. His monthly retirement pay totaled $552.63, which did not pay all his bills. "Now, you get the light bill outta there," he explained in 1986. "You get the water bill outta there. Buy some food outta that plus $131 we get in food stamps. You're about $40 short." During the 1970s, the region around Gary had lost 65,000 manufacturing jobs, including 12,000 at US Steel. "Foreign steel was takin' our man-hours away from us, " Morse explained. "And it ain't no racial thing either. That blue-eyed soul brother is catchin' jes' as much hell as I'm catching." Actually, black workers were catching more than their share of hell. In the ranks of this new army of displaced workers was a disproportionately large number of blacks. A study of 2,380 firms which were shut down in Illinois between 1975 and 1978 found that while blacks constituted only 14 percent of the state's workforce, they totaled 20 percent of the laidoff laborers. Of the black workers displaced between 1979 and 1984, only 42 percent were able to secure new employment. They were forced to become the "truly disadvantaged."[37]

Staring at the boarded-up factories, many young blacks were unable to get even their first jobs — work experience essential for acquiring skills as well as self-esteem. One of them, Darryl Swafford, grew up around Gary. Unemployed and dependent on food stamps, he had the same dream as most Americans: "I always had that goal, working in the mill. Have a home, a big car. But now there's no mill and I'm down. Just trying to make it, trying to survive." Many of the jobs available to young blacks were in the fast-food services like Burger King and McDonald's. But these jobs paid very low wages and led nowhere. "They treat you like a child on those minimum-wage jobs," complained Danny Coleman, who had worked in a fast-food restaurant. "And there is no

way you can make it on that kind of salary. It is just a dead end."
Young workers like Coleman faced an economy that said: "Let
them flip hamburgers."[38]

In the midst of this economic crisis, America's inner cities became
tinderboxes for violent explosions. On April 29, 1992, immediately
after four white police officers were found not guilty of assault
against black motorist Rodney King, racial rage engulfed Los
Angeles. The governor declared a state of emergency and ordered
6,000 National Guard troops into the city to restore order. When
the unrest finally came to an end days later, the devastation was
immense: 52 deaths, 2,499 injuries, and 6,559 arrests. More than
3,000 businesses had been damaged by fire, vandalism, and looting, and losses totaled $800 million. The live televised images
mesmerized America. The thousands of fires burning out of control and the dark smoke filling the skies made Los Angeles look
like a bombed-out city.

"It took a brutal beating, an unexpected jury verdict, and the
sudden rampage of rioting, looting, and indiscriminate violence
to bring this crisis [of urban America] back to the forefront,"
Business Week reported. "Racism surely explains some of the carnage in Los Angeles. But the day-to-day living conditions with
which many of America's urban poor must contend is an equally
compelling story—a tale of economic injustice." The riot was
a cry of rage against the poverty of the inner city. "South Central Los Angeles is a Third World country," declared Krashaun
Scott, a former member of the Los Angeles Crips gang. "There's
a South Central in every city, in every state." Describing the
desperate conditions in his community, he continued: "What we
got is inadequate housing and inferior education. I wish someone would tell me the difference between Guatemala and South
Central." This comparison vividly illustrated the squalor and
poverty present within one of America's wealthiest and most
modern cities. Like a Third World country, South Central Los
Angeles had become extremely volatile. A gang member known
as Bone explained that the recent violence was "not a riot—it
was a class struggle. When Rodney King asked, 'Can we get
along?' it ain't just about Rodney King. He was the lighter and it
blew up."[39]

What exploded was anguish born of despair. "What happens
to a dream deferred?" asked Langston Hughes in Harlem during
the 1920s.

Does it dry up
Like a raisin in the sun?
... Or does it explode?[40]

"Once again, young blacks are taking to the streets to express their outrage at perceived injustice," *Newsweek* reported, "and once again, whites are fearful that The Fire Next Time will consume them." But this time, the magazine noticed, the situation was different from the earlier riot: the recent conflict was not just between blacks and whites. "The nation is rapidly moving toward a multiethnic future in which Asians, Hispanics, Caribbean islanders, and many other immigrant groups compose a diverse and changing social mosaic that cannot be described by the old vocabulary of race relations in America." The terms "black" and "white," *Newsweek* concluded, no longer "depict the American social reality."[41]

The fire this time consumed the stores and dreams of Korean-American shopkeepers. "April 29, 1992, the night the store burned down," merchant Young Soon Han recalled, "I didn't even know what was happening. I hadn't been paying much attention to the Rodney King verdict. I didn't think the issue was so serious." Warned trouble was coming, Han went home. Later he was told that his store had been burned to the ground. During the days of fury and fire, recalled Sun Soon Kim, another storeowner, Koreatown "looked like it went to war." Smoke was rising from the buildings, and Korean merchants were frantically trying to "salvage any remains of a dream." What she saw resembled a surrealistic scene from hell. "I couldn't believe what I was seeing—like something from the movies. I felt like I was on the movie screen walking through a war zone and people in the movie theater were watching this." But she was not watching a Hollywood fantasy. "I honestly wasn't prepared for what I was about to see. In front of me was the remaining rubbles of the stores that I had poured my money, sweat, and time into. Everything I had worked so hard to build was crumbled in front of me." Kim felt that she had "died, not physically but emotionally."[42]

Out of the conflagration, however, arose an awareness of multiracial connectedness and an affirmation of interdependency. Shortly after the 1992 explosion, social critic Richard Rodriguez reflected: "The Rodney King riots were appropriately multiracial in this multicultural capital of America. We cannot settle for black and white conclusions when one of the most important conflicts the riots revealed was the tension between Koreans and African Americans." He also noted that "the majority of looters who were arrested...turned out to be Hispanic." Out of the Los Angeles conflict came a sense of community. "Here was a race riot that had no border," Rodriguez wrote, "a race riot without nationality. And, for the first time, everyone in the city realized—if only in fear—that they were related to one another." "I think good will come of [the riot]," stated Janet Harris, a chaplain at Central Juvenile Hall. "People need to take off their rose-colored glasses," she added, "and take a hard look at what they've been doing. They've been living in invisible cages. And they've shut out that world. And maybe the world came crashing in on them and now people will be moved to do something."[43]

Asian Americans: A "Model Minority" for Blacks?

As inner-city African Americans struggled to get by, news pundits and policymakers celebrated Asian-American success. Five years before the 1992 Los Angeles riot, CBS's *60 Minutes* presented a glowing report on the stunning achievements of Asian Americans in the academy. "Why are Asian Americans doing so exceptionally well in school?" Mike Wallace asked and quickly added, "They must be doing something right. Let's bottle it." Wallace then suggested that failing black students should try to pursue the Asian-American formula for academic success. At the same time, President Ronald Reagan joined the chorus trumpeting Asian-American achievements. While congratulating Asian Americans for their family values, hard work, and high incomes, Reagan chastised blacks for their dependency on the "spider's web of welfare" and their failure to recognize that the "only barrier" to success was "within" them. Reagan had skillfully set the stage for the battle between "meritocracy" and affirmative action.[44]

In the spring of 1995, Governor Pete Wilson of California announced his opposition to affirmative action when he launched his campaign for the Republican nomination for the presidency. Following Wilson that summer, African-American Ward Connerly began his attack on what he scorned as "preferential treatment" for blacks. As a member of the Board of Regents of the University of California, he successfully engineered a ban on affirmative action for university admissions. Connerly argued that affirmative action represented "reverse discrimination": it discriminated in favor of African Americans and Latino Americans, not only at the expense of whites but also of Asian Americans. Pitting Asian Americans against African Americans, Connerly declared that African-American students should be like Asian-American students, and that they should study hard, get excellent test scores and grades, and seek admission to the university based solely on their merit. Buoyed by his victory, Connerly took his crusade to the 1996 election. On the ballot, he placed Proposition 209, an initiative to prohibit affirmative action in the entire state. His proposal was called the California Civil Rights Initiative. The proposition was approved by 54 percent of the voters. But exit polls revealed that 25 percent of those who voted for it were also for affirmative action. They did not clearly understand that the "civil rights" initiative would prohibit race and gender considerations for hiring, contracting, and university admissions. In the wake of Prop. 209, diversity on university campuses declined sharply for African-American and Latino enrollments, from 5 and 15 percent to 2 and 8 percent, respectively. Yet together the two minorities totaled 40 percent of the state's population, paying taxes to subsidize the University of California.

The news media and political hype over Asian-American "success" and black "failure" shrouded the impact of the Cold War economy on the problems of unemployment and poverty in the inner city. The strategic nuclear weapons program under the Reagan presidency was financed by enormous deficits. Defense expenditures under the Reagan administration more than doubled from $134 billion in 1980 to $282 billion in 1987. In that year, defense spending amounted to 60 cents out of every dollar received by the federal government in income tax. Meanwhile, resources were being diverted from social needs: defense spending was $35 billion greater in 1985 than in 1981, while funds for entitlement programs such as food stamps and welfare were cut by $30 billion. Moreover, the focus of research and development on strategic nuclear weapons was detrimental to the general economy. Between 1955 and 1990, the federal government spent more than $1 trillion on nuclear arms and other weaponry for the Cold War—a sum representing 62 percent of all federal research expenditures. This concentration on atomic arms research and production drained national resources and at the same time undermined America's capacity to produce competitive consumer goods, which, in turn, generated trade imbalances and contributed to a decline in commercial manufacturing, especially for those sectors of the industrial economy where many blacks had been employed. The United States won the atomic arms race, but the victory was enormously costly.[45]

Still, there were new prospects for change and progress. The end of the Cold War gave the country a "peace dividend." Resources devoted to nuclear-weapons production could now be shifted to the production of consumer goods, helping revitalize the economy and making it more competitive with Japan and Germany. "It's as though America just won the lottery," the *New York Times* editorialized exuberantly in March 1990. "With Communism collapsing, the United States, having defended the free world for half a century, now stands to save a fortune. Defense spending could drop by $20 billion next year and $150 billion a year before the decade ends." This tremendous resource could now be directed into the consumer-goods economy. What was needed, proposed Ann Markusen of Rutgers University, was "an independent Office of Economic Conversion, designed to be self-liquidating by the year 2000 and accountable to the President."[46]

The United States found itself perched on the threshold of a new era of economic expansion. To meet the research needs of the military over the prior half century, the government had educated and supported an impressive array of brilliant engineers and scientists. "These wizards of the cold war comprise the greatest force of scientific and engineering talent ever assembled," observed journalist William J. Broad in 1992. "Over the decades this army of government, academic and industry experts made the breakthroughs that gave the West its dazzling military edge." Released from military R&D, these "wizards" could now concentrate on the consumers-goods market. Under the guidance of a comprehensive national industrial strategy, giant American corporations like Rockwell International, Grumman, Northrup, Martin Marietta, and Lockheed could now start designing and producing "smart" consumer goods rather than "smart" bombs. More important, vital resources could now be redirected to the rebuilding of the manufacturing base in the inner cities as well as to schools and job-training programs.[47]

A bright future seemed ahead for America. But then came September 11, 2001, with the terrorist attack on the World Trade Center. And the hopes of the rising wind for social justice again became "dreams deferred."

16

AGAIN, THE
"TEMPEST-TOST"

IN SHAKESPEARE'S STORY *The Tempest*, Prospero commands the spirit Ariel to stir the seas in order to create a storm that will blow to his enchanted island the ship carrying the King of Naples and his entourage. The tempest terrifies all on board. "Now I would give a thousand furlongs of sea for an acre of barren ground—long heath, brown furze, anything," cries Gonzalo, the king's adviser. "The wills above be done, but I would fain die a dry death." Ariel lands them gently on the island's shore.

On the pedestal of the Statue of Liberty is also emblazoned a reference to a storm:

> *"Keep ancient lands, your storied pomp!" cries she*
> *With silent lips. "Give me your tired, your poor,*
> *Your huddled masses yearning to breathe free,*
> *The wretched refuse of your teeming shore.*
> *Send these, the homeless, tempest-tost to me,*
> *I lift my lamp beside the golden door!"* [1]

Fleeing the "tempests" of political strife, wars, and poverty during the recent decades, the world has rushed into America once more, and transformed our society into a more complex multicultural tapestry.

From a "Teeming Shore": Russia, Ireland, and China

The global context of the Cold War conditioned immigration from what had been the Soviet Union. Refugees fleeing from religious oppression, Jews began arriving in America again. The collapse of Communism in Eastern Europe and Russia in the 1990s unleashed a new wave of anti-Semitism, and many Jews were afraid of what would happen to them. "Anti-Semitism and all the other old national hatreds were never really extinguished by Communism, merely frozen in time," James E. Young noted in his review of Charles Hoffman's study of the Jews of Eastern Europe in the postcommunist era. "When the thaw came, the traditional conflicts bloomed with a vengeance, picking up exactly where they left off 45 years ago." The unraveling of communist controls unleashed old, pent-up nativist passions. "The country is experiencing a process of 'decivilization,'" explained a Moscow lawyer in 1990. "The layers of civilization are being peeled off, and underneath there is this ugliness, including fascism and anti-Semitic hatred. Jews are trying to get out of Russia as fast as they can." An old Jewish man in a village near Minsk told two American visitors: "It's time now. We have to go. It wouldn't be safe for us to stay." He was not religiously Jewish: for lunch he served ham. Prohibited from practicing their religion, many Jews had become Jewish mainly in terms of their ethnic origins. "The last of the [Jewish] culture-bearers were executed 40 years ago," explained Aleksandr Z. Burakovsky, chair of the Kiev Sholom Aleichem Society. "Schools, synagogues, libraries were all abolished." Aleksandr A. Shlayen, director of the Babi Yar Center, added: "They started to beat the Jewishness out of Jews a long time ago, under the czars."[2]

Though many Jews in what had been the Soviet Union did not feel a strong identity as Jews, they encountered hatred from their neighbors and fellow citizens. In schools, Jewish children were beaten and called names. Resentment spread to the workplace: professional Jews experienced discrimination in employment. Graffiti on walls warned: "Jews get out." "My husband wanted to emigrate, but I didn't want to leave," recounted a young Jewish woman. "My parents are old and need to be cared for. I also thought of myself as a Soviet citizen." Many people saw her only as a "Jew," however, and the harassment became "awful." Seeking sanctuary, half a million Jews fled to Israel and also to America.[3]

Like the Jewish immigrants of the late nineteenth century, they sold their houses and furniture, giving away almost everything and leaving with only what they could carry. After their arrival, they had to start all over again. Describing the plight of a Jewish refugee family, Barbara Budnitz of Berkeley, California, explained: "These people have nothing. I offered them an old desk. They said they wanted it, but what they really needed was a bed." Many of these refugees had been engineers in the old country, but here they suffered from unemployment. Lacking English-language skills and possessing technical knowledge that had limited transferability, many were forced to find jobs as apartment managers, janitors, or even as helpers at McDonald's. According to Barbara Nelson of the Jewish Family Services in Oakland, California, about 80 percent of the Jewish refugee families were compelled to seek welfare support.[4]

Still, the Jews were glad to be in America, where there was religious freedom. "My five-year-old daughter is attending school at the synagogue—something she could not do in the Ukraine," explained Sofiya Shapiro, who came with her family in 1991. "I am glad she can get to know Jewish tradition." Indeed, many of the refugees were learning about Judaism for the first time. Like the Jewish immigrants of earlier times, the recent refugees embraced the hope that this country would offer them an opportunity to begin again. "That's what America is," commented Budnitz. "We need to keep it that way."[5]

America's continuing allure has also been as a place for a fresh economic start. This was particularly true for the most recent wave from Ireland. Like the nineteenth-century Irish immigrants fleeing hunger and the ravages of the Potato Famine, these newcomers were pushed by grim economic conditions at home: in 1990, unemployment in Ireland was a staggering 18 percent. Seeking work in America, many entered legally with a student, work, or tourist visa, and simply stayed after it expired. Undocumented Irish workers totaled as many as 120,000. "It's an anonymous floating population," stated Lena Deevy, director of the Irish Immigration Reform Movement office in Boston. "It's like counting the homeless." These illegal aliens constituted what one of them described as "an underclass," forced to take "the crummiest jobs at the lowest wages." The 1986 Immigration Reform Act, which made it unlawful for employers to hire undocumented workers, created economic and social borders for many Irish. "You can't apply for a job," explained an Irish waitress who came to Boston in 1986. "You can't answer a want ad. It's all word of mouth." Undocumented Irish workers had to keep a low profile, she added: "My social life is limited to the Irish sector. I can't talk to Americans—you just have to tell too many lies." Deevy described their nervousness: "It's like living on the edge. There's a lot of fear that someone will squeal to the INS [Immigration and Naturalization Service]." In 1990, a new immigration law provided for the distribution of 40,000 green cards to be awarded by lottery, with 16,000 of them reserved for Irish. "I plan to fill out at least a thousand applications," said Joanne O'Connell of Queens, New York, as she looked forward to this "Irish Sweepstakes."[6]

Facing a rising nativist backlash against illegal immigrants, many Irish newcomers joined Mexican Americans in demanding comprehensive immigration reform that would enable all of them to become legalized. In February 2006, fifteen hundred Irish participated in an immigration reform rally in San Francisco. One of them, Elaine, worked as a nanny. "We're all in the same boat," she told a reporter. "The Irish are lucky because we speak English and we're white. We do get treated better. But we [undocumented immigrants] are all hard workers. We all want a better life." Elaine explained that she would like to become a legal permanent resident so that she could build a stable life in her adopted country without fear of being picked up by immigration authorities. She also would like to take her six-year-old son to Ireland so he can maintain his ties to his grandparents and his Irish heritage.[7]

Joining the Jews and the Irish were also immigrants from China. In the wake of civil rights legislation for African Americans in the 1960s, the question surfaced: if discrimination is immoral and illegal, why was there an immigration restriction law based on racial exclusion? "Just as we sought to eliminate discrimination in our land through the Civil Rights Act," declared a congressman, "today we seek by phasing out the national origins quota system to eliminate discrimination in immigration to this nation composed of the descendants of immigrants." All groups should have equal opportunity to enter America. "Everywhere else in our national life, we have eliminated discrimination based on national origins," Attorney General Robert Kennedy told Congress. "Yet, this system is still the foundation of our immigration law." In 1965, Congress legislated the removal of all restrictions to Asian immigration—an injustice of exclusion that Asian Americans had struggled for decades to overcome.[8]

For the Chinese, the new law reopened the gates to the country they had affectionately called Gold Mountain. In 1960 the Chinese population was only 237,000; twenty years later it had jumped to 812,200. The Chinese-American community had been radically transformed from 61 percent American-born to 63 percent foreign-born, becoming once more mainly an immigrant community. This tide of new immigrants from China was not anticipated at all when Congress passed the 1965 immigration law. The early immigrants had been here a long time, and most of them did not have immediate family members to bring to America. But the family unification provision of the law opened the way for new immigrants who came here initially as students. "My brother-in-law left his wife in Taiwan and came here as a student to get a Ph.D. in engineering," explained Subi Lin Felipe. "After he received his degree, he got a job in San Jose. Then he brought in a sister and his wife, who brought over one of her brothers and me. And my brother's wife then came."[9]

During the 1960s, Chinese students flocked to the United States to pursue their education; in 1980 half of the 300,000 foreign students here were from China and other Asian countries. Thousands of Chinese students were able to find employment and then acquire Labor Department certification as immigrants under the sixth preference for skilled workers. In this way large numbers of Chinese were able to change their status from foreign students to immigrants. Once they became immigrants, they could develop an expanding immigrant kin network under the family preferences of the 1965 law. They could bring their wives and children here; then as U.S. citizens a few years later, they could bring their parents as well as their brothers and sisters, who, in turn, could arrange for the entry of their spouses and children. Thus one immigrant coming originally as a student could bring to America a chain migration of family members.

Not all of the new immigrants were educated. They included low-wage laborers, employed as service workers and operatives in Chinatowns. Most of them did not have a high school certificate, or English-language skills. The problems of limited English and limited employment opportunities were self-reinforcing. "Chinese people have lower incomes because first, the language problem," explained Wing Ng. "If you know just a little English, you can go to an office and get a job cleaning up. It has more security, more benefits. But how are you going to get a job like that if you don't know a little English? And how are you going to learn English if you have to work twelve hours a day, six days a week, and then come home and take care of your family?"[10]

Unable to speak English, many Chinese immigrant women had no choice but to work as seamstresses. In the 1980s, they became a major source of labor for New York's garment industry, which had earlier employed Jewish immigrants. "These factories are one of New York City's unknown industrial success stories," said Harry Schwartz, president of the Garment Industry Development Corporation. "You walk around the Garment District and ask, 'Where have the production shops gone?' Well, they've gone to Chinatown." In San Francisco, Chinese women were producing almost half of the total volume of manufactured apparel, usually working for minimum wages in a sweatshop environment. "The conditions in the factories are terrible," reported a Chinatown resident. "Dirty air, long hours, from eight in the morning to eight at night, six days! They are paid by the piece and only a few can make good money. They don't protest because they don't know how to talk back and they don't know the law."[11]

While the women in Chinatown were located largely in the garment industry, many of the men were employed in the restaurants. S. L. Wong, the director of an English-language school in San Francisco's Chinatown, explained how the newcomers were locked in a low-wage restaurant-labor market: "Most immigrants coming into Chinatown with a language barrier cannot go outside this confined area into the mainstream of American industry." Danny Lowe described his predicament: "Before I was a painter in Hong Kong, but I can't do it here. I got no license, no education. I want a living, so it's dishwasher, janitor, or cook."[12]

The low-wage workers included immigrants who had been professionals in China. Winnie Wu had been a mathematics teacher and her husband a professor of Chinese at a university; in San Francisco, she worked as an office clerk and he as a janitor in a hotel. Both wanted to get ahead and they studied English late into the night, until 2 A.M. Wah Tom Wing had been a professional with a college degree in physics. She arrived here in 1976 and went to work on an assembly line. "We are college graduates," she said, "but are working in sewing or electronic factories. We all have taken a big step backwards in our profession or work. Life cannot forever be like this—work, work, and work."[13]

Similarly Wei-Chi Poon and her husband, Boon-Pui Poon, experienced the problem of underemployment. Before they came in 1968, she had been a young biology professor, and he had been an architect in the People's Republic of China. "We had a really hard time right after we got here," she said. "My husband was a very good architect, but because he couldn't speak English he could work only as a draftsman. His pay was so low that he had to work at two jobs, from eight in the morning till eleven o'clock at night." She worked in a laundry factory, packing uniforms into bags to be sent to Vietnam, while earning only the minimum wage. "The bags were at least one hundred pounds each. At the time, I was one of the younger workers, so I had more strength than some of the others. I got scared, wondering, 'Will I be doing this for the rest of my life?'" She knew she would be trapped in this dead-end job unless she learned English. "We were so busy working and so tired we had no time and energy to study English." A program funded by the Comprehensive Employment Training Act enabled her to take English classes and work as a library assistant in the Chinatown branch of the San Francisco Library. She enrolled in the city's junior college and did so well she was able to be admitted directly to graduate study in library science at San Jose State University. In the 1990s, Wei-Chi Poon became the head of the Asian American Studies Library of the University of California at Berkeley. One of her tasks was to collect books and materials on a new group of Asian Americans—the refugees from Vietnam.[14]

Dragon's Teeth of Fire: Vietnam

Unlike the immigrants from China, the Vietnamese were refugees fleeing for their lives. Their country had been a French colony since the late nineteenth century; during World War II, the Vietminh, under the leadership of Ho Chi Minh, fought the French to regain their country's independence. This war ended in 1954 when the French forces were defeated at the battle of Dien Bien Phu. At Geneva shortly afterward, the French and Vietminh signed an agreement that provided for a temporary partition of Vietnam at the Seventeenth Parallel and for an all-Vietnamese election in 1956. But a year after the Geneva conference, a new government was formed in the south headed by Ngo Dinh Diem, with the support of the United States, to counter the government in the north backed by China and the Soviet Union. The partition of Vietnam became permanent: the election was never held, and civil war erupted. U.S. involvement in the conflict began to expand significantly in the early sixties when President John Kennedy sent special forces to Vietnam and when President Lyndon Johnson asked Congress to give him war powers in the 1964 Gulf of Tonkin Resolution. The war ended disastrously for South Vietnam and for the United States eleven years later, precipitating a massive exodus of Vietnamese to the United States.

Unlike the other Asian groups already in America, the 1975 wave of Vietnamese migrants did not choose to come here. In fact, they had no decision to make, for they were driven out by the powerful events surrounding them. Most of them were military personnel and their families, in flight from the North Vietnamese troops. A week before the collapse of the South Vietnamese government on April 29, ten to fifteen thousand people were evacuated; then in a frenzy during the last days of April, eighty-six thousand Vietnamese fled from the besieged country.

At the street level, panic gripped the people. "On those last days of April," remembered a refugee, "[there was] a lot of gunfire and bombing around the capital. People were running on chaotic streets. We got scared. We went to an American building where a lot of Americans and their Vietnamese associates were ready to be picked up by American helicopters." They could "feel" the bombing. "Our houses were shaking," said Thai Dang. "Then afterward we went outside and saw abandoned guns and army uniforms on the streets. The soldiers in flight had thrown away their weapons and taken off their clothes. Here and there we saw bodies."[15]

The city shuddered under relentless missile bombardments. Homes and buildings were burning everywhere. A poem captured the horrifying experience:

> *Fires spring up like dragon's teeth*
> *A furious, acrid wind sweeps them toward us*
> > *from all sides*
> *All around, the horizon burns with the color*
> > *of death.*

Fleeing from death, frightened people rushed to get out of Saigon. From the roof of the American embassy, hundreds climbed frantically onto helicopters. Others drove to the airport, where they abandoned their cars with notes on the windshields: "For those who are left behind."[16]

The refugees had no time to prepare psychologically for departure; more than half of them were given less than ten hours. "I was afraid of the killings when the Communists came to town," one of them explained. "Mother came along to the airport. Then at the last minute she stayed behind because the number of children staying was larger than those leaving." Many thought they would be gone for only a month or two: "My mother would never have left her other six children behind if she thought she wasn't coming back." Others did not even know they were leaving or where they were going. "I saw everyone running to the harbor, so I decided to go along," recalled a Vietnamese. After reaching the Philippines, a family learned they were bound for the United States; later they said: "We did not plan on taking this trip."[17]

Altogether some 130,000 Vietnamese refugees found sanctuary in the United States in 1975. The first-wave refugees generally came from the educated classes: 37 percent of the heads of households had completed high school and 16 percent had been to college. Almost two-thirds could speak English well or with some fluency. Coming from the urban areas, especially Saigon, they were more westernized than the general population. They had worked with the French and then the Americans. About half of them were Christian, a group that represented only 10 percent of the country's population. Unlike the earlier waves of Asian immigrants, they came as family units rather than as young single men; almost half were female. After their arrival in the United States, the 1975 refugees were initially placed in processing camps like Pendleton in California and Fort Chaffee in Arkansas. From the camps they were spread throughout the country, but they soon began to gather in communities such as Orange County, California.[18]

Meanwhile, in Vietnam, the fighting had stopped, and "everything had fallen into absolute silence, a silence that was so unusual." Then the new communist government began the reconstruction of society. Businesses were nationalized, and reeducation camps were instituted for individuals associated with the old regime. "New Economic Zones" were developed for the movement of the population to the countryside. Thousands of Vietnamese, particularly urban businessmen and professional elites, were ordered to "go to the country to do labour, the hard jobs, to make the irrigation canals, sometimes for one month, sometimes for two, or three months." "I remember the choked mute lines of families trudging out of the cities to begin agricultural work in the countryside," said an ethnic Chinese businessman. "They had no prior knowledge of how to do that job, yet they had no choice." One of them said: "Life was very hard for everybody. All had changed! I could see no future for me in Vietnam, no better life! I wanted to escape."[19]

Thousands did escape—21,000 in 1977, 106,500 in 1978, over 150,000 in 1979, and scores of thousands later. The second-wave Vietnamese refugees took their wives and children and boarded crowded, leaky boats, risking their lives at sea, where storms threatened to drown them and pirates waited to rob them and rape the women. Two-thirds of the boats were attacked by pirates, each boat an average of more than two times. Luong Bot Chau told the terrifying story of what happened to her. She and her husband, along with more than two dozen refugees, sailed away on a small thirty-foot vessel; off the coast of Thailand, their boat was attacked by Thai pirates. The pirates chopped off one of her husband's fingers to get his ring and then tried to slit his throat. "But the knife they had was too blunt," she said later. Instead they clubbed him to death and threw his body into the sea. Then they dragged the young girls up to the deck and systematically raped them. "We heard them scream and scream," Luong Bot Chau cried. "We could not get out, because the pirates had nailed down the hatch."[20]

The survivors floated to Thailand, where they were forced to live in squalid refugee camps for months and often years. From the camps, they went to countries like Australia, Canada, and France, but most of them came to the United States. "In 1978 my sister, Nguyet, my brothers Tinh, Hung, my father, and I left the country," wrote Tuyet Anh Nguyen in a letter to me. "My mom and sister and couple of brothers stayed in Vietnam. It was so hard for my family to suffer the separation." The second-wave refugees were diverse, including educated professionals as well as fishermen, farmers, and storekeepers from the rural areas and small coastal cities and villages. Unlike the earlier refugees from Saigon, most of them did not speak English. Approximately 40 percent of the second wave were ethnic Chinese Vietnamese. They had experienced hostility from Vietnamese society for decades and became targets of discrimination under the new communist regime. The government's program of nationalizing the economy focused heavily on the ethnic Chinese: constituting 7 percent of the country's population, they controlled about 80 percent of its retail trade. Furthermore, military conflict had broken out between China and Vietnam in 1979, and the ethnic Chinese in Vietnam found themselves caught in the political crossfire.[21]

In 1985 there were 643,200 Vietnamese in the United States.

"Remember these are the people who were on our side," an American veteran of the Vietnam War said. "They have a right to come to this country as refugees. They just need a home." But often they did not feel welcome. Like earlier Asian immigrants, the Vietnamese felt the stings of racial slurs and were sometimes called names like "Chink" and told to "go back to China." "It's really hard for you [Americans] to understand us," said a Vietnamese immigrant, "and we don't expect you to, but we do expect you to treat us as human beings and not be prejudiced."[22]

Many Vietnamese, especially those who fought in the army, fiercely refused to abandon their country to the communists. At Tet New Year celebrations, they gathered under a banner trumpeting the slogan To Quoc Ten Het, "Country Above All." "We shall return," they shouted as they pledged themselves to the "liberation of Vietnam." Many refugees nurtured strong attachments to their homeland. "Vietnam is my home," said a refugee in 1988 as she described her determination to go back. She had been in the United States for ten years and had even become a naturalized citizen, but she adamantly claimed her Vietnamese identity. "I get angry, mad," she argued, "when I see Vietnamese children who can't speak Vietnamese." They included her own, born in the United States. When asked what would happen to her children when she returned to Vietnam, she answered: "They will have to choose between the two countries."[23]

But the choice was saturated with ambivalence. "If Vietnam were a free country," said Loan Vo Le, who had fled from Saigon in April 1975, "I would like to go back. I miss my family so much. But we couldn't stay. I'm afraid we are too spoiled by life here, the conveniences, the opportunities, the education and the freedom. I feel like a Vietnamese American, but inside I'm still Vietnamese."[24]

In their adopted country, many refugees realized that Vietnamese culture could not be strictly maintained, particularly in terms of gender roles. "In Vietnam, the women usually were dependent on the husband a great deal," a husband explained. "Then when we came here, the Vietnamese women had jobs. This made the men feel extremely insecure." But he himself had overcome this problem. "My wife didn't work in Vietnam. Now because she is working, I start to help her with the dishes and chores around the house. Sometimes when I am on vacation and she is working, I try new recipes so that when she comes home the meals are ready. She never tells me that I should help her, but I think because she is working like me too, I should give her a hand."[25]

Finding new opportunities in America, many women re-invented themselves. Winnie Che, for example, began working as a waitress in 1981. "My first job I felt so happy," she said. "I can work! Somebody will hire me here." Che saved her money and took loans from family and friends and in 1983 opened a restaurant, the Little Sai-Gon, in Carnation, Washington. "In Vietnam, I would be just a housewife: clean up, cook dinner. Here, if you work hard, you can do what you want." Vietnamese women like Winnie Che began to stretch and feel the arches of their backs, freeing themselves for new activities and identities. But this exercise of new freedom was often accompanied by conflict within the family as college-educated Vietnamese women seeking professional careers tried to break from the traditions of arranged marriages and female subservient roles.[26]

Thrust abruptly into a very different culture, the Vietnamese found their traditional family ties severely strained. "Back in Vietnam the family is something precious for us — father, mother, children," explained Tran Xuan Quang. "But in coming here, we saw that the family here is too loose. The father works in one place, the mother works in another, and they don't see each other at all. Sometimes the father works in the morning and the mother works in the afternoon and the children go to school. When they get home, they hardly see each other at all." Many children began to lose their Vietnamese language. "I hated it when Americans teased me about my language," complained Mai Khanh Tran. "Maybe that's why I don't talk in Vietnamese in front of an American anymore. When I first came here, I used to talk in Vietnamese, but ever since they teased me I don't feel comfortable doing it anymore. At home I do because my parents always talk Vietnamese and I'm trying to preserve what I have for as long as possible. But I can feel it's slipping away."[27]

Most refugees began to realize that their stay in America would be permanent. "In their heart, they want to go back," observed San Francisco State University professor Chuong Hoang Chung. "But reality has crept in and they know they will be here for a long time. They receive letters from home saying the conditions are terrible and don't come back. They are also having children born here." Many Vietnamese would like to become part of American society. "I think it's necessary to acculturate to some degree in order to move up and most important to live within the society in harmony," said one of them. "For example, if we are strangers in the neighborhood, there might be some resistance from the natives. But if we become their friends and show them that we are nice people too, then their anti-Vietnamese attitude would alter. In fact, if different people understand each other, then there will be a lot less hatred between races." He hoped the understanding would be based on accepting and appreciating them as Vietnamese as well as Americans.[28]

Meanwhile, the refugees concentrated on more immediate economic needs. Many of them secured new jobs that did not have the remunerative rewards and status of the work they had done in Vietnam. There many of the refugees had been professionals and managers; here they became workers in craft, operative, and service employment. "In Vietnam I was a history and geography teacher," a refugee told an interviewer. "Here I worked on many different jobs — bricklayer, carpenter, clerk typist, salesman, truck driver, delivery man. I felt frustrated and depressed because I had social status and possessions in Vietnam. Here I didn't have anything." "I am a patient man," another Vietnamese refugee said. "If I have to start over again, I believe I will make it someday. I believe I will become self-sufficient as an auto mechanic. Most refugees have only one hope: to have a job and become a taxpayer."[29]

Actually, many Vietnamese have achieved much more. In California, where the Vietnamese have concentrated and where 40 percent have made their homes, they have created their own Vietnamese colonies or ethnic enclaves. In 1988 the city council of Westminster, Orange County, officially designated the area along Bolsa Avenue from Magnolia to Bushard as "Little Saigon." This section constitutes a "large language island." "A walk down the Bolsa Avenue can testify to the extensive use and importance of Vietnamese," observed Chuong Hoang Chung. "A look at directories published in Vietnamese and distributed free to Vietnamese shoppers shows that any Vietnamese resident of Orange County can obtain all necessary services without ever having to use English."[30]

Over the years, in Orange and Los Angeles counties, Vietnamese-owned businesses have proliferated. Vietnamese professionals have become doctors and dentists, and ethnic Chinese Vietnamese have become almost ubiquitous in restaurants and grocery stores. Their businesses have not been just mom-and-pop stores. In fact, many of the retailers had been big merchants in Vietnam and had brought capital with them to the United States: here they opened supermarket chains like Wai Wai Supermarkets and Man Wah Supermarkets. "For people who do business here, they feel as if they are doing business at home," said Hoang Giao of the Vietnamese Chamber of Commerce in Los Angeles. Most of the shop signs in Westminster were in Vietnamese only. But the merchants of Little Saigon have begun to reach out for a larger customer market. In some Vietnamese stores, signs announce: "Se habla español."[31]

In northern California, Vietnamese entrepreneurs have been flourishing in San Jose. "Vietnamese now constitute 10 percent of San Jose's population and have moved into its commercial life in an aggressive way," reported T. T. Nhu in 1988. "Nearly forty percent of the retail business in downtown San Jose is Vietnamese.... The fact is that the Vietnamese have become an inescapable presence in San Jose. They want to become part of San Jose because they are here to stay." Downtown San Jose had been in decline until the arrival of the Vietnamese newcomers. "There's a new vitality downtown and it's the Vietnamese who have made it what it is today," stated Doanh Chau, executive director of the Vietnamese Chamber of Commerce. "It was abandoned. But the past few years has brought a new life to the area."[32]

Signs of Vietnamese-American settlement are certainly evident. Significantly, more Vietnamese have recently begun coming to America as immigrants: they are entering under the Orderly Departure Program, an agreement between Vietnam and the United States begun in 1982 which encourages family reunification by allowing twenty thousand Vietnamese to enter the United States annually. In 2000, the Vietnamese-American population totaled 1,388,000. Their presence has been folded into the larger social landscape: their favorite noodle soup, pho, has become an American dish.[33]

Wars of Terror: Afghanistan

Like the Vietnamese, they came as refugees, but from another region of the world—from Afghanistan, a landlocked Muslim country nearly the size of Texas, wedged between Pakistan, Iran, and the Soviet Union (the area now comprising the countries of Turkmenistan, Uzbekistan, and Tajikistan). Ruled by a monarchy and then a constitutional monarchy, the nation became a republic in 1973, when Mohammed Daoud Khan staged a coup and forced King Zahir Shah into exile. Five years later, Daoud himself was deposed. In 1979, the Soviet Union invaded Afghanistan and installed procommunist Babrak Karmal as the new leader.

Like Vietnam, Afghanistan became a battleground of the Cold

War. Concerned that Russian domination of Afghanistan could threaten U.S. access to the oil resources of Central Asia, the American government helped finance and arm the mujahideen—- the anti-Soviet "freedom fighters." An Afghan refugee now living in California recalled: "They were helping the mujahideen. The mujahideen were bad." The fighting turned into a civil war. "Bloody battles were everywhere. Communists and religious people, and many different groups inside Afghanistan were fighting with each other. Cousins turned on cousins, brothers turned on brothers. Sometimes, fathers turned on their sons." The bloody fighting lasted for ten years, ending with the withdrawal of Soviet troops in 1989. "We beat the Russians!" exclaimed Afghan refugees in America as many of them prepared to return to their homeland.[34]

Then, before the exiles could buy their plane tickets, civil war broke out between rival anti-Soviet factions, with Iran and Pakistan playing major support roles. In 1996, the Pakistan-backed Taliban faction took control of the capital city of Kabul, which became the base for extending its domination over the rest of Afghanistan. Refugee Sediqullah Rahi said: "The Taliban are very primitive, closed-minded people. They are not allowing anything progressive in Afghanistan. Our economy is destroyed, our social life is destroyed, our people's lives are nothing. And, now, they're destroying our cultural life, too."[35]

Before the Taliban came to power, Kabul resembled a modern Paris. "I grew up in Kabul City during the 1960s," recalled a mother now living in Fremont, California. "Girls wore make-up, miniskirts, and went to school. Some of us even flirted with boys." Such Western lifestyles were suddenly banned. Imposing their fundamentalist version of Islam, the Taliban forced women to cover themselves in burqas, garments that covered their entire bodies, with nets hiding their faces. "One day," recalled Asia Miskeenyar, now also in Fremont, "I went to buy shoes for my son and found it hard to breathe under the afternoon sun so I removed the burqa from covering my face. A Taliban soldier spotted me in the crowded marketplace and demanded that I cover myself again. I explained that I couldn't breathe and he fired his gun in the open air. My heart was pounding and my crying son was squeezing my thighs." After Miskeenyar escaped with her children to Pakistan, she pulled off the burqa that had kept her "in the shadows for so long. I handed it to some other woman in the street. I hated that thing!"[36]

Then came September 11, 2001. The hijackers who attacked the World Trade Center and the Pentagon were traced to Al-Qaeda, a terrorist organization based in Afghanistan and headed by Osama bin Laden, a Saudi Arabian. In 2002, Western powers, led by the United States, invaded Afghanistan; with the help of anti-Taliban factions, the coalition quickly routed the Taliban. But the Taliban had not been vanquished.

Memories of the wars and their harrowing escape from their homeland remain alive for Afghan refugees. Now living in the United States, Farhad Ahad wrote a story, "My Mother's Courage," published in 2003 in *Afghan Journal: An Inter-Generational Afghan American Voice*. In 1984, his parents had become convinced that the end of the war between the Russian-backed government forces and Western-backed rebels was not in sight. So in December his mother left for Pakistan with his five sisters and baby brother. "My mother had been gone for three months, and we had no news of her whatsoever, when miraculously one day she appeared at the door." She had successfully crossed the border and delivered all of his siblings to her cousins; then she had returned for her husband and Farhad. His father took his time getting ready to depart. "One of the clearest quotes I remember from my mother," he wrote, "was 'We have to go. I will not wait one more day not knowing how my children are doing over there.'" They went. "We started riding on top of camels, mules, and donkeys, but ended up traversing most of the otherwise impassable terrain on foot." His mother never lost her "cool, calm demeanor, and would press on, almost leading the entire caravan of escapees."[37]

Another refugee, a teacher in her homeland, was not able to save everyone in her family. Recently widowed, she was living in Kabul with four daughters, ranging in age from three to fifteen, and an eleven-year-old son. In 1996, after a rocket destroyed their home, she decided that the time had come to escape. She and her children joined a group of strangers preparing to trek to Pakistan. Covering herself and her daughters with burqas, she commanded them not to speak, for to do so would betray their educated accents at the Taliban checkpoints; they were trying to sneak by as illiterate nomadic tribal people. "One day," this mother recalled, "as we were crossing the mountains on foot, my 13-year-old daughter had an asthma attack. When we came upon a Taliban check post, my daughter began gasping for air. In a panic to breathe, she lifted her burqa to try to get some air. The Taliban started beating my daughter with rubber tubes." Her young son then threw a stone and hit the Taliban commander. The soldiers turned on him. "I screamed and screamed and screamed as they beat him unconscious then dragged him away to one of the camps hidden in the caves in the mountains. That was the last time I saw my son." The mother knew she had to keep walking to Pakistan to save her daughters.[38]

For this mother and 2 million other refugees, Pakistan turned out to be a hellhole. After they successfully trekked across the mountains into Pakistan, they were herded into crowded, dangerous, and disease-infested camps. In the midst of grinding poverty, many parents were forced to make their children work in brick and carpet-weaving factories where they were beaten, sexually abused, and given opium to stimulate them to work harder. In the chaotic misery of the camps, hunger prevailed, and a grim future awaited them. The lucky ones escaped from the nightmarish camps, making their way to Europe and the United States. In 2007, the Afghan newcomers totaled about 240,000 people in America.

In the beginning, the refugees found life in their new homeland confusing and challenging. "Two months after leaving Kabul," one of them recalled, "my husband and my children and I were living in an apartment in Alameda, California. It was 1980. We had one bed for the entire family, and used a cardboard box as our dining table." They quickly ran out of money. "We didn't know the language. We did not know the culture. We were scared. What was this thing called America? we asked ourselves." There were no mosques, and they were afraid to go outside their apartment. "But I was lucky, we were lucky. My little girl, and my baby boy, and my husband. We escaped. We were safe."[39]

Like this woman and her family, some sixty thousand Afghan refugees settled in the San Francisco Bay Area, most of them in Fremont. There they found hills that reminded them of their homeland and were attracted to the city's growing diversity. The population of this bedroom community was being transformed: once predominantly white, the community had come to include Chinese, South Asians, Mexicans, and Afghans. The refugees were also pulled to Fremont by word-of-mouth tales about an emerging Afghan community, with refugee social services, educational support such as ESL (English as a Second Language), and Afghan-American organizations and businesses.

"As they say, Fremont is happening," observed Feraidoon

Mojadidi, owner of the Rumi Bookstore, where people can find Afghan magazines, newspapers, and books. Close to his bookstore are Afghan restaurants that feature kabobs, *pallow* (a rice dish similar to pilaf), and fragrant bread. Nearby are grocery stores that sell halal meats and sweet green melons native to Afghanistan. "We have many Afghan-owned businesses here, in fact this area [of Fremont] is dubbed Little Kabul," explained Homoyoun Kharmosh, a "freedom fighter" and physician who had left his homeland in 1991. Without the credentials to practice medicine in the United States, he operates a grocery store that sells Afghan breads and other Afghan foods. "I'm married and trying to support my family, so if business continues to be good I plan to buy another business. Many of my countrymen have businesses that range from hot-dog stands and gas stations to high-tech work in giant Silicon Valley corporations."[40]

As they settle in Little Kabul, Afghan Americans are transplanting their traditions. They celebrate the Afghan New Year—Now-ruz. As their ancestors did for thousands of years, they dress up, eat homeland foods, and dance to Afghan music. "We will celebrate our tradition over here," said Suraya Ahmadzai, who had arrived in Fremont with her two daughters and three sons in 2000. "We're not going to forget about it." The new Americans also built a $2 million mosque, attended by Afghan men in traditional turbans as well as by younger men in designer jeans and baseball caps.[41]

Beneath the surface of Little Kabul's prosperity and progress have been overwhelming economic and personal difficulties. The host of Lemar-TV, a television program for the Afghan community in Fremont, Naseem Yar, told me: "Here in America, many refugee men find they have no status in the home. They don't work. They don't want to work at a gas station." Many of the women also do not work. Unable to speak English and unable to work, widows find themselves on welfare, with their eldest sons working to help pay the bills. They stay at home, keeping the curtains drawn out of fear of being seen.[42]

Fear became widespread among Afghan Americans in the days after the 9/11 terrorist attacks. Upon waking up that morning, Nadia Ali Maiwandi found a message from her mother on her answering machine. "My mom was nervous and stuttering about what she had seen on TV. I caught something about twin towers falling before the machine cut her off. I called and got the details. Thousands dead, she told me, the towers are gone." In the following days and weeks, Maiwandi noticed anxiety sweeping through the Afghan community. "Some Afghans claimed Greek, Italian or Hispanic heritage to prevent abuse and hid their 'Allah' pendants under their clothes." Some Afghans tried to demonstrate their American patriotism by hanging U.S. flags from their porches.[43]

"When 9/11 happened," wrote Nadeem Saaed in an e-mail to me dated September 11, 2007, "I remember being in my English class at Ohlone College in Fremont. The teacher walked in very sad, so sad that she was almost about to cry." She canceled the class to let the students be with their families. Leaving campus, Nadeem and his fellow countrymen were afraid that since they were Afghans, they would be attacked and arrested. "My father told me to be extra careful now because the law is going to be much stricter on us." Nadeem saw the events of 9/11 as an anxious turning point for Afghan Americans. "I really felt like that's it, the world is not a world that we once knew anymore, but rather a world that we will never know again. It was at this moment that I realized that everything is going to change. Being Afghan American is not what people think it was before; now it's what people want to know about you and who you really are inside, an American or a terrorist."[44]

"After 9/11," recalled Zarpana Reitman, an Afghan-American teacher in a nearby school, "Afghan children were asked by their fellow students. 'Are you Muslim?' 'Do you know Osama bin Laden?' The Afghan children became subselves. Some of them pretended they were Mexican. The source of the problem of ignorance of Muslims is the curriculum. Children are taught about the heroic Crusaders who defended Europe against the evil Muslim invaders."[45]

That morning was also vividly remembered by Dr. Mohammad Qayoumi, the current president of California State University, East Bay. Years earlier, he had been a student in the U.S. Midwest, when the Soviets invaded his homeland and forced his family to flee to Pakistan. On September 11, 2001, he was driving from Northridge to Long Beach, California, and was listening to the radio. Suddenly came the reports of the attacks on the World Trade Center. He wondered who might have done it and hoped it was not any Muslim terrorists. In the days that followed, Dr. Qayoumi noted that most Muslim Americans spoke out against the atrocity committed by a handful of terrorists. He also found "heartwarming" the support they received from many Americans. "When some Muslims were attacked by thugs in various

U.S. cities, many Americans spoke out against such travesties." But still Dr. Qayoumi was concerned that "there were those who questioned whether Muslims like me could be true to their religion and be patriotic Americans as well."[46]

In the wake of 9/11, what did it mean to be an Afghan American? This was the foremost question addressed at a conference organized by Melanie Gadener, an activist in Fremont's Afghan-American community. Entitled "East Meets West: Awakening to the Challenges of Afghans in Fremont, California," the conference was held in Little Kabul on June 23, 2007, and attended by more than three hundred people from the community, young and old. To assist in the communication between the generations, headsets were distributed for people to listen to instant translations from English into Farsi and Dari, two Afghan languages.

In her welcoming remarks, the master of ceremonies, Zarpana Reitman, asked the participants to think about their identity—what it means for "East to meet West" in the Afghan-American community.

One of the participants, Layma Murtaza, told a reporter about her struggle to be both "East" and "West." Her parents had left Afghanistan after the Soviet invasion; born and raised in Fremont, she has never been to Afghanistan but feels a strong bond with her cultural heritage. "There are a lot of kids my age," the twenty-four-year-old Murtaza said, "who don't understand or appreciate what their parents went through. We are half American. It's not a bad thing or a good thing. It's who we are. But Afghanistan is also embedded in me—it is who I am, at least a part of me."[47]

Still, to be both American and Afghan has not been easy. A panelist at the conference, Tamim Ansary, author of *West of Kabul, East of New York: An Afghan American Story,* declared: "It is very difficult to live on two sides because the border runs up through you, and that is uncomfortable."[48]

One of the conference organizers, Nadeem Saaed, offered his own metaphor for the dual identity many young people feel. His parents had fled from their homeland after the Russian invasion, and he was born in Dubai, United Arab Emirates. "I identify myself as being an Afghan American," he said. "I am Afghan because that is what my parents are and that's the blood running through my veins. And I am an American because that's what makes most of my character and style. I guess you can call me a grilled cheese sandwich, except the cheese is Afghan and the toast is American. But nonetheless, a proud American I am and very thankful for the freedom this country has given me to pursue my goals and dreams."[49]

Nadeem recently graduated with a degree in public health. When asked, "What are your dreams?" Nadeem answered: "I want to go back to Afghanistan, to open a hospital." Asked the same question, Zarpana Reitman replied: "I was six months old when my parents left Afghanistan because of the Russian invasion. It has always been a dream of mine to go back to Afghanistan, and to open a school there. But would it be good for my two-year-old child to be there, with all the bombings?"[50]

One purpose of the "East Meets West" conference was to offer a common ground for the older and younger generations to interact and try to resolve their differences in culture and identity. During the Q&A, a young man commented that "cross-generational education has to be two-way. The elders want cultural retention. The young people are uncertain about what to do. There has to be change on both sides." A father of four children and grandfather of five told a reporter for the *San Francisco Chronicle:* "No one really taught us about the cross-cultural differences. We've had to learn them ourselves. They've created some problems between parents and children. In our country, children do not speak in front of their elders. But here they express themselves. Back when we first started immigrating to the U.S., conferences like this should have been arranged."[51]

One of the young people attending the conference was Fatema Nourzaie. Her parents had fled Afghanistan after the Soviet invasion, and she was born in California. The 9/11 terrorist attack was an experience she would never forget. "I started hearing how girls in hijab were being attacked," Fatema recalled. "Indians were getting shot because they 'looked' Middle Eastern, and mosques were getting burned down. That was the only time ever I was afraid to be a Muslim."

Even before that world-shattering event, Fatema had been struggling over her identity as an Afghan American. "I don't think I could ever completely label myself as either one or the other," she explained. "I am just as much American as I am Afghan." She was raised in the United States and did not know what it was like for her parents and brothers to come here from "a different world." But she had to face the fact that she was a daughter in a Muslim family. "It was hard to convince my parents to let me go to the football games or dances. It's a hard thing for Afghan parents to let their daughter go out no matter what the reason." Still Fatema understood that Muslim parents in America felt they needed to preserve many of the old ways.

Fatema would like to be both Afghan and American. "Afghans have integrated instead of assimilated," she explained. "Fremont would be a good example. Afghans have managed to keep their culture and identity. It hasn't been lost in the idea of assimilation. That's when you totally and completely become the culture that you have immigrated to and completely lose your people's original identity. Afghans have kept their uniqueness, the beauty of their culture, and at the same time have thoroughly functioned in today's society. I think that's what integration means."[52]

Fatema's brother Omar summed up the challenge facing Afghan Americans: "The refugees know that a return to Afghanistan is not in their near future. They will have to change and make do in America."[53] Indeed, Afghan Americans, refugees and their U.S.-born children, are "making do": they have begun to sort out and blend old and new cultures and identities. Across generations, they are, in one way or another and to varying degrees, reinventing themselves. They are also helping to change their adopted country, making America a nation of many religions, including Islam.

Beckoned North: Mexico

Joining the newcomers from Russia, Ireland, China, Vietnam, and Afghanistan are 12 million undocumented immigrants, mostly from Mexico.

What should be done about them? Arrest them and deport them to Mexico, argue the opponents of Mexican immigration. Build bigger fences and send troops to guard the border in order to keep them out of America; prohibit them from taking jobs away from American citizens; deny them driver's licenses, access to schools and medical services; and refuse to offer them English-language classes. Tell them to stay home in Mexico. Beneath this nativist clamor is a fear of the "Browning of America," one that can be found not only in television and radio talk shows, but also print news media and anti-immigrant legislation.

Give them "amnesty," answered *Time* magazine in its June 18, 2007, cover story, "Immigration: Why Amnesty Makes Sense." The "illegals are by their sheer numbers undeportable. More important, they are too enmeshed in a healthy U.S. economy to be extracted." America is "the only industrialized nation with a population that is growing fast enough...to provide the kind of workforce that a dynamic economy needs. The illegals are part of the reason for that, and amnesty ensures that competitive advantage." *Time* also argued that the Mexican immigrants would eventually be incorporated into the culture of their new homeland. "Assimilation is slow, but inevitable." We must have "faith in America's undimmed ability to metabolize immigrants from around the world, to change them more than they change the U.S."[54]

Like the earlier waves of immigrants crossing our southern border, Mexicans are being pushed by intensifying poverty. But this time it is different. The illegal border crossings from Mexico spiked upward after 1994, the year the North American Free Trade Agreement became U.S.-Mexican policy. Under NAFTA, government-subsidized corn grown in Iowa and shipped to Mexico as cheap corn bankrupted 1.5 million farmers there, forcing them to migrate to the cities and also northward across the border. Free trade has also destabilized the Mexican economy and led to increases in unemployment. "The real, dirty secret of trade agreements is displacement," wrote journalist David Bacon. "During the years NAFTA has been in effect, more than 6 million people from Mexico have come to live in the United States. They didn't abandon their homes, families, and farms and jobs willingly. They had no other option for survival."[55]

Pushed by the need to survive, the migrants have also been pulled by a pursuit of happiness. "Back where we're from it was a very poor community," an immigrant explained. "There was no work there. We just planted corn. So, when we saw that we could not support ourselves, well, we said we have to start looking elsewhere." "Elsewhere" has become "El Norte." "You can see why people go to America," a Mexican stated. "They come back with brand-new trucks, with videos; they have dollars. And it has an impact. You say, 'Wow, there's the good life.'" One of the immigrants recalled that her friend had first migrated to the United States. "She would always write and tell me it was very pretty and that you could live here better. And that people don't have to be very skilled to live better." Women sometimes came alone, or with only their children. "My husband left me," one said, "and there was an opportunity for me to come. I decided to come here because I wanted to try living here, know what it is like here. I saw that it was easy for me, although I had to struggle because it was hard to understand people. But I've struggled for my children more than anything else."[56]

But crossing the northern border is enormously stressful. One of their songs gives an eye-level view of the experience:

> *Now boys, to earn lots of dollars,*
> *They left Mexico.*
> *Since they didn't bring any papers,*
> *They crossed as "wire fence jumpers."*
> *They crossed over the hills.*
> *They turned and twisted on the paths.*
> *It was night.*
> *A helicopter searched attempting to find*
> *   them,*
> *But with all the bushes, they couldn't see*
> *   anything.*

On this side of the border, Mexicans have often had to run across busy freeways, where scores of them have been killed. Signs have been posted: "CAUTION — WATCH FOR PEOPLE CROSSING ROAD." One sign has the word "CAUTION," with a silhouette of a man, woman, and child. Forced by the border patrol to find alternate routes, many of them have died in hot deserts, their bodies rotting in desolate canyons.[57]

The illegal immigrants have kept coming because they know that employers are willing and ready to hire them. Like earlier farm laborers, they are laboring in the fields and orchards of America. Without them, California's agriculture would shut down, warned Senator Dianne Feinstein. There would be sharp increases in the prices of fruits and vegetables, and a revolt by consumers if food costs skyrocketed. At stake, she stated, is the future of California's $32 billion agriculture industry, with its seventy-six thousand farms and 1 million laborers.

To meet California's need for agricultural workers, President George W. Bush proposed a guest worker program. But his proposal had a definite downside. "Guest workers would have to return home and stay there for up to one year before they would be eligible to come back again," wrote conservative activist Linda Chavez and union leader John W. Wilhelm. "And while working as 'guests,' they would constitute a second class of workers with few rights on the job. It hearkens back to the dark period in the 1860s when we admitted tens of thousands of Chinese male laborers to help build our railroads and then prevented them from ever naturalizing or bringing their families into America. Do we really want to repeat this experiment?"[58]

In order to stop the flow of illegal immigrants from Mexico, President Bush sent six thousand National Guard troops to the border in 2006. His action provoked the *San Francisco Chronicle* to issue an editorial entitled "The Border Is Not a Military Zone." "The reality is that he is chasing a mirage that will always be out of reach as long as U.S. immigration policy is detached from reality." Since the early 1990s, the number of border patrol agents has doubled. "The result? There are three times as many illegal immigrants in the United States as a decade ago." One reason is revealed in statistics: "In the early 1980s, half of all undocumented migrants returned home within a year of entering the United States. By 2000 only 25 percent did."[59]

Years earlier, a conservative Republican leader had raised his voice in support of the illegal immigrants. In a radio broadcast in 1977, Ronald Reagan noted the apples rotting on the trees in New England for lack of workers. "It makes one wonder about the illegal-alien fuss. Are great numbers of our unemployed really victims of the illegal-alien invasion or are those illegal tourists actually doing the work our own people won't do?" he asked. "One thing is certain in this hungry world: no regulation or law should be allowed if it results in crops rotting in the fields for lack of harvesters." Nine years later, as president of the United States, Reagan signed the Immigration and Control Act, which gave many illegal immigrants immediate permanent residency—green cards, granted in a fast-track application process for a small fee.[60]

In addition to agriculture, undocumented Mexican immigrants are working in poultry processing plants, garment factories, construction, hotels, and restaurants. They also labor in homes, cleaning houses and babysitting, often being paid extremely low wages. Though the undocumented newcomers usually earn very little money, they rarely seek publicly financed medical assistance, food stamps, or welfare, for fear they will be apprehended and deported. Yet they pay taxes. A 2006 report of the Public Policy Institute of California pointed out that many illegal immigrants pay social security taxes but never collect benefits. A young and working population, they help to subsidize the Social Security retirement program benefiting mainly an aging white population.[61]

Individual stories humanize the experiences of these undocumented immigrants. One of them is Carmen Diera Trujillo. "I was born in a small town called Jerez," she recalled. "I began to work when I was eight years old. Since my family was always short on money, we did not have money to pay for rent and food. So I began to work cleaning houses for the wealthy." At the age of sixteen, Carmen was told by her sister that she would have to go to the United States to work. "I had a boyfriend, and I did not want to leave my friends." But Carmen crossed the border, and initially worked as a housecleaner. "I started my life here living behind closed doors. I was not allowed to leave all week until Saturday. I cleaned the house, took care of the children, and since they knew I had come from Mexico, they would want me to cook Mexican food. They gave me videos, cassettes, and books so that at night I can study English. But since I never went to school, it was difficult to learn English because I did not know how to even write in Spanish."

But Carmen was able to get a Social Security card and began working as a seamstress in the garment factories of Los Angeles. "None of my employers ever asked me for my papers. A lot of employers liked the way I worked so they would look for me whenever they needed to complete a job. I even began to work two shifts because they knew that I was a hard worker. Sometimes it was 2:00 A.M. and I was still in downtown working."

After the enactment of the 1986 immigration law, Carmen was allowed to stay permanently. "I had done my taxes every year since I began working in the garment factories. I had all the papers as proof of being a qualified applicant for amnesty. I always hoped to become legalized since all of my children were already here in the U.S. and they were by birth legal." Though she had no opportunity for schooling in Mexico, she is proud that her children have fulfilled her hopes—a master's degree in school counseling, an emergency medical technician, and two future teachers.[62]

Camelia Palafox also has an inspiring story. "Ever since I was little," she revealed, "I used to tell myself that I would be a singer. I have always loved music. Everywhere there was a party, I used to sing." Camelia began singing with a small theater group in Tijuana and toured the state of Baja California. "I got a scholarship for being the best actress of all Baja California. The scholarship was a full-paid tuition for study in Mexico City. I remember when I got the scholarship, the theater group director, Professor Orozco, looked at me with a happy and sad face. He was happy for my achievements, but he was upset because he knew that at the time I [was pregnant] with my first child." The father abandoned the family. "I was eighteen when I had Jose. I worked and took care of my son by myself. I don't regret my decision, but I would have liked to have traveled to Mexico City and see many things there."

After working as a sales clerk in Tijuana, Camelia realized that in order to make more money, she needed to work in the United States. With her sister, she began doing housework in San Diego. "Cleaning houses for one or two days in San Diego would earn us the same amount of money that we would get if we worked in Tijuana for one whole week." The work was hard, and sometimes she was cheated by her employers; at other times she found that men advertising for domestic work wanted "other things and not really housecleaning."

Camelia then started working as a waitress in a Mexican-owned restaurant. "Most of the customers there were Mexicans. Every once in a while *la migra* [the Immigration and Natural-ization Service, or INS] would arrest a busload of undocumented people. Sometimes they would go undercover and check out the scene. Next thing you knew, people were running all over the place." Camelia was always afraid that she would be arrested and deported. "I felt ashamed that I didn't have papers. I felt inferior. I was scared that I would get put in a van with other people. I felt like we would be treated like animals, as if we were the dogs, and they [the INS] were the dogcatchers." In 1979, Camelia decided that it was time to sneak her five-year-old son, Jose, across the border. "I missed him a lot. It was luck that a friend's husband was able to cross him as a U.S. citizen with no problems at all."

Many years after she crossed the border, Camelia was allowed to stay permanently. She took special classes and passed an examination to qualify her to work in a retirement home. "What I really like about my job is that I'm helping others. I love doing that. I come home from work, and I feel good because I know I did something to help somebody." Reflecting on her life, Camelia said: "Now that I'm a U.S. citizen, I feel a little safer. Also, as a citizen, one can vote and have their voice heard. I also got Jose to get his U.S. citizenship. When I found out that my son had been accepted to UC Berkeley, I was really happy."[63]

Today, young Mexican Americans are striving to find a place for themselves in the America of their dreams. One of them is Alexis Lopez. In 1950, when his grandfather Juan Frias was seventeen years old, he left his village in Mexico to find work. "During this time," Alexis wrote, "a craze of making it big in the United States sparked throughout most of the 31 Mexican states." Juan worked in the fields of California, visiting his homeland to get married and have children but returning to the United States to work. In 1976, he decided to make his home permanently in San Francisco and brought his wife and two of his older children. One of them was Alexis's mother, Griselda. After graduation from high school, she worked as a cashier and cook at a Mexican restaurant, where she met Leonardo Lopez. Her parents disapproved of Leoardo, but she married him. Though he had been angry, her father finally came around with the birth of Alexis—"Juan's first grandchild and the first real Mexican American."

Alexis has had to navigate between his two identities. "I grew up speaking Spanish because that is the main language my parents spoke at home." But "I also had a television along with Nickelodeon and the Disney Channel teaching me English, along with the English-speaking children at Woodrow Wilson Elementary School." In high school, Alexis joined the Puente Program—an outreach program for educationally and financially underserved Latinos. "This program allowed me to interact with other Mexican American students and to become more college bound. Education was not something that was necessarily promoted throughout any of the generations that came before me. My grandfather worked in the fields of California. My mother spent her childhood in Mexico, and then was taken to the U.S., where she worked and began having children as a young woman. I have the opportunity to do something else, not that it is necessarily better, but different. It is because of these generations that I am able to want something 'more'—that I am privileged to have these opportunities. They came to this country to make a better life and the only thing they would want is for those that come after them, like me, to make them proud."[64]

Alexis knows he is one of a fortunate few among Mexican-American students. In June 2007, the *San Francisco Chronicle* reported that Latinos have the lowest level of education of any racial group in the state. Just one in seven Latino high school graduates attends college, although they represent 48 percent of all high school students. "At stake is not only the future success of these young people in a job market that increasingly requires a college degree, but the viability of the California economy. If the majority of the state's future population lacks a good education, California will have too few skilled workers to meet the needs of the information-driven economy and too few middle-class taxpayers to keep the state afloat fiscally as baby boomers retire."[65]

However, Mexican-American students who qualify for college admissions often encounter an additional hurdle. Belonging to families here illegally, they must pay exorbitant out-of-state tuition in many states. Criticizing this policy, columnist Cynthia Tucker wrote: "Having taken advantage of their cheap labor for decades now—eagerly employing them to water our lawns, wash our cars and pluck our chickens—we shouldn't hesitate to make it easy for their children to attend college. It isn't merely a matter of fairness or compassion, but also one of economic self-interest. Any student dedicated enough to learn a new language, excel in high school and start college is going to be successful *somewhere*. I'd rather it be here."[66]

Many of these Mexican-American students participated in the massive demonstrations on May 1, 2006. Facing an exploding racially tinged nativism, Mexican Americans realized they needed to take to the streets, but not in riots. Marching in cities across America, they protested against the draconian anti-Latino legislation pending in Congress. They called their action "A Day Without a Mexican" to send a message to America: the economy needs their labor.[67]

The future for the Mexican newcomers is promising. According to the 2006 U.S. Census figures, 70 percent of California's Mexican population are U.S. citizens. This incline in citizenship is due to births in the United States and also to the recent spike in naturalized citizenship for their parents. About half of the 460,766 Mexican immigrants who became naturalized citizens between 2000 and 2006 were in California. One of them was Roselia Aguilar, a twenty-nine-year-old immigrant who has lived in San Jose for a dozen years and was worried about the backlash against immigrants from Mexico. As she stood with 450 individuals from fifty-seven nations and solemnly took an oath to "bear true faith and allegiance to the Constitution," she felt exuberant. "I feel it's one of the most important things that ever happened to me," she said moments after the ceremony. "It's just different. I feel something nice inside me. I feel like I was born again."[68]

17

"WE WILL ALL
BE MINORITIES"

ON A MONDAY morning in June 1997, I was writing in my study at home when I received a call from Doris Matsui, an assistant to President Bill Clinton. She told me that the president wanted me to come to Washington to help him write a major speech on race. "He would like to take the national dialogue on race beyond the black/white binary," she said. "So it's very important for you to be here." Within hours, I was flying to Washington.

The next day, at the White House, President Clinton facilitated the meeting of a small gathering of civil rights leaders and intellectuals. After raising my hand, I said: "I think your speech is timely. Sometime in the twenty-first century, whites will become a minority in the U.S. population. They already are in California. So when you come to my state to give your speech, you will be a minority." Then I tried to crack a joke: "Welcome to the club, Mr. President." Instantly, he winked at me: "Yes, I know! Why do you think I am doing all of this?" "Yes," I answered, "we will all be minorities."

That Saturday, President Clinton gave his address, "One America in the Twenty-first Century: The President's Initiative on Race." To the graduating class of the University of California at San Diego, he declared: "A half-century from now, when your own grandchildren are in college, there will be no majority race in America." He then presented highlights from our multicultural past:

> Consider this: we were born with a Declaration of Independence which asserted that we were all created equal and a Constitution that enshrined slavery. We fought a bloody civil war to abolish slavery and preserve the union, but we remained a house divided and unequal by law for another century. We advanced across the continent in the name of freedom, yet in so doing we pushed Native Americans off their land, often crushing their culture and their livelihood.... In World War II, Japanese Americans fought valiantly for freedom in Europe, taking great casualities, while at home their families were herded into internment camps. The famed Tuskegee Airmen lost none of the bombers they guarded during the war, but their African American heritage cost them a lot of rights when they came back home in peace.

In his conclusion, President Clinton identified the challenge we faced: "More than 30 years ago, at the high tide of the civil rights movement, the Kerner Commission said we were becoming two Americas, one white, one black, separate but unequal. Today, we face a different choice: will we become not two, but many Americas, separate, unequal and isolated? Or will we draw strength from all our people and the ancient faith in the quality of human dignity, to become the world's first truly multiracial democracy?"[1]

The future is in our hands. The choices we make will be influenced by whether our memory of the past is the Master Narrative of American History or the narrative of "a different mirror." A history that leaves out minorities reinforces separation, but an inclusive history bridges the divide.

We have the opportunity to redefine the "errand into the wilderness"—to write our own ending to Shakespeare's play about America. The bard need not be prophetic, for we have the advantage of hindsight: we know what happened not only to Prospero but also to Caliban in American history.

This epic story was illuminated by Herman Melville in his great American novel *Moby-Dick*. The crew of the *Pequod* represents the races and cultures of the world. On deck, Captain Ahab and his officers are all white men. Below deck, there are whites like

Ishmael, Africans like Daggoo, Pacific Islanders like Queequeg, American Indians like Tashtego, and Asians like Fedallah. There is a noble class unity among the workers: they possess "democratic dignity," and an "ethereal light" shines on the "workman's arm."[2]

On their voyage through history, the people on board the *Pequod* known as America found their paths crisscrossing one another in events and developments such as Bacon's Rebellion, the Market Revolution, the Civil War, and World War II. Their lives and cultures have swirled together in the settling and building of America from the first meeting of Powhatans and English on the Virginia shore to the last Mexican immigrants crossing the border.

Together, they have been creating what Gloria Anzaldúa calls a "borderland" — a place where "two or more cultures edge each other, where people of different races occupy the same territory." How can all of us meet on communal ground? "The struggle," Anzaldúa responds, "is inner: Chicano, *indio*, American Indian, *mojado*, *mexicano*, immigrant Latino, Anglo in power, working class Anglo, Black, Asian — our psyches resemble the border-towns and are populated by the same people.... Awareness of our situation must come before inner changes, which in turn come before changes in society."[3]

Such awareness must come from a "re-visioned" history. What Gloria Steinem termed "revolution from within" must ultimately be grounded in "unlearning" much of what we have been told about America's past and substituting a more inclusive and accurate history of all the peoples of America.[4]

A cutting edge of this "unlearning" can be found on the continent's western shore. "California, and especially Los Angeles, a gateway to both Asia and Latin America," Carlos Fuentes observed, "poses the universal question of the coming century: how do we deal with the Other?"[5]

Asked whether California, with its multiethnic society, represented the America of the twenty-first century, Alice Walker replied: "If that's not the future reality of the United States, there won't be any United States, because that's who we are." Walker's own ancestry is a combination of Native American, African American, and European American.[6]

King of golf Tiger Woods is a mixture of different races. "All the media try to put black in him," protested his mother, Kultida Woods. "Why don't they ask who half of Tiger is from? In the United States, one little part black is all black. Nobody wants to listen to me. I've been trying to explain to people, but they don't understand. To say he is 100 percent black is to deny his heritage. To deny his grandmother and grandfather. To deny me!" Tiger Woods himself declared to the media: "My parents have taught me to always be proud of my ethnic background. Yes, I am the product of two great cultures, one African American and the other Asian. On my father's side I'm African American. On my mother's side I am Thai. Truthfully, I feel very fortunate, and equally proud to be both African American and Asian."[7]

Barack Obama is proud of his biracial identity. "We've got a tragic history when it comes to race in this country," he said, noting "pent-up anger and mistrust and bitterness." "I continue to believe that this country wants to move beyond these kinds of things." Pointing out that his father is black and his mother white, he declared: "Born into a diverse family, I have little pieces of America all in me."

One of those "pieces" is Asian American. Obama was born and raised in Hawaii, the only state with an Asian-American majority. His stepfather, Lolo Soetoro, was Indonesian; his half-sister, Maya Soetoro-Ng, is married to a Chinese Canadian. Obama's legislative director is Chris Lu, the daughter of Chinese immigrants. "A lot of aspects of the senator's story will be recognizable to many Asian Americans," she said. "He talks about feeling somewhat of an outsider, about coming to terms with his self-identity, about figuring out how to reconcile the values from his unique heritage with those of the larger U.S. society. These are tensions and conflicts that play out in the lives of all children of immigrants."[8]

Native-American writer Paula Gunn Allen prizes the "little pieces" in herself—American Indian, Scotch, Jewish, and Lebanese. "Just people from everywhere are related to me by blood," she explained, "and so that's why I say I'm a multicultural event. It's beautiful, it's a rainbow. It reflects light, and I think that's what a person like me can do."[9] Imagine what "light" a "multicultural event" called America can reflect.

America's dilemma has been the denial of our immensely varied selves. Asked whether she had a specific proposal for improving the current racial climate in America, Toni Morrison answered: "Everybody remembers the first time they were taught that part of the human race was Other. That's a trauma. It's as though I told you that your left hand is not part of your body."[10]

We need not repeat what Prospero did to Caliban. Instead, we can heed the lesson of Black Elk. In his vision of the "whole hoop of the world," the Sioux holy man saw "in a sacred manner the shapes of all things in the spirit, and the shape of all shapes as they must live together like one being." The "sacred hoop" of his people was "one of many hoops that made one circle, wide as daylight and as starlight, and in the center grew one mighty flowering tree to shelter all the children of one mother and one father."[11] Today, we need to stop denying our wholeness as members of one humanity as well as one nation.

We originally came from many different shores, and our diversity has been at the center of the making of America. Composed of many colors and cultures, we have been "singing with open mouths their strong melodious songs" from the tobacco fields of Virginia, the textile mills of Lowell, the "Trail of Tears," the cotton fields of Mississippi, the battlefields of the Civil War, the Indian reservations of South Dakota, the railroad tracks in the Sierras of California, the snow-covered ground of Wounded Knee, the garment factories of the Lower East Side, the canefields of Hawaii, the internment camp of Manzanar, South Central Los Angeles, the Lincoln Memorial in Washington, D.C., and a thousand other places.[12]

Signs of our ethnic diversity can also be found across America — Ellis Island, Angel Island, Chinatown, Harlem, South Boston, the Lower East Side, places with Spanish names like Los Angeles and San Antonio or Indian names like Massachusetts and Iowa. Much of what is familiar in America's cultural landscape has ethnic origins. The Bing cherry was developed by an early Chinese immigrant named Ah Bing. American Indians were cultivating corn, potatoes, tomatoes, and tobacco long before the arrival of Columbus. The term "okay" was derived from the Choctaw word, *oke,* meaning "it is so." There is evidence indicating that the name "Yankee" came from Indian terms for the English — from *eankke* in Cherokee and *Yankwis* in Delaware. Jazz and blues as well as rock and roll have African-American origins. The "Forty-Niners" of the gold rush learned mining techniques from the Mexicans; American cowboys acquired herding skills from Mexican *vaqueros* and adopted their range terms — such as "lariat" from *la reata,* "lasso" from *lazo,* and "stampede" from *estampida.* Songs like "God Bless America," "Easter Parade," and "White Christmas" were written by a Russian-Jewish immigrant named Israel Baline, more popularly known as Irving Berlin.[13]

Like Caliban and Stephano, marginalized minorities have been chanting, "Freedom, highday! highday, freedom! freedom, highday, freedom!" They have been singing: "We shall overcome. We shall overcome." While their struggle must continue, they have won a multitude of victories—the abolishing of slavery, the integrating of the U.S. Armed Forces, the outlawing of segregated schooling for Mexican Americans and African Americans, the ending of Jim Crow in the South, the extending of naturalized citizenship to all immigrants regardless of race, the overturning of anti-miscegenation laws, the guaranteeing of voting rights for minorities, the reopening of immigration from Asia, the granting of redress and reparations to Japanese internees, and the awakening of America to our amazing diversity. Indeed, in many significant ways, we have "overcome."

What does the future hold for America? Over one hundred years ago, Herman Melville wrote: America is not a nation "so much as a world." In this new society, the "prejudices of national dislikes" could be "forever extinguished." Walt Whitman chimed: All of us belonged to "a teeming Nation of nations" where "all races and cultures" could be "accepted" and "saluted," not "controlled or placed in hierarchy," and all could be welcomed—"Chinese, Irish, German, pauper or not, criminal or not—all, all, without exceptions." "Of every hue and caste am I, I resist any thing better than my own diversity."[14]

"The problem of the twentieth century," as W. E. B. Du Bois observed, was "the problem of the color line." However, the promise of the twenty-first century is the promise of the changing colors of the American people. Demography is redefining who is an American. The time has come for us to embrace our varied selves. A new America is approaching, a society where diversity is destiny. How can we prepare ourselves for this "brave new world that has such people in't"? Here, history matters. Offering our "mystic chords of memory" more inclusively, *A Different Mirror* tells the story of America as a diversely peopled nation, "dedicated to the proposition that all men are created equal." Woven into the multicultural tapestry of our national narrative is the fervent and felicitous message of Langston Hughes: "Let America be America again.... Let America be the dream the dreamers dreamed... [where] equality is in the air we breathe."[15]

AUTHOR'S NOTE: EPISTEMOLOGY AND EPIPHANY

AS IT TURNS out, the history I have written is reflected in my own life: my personal experiences have resonated with those of America's multicultural people — their disappointments but also their dreams, their tribulations but also their triumphs, and their separate but also their shared identities. What happened to me and what happened in history illustrate and illuminate one another.

Born in Hawaii in 1939, the son of a Japanese immigrant father and an American-born Japanese mother, I grew up in the working-class community of Palolo Valley, Oahu. My neighbors were Japanese, Chinese, Portuguese, Korean, and Hawaiian. As children we visited each other's homes, where we heard a rich diversity of languages. Playing together, we spoke pidgin English. "Hey, da kine *tako ono*, you know," we would say, combining English, Japanese, and Hawaiian. My father died when I was five years old, and shortly afterward, my mother married an immigrant from China, Koon Keu Young.

I attended the nearby public elementary school, where the students said the Pledge of Allegiance to the flag every morning. I did not realize then that I had been assigned to a non-English standard school, a system that tracked Asian and Hawaiian students to a high school without a college prep curriculum.

My mother had been born on a sugarcane plantation and had only an eighth-grade education, and my stepfather also had very little schooling. They were determined to give me the opportunity to be college educated. At the beginning of fifth grade, they pulled me out of the public school and, sacrificing the family finances, enrolled me in a private school, Iolani.

As a teenager, I developed a passion for surfing. My nickname was "Ten Toes Takaki." My parents operated a Chinese takeout restaurant in Waikiki, and every day after school I went there to help wash pots and cut vegetables; after finishing my chores, I ran to the beach with my surfboard. I idolized and befriended the beachboy surfers like Jama Kekai, Steamboat, and Blackie. Sitting on my board and gazing at the rainbows over the Koolau Mountains and the spectacular sunsets over the Pacific, I wanted to be a surfer forever.

During my senior year, however, I had a teacher who changed my life. At the first class meeting, he introduced himself as Dr. Shunji Nishi, Ph.D. Most of the students at Iolani were Asian American, and we knew other Asian-American doctors, but they were all M.D.s. Impressed with my new teacher's unusual credentials, I went home and asked my mother: "Mom, my teacher's name is Dr. Shunji Nishi, Ph.D. Mom, what's a Ph.D.?" She replied: "I don't know. But he must be very smart."

Dr. Nishi required his students to read *The Screwtape Letters* by C. S. Lewis. These were letters that the chief devil wrote to his nephew, Wormword, giving instructions on how to entrap Christians into committing sins; for example, convince them that the ends justify the means, including lying and warfare. Dr. Nishi's writing assignments were challenging: we had to read a letter and then write an essay on the problems of the world and the human condition. Like a Screwtape letter, each essay had to open with the greeting: "Dear Wormwood." Dr. Nishi returned my essays with extensive marginal comments, many of them asking questions of epistemology: How do you know what you know? The "how" includes evidence, approaches, and assumptions. The "how" of knowing something is more important than the "what," for the "how" determines the "what."

A relationship blossomed between the two of us through my essays and his marginal comments. In April of the spring semester, Dr. Nishi stopped me as I was walking across campus. "Ronald," he said, "I think you should go away for college. It would be good for your personal growth and intellectual development. There's a fine liberal arts college in Ohio called the College of Wooster. Would you like to go to the College of Wooster?" Immediately, I replied, "No." I had already been accepted to the University of Hawaii, and the idea of transplanting myself so far away was intimidating. "Well," said Dr. Nishi, "would be it okay for me to write a letter to the college and tell them about you?" I agreed, and a month later, I received a letter informing me that I had been accepted. That one teacher and that one letter put me on a new path.

At college in the fall of 1957, I experienced a culture shock. The student body was very homogeneous, and my fellow students would ask me: How long have you been in this country? Where did you learn to speak English? To them, I did not look like an American and did not have an American-sounding name.

I was extremely homesick. Almost weekly, my mother sent me beautifully written letters. In one of them, she described her day: "It's 8:00 P.M. as I sit writing to you. About 1 A.M. in Ohio and I imagine you are snug in bed. We are still down at the store since Dad has to catch up soaking the teriyaki steak, etc. This week has been very busy and I am exhausted." In another letter, she wrote: "I never went to school much and you can say that again. What I do know is from reading. In my small way I am trying and doing my best (working) so that you being an exception *can and must* be above our intellectual level. At times I yearn for rest (6 years without a vacation)."

During the spring semester of my sophomore year, I was introduced to a fellow student — Carol Rankin, from New Jersey. I asked her to be my date for my fraternity spring prom. Soon we were in love. But then Carol told me that her parents would never approve of our relationship: the problem was my race. When her parents found out about us, they reacted furiously, calling me a "Jap." When she insisted that I was American, her father snapped back, "Impossible!" Claiming that the Japanese people were "treacherous" by nature, he pointed to the attack on Pearl Harbor. Her parents also feared that if she married me, she would be ostracized by white society and interned if there was another war with Japan.

Carol and I decided to do what was right for us. We were married in June 1961, with her parents reluctantly in attendance.

That fall, I entered the Ph.D. program in American history at the University of California, Berkeley. Like thousands of Berkeley students, I was inspired by the moral vision of Martin Luther King, Jr. During Freedom Summer of 1964, students of many races went into the South to register black voters. I was horrified by the news that three young civil rights workers had been murdered in Mississippi. My outrage at this racial hatred and violence led me to study slavery for my dissertation.

In 1965 our first child was born. When Carol's parents arrived at our home in California to welcome her birth, I greeted them in the driveway. "Let me help you with the luggage, Mr. Rankin," I said, and he replied: "You can call me Dad." As it turned out, his racist attitudes were not fixed and frozen.

Also in 1965, while I was working on my dissertation, the Watts riot exploded. The days of rage and burning led UCLA's history department to create a new position in black history. I applied for the opening, and in the fall of 1967, I joined the faculty as a young assistant professor.

I vividly remember my first class meeting. When I entered the enormous classroom, I found a packed crowd of three hundred excited students. Those were the days of black student militancy, when students wore dashikis and sported Afros. Before I could begin my lecture, a tall black student stood up in the middle of the classroom and raised his hand. "Well, Professor Taa-ka-ki," he declared, "what revolutionary tools are we going to learn in this class?" After hesitating for a moment, I replied, "We will be studying the history of the United States as it relates to black people. We will also be strengthening and sharpening our critical thinking skills and our writing skills. And these can be revolutionary tools, if you want to make them so."

As I taught my courses, I noted that my students had roots reaching back not only to Europe and Africa, but also to Latin America and Asia. Awareness of this diversity led me to ask an epistemological question: How do I really know what I know about American history? Even though I had a Ph.D., I realized I would have to reteach myself and began to conceptualize a comparative approach to the study of racial inequality. Meanwhile, I actively joined students in demanding a more diverse faculty and curriculum.

In 1971, however, I was denied tenure by the history department. This was a decision I had not expected: my teaching had been rated outstanding, and my dissertation had been accepted by the Free Press for publication as *A Pro-Slavery Crusade: The Agitation to Reopen the African Slave Trade*. Fortunately, Berkeley offered me an appointment as an associate professor with tenure in the newly instituted Department of Ethnic Studies. In 1972, I began teaching what would become Ethnic Studies 130, "The Making of Multicultural America: A Comparative Historical Perspective." This course provided the conceptual framework for the Comparative Ethnic Studies B.A. in 1974, the Comparative Ethnic Studies Ph.D. in 1984, and the American Cultures graduation requirement in 1987, which explores our society's racial and ethnic diversity comparatively. Out of my pursuit for a more inclusive and hence more accurate history came the writing of an abundance of books, including *Iron Cages: Race and Culture in Nineteenth-Century America* (Knopf, 1979) and *Strangers from a Different Shore: A History of Asian Americans* (Little, Brown, 1989).

During this time, my family became increasingly multiracial. Our daughter's husband has Anglo-Saxon ancestry, and our sons' wives have Jewish roots. We have seven grandchildren, including our son's adopted daughter, whose biological father is Mexican. Our family belongs to a rapidly growing population of mixed-race Americans. Indeed, like Melville's America, we are "not a narrow tribe."

My surfer-to-scholar story belongs to what Walt Whitman celebrated as "the varied carols" of America. In the vibrant sharing of our "melodious songs," we are creating a larger memory of a nation peopled by the world. As the time approaches when all Americans are minorities, we are facing a challenge: The task for us is not only to comprehend the world, but also to change the world. In our very comprehending, we are in fact changing the world. *A Different Mirror* seeks to study the past for the sake of the future.

NOTES

Chapter 1: A Different Mirror

1. Toni Morrison, *Playing in the Dark: Whiteness in the Literary Imagination* (Cambridge, Mass., 1992), p. 47.

2. Frederick Jackson Turner, "The Significance of the Frontier in American History," in *The Early Writings of Frederick Jackson Turner* (Madison, Wis., 1939), pp. 185–198.

3. Oscar Handlin, *The Uprooted: The Epic Story of the Great Migrations That Made the American People* (New York, 1951), p. 3.

4. Nick to Grandpa Ron, e-mail, June 17, 2007.

5. Edward Fiske, "Lessons," *New York Times*, February 7, 1990; "University of Wisconsin–Madison: The Madison Plan," February 9, 1988; interview with Dean Fred Lukermann, University of Minnesota, 1987.

6. Walt Whitman, Preface, *Leaves of Grass* (New York, 1958), p. 453.

7. David Herbert Donald, *Lincoln* (New York, 1995), p. 527; W. E. B. Du Bois, *The Souls of Black Folk: Essays and Sketches* (New York, 1965), p. v; Martin Luther King, Jr., *Why We Can't Wait* (New York, 1964), pp. 92–93.

8. Interview with old laundryman, in "Interviews with Two Chinese," circa 1924, Box 326, folder 325, Survey of Race Relations, Stanford University, Hoover Institution Archives; Congressman Robert Matsui, speech in the House of Representatives on the 442 bill for redress and reparations, September 17, 1987, *Congressional Record* (Washington, D.C., 1987), p. 7584.

9. Lawrence J. McCaffrey, *The Irish Diaspora in America* (Washington, D.C., 1984), pp. 6, 62.

10. John Murry Cuddihy, *The Ordeal of Civility: Freud, Marx, Levi Strauss, and the Jewish Struggle with Modernity* (Boston, 1987), p. 165; Jonathan Kaufman, *Broken Alliance: The Turbulent Times between Blacks and Jews in America* (New York, 1989), pp. 28, 82, 83–84, 91, 93, 106.

11. Albert Camarillo, *Chicanos in a Changing Society: From Mexican*

Pueblos to American Barrios in Santa Barbara and Southern California, 1848–1930 (Cambridge, Mass., 1979) p. 2; Juan Nepomuceno Seguin, in David J. Weber (ed.), *Foreigners in Their Native Land: Historical Roots of the Mexican Americans* (Albuquerque, N.M., 1973), p. vi; Jesus Garza, in Manuel Gamio, *The Mexican Immigrant: His Life Story* (Chicago, 1931), p. 15; "Immigration: Why Amnesty Makes Sense," *Time*, June 18, 2007, pp. 42, 39.

12. Nadeem Saaed, e-mail to Professor Takaki, September 11, 2007.

13. Omar Nourzaie, conversation in Fremont, California, June 23, 2007.

14. Andrew Jackson, Second Annual Message, James D. Richardson (ed.), *A Compilation of the Messages and Papers of the Presidents, 1789–1897* (Washington, D.C., 1897), vol. 2, pp. 520–522; Luther Standing Bear, "What the Indian Means to America," in Wayne Moquin (ed.), *Great Documents in American Indian History* (New York, 1973), p. 307.

15. Jefferson to Monroe, November 24, 1801, in Paul L. Ford (ed.), *The Works of Thomas Jefferson*, 10 vols. (New York, 1892–1899), vol. 9, p. 317.

16. Whitman, *Leaves of Grass*, p. 284.

17. David R. Roediger, *The Wages of Whiteness: Race and the Making of the American Working Class* (London, 1991) p. 137; Leon Litwack, *North of Slavery: The Negro in the Free States, 1790–1860* (Chicago, 1961), p. 163.

18. Mathilde Bunton, "Negro Work Songs" (1940), 1 typescript in Box 91 ("Music"), Illinois Writers Project, U.S.W.P.A., in James R. Grossman, *Land of Hope: Chicago, Black Sojourners, and the Great Migration* (Chicago, 1989), p. 192; Carl Wittke, *The Irish in America* (Baton Rouge, 1956), p. 39; Kazuo Ito, *Issei: A History of Japanese Immigrants* (Seattle, 1973), p. 343; Manuel Gamio, *Mexican Immigration to the United States* (Chicago, 1930), pp. 84–85.

19. Tomas Almaguer, "Racial Domination and Class Conflict in Capitalist Agriculture: The Oxnard Sugar Beet Workers' Strike of 1903," *Labor History*, vol. 25, no. 3 (Summer 1984), p. 347; Howard M. Sachar, *A History of the Jews in America* (New York, 1992), p. 183.

20. Takashi Tsutsumi, *History of Hawaii Laborers' Movement* (Honolulu, 1922), pp. 12, 44, 17, 13, 22.

21. Harvard Sitkoff, *A New Deal for Blacks: The Emergence of Civil Rights as a National Issue* (New York, 1978), pp. 251, 252, 254, 179–186; Raymond Wolters, *Negroes and the Great Depression: The Problem of Economic Recovery* (Westport, Conn., 1970), pp. 236–40, 258.

22. Ito, *Issei*, p. 497.

23. Arnold Schrier, *Ireland and the American Emigration, 1850–1900* (New York, 1970), p. 24; "The Celestials at Home and Abroad," in *Littel's Living Age*, August 14, 1852, p. 294.

24. Ito, *Issei*, pp. 20, 33; Abraham Cahan, *The Rise of David Levinsky*

(New York, 1960, originally published in 1917), pp. 59–61; song, in Mark Slobin, *Tenement Songs: The Popular Music of the Jewish Immigrants* (Urbana, Ill., 1982), p. 155; Lawrence A. Cardoso, *Mexican Emigration to the United States, 1897–1931* (Tucson, 1981), p. 80.

25. Abraham Lincoln, "First Inaugural Address," in *The Annals of America*, vol. 9, *1861–1865: The Crisis of the Union* (Chicago, 1968), p. 255.

26. Donald, *Lincoln*, pp. 429–431.

27. Ibid.

28. Leon Litwack, *Been in the Storm So Long: The Aftermath of Slavery* (New York, 1979), p. 64.

29. Donald, *Lincoln*, pp. 526–527.

30. Abraham Lincoln, "The Gettysburg Address," in *The Annals of America*, pp. 462–463.

31. *Pittsburgh Courier*, January 31, 1942.

32. Andrew Lind, *Hawaii's Japanese: An Experiment in Democracy* (Princeton, 1946), p. 158.

33. Chester Tanaka, *Go for Broke: A Pictorial History of the Japanese American 100th Infantry Battalion and the 442d Regimental Combat Team* (Richmond, California, 1982), p. 171.

34. Poem by Kiyoko Nieda, in Lucille Nixon and Tomoe Tana (eds. and trans.), *Sounds from the Unknown: A Collection of Japanese American Tanka* (Denver, 1963), p. 49.

35. Martin Luther King, Jr., "I Have a Dream," reprinted in Francis L. Broderick and August Meier (eds.), *Negro Protest Thought in the Twentieth Century* (New York, 1965), pp. 400–405.

36. Dionne Walker, "Mildred Loving—Challenged Marriage Ban," *San Francisco Chronicle*, May 6, 2008.

37. "Text of Reagan's Remarks," reprinted in *Pacific Citizen*, August 19–26, 1988, p. 5; *San Francisco Chronicle*, August 5, 1988 and August 11, 1988.

38. Weber (ed.), *Foreigners in Their Native Land*, p. vi; Hamilton Holt (ed.), *The Life Stories of Undistinguished Americans As Told by Themselves* (New York, 1906), p. 143.

39. Leslie Marmon Silko, *Ceremony* (New York, 1978), p. 2; Harriet A. Jacobs, *Incidents in the Life of a Slave Girl* (Cambridge, Mass., 1987; originally published in 1857), p. xiii.

40. "Social Document of Pany Lowe, interviewed by C. H. Burnett, Seattle, July 5, 1924," p. 6, Survey of Race Relations, Stanford University, Hoover Institution Archives; Minnie Miller, "Autobiography," private manuscript, copy from Richard Balkin; Tomo Shoji, presentation, Ohana Cultural Center, Oakland, California, March 4, 1988; Keiko Teshirogi, poem, in Kazuo Ito, *Issei* (Seattle, 1973), p. 480.

41. Adrienne Rich, *Blood, Bread, and Poetry: Selected Prose, 1979–1985* (New York, 1986), p. 199; Audre Lorde, "Good Mirrors Are Not

Cheap," in Henry Louis Gates, Jr., *Loose Canons: Notes on the Culture Wars* (New York, 1992), p. 192.

42. Ishmael Reed, "America: The Multinational Society," in Rick Simonson and Scott Walker (eds.), *Multi-Cultural Literacy* (St. Paul, 1988), p. 160.

43. Langston Hughes, in Hughes and Arna Bontemps (eds.), *The Poetry of the Negro, 1746–1949* (Garden City, N.Y., 1951), p. 106.

44. John Locke, *Of Civil Government: Second Treatise* (rpt., Chicago, 1955), p. 19; F. Scott Fitzgerald, *The Great Gatsby* (New York, 1953), p. 182.

45. Herman Melville, *Redburn* (Chicago, 1969), p. 169; also quoted in Henry Louis Gates, Jr., *Loose Canons: Notes on the Culture Wars* (New York, 1992), pp. 116–117.

Part One: Foundations

1. "The Saga of the Greenlanders: Eirik the Red Takes Land in Iceland" and "The Saga of Eirik the Red: Leif Eiriksson Discovers Vinland," in *Vinland the Good: The Saga of Leif Eiriksson and the Viking Discovery of America, with a Preface by Helge Ingstad* (Oslo, 1986). The Greenland saga was written down in the fourteenth century and the saga of Erik in the fifteenth century.

2. *Vinland the Good*, pp. 20, 26, 28.

3. *Vinland the Good*, pp. 65–66, 34, 71–72. The name "Skraelinger" was applied by the Norsemen to Indians in Vinland and may be related to the modern Norwegian term *skraela*, or "scream." See Gwyn Jones, *The Norse Atlantic Saga: Being the Norse Voyages of Discovery and Settlement to Iceland, Greenland, America* (New York, 1964), pp. 59–60. My thanks to my former graduate student, Amy Lonetree, for informing me that they were Beothuk.

4. *Vinland the Good*, pp. 66, 68, 36, 69.

5. Christopher Columbus, Journal, October 21 and 23, 1492, in Samuel Eliot Morison (ed.), *Journals and Other Documents on the Life and Voyages of Christopher Columbus* (New York, 1963), pp. 78, 79.

Chapter 2: The "Tempest" in the Wilderness

1. John Winthrop, *Winthrop Papers*, vol. 2 (1623–1630), Massachusetts Historical Society (1931), p. 139; Perry Miller, "Errand into the Wilderness," in Miller, *Errand into the Wilderness* (New York, 1964), pp. 1–15; Miller's metaphor and theme originally came from Samuel Danforth's sermon, delivered on May 11, 1670, entitled, "A Brief Recognition of New England's Errand into the Wilderness"; John Winthrop, "A Model of Christian Charity," in Perry Miller (ed.), *The American Puritans: Their Prose and Poetry* (New York, 1956), pp. 79–84.

2. Frank G. Speck, "Penobscot Tales and Religious Beliefs," *Journal of American Folklore*, vol. 48, no. 187 (January–March, 1915), p. 19; William Wood, quoted in William S. Simmons, *Spirit of New England Tribes: Indian History and Folklore, 1620–1984* (Hanover, N.H., 1986), p. 66; Edward Johnson, *Wonder-working Providence, 1628–1651*, edited by F. Franklin Jameson (New York, 1910, originally published in 1654), p. 39; Colin G. Calloway (ed.), *Dawnland Encounters: Indians and Europeans in Northern New England* (Hanover, N.H., 1991), pp. 30, 50; Roger Williams, *A Key into the Language of America* (Detroit, 1973), p. 191. See also James Axtell, "Through Another Glass Darkly: Early Indian Views of Europeans," in Axtell, *After Columbus: Essays in the Ethnohistory of Colonial North America* (New York, 1988), pp. 125–143.

3. Simmons, *Spirit of New England Tribes*, pp. 71, 72; Axtell, *After Columbus*, p. 129; James Axtell, *The Invasion Within: The Contest of Cultures in Colonial North America* (New York, 1985), p. 8.

4. William Shakespeare, *The Tempest*, ed. by Louis B. Wright and Virginia A. Lamar (New York, 1971), p. 81. *The Tempest* has recently been swept into the storm over "political correctness." In *Newsweek* on April 15, 1991, George Will issued a scathing attack on "left" scholars and their "perverse" "liberation" of literature, especially their interpretation of this play as a reflection of "the imperialist rape of the Third World." Shakespeare specialist Stephen Greenblatt responded: "This is a curious example — since it is very difficult to argue that *The Tempest* is *not* about imperialism." Such an authoritative counter-statement clears the way for a study of this story in relationship to its historical setting. See George Will, "Literary Politics: 'The Tempest'? It's 'really' about imperialism. Emily Dickinson's poetry? Masturbation," *Newsweek*, April 15, 1991, p. 72, and Stephen Greenblatt, "The Best Way to Kill Our Literary Inheritance Is to Turn It into a Decorous Celebration of the New World Order," *Chronicle of Higher Education*, vol. 37, no. 39 (June 12, 1991), p. B1, 3. As Adam Begley has noted, Stanley Fish reminds us that "the circumstances of an utterance determine its meaning." See Begley, "Souped-Up Scholar," *New York Times Magazine*, May 3, 1992, p. 52. My appreciation to Frederick E. Hoxie and David Thelen for helping me develop the critical contours of my analysis.

5. Winthrop Jordan chose *Othello* for his play in *White Over Black: American Attitudes Toward the Negro, 1550–1812* (Chapel Hill, N.C., 1968), pp. 37–40. *Othello* was first performed in 1604, before the founding of Jamestown. Jordan overlooked the rich possibility of studying *The Tempest*.

6. Nicholas P. Canny, "The Ideology of English Colonization: From Ireland to America," *William and Mary Quarterly*, 3rd series, vol. 30, no. 4 (October 1973), p. 585; David B. Quinn, *The Elizabethans and the Irish* (Ithaca, N.Y., 1966), p. 161; Francis Jennings, *The Invasion of America: Indians, Colonialism, and the Cant of Conquest* (New York, 1976), p. 7.

In *White Supremacy: A Comparative Study in American & South African History* (New York, 1971), George Frederickson describes the conquest of Ireland as a "rehearsal," p. 13.

7. Canny, "Ideology," pp. 585, 588; Howard Mumford Jones, *O Strange New World: American Culture, the Formative Years* (New York, 1965), p. 169; Keith Thomas, *Man and the Natural World: A History of the Modern Sensibility* (New York, 1983), p. 42; Jennings, *Invasion of America*, pp. 46, 49; James Muldoon, "The Indian as Irishman," *Essex Institute Historical Collections*, vol. 111 (October 1975), p. 269; Quinn, *Elizabethans and the Irish*, p. 76.

8. Muldoon, "Indian as Irishman," p. 284; Quinn, *Elizabethans and the Irish*, p. 108.

9. Canny, "Ideology," pp. 593, 582; Jennings, *Invasion of America*, p. 153; Frederickson, *White Supremacy*, p. 15.

10. Canny, "Ideology," p. 582; Jennings, *Invasion of America*, p. 168; Quinn, *Elizabethans and the Irish*, p. 44.

11. Quinn, *Elizabethans and the Irish*, pp. 132–133.

12. Quinn, *Elizabethans and the Irish*, p. 121; William Christie MacLeod, "Celt and Indian: Britain's Old World Frontier in Relation to the New," in Paul Bohannan and Fred Plog (eds.), *Beyond the Frontier: Social Process and Cultural Change* (Garden City, N.Y., 1967), pp. 38–39; Jennings, *Invasion of America*, p. 312.

13. Quinn, *Elizabethans and the Irish*, p. 121; Muldoon, "Indian as Irishman," p. 270; MacLeod, "Celt and Indian," p. 26; see also Canny, "Ideology," p. 576.

14. Shakespeare, *Tempest*, pp. 13, 81; Frank Kermode, "Introduction," *The Tempest*, The Arden Edition of the Works of William Shakespeare (London, 1969), p. xxvii; Robert R. Cawley, "Shakespeare's Use of the Voyagers in *The Tempest*," *Publications of the Modern Language Association of America*, vol. 41, no. 3 (September 1926), pp. 699–700, 689; Frederickson, *White Supremacy*, p. 22. See also Leo Marx, *The Machine in the Garden: Technology and the Pastoral Ideal in America* (New York, 1964), pp. 34–75.

15. Shakespeare, *Tempest*, pp. 27–28, 31; Cawley, "Shakespeare's Use," pp. 702, 703, 704; Kirkpatrick Sale, *The Conquest of Paradise: Christopher Columbus and the Columbian Legacy* (New York, 1990), p. 102. For analysis of America imaged as a woman, see Carolyn Merchant, *Ecological Revolutions: Nature, Gender, and Science in New England* (Chapel Hill, N.C., 1989), p. 101; Annette Kolodny, *The Lay of the Land: Metaphor as Experience and History in American Life and Letters* (Chapel Hill, N.C., 1975).

16. Shakespeare, *Tempest*, p. xxxviii; Kermode (ed.), introduction, *Tempest*, p. xxiv. For anagram of Hamlet, see dedication to William Shakespeare at Kronborg Castle, Denmark.

17. Christopher Columbus, Journal, November 12, 1492, in Samuel Eliot

Morison (ed.), *Journals and Other Documents on the Life and Voyages of Christopher Columbus* (New York, 1963), p. 126; Sale, *Conquest of Paradise*, p. 126; Guillermo Coma to the Duke of Milan, December 13, 1494, in Morison (ed.), *Journals of Columbus*, 238; Cuneo to Lord Hieronymo Annari, October 15, 1495, in Morison (ed.), *Journals of Columbus*, pp. 226–227.

18. Kenneth M. Morrison, *The Embattled Northeast: The Elusive Ideal of Alliance in Abenaki-Euramerican Relations* (Berkeley, Calif., 1984), pp. 22–23; Leonard A. Adolf, "Squanto's Role in Pilgrim Diplomacy," *Ethnohistory*, vol. 11, no. 4 (fall 1964), pp. 247–248; Cawley, "Shakespeare's Use," pp. 720, 721; Shakespeare, *Tempest*, pp. 41, 40; Kermode (ed.), text explanation, *Tempest*, p. 62.

19. William Bradford, *Of Plymouth Plantation: 1620–1647* (New York, 1967), p. 26; Frederickson, *White Supremacy*, p. 11; Roy Harvey Pearce, *Savagism and Civilization: A Study of the Indian and the American Mind* (Baltimore, 1967), p. 12; Colin G. Calloway (ed.), *Dawnland Encounters: Indians and Europeans in Northern New England* (Hanover, N.H., 1991), p. 33.

20. Washburn (ed.), *Indian and White Man*, pp. 4, 5, 7.

21. Shakespeare, *Tempest*, p. 19; Cawley, "Shakespeare's Use," p. 715; Frederickson, *White Supremacy*, p. 12; Pearce, *Savagism and Civilization*, pp. 9, 10.

22. Axtell, *After Columbus*, p. 190; Helen C. Rountree, *The Powhatan Indians of Virginia: Their Traditional Culture* (Norman, Okla., 1990), pp. 44, 45, 46, 49, 60, 63.

23. Mortimer J. Adler (ed.), *Annals of America*, vol. 1, *Discovering a New World* (Chicago, 1968), pp. 21, 26, 22.

24. Gary Nash, *Red, White, and Black: The Peoples of Early America* (Englewood Cliffs, N.J., 1974), p. 58; Adler (ed.), *Annals of America*, vol. 1, p. 26.

25. Cotton Mather, *Magnalia Christi Americana*, books 1 and 2 (Cambridge, Mass., 1977), p. 116; Frederickson, *White Supremacy*, p. 24; Sale, *Conquest of Paradise*, p. 277.

26. Jennings, *Invasion of America*, p. 66; Nash, *Red, White, and Black*, p. 57.

27. Merchant, *Ecological Revolutions*, p. 22; Shakespeare, *Tempest*, pp. 29, 80, 52; Thomas, *Man and the Natural World*, p. 42; Cawley, "Shakespeare's Use," p. 715.

28. Jennings, *Invasion of America*, pp. 78, 80; Sale, *Conquest of Paradise*, p. 295; Nash, *Red, White, and Black*, pp. 62, 63; Sale, *Conquest of Paradise*, pp. 293, 294; Jennings, *Invasion of America*, p. 153.

29. Shakespeare, *Tempest*, pp. 70, 15–16, 18, 19, 29, 50; Kermode (ed.), text explanation, *Tempest*, p. 63.

30. Howard S. Russell, *Indian New England Before the Mayflower* (Hanover, N.H., 1980), p. 11; John Smith, "A Description of New England," in Adler (ed.), *Annals of America*, vol. 1, p. 39.

31. Eva L. Butler, "Algonkian Culture and the Use of Maize in Southern New England," *Bulletin of the Archeological Society of Connecticut*, no. 22 (December 1948), p. 6; Speck, "Penobscot Tales and Religious Beliefs," *Journal of American Folklore*, vol. 48, no. 187 (January–March 1915), p. 75; Merchant, *Ecological Revolutions*, p. 72.

32. Russell, *Indian New England*, pp. 10, 11, 166; Merchant, *Ecological Revolutions*, p. 80; Peter A. Thomas, "Contrastive Subsistence Strategies and Land Use as Factors for Understanding Indian-White Relations in New England," *Ethnohistory*, vol. 23, no. 1 (winter 1976), p. 10; Roger Williams, *A Key into the Language of America* (Detroit, 1973), p. 170; Eva L. Butler, "Algonkian Culture," pp. 15, 17. For a study of the Abenakis as hunters, see Merchant, *Ecological Revolutions*, pp. 29–68.

33. Thomas, "Contrastive Subsistence Strategies and Land Use," p. 4.

34. Bradford, *Of Plymouth Plantation*, pp. 270–271; Alfred W. Crosby, "Virgin Soil Epidemics as a Factor in the Aboriginal Depopulation in America," *William and Mary Quarterly*, vol. 33, no. 2 (April 1976), p. 289; Dean R. Snow, "Abenaki Fur Trade in the Sixteenth Century," *Western Canadian Journal of Anthropology*, vol. 6, no. 1 (1976), p. 8; Merchant, *Ecological Revolutions*, p. 90.

35. Roy Harvey Pearce, "The 'Ruines of Mankind': The Indian and the Puritan Mind," *Journal of the History of Ideas*, vol. 13 (1952), p. 201; Peter Carroll, *Puritanism and the Wilderness: The Intellectual Significance of the Frontier, 1629–1700* (New York, 1969), p. 13; Johnson, *Wonder-working Providence*, p. 40.

36. Cronon, *Changes in the Land*, p. 90; Alfred W. Crosby, "God...Would Destroy Them, and Give Their Country to Another People," *American Heritage*, vol. 29, no. 6 (October–November 1978), p. 40; Bradford, *Of Plymouth Plantation*, pp. 65–66.

37. Johnson, *Wonder-working Providence*, p. 262; William Cronon, *Changes in the Land: Indians, Colonists, and the Ecology of New England* (New York, 1983), pp. 55, 56; William Wood, *New England's Prospect*, ed. by Alden T. Vaughn (Amherst, Mass., 1977), p. 96.

38. Jill Lepore, *The Name of War: King Philip's War and the Origins of American Identity* (New York, 1998), pp. xii, xvi.

39. Charles M. Segal and David C. Stineback (eds.), *Puritans, Indians & Manifest Destiny* (New York, 1977), pp. 136–137, 111; Sherburne F. Cook, "Interracial Warfare and Population Decline among the New England Indians," *Ethnohistory*, vol. 20 (winter 1973), pp. 19–21; Simmons, "Cultural Bias," p. 67; Segal and Stineback (eds.), *Puritans, Indians & Manifest Destiny*, p. 182.

40. Kai Erikson, *Wayward Puritans: A Study in the Sociology of Deviance* (New York, 1966), pp. 13, 64; see also Pearce, *Savagism and Civilization*, p. 8.

41. Cotton Mather, *On Witchcraft: Being, The Wonders of the Invisible World* (New York, n.d.; originally published in 1692), p. 53; Simmons, "Cultural Bias," p. 71.

42. Richard Slotkin, *Regeneration Through Violence: The Mythology of the American Frontier, 1600–1860* (Middletown, Conn., 1973), pp. 132, 142, 65.

43. Johnson, *Wonder-working Providence*, p. 263; Bradford, *Of Plymouth Plantation*, p. 205.

44. Johnson, *Wonder-working Providence*, pp. 71, 168, 211, 247–248; see Cronon, *Changes in the Land*, pp.166–167.

45. My thanks to David R. Ford for pointing out the complexity of Rowlandson's narrative. David R. Ford, "Mary Rowlandson's Captivity Narrative: A Paradigm of Puritan Representations of Native Americans?" Ethnic Studies 299 paper, fall 1996, University of California, Berkeley.

46. Axtell, *Invasion Within*, p. 167.

47. Thomas Jefferson to Brother John Baptist de Coigne, chief of Kaskaskia, June 1781, and to John Page, August 5, 1776, in Andrew A. Lipscomb and Albert E. Bergh (eds.), *Writings of Thomas Jefferson*, 20 vols. (Washington, D.C., 1904), vol. 16, p. 372; vol. 4, pp. 270–271.

48. Jefferson to chiefs of the Shawnee Nation, February 19, 1807, in Lipscomb and Bergh (eds.), *Writings of Jefferson*, vol. 16, p. 424.

49. Thomas Jefferson, *Notes on the State of Virginia* (New York, 1964, written in 1781), p. 91.

50. Jefferson to chiefs of the Upper Cherokees, May 4, 1808, in Lipscomb and Bergh (eds.), *Writings of Jefferson*, vol. 16, p. 434; Jefferson to John Baptist de Coigne, June 1781, in Julian Boyd (ed.), *The Papers of Thomas Jefferson*, 18 vols. (Princeton, N.J., 1950–1965), vol. 6, pp. 60–63; Jefferson to Choctaw Nation, December 17, 1803, and to chiefs of the Ottawas, Chippewas, Powtewatamies, Wyandots, and Senecas of Sandusky, April 22, 1808, in Lipscomb and Bergh (eds.), *Writings of Jefferson*, vol. 16, pp. 401, 429.

51. Jefferson, "Confidential Message Recommending a Western Exploring Expedition," January 18, 1803, in Lipscomb and Bergh (eds.), *Writings of Jefferson*, vol. 3, pp. 489–490; Jefferson to Governor William H. Harrison, February 27, 1803, in Lipscomb and Bergh (eds.), *Writings of Jefferson*, vol. 10, pp. 370–373; Jefferson to John Adams, June 11, 1812, in Lester J. Cappon (ed.), *The Adams-Jefferson Letters*, 2 vols. (Chapel Hill, N.C., 1959), vol. 2, pp. 307–308.

52. Jefferson to William Ludlow, September 6, 1824, in Lipscomb and Bergh (eds.), *Writings of Jefferson*, vol. 16, pp. 74–75.

Chapter 3: The Hidden Origins of Slavery

1. William Shakespeare, *The Tempest* (New York, 1971), p. 15.

2. Winthrop Jordan, *White Over Black: American Attitudes Toward the Negro, 1550–1812* (Chapel Hill, N.C., 1968), pp. 4–7. Jordan's study is monumental, truly a classic.

3. Jordan, *White Over Black*, p. 15.

4. Shakespeare, *Tempest*, p. 19; Jordan, *White Over Black*, pp. 24, 25.

5. Shakespeare, *Tempest*, pp. 85, 62, 18, 19.

6. Jordan, *White Over Black*, p. 579.

7. Shakespeare, *Tempest*, p. 15.

8. Jordan, *White Over Black*, p. 73.

9. Olaudah Equiano, "Early Travels of Olaudah Equiano," in Philip D. Curtain, *Africa Remembered: Narratives by West Africans from the Era of the Slave Trade* (Madison, Wis., 1968), pp. 92–97.

10. Edmund Morgan, *American Slavery American Freedom: The Ordeal of Colonial Virginia* (New York, 1975), p. 154. This is the most important study of class and race relations in early Virginia.

11. Abbot Emerson Smith, *Colonists in Bondage: White Servitude and Convict Labor in America, 1607–1776* (Gloucester, Mass., 1965), p. 29.

12. T. H. Breen and Stephen Innes, *"Myne Owne Grounde": Race and Freedom on Virginia's Eastern Shore, 1640–1676* (New York, 1980), p. 59; *Colonists in Bondage*, pp. 4, 13.

13. Smith, *Colonists in Bondage*, pp. 3, 45.

14. Smith, *Colonists in Bondage*, pp. 68–69, 163, 166–167; Marcus W. Jernegan, *Laboring and Dependent Classes in Colonial America, 1607–1783* (New York, 1960), p. 50.

15. Smith, *Colonists in Bondage*, pp. 256, 253.

16. William W. Hening, *The Statutes at Large: Being a Collection of All the Laws of Virginia*, 13 vols. (Richmond, Va., 1809–23), vol. 2, p. 26; Helen Catterall (ed.), *Judicial Cases concerning American Slavery and the Negro*, vol. 1, *Cases from the Courts of England, Virginia, West Virginia, and Kentucky* (New York, 1968), p. 80.

17. Catterall, *Judicial Cases*, pp. 77, 78; Morgan, *American Slavery American Freedom*, pp. 155, 336; Winthrop Jordan, "Modern Tensions and the Origins of American Slavery," *Journal of Southern History*, vol. 28, no. 1 (February 1962), p. 28; Breen and Innes, *"Myne Owne Grounde,"* p. 96.

18. Hening, *Statutes*, vol. 1, p. 226; Breen and Innes, *"Myne Owne Grounde,"* pp. 25, 29; Catterall, *Judicial Cases*, p. 77.

19. "Inventory of the goods Cattle and Chattles of and belonging unto the estate of Mr. William Burdett," November 13, 1643, reprinted in Susie M. Ames (ed.), *County Court Records of Accomack-Northampton, Virginia, 1640–1645* (Charlottesville, Va., 1973), pp. 419–425.

20. Ames (ed.), *Court Records*, pp. 324, 255, 433–434; Jordan, *White Over Black*, p. 75; Morgan, *American Slavery American Freedom*, p. 154; Carl Degler, *Out of Our Past: The Forces That Shaped Modern America* (New York, 1962), p. 34; Alden T. Vaughan, "The Origins Debate: Slavery and Racism in Seventeenth-Century Virginia," *Virginia Magazine of History and Biography*, vol. 97, no. 3 (July 1989), p. 354.

21. Hening, *Statutes*, vol. 2, pp. 26, 270.

22. Russell Menard, "From Servants to Slaves: The Transformation of the Chesapeake Labor System," *Southern Studies,* vol. 5 (winter 1977), p. 363; Morgan, *American Slavery American Freedom,* p. 299.

23. Shakespeare, *The Tempest,* pp. 44, 45, 52, 54, 55, 68, 73.

24. T. H. Breen, "A Changing Labor Force and Race Relations in Viriginia, 1660–1710," *Journal of Social History,* vol. 7 (fall 1973), p. 4.

25. Morgan, *American Slavery American Freedom,* pp. 215–220.

26. Breen, "Changing Labor Force," pp. 3, 8, 9; Breen and Innes, *"Myne Owne Grounde,"* p. 60; Smith, *Colonists in Bondage,* p. 138. The House of Burgesses used the term "giddy multitude" to describe the followers of Nathaniel Bacon. H. R. McIlwaine (ed.), *Journals of the House of Burgesses of Virginia, 1659/60–1693* (Richmond, Va., 1914). See Breen, "Changing Labor Force," p. 18.

27. Breen, "Changing Labor Force," pp. 3–4; Morgan, *American Slavery American Freedom,* pp. 241–242.

28. Morgan, *American Slavery American Freedom,* pp. 257, 258, 260.

29. Breen, "Changing Labor Force," p. 10.

30. Breen, "Changing Labor Force," p. 11.

31. Morgan, *American Slavery American Freedom,* p. 308; Breen, "Changing Labor Force," p. 12. Morgan is reluctant to press his analysis as far as I do. "The substitution of slaves for servants gradually eased and eventually ended the threat that the freedmen posed," he wrote. "As the annual number of imported servants dropped, so did the number of men turning free.... Planters who bought slaves instead of servants did not do so with any apparent consciousness of the social stability to be gained thereby." Perhaps not, but perhaps they did, though not "apparently." See Theodore Allen, "'...They Would Have Destroyed Me': Slavery and the Origins of Racism," *Radical America,* vol. 9, no. 3 (May–June 1975), pp. 41–63, which I read after completing my analysis of Bacon's Rebellion, for an argument that the planters acted deliberately and consciously.

32. Darrett B. and Anita H. Rutman, *A Place in Time: Middlesex County, Virginia, 1650–1750* (New York, 1984), p. 165; Morgan, *American Slavery American Freedom,* p. 306.

33. Breen, "Changing Labor Force," pp. 16, 17; Morgan, *American Slavery American Freedom,* pp. 404, 423; Degler, *Out of Our Past,* p. 27; Russell Menard, "From Servants to Slaves: The Transformation of the Chesapeake Labor System," *Southern Studies,* vol. 5 (winter 1977), p. 370; Hening, *Statutes,* vol. 3, pp. 447–478.

34. Hening, *Statutes,* vol. 2, pp. 481, 493.

35. Allen, "'They Would Have Destroyed Me,'" p. 55; Hening, *Statutes,* vol. 3, pp. 86–87; Morgan, *American Slavery American Freedom,* pp. 333, 335–357.

36. The subheading comes from Winthrop Jordan's magisterial book, *White Over Black;* Jefferson, *Notes on the State of Virginia* (New York, 1861), p. 167; Jefferson to John Jordan, December 21, 1805, and Jefferson

to W. Eppes, June 30, 1820, in Edwin M. Betts (ed.), *Thomas Jefferson's Farm Book* (Princeton, N.J., 1953), pp. 21, 43.

37. Jefferson to Daniel Bradley, October 6, 1805, and Jefferson to Thomas M. Randolph, June 8, 1803, in Betts, *Jefferson's Farm Book*, pp. 21, 19.

38. Jefferson to Edward Coles, August 25, 1814, in Paul L. Ford (ed.), *The Works of Thomas Jefferson*, 20 vols. (New York, 1892–99), vol. 11, p. 416; Jefferson, *Notes*, p. 132; Jefferson to Brissot de Warville, February 11, 1788, in Julian Boyd (ed.), *The Papers of Thomas Jefferson*, 18 vols. (Princeton, N.J., 1950–65), vol. 12, pp. 577–578.

39. Jefferson to Francis Eppes, July 30, 1787, in Boyd (ed.), *Papers*, vol. 10, p. 653; Jefferson to Nicholas Lewis, July 29, 1787, in Boyd (ed.), *Papers*, vol. 10, p. 640.

40. Jefferson, *Notes*, p. 155.

41. Jefferson, *Notes*, pp. 85–86; Jefferson to John Holmes, April 22, 1820, in Ford (ed.), *Works*, vol. 12, p. 334.

42. Jefferson to Jared Sparks, February 4, 1824, in Ford (ed.), *Works*, vol. 13, p. 159.

43. Jefferson, *Notes*, pp. 127, 138.

44. Jordan, *White Over Black*, pp. 283–284; Phillis Wheatley, *The Poems of Phillis Wheatley*, edited by Julian Mason (Chapel Hill, N.C., 1966), pp. 7, 34.

45. Jordan, *White Over Black*, p. 437; Jefferson, *Notes*, p. 135.

46. Banneker to Jefferson, August 19, 1791, reprinted in George Ducas, with Charles Van Doren (eds.), *Great Documents in Black American History* (New York, 1970), pp. 23–26.

47. Banneker to Jefferson.

48. Jefferson to Banneker, August 30, 1791, in Ford (ed.), *Works*, vol. 6, pp. 309–310; Jefferson to Joel Harlow, October 8, 1809, in Ford (ed.), *Works*, vol. 11, p. 121.

49. Shakespeare, *The Tempest*, p. 70; Jefferson, *Notes*, pp. 137–141.

50. Jefferson, *Notes*, pp. 138–139, 127; Jefferson to Edward Coles, August 25, 1814, in Ford, *Works*, vol. 11, pp. 417–418.

51. Callender, in *Richmond Recorder*, September 1, 1802, quoted in Fawn Brodie, *Thomas Jefferson: An Intimate History* (New York, 1974), p. 349; *Richmond Examiner*, September 18, 25, 1802.

52. *Boston Gazette*, reprinted in *Richmond Recorder*, December 1, 1802, quoted in Jordan, *White Over Black*, p. 468.

53. *Boston Gazette*, reprinted in *New York Evening Post*, December 8, 1802.

54. Jefferson to James Madison, May 29, 1801, in W. C. Ford, "Thomas Jefferson and James Thomson Callener," *New England Historical and Genealogical Register* (1896–97), vol. 2, p. 157; Thomas J. Randolph, in appendix, Milton E. Flower, *James Parton: The Father of Modern Biography* (Durham, N.C., 1951), pp. 236–239.

55. Brodie, *Jefferson,* p. 216.

56. "Jefferson's Other Family," *Newsweek,* February 7, 2000, p. 57; "Reminiscences of Madison Hemings," published as "Life Among the Lowly, No. 1," *Pike County (Ohio) Republican,* March 13, 1873, reprinted in appendix, Brodie, *Jefferson,* pp. 272–273; "Jefferson Fathered Slave's Last Child," *Nature* 196 (November 5, 1998), pp. 27–28; see also Ronald Takaki, *Iron Cages: Race and Culture in 19th-Century America* (New York, 1979), pp. 42–55. My thanks to Ted Fang, "Jeffersonian Rites," paper for Ethnic Studies 250, University of California, Berkeley, 2002. His research restirred my interest in the controversy over Jefferson and Hemings.

57. Jefferson, *Notes,* pp. 132–133.

58. Jefferson to James Monroe, July 14, 1793, and Jefferson to St. George Tucker, August 28, 1797, in Ford (ed.), *Works,* vol. 7, pp. 449–459; vol. 8, p. 335; Jefferson to James Monroe, September 20, 1800, in Ford (ed.), *Works,* vol. 9, p. 147; Jefferson to William Burwell, January 28, 1805, in Betts (ed.), *Jefferson's Farm Book,* p. 20.

59. Jefferson to John Holmes, April 22, 1820, in Ford (ed.), *Works,* vol. 13, p. 159.

60. Shakespeare, *The Tempest,* p. 78.

Part Two: Contradictions

1. Douglass C. North, *The Economic Growth of the United States, 1790–1860* (New York, 1966).

2. See George R. Taylor, *The Transportation Revolution, 1815–1860* (New York, 1962).

3. North, *Economic Growth,* pp. 136, 141, 151, 129.

4. North, *Economic Growth,* pp. 59, 250, 233, 257, 262,124, 256, 257, 232, 233.

Chapter 4: Toward "the Stony Mountains"

1. Jefferson to Andrew Jackson, February 16, 1803, in Andrew A. Lipscomb and Albert E. Bergh (eds.), *Writings of Thomas Jefferson,* 20 vols. (Washington, D.C., 1904), vol. 10, pp. 357–359. The title for this subchapter challenges John William Ward, *Andrew Jackson: Symbol for an Age* (New York, 1955). Jackson was also the symbol of destruction and death for Native Americans.

2. Michael Paul Rogin, *Fathers and Children: Andrew Jackson and the Subjugation of the American Indian* (New York, 1975), pp. 140–141.

3. Jackson to Thomas Pinckney, February 16 and 17, 1814, May 18, 1814, in John Spencer Bassett (ed.), *Correspondence of Andrew Jackson,* 6 vols. (Washington, D.C., 1926), vol. 1, pp. 463–465, vol. 2, pp. 2–3; Jackson to Mrs. Jackson, April 1, 1814, in Bassett (ed.), *Correspondence,* vol. 1, p. 493.

4. Jackson, Proclamation, April 2, 1814, Fort Williams, in Bassett (ed.), *Correspondence,* vol. 1, p. 494.

5. Jackson, Special Message to the Senate, February 22, 1831, in James D. Richardson (ed.), *A Compilation of the Messages and Papers of the Presidents, 1789–1897* (Washington, D.C., 1897), vol. 2, p. 541; Rogin, *Fathers and Children,* p. 213.

6. Mary E. Young, "Indian Removal and Land Allotment: The Civilized Tribes and Jacksonian Justice," *American Historical Review,* vol. 64 (October 1958), p. 36.

7. Jackson, speech to the Chickasaws; Jackson, First Annual Message to Congress, in Richardson (ed.), *Papers of the Presidents,* vol. 2, pp. 241, 456–458.

8. Jackson to Captain James Gadsden, October 12, 1829, in Bassett (ed.), *Correspondence,* vol. 4, p. 81; Jackson to Major David Haley, October 15, 1829, quoted in Annie Heloise Abel, *The History of Events Resulting in Indian Consolidation West of the Mississippi* (Washington, D.C., 1906), p. 373; Jackson, speech to Chickasaws, Special Message to Senate, in Richardson (ed.), *Papers of the Presidents,* vol. 2, pp. 241, 541.

9. Jackson, Proclamation, April 2, 1814, Fort Williams, in Bassett (ed.), *Correspondence,* vol. 1, p. 494; Jackson, Second Annual Message, in Richardson (ed.), *Papers of the Presidents,* vol. 2, pp. 520–522.

10. Rogin, *Fathers and Children,* p. 231.

11. F. P. Prucha, "Introduction," in D. S. Otis, *The Dawes Act and the Allotment of Indian Lands* (Norman, Okla., 1973), p. ix.

12. T. N. Campbell, "Choctaw Subsistence: Ethnographic Notes from the Lincecum Manuscript," *Florida Anthropologist,* vol. 12 (1959), pp. 16–19; John R. Swanton (ed.), "An Early Account of the Choctaw Indians," *Memoirs of the American Anthropological Association,* vol. 5 (April–June 1918), pp. 58–59.

13. Richard White, *Roots of Dependency: Subsistence, Environment, and Social Change among the Choctaws, Pawnees, and Navajos* (Lincoln, Nebr., 1983), pp. 41, 42.

14. White, *Roots of Dependency,* pp. 102, 133–135.

15. Arthur H. DeRosier, Jr., *The Removal of Choctaw Indians* (New York, 1972), pp. 104, 126, 122; White, *Roots of Dependency,* p. 143.

16. DeRosier, *Removal of Choctaw Indians,* p. 128; Angie Debo, *The Rise and Fall of the Choctaw Republic* (Norman, Okla., 1934), p. 70.

17. DeRosier, *Removal of Choctaw Indians,* p. 124.

18. Grant Foreman, *Indian Removal: The Emigration of the Five Civilized Tribes of Indians* (Norman, Okla., 1972), p. 73.

19. Rogin, *Fathers and Children,* p. 230; Jackson to General John Coffee, April 7, 1832, in Bassett (ed.), *Correspondence,* vol. 4, p. 430.

20. Foreman, *Indian Removal,* pp. 56, 64, 98.

21. Alexis de Tocqueville, *Democracy in America,* 2 vols. (New York, 1945), vol. 1, pp. 352–353, 364.

22. Debo, *Choctaw Republic* (Norman, Okla., 1972), p. 56; Wayne Moquin (ed.), *Great Documents in American Indian History* (New York, 1973), pp. 151–153.

23. DeRosier, *Removal of Choctaw Indians,* p. 163.

24. James Mooney, *Myths of the Cherokee,* published in United States Bureau of Ethnology, *Nineteenth Annual Report, 1897–98* (Washington, D.C., 1900), pp. 239–240.

25. Foreman, *Indian Removal,* p. 229.

26. John Ross to General Council, July 10–16, 1830, in Gary E. Moulton (ed.), *The Papers of Chief John Ross,* 2 vols. (Norman, Okla., 1985), vol. 1, p. 190; Ross, "To the Cherokees," April 14, 1831, in Moulton (ed.), *Papers of Ross,* vol. 1, p. 218; Ross to Cass, February 6, 1834, in Moulton (ed.), *Papers of Ross,* vol. 1, p. 275; Ross to Jackson, March 12, 1834, in Moulton (ed.), *Papers of Ross,* vol. 1, p. 277.

27. Rogin, *Fathers and Children,* p. 227; Ross, "Annual Message," October 12, 1835, in Moulton (ed.), *Papers of Ross,* vol. 1, p. 358.

28. Ross, "To the Senate," March 8, 1836, in Moulton (ed.), *Papers of Ross,* vol. 1, p. 394; Mooney, *Myths of the Cherokee,* p. 126–127.

29. Mooney, *Myths of the Cherokee,* p. 127.

30. Foreman, *Indian Removal,* p. 283.

31. Foreman, *Indian Removal,* pp. 286–288.

32. George Hicks to John Ross, November 4, 1838, in Moulton (ed.), *Papers of Ross,* vol. 1, p. 687.

33. Foreman, *Indian Removal,* pp. 309, 296; Thurman Wilkins, *Cherokee Tragedy: The Story of the Ridge Family and of the Decimation of a People* (New York, 1970), p. 314.

34. Gloria Levitas, Frank Vivelo, and Jacquelien Vivelo (eds.), *American Indian Prose and Poetry* (New York, 1974), p. 180; Wilkins, *Cherokee Tragedy,* p. 314.

35. George A. Dorsey, *The Pawnee Mythology* (Washington, D.C., 1906), pp. 21–28.

36. Frances Densmore, *Pawnee Music,* in Smithsonian Institution, *Bureau of Ethnology,* Bulletin 93 (Washington, D.C., 1929), p. 32; Gene Weltfish, *The Lost Universe* (New York, 1965), p. 203; Dorsey, *Pawnee Mythology,* p. 213.

37. Martha Royce Blaine, *Pawnee Passage: 1870–1875* (Norman, Okla., 1990), p. 81.

38. David J. Wishart, "The Dispossession of the Pawnee," in *Annals of the Association of American Geographers,* vol. 69, no. 3 (September 1979), p. 386; John B. Dunbar, "The Pawnee Indians: Their Habits and Customs," *Magazine of American History,* vol. 5, no. 5 (November 1880), pp. 327–328, 331; White, *Roots of Dependency,* p. 188.

39. Levitas et al. (eds.), *American Indian Prose and Poetry,* p. 41; John B. Dunbar, "The Pawnee Indians: Their History and Ethnology," *Magazine of American History,* vol. 4, no. 4 (April 1880), p. 275; James R.

Murie, *Ceremonies of the Pawnee,* in Douglas R. Parks (ed.), *Smithsonian Contributions to Anthropology,* no. 27 (Washington, D.C., 1981), pp. 80–82.

40. Dunbar, "Pawnee Indians," p. 276.

41. White, *Roots of Dependency,* pp. 191–192; Wishart, "Dispossession of the Pawnee," p. 387.

42. Jackson, Third Annual Message to Congress, 1831, in Richardson (ed.), *Papers of the Presidents,* vol. 2, p. 545.

43. "The Spirit of the Times; or the Fast Age," *Democratic Review,* vol. 33 (September 1853), pp. 260–261.

44. Alfred L. Riggs, "What Shall We Do with the Indians?" *The Nation,* vol. 67 (October 31, 1867), p. 356.

45. Ulysses S. Grant, First Annual Message, 1869, in Richardson (ed.), *Papers of the Presidents,* vol. 9, p. 3993.

46. Robert G. Athearn, *William Tecumseh Sherman and the Settlement of the West* (Norman, Okla., 1956), pp. 324–325.

47. Francis Amasa Walker, *The Indian Question* (Boston, 1874), p. 5; Ira G. Clark, *Then Came the Railroads: The Century from Steam to Diesel in the Southwest* (Norman, Okla., 1958), pp. 121, 128.

48. Levitas et al. (eds.), *American Indian Prose and Poetry,* p. 229.

49. Wishart, "Dispossession of the Pawnee," p. 392.

50. White, *Roots of Dependency,* p. 201; Blaine, *Pawnee Passage,* p. 215; Dunbar, "Pawnee Indians," p. 251; Weltfish, *Lost Universe,* p. 4.

51. Densmore, *Pawnee Music,* p. 90; White, *Roots of Dependency,* p. 210; Blaine, *Pawnee Passage,* p. 143; Peter Nabokov (ed.), *Native American Testimony: A Chronicle of Indian-White Relations from Prophecy to the Present, 1492–1992* (New York, 1991), p. 40.

52. E. L. Sabin, *Building the Pacific Railway* (Philadelphia, 1919), p. 233.

Chapter 5: *"No More Peck o' Corn"*

1. James Madison, quoted in Michael Paul Rogin, *Fathers and Children: Andrew Jackson and the Subjugation of the American Indian* (New York, 1975), p. 319.

2. David Walker, *Appeal to the Colored Citizens of the World* (New York, 1965; originally published in 1829), pp. 72, 93, 34.

3. Leon Litwack, *North of Slavery: The Negro in the Free States, 1790–1860* (Chicago, 1965), p. 234; William Chambers, *Things as They Are in America* (Philadelphia, 1854), p. 354. Litwack's study is the standard work on this subject.

4. Alexis de Tocqueville, *Democracy in America,* 2 vols. (New York, 1945; originally published in 1835), vol. 1, pp. 373–374.

5. Litwack, *North of Slavery,* p. 120.

6. Robert A. Warner, *New Haven Negroes: A Social History* (New

Haven, Conn., 1940), p. 34; Tocqueville, *Democracy,* vol. 1, p. 373; Litwack, *North of Slavery,* pp. 66, 98, 155–156; Frank U. Quillan, *The Color Line in Ohio: A History of Race Prejudice in a Typical Northern State* (Ann Arbor, Mich., 1913), p. 55; Thomas F. Gossett, *Race: The History of an Idea in America* (Dallas, 1963), p. 74.

7. Litwack, *North of Slavery,* p. 164; *Richmond Jeffersonian,* in Emma Lou Thornbrough, *The Negro in Indiana: A Study of a Minority* (n.p., 1957), p. 62.

8. Tocqueville, *Democracy in America,* vol. I, p. 373; Eugene H. Berwanger, *The Frontier against Slavery: Western Anti-Negro Prejudice and the Slavery Extension Controversy* (Urbana, Ill., 1967), pp. 20, 36; Litwack, *North of Slavery,* p. 77.

9. Thornbrough, *Negro in Indiana,* p. 163; Litwack, *North of Slavery,* pp. 149–150.

10. Litwack, *North of Slavery,* pp. 153–154.

11. Kenneth Stampp, *The Peculiar Institution: Slavery in the Antebellum South* (New York, 1956), p. 44; Frederick Law Olmsted, *The Slave States* (New York, 1959; originally published as *A Journey in the Back Country* in 1860), pp. 176–177. Stampp's study is essential for an understanding of the institution of slavery.

12. Stampp, *Peculiar Institution,* pp. 44, 74.

13. Stampp, *Peculiar Institution,* pp. 163, 146.

14. George Fitzhugh, *Sociology for the South,* in Harvey Wish (ed.), *Antebellum: Writings of George Fitzhugh and Hinton Rowan Helper on Slavery* (New York, 1960), pp. 88, 89; Bertram W. Doyle, *Etiquette of Race Relations in the South* (Chicago, 1931), p. 54.

15. John Hope Franklin, "The Enslavement of Free Negroes in North Carolina," *Journal of Negro History,* vol. 29 (October 1944), p. 405; William Gilmore Simms, *The Yamassee* (New York, 1962), p. 392.

16. Edward Pollard, *Black Diamonds Gathered in the Darkey Homes of the South* (New York, 1859), pp. 57–58; Benjamin F. Perry, in Lillian Kibler, *Benjamin F. Perry: South Carolina Unionist* (Durham, N.C., 1946), p. 282; *Natchez Free Trader,* September 20, 1858; Gustave A. Breaux, Diary, January 1, 1859, Breaux Papers, Tulane University Library, New Orleans, Louisiana.

17. J. J. Pettigrew, in *De Bow's Review,* vol. 25 (September 1858), p. 293; Roger Pryor, in *De Bow's Review,* vol. 24 (June 1858), p. 582; *Galveston News,* December 6, 1856; *Charleston Mercury,* October 20, 1858; J. G. M. Ramsey to L. W. Spratt, April 23, 1858, Ramsey Papers, University of North Carolina Library.

18. Percy Lee Rainwater, *Mississippi, Storm Center of Secession, 1856–1861* (Baton Rouge, La., 1938), p. 12; Charles G. Sellers, Jr., *The Southerner as American* (Chapel Hill, N.C., 1960), p. 48; Ernest T. Thompson, *Presbyterians in the South, 1607–1861* (Richmond, 1963), p. 533; *Galveston News,* December 5, 1856.

19. *De Bow's Review,* vol. 14 (1853), p. 276, italics added; William W. Freehling, *Prelude to Civil War: The Nullification Controversy in South Carolina, 1816–1832* (New York, 1966), p. 59.

20. Fredericka Bremer, *The Homes of the New World: Impressions of America,* 3 vols. (London, 1853), vol. 2, p. 451; Frances A. Kemble, *Journal of a Residence on a Georgia Plantation in 1838–1839* (New York, 1961; originally published in 1863), p. 342; *New Orleans Picayune,* December 24, 1856.

21. Stampp, *Peculiar Institution,* p. 87; U. B. Phillips, *Life and Labor in the Old South* (Boston, 1929), p. 276.

22. William Francis Allen et al., *Slave Songs of the United States* (New York, 1867), p. 48; Raymond and Alice H. Bauer, "Day to Day Resistance to Slavery," *Journal of Negro History,* vol. 27 (1942), pp. 388–419; Stampp, *Peculiar Institution,* pp. 88, 90.

23. John Dollard, *Caste and Class in a Southern Town* (New York, 1949), p. 390; Leon Litwack, *Been in the Storm So Long: The Aftermath of Slavery* (New York, 1979), p. 221.

24. Sarah Logue to "Jarm," February 20, 1860, and J. W. Loguen to Mrs. Sarah Logue, reprinted in *Boston Liberator,* April 27, 1860.

25. Stampp, *Peculiar Institution,* p. 132; Phillips, *Life and Labor in the South,* p. 209; Nat Turner and T. R. Gray, *The Confessions of Nat Turner,* in Herbert Aptheker, *Nat Turner's Rebellion* (New York, 1968), appendix, pp. 136, 138, 130–131.

26. Quoted in Stampp, *Peculiar Institution,* pp. 100, 127; Eugene Genovese, *Roll, Jordan, Roll: The World the Slaves Made* (New York, 1974), pp. 300, 318, 602. Genovese's study offers an understanding of slavery from the viewpoint of the slaves as men and women.

27. Richard Wade, *Slavery in the Cities: The South, 1820–1860* (New York, 1964), p. 39.

28. Wade, *Slavery in the Cities,* p. 49.

29. Wade, *Slavery in the Cities,* p. 279.

30. Wade, *Slavery in the Cities,* pp. 245–246; Eugene Genovese, *The Political Economy of Slavery* (New York, 1965), p. 226.

31. Litwack, *Been in the Storm So Long,* pp. 6, 21. This is the best book on what it felt like to be suddenly free.

32. Litwack, *Been in the Storm So Long,* p. 7; E. Franklin Frazier, *The Negro Family in the United States* (Chicago, 1939), p. 79; Genovese, *Roll, Jordan, Roll,* p. 133.

33. Litwack, *Been in the Storm So Long,* p. 21; Bell Wiley, *Southern Negroes, 1861–1865* (New Haven, Conn., 1938), pp. 72, 70.

34. Litwack, *Been in the Storm So Long,* p. 12; Genovese, *Roll, Jordan, Roll,* pp. 105, 581.

35. Litwack, *Been in the Storm So Long,* pp. 19, 59; Edwin D. Hoffman, "From Slavery to Self-Reliance," *Journal of Negro History,* vol. 41 (January 1956), pp. 13–14.

36. Litwack, *Been in the Storm So Long*, pp. 144, 135; Wiley, *Southern Negroes*, p. 83; Eugene Genovese, *Roll, Jordan, Roll*, p. 101.

37. Harriet A. Jacobs, *Incidents in the Life of a Slave Girl, written by herself* (Cambridge, Mass., 1987; originally published in 1857), pp. 77, 27, 55; Mary B. Chestnut, *A Diary from Dixie* (Cambridge, Mass., 1961), pp. 21–22.

38. Frederick Douglass, *Narrative of the Life of Frederick Douglass* (New York, 1968; originally published in 1845), p. 26.

39. Douglass, *Life and Times*, pp. 27–30.

40. Douglass, *Life and Times*, pp. 76–78.

41. Douglass, *Life and Times*, pp. 78–82.

42. Frederick Douglass, *My Bondage and My Freedom* (New York, 1969; originally published in 1855), pp. 315–316.

43. Douglass, *Life and Times*, pp. 75–94.

44. Douglass, *Life and Times*, pp. 112, 186.

45. Douglass, *Life and Times*, pp. 124–125.

46. Douglass, *Life and Times*, pp. 125–134.

47. Douglass, *Life and Times*, pp. 140, 142–143.

48. Douglass, *Life and Times*, pp. 271–275; Douglass, in *Boston Liberator*, June 8, 1849; *Douglass's Monthly*, November 1859; Douglass, letter to John Brown, in *Boston Liberator*, November 11, 1859.

49. Douglass, in *Boston Liberator*, November 11, 1859.

50. Douglass, *Life and Times*, pp. 440–452.

51. Douglass, letter to H. G. Warner, in *Boston Liberator*, October 6, 1848; Douglass, in Philip S. Foner, *The Life and Writings of Frederick Douglass*, 4 vols. (New York, 1950), (ed.) vol. 1, p. 423, vol. 2, p. 421, vol. 4, pp. 116, 427; *Rochester North Star*, September 15, 1848; Douglass, quoted in Benjamin Quarles, *Frederick Douglass* (New York, 1968), p. 35; Douglass, *Life and Times*, p. 534; Douglass to Francis Jackson, January 29, 1846, Anti-Slavery Collection, Boston Public Library.

52. Douglass, *Life and Times*, pp. 284–290; Douglass, "The Future of the Colored Race," in *The North American Review*, in Foner (ed.), *Life and Writings*, vol. 4, pp. 193–196.

53. Douglass, quoted in Frank A. Rollin, *Life and Public Services of Martin R. Delany* (Boston, 1883), p. 19; Martin Delany, *Official Report of the Niger Valley Exploring Party*, reprinted in Howard H. Bell, *Search for a Place: Black Separatism and Africa, 1860* (Ann Arbor, Mich., 1969), p. 121.

54. Bell, *Search for a Place*, p. 121.

55. Martin Delany, "American Civilization—Treatment of the Colored People in the United States," *Rochester North Star*, March 30, 1849.

56. Student petition to the faculty, December 10, 1850, Countway Library, Harvard Medical School.

57. Records of the Medical Faculty, vol. 2, Minutes for December 16, 1859; drafts of letters to the Massachusetts Colonization Society and to Abraham R. Thompson, Countway Library.

58. Delany, *The Condition, Elevation, Emigration, and Destiny of the Colored People of the United States* (New York, 1969; originally published in 1852), pp. 42, 47–48, 190, 197–198; Delany, "Political Destiny," in Rollin, *Delany,* p. 358.

59. Delany, "Domestic Economy," in *Rochester North Star,* March 23, 1849; Delany, in *Rochester North Star,* April 28, 1848; Delany, *Condition, Elevation, Emigration,* pp. 44–46, 192–195.

60. Delany, "Political Destiny," pp. 330–335, 355.

61. Delany, *Condition, Elevation, Emigration,* p. 44.

62. Delany, *Condition, Elevation, Emigration,* pp. 329–334; 183, 191, 205, 210.

63. Delany, *Condition, Elevation, Emigration,* pp. 48, 49, 67–84, 109, 203; "Platform: or Declaration of Sentiments of the Cleveland Convention," in Herbert Aptheker (ed.), *A Documentary History of the Negro People in the United States,* 2 vols. (New York, 1967), vol. 1, p. 365; Delany, *Official Report,* p. 32.

64. Delany, *Official Report,* p. 64.

65. Douglass, *Life and Times,* pp. 335–336; Delany, in Victor Ullman, *Martin R. Delany: The Beginnings of Black Nationalism* (Boston, 1971), p. 312.

66. Leon Litwack, *Been in the Storm So Long,* p. 64.

67. James McPherson (ed.), *The Negro's Civil War: How American Negroes Felt and Acted during the War for the Union* (New York, 1965), p. 298.

68. Litwack, *Been in the Storm So Long,* p. 117.

69. Litwack, *Been in the Storm So Long,* p. 399; McPherson (ed.), *Negro's Civil War,* p. 294.

70. Litwack, *Been in the Storm So Long,* pp. 401–402.

71. La Wanda Cox, "The Promise of Land for the Freedmen," *Mississippi Valley Historical Review,* vol. 45 (December 1958), p. 429; James McPherson, *The Struggle for Equality: Abolitionists and the Negro in the Civil War and Reconstruction* (Princeton, N.J., 1964), p. 409; Hoffman, "From Slavery to Self-Reliance," pp. 22, 27.

72. Joel Williamson, *After Slavery: The Negro in South Carolina during Reconstruction, 1861–1877* (Chapel Hill, N.C., 1965), p. 54; McPherson, *Struggle for Equality,* p. 416; Ullman, *Delany,* p. 342.

73. Jacqueline Jones, *Labor of Love, Labor of Sorrow: Black Women, Work, and the Family from Slavery to the Present* (New York, 1985), p. 54.

74. "The Life Story of a Negro Peon," in Hamilton Holt (ed.), *The Life Stories of Undistinguished Americans as Told by Themselves* (New York, 1906), pp. 183–199; Negro folk song, in Edmund David Cronon, *Black Moses: The Story of Marcus Garvey and the Universal Improvement Association* (Madison, Wis., 1966), p. 21.

75. C. Vann Woodward, *Origins of the New South, 1877–1913* (Baton Rouge, La., 1951), p. 112.

76. Paul M. Gaston, *The New South Creed: A Study in Southern Mythmaking* (New York, 1970), p. 147; Broadus Mitchell, *The Rise of Cotton Mills in the South* (Baltimore, 1921), p. 214; Sterling D. Spero and Abram L. Harris, *The Black Worker: The Negro and the Labor Movement* (Port Washington, N.Y., 1966), p. 246; Woodward, *Origins of the New South,* p. 360; Paul B. Worthman, "Working Class Mobility in Birmingham, Alabama, 1880–1914," in Tamara K. Hareven (ed.), *Anonymous Americans: Explorations in Nineteenth-Century Social History* (Englewood Cliffs, N.J., 1971), p. 175.

77. James Creelman, in *New York World,* September 18, 1895, reprinted in Louis R. Harlan (ed.), *The Booker T. Washington Papers,* 4 vols. (Urbana, Ill., 1975), vol. 4, pp. 13, 14.

78. Booker T. Washington, "Atlanta Address," in *Up from Slavery* (New York, 1963; originally published in 1901), pp. 153–158.

79. James Creelman, in *New York World,* reprinted in Louis R. Harlan (ed.), *The Booker T. Washington Papers,* 4 vols. (Urbana, Ill., 1975), vol. 4, p. 3.

80. August Meier, *Negro Thought in America, 1880–1915* (Ann Arbor, Mich., 1966), p. 107.

81. Washington, *Up from Slavery,* pp. 27, 83, 146; Booker T. Washington, "The Educational Outlook in the South," *Journal of the Proceedings and Addresses of the National Educational Association, Session of the Year 1884, at Madison, Wis.* (Boston, 1885), pp. 125–130.

82. Litwack, *Been in the Storm So Long,* p. 399; Rayford Logan, *The Negro in American Life and Thought: The Nadir, 1877–1901* (New York, 1954).

Chapter 6: Fleeing "the Tyrant's Heel"

1. Leon Litwack, *North of Slavery: The Negro in the Free States, 1790–1860* (Chicago, 1965), p. 163; David R. Roediger, *The Wages of Whiteness: Race and the Making of the American Working Class* (London, 1991), p. 134.

2. Kerby A. Miller, *Emigrants and Exiles: Ireland and the Irish Exodus to North America* (New York, 1985), p. 105; Kerby Miller, Bruce Boling, and David Doyle, "Emigrants and Exiles: Irish Cultures and Irish Emigration to North America, 1790–1922," *Irish Historical Studies,* vol. 40 (1980), p. 112; Oliver MacDonagh, "The Irish Famine Emigration to the United States," in *Perspectives in American History,* vol. 10 (1976), p. 358; Robert L. Wright (ed.), *Irish Emigrant Ballads and Songs* (Bowling Green, Ohio, 1975), pp. 35, 37. Miller's book is filled with archivally based information. Miller has done for the Irish immigrants what Irving

Howe has done for the Jewish immigrants in *World of Our Fathers* (New York, 1976). The theme of "exile" is emphasized in Miller's study.

3. Miller, *Emigrants and Exiles,* pp. 100, 99; Wright (ed.), *Irish Emigrant Ballads,* pp. 592, 165, 129.

4. Lawrence J. McCaffrey, *The Irish Diaspora in America* (Washington, D.C., 1984), pp. 17–18; Wright (ed.), *Irish Emigrant Ballads,* p. 70; Arnold Schrier, *Ireland and the American Emigration, 1850–1900* (New York, 1970), p. 45.

5. Owen Dudley Edwards, "The American Image of Ireland: A Study of Its Early Phases," *Perspectives in American History,* vol. 4 (1970), p. 236; Miller, *Emigrants and Exiles,* p. 32; Wright (ed.), *Irish Emigrant Ballads,* pp. 96, 50.

6. MacDonagh, "Irish Famine Emigration," p. 366; Miller, *Emigrants and Exiles,* p. 241.

7. Miller, *Emigrants and Exiles,* pp. 139, 197, 202; Schrier, *Ireland and the American Emigration,* p. 95.

8. Miller, *Emigrants and Exiles,* pp. 34, 53; Hamilton Holt, "Life Story of an Irish Cook," in Holt (ed.), *Life Stories of Undistinguished Americans as Told by Themselves* (New York, 1906), p. 144.

9. Miller, *Emigrants and Exiles,* p. 281.

10. Hasia R. Diner, *Erin's Daughters in America: Irish Immigrant Women in the Nineteenth Century* (Baltimore, Md., 1983), p. 2; Wright, *Irish Emigrant Ballads,* p. 46. Diner's study is an excellent example of the ways women's history can illuminate general understanding of immigration.

11. Miller, *Emigrants and Exiles,* pp. 285–287; Michael Kraus, *Immigration: The American Mosaic* (New York, 1966), p. 130; Schrier, *Ireland and the American Emigration,* p. 42; Wright (ed.), *Irish Emigrant Ballads,* p. 3.

12. Oscar Handlin, *Boston's Immigrants: A Study in Acculturation* (New York, 1968), p. 51; MacDonagh, "Irish Famine Emigration," pp. 431, 407; Miller, *Emigrants and Exiles,* p. 298.

13. McCaffrey, *Irish Diaspora,* pp. 71, 72; Wright (ed.), *Irish Emigrant Ballads,* p. 126.

14. MacDonagh, "Irish Famine Emigration," pp. 403, 410–411.

15. Diner, *Erin's Daughters,* p. 8; Miller, *Emigrants and Exiles,* p. 360.

16. Carl Wittke, *The Irish in America* (Baton Rouge, 1956), pp. 32–33; Buckley, *Tour in America,* p. 164; Wright (ed.), *Irish Emigrant Ballads,* p. 533.

17. Wright (ed.), *Irish Emigrant Ballads,* p. 539; Wittke, *Irish in America,* p. 3.

18. Wittke, *Irish in America,* p. 37; Diner, *Erin's Daughters,* p. 60; Elizabeth Gurley Flynn, *I Speak My Own Piece* (New York, 1955), p. 20; Miller, *Emigrants and Exiles,* pp. 267, 318; Stephan Thernstrom, *Poverty and Progress: Social Mobility in a Nineteenth Century City* (Cambridge,

Mass., 1964), p. 27; Michael B. Buckley, *Diary of a Tour in America* (Dublin, 1886), p. 142; McCaffrey, *Irish Diaspora*, p. 71.

19. Miller, *Emigrants and Exiles*, p. 318; Anne Halley, "Afterword," in Mary Doyle Curran, *The Parish and the Hill* (New York, 1986), pp. 230–231; Kerby Miller, "Assimilation and Alienation: Irish Emigrants' Responses to Industrial America, 1871–1921," in Drudy (ed.), *Irish in America,* p. 105.

20. Frederick Rudolph, "Chinamen in Yankeedom: Anti-Unionism in Massachusetts in 1870," *American Historical Review*, vol. 53, no. 1 (October 1947), p. 10.

21. *The Nation*, vol. 10 (June 23, 1870), p. 397.

22. William Shanks, "Chinese Skilled Labor," *Scribner's Monthly*, vol. 2 (September 1871), pp. 495–496.

23. *The Nation*, vol. 10 (June 30, 1870), p. 412; Rudolph, "Chinamen in Yankeedom," p. 23.

24. Frank Norton, "Our Labor System and the Chinese," *Scribner's Monthly*, vol. 2 (May 1871), p. 70.

25. Roediger, *The Wages of Whiteness*, pp. 133, 146; Michael B. Katz, *The Irony of School Reform: Educational Innovation in Mid-Nineteenth Century Massachusetts* (Boston, 1972), pp. 124, 120–121, 123, 41–43, 172, 88; Herbert G. Gutman, *Work, Culture and Society in Industrializing America* (New York, 1977), pp. 1–27, 71; Stanley K. Schultz, *The Culture Factory: Boston Public Schools, 1789–1860* (New York, 1973), p. 243; Herbert G. Gutman, *The Black Family in Slavery and Freedom, 1750–1925* (New York, 1976), p. 299; Litwack, *North of Slavery*, p. 163.

26. Halley, "Afterword," p. 27; Thernstrom, *Poverty and Progress*, p. 27; Schultz, *Culture Factory*, p. 289; Katz, *Irony of Early School Reform*, pp. 182–183, 43.

27. Roediger, *Wages of Whiteness*, pp. 136–137.

28. Frederick Law Olmsted, *The Slave States Before the Civil War* (New York, 1859), p. 76; Litwack, *North of Slavery*, p. 166.

29. Roediger, *Wages of Whiteness*, p. 137.

30. Litwack, *North of Slavery*, p. 163; Gutman, *Black Family*, p. 301; "Folk-Lore Scrap-Book," in *Journal of American Folk-Lore*, vol. 12, no. 46 (July–September 1899), p. 227.

31. Litwack, *North of Slavery*, p. 163; Roediger, *Wages of Whiteness*, p. 137.

32. Gilbert Osofsky, *Harlem: The Making of a Ghetto, Negro New York, 1890–1930* (New York, 1966), p. 45.

33. Schultz, *Culture Factory*, p. 193; Eugene Genovese, *Roll, Jordan, Roll: The World the Slaves Made* (New York, 1974), p. 24; Litwack, *North of Slavery*, p. 163; Handlin, *Boston's Immigrants*, p. 133.

34. Schultz, *Culture Factory*, p. 193; Wittke, *Irish in America*, p. 143; Albon P. Man, Jr., "Labor Competition and the New York Draft Riots of

1863," *Journal of Negro History,* vol. 36, no. 4 (October 1951), pp. 386, 377, 378.

35. Adrian Cook, *Armies of the Streets: The New York City Draft Riots of 1863* (Lexington, Ky., 1974), p. 205; Stephen Steinberg, *The Ethnic Myth: Race, Ethnicity, and Class in America* (New York, 1981), p. 177.

36. Cook, *Armies in the Streets,* pp. 80, 123, 97; Iver Bernstein, *The New York City Draft Riots: Their Significance for American Society and Politics in the Age of the Civil War* (New York, 1990), pp. 17–42. Man, "Labor Competition," p. 401; Wittke, *Irish in America,* p. 146.

37. Litwack, *North of Slavery,* pp. 158–159; Diner, *Erin's Daughters,* pp. 31, 30; Steinberg, *Ethnic Myth,* p. 162.

38. Janet A. Nolan, *Ourselves Alone: Women's Emigration from Ireland, 1885–1920* (Lexington, Ky., 1989), pp. 23, 22; Diner, *Erin's Daughters,* p. 10; Lynn H. Lees and John Model, "The Irish Countryman Urbanized: A Comparative Perspective on the Famine Migration," *Journal of Urban History,* vol. 3, no. 4 (August 1977), p. 392; Miller, *Emigrants and Exiles,* p. 408.

39. Miller, *Emigrants and Exiles,* p. 407.

40. Miller, *Emigrants and Exiles,* p. 408; Schrier, *Ireland and American Emigration,* p. 26; Diner, *Erin's Daughters,* p. 90; Wright (ed.), *Irish Emigrant Ballads,* p. 100.

41. Diner, *Erin's Daughters,* p. 92.

42. Steinberg, *Ethnic Myth,* pp. 154, 155; Lucy Maynard Salmon, *Domestic Service* (New York, 1897), p. 79; Diner, *Erin's Daughters,* p. 83.

43. Diner, *Erin's Daughters,* p. 90; Schrier, *Ireland and American Emigration,* p. 29.

44. Diner, *Erin's Daughters,* p. 94.

45. Holt, "Life Story of an Irish Cook," p. 146; Steinberg, *Ethnic Myth,* p. 158; Helen Campbell, *Prisoners of Poverty: Women Wage-Workers, Their Trades and Their Lives* (Boston, 1900), p. 226.

46. Campbell, *Prisoners of Poverty,* pp. 227, 229, 226, 15–16.

47. Steinberg, *Ethnic Myth,* p. 157; Campbell, *Prisoners of Poverty,* p. 224.

48. Steinberg, *Ethnic Myth,* p. 157; Diner, *Erin's Daughters,* p. 75; Flynn, *I Speak My Own Piece,* p. 24.

49. Miller, *Emigrants and Exiles,* p. 505; Philip S. Foner (ed.), *The Factory Girls* (Urbana, Ill., 1977), pp. 6–7; Diner, *Erin's Daughters,* p. 75.

50. Schrier, *Ireland and American Emigration,* p. 28; Diner, *Erin's Daughters,* pp. 77, 78.

51. Schrier, *Ireland and American Emigration,* p. 24; Carol Groneman, "Working-Class Immigrant Women in Mid-Nineteenth-Century New York: The Irish Woman's Experience," *Journal of Urban History,* vol. 4, no. 3 (May 1978), p. 269.

52. Schrier, *Ireland and American Emigration,* p. 38; Miller, "Assimilation and Alienation," p. 97.

53. David M. Katzman, *Seven Days a Week: Women and Domestic Service in Industrializing America* (New York, 1978), pp. 70, 231.

54. Thernstrom, *Poverty and Progress*, pp. 132–133; Miller, *Emigrants and Exiles*, pp. 496, 508.

55. Marcia Graham Synnott, *The Half-Opened Door: Discrimination and Admissions at Harvard, Yale, and Princeton, 1900–1970* (Westport, Conn., 1979), pp. 40–44, 245.

56. Steven P. Erie, *Rainbow's End: Irish-Americans and the Dilemmas of Urban Machine Politics, 1840–1985* (Berkeley, 1988), p. 28; David M. Emmons, *The Butte Irish: Class and Ethnicity in an American Mining Town, 1875–1925* (Urbana, Ill., 1989), p. 6; Schrier, *Ireland and American Emigration*, p. 130; Flynn, *I Speak My Own Piece*, p. 19.

57. Wittke, *Irish in America*, p. 26.

58. Erie, *Rainbow's End*, pp. 248, 2, 5, 8, 87; Nathan Glazer and Daniel P. Moynihan, *Beyond the Melting Pot* (Cambridge, Mass., 1963), pp. 218, 223–230.

59. Miller, *Emigrants and Exiles*, p. 500; David Montgomery, "The Irish and the American Labor Movement," in David N. Doyle and Owen D. Edwards (eds.), *America and Ireland, 1776–1976* (Westport, Conn., 1980), pp. 211–212.

60. Roediger, *Wages of Whiteness*, pp. 133–166.

61. Douglas V. Shaw, *The Making of an Immigrant City: Ethnic and Cultural Conflict in Jersey City, New Jersey, 1850–1877* (New York, 1976), p. 2; Kathleen Donovan, "Good Old Pat: An Irish-American Stereotype in Decline," *Eire-Ireland: A Journal of Irish Studies*, vol. 15, no. 2 (fall 1980), p. 9; Flynn, *I Speak My Own Piece*, p. 13.

62. Miller, *Emigrants and Exiles*, pp. 508, 511, 512.

Chapter 7: "Foreigners in Their Native Land"

1. Thomas Jefferson to James Monroe, November 24, 1801, in Paul L. Ford (ed.), *The Works of Thomas Jefferson*, 20 vols. (New York, 1892–1899), vol. 9, p. 317. For the title of this chapter, see Juan Nepomuceno Seguin who described himself as "*a foreigner in my native land*," in David J. Weber (ed.), *Foreigners in Their Native Land: Historical Roots of the Mexican Americans* (Albuquerque, N. Mex., 1973), p. 176.

2. David J. Weber (ed.), *Foreigners in Their Native Land: Historical Roots of the Mexican Americans* (Albuquerque, N.Mex., 1973), pp. 30, 102, 104–105.

3. Weber (ed.), *Foreigners in Their Native Land*, p. 84.

4. Weber (ed.), *Foreigners in Their Native Land*, p. 89; Arnold De Leon, *They Called Them Greasers: Anglo Attitudes toward Mexicans in Texas, 1821–1900* (Austin, Tex., 1983), pp. 3, 12; Rodolfo Acuña, *Occupied America: A History of Chicanos* (New York, 1981), pp. 6–7, 8.

5. Acuña, *Occupied America*, p. 9.

6. Weber (ed.), *Foreigners in Their Native Land,* p. 92; Acuña, *Occupied America,* p. 10.

7. Reginald Horsman, *Race and Manifest Destiny: The Origins of American Racial Anglo-Saxonism* (Cambridge, Mass., 1981), pp. 213–214.

8. Weber, *Foreigners in Their Native Land,* p. 95.

9. James K. Polk, quoted in Norman Graebner, *Empire on the Pacific: A Study in American Continental Expansion* (New York, 1955), pp. 48–50.

10. Ben Kelsey, quote, in exhibit on the Bear Flag Republic, in Sonoma Mission Museum, Sonoma, California; Leonard Pitt, *The Decline of the Californios: A Social History of the Spanish-Speaking Californians, 1846–1890* (Berkeley, Calif., 1970), p. 29.

11. Pitt, *Decline of the Californios,* p. 27.

12. Vallejo to Thomas Larkin, September 15, 1846, in Myrtle McKittrick, *Vallejo: Son of California* (Portland, Oreg., 1944), pp. 275–276.

13. Walton Bean, *California: An Interpretive History* (New York, 1978), pp. 32, 36, 40, 38.

14. Douglas Monroy, *Thrown Among Strangers,* pp. 101–102, 22, 151, 153; exhibit on the Californios, Sonoma Mission Museum, Sonoma, California.

15. Bean, *California,* pp. 65–66; Pitt, *Decline of the Californios,* p. 19; Monroy, *Thrown Among Strangers,* p. 161.

16. Richard Henry Dana, *Two Years Before the Mast* (New York, 1963; originally published in 1840), pp. 136–137, 60–61, 188.

17. Monroy, *Thrown Among Strangers,* pp. 163, 164.

18. Pitt, *Decline of the Californios,* p. 29; John Bidwell, "Fremont in the Conquest of California," *Century Magazine,* reprinted by the California Department of Parks and Recreation (Sacramento, 1987), p. 522.

19. Acuña, *Occupied America,* p. 15; Carey McWilliams, *North from Mexico: The Spanish-Speaking People of the United States* (New York, 1968), pp. 102–103. McWilliams's study is a classic.

20. Albert K. Weinberg, *Manifest Destiny: A Study of Nationalist Expansionism in American History* (Chicago, 1963), p. 112.

21. Horsman, *Race and Manifest Destiny,* p. 235; Weinberg, *Manifest Destiny,* p. 111; David Montejano, *Anglos and Mexicans in the Making of Texas, 1836–1986* (Austin, Tex., 1987), pp. 14, 18. Montejano's work is an excellent and nuanced study based on original research.

22. "The Conquest of California," *Southern Quarterly Review,* vol. 15 (July 1849), pp. 411–415.

23. Weber (ed.), *Foreigners in Their Native Land,* p. 199; Acuña, *Occupied America,* p. 19. The Treaty of Guadalupe Hidalgo described the newly acquired territory as places "occupied" by U.S. forces. See the terms of the treaty in Wayne Moquin (ed.), *A Documentary History of the Mexican Americans* (New York, 1972), pp. 182–187.

24. Acuña, *Occupied America*, p. 20; Weber (ed.), *Foreigners in Their Native Land*, p. 176.

25. Robert F. Heizer and Alan F. Almquist, *The Other Californians: Prejudice and Discrimination under Spain, Mexico, and the United States to 1920* (Berkeley, Calif., 1971), p. 151.

26. Heizer and Almquist, *Other Californians*, p. 143; Weber (ed.), *Foreigners in Their Native Land*, pp. 171–173.

27. Albert Camarillo, *Chicanos in a Changing Society: From Mexican Pueblos to American Barrios in Santa Barbara and Southern California, 1848–1930* (Cambridge, Mass., 1979), pp. 23, 46, 41, 187. This is an important community study that provides insights into larger patterns of Chicano experiences.

28. Montejano, *Anglos and Mexicans*, pp. 39, 143; Weber (ed.), *Foreigners in Their Native Land*, pp. 146, 147.

29. Acuña, *Occupied America*, p. 19.

30. Mario Barrera, *Race and Class in the Southwest: A Theory of Racial Inequality* (Notre Dame, Ind., 1979), pp. 26–27. This is a very useful integration of theories of race and class and the history of Chicanos; Monroy, *Thrown Among Strangers*, p. 114; Bean, *California*, pp. 132–133.

31. Barrera, *Race and Class*, pp. 20, 19; Bean, *California*, p. 135; Heizer and Almquist, *Other Californians*, p. 150; Pitt, *Decline of the Californios*, p. 118; Weber (ed.), *Foreigners in Their Native Land*, pp. 197–199.

32. Pitt, *Decline of the Californios*, pp. 96–97; McKittrick, *Vallejo*, pp. 316, 318, 322, 324, 347; M. G. Vallejo, "What the Gold Rush Brought to California," in Valeska Bari (ed.), *The Course of Empire: First Hand Accounts of California in the Days of the Gold Rush of '49* (New York, 1931), p. 53.

33. Montejano, *Anglos and Mexicans*, p. 68.

34. Montejano, *Anglos and Mexicans*, pp. 61, 62.

35. McWilliams, *North from Mexico*, p. 77; Camarillo, *Chicanos in a Changing Society*, pp. 45–46, 34, 35–36.

36. Weber (ed.), *Foreigners in Their Native Land*, p. 199; Camarillo, *Chicanos in a Changing Society*, p. 36.

37. Montejano, *Anglos and Mexicans*, p. 158; Camarillo, *Chicanos in a Changing Society*, p. 191.

38. Montejano, *Anglos and Mexicans*, p. 113.

39. McWilliams, *North from Mexico*, p. 154; Arnold De Leon, *The Tejano Community, 1836–1900* (Albuquerque, N.Mex., 1982), pp. 55–56.

40. Montejano, *Anglos and Mexicans*, p. 114.

41. De Leon, *Greasers*, p. 62; McWilliams, *North from Mexico*, pp. 176, 158.

42. Mario T. Garcia, *Desert Immigrants: The Mexicans of El Paso, 1880–1920* (New Haven, Conn., 1981), p. 37; Camarillo, *Chicanos in a*

Changing Society, p. 97. Garcia's excellent study is based on primary sources, showing the ways the immigrants continued to think of themselves as Mexicans.

43. McWilliams, *North from Mexico,* p. 167; "Los Enganchados — the Hooked Ones," in Manuel Gamio, *Mexican Immigration to the United States* (Chicago, 1930), pp. 84–85.

44. Moquin (ed.), *A Documentary History,* p. 212; McWilliams, *North from Mexico,* p. 144.

45. Barrera, *Race and Class,* pp. 45, 46; Camarillo, *Chicanos in a Changing Society,* p. 139; Montejano, *Anglos and Mexicans,* p. 73.

46. Garcia, *Desert Immigrants,* p. 90; Barrera, *Race and Class,* p. 41.

47. Andres E. Jimenez Montoya, "Political Domination in the Labor Market: Racial Division in the Arizona Copper Industry," Working Paper 103, Institute for the Study of Social Change, University of California, Berkeley (1977), p. 20.

48. De Leon, *Tejano Community,* p. 202.

49. Tomas Almaguer, "Racial Domination and Class Conflict in Capitalist Agriculture: The Oxnard Sugar Beet Workers' Strike of 1903," *Labor History,* vol. 25, no. 3 (summer 1984), p. 334.

50. Almaguer, "Racial Domination," pp. 346, 347.

51. McWilliams, *North from Mexico,* p. 197; Weber (ed.), *Foreigners in Their Native Land,* p. 219.

52. Acuña, *Occupied America,* p. 88.

53. De Leon, *Tejano Community,* pp. 194–196; Garcia, *Desert Immigrants,* p. 224.

54. Weber (ed.), *Foreigners in Their Native Land,* pp. 248–250.

Chapter 8: Searching for Gold Mountain

1. William Shakespeare, *The Tempest* (New York, 1904), act 2, sc. 2, 60–63; Thomas Hart Benton, *Selections of Editorial Articles from the St. Louis Enquirer, on the Subject of Oregon and Texas, as Originally Published in that Paper in the Years 1818–1819* (St. Louis, 1844), pp. 5, 23; Thomas Hart Benton, Speech on the Oregon Question, May 28, 1846, U.S. Congress, Senate, *Congressional Globe,* 29th Cong., 1st sess. (Washington, D.C., 1846), pp. 915–917; Thomas Hart Benton, Speech on railroad bill, U.S. Congress, Senate, *Congressional Globe,* 30th Cong., 2nd sess. (Washington, D.C., 1849), pp. 473–474; Edward Said, *Orientalism* (New York, 1978), p. 1.

2. Aaron H. Palmer, *Memoir, geographical, political, and commercial, on the present state, productive resources, and capabilities for commerce, of Siberia, Manchuria, and the Asiatic Islands of the Northern Pacific Ocean; and on the importance of opening commercial intercourse with those countries, March 8, 1848.* U.S. Congress, Senate, 30th Cong., 1st sess., Senate misc. no. 80, pp. 1, 52, 60, 61.

3. June Mei, "Socioeconomic Origins of Emigration: Guandong to California, 1850–1882," in Lucie Cheng and Edna Bonacich (eds.), *Labor Immigration under Capitalism: Asian Workers in the United States before World War II* (Berkeley, Calif., 1984), p. 232.

4. Kil Young Zo, *Chinese Emigration into the United States, 1850–1880* (New York, 1971), p. 62; "The Celestials at Home and Abroad," *Littel's Living Age,* August 14, 1852, p. 294; Clarence E. Glick, *Sojourners and Settlers: Chinese Migrants in Hawaii* (Honolulu, 1980).

5. Circular, translation, in Diane Mei Lin Mark and Ginger Chih, *A Place Called Chinese America* (Dubuque, Iowa, 1982), p. 5; Lee Chew, interview, "Life Story of a Chinaman," in Hamilton Holt (ed.), *The Life Stories of Undistinguished Americans as Told by Themselves* (New York, 1906), pp. 287–288.

6. Folk song, translation, in Marlon K. Hom, *Songs of Gold Mountain: Cantonese Rhymes from San Francisco Chinatown* (Berkeley, Calif., 1987), p. 39.

7. "Letter of the Chinamen to His Excellency, Gov. Bigler," San Francisco, April 28, 1852, reprinted in *Littel's Living Age,* July 3, 1852, pp. 32–34; message from Dr. Bowring to Lord Malmesbury, January 5, 1853, in Zo, *Chinese Emigration,* p. 86; William Speer, *The Oldest and the Newest Empire: China and the United States* (Hartford, Conn., 1870), pp. 475–478.

8. *Daily Alta California,* May 12, 1852; Lai Chun-Chuen, *Remarks of the Chinese Merchants of San Francisco, upon Governor Bigler's Message* (San Francisco, 1855), p. 4.

9. Charles J. McClain, Jr., "The Chinese Struggle for Civil Rights in Nineteenth Century America: The First Phase, 1850–1870," *California Law Review,* vol. 72 (1984), pp. 544, 555.

10. Sucheng Chan, "Chinese Livelihood in Rural California: The Impact of Economic Change, 1860–1880," *Pacific Historical Review,* vol. 53, no. 3 (1984), pp. 281–282; Gunther Barth, *Bitter Strength: A History of the Chinese in the United States, 1850–1870* (Cambridge, Mass., 1964), pp. 114, 115; Otis Gibson, *The Chinese in America* (Cincinnati, 1877), p. 234.

11. E. L. Sabin, *Building the Pacific Railway* (Philadelphia, 1919), p. 111; Corinne K. Hoexter, *From Canton to California: The Epic of Chinese Immigration* (New York, 1976), p. 73; Jack Chen, *The Chinese in America* (New York, 1981), p. 67.

12. Thomas Chinn, H. M. Lai, and Philip Choy, *A History of the Chinese in California* (San Francisco, 1969), p. 45; Albert P. Richardson, *Beyond the Mississippi* (Hartford, Conn., 1867), p. 462; Alexander Saxton, *The Indispensable Enemy: Labor and the Anti-Chinese Movement in California* (Berkeley, Calif., 1971), p. 65.

13. Thomas W. Chinn, ed., *A History of the Chinese in California* (San Francisco, 1969), p. 46; *San Francisco Alta,* July 1 and 3, 1867; Sabin, *Building the Pacific Railway,* p. 111.

14. Paul M. Ong, "Chinese Labor in Early San Francisco: Racial Segmentation and Industrial Expansion," *Amerasia,* vol. 8, no. 1 (1981), pp. 70–75.

15. Chan, "Chinese Livelihood in Rural California," pp. 288–289, 296, 300–307; A. W. Loomis, "How Our Chinamen Are Employed," *Overland Monthly,* March 1869, p. 234.

16. Carey McWilliams, *Factories in the Field* (Santa Barbara, Calif., 1971), pp. 67, 71.

17. Loomis, "How Our Chinamen Are Employed," p. 237; Sandy Lydon, *Chinese Gold: The Chinese in the Monterey Bay Region* (Capitola, Calif., 1985), p. 286.

18. Loomis, "How Our Chinamen Are Employed," pp. 233–234; calculations in Sucheng Chan, *This Bitter-Sweet Soil: The Chinese in California Agriculture, 1860–1910* (Berkeley, Calif., 1986), pp. 305, 306, 307, 316, 317.

19. Chan, *Bitter-Sweet Soil,* pp. 332–333.

20. McWilliams, *Factories in the Field,* p. 74.

21. Paul Ong, "Chinese Laundries as an Urban Occupation in Nineteenth Century California," *The Annals of the Chinese Historical Society of the Pacific Northwest* (Seattle, 1983), p. 72.

22. Lee Chew, "Life Story of a Chinaman," pp. 289–290; Wong Chin Foo, "The Chinese in New York," *The Cosmopolitan,* vol. 5, no. 4 (June 1888), p. 298.

23. Paul Siu, *The Chinese Laundryman: A Study of Social Isolation* (New York, 1987), pp. 52, 119–123.

24. Lee Chew, "Life Story of a Chinaman," p. 296; Ong, "Chinese Laundries as an Urban Occupation," pp. 69, 70, 74; Victor and Brett de Bary Nee, *Longtime Californ': A Documentary Study of an American Chinatown* (New York, 1972), p. 22; Ng Poon Chew, "The Chinaman in America," *Chautauquan,* vol. 9, no. 4 (January 1889), p. 802.

25. Dan Caldwell, "The Negroization of the Chinese Stereotype in California," *Southern California Quarterly,* vol. 53 (June 1971), pp. 123–131; planter, quoted in Stephen Steinberg, *The Ethnic Myth: Race, Ethnicity, and Class in America* (New York, 1981), p. 184; *Vicksburg Times,* June 30, 1869, in James W. Loewen, *The Mississippi Chinese: Between Black and White* (Cambridge, Mass., 1971), p. 22; planters' convention report, reprinted in John R. Commons et al. (eds.), *A Documentary History of American Industrial Society* (Cleveland, 1910/11), vol. 9, p. 81.

26. John Todd, *The Sunset Land* (Boston, 1870), pp. 284–285; Lucy M. Cohen, *Chinese in the Post–Civil War South: A People Without a History* (Baton Rouge, La., 1984), pp. 109, 123–124; Loewen, *The Mississippi Chinese,* pp. 23, 24; Barth, *Bitter Strength,* p. 189; Ralph Keeler, "The 'Heathen Chinee' in the South," *Every Saturday,* vol. 3, no. 83 (July 29, 1871), p. 117.

27. Cohen, *Chinese in the Post–Civil War South,* p. 136.

28. Samuel Bowles, *Our New West* (Hartford, Conn., 1869), p. 414.

29. *Report of the Joint Special Committee to Investigate Chinese Immigration,* Senate Report No. 689, 44th Cong., 2nd sess., 1876/7, pp. 679, 680.

30. Henry Robinson, "Our Manufacturing Era," *Overland Monthly,* vol. 2 (March 1869), p. 282; *Report of the Committee to Investigate Chinese Immigration,* p. 667.

31. Said, *Orientalism,* p. 477.

32. *San Francisco Alta,* June 4, 1853; *Hutching's California Magazine,* vol. 1 (March 1857), p. 387; *New York Times,* December 26, 1873; *The Wasp Magazine,* vol. 30 (January–June 1893), pp. 10–11; *Report of the Committee to Investigate Chinese Immigration,* p. vi; Caldwell, "The Negroization of the Chinese Stereotype," pp. 123–131.

33. Megumi Dick Osumi, "Asians and California's Anti-Miscegenation Laws," in Nobuya Tsuchida (ed.), *Asian and Pacific American Experiences: Women's Perspectives* (Minneapolis, 1982), pp. 2, 6.

34. *California Marin Journal,* April 13, 1876; Seymour, in *New York Times,* August 6, 1870; *The Nation,* vol. 9 (July 15, 1869), p. 445; *Congressional Record,* 47th Cong., 1st sess., p. 3267.

35. California Supreme Court, *The People v. Hall,* October 1, 1854, in Robert F. Heizer and Alan F. Almquist, *The Other Californians: Prejudice and Discrimination under Spain, Mexico, and the United States to 1920* (Berkeley, Calif., 1971), p. 229.

36. Stuart C. Miller, *The Unwelcome Immigrant: The American Image of the Chinese, 1752–1882* (Berkeley, Calif., 1969), p. 190.

37. John A. Garraty, *Unemployment in History: Economic Thought and Public Policy* (New York, 1978), pp. 103–109.

38. *The Nation* (March 16, 1882), p. 222; *Congressional Record,* 47th Cong., 1st sess., pp. 2973–2974, 2033, 3310, 3265, 3268; appendix, pp. 48, 89, 21; Chinese Exclusion Act of 1888, reprinted in Cheng-Tsu Wu, *"Chink!" A Documentary History of Anti-Chinese Prejudice in America* (New York, 1972), pp. 82–83.

39. Hoexter, *From Canton to California,* p. 44; McClain, "Chinese Struggle for Civil Rights," pp. 555–557, 564–567; Fung Tang, "Address to the Committee by the Chinese Merchants," *Daily Alta California,* June 26, 1869.

40. Kwang Chang Ling, *Why Should the Chinese Go? A Pertinent Inquiry from a Mandarin High in Authority* (San Francisco, 1878), p. 16; "Life History as a Social Document of Mr. J. S. Look," August 13, 1924, p. 1, Survey of Race Relations, Stanford University, Hoover Institution Archives; "Life History as Social Document of Law Yow," August 12, 1924, p. 3, Survey of Race Relations; "Life History and Social Document of Andrew Kan," August 22, 1924, p. 2, Survey of Race Relations; Huie Kin, *Reminiscences* (Peiping, 1932), p. 27.

41. Lai Chun-Chuen, *Remarks of the Chinese Merchants,* pp. 3, 6.

42. For a study of gender and race discrimination related to Chicanas, see Margarita Melville (ed.), *Twice a Minority: Mexican American Women* (St. Louis, 1980); Ginger Chih, *Immigration of Chinese Women to the U.S.A., 1900–1940*, unpublished M.A. thesis, Sarah Lawrence College, 1977, p. 11.

43. Victor Nee and Herbert Y. Wong, "Asian American Socioeconomic Achievement: The Strength of the Family Bond," *Sociological Perspectives*, vol. 28, no. 3 (July 1985), pp. 288–289; Mau Yun Len, interview, July 13, 1988.

44. *The Friend*, January 1880, p. 6; *In Re Ah Moy, on Habeas Corpus*, Circuit Court, District of California, in Robert Desty (ed.), *Federal Reporter: Circuit and District Courts of the United States, August–November, 1884* (St. Paul, 1884), pp. 785–789. On the exclusion of Chinese wives, see Megumi Dick Osumi, "Asians and California's Anti-Miscegenation Laws," p. 7; the 1882 and 1888 acts are reprinted in Cheng-Tsu Wu, *"Chink!" A Documentary History*, pp. 70–75, 80–85.

45. Jack Chew, interview, in appendix of Peter C. Y. Leung, *One Day, One Dollar: Locke, California and the Chinese Farming Experience in the Sacramento Delta* (El Cerrito, Calif., 1984), p. 68; Willard G. Jue, "Chin Gee-Hee, Chinese Pioneer Entrepreneur in Seattle and Toishan," in Douglas W. Lee (ed.), *The Annals of the Chinese Historical Society of the Pacific Northwest* (Seattle, 1983), p. 32; A. W. Loomis, "Chinese Women in California," *Overland Monthly* (April 1869), pp. 349–350; Lydon, *Chinese Gold*, pp. 156–158; "Memorial of the Chinese Six Companies," 1876, reprinted in Gibson, *Chinese in America*, p. 318.

46. "Story of Wong Ah So," in Social Science Institute, Fiske University, "Orientals and Their Cultural Adjustment" (Nashville, 1946), pp. 31–33.

47. Hom, *Songs of Gold Mountain*, p. 309; Lilac Chen, in Nee, *Longtime Californ'*, p. 85; Judy Yung, *Chinese Women of America: A Pictorial History* (Seattle, 1986), p. 23; Hirata, "Chinese Immigrant Women," p. 234.

48. Perrin, *Coming to America*, p. 19; Sing Kum, "Letter by a Chinese Girl," reprinted in Gibson, *Chinese in America*, pp. 220–221, "Story of Wong Ah So," pp. 31–32; "Story of Exslave, and Slave Owner," in "Two Schools for Chinese" by Mrs. Park, August 1924, pp. 3–4, Survey of Race Relations, Stanford University, Hoover Institution Archives.

49. Lucie Cheng Hirata, "Chinese Immigrant Women in Nineteenth-Century California," in Carol Berkin and Mary Norton (eds.), *Women of America* (Boston, 1979), pp. 243–244; folk song, translation, Hom, *Songs of Gold Mountain*, p. 321.

50. Lee Chew, "Life Story of a Chinaman," p. 295; "Life History of Mr. Woo Gen," July 29, 1924, p. 16, Survey of Race Relations, Stanford University, Hoover Institution Library; "Conversation with waiter, International Chop Suey," February 2, 1924, Survey of Race Relations.

51. Chinn et al., *Chinese in California*, p. 10; Huie, *Reminiscences*,

pp. 25, 28; A. W. Loomis, "The Old East in the New West," in *Overland Monthly* (October 1868), p. 364.

52. Gibson, *Chinese in America*, p. 14; A. W. Loomis, "Chinese in California: Their Sign-Board Literature," *Overland Monthly* (August 1868), pp. 152–155.

53. Based on tables in appendix of Chan, "Chinese Livelihood in Rural California," pp. 300–307.

54. "Interview with Chinese Tong Members in Chicago, January 1925," and letter by C. O. M., a laundry worker, December 14, 1913, "Segregation folder," Box 1, Survey of Race Relations, Stanford University, Hoover Institution Archives; interview by C. H. Burnett, August 9, 1924, p. 5, Survey of Race Relations.

55. A. W. Loomis, "Holiday in the Chinese Quarter," *Overland Monthly* (February 1869), pp. 148, 149, 151; poem, in Hom, *Songs of Gold Mountain*, p. 195.

56. Chinese rhyme, in Hom, *Songs of Gold Mountain*, p. 90; Gibson, *Chinese in America*, pp. 15–16; A. W. Loomis, "The Old East in the New West," p. 364; Lee Chew, "Life Story of a Chinaman," p. 294; "Conversation with waiter, International Chop Suey," February 2, 1924, Survey of Race Relations, Stanford University, Hoover Institution Archives; "Interview with Tom Lee, Cook for Dr. N. C. Peterson," circa 1924, p. 2, Survey of Race Relations, Stanford University, Hoover Institution Archives.

57. Mark and Chih, *A Place Called Chinese America*, p. 52; Robert Stewart Culin, in Stanford M. Lyman, *Chinatown and Little Tokyo* (Millwood, N.Y., 1986), p. 123; Robert Culin, "Customs of the Chinese in America," *Journal of American Folklore* (July–September 1890) pp. 191, 193; Pardee Lowe, *Father and Glorious Descendant* (Boston, 1943), p. 98; Wong Chin Foo, "Chinese in New York," p. 301; folk song, in Him Mark Lai, Joe Huang, and Don Wong, *The Chinese of America, 1785–1980* (San Francisco, 1980), p. 51; translated and reprinted in Loomis, "The Old East in the New West," p. 362.

58. Chinese rhyme, in Hom, *Songs of Gold Mountain*, p. 124; letter by unknown Chinese migrant, in the Kam Wah Chung Company, John Day, Oregon, Papers.

59. Chu-chia to Lung On, July 1899; wife to Lung On, undated; Lung On to Liang Kwan-jin, March 2, 1905; Liang Kwang-jin to Lung On, March 4, 1905; Ing Du-hsio to Ing Hay, April 9, no year, translations by Chia-Lin Chen, Kam Wah Chung Company Papers.

60. Hom, *Songs of Gold Mountain*, p. 294.

61. Rose Hum Lee, "Chinese Dilemma," *Phylon* (1949), p. 139; Lai, Lim, and Yung, *Island*, p. 12; interview with old laundryman, in "Interviews with Two Chinese," circa 1924, box 326, folder 325, Survey of Race Relations, Stanford University, Hoover Institution Archives; "Life History and Social Document of Andrew Kan," p. 11, Survey of Race Relations, Hoover Institution Archives.

62. Folk song, translation, in Hom, *Songs of Gold Mountain*, p. 96.

63. Esther Wong, "The History and Problem of Angel Island," March 1924, pp. 7–8, Survey of Race Relations, Stanford University, Hoover Institution Archives; "Interview with Mr. Faris, Deputy Commissioner of Immigration in Seattle," pp. 2–11, Survey of Race Relations.

64. H. K. Wong, *Gum Sahn Yun: Gold Mountain Men* (San Francisco, 1987), p. 187; Alice Fun, interview, February 28, 1982, Chinese Women of America Research Project, Chinese Culture Foundation of San Francisco, p. 3; Nee, *Longtime Californ'*, p. 63.

65. Eliot G. Mears, *Resident Orientals on the American Pacific Coast* (Chicago, 1928), p. 408.

66. Richard Kock Dare, "The Economic and Social Adjustment of the San Francisco Chinese for the Past Fifty Years," unpublished M.A. thesis, University of California, Berkeley, 1959, p. 54.

67. Esther Wong, "The History and Problem of Angel Island," pp. 1–4, Survey of Race Relations, Stanford University, Hoover Institution Archives; Mary Naka, "Angel Island Immigration Station," 1922, Survey of Race Relations, Stanford University, Hoover Institution Archives.

68. Him Mark Lai, Genny Lim, and Judy Yung (eds.), *Island: Poetry and History of Chinese Immigrants on Angel Island, 1910–1940* (San Francisco, 1980), p. 44; Diane Mei Lin Mark and Ginger Chih, *A Place Called Chinese America* (Dubuque, Iowa, 1982), pp. 47–48; Shih-Shan Henry Tsai, *The Chinese Experience in America* (Bloomington, Ind., 1986), p. 101.

69. Lai et al., *Island*, pp. 126, 150, 94.

70. Rose Hum Lee, "The Decline of Chinatowns in the U.S.," *American Journal of Sociology,* vol. 54, no. 5 (March 1949), pp. 425, 427, 428; Nee, *Longtime Californ'*, p. 62; Rose Hum Lee, "Chinese in the U.S. Today: The War Has Changed Their Lives," *Survey Graphic* (October 1942), p. 419.

71. Kian Moon Kwan, "Assimilation of the Chinese in the United States: An Exploratory Study in California," unpublished Ph.D. thesis, University of California, Berkeley, 1958, p. 62; Nee, *Longtime Californ'*, p. 148; Wong, "Chinese in New York," p. 308; Rose Hum Lee, *The Chinese in the U.S.A.* (Hong Kong, 1960), pp. 40, 41; Ling-chi Wang, "Politics of Assimilation and Repression: History of the Chinese in the United States, 1940 to 1970," unpublished manuscript, Asian American Studies Library, University of California, Berkeley), p. 47. Even the 52 percent figure would not have been reached had it not also been for the 90,299 Chinese who returned to their homeland between 1908 and 1943. See S. W. Kung, *Chinese in American Life: Some Aspects of Their History, Status, Problems, and Contributions* (Seattle, 1962), p. 94.

72. Nee, *Longtime Californ'*, pp. 150, 180; Nee, "Growing Up in a Chinatown Grocery Store," p. 346; Victor Wong, "Childhood 1930s," in Nick Harvey (ed.), *Ting: The Cauldron: Chinese Art and Identity in San Fran-*

cisco (San Francisco, 1970), p. 15; Mark and Chih, *A Place Called Chinese America*, p. 75.

73. Kit King Louis, "Problems of Second Generation Chinese," *Sociology and Social Research* (January–February 1932), p. 257. Betty Lee Sung, interview, January 4, 1982, Chinese Women of America Research Project, Chinese Culture Foundation of San Francisco, p. 4; Victor Wong, "Childhood II," in Harvey (ed.), *Ting*, p. 71.

74. Jade Snow Wong, *Fifth Chinese Daughter* (New York, 1950), p. 178.

Part Three: Transitions

1. Max Weber, *The Protestant Ethic and the Spirit of Capitalism* (New York, 1958), pp. 181–182. For the industrial revolution, see George R. Taylor, *The Transportation Revolution, 1800–1860* (New York, 1962), pp. 63–64, 207, 212, 228, 249; Marvin M. Fisher, *Workshops in the Wilderness: The European Response to American Industrialism, 1830–1860* (New York, 1967), pp. 5, 12; Edward Kirkland, *Industry Comes of Age: Business, Labor, and Public Policy, 1860–1897* (New York, 1961), p. 46; Robert Higgs, *The Transformation of the American Economy, 1865–1914: An Essay in Interpretation* (New York, 1971), pp. 47, 59; Peter Temin, *Iron and Steel in Nineteenth-Century America: An Economic Inquiry* (Cambridge, Mass., 1964), pp. 166–167, 274.

2. Walter La Feber, *The New Empire: An Interpretation of American Expansion, 1860–1898* (Ithaca, N.Y., 1967), pp. 17, 200; Josiah Strong, *Expansion Under New World Conditions* (New York, 1900), p. 80; Richard B. Du Boff, "Unemployment in the United States: An Historical Summary," *Monthly Review*, vol. 29, no. 6 (November 1977), p. 11.

3. Josiah Strong, *Our Country: Its Possible Future and Its Present Crisis* (New York, 1885), pp. 76, 174–175, 30, 40, 43, 44, 53, 57, 84–85, 94, 106, 126, 119, 139, 153, 14.

4. Alfred T. Mahan, *The Influence of Sea Power Upon History, 1660–1783* (Boston, 1890), pp. 1, 25, 27–33, 57–58, 82–87.

5. Mahan, *The Problem of Asia and Its Effect upon International Policies* (Boston, 1900), pp. 15, 98; Mahan, *Influence of Sea Power,* pp. 165–167; Mahan, *The Harvest Within: Thoughts on the Life of a Christian* (Boston, 1902), pp. 44, 34.

6. Mahan to Samuel Ashe, April 30, 1879; May 19, 1876; November 13, 1880, December 21, 1882; and March 11, 1885, Mahan-Ashe Papers, Duke University Library; Mahan, quoted in Peter Karsten, *The Naval Aristocracy: The Golden Age of Annapolis and the Emergence of Modern American Navalism* (New York, 1972), p. 189.

7. Theodore Roosevelt to Mahan, May 12, 1890, Alfred Thayer Mahan Papers, Library of Congress, Washington, D.C; Mahan to Roosevelt, May 1, 1897, quoted in William E. Livezey, *Mahan on Sea Power* (Norman,

Okla., 1947), p. 114; Mahan to Roosevelt, March 14, 1898, and Roosevelt to Mahan, March 21, 1898, Alfred Mahan Papers, Library of Congress.

Chapter 9: The "Indian Question"

1. James Mooney, *The Ghost-Dance Religion and the Sioux Outbreak of 1890*, Fourteenth Annual Report of the Bureau of Ethnology, 1892–93, Part 2 (Washington, D.C., 1896), p. 26.

2. Dee Brown, *Bury My Heart at Wounded Knee: An Indian History of the American West* (New York, 1970), p. 436.

3. Brown, *Bury My Heart*, p. 437.

4. James H. McGregor, *The Wounded Knee Massacre from the Viewpoint of the Sioux* (Minneapolis, 1950), p. 105.

5. McGregor, *Wounded Knee Massacre*, p. 118; Brown, *Bury My Heart*, p. 42; Black Elk, *Black Elk Speaks: Being the Life Story of a Holy Man of the Oglala Sioux*, as told to John G. Neihardt (Lincoln, Neb., 1961), pp. 261–262.

6. McGregor, *Wounded Knee Massacre*, pp. 128, 111; Mooney, *Ghost-Dance Religion*, pp. 132, 118.

7. McGregor, *Wounded Knee Massacre*, p. 128; Black Elk, *Black Elk Speaks*, p. 259.

8. Black Elk, *Black Elk Speaks*, p. 262; Mooney, *Ghost-Dance Religion*, p. 130.

9. Buffalo Bill, quoted in Jay Monaghan, *Custer: The Life of General George Armstrong Custer* (Boston, 1959), p. 395; *Bismarck Weekly Tribune*, quoted in Henry E. Fritz, *The Movement for Indian Assimilation, 1860–1890* (Philadelphia, 1963), p. 176.

10. George A. Custer, *Wild Life on the Plains and Horrors of Indian Warfare* (St. Louis, 1891), pp. 31, 28, 13, 21–22, 215, 226; Custer to Mrs. Custer, April 14, 1867, in Elizabeth Custer, *Tenting on the Plains, or General Custer in Kansas and Texas* (New York, 1889), pp. 556–59, 628–629; Elizabeth Custer, *"Boots and Saddles"; or Life in Dakota with General Custer* (New York, 1885), p. 245; Custer, "The Red Man," Custer Papers, Custer Battlefield National Monument, Crow Agency, Montana; Custer, *Wild Life*, p. 28.

11. Custer, *Wild Life*, p. 31.

12. Custer, *Wild Life*, pp. 139–140.

13. Custer, *Wild Life*, pp. 70, 98; Custer, quoted in Monaghan, *Custer*, p. 266; Custer, *"Boots and Saddles,"* p. 278; Custer, *Tenting on the Plains*, pp. 111–112, 592, 528, 579.

14. Custer to Libbie Custer, July 19, 1873, in Custer, *"Boots and Saddles,"* p. 278; Custer, *Wild Life*, pp. 21, 14; Custer, *Tenting on the Plains*, p. 694.

15. Francis Amasa Walker, *The Indian Question* (Boston, 1874), pp. 34–35, 99.

16. Francis Amasa Walker, *Political Economy* (New York, 1888), p. 9.

17. Walker, *Indian Question*, pp. 113–14, 38, 91–92.

18. Francis Amasa Walker, "Our Indians and Mr. Wells," *The Nation*, vol. 15 (August 1, 1872), p. 73; Walker, *Indian Question*, pp. 10, 62–63, 64–67; Robert F. Berkhofer, Jr., *The White Man's Indian: Images of the American Indian from Columbus to the Present* (New York, 1979), p. 168.

19. Francis Amasa Walker, *Annual Report of the Commissioner of Indian Affairs to the Secretary of the Interior for the Year 1872* (Washington, D.C., 1872), pp. 11, 63, 64, 77–79, 94–95.

20. James P. Munroe, *A Life of Francis Amasa Walker* (New York, 1923), pp. 135, 25; Walker, *Annual Report*, p. 11; Walker, *Indian Question*, pp. 79–80.

21. D. S. Otis, *The Dawes Act and the Allotment of Indian Lands* (Norman, Okla., 1973), pp. x, 57, 4, 5, 9, 10, 38, 55; *U.S. Statutes at Large*, vol. 24, pp. 388–391.

22. Frederick E. Hoxie, *A Final Promise: The Campaign to Assimilate the Indians, 1880–1920* (Lincoln, Neb., 1984), pp. 76, 77.

23. *Congressional Record*, 49th Cong., 2nd sess., 1887, vol. 18, pp. 189–192, 224–226, 973–974; *Congressional Record*, 49th Cong., 1st sess., 1887, vol. 17, p. 1634.

24. Hoxie, *Final Promise*, p. 180.

25. Francis Prucha, *Americanizing the American Indians: Writings by the "Friends of the Indian": 1800–1900* (Cambridge, Mass., 1973), pp. 108–109.

26. Otis, *Dawes Act*, pp. 17, 18, 86, 87; Loring Benson Priest, *Uncle Sam's Stepchildren: The Reformation of United States Indian Policy, 1865–1887* (New York, 1972), p. 223.

27. Leonard A. Carlson, *Indians, Bureaucrats, and Land: The Dawes Act and the Decline of Indian Farming* (Westport, Conn., 1981), pp. 11–12.

28. Hoxie, *Final Promise*, pp. 160, 165.

29. Hoxie, *Final Promise*, pp. 155, 158.

30. Hoxie, *Final Promise*, pp. 163, 168.

31. James S. Olson and Raymond Wilson, *Native Americans in the Twentieth Century* (Provo, Utah, 1984), p. 86.

32. Graham D. Taylor, *The New Deal and American Indian Tribalism: The Administration of the Indian Reorganization Act, 1934–45* (Lincoln, Neb., 1980), p. 6; Michael T. Smith, "The Wheeler-Howard Act of 1934: The Indian New Deal," *Journal of the West*, vol. 10, no. 3 (July 1971), p. 521; Clayton R. Koppes, "From New Deal to Termination: Liberalism and Indian Policy, 1933–1953," *Pacific Historical Review*, vol. 46, no. 4 (November 1977), p. 546.

33. John Collier, *From Every Zenith: A Memoir and Some Essays on Life and Thought* (Denver, 1963), pp. 126, 203; Taylor, *New Deal*

and American Indian Tribalism, p. x; see also Lawrence C. Kelley, *The Navajo Indians and Federal Indian Policy, 1900–1935* (Tucson, Ariz., 1968), p. 150; Donald L. Parman, *The Navajos and the New Deal* (New Haven, Conn., 1976), pp. 30–31.

34. Collier, *From Every Zenith*, pp. 129–130; Kelley, *Navajo Indians*, p. 157; Smith, "Wheeler-Howard Act," p. 525.

35. Koppes, "From New Deal to Termination," p. 551; Smith, "Wheeler-Howard Act," pp. 526, 531; Kelley, *Navajo Indians*, p. 298; Collier, *From Every Zenith*, p. 176.

36. Olson and Wilson, *Native Americans*, p. 123.

37. Peter Nabokov (ed.), *Native American Testimony* (New York, 1978), p. 203; Richard White, *The Roots of Dependency: Subsistence, Environment, and Social Change among the Choctaws, Pawnees, and Navajos* (Lincoln, Neb., 1983), pp. 212–215.

38. Peter Iverson, *The Navajo Nation* (Westport, Conn., 1981), p. 9.

39. John Collier, *The Indians of the Americas* (New York, 1947), p. 280; Taylor, *New Deal and American Indian Tribalism*, p. 32.

40. Phelps-Stokes Fund, *The Navajo Indian Problem* (New York, 1939), pp. 8–9; David F. Aberle, *The Peyote Religion Among the Navaho* (Chicago, 1966), pp. 55–64; Collier, *Indians of the Americas*, p. 276; Iverson, *Navajo Nation*, pp. 27, 28.

41. White, *Roots of Oppression*, pp. 251, 258; Edward H. Spicer, "Sheepmen and Technicians: A Program of Soil Conservation on the Navajo Indian Reservation," in Edward H. Spicer (ed.), *Human Problems in Technological Change* (New York, 1952), p. 185.

42. Collier, *From Every Zenith*, p. 252.

43. Parman, *Navajos and New Deal*, p. 44.

44. Collier, *From Every Zenith*, p. 252; Taylor, *New Deal and American Indian Tribalism*, p. 130.

45. Walter Dyk (ed.), *Son of Old Man Hat: A Navajo Autobiography* (New York, 1938), pp. 78, 103.

46. Evon Z. Vogt, *Navaho Veterans: A Study of Changing Values* (Cambridge, Mass., 1951), pp. 71, 156, 79.

47. Aberle, *Peyote Religion Among the Navaho*, pp. 63–64.

48. Spicer, "Sheepmen and Technicians," p. 194; White, *Roots of Oppression*, pp. 265, 313; Spicer, "Sheepmen and Technicians," p. 193; Nabokov, *Native American Testimony*, p. 330.

49. White, *Roots of Oppression*, pp. 272, 282.

50. Aberle, *Peyote Religion Among the Navaho*, p. 64; Iverson, *Navajo Nation*, p. 23.

51. White, *Roots of Oppression*, pp. 229, 313; Parman, *Navajos and New Deal*, p. 45; White, *Roots of Oppression*, p. 260; "Night Chant," in Paul Jacobs and Saul Landau (eds.), *To Serve the Devil: Natives and Strangers*, vol. 1 (New York, 1971), p. 41.

Chapter 10: Pacific Crossings

1. *Japan Weekly Mail*, December 20, 1884, reprinted in Nippu Jiji, *Golden Jubilee of the Japanese in Hawaii, 1885–1935* (Honolulu, 1935), n.p.; Yuji Ichioka, *The Issei: The World of the First Generation Japanese Immigrants, 1885–1924* (New York, 1988), p. 45. Ichioka's is the best book on the subject.

2. Kazuo Ito, *Issei: A History of the Japanese Immigrants in North America* (Seattle, 1973), pp. 27, 38, 29. Ito's study is a massive and wonderful compilation of stories, oral histories, and poems. It is indispensable.

3. Robert Wilson and Bill Hosokawa, *East to America: A History of the Japanese in the United States* (New York, 1980), pp. 47, 113–114.

4. Eileen Sunada Sarasohn (ed.), *The Issei: Portrait of a Pioneer, an Oral History* (Palo Alto, Calif., 1983), pp. 44, 31–32.

5. Thomas C. Smith, *Nakahara: Family Farming and Population in a Japanese Village, 1717–1830* (Palo Alto, Calif., 1977), pp. 134, 152, 153; Sheila Matsumoto, "Women in Factories," in Joyce Lebra, et al. (eds.), *Women in Changing Japan* (Boulder, Colo., 1976), pp. 51–53; Sharon L. Sievers, *Flowers in Salt: The Beginnings of Feminist Consciousness in Modern Japan* (Palo Alto, Calif., 1983), pp. 55, 62, 66, 84; Yukiko Hanawa, "The Several Worlds of Issei Women," unpublished M.A. thesis, California State University, Long Beach, 1982, pp. 31–34; Yasuo Wakatsuki, "Japanese Emigration to the United States, 1866–1924," *Perspectives in American History*, vol. 12 (1979), pp. 401, 404; Wilson and Hosokawa, *East to America*, p. 42.

6. Hanawa, *Several Worlds*, pp. 13–16; Emperor Meiji is quoted in Susan McCoin Kataoka, "Issei Women: A Study in Subordinate Status," unpublished Ph.D. dissertation, University of California, Los Angeles, 1977, p. 6; Akemi Kikumura, *Through Harsh Winters: The Life of a Japanese Immigrant Woman* (Novato, Calif., 1981), pp. 18, 25; Emma Gee, "Issei: The First Women," in Emma Gee (ed.), *Asian Women* (Berkeley, Calif., 1971), p. 11.

7. Tsuru Yamauchi is quoted in Ethnic Studies Oral History Project (ed.), *Uchinanchu: A History of Okinawans in Hawaii* (Honolulu, 1981), pp. 490, 491.

8. Tadashi Fukutake, *Japanese Rural Society* (Ithaca, N.Y., 1967), pp. 6, 7, 39, 40, 42.

9. Katherine Coman, *The History of Contract Labor in the Hawaiian Islands* (New York, 1903), p. 42; Alan Moriyama, "Causes of Emigration: The Background of Japanese Emigration to Hawaii, 1885–1894," in Edna Bonacich and Lucie Cheng (eds.), *Labor Immigration Under Capitalism: Asian Workers in the United States before World War II* (Berkeley, Calif., 1984), p. 273; Republic of Hawaii, Bureau of Immigration, *Report*

(Honolulu, 1886), p. 256; manager of the Hutchinson Sugar Company to W. G. Irwin and Company, February 5, 1902, and January 25, 1905, Hutchinson Plantation Records; for terms of the Gentlemen's Agreement, see Frank Chuman, *The Bamboo People: The Law and Japanese-Americans* (Del Mar, Calif., 1976), pp. 35–36.

10. H. A. Millis, *The Japanese Problem in the United States* (New York, 1915), p. 86.

11. Sarasohn, *The Issei*, p. 34; Yuriko Sato, "Emigration of Issei Women" (Berkeley, Calif., 1982), in the Asian American Studies Library, University of California, Berkeley; Ito, *Issei*, p. 34.

12. *Pacific Commercial Advertiser*, April 25, 1874; Theo. H. Davies and Company to C. McLennan, July 2, 1890; January 3, 1898, Laupahoehoe Plantation Records, microfilm, University of Hawaii Library; William G. Irwin and Company to George D. Hewitt, October 12, 1894, Hutchinson Plantation Records, microfilm, University of Hawaii Library; vice president of H. Hackfeld and Company to G. N. Wilcox, May 5, 1908, Grove Farm Plantation Records, Grove Farm Plantation, Kauai.

13. G. C. Hewitt to W. G. Irwin and Company, March 16, 1896, Hutchinson Plantation Records; Robert Hall, George F. Renton, and George H. Fairfield, in Republic of Hawaii, *Report of the Labor Commission on Strikes and Arbitration* (Honolulu, 1895), pp. 23–24, 28, 36; H. Hackfeld and Company to George Wilcox, September 26, 1896, Grove Farm Plantation Records.

14. *Report of the Commission of Labor*, in *Planters' Monthly*, vol. 22, no. 7 (July 1903), p. 296; Walter Giffard to manager of the Hutchinson Sugar Plantation, October 3, 1898, in Wayne K. Patterson, "The Korean Frontier in America: Immigration to Hawaii, 1896–1910," unpublished Ph.D. thesis, University of Pennsylvania, 1977, p. 100; manager of the Hutchinson Sugar Plantation to W. G. Irwin and Company, April 11, 1905, Hutchinson Plantation Records.

15. Labor committee of the Hawaiian Sugar Planters Association to the trustees, July 28, 1909, Grove Farm Plantation Records; manager of the Hawaiian Agricultural Company to C. Brewer and Company, August 7 and 27, 1913, Hawaiian Agricultural Company Records, microfilm, University of Hawaii Library.

16. Hawaiian Sugar Planters' Association, resolution of trustees, November 18, 1904, Grove Farm Plantation Records; *Planters' Monthly*, vol. 1, no. 7 (October 1882), p. 242; Bureau of Labor Statistics, *Report of the Commissioner of Labor on Hawaii* (Washington, 1916), pp. 120–153; Machiyo Mitamura, "Life on a Hawaiian Plantation: An Interview," in *Social Process in Hawaii*, vol. 6 (1940), p. 51.

17. "The Five O'Clock Whistle," in the *Kohala Midget*, April 27, 1910.

18. Korean woman, in Eun Sik Yang, "Korean Women of America: From Subordination to Partnership, 1903–1930," *Amerasia Journal*, vol. 11, no. 2 (1984), p. 5; Ethnic Studies Oral History Project, *The 1924 Filipino Strike on Kauai* (Honolulu, 1979), vol. 2, p. 662.

19. "Plantation Work Begins, Silently, in Early Morn," *Honolulu Star Bulletin*, January 13, 1934; Minnie Caroline Grant, *Scenes in Hawaii* (Toronto, 1888), pp. 140–142.

20. Lillian Ota Takaki, daughter of Yukino Takaki, letter to the author, August 10, 1985.

21. Ethnic Studies Oral History Project, *Uchinanchu*, pp. 360, 520, 513.

22. Ethnic Studies Oral History Project, *Waialua and Haleiwa: The People Tell Their Story* (Honolulu, 1977), vol. 8, p. 149.

23. Ethnic Studies Oral History Project, *Uchinanchu*, p. 488; Andrew Lind, *An Island Community* (Chicago, 1938), pp. 240–241; song, in *Hawaii Herald*, February 2, 1973.

24. H. Brett Melendy, *Asians in America* (Boston, 1977), pp. 86–87; Mary H. Drout, *Hawaii and a Revolution* (New York, 1898), pp. 237–238.

25. Ethnic Studies Oral History Project, *Waialua and Haleiwa*, vol. 8, p. 167; Yako Morishita, poem, in Jiro Nakano, *History of Japanese Short Poems (Tanka, Haiku and Senryu) in Hawaii*, unpublished manuscript, 1986, p. 46.

26. Song, in Yukuo Uyehara, "The Horehore-Bushi: A Type of Japanese Folksong Developed and Sung Among the Early Immigrants in Hawaii," in *Social Process in Hawaii*, vol. 28 (1980–1981), p. 114.

27. Ethnic Studies Oral History Project, *Uchinanchu*, p. 369.

28. *The Higher Wage Question*, excerpts reprinted in Bureau of Labor Statistics, *Report of the Commissioner of Labor on Hawaii* (Washington, 1910), p. 76.

29. Soga, in *Honolulu Record*, July 7, 1949; Allan Beekman, "Hawaii's Great Japanese Strike," reprinted in Dennis Ogawa (ed.), *Kodomo no tame ni* (Honolulu, 1978), p. 158.

30. Letter to plantation manager E. K. Bull, signed by ninety-two strikers, May 19, 1909, reprinted in Bureau of Labor Statistics, *Report*, p. 80; Higher Wage Association, statement, in Bureau of Labor Statistics, *Report*, p. 68; *Higher Wage Question*, in Bureau of Labor Statistics, *Report*, pp. 77–78.

31. Takashi Tsutsumi, *History of Hawaii Laborers' Movement* (Honolulu, 1922), p. 175.

32. Tsutsumi, *Hawaii Laborers' Movement*, pp. 217, 224, 238, 240, 241, 242, 243.

33. Tsutsumi, *Hawaii Laborers' Movement*, pp. 12, 44, 17, 13, 22.

34. Hawaii Laborers' Association, *Facts About the Strike on Sugar Plantations in Hawaii* (Honolulu, 1920), p. 1.

35. President of C. Brewer and Company to James Campsie, manager of the Hawaiian Agricultural Company, February 3, 1920, Hawaiian Agricultural Company Records; R. D. Mead, director of the Labor Bureau, to manager of Grove Farm Plantation, February 13, 1920, Grove Farm Plantation Records.

36. Interview with Tadao Okada by the author, July 1980.

37. Milton Murayama, *All I Asking for Is My Body* (San Francisco, 1975), pp. 28, 96.

38. Richard Okawa, interviews, February 1978 and July 1980; Minoru Takaki, interview, July 1985.

39. Yasutaro Soga, *Looking Backward 50 Years in Hawaii*, reprinted in *Honolulu Record*, March 31, 1949; Ethnic Studies Oral History Project, *Uchinanchu*, pp. 363, 489.

40. C. Brewer and Company to W. G. Ogg, August 2, 1916, Hawaiian Agricultural Company Records; Donald S. Bowman to Grove Farm Plantation, September 15, 1920, Grove Farm Plantation Records; W. Pfotenhauser, "President's Address," in *The Hawaiian Planters' Record*, vol. 4, no. 1 (January 1911), p. 4; Donald S. Bowman, "Housing the Plantation Worker," in *The Hawaiian Planters' Record*, vol. 22, no. 4 (April 1920), pp. 202–203.

41. Ethnic Studies Oral History Project, *Uchinanchu*, p. 382; Ito, *Issei*, p. 21.

42. Murayama, *All I Asking for Is My Body*, p. 45.

43. Manager of the Hawaiian Agricultural Company to C. Brewer and Company, October 17 and November 2, 1911, Hawaiian Agricultural Company Records; H. Hackfield and Company to George Wilcox, April 25, 1900, Grove Farm Plantation Records.

44. Ethnic Studies Oral History Project, *Uchinanchu*, p. 387; Mrs. Joe Rapozo, in *Honolulu Advertiser*, July 6, 1973; Ethnic Studies Oral History Project, *Waialua and Haleiwa*, vol. 8, p. 64, and vol. 9, p. 223.

45. Manager of the Hawaiian Agricultural Company to Bureau of Labor, Hawaiian Sugar Planters' Association, April 5, 1919, Hawaiian Agricultural Company Records; interviews, in Ethnic Studies Oral History Project, *Uchinanchu*, pp. 415, 470; William C. Smith, "Pidgin English in Hawaii," *American Speech*, vols. 8–9, February 1933, pp. 15–19; Ethnic Studies Oral History Project, *Waialua and Haleiwa*, vol. 3, p. 11.

46. Daniel K. Inouye, *Journey to Washington* (Englewood Cliffs, N.J., 1967), pp. 24–25; Aiko Mifune, interview, February 18, 1988; Minoru Takaki and Susumu Takaki, interview on the Puunene Plantation, July 1985; Jeanette Takaki Watanabe, interview, March 14, 1987.

47. Ray Stannard Baker, "Human Nature in Hawaii: How the Few Want the Many to Work for Them — Perpetually, and at Low Wages," *American Magazine*, vol. 73 (January 1912), p. 330.

48. Curtis Aller, "The Evolution of Hawaiian Labor Relations: From Benevolent Paternalism to Mature Collective Bargaining," unpublished Ph.D. thesis, Harvard University, 1958, p. 39.

49. William C. Smith, *Americans in Process: A Study of Our Citizens of Oriental Ancestry* (Ann Arbor, Mich., 1937), p. 52.

50. Lillian Takaki Ota, interview with her nephew and author, May 1986; Ellen Kasai, interview with author, August 1986.

51. Song, in *Hawaii Herald*, February 2, 1973.

52. William C. Smith, *The Second Generation Oriental in America* (Honolulu, 1927), p. 21.

53. Ito, *Issei*, p. 446.

54. Immigration Commission, *Japanese and Other Immigrant Races*, vol. 1, p. 80.

55. Ichioka, *Issei*, p. 121.

56. Paul S. Taylor and Tom Vasey, "Historical Background of California Farm Labor," *Rural Sociology*, vol. 1 (September 1936), p. 286; Gerald D. Nash, "Stages of California's Economic Growth, 1870–1970: An Interpretation," *California Historical Quarterly* (winter 1972), pp. 318–319.

57. Ito, *Issei*, pp. 250, 280.

58. Ito, *Issei*, pp. 251, 442, 255; Yukiko Hanawa, *The Several Worlds of Issei Women*, unpublished M.A. thesis, California State University, Long Beach, 1982, p. 86.

59. "Interview with Mr. S. Nitta," 1924, p. 2, Survey of Race Relations, Stanford University, Hoover Institution Library; Bill Hosokawa, *Nisei: The Quiet Americans* (New York, 1969), p. 61.

60. Kiyoshi K. Kawakami, *Asia at the Door: A Study of the Japanese Question in Continental United States, Hawaii and Canada* (New York, 1914), p. 99; *San Francisco Chronicle*, June 25, 1912; Kiyoshi Kawakami, "How California Treats the Japanese," *The Independent*, vol. 74 (May 8, 1913), p. 1020; "Visit with Mr. George Shima, 'Potato King' of California," interview, July 14, 1924, pp. 1–3, Survey of Race Relations, Stanford University, Hoover Institution Library.

61. Ichioka, *Issei*, p. 61.

62. Ichioka, *Issei*, pp. 147, 148.

63. Kesa Noda, *Yamato Colony, 1906–1960* (Livingston, Calif., 1981), p. 18.

64. Noda, *Yamato Colony*, p. 18.

65. Ichioka, *Issei*, p. 148; Noda, *Yamato Colony*, pp. 10, 18, 40, 65, 174; Ito, *Issei*, p. 132.

66. Yuji Ichioka, "The Early Japanese Immigrant Quest for Citizenship: The Background of the 1922 Ozawa Case," *Amerasia Journal*, vol. 4, no. 2 (1977), p. 12; Ichioka, "Early Japanese Immigrant Quest for Citizenship," pp. 10, 11, 17; Yamato Ichihashi, *Japanese in the United States* (New York, 1969), p. 298; *Ozawa vs. United States, Decision of the Court*, November 13, 1922, reprinted in appendix, Mears, *Resident Orientals*, pp. 509, 513, 514.

67. *Japanese American Courier*, January 21, 1933; Ichioka, *Issei*, p. 247; "Message from Japan to America," *Japan Times and Mail*, October 1, 1924, reprinted in appendix, Mears, *Resident Orientals*, pp. 516–518; "Interview with R. Ode, Japanese foreman," pp. 12, 18, Survey of Race Relations, 1924, Stanford University, Hoover Institution Library; "Life History of a Japanese Man at Santa Paula, California," December 29, 1924, p. 4, Survey of Race Relations, Stanford University.

68. Ito, *Issei*, pp. 884, 429, 491, 889.

69. Ichihashi, *Japanese in the United States*, pp. 321–322; Jerrold Takahashi, "Changing Responses to Racial Subordination: An Exploratory Study of Japanese American Political Styles," unpublished Ph.D. thesis, University of California, Berkeley, 1980, p. 107.

70. *Japanese American Courier*, January 21, 1933; Ito, *Issei*, pp. 274, 449, 497; "Life History of Dr. Peter S___ of Los Angeles," pp. 2–3, 1925, Survey of Race Relations, Stanford University, Hoover Institution Library; "Interview with Yamato Ichihashi," p. 1, in Survey of Race Relations; "Life History of a Japanese Man at Santa Paula, California," December 29, 1924, p. 2, in Survey of Race Relations; S. Morris Morishita, in William C. Smith, *Americans in Process: A Study of Our Citizens of Oriental Ancestry* (Ann Arbor, Mich., 1937), p. 112; Hosokawa, *Nisei*, p. 136.

71. Fred Korematsu, "Views from Within," A Symposium on the Japanese American Internment Experience, University of California, Berkeley, September 19, 1987; Kay Yasui, "'Jap!' 'Jap!' 'Jap!'" *Pacific Citizen*, January 15, 1931; interviews with Mary Tsukamoto and Donald Nakahata, in John Tateishi, *And Justice for All: An Oral History of the Japanese American Detention Camps* (New York, 1984), pp. 5, 36; Toyo Tanaka, "How to Survive Racism in America's Free Society," in Arthur A. Hansen and Betty F. Mitson (eds.), *Voices Long Silent: An Oral Inquiry into the Japanese American Evacuation* (Fullerton, Calif., 1974), pp. 84, 90; "An American Born Japanese in America," an interview with J. Sato, pp. 2–3, Survey of Race Relations, Stanford University, Hoover Institution Library.

72. Report on Vocational Guidance Issue by Kojiro Unoura, in *Japanese American Courier*, September 10, 1938; Eliot G. Mears, *Resident Orientals on the American Pacific Coast: Their Legal and Economic Status* (New York, 1927), pp. 199, 200; John Modell, *Economics and Politics of Racial Accommodation*, pp. 132, 137–138; Yori Wada, "Growing Up in Central California," *Amerasia*, vol. 13, no. 2 (1986/7), p. 12; "Interview with Miss Esther B. Bartlett of Y.W.C.A.," December 12, 1924, p. 5, Survey of Race Relations, Stanford University, Hoover Institution Library.

73. Monica Sone, *Nisei Daughter* (Boston, 1953), pp. 8–10, 11, 22, 60–63.

74. Sone, *Nisei Daughter*, pp. 70, 52.

75. Sone, *Nisei Daughter*, pp. 38, 114, 115, 119, 122.

76. Sone, *Nisei Daughter*, pp. 121, 133.

Chapter 11: The Exodus from Russia

1. Abraham Cahan, *The Education of Abraham Cahan*, translated by Leon Stein, Abraham P. Conan, and Lynn Davison (Philadelphia, 1969),

p. 184. The phrase "two endless days" comes from the definitive study and classic by Irving Howe, *World of Our Fathers: The Journey of the East European Jews to America and the Life They Found and Made* (New York, 1983), p. 12, which I found indispensable and inspirational. For important analyses that focus on Jewish women, see Sidney Stahl Weinberg, *The World of Our Mothers: The Lives of Jewish Immigrant Women* (New York, 1988), and Susan A. Glenn, *Daughters of the Shtetl: Life and Labor in the Immigrant Generation* (Ithaca, N.Y., 1990).

2. Mary Antin, *The Promised Land* (New York, 1980; originally published in 1911), pp. 5, 22; Irving Howe, *World of Our Fathers*, p. 10.

3. Sydelle Kramer and Jenny Masur (eds.), *Jewish Grandmothers* (Boston, 1976), p. 64; Golda Meir, in Maxine Schwartz Seller (ed.), *Immigrant Women* (Philadelphia, 1981), p. 37; Glenn, *Daughters of the Shtetl*, p. 43; Ronald Sanders, *Shores of Refuge: A Hundred Years of Jewish Emigration* (New York, 1988), p. 213; Cahan, *Education,* pp. 158, 182.

4. Song, "Purim Gifts," in Mark Slobin, *Tenement Songs: The Popular Music of the Jewish Immigrants* (Urbana, Ill., 1982), p. 155.

5. Abraham Cahan, *Rise of David Levinsky* (New York, 1960; originally published in 1917), pp. 59–61; Anzia Yezierska, *Children of Loneliness* (New York, 1923), p. 152; Mary Antin, quoted in Howe, *World of Our Fathers*, p. 27; Antin, *Promised Land*, p. 142.

6. Cahan, *Education,* pp. 187, 186; Glenn, *Daughters of the Shtetl*, pp. 46, 47; Weinberg, *World of Our Mothers*, p. 73; Elizabeth Ewen, *Immigrant Women in the Land of Dollars: Life and Culture on the Lower East Side, 1890–1925* (New York, 1985), p. 54.

7. Antin, *Promised Land*, pp. 168–169; Cahan, *Education,* pp. 195, 188.

8. Sanders, *Shores of Refuge*, p. 66; Milton Meltzer, *Taking Root: Jewish Immigrants in America* (New York, 1976), p. 36; Cahan, *Education,* pp. 214, 215, 196; see also Howe, *World of Our Fathers*, pp. 39–41.

9. Howe, *World of Our Fathers*, p. 12; Cahan, *Education,* p. 196. My thanks to my friend Larry Friedman for the phrase "countryless people."

10. "The Life Story of a Polish Sweatshop Girl," in Hamilton Holt (ed.), *The Life Stories of Undistinguished Americans as Told by Themselves* (New York, 1906), p. 36; Cahan, *Rise of David Levinsky*, pp. 86, 87; Sanders, *Shores of Refuge*, p. 161.

11. Klaperman, quoted in Stephen Steinberg, *The Ethnic Myth: Race, Ethnicity, and Class in America* (New York, 1981), p. 82.

12. For statistics, see Glenn, *Daughters of the Shtetl,* p. 47; Thomas Kessner, *The Golden Door: Italian and Jewish Immigrant Mobility in New York City, 1880–1915* (New York, 1977), p. 33; and Sydney Stahl Weinberg, *The World of Our Mothers: The Lives of Jewish Immigrant Women* (New York, 1988), p. 76; Howe, *World of Our Fathers*, p. 59.

13. Glenn, *Daughters of the Shtetl*, pp. 54, 137–138; Deborah Dash Moore, *At Home in America: Second Generation New York Jews* (New York, 1981), p. 29; Meltzer, *Taking Roots*, p. 65; Cahan, *Rise of David Levinsky*, p. 93.

14. Cahan, *Rise of David Levinsky*, pp. 512, 93; Meltzer, *Taking Root*, p. 64; Kramer and Masur (eds.), *Jewish Grandmothers*, pp. 131, 132.

15. Isaac Raboy, in Irving Howe and Kenneth Libo (eds.), *How We Lived: A Documentary History of Immigrant Jews in America, 1880–1930* (New York, 1979), p. 29.

16. Moses Rischin, *The Promised City: New York's Jews, 1870–1914* (Cambridge, Mass., 1977; originally published in 1962), pp. 79, 82–83.

17. Rischin, *Promised City*, pp. 84, 87; Howe, *World of Our Fathers*, p. 152.

18. Howe, *World of Our Fathers*, p. 212.

19. Howe, *World of Our Fathers*, pp. 72, 184, 239, 213; Cahan, *Rise of David Levinsky*, p. 459.

20. Isaac Raboy, in Howe and Libo, *How We Lived*, p. 26; Rischin, *Promised City*, p. 55; Michael Kraus, *Immigration, The American Mosaic* (New York, 1966), p. 168.

21. Anzia Yezierska, in Howe and Libo, *How We Lived*, p. 19; Rischin, *Promised City*, p. 55.

22. Cahan, *Rise of David Levinsky*, pp. 97, 107.

23. Howe, *World of Our Fathers*, p. 80.

24. Howe, *World of Our Fathers*, p. 60.

25. Glenn, *Daughters of the Shtetl*, p. 92; Rischin, *Promised City*, pp. 63, 67.

26. Glenn, *Daughters of the Shtetl*, p. 95; Cahan, *Rise of David Levinsky*, p. 443.

27. Glenn, *Daughters of the Shtetl*, pp. 90, 94, 64; Rischin, *Promised City*, p. 61; Howe, *World of Our Fathers*, p. 81.

28. Cahan, *Rise of David Levinsky*, p. 151; Glenn, *Daughters of the Shtetl*, p. 94; Ray Stannard Baker, in Howe and Libo, *How We Lived*, p. 153.

29. Glenn, *Daughters of the Shtetl*, pp. 100, 104, 101; Meltzer, *Taking Root*, pp. 111–112; Bella Feiner, in Ewen, *Immigrant Women in the Land of Dollars*, p. 245.

30. Glenn, *Daughters of the Shtetl*, pp. 101, 152; Marie Ganz, in Howe and Libo, *How We Lived*, p. 136; Anzia Yezierska, *Children of Loneliness* (New York, 1923), p. 158.

31. Mollie Linker, in Sydelle Kramer and Jenny Masur (eds.), *Jewish Grandmothers* (Boston, 1976), p. 95; "Life Story of a Polish Sweatshop Girl," in Holt, *Life Stories*, p. 43.

32. Glenn, *Daughters of the Shtetl*, p. 103; Anzia Yezierska, in Kramer and Masur, *Jewish Grandmothers*, p. 45; Morris Rosenfield, poem, in Howe and Libo, *How We Lived*, p. 157.

33. Meltzer, *Taking Root*, pp. 111–112; "Life Story of a Polish Sweatshop Girl," in Holt, *Life Stories*, p. 44.

34. Glenn, *Daughters of the Shtetl*, pp. 49, 19, 21, 22, 26; Fannie Shapiro, in Kramer and Masur, *Jewish Grandmothers*, p. 10.

35. "Life Story of a Polish Sweatshop Girl," in Holt, *Life Stories*, pp. 42, 46.

36. Glenn, *Daughters of the Shtetl*, pp. 80, 87, 138–139.

37. *Forward*, March 26, 1911, in Howe and Libo, *How We Lived*, p. 185; Rischin, *Promised City*, p. 253; Meltzer, *Taking Roots*, pp. 231, 233.

38. Mothers' laments, "Mamenyu! Including an Elegy to the Triangle Fire Victims," in Mark Slobin, *Tenement Songs: The Popular Music of the Jewish Immigrants* (Urbana, Ill., 1982), p. 134; poem by Morris Rosenfeld, in Howe, *World of Our Fathers*, p. 305.

39. Glenn, *Daughters of the Shtetl*, p. 49; reporter, in Ewen, *Immigrant Women in the Land of Dollars*, p. 260.

40. Clara Lemlich, in Howe, *World of Our Fathers*, p. 298, and in Howard M. Sachar, *A History of the Jews in America* (New York, 1992), p. 183; Benjamin Feigenbaum, in Glenn, *Daughters of the Shtetl*, p. 187.

41. Glenn, *Daughters of the Shtetl*, p. 205.

42. Glenn, *Daughters of the Shtetl*, p. 172; Howe, *World of Our Fathers*, pp. 299–300; poem "The Uprising of the 20,000" in Ewen, *Immigrant Women in the Land of Dollars*, p. 242.

43. Howe, *World of Our Fathers*, p. 302.

44. Glenn, *Daughters of the Shtetl*, p. 169.

45. Immigrant's recollection, in Glenn, *Daughters of the Shtetl*, p. 204; Paul Novick, in Howe, *World of Our Fathers*, pp. 306, 302.

46. Immigrant, in Weinberg, *World of Our Mothers*, p. 83; Howe, *World of Our Fathers*, p. 121.

47. John Murray Cuddihy, *The Ordeal of Civility: Freud, Marx, Levi Strauss, and the Jewish Struggle with Modernity* (Boston, 1987), pp. xi, 13, 165, 166; Andrew R. Heinze, *Adapting to Abundance: Jewish Immigrants, Mass Consumption, and the Search for American Identity* (New York, 1990), p. 98.

48. Cuddihy, *Ordeal of Civility*, p. 13; Ewen, *Immigrant Women in the Land of Dollars*, p. 68; Cahan, *Rise of David Levinsky*, pp. 93, 94, 101; "Life Story of a Polish Sweatshop Girl," in Holt, *Life Stories*, p. 46.

49. Howe, *World of Our Fathers*, p. 128; Jewish mother, in Ewen, *Immigrant Women in the Land of Dollars*, p. 72; Cahan, *Rise of David Levinsky*, pp. 172, 93, 94, 101, 129, 176.

50. Howe, *World of Our Fathers*, pp. 128, 181; Heinze, *Adapting to Abundance*, p. 43; Weinberg, *World of Our Mothers*, p. 114; Meltzer, *Taking Root*, pp. 142–143; Antin, *Promised Land*, p. 188.

51. Heinze, *Adapting to Abundance*, pp. 4, 15, 126, 42, 77.

52. Heinze, *Adapting to Abundance*, p. 116; *Commercial Advertiser*, September 25, 1899, and the *Forward* in Howe and Libo, *How We Lived*,

pp. 77, 78; Maurice Samuel, poem, in Howe and Libo, *How We Lived*, p. 115.

53. Cahan, *Rise of David Levinsky*, pp. 404, 337.

54. Statistics and quote from immigrant woman, in Glenn, *Daughters of the Shtetl*, pp. 74, 75.

55. Immigrant daughter, in Weinberg, *World of Our Mothers*, p. 105; Glenn, *Daughters of the Shtetl*, p. 67; Heinze, *Adapting to Abundance*, pp. 108, 106; Mollie Linker, in Glenn, *Daughters of the Shtetl*, p. 1, and in Kramer and Masur, *Jewish Grandmothers*, p. 100; Ruth Katz, in Kramer and Masur, *Jewish Grandmothers*, pp. 148, 149.

56. Glenn, *Daughters of the Shtetl*, p. 77; Heinze, *Adapting to Abundance*, p. 108.

57. Selma C. Berrol, "Education and Economic Mobility: The Jewish Experience in New York City, 1880–1920," *American Jewish Historical Quarterly*, vol. 65 (March 1976), p. 271; Heinze, *Adapting to Abundance*, p. 102.

58. *Daily Forward*, in Steinberg, *Ethnic Myth*, p. 226.

59. Thomas Kessner, *The Golden Door: Italian and Jewish Immigrant Mobility in New York City, 1880–1915* (New York, 1977), p. 170; Glenn, *Daughters of the Shtetl*, pp. 83, 84.

60. Kessner, *Golden Door*, p. 98; Steinberg, *Ethnic Myth*, p. 228.

61. Steinberg, *Ethnic Myth*, pp. 234, 242.

62. A. Lawrence Lowell, to Professor William E. Hocking, May 19, 1922, and A. Lawrence Lowell, to Judge Julian Mack, March 29, 1922, in Steinberg, *Ethnic Myth*, pp. 245, 241. See also Marcial Graham Synnott, *The Half-Opened Door: Discrimination and Admissions at Harvard, Yale, and Princeton, 1900–1970* (Westport, Conn., 1979), pp. 27, 36, 112.

63. A. Lawrence Lowell, *New York Times*, June 17, 1922, in Steinberg, *Ethnic Myth*, pp. 241, 240; Sachar, *History of the Jews in America*, pp. 322–324.

64. Steinberg, *Ethnic Myth*, p. 248; Synnott, *Half-Opened Door*, pp. 109–110, 112.

65. Mayor James Michael Curley, in Synnott, *Half-Opened Door*, p. 77.

66. Howe, *World of Our Fathers*, p. 126.

67. John Higham, *Send These to Me: Immigrants in Urban America* (Baltimore, 1984), p. 158.

68. Higham, *Send These to Me*, pp. 109, 166, 114; Sachar, *History of the Jews in America*, p. 321; John Higham, *Strangers in the Land: Patterns of American Nativism, 1860–1925* (New York, 1966), pp. 67, 93.

69. Horace Kallen, in Steinberg, *Ethnic Myth*, p. 246; Higham, *Send These to Me*, pp. 169, 145, 135; Sachar, *History of the Jews in America*, p. 331.

70. Quoted in Gilbert Osofsky, *Harlem: The Making of a Ghetto, Negro New York, 1890–1930* (New York, 1966), pp. 88–89.

71. Deborah Dash Moore, *At Home in America: Second Generation New York Jews* (New York, 1981), pp. 24, 42, 43.

72. Moore, *At Home in America*, pp. 20, 23, 28.

73. Moore, *At Home in America*, pp. 30, 38; Cahan, *Rise of David Levinsky*, p. 512.

74. F. Scott Fitzgerald, *The Great Gatsby* (New York, 1953), p. 182.

Chapter 12: El Norte

1. Mario T. Garcia, *Desert Immigrants: The Mexicans of El Paso, 1880–1920* (New Haven, Conn., 1981), pp. 37, 39.

2. Ricardo Romo, *East Los Angeles: History of a Barrio* (Austin, Tex., 1983), p. 48; Lawrence A. Cardoso, *Mexican Emigration to the United States, 1897–1931* (Tucson, Ariz., 1980), p. 80.

3. Albert Camarillo, *Chicanos in a Changing Society: From Mexican Pueblos to American Barrios in Santa Barbara and Southern California, 1848–1930* (Cambridge, Mass., 1979), p. 146; Manuel Gamio, *The Mexican Immigrant: His Life Story* (Chicago, 1931), p. 15.

4. Romo, *East Los Angeles*, p. 45.

5. Romo, *East Los Angeles*, pp. 32, 37, 36, 52; Cardoso, *Mexican Emigration*, pp. 6, 75.

6. Romo, *East Los Angeles*, p. 48; Garcia, *Desert Immigrants*, p. 41; Gamio, *Mexican Immigrant*, pp. 2, 46, 67.

7. Gamio, *Mexican Immigrant*, pp. 69–70; Camarillo, *Chicanos in a Changing Society*, p. 156; Garcia, *Desert Immigrants*, p. 39; Romo, *East Los Angeles*, pp. 57, 40.

8. Romo, *East Los Angeles*, pp. 32, 36; David J. Weber, *Foreigners in Their Native Land: Historical Roots of the Mexican Americans* (Albuquerque, N.Mex., 1973), p. 260; Mario Barrera, *Race and Class in the Southwest: A Theory of Racial Inequality* (Notre Dame, Ind., 1979), p. 71.

9. Manuel Gamio, *Mexican Immigration to the United States* (Chicago, 1930), pp. 91–92.

10. Cardoso, *Mexican Emigration*, p. 82; Romo, *East Los Angeles*, p. 52; Barrera, *Race and Class in the Southwest*, p. 75; Mark Reisler, *By the Sweat of Their Brow: Mexican Immigrant Labor in the United States, 1900–1940* (Westport, Conn., 1976), p. 269; Ernesto Galarza, *Barrio Boy: The Story of a Boy's Acculturation* (Notre Dame, Ind., 1971), p. 200.

11. Marilyn P. Davis, *Mexican Voices, American Dreams: An Oral History of Mexican Immigration to the United States* (New York, 1990), p. 8; Cardoso, *Mexican Emigration*, pp. 76–77.

12. Gamio, *Mexican Immigrant*, p. 124.

13. Barrera, *Race and Class in the Southwest*, p. 86; Camarillo, *Chicanos in a Changing Society*, p. 172; Gamio, *Mexican Immigrant*, pp. 97–98.

14. Barrera, *Race and Class in the Southwest*, p. 89; Camarillo,

Chicanos in a Changing Society, pp. 211–212, 176; Garcia, *Desert Immigrants*, p. 87.

15. Vicki L. Ruiz, "A Promise Fulfilled: Mexican Cannery Workers in Southern California," in Ellen Carol DuBois and Vicki L. Ruiz (eds.), *Unequal Sisters: A Multi-Cultural Reader in U.S. Women's History* (New York, 1990), p. 265; Edith Summers Kelley, "The Head-Cutters," in appendix, Vicki L. Ruiz, *Cannery Women, Cannery Lives: Mexican Women, Unionization, and the California Food Processing Industry, 1930–1950* (Albuquerque, N.Mex., 1987), pp. 125–127.

16. Barrera, *Race and Class in the Southwest*, p. 91; Reisler, *Sweat of Their Brow*, pp. 101, 100–102, 97; Garcia, *Desert Immigrants*, pp. 57, 68.

17. Reisler, *Sweat of Their Brow*, pp. 176, 175, 87; Carey McWilliams, *Factories in the Field: The Story of Migratory Farm Labor in California* (Santa Barbara, Calif., 1971), pp. 127–128, 131; Abraham Hoffman, *Unwanted Americans in the Great Depression: Repatriation Pressures, 1929–1939* (Tucson, Ariz., 1974), p. 10; Cardoso, *Mexican Emigration*, p. 25.

18. David Montejano, *Anglos and Mexicans in the Making of Texas, 1836–1986* (Austin, Tex., 1987), pp. 172, 184–185, 199; Reisler, *Sweat of Their Brow*, pp. 77, 11.

19. Devra A. Weber, "Mexican Women on Strike: Memory, History and Oral Narrative," in Alelaida R. Del Castillo (ed.), *Between Borders: Essays on Mexicana/Chicana History* (Encino, Calif., 1990), p. 183.

20. Galarza, *Barrio Boy*, pp. 261–262; Gamio, *Mexican Immigrant*, p. 56.

21. Reisler, *Sweat of Their Brow*, pp. 84, 85.

22. Reisler, *Sweat of Their Brow*, p. 235.

23. Reisler, *Sweat of Their Brow*, p. 240.

24. Weber, "Mexican Women on Strike," pp. 186, 192.

25. Gamio, *Mexican Immigrant*, pp. 149, 147.

26. Leonard Greenwood, "El Centro's Community of Sikhs Dying Out," *Los Angeles Times,* December 28, 1966; Agnes Foster Buchanan, "The West and the Hindu Invasion," in *Overland Monthly*, vol. 51, no. 4 (April 1908), pp. 308–313; H. A. Millis, "East Indian Immigration to the Pacific Coast," in *Survey*, vol. 28 (1912), p. 379; Herman Scheffauer, "The Tide of Turbans," *Forum*, vol. 43 (June 1910), pp. 616–618.

27. H. Brett Melendy, *Asians in America: Filipinos, Koreans, and East Indians* (Boston, 1977), p. 227; Millis, "East Indian Immigration," pp. 384–385.

28. Annette Thackwell Johnson, "'Ragheads'—A Picture of America's East Indians," in the *Independent*, vol. 109 (October 28, 1922), p. 234; Bruce La Brack, "Occupational Specialization among Rural California Sikhs: The Interplay of Culture and Economics," in *Amerasia*, vol. 9, no. 2 (1982), p. 39; Dhan Gopal Mjkerji, *Caste and Outcast* (New York, 1923), pp. 269–270.

29. Bruce La Brack, "Immigration Law and the Revitalization Process: The Case of the California Sikhs," in S. Chandrasekhar, *From India to America* (La Jolla, Calif., 1982), p. 60; United States Immigration Commission, *Japanese and East Indians* (Washington, D.C., 1911), p. 339; Saint Nihal Singh, "The Picturesque Immigrant from India's Coral Strand," in *Out West*, vol. 30 (1909), p. 45; Bill Strobel, "California's Sikhs: The Pride and the Prejudice," in *California Today*, the magazine of the *San Jose Mercury News*, May 27, 1979; Greenwood, "El Centro's Community of Sikhs Dying Out"; Sucheta Mazumdar, "Punjabi Agricultural Workers in California, 1905–1945," in Lucie Cheng and Edna Bonacich (eds.), *Labor Immigration Under Capitalism: Asian Workers in the United States before World War II* (Berkeley, Calif., 1984), p. 572.

30. Rajani Kanta Das, *Hindustani Workers on the Pacific Coast* (Berlin, 1923), p. 110; information about Lohar Bupara from Roberto Haro, interview, September 6, 1988; "Interview with Inder Singh," p. 1, Survey of Race Relations, Stanford University, Hoover Institution Archives; Salim Khan, "A Brief History of Pakistanis in the Western United States," unpublished M.A. thesis, Sacramento (Calif.) State University, 1981, p. 46; "Moola Singh: Segments from His Life Story," in appendix, Karen Leonard, "Changes in Meaning for Immigrant Punjabis in Early 20th Century California" (paper for Conference on Anthropology of Experience, Feelings, and Emotion in South Asia; Houston, Texas, December 1985), p. 19; Sucha Singh, interview, August 8, 1924, Survey of Race Relations, Stanford University, Hoover Institution Library.

31. Karen Leonard, "Marriage and Family Life Among Early Asian Indian Immigrants," in S. Chandrasekhar, *From India to America,* p. 73; Roberto Haro, interview, September 6, 1988; Bruce La Brack and Karen Leonard, "Conflict and Compatibility in Punjabi-Mexican Immigrant Families in Rural California, 1915–1965," *Journal of Marriage and the Family*, vol. 46 (August 1984), p. 530; "Moola Singh: Segments from His Life Story," in appendix, Leonard, "Changes in Meaning for Immigrant Punjabis," p. 25; Sucha Singh, interview, Survey of Race Relations, Stanford University, Hoover Institution Archives.

32. Gamio, *Mexican Immigrant*, p. 177.

33. Montejano, *Anglos and Mexicans*, pp. 226–227, 221, 194.

34. Sarah Deutsch, *No Separate Refuge: Culture, Class, and Gender on an Anglo-Hispanic Frontier in the American Southwest, 1880–1940* (New York, 1987), p. 141; Rosalinda M. Gonzalez, "Chicanas and Mexican Immigrant Familes, 1920–1940: Women's Subordination and Family Exploitation," in Lois Scharf and Joan M. Jensen (eds.), *Decades of Discontent: The Women's Movement, 1920–1940* (Westport, Conn., 1983), p. 66.

35. Montejano, *Anglos and Mexicans*, pp. 192–193.

36. Gamio, *Mexican Immigrant*, pp. 222–223; Garcia, *Desert Immigrant*, p. 125.

37. Galarza, *Barrio Boy*, p. 211.

38. Gamio, *Mexican Immigrant*, pp. 44, 132; Deutsch, *No Separate Refuge*, p. 139.

39. Reisler, *Sweat of Their Brow*, pp. 152, 155, 153, 155, 156, 205.

40. Reisler, *Sweat of Their Brow*, p. 156.

41. Reisler, *Sweat of Their Brow*, pp. 154, 182–183.

42. Garcia, *Desert Immigrants*, pp. 104, 101.

43. Cardoso, *Mexican Emigration*, p. 146.

44. Camarillo, *Chicanos in a Changing Society*, p. 163; Hoffman, *Unwanted Americans*, p. 95; Carey McWilliams, "Getting Rid of the Mexican," in Wayne Moquin (ed.), *A Documentary History of the Mexican Americans* (New York, 1971), p. 297; Reisler, *Sweat of Their Brow*, p. 203.

45. Galarza, *Barrio Boy*, p. 200.

46. Camarillo, *Chicanos in a Changing Society*, p. 62; Galarza, *Barrio Boy*, p. 206; Arnold De Leon, *The Tejano Community, 1836–1900* (Albuquerque, N.Mex., 1982), pp. 180–181.

47. Gamio, *Mexican Immigrant*, p. 28; De Leon, *Tejano Community*, p. 160.

48. Camarillo, *Chicanos in a Changing Society*, p. 169; Galarza, *Barrio Boy*, p. 201.

49. De Leon, *Tejano Community*, p. 65; Galarza, *Barrio Boy*, p. 201.

50. Gamio, *Mexican Immigrant*, p. 26.

51. Galarza, *Barrio Boy*, p. 239.

52. Galarza, *Barrio Boy*, pp. 12, 19, 23, 42.

53. Montejano, *Anglos and Mexicans*, p. 31; Gamio, *Mexican Immigrant*, pp. 13, 182, 104; Reisler, *Sweat of Their Brow*, p. 113.

54. Galarza, *Barrio Boy*, p. 12.

Chapter 13: To "the Land of Hope"

1. Zora Neale Hurston, *Jonah's Gourd Vine* (New York, 1990; originally published in 1934), pp. 147–148; Florette Henri, *Black Migration: Movement North, 1900–1920* (New York, 1976), p. 49.

2. Gilbert Osofsky, *Harlem: The Making of a Ghetto, Negro New York, 1890–1930* (New York, 1965), p. 17. This is the best book on the subject.

3. Emmett J. Scott, *Negro Migration During the War* (London, 1920), pp. 41, 48; Henri, *Black Migration*, p. 72; Arna Bontemps and Jack Conroy, *Anyplace But Here* (New York, 1945), p. 163.

4. Scott, *Negro Migration*, pp. 42–43.

5. Bontemps and Conroy, *Anyplace But Here*, p. 163; Zora Neale Hurston, *Dust Tracks on a Road* (New York, 1991; originally published in 1942), p. 7; Osofsky, *Harlem*, p. 23; Henri, *Black Migration*, p. 51.

6. St. Claire Drake and Horace R. Cayton, *Black Metropolis: A Study of Negro Life in a Northern City* (New York, 1962), vol. 1, p. 60; Ray Stannard Baker, "The Negro Goes North," *World's Work*, vol. 34 (July 1917), p. 315.

7. Allan H. Spear, *Black Chicago: The Making of a Negro Ghetto, 1890–1920* (Chicago, 1967), p. 135; Scott, *Negro Migration*, pp. 17–18.

8. Emmett J. Scott (ed.), "Letters of Negro Migrants of 1916–18," *Journal of Negro History*, vol. 4 (July and October 1919), p. 413.

9. Scott (ed.), "Letters of Negro Migrants," p. 459; Spear, *Black Chicago*, p. 133; Baker, "Negro Goes North," p. 314.

10. Osofsky, *Harlem*, pp. 24, 26.

11. Osofsky, *Harlem*, pp. 21, 24–25.

12. Spear, *Black Chicago*, p. 137.

13. Osofsky, *Harlem*, pp. 21, 22; Ray Stannard Baker, *Following the Color Line* (New York, 1964; originally published in 1908), p. 112; Baker, "Negro Goes North," p. 316; Bontemps and Conroy, *Anyplace But Here*, p. 163.

14. Osofsky, *Harlem*, p. 23; Scott, *Negro Migration*, p. 31; Scott, "Letters of Negro Migrants," pp. 329, 438, 298.

15. Osofsky, *Harlem*, p. 21; Richard Wright, "Introduction," in Drake and Cayton, *Black Metropolis*, xvii; Toni Morrison, *Jazz* (New York, 1992), pp. 33, 7.

16. Baker, "Negro Goes North," p. 319.

17. Spear, *Black Chicago*, pp. 136–137.

18. Hurston, *Jonah's Gourd Vine*, p. 151.

19. James R. Grossman, *Land of Hope: Chicago, Black Southerners, and the Great Migration* (Chicago, 1989), p. 110; Osofsky, *Harlem*, p. 31. Grossman's is a human portrait of these migrants in Chicago.

20. Scott, *Negro Migration*, p. 102.

21. Drake and Cayton, *Black Metropolis*, p. 177. This book and also Spear, *Black Chicago*, are the standard works.

22. Spear, *Black Chicago*, pp. 22, 140, 202.

23. Spear, *Black Chicago*, pp. 209, 210.

24. Drake and Cayton, *Black Metropolis*, p. 181.

25. Spear, *Black Chicago*, pp. 29, 39.

26. Spear, *Black Chicago*, pp. 151, 157–158.

27. Drake and Cayton, *Black Metropolis*, p. 305.

28. Drake and Cayton, *Black Metropolis*, p. 306.

29. Spear, *Black Chicago*, p. 163.

30. Spear, *Black Chicago*, p. 211.

31. Spear, *Black Chicago*, p. 213.

32. Drake and Cayton, *Black Metropolis*, p. 66.

33. Spear, *Black Chicago*, p. 221; Drake and Cayton, *Black Metropolis*, p. 80.

34. Osofsky, *Harlem*, pp. 94, 95.

35. Osofsky, *Harlem*, pp. 105–110.

36. Osofsky, *Harlem*, pp. 105, 130, 122.

37. Osofsky, *Harlem*, p. 136.

38. Osofsky, *Harlem*, pp. 127, 122; Edmund David Cronon, *Black*

Moses: The Story of Marcus Garvey and the Universal Negro Improvement Association (Madison, Wis., 1966), p. 70. Cronon's biography is a useful narrative.

39. Marcus Garvey, "The Negro's Greatest Enemy," *Current History*, vol. 18 (September 1923), pp. 951–953.

40. Garvey, "Negro's Greatest Enemy," pp. 953–954.

41. Cronon, *Black Moses*, p. 206.

42. Cronon, *Black Moses*, pp. 176, 39, 65, 68; see also Amy Jacques-Garvey (ed.), *The Philosophy and Opinions of Marcus Garvey* (New York, 1969), pp. 79, 93.

43. Cronon, *Black Moses*, pp. 52, 114.

44. Garvey, "Negro's Greatest Enemy," p. 955; Cronon, *Black Moses*, pp. 136, 142.

45. Cronon, *Black Moses*, p. 136.

46. Nathan Huggins, *Harlem Renaissance* (New York, 1971), p. 24; Osofsky, *Harlem*, p. 181.

47. Robert Bone, *The Negro Novel in America* (New Haven, Conn., 1958), pp. 45, 33, 53; Langston Hughes, *The Langston Hughes Reader* (New York, 1958), p. 341; Huggins, *Harlem Renaissance*, p. 58.

48. Langston Hughes, "The Negro Artist and the Racial Mountain," *The Nation*, vol. 122, no. 3181 (June 23, 1926), pp. 692–694.

49. Hughes, "Negro Artist and Racial Mountain," pp. 692–694.

50. Hughes, "Afro-American Fragment," in Hughes, *Poetry of the Negro*, p. 102; Huggins, *Harlem Renaissance*, pp. 179, 82.

51. Hughes, "The Negro Speaks of Rivers," in Hughes, *Poetry of the Negro*, pp. 105–106.

52. Arna Bontemps, "Introduction," in Jean Toomer, *Cane* (New York, 1969), p. viii.

53. Toomer, *Cane*, pp. 10, 107–116.

54. Darwin Turner, "Introduction," in Jean Toomer, *Cane* (New York, 1975), p. x; Bontemps, "Introduction," pp. xiii–xv; Hughes, *Hughes Reader*, p. 380.

55. Zora Neale Hurston, *Dust Tracks on a Road*, p. 121; Robert E. Hemenway, *Zora Neale Hurston: A Literary Biography* (Urbana, Ill., 1977), p. 31.

56. Hurston, *Their Eyes Were Watching God*, pp. 48, 49, 87, 110, 111.

57. Hurston, *Dust Tracks on a Road*, p. 151.

58. Hughes, *Hughes Reader*, p. 383.

59. Harvard Sitkoff, *A New Deal for Blacks: The Emergence of Civil Rights as a National Issue* (New York, 1978), pp. 35, 36. Sitkoff's study and Raymond Wolters, *Negroes and the Great Depression: The Problem of Economic Recovery* (Westport, Conn., 1970), are the two most useful books on the subject.

60. Sitkoff, *New Deal for Blacks*, pp. 37, 39.

61. Wolters, *Negroes and the Great Depression*, pp. 91, 92.

62. Sitkoff, *New Deal for Blacks*, pp. 54, 55, 56–57.

63. Francis L. Broderick, *W. E. B. Du Bois: Negro Leader in a Time of Crisis* (Palo Alto, Calif., 1959), p. 189; Wolters, *Negroes and the Great Depression*, p. 250.

64. Broderick, *Du Bois*, pp. 165–179; Sitkoff, *New Deal for Blacks*, pp. 251, 252, 254, 179–186; Wolters, *Negroes and the Great Depression*, pp. 236–240, 258.

65. Sitkoff, *New Deal for Blacks*, pp. 69, 72, 97, 95.

Part Four: Transformations

1. W. E. B. Du Bois, *The Souls of Black Folk: Essays and Sketches* (New York, 1965), p. v.

2. M. F. Ashley Montagu, *Man's Most Dangerous Myth: The Fallacy of Race* (New York, 1942), pp. 179–180; Ruth Benedict and Gene Weltfish, *The Races of Mankind* (New York, 1943), p. 31.

3. Richard Pollenberg, *One Nation Divisible: Class, Race, and Ethnicity in the United States Since 1938* (New York, 1980), pp. 47, 71; Gunnar Myrdal, *An American Dilemma: The Negro Problem and Modern Democracy* (New York, 1962; originally published in 1944), p. 1009; Harvard Sitkoff, *A New Deal for Blacks: The Emergence of Civil Rights as a National Issue: The Depression Decade* (New York, 1978), p. 311.

4. Myrdal, *American Dilemma*, pp. 1004, 1021.

Chapter 14: World War II

1. Franklin D. Roosevelt, "The Four Freedoms," Address to Congress, January 6, 1941, *Congressional Record*, 1941, vol. 87, pt. 1 (Washington, D.C., 1941).

2. Franklin D. Roosevelt, Joint Address to Congress Leading to a Declaration of War Against Japan, December 8, 1941, Franklin D. Roosevelt Presidential Library and Museum.

3. Robert A. Wilson and Bill Hosokawa, *East to America: A History of the Japanese in the United States* (New York, 1980), p. 154; Commission on Wartime Relocation and Internment of Civilians, *Personal Justice Denied: Report of the Commission on Wartime Relocation and Internment of Civilians* (Washington, D.C., 1982), p. 264.

4. Commission on Wartime Relocation, *Personal Justice Denied*, p. 265.

5. Commission on Wartime Relocation, *Personal Justice Denied*, pp. 270, 272, 274.

6. Commission on Wartime Relocation, *Personal Justice Denied*, p. 272.

7. Commission on Wartime Relocation, *Personal Justice Denied*, p. 55.

8. Roger Daniels, *Concentration Camps USA: Japanese Americans*

and World War II (New York, 1971), pp. 45–46; Commission on Wartime Relocation, *Personal Justice Denied*, pp. 75, 78.

9. Commission on Wartime Relocation, *Personal Justice Denied*, pp. 78, 79.

10. Commission on Wartime Relocation, *Personal Justice Denied*, pp. 66, 85.

11. Commission on Wartime Relocation, *Personal Justice Denied*, pp. 111, 121; Robert Matsui, speech in the House of Representatives on the 442 bill for redress and reparations, September 7, 1987, *Congressional Record* (Washington, D.C., 1987), p. 7584; poem by Sojin, in Constance Hayashi and Keiho Yamanaka, "Footprints: Poetry of the American Relocation Camp Experience," *Amerasia Journal*, vol. 3, no. 2 (1976), p. 115.

12. Minoru Yasui, interview, in John Tateishi, *And Justice for All: An Oral History of the Japanese American Detention Camps* (New York, 1984), pp. 70–71; Gordon Hirabayashi, "Growing Up American in Washington," the spring 1988 Pettyjohn Distinguished Lecture, Washington State University, March 24, 1988; Hirabayashi, interview by author, March 24, 1988.

13. Poem by Keiho Soga, in Jiro Nakano and Kay Nakano (eds. and translators), *Poets Behind Barbed Wire* (Honolulu, 1983), p. 19; letter by Congressman Norman Mineta's father, quoted in his speech to the House of Representatives, September 17, 1987, *Congressional Record* (Washington, D.C., 1987), p. 7585; Commission on Wartime Relocation, *Personal Justice Denied*, p. 135.

14. Yasui and Tsukamoto, interviews, in Tateishi, *And Justice for All*, pp. 73, 12, 74; poem by Hakujaku, in Hayashi and Yamanaka, "Footprints," p. 116; Commission on Wartime Relocation, *Personal Justice Denied*, pp. 139, 142, 147.

15. Yasui, interview, in Tateishi, *And Justice for All*, p. 76.

16. Commission on Wartime Relocation, *Personal Justice Denied*, p. 160; poem by Nikaido Gensui, in Hayashi and Yamanaka, "Footprints," p. 116.

17. Commission on Wartime Relocation, *Personal Justice Denied*, pp. 172, 176.

18. Miyo Senzaki, interview, in Tateishi, *And Justice for All*, p. 104.

19. Jacobus tenBroek, Edward Barnhart, and Floyd Matson, *Prejudice, War, and the Constitution: Causes and Consequences of the Evacuation of the Japanese Americans in World War II* (Berkeley, 1970), p. 150; Commission on Wartime Relocation, *Personal Justice Denied*, pp. 189, 191.

20. Commission on Wartime Relocation, *Personal Justice Denied*, pp. 191–192; poem by Sunada Toshu, in Hayashi and Yamanaka, "Footprints," p. 116.

21. Andrew Lind, *Hawaii's Japanese: An Experiment in Democracy* (Princeton, 1946), p. 161.

22. Minoru Hinahara, interview by author, July 3, 1988; Chester Tanaka, *Go For Broke: A Pictorial History of the Japanese American 100th Infantry Battalion and the 442d Regimental Combat Team* (Richmond, Calif., 1982), p. 100.

23. Daniel K. Inouye, *Journey to Washington* (Englewood Cliffs, N.J., 1967), pp. 151–152.

24. Lind, *Hawaii's Japanese*, p. 158.

25. Tanaka, *Go For Broke*, p. 171; Frank Chuman, *The Bamboo People: The Law and Japanese-Americans* (Del Mar, Calif.), pp. 343–344.

26. Aiko Mifune, interviews by author, February 18, 1988, and March 29, 1988; Commission on Wartime Relocation, *Personal Justice Denied*, p. 242; poem by Keiho Soga, in Nakano and Nakano, *Poets Behind Barbed Wire*, p. 64.

27. Philip McGuire (ed.), *Taps for a Jim Crow Army: Letters from Black Soldiers in World War II* (Lexington, Ky., 1993), p. xxiii; Brenda L. Moore, *To Serve My Country, To Serve My Race: The Story of the Only African American WACs Stationed Overseas During World War II* (New York, 1996), p. 29.

28. Herbert Shapiro, *White Violence and Black Response: From Reconstruction to Montgomery* (Amherst, Mass., 1988), p. 303; *Crisis*, October 9, 1940.

29. Adam Clayton Powell, Jr., "Is This a White Man's War?" *Common Sense*, April 1942, p. 112; Gunnar Myrdal, *An American Dilemma: The Negro Problem and Modern Democracy* (New York, 1944), p. 1007; Harvard Sitkoff, *A New Deal for Blacks: The Emergence of Civil Rights as a National Issue* (New York, 1978), pp. 301, 324.

30. Private Bert Babero, letter to Truman K. Gibson, February 13, 1994, in McGuire (ed.), *Taps for a Jim Crow Army*, p. 50; letter to NAACP quoted in Lucille B. Milner, "Jim Crow in the Army," *New Republic* 110 (March 13, 1944), p. 339; Horace R. Cayton, "Fighting for White Folks?" *The Nation*, vol. 155 (September 26, 1942), p. 268.

31. Babero, letter to Gibson, February 13, 1994, in McGuire (ed.), *Taps for a Jim Crow Army*, p. 52; "A Negro Soldier," letter dated September 27, 1943, published in the *Baltimore Afro-American*, reprinted in McGuire (ed.), *Taps for a Jim Crow Army*, pp. 19–20.

32. 328th Aviation Squadron, letter to the *Richmond Afro-American*, November 22, 1943, reprinted in McGuire (ed.), *Taps for a Jim Crow Army*, pp. 67–69.

33. Timeul Black, interview, in Studs Terkel, *"The Good War": An Oral History of World War Two* (New York, 1984), pp. 274–279.

34. Stanley Sandler, *Segregated Skies: All-Black Combat Squadrons of WW II* (Washington, D.C., 1992), p. 13; Fred Smith, interview with author, August 30, 1998.

35. *Pittsburgh Courier*, January 31, 1942; William H. Hastie, "Why I Resigned," *Chicago Defender*, February 6, 1943.

36. Sandler, *Segregated Skies,* p. 60.

37. Coleman Young, interview, in Terkel, *"The Good War,"* p. 344.

38. Lou Potter, *Liberators: Fighting on Two Fronts in World War II* (New York, 1992), p. 111.

39. Potter, *Liberators,* pp. 185, 195–196.

40. Moore, *To Serve My Country,* p. 13.

41. Lucia M. Pitts, *One Negro WAC's Story* (Los Angeles, 1968; privately published, copy in the Bancroft Library, University of California, Berkeley), p. 4; Martha S. Putney, *When the Nation Was in Need: Blacks in the Women's Army Corps During World War II* (Metuchen, N.J., 1992), pp. 100–101; Charity Adams Early, *One Woman's Army: A Black Officer Remembers the WAC* (College Station, Tex., 1989), p. 151.

42. Sitkoff, *A New Deal for Blacks,* p. 314; Jacqueline Jones, *Labor of Love, Labor of Sorrow: Black Women, Work, and the Family from Slavery to the Present* (New York, 1985), p. 233; A. Philip Randolph, "Let the Negro Speak," in *The Black Worker,* March 1941. A. Philip Randolph, "The Call to the March on Washington," in *The Black Worker,* July 1941.

43. Jervis Anderson, *A. Philip Randolph: A Biographical Portrait* (Berkeley, 1986), pp. 256–257.

44. Franklin D. Roosevelt, Executive Order 8802, in *The Federal Register,* 6 (July 27, 1941).

45. Karen Tucker Anderson, "Last Hired, First Fired: Black Women Workers During World War II," in *Journal of American History,* vol. 69, no. 1, June 1982, pp. 84–85; Richard Polenberg, *One Nation Divisible: Class, Race, and Ethnicity in the United States Since 1933* (New York, 1980), p. 75.

46. Eugene Katz to Cornelius Du Bois, July 14, 1942, Special Services Division, Office of War Information, National Archives, Washington, D.C.; Anderson, "Last Hired, First Fired," pp. 82, 87; Mary Anderson, "Negro Women on the Production Front," *Opportunity: Journal of Negro Life,* vol. 21, 1943, p. 38.

47. Miriam Frank, Marilyn Ziebarth, and Connie Field, *The Life and Times of Rosie the Riveter: The Story of Three Million Working Women During World War II* (Emeryville, Calif., 1982), pp. 49, 54.

48. Sherna Berger Gluck, *Rosie the Riveter Revisited: Women, the War, and Social Change* (New York, 1987), pp. 37, 38, 23.

49. Carl T. Rowan, *Dream Makers, Dream Breakers: The World of Thurgood Marshall* (New York, 1993), pp. 98–99.

50. "Special Report on Negro Housing Situation in Detroit," March 5, 1942, marked "Confidential," prepared by Nelson Foote, Office of Facts and Figures, Bureau of Intelligence, National Archives, Washington, D.C.

51. *Chicago Defender,* June 26, 1943; Nat Brandt, *Harlem at War: The Black Experience in WWII* (Syracuse, 1996), p. 151; Doris Kearns Goodwin, *No Ordinary Time: Franklin and Eleanor Roosevelt: The Home Front in World War II* (New York, 1994), p. 447.

52. Adam Clayton Powell, Jr., *Marching Blacks* (New York, 1945), p. 125.

53. Lonnie Quan, interview, October 15, 1982, Chinese Women of America Research Project, Chinese Culture Foundation of San Francisco, p. 11.

54. Victor and Brett de Bary Nee, *Longtime Californ': A Documentary Study of an American Chinatown* (New York, 1972), pp. 154–155; Diane Mark and Ginger Chih, *A Place Called Chinese America* (Dubuque, Iowa, 1982), pp. 97–98.

55. Rose Hum Lee, "Chinese in the U.S. Today: The War Has Changed Their Lives," *Survey Graphic*, October 1942, p. 419; "Give 'Em Wings: The Story of the Part Played in Aircraft by L.A. Chinese," *Chinese Press*, April 2, 1943; Arthur Wong, oral history, in Joan Morrison and Charlotte Fox Zabusky, *American Mosaic: The Immigrant Experience in the Words of Those Who Lived It* (New York, 1980), p. 78.

56. "All Chinatown Responds to War Needs," *Chinese Press*, January 2, 1942, "Chinese Career Girls: They Help Run the Vital 'Behind-the-Line' Business of the United States at War," *Chinese Press*, May 29, 1942; "Women in the War," *Chinese Press*, March 26, 1943.

57. John W. Dower, *War Without Mercy: Race and Power in the Pacific War* (New York, 1986), p. 167; Fred Riggs, *Pressures on Congress: A Study of the Repeal of Chinese Exclusion* (New York, 1950), pp. 161–162.

58. Dower, *War Without Mercy*, pp. 164–169; *Congressional Record*, 78th Congress, 1st session, 1943, vol. 89, part 6, pp. 8580, 8581, 8597.

59. Lee, "Chinese in the U.S. Today," p. 444; Franklin D. Roosevelt, "Message From the President of the United States Favoring Repeal of the Chinese Exclusion Laws," October 11, 1943, in appendix, Riggs, *Pressures on Congress*, pp. 210–211.

60. Roberto Haro, interview, July 25, 1998.

61. Richard Santillán, "Rosita the Riveter: Midwest Mexican American Women during World War II," in *Perspectives in Mexican American Studies*, vol. 2, 1989 (Tucson), p. 120; Raul Morin, *Among the Valiant: Mexican Americans in WW II and Korea* (Alhambra, Calif., 1966), p. 21.

62. Socorro Díaz Blanchard, *Recuerdos (Memories)*, vol. 1, December 1992, unpublished autobiography, loaned to the author by her grandson, Sean O'Shea, p. 108; Patricia Preciado Martin, *Songs My Mother Sang to Me: An Oral History of Mexican-American Women* (Tucson, Ariz., 1996), p. 70.

63. Santillán, "Rosita the Riveter," pp. 124, 135.

64. Carey McWilliams, *North from Mexico: The Spanish-Speaking People of the United States* (New York, 1968), p. 260; Morin, *Among the Valiant*, pp. 153–154.

65. *La Opinión*, June 1, 1945; August 15, 1945; March 25, 1945.

66. Martha Nakagawa, "Supporters Rally for Latino Legend Who Captured 1000 Japanese Soldiers," *Pacific Citizen Weekly*, August 6–12, 1999, pp. 1,8.

67. Morin, *Among the Valiant,* pp. 232–233; David Reyes, "Taking a Stand for a Peaceful Hero," *Los Angeles Times,* August 31, 1998.

68. *La Opinión,* March 21, 1942; Maria Herrera-Sobek, *Northward Bound: The Mexican Immigrant Experience in Ballad and Song* (Bloomington, Ind., 1993), pp. 147–148; McWilliams, *North from Mexico,* pp. 266–267.

69. Matt S. Meier and Felicino Ribera, *Mexican Americans/American Mexicans* (New York, 1993), p. 175; Erasmo Gamboa, *Mexican Labor and World War II: Braceros in the Pacific Northwest, 1942–1947* (Austin, Tex., 1990), p. 62; Bracero, interview, in Henry Anderson, *Fields of Bondage: The Mexican Contract Labor System in Industrialized Agriculture* (Martinez, Calif., 1963), p. 53.

70. *La Opinión,* November 2, 1943; February 12, 1943; January 23, 1944.

71. *La Opinión,* April 1, 1942; Richard Santillán, "Midwestern Mexican American Women and the Struggle for Gender Equality," in *Perspectives in Mexican American Studies,* vol. 5 (1995), p. 95; Santillán, "Rosita the Riveter," p. 125.

72. Gluck, *Rosie the Riveter Revisited: Women, the War, and Social Change* (New York, 1987), pp. 85–86.

73. Gluck, *Rosie the Riveter,* p. 85.

74. Gluck, *Rosie the Riveter,* p. 86; Santillán, "Rosita the Riveter," p. 128.

75. Vicki Ruiz, *From Out of the Shadows: Mexican Women in Twentieth-Century America* (New York, 1998), p. 82.

76. Santillán, "Rosita the Riveter," pp. 123–124; Santillán, "Midwestern Mexican American Women," pp. 98–99.

77. Harold Foster, interview, number 1164, American Indian History Project, Western History Center, University of Utah, p. 11; Bruce Watson, "Navajo Code Talkers: A Few Good Men," *Smithsonian,* vol. 24, no. 5 (August 1993), p. 40.

78. Jere Franco, "Bringing Them Alive: Selective Service and Native Americans," *Journal of Ethnic Studies,* vol. 18, no. 3 (fall 1990), p. 18; Evon Z. Vogt, *Navaho Veterans: A Study of Changing Values* (Cambridge, Mass., 1951), p. 64.

79. Kenji Kawano, *Warriors: Navajo Code Talkers* (Flagstaff, Ariz., 1990), p. 56; S. McClain, *Navajo Weapon* (Boulder, Colo., 1994), p. 38.

80. Cozy Stanley Brown, interview, in Broderick H. Johnson (ed.), *Navajos and World War II* (Tsaile, Navajo Nation, Ariz., 1977), p. 54.

81. Interview with Jimmy King, tape number 2, pp. 6, 8–9, American Indian Oral History Project, Western History Center, University of Utah.

82. Cozy Stanley Brown, interview, in Johnson (ed.), *Navajos and World War II,* p. 54; Isabel Simmons, "The Unbreakable Code," *Marine Corps Gazette,* November 1971, pp. 4–6.

83. Watson, "Navajo Code Talkers," p. 40.

84. McClain, *Navajo Weapon*, p. 180; Watson, "Navajo Code Talkers," p. 35.

85. Watson, "Navajo Code Talkers," p. 40.

86. Watson, "Navajo Code Talkers," p. 41; Claude Hatch, interview, in Johnson (ed.), *Navajos and World War II*, pp. 124–125; Keats Begay, interview, in Johnson (ed.), *Navajos and World War II*, p. 44.

87. Letter from Mrs. B, reprinted in Doris A. Paul, *The Navajo Code Talkers* (Bryn Mawr, Pa., 1973), p. 112.

88. Oliver La Farge, "They Were Good Enough for the Army," *Harper's Magazine*, November 1947, p. 445.

89. Alison R. Bernstein, *American Indians and World War II* (Norman, Okla., 1991), p. 152.

90. Kawano, *Warriors*, p. 16; Symposium on the Navajo Code Talkers, University of California, Berkeley, November 17, 1995; McClain, *Navajo Weapon*, p. v.

91. Rafael Medoff, *The Deafening Silence* (New York, 1987); Joseph Conrad, *Heart of Darkness* (New York, 1981); Isaac Metzker (ed.), *A Bintel Brief: Sixty Years of Letters from the Lower East Side to the Jewish Daily Forward* (Garden City, N.Y., 1971), pp. 189–190.

92. David Brody, "American Jewry, the Refugees and Immigration Restriction (1932–1942)," *Publication of the American Jewish Historical Society*, vol. 45, no. 4 (June 1956), p. 241.

93. Ronald Sanders, *Shores of Refuge: A Hundred Years of Jewish Emigration* (New York, 1988), pp. 448, 449.

94. Saul S. Friedman, *No Haven for the Oppressed: United States Policy Toward Jewish Refugees, 1938–1945* (Detroit, 1973), pp. 86–87; Haskell Lookstein, *Were We Our Brothers' Keepers? The Public Response of American Jews to the Holocaust, 1938–1944* (New York, 1985), p. 43; David S. Wyman, *Paper Walls: America and the Refugee Crisis, 1939–1941* (New York, 1985), p. 67.

95. Wyman, *Paper Walls,* p. 78.

96. Arthur D. Morse, *While Six Million Died: A Chronicle of American Apathy* (New York, 1968), p. 256; Wyman, *Paper Walls,* p. 97; Friedman, *No Haven,* p. 102.

97. Marie Syrkin, "What American Jews Did During the Holocaust," *Midstream: A Monthly Jewish Review*, vol. 28, no. 8 (October 1982), p. 9; Eleanor Roosevelt, *This I Remember* (New York, 1949), p. 161.

98. Medoff, *The Deafening Silence,* p. 58.

99. Lookstein, *Were We Our Brothers' Keepers?*, pp. 84, 86.

100. Arthur Hertzberg, *The Jews in America: Four Centuries of an Uneasy Encounter* (New York, 1989), p. 293.

101. Lookstein, *Were We Our Brothers' Keepers?*, pp. 46, 65.

102. Medoff, *The Deafening Silence,* p. 64.

103. Henry L. Feingold, "'Courage First and Intelligence Second':

The American Jewish Secular Elite, Roosevelt, and the Failure to Rescue," in Verne W. Newton (ed.), *FDR and the Holocaust* (New York, 1966), p. 72.

104. Stephen Wise, *Challenging Years: The Autobiography of Stephen Wise* (New York, 1949), p. 227; David Wyman, *The Abandonment of the Jews: America and the Holocaust, 1941–1945* (New York, 1984), p. 25.

105. Zygmunt Bauman, *Modernity and the Holocaust* (Ithaca, N.Y., 1991); Sanders, *Shores of Refuge,* p. 515.

106. Wise to John Haynes Holmes, 1942, in Justine Wise Polier and James Waterman Wise (eds.), *The Personal Letters of Stephen Wise* (Boston, 1956), pp. 260–261.

107. Wise, *Challenging Years,* pp. 275–276.

108. *New York Times,* December 2, 1942, p. 24.

109. Morse, *While Six Million Died,* pp. 26–27.

110. Feingold, "'Courage First and Intelligence Second,'" in Newton (ed.), *FDR and the Holocaust,* p. 76; Medoff, *The Deafening Silence,* pp. 115, 121.

111. *New York Times,* May 4, 1943, p. 17; Monty Noam Penkower, "In Dramatic Dissent: The Bergson Boys," *American Jewish History,* vol. 7 (March 1981), p. 288.

112. Lucy Dawidowicz, "American Jews and the Holocaust," *New York Times Magazine,* April 18, 1982, p. 114; Morse, *While Six Million Died,* p. 92.

113. *New York Times,* January 23, 1944, p. 11.

114. Medoff, *The Deafening Silence,* pp. 143, 144; Wyman, *Abandonment,* p. 263.

115. Henry Feingold, "The Roosevelt Administration and the Effort to Save the Jews of Hungary," *Hungarian-Jewish Studies,* vol. 2 (1969), p. 231; Medoff, *While Six Million Died,* p. 145.

116. Jonathan Kaufman, *Broken Alliance: The Turbulent Times Between Blacks and Jews in America* (New York, 1989), p. 50.

117. Tanaka, *Go For Broke,* p. 117; "Report on Japanese Americans in Jerusalem, reunion between members of the 442nd Regiment and former Dachau inmates," CBS News, May 3, 1992.

118. Brewster Chamberlain and Marcia Feldman, *The Liberation of the Nazi Concentration Camps 1945* (Washington, D.C.: Government Printing Office, 1987), p. 36.

119. Chamberlain and Feldman, *Liberation of the Nazi Concentration Camps,* pp. 37–39, 98.

120. Medoff, *The Deafening Silence.*

121. Aaron Berman, "American Zionism and the Rescue of European Jewry: An Ideological Perspective," *American Jewish History,* vol. 30, March 1981, p. 316; Naomi W. Cohen, *American Jews and the Zionist Idea* (Hoboken, 1975), pp. 6, 31, 35; Henry L. Feingold, *A Time for Searching: Entering the Mainstream, 1920–1945* (Baltimore, 1992), p. 185; Paul

Masserman and Max Baker, *The Jews Come to America* (New York, 1932), p. 334; Dawidowicz, "American Jews and the Holocaust," p. 48; Michael Beschloss, "A Case of Courage," excerpt from his book *Presidential Courage: Brave Leaders and How They Changed America,* in *Newsweek,* May 14, 2007, p. 34.

122. Robert Frost, *Complete Poems of Robert Frost, 1949* (New York, 1949), p. 569.

123. Truman, *Diary,* in Robert H. Ferrell (ed.), *Off the Record: The Private Papers of Harry S. Truman* (New York, 1982), p. 16.

124. Robert J. Donovan, *Conflict and Crisis: The Presidency of Harry S. Truman, 1945–1948* (New York, 1977), p. 15; David McCullough, *Truman* (New York, 1992), p. 349; Margaret Truman (ed.), *Where the Buck Stops: The Personal and Private Writings of Harry S. Truman* (New York, 1989), pp. 221, 192, 58; Lisle A. Rose, *Dubious Victory: The United States and the End of World War II* (Akron, Ohio, 1973), p. 84.

125. Truman to Bess, June 22, 1911, reprinted in Robert H. Ferrell (ed.), *Dear Bess: The Letters from Harry to Bess Truman, 1910–1959* (New York, 1983), p. 39.

126. Dower, *War Without Mercy,* pp. 217, 242–245; George E. Hopking, "Bombing and the American Conscience During World War II," *The Historian,* vol. 28, no. 3 (May 1966), p. 470; Truman, quoted in Barton J. Bernstein, "The Atomic Bomb and American Foreign Policy: The Route to Hiroshima," in Barton J. Bernstein (ed.), *The Atomic Bomb: The Critical Issues* (Boston, 1976), p. 113; Truman, *Diary,* in Ferrell (ed.), *Off the Record,* p. 53.

127. Truman, *Diary,* in Ferrell (ed.), *Off the Record,* pp.53–56.

128. Truman, *Diary,* in Ferrell (ed.), *Off the Record,* pp.53–56.

129. Richard Rhodes, *The Making of the Atomic Bomb* (New York, 1986), p. 742; Henry A. Wallace, *Diary,* August 10, 1945, reprinted in Michael B. Stoff, Jonathan F. Fanton, and R. Hal Williams (eds.), *The Manhattan Project* (Philadelphia, 1991), p. 245.

130. W. E. B. Du Bois, "The Winds of Time: Negroes War Gains and Losses," *Chicago Defender,* September 15, 1945; W. E. B. Du Bois, *The Souls of Black Folk: Essays and Sketches* (New York, 1965), p. v.

131. Abraham Lincoln, "First Inaugural Address," in *The Annals of America,* vol. 9, *The Crisis of the Union: 1858–1865* (New York, 1968), p. 255; Francis L. Broderick, *W. E. B. Du Bois: Negro Leader in a Time of Crisis* (Stanford, 1966), p. 196.

Chapter 15: Out of the War

1. Walter White, *A Rising Wind* (Garden City, N.Y., 1945), p. 155.

2. Maya Angelou, *I Know Why the Caged Bird Sings* (New York, 1971), pp. 224–229.

3. "Mela — Queen of the 12-Inch (Inland Steel Company)," in *Mexican*

American Harbor Lights, published by the Señoras of Yesteryear, Indianapolis Humanities Council, Indianapolis, 1992, pp. 34–35.

4. Judy Yung, *Unbound Feet: A Social History of Chinese Women in San Francisco* (Berkeley, 1995), pp. 254, 259.

5. Brenda L. Moore, *To Serve My Country, To Serve My Race: The Story of the Only African-American WACs Stationed Overseas During World War II* (New York, 1996), pp. 12–13, 171.

6. Philip McGuire (ed.), *Taps for a Jim Crow Army: Letters from Black Soldiers in World War II* (Lexington, Ky., 1993), pp. 248–251.

7. Frank Chuman, *The Bamboo People: The Law and Japanese-Americans* (Del Mar, Calif., 1967), pp. 209–218; Kazuo Ito, *Issei: A History of Japanese Immigrants in North America* (Seattle, 1973), p. 585; Robert Wilson and Bill Hosokawa, *East to America: A History of the Japanese in the United States* (New York, 1980), p. 279; poem by Kiyoko Nieda, in Lucille Nixon and Tomoe Tana (eds. and trans.), *Sounds from the Unknown: A Collection of Japanese-American Tanka* (Denver, 1963), p. 49.

8. Congressman Robert Matsui, speech in the House of Representatives on bill 442 for redress and reparations, September 17, 1987, *Congressional Record* (Washington, D.C., 1987), p. 7584; Congressman Norman Mineta, interview, March 26, 1988; Warren Furutani, testimony, reprinted in *Amerasia*, vol. 8, no. 2, p. 104; Alice Tanabe Nehira, testimony, reprinted in ibid., p. 93.

9. "Text of Reagan's Remarks," reprinted in *Pacific Citizen*, August 19–26, 1988, p. 5; *San Francisco Chronicle*, August 5, 1988, and August 11, 1988.

10. Richard Santillán, "Midwestern Mexican American Women and the Struggle for Gender Equality," in *Perspectives in Mexican American Studies*, vol. 5 (1995), p. 98; Rodolpho Acuña, *Occupied America: A History of Chicanos* (New York, 1981), p. 332.

11. Richard Griswold del Castillo and Richard A. Garcia, *Cesar Chavez: A Triumph of Spirit* (Norman, Okla., 1995), p. 87; Sabine R. Ulibarri, *Mayhem Was Our Business: Memorias de un Veterano* (Tempe, Ariz., 1997), pp. 115, 31; Richard Santillán, "Rosita the Riveter: Midwest Mexican American Women During World War II," in *Perspectives in Mexican American Studies* , vol. 2 (1989), p. 138.

12. Acuña, *Occupied America: A History of Chicanos*, p. 330; Mario Garcia, "Americans All: The Mexican American Generation and the Politics of Wartime Los Angeles, 1941–45," *Social Science Quarterly*, vol. 65, no. 2 (June 1984), pp. 282–283.

13. Carl T. Rowan, *Dream Makers, Dream Breakers: The World of Thurgood Marshall* (New York, 1993), pp. 102–103.

14. *Brown et al. v. Board of Education of Topeka et al.,* reprinted in Clayborne Carson et al. (eds.), *The Eyes on the Prize Civil Rights Reader* (New York, 1991), pp. 64–74; "The Atlanta Declaration" of the NAACP,

reprinted in ibid., p. 82; Robert Williams, quoted in ibid., p. 36; the implementation decision, in ibid., pp. 95–96.

15. Harvard Sitkoff, *The Struggle for Black Equality, 1954–1980* (New York, 1981), pp. 41–42, 52; Stephen B. Oates, *Let the Trumpet Sound: The Life of Martin Luther King, Jr.* (New York, 1982), p. 84.

16. Martin Luther King, Jr., *Stride Toward Freedom: The Montgomery Story* (New York, 1958), pp. 12–13; Oates, *Let the Trumpet Sound*, p. 16.

17. King, *Stride Toward Freedom*, pp. 47–48; Oates, *Let the Trumpet Sound*, p. 112. See Gloria Steinem, *Revolution from Within* (Boston, 1992).

18. Sitkoff, *Struggle for Black Equality*, pp. 86, 90; student quoted by James Farmer, in Francis L. Broderick and August Meier, *Negro Protest Thought in the Twentieth Century* (New York, 1965), p. 372; Oates, *Let the Trumpet Sound*, p. 154; Clayborne Carson, *In Struggle: SNCC and the Black Awakening of the 1960s* (Cambridge, Mass., 1981), p. 64.

19. Sitkoff, *Struggle for Black Equality*, p. 109; Fred Powledge, *Free at Last? The Civil Rights Movement and the People Who Made It* (Boston, 1991), pp. 256, 262.

20. Jervis Anderson, *A. Philip Randolph: A Biographical Portrait* (Berkeley, 1986), pp. 328–329.

21. Martin Luther King, Jr., "I Have a Dream," reprinted in Francis L. Broderick and August Meier (eds.), *Negro Protest Thought in the Twentieth Century* (New York, 1965), pp. 400–405.

22. Arthur Hertzberg, *The Jews in America* (New York, 1989), pp. 348–349.

23. Jonathan Kaufman, *Broken Alliance: The Turbulent Times Between Blacks and Jews in America* (New York, 1989), pp. 14, 17. For this discussion on Jews, I am indebted to this informed and passionate study of the Jewish involvement in the Civil Rights Movement.

24. Kaufman, *Broken Alliance*, pp. 20, 17, 28, 63, 64, 81, 91.

25. Kaufman, *Broken Alliance*, pp. 95, 83, 84, 96, 212; see Alan M. Dershowitz, *Chutzpah* (Boston, 1991), pp. 65–80.

26. Kaufman, *Broken Alliance*, pp. 96, 30, 63.

27. Kaufman, *Broken Alliance*, pp. 104, 130, 132, 77.

28. See Stokely Carmichael and Charles Hamilton, *Black Power: The Politics of Liberation* (New York, 1967); Frantz Fanon, *The Wretched of the Earth* (New York, 1966); Martin Luther King, Jr., *Where Do We Go from Here: Chaos or Community?* (New York, 1967), p. 55.

29. Lyndon B. Johnson, Commencement Address at Howard University, June 4, 1965, reprinted in Clayborne Carson et al. (eds.), *The Eyes on the Prize Civil Rights Reader*, pp. 611–613.

30. Kenneth B. Clark, *Dark Ghetto: Dilemmas of Social Power* (New York, 1965), pp. 1, 12.

31. Clark, *Dark Ghetto*, p. 10.

32. James H. Cone, *Martin & Malcolm & America: A Dream or a Nightmare* (Maryknoll, N.Y., 1991), p. 223; Martin Luther King, Jr., *Why*

We Can't Wait (New York, 1964), pp. 80, ix; King, *Where Do We Go from Here?*, p. 6.

33. Cone, *Martin & Malcolm & America*, pp. 1, 42, 213, 222.

34. William Julius Wilson, *The Truly Disadvantaged: The Inner City, the Underclass, and Public Policy* (Chicago, 1987), p. 109; King, *Stride Toward Freedom*, p. 72; Nicholas Lemann, *The Promised Land: The Great Black Migration and How It Changed America* (New York, 1991), p. 6; Leslie Dunbar, *The Common Interest: How Our Social Welfare Policies Don't Work and What We Can Do About Them* (New York, 1988), p. 103.

35. Dunbar, *Common Interest*, pp. 165–167.

36. John Reid, *Black America in the 1980s, Population Bulletin*, vol. 37, no. 4 (December 1982), p. 7; Barry Bluestone and Bennett Harrison, *The Deindustrialization of America: Plant Closings, Community Abandonment, and the Dismantling of Basic Industry* (New York, 1982), p. 270; Wilson, *Truly Disadvantaged*, pp. 12, 90–91.

37. Jimmy Morse, interview, in Dunbar, *Common Interest*, pp. 89–94; Illinois Advisory Committee to the United States Commission on Civil Rights, *Shutdown: Economic Dislocation and Equal Opportunity* (Washington, D.C., 1980), pp. 8, 32–34; Report of the Congressional Office of Technology Assessment, reported in *New York Times*, February 7, 1986; Wilson, *Truly Disadvantaged*. For the welfare argument, see Charles Murray, *Losing Ground* (New York, 1984).

38. Darryl Swafford and Danny Coleman, quoted in Jacob Lamar, "Today's Native Sons," *Time*, December 1, 1986, pp. 28, 29.

39. "The Economic Crisis of Urban America," cover story, *Business Week*, May 18, 1992, pp. 38, 40, 43; Gregory Lewis, "L.A. Riot Area Likened to Third World Nation," *San Francisco Examiner*, May 31, 1992; April Lynch, "Southland's Hopes Turn to Ashes: Promise Eroded by Recession, Ethnic Tensions," *San Francisco Chronicle*, May 22, 1992.

40. Langston Hughes, "Lennox Avenue Mural," in Langston Hughes, *The Langston Hughes Reader* (New York, 1958), p. 123.

41. "Beyond Black and White," cover story, *Newsweek*, May 18, 1992, p. 28.

42. *Sa-I-Gu*, documentary film, national PBS broadcast on *P.O.V.*, September 10, 1993; Samantha Lee, " 'Not Going to Let the Riots Beat Me': Sun Soon Kim" paper originally written for *Asian American Studies 120*, Berkeley, California, 1997, in Ronald Takaki, *A Larger Memory: A History of Our Diversity, with Voices* (New York, 1998), pp. 313–315.

43. Richard Rodriguez, "Horizontal City," *This World*, San Francisco *Chronicle*, May 24, 1992, p. 16; Martin Luther King, Jr., quoted in Willie L. Brown, "Riots Echo Decades-old Anguish of Dispossessed," *San Francisco Examiner*, May 3, 1992, p. A13; interview with Sister Janet Harris, in *Los Angeles Times*, May 13, 1992, p. T11.

44. CBS, *60 Minutes*, "The Model Minority," February 1, 1987; President Ronald Reagan, speech to a group of Asian and Pacific Americans

in the White House, February 23, 1984, reprinted in *Asian Week*, March 2, 1984; Ronald Takaki, "Poverty Is Thriving Under Reagan," *New York Times*, March 3, 1986.

45. William Broad, "Swords Have Been Sheathed but Plowshares Lack Design," *New York Times*, February 5, 1992, pp. A1, A8.

46. "$150 Billion a Year: Where to Find It," *New York Times*, March 8, 1990; Ann Markusen, "Department of the Peace Dividend," *New York Times*, May 18, 1992.

47. Broad, "Swords Have Been Sheathed."

Chapter 16: Again, the "Tempest-Tost"

1. Emma Lazarus, "The New Colossus" (1883).

2. James E. Young, "Living at the Scene of the Crime," review of Charles Hoffman's *Gray Dawn: The Jews of Eastern Europe in the Post-Communist Era* (New York, 1992), *New York Times Book Review*, September 6, 1992, pp. 12–13; interview with Soviet lawyer in Moscow, June 1990; interview with Barbara Budnitz, August 22, 1992; Steven Erlanger, "As Ukraine Loses Jews, the Jews Lose a Tradition," *New York Times*, August 27, 1992.

3. Interview with Sofiya Shapiro (pseudonym), August 30, 1992.

4. Interview with Barbara Budnitz, August 22, 1992.

5. Interview with Sofiya Shapiro (pseudonym), August 30, 1992; interview with Barbara Budnitz, August 22, 1992.

6. Al Kamen, "Irish Will Win 'Green Card' Sweepstakes," *San Francisco Chronicle*, July 29, 1991; Richard Lacayo, "Give Me Your Rich, Your Lucky...," *Time*, October 14, 1991, p. 27.

7. Tyche Hendricks, "Irish Make Their Presence Felt in Fight over Illegal Immigration," *San Francisco Chronicle*, February 9, 2007.

8. David Reimers, *Still the Golden Door: The Third World Comes to America* (New York, 1985), pp. 83, 70, 67, 71.

9. Subi Lin Felipe, interview with author, July 24, 1988.

10. Wing Ng, in Thomas Kessner and Betty Boyd Caroli, *Today's Immigrants, Their Stories* (New York, 1981), p. 256.

11. Alexander Reid, "New Asian Immigrants, New Garment Center," *New York Times*, October 5, 1986; Kessner and Caroli, *Today's Immigrants*, p. 257.

12. Victor and Brett de Bary Nee, *Longtime Californ': A Documentary Study of an American Chinatown* (New York, 1972), pp. 282, 285.

13. Karen Ringuette, "Asian Immigrants: Debunking the Myths," *East/West News,* October 23, 1986; Tom Wing Wah, interview, September 5, 1982, Chinese Women of America Research Project, Chinese Cultural Foundation of San Francisco, pp. 3–4.

14. Wei-Chi Poon, interviews with author, January 27 and February 2, 1988.

15. Student paper, name withheld, "Vietnamese Refugee," *Asian American Studies* 126, spring 1987, University of California at Berkeley, pp. 1–2; Thai Dang, interviewed by author, April 28, 1988.

16. Thai Dang, interviewed by author, April 28, 1988; Thich Nhat Hanh, "The Cry of Vietnam," in Thomas Bentz, *New Immigrants: Portraits in Passage* (New York, 1981), p. 145; William Liu, *Transition to Nowhere: Vietnamese Refugees in America* (Nashville, 1979), p. 78.

17. "New Immigrants' Quest: Refugees from Saigon," *New York Times*, July 2, 1986; Liu, *Transition to Nowhere*, pp. 21, 15, 19.

18. Liu, *Transition to Nowhere*, p. 55; Kenneth Skinner, "Vietnamese in America: Diversity in Adaptation," *California Sociologist*, vol. 3, no. 2 (Summer 1980), p. 105; Barry N. Stein, "Occupational Adjustment of Refugees: The Vietnamese in the United States," *International Migration Review*, vol. 13, no. 1 (Spring, 1979), p. 40.

19. Lesleyanne Hawthorne, *Refugee: The Vietnamese Experience* (Melbourne, Australia, 1982), pp. 97, 214, 221, 237.

20. Barry Wain, *The Refused: The Agony of the Indochina Refugees* (New York, 1981), pp. 72, 73; Michael Dorgan, "Attacks Leave Scars that Will Not Fade," *San Jose Mercury News*, April 10, 1987; Bruce Grant, *The Boat People: An "Age" Investigation* (New York, 1979), pp. 65, 66.

21. Tuyet Anh Nguyen, letter to the author, May 2, 1988; Chuong Hoang Chung, "The Language Situation of Vietnamese Americans," in Sandra McKay and Sau Ling Wong (eds.), *Language Diversity: Problem or Resource* (New York, 1988), p. 277.

22. Alan Hope, "Language, Culture Are Biggest Hurdles for Vietnamese," *Gainesville Times* (Ga.), March 31, 1985; Edward Iwata, "Ugly Tangle over Foreign Fishing Ways," *San Francisco Chronicle,* September 10, 1983, p. 28; Karen Ringuette, "Asian Immigrants," p. 9; Tricia Knoll, *Becoming Americans: Asian Sojourners, Immigrants, and Refugees in the Western United States* (Portland, Ore., 1982), pp. 196, 192.

23. T. T. Nhu, "Old Feuds Still Disrupt Peace Among Vietnamese," *San Jose Mercury News*, March 2, 1988; Katherine Bishop, "Refugees Press On with Vietnam War," *New York Times*, August 3, 1987, pp. 1, 8; Cheryl Romo, "The War Away from Home," *In These Times*, August 10–23, 1983, pp. 12–13, 22; Marvine Howe, "Vietnamese Celebrate Traditional New Year," *New York Times*, February 1, 1987; Joanne Omang, "Dreaming of a Return to Vietnam," *San Francisco Chronicle*, March 9, 1983; interview with Vietnamese woman, name withheld, field notes, February 27, 1988.

24. Thomas Bentz, *New Immigrants: Portraits in Passage* (New York, 1981), p. 154.

25. Student paper, name withheld, "Vietnamese Refugee," *Asian American Studies* 126, spring 1987, University of California at Berkeley, pp. 7–8.

26. Ashley Dunn, "Legacy Comes Home: The Land of Opportunity Offers Refugees a New Life," *Seattle Times Post-Intelligencer*, April 28, 1985.

27. Michael McCabe and L. A. Chung, "Facing the Hopes and Fears of Assimilation," *San Francisco Chronicle*, July 25, 1988; Knoll, *Becoming Americans*, pp. 188, 186.

28. Chuong Hoang Chung, interview, March 24, 1988; student paper, name withheld, "Vietnamese Refugee," p. 10.

29. Stein, "Occupational Adjustment of Refugees," p. 29; "Duke Points the Way to Little Saigon," *East/West News*, June 30, 1988.

30. Chung, "Language Situation of Vietnamese Americans," in McKay and Wong (eds.), *Language Diversity*, pp. 276, 285, 289.

31. Liu, *Transition to Nowhere*, p. 170; Anh K. Tran, "Adaptational Strategy of Chinese-Vietnamese in the United States," paper presented at the Fifth National Conference of the Association for Asian American Studies, March 24–27, 1988, Washington State University, p. 30; Julie Rees, "Striving for the American Dream," *Long Beach Press-Telegram*, May 6, 1985.

32. Patrick Anderson, "Asians Revive Tenderloin," *AsianWeek*, April 17, 1987; Raymond Lou, "The Vietnamese Business Community of San Jose," paper presented at the Fifth National Conference of the Association for Asian American Studies, March 24–27, 1988, Washington State University, pp. 3, 4; Judith Lyons, "72,000 Viets with 320 Firms Spark New Life in San Jose," *AsianWeek*, June 19, 1987.

33. "'New Face of Asian Pacific American' Debuts," *AsianWeek*, May 8, 2003.

34. Afghan refugee, quoted in Melanie Gadener, "In Memory of My Father," Ethnic Studies 201 paper, Spring 2007, University of California, Berkeley, p. 6. Thanks to Ms. Gadener for letting me quote from the research papers she did in my seminars. Fariba Nawa, "Afghan Exiles—Grasping at a Thread of Hope," *Pacific News Service*, July 30, 1996.

35. Jonathan Curiel, "Afghan Angst: Bay Area Community Watches Taliban Depredations from Afar," *San Francisco Chronicle*, March 18, 2001.

36. Afghan refugee, quoted in Gadener, "In Memory of My Father," p. 4; Meg Dixit, "Stories of Afghan American Women," *AsianWeek*, May 17, 2002.

37. Farhad Ahad, "My Mother's Courage," in *Afghan Journal: An Inter-Generational Afghan American Voice*, Winter/Spring 2003 (San Francisco), p. 10.

38. Mother, quoted in Melanie L. Gadener, "Tragedy of the Running Brains: The Making of the Afghan Community in Fremont, California," Ethnic Studies 190 paper, Spring 2005, University of California, Berkeley, pp. 52–53.

39. Afghan refugee, quoted in Melanie Gadener, "In Memory of My Father," pp. 8–9.

40. Curiel, "Afghan Angst"; Julia Hollister, "Fewer Immigrants Are Choosing California," *California Job Journal*, March 21, 2004.

41. Curiel, "Afghan Angst."

42. Naseem Yar, interview, May 27, 2007.

43. Nadia Ali Maiwandi, "The Afghan-American Response," *Afghan Magazine*, January–December 2001.

44. Nadeem Saaed, e-mail to Professor Takaki, September 11, 2007.

45. Zarpana Reitman, interview, May 27, 2007.

46. Mohammad H. Qayoumi, "From Silk Road to Route 66: My American Journey," in Myron W. Lustig and Jolene Koester, *Among Us: Essays on Identity, Belonging, and Intercultural Competence* (Upper Saddle River, N.J., 2003), p. 106.

47. Elizabeth Fernandez, "Afghan Cultural Issues Subject of Panel, Book," *San Francisco Chronicle*, June 24, 2007.

48. Tamim Ansary, speech, East Meets West conference, Fremont, California, June 23, 2007.

49. Nadeem Saaed, e-mail to Professor Takaki, September 11, 2007.

50. Nadeem Saaed, interview, May 27, 2007; Zarpana Reitman, interview, May 27, 2007.

51. Young man in the audience, East Meets West conference, Fremont, California, June 23, 2007; Fernandez, "Afghan Cultural Issues Subject of Panel, Book."

52. Fatema Nourzaie, e-mail to Professor Takaki, September 15, 2007.

53. Omar Nourzaie, conversation in Fremont, California, June 23, 2007.

54. "Immigration: Why Amnesty Makes Sense," *Time,* June 18, 2007, pp. 42, 39.

55. David Bacon, "What a Vote for Free Trade Means for the U.S.," *San Francisco Chronicle,* November 20, 2007.

56. Leo Chavez, *Shadowed Lives: Undocumented Immigrants in American Society* (New York, 1998), pp. 28, 34.

57. Chavez, *Shadowed Lives*, pp. 53, 63.

58. Linda Chavez and John W. Wilhelm, "Permanent, Not Temporary Workers," *San Francisco Chronicle*, May 10, 2007.

59. "The Border Is Not a Military Zone," *San Francisco Chronicle*, May 16, 2006.

60. Ronald Reagan, quoted in Fareed Zakaria, "America's New Know-Nothings," *Newsweek*, May 28, 2007, p. 39.

61. Hans P. Johnson, "Illegal Immigration," *At Issue: Public Policy Institute of California*, April 2006 (San Francisco), p. 10.

62. Claudia Diera, "My Story, Our History: From Mexico to Los Angeles," Ethnic Studies 195 paper, Fall 2006, University of California, Berkeley.

63. José Palafox, "A Song of El Norte: Camelia Palafox," in Ronald

Takaki, *A Larger Memory: A History of Our Diversity, with Voices* (New York, 1997), pp. 248–261, paper originally written in Ethnic Studies 195, Fall 1997, University of California, Berkeley.

64. Alexis Lopez, "Generaciones: A Mosaic of Mexican American Identity," paper for Ethnic Studies 195, Fall 2006, University of California, Berkeley. Interview with author, June 5, 2007.

65. Tyche Hendricks, "College Seems Out of Reach to Most Latinos," *San Francisco Chronicle*, June 24, 2007.

66. Cynthia Tucker, "An Investment in Our Future," *San Francisco Chronicle*, May 28, 2007.

67. Raul Reyes, "Latinos: Can You Hear Us Now?" *USA Today*, December 29, 2006.

68. Javier Erik Olvera and Mike Swift, "The Immigration Debate: 70 Percent of Mexicans in California are U.S. Citizens," *San Jose Mercury News*, November 5, 2007.

Chapter 17: "We Will All Be Minorities"

1. President Bill Clinton, "One America in the Twenty-first Century: The President's Initiative on Race" (Washington, D.C., White House, June 16, 1997). On July 10, Minyon Moore, deputy assistant to the president for political affairs, wrote to me: "Thank you for the valuable input you provided President Clinton in preparation for his speech on Race and Reconciliation in San Diego. The ideas you shared with the President meant a great deal to him."

2. Herman Melville, *Moby-Dick* (Boston, 1956; originally published in 1851), pp. 105, 182, 253, 322–323.

3. Gloria Anzaldúa, *Borderlands, La Frontera: The New Mestiza* (San Francisco, 1987), first page of preface, p. 87.

4. Gloria Steinem, *Revolution from Within* (Boston, 1990), p. 107.

5. Carlos Fuentes, *The Buried Mirror: Reflections on Spain and the New World* (New York, 1992), p. 348.

6. Reese Erlich, "Alice's Wonderland," an interview with Alice Walker, Image, *San Francisco Examiner*, July 19, 1992, p. 12.

7. Greg Mayeda, "Golf Phenomenon Asserts Mixed Race Identity," *What's Hapa'ning: The Hapa Issues Forum Newsletter*, vol. 3, no. 2, summer 1995 (Berkeley, Calif.).

8. Johanna Neuman, "Obama Decries Rash of Divisive Campaigning," *San Francisco Chronicle*, March 16, 2008; Jeff Yang, "Another First for Obama If Elected?" *San Francisco Chronicle*, July 21, 2008.

9. Paula Gunn Allen, interview, in Laura Coltelli (ed.), *Winged Words: American Indian Writers Speak* (Lincoln, Neb., 1990), p. 17.

10. Interview with Toni Morrison, *Time,* May 22, 1989, p. 121.

11. John G. Neihardt (ed.), *Black Elk Speaks: Being the Life Story of a Holy Man of the Oglala Sioux* (Lincoln, Neb., 1988), p. 43.

12. Walt Whitman, Leaves of Grass and Selected Prose (New York, 1958), p. 10.

13. Ronald Takaki, *Strangers from a Different Shore: A History of Asian Americans* (Boston, 1989), pp. 88–89; Jack Weatherford, *Native Roots: How the Indians Enriched America* (New York, 1991), pp. 210, 212; Carey McWilliams, *North from Mexico: The Spanish-Speaking People of the United States* (New York, 1968), p. 154; Stephan Thernstrom (ed.), *Harvard Encyclopedia of American Ethnic Groups* (Cambridge, Mass., 1980), p. 22; Howard Sachar, *A History of the Jews in America* (New York, 1992), p. 367.

14. Herman Melville, *Redburn* (Chicago, 1969; originally published in 1849), p. 169; also quoted in Henry Louis Gates, Jr., *Loose Canons: Notes on the Culture Wars* (New York, 1992), pp. 116–117; Walt Whitman, *Leaves of Grass and Selected Prose* (New York, 1958), pp. 284, 9, 10, 38.

15. W. E. B. Du Bois, *The Souls of Black Folk: Essays and Sketches* (New York, 1965), p. v; Abraham Lincoln, "First Inaugural Address," in *The Annals of America*, vol. 9, *1861–1865: The Crisis of the Union* (Chicago, 1968), p. 255; Abraham Lincoln, "The Gettysburg Address," in ibid. pp. 462–463; Langston Hughes, "Let America Be America Again," in Langston Hughes and Arna Bontemps (eds.), *The Poetry of the Negro, 1746–1949* (Garden City, N.Y., 1951), p. 106.

INDEX

ABOUT THE AUTHORS

Ronald Takaki (1939–2009) was one of the preeminent scholars of our nation's diversity. He was a Professor Emeritus of Ethnic Studies at the University of California, Berkeley, where he taught more than twenty thousand students during thirty-six years of teaching.

The grandson of immigrant Japanese plantation laborers in Hawaii, Takaki graduated from the College of Wooster, Ohio, in 1961. Six years later, after receiving his PhD in American History from UC Berkeley, he went to UCLA to teach its first Black History course.

In 1972, Professor Takaki returned to Berkeley to teach in the newly instituted Department of Ethnic Studies. His comparative approach to the study of race and ethnicity provided the conceptual framework for the BA program and the PhD program in Comparative Ethnic Studies as well as for the university's multicultural requirement for graduation, known as the American Cultures Requirement.

Clint Smith is a staff writer at *The Atlantic*. He is the author of *How the Word Is Passed: A Reckoning with the History of Slavery Across America,* a #1 *New York Times* bestseller for which he received the National Book Critics Circle Award, the Stowe Prize, and the Hillman Prize for Book Journalism, among other honors. He is also the author of two poetry collections, the award-winning *Counting Descent* and *Above Ground*. His writing has been published in *The New Yorker,* the *New York Times Magazine, Poetry, The Paris Review,* and elsewhere. Born and raised in New Orleans, he received his BA in English from Davidson College and his PhD in education from Harvard University.